Chile: The Carretera Austral

A guide to one of the world's most scenic road trips

the Bradt Guide

Hugh Sinclair
& Edward Menard

edition
2

www.bradtguides.com

Bradt Guides Ltd, UK
The Globe Pequot Press Inc, USA

NORTHERN SECTION
map, page 76

Ensenada

47km

Paso Río Manso → *Argentina*

Cochamó

32km

Paso Río Puelo → *Argentina*

15km

14km

Segundo Coral

12km

Río Puelo

Puerto Canelo

20km

Primer Coral

Llanada Grande

36km

Caleta Puelche

54km

Puerto Maldonado

34km

45km

Puerto Montt

Caleta La Arena

77km

Hornopirén

Caleta Gonzalo

44km

Chaitén

24km

El Amarillo

52km

Futaleufú ⚡ → *Argentina*

48km

Puerto Ramírez

30km

Palena ⚡ → *Argentina*

43km

Villa Santa Lucía

Lago Verde → *Argentina*

68km

Raúl Marín Balmaceda

75km

La Junta ⚡

78km

47km

Puyuhuapi

56km

Cisnes Junction

35km

Puerto Cisnes

34km

Villa Amengual

51km

55km

La Tapera

Paso Río Frías → *Argentina*

45km

Mañihuales

12km

28km

Puerto Aysén ⚡

14km

18km

Coyhaique

46km

28km

30km

32km

Nirehuao

32km

Paso Puesto Viejo → *Argentina*

45km

Paso Coyhaique → *Argentina*

CLASSIC SECTION
map, page 142

KEY

Paved road

Gravel road

Poor gravel road

Non-vehicular access

Vehicular border crossing *(page 329)*

Bradt

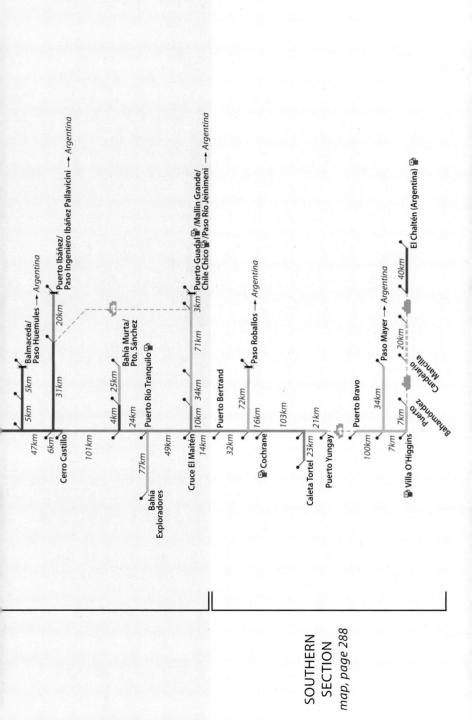

Balmaceda/
Paso Huemules → Argentina

Puerto Ibáñez/
Paso Ingeniero Ibáñez Pallavicini → Argentina

Puerto Guadal / Mallin Grande/
Chile Chico / Paso Río Jeinimeni → Argentina

5km

5km

47km

6km

31km

20km

Cerro Castillo

101km

4km

25km

24km

Bahía Murta/
Pto. Sánchez

Puerto Río Tranquilo

49km

77km

Bahía
Exploradores

Cruce El Maitén

14km

10km   34km   71km   3km

Puerto Bertrand

32km

72km

Paso Roballos → Argentina

16km

Cochrane

103km

Caleta Tortel

23km

21km

Puerto Yungay

Puerto Bravo

100km

34km

Paso Mayer → Argentina

7km

Villa O'Higgins

7km

20km

40km

El Chaltén (Argentina)

Puerto
Bahamóndez

Candelario
Mancilla

SOUTHERN
SECTION
map, page 288

Chile: The Carretera Austral Don't miss...

National parks and reserves
Marvel at giant alerce trees at the Parque Nacional Alerce Andino (GR/ML/A) page 99

Glaciers
It's hard to traverse the Carretera Austral without seeing a glacier, but if you only make the effort to visit one, make it the Ventisquero San Rafael (HS) page 267

Trekking

Cerro Castillo is one of the key trekking areas in southern Chile, with options for gentle hikes and challenging climbs
(G/S) page 251

History

The history of the Carretera Austral is fascinating but relatively undocumented — pictured here are the Puyuhuapi pioneers, whose legacy is still visible in the town today
(LL) page 179

Wildlife

Raúl Marín Balmaceda is a paradise for wildlife watchers, where penguins, cormorants, dolphins and sea lions vastly outnumber people
(HS) page 167

above The ferry ride from Hornopirén to Caleta Gonzalo through the Fiordo Comau is a dramatic introduction to what lies in store further south (HS) page 122

left The pretty cemetery of the San Miguel de Aulen chapel, along the coastal road towards Hornopirén (HS) page 111

below The quaint church in Villa Santa Lucía (A/S) page 136

above & below **A private initiative pioneered by conservationist Doug Tompkins, Parque Pumalín has two volcanoes, plenty of well-marked walking trails, waterfalls, lakes, alerce trees and campgrounds** (HS) and (EB/S) page 132

AUTHOR

Hugh Sinclair lives in Bariloche (Argentina) with his Dutch wife and two daughters. He is a reformed investment banker, author and economist. In 2001 he successfully established the Guinness World Record for the fastest traverse of the Americas by motorcycle, developing an obsession with Latin America in the meantime. He has lived and worked in countless countries, from Mongolia to Liberia, Mexico to Mozambique, but his true passion is Patagonia.

CO-AUTHOR

Edward Menard lives in the UK, where he attended Winchester College and took A-levels in Economics, German and History. He began studying at UCL in 2020. He worked in Vienna with Big Bus for the summer of 2018, and spent late 2019 and 2020 in Argentina and Chile, researching this book and learning Spanish.

CONTRIBUTOR

Warren Houlbrooke co-authored the first edition of this guide. He is originally from New Zealand, where he worked predominantly in agriculture, both on farms and as a sales rep for international agricultural companies. He has lived in Bariloche for 15 years with his wife and daughter, working in agriculture, property development and real estate. He has travelled extensively in Latin America, in particular across both Chilean and Argentine Patagonia. He is a highly proficient motorcyclist, scuba-diver, skier, equestrian, cyclist and sailor. He has traversed the entire Carretera Austral seven times.

COVID-19

Please note that research for this guide was carried out during the Covid-19 pandemic. Because of the impact of the crisis on tourism, some businesses or services listed in the text may no longer operate. We will post any information we have about these on w bradtguides.com/updates. And we'd of course be grateful for any updates you can send us during your own travels, which we will add to that page for the benefit of future travellers.

Second edition published October 2022
First published 2016
Bradt Guides Ltd
31a High Street, Chesham, Buckinghamshire, HP5 1BW, England
www.bradtguides.com
Print edition published in the USA by The Globe Pequot Press Inc,
PO Box 480, Guilford, Connecticut 06437-0480

Text copyright © 2022 Hugh Sinclair
Maps copyright © 2022 Bradt Guides Ltd; includes map data © OpenStreetMap contributors
Photographs copyright © 2022 Individual photographers (see below)
Project Manager: Susannah Lord
Cover research: Pepi Bluck, Perfect Picture

ISBN: 9781784774752

British Library Cataloguing in Publication Data
A catalogue record for this book is available from the British Library

Photographs Alamy Stock Photos: Galen Rowell/Mountain Light (GR/ML/A); Dreamstime. com: Galyna Andrushko (GA/D); Warren Houlbrooke (WH); Luisa Ludwig (LL); Hugh Sinclair (HS); Shutterstock.com: Adwo (A/S), Ammit Jack (AJ/S), Alberto Loyo (AL/S), Dudarev Mikhail (DM/S), ecerovi2016 (e/S), Emiliano Barbieri (EB/S), Guaxinim (G/S), Idan Ben Haim (IBH/S), Jorge Leon Cabello (JLC/S), Jeremy Richards (JR/S), Luciano Queiroz (LQ/S), Manon van Goethem (MVG/S), reisegraf.ch (r/S), Rich Lindie (RL/S), sunsinger (S/S), Tanja Gavrilovic (TG/S); SuperStock.com (SS)
Front cover Carretera Austral in southern Patagonia, Chile (GA/D)
Back cover Ventisquero Colgante (hanging glacier), Parque Nacional Queulat (S/S); Trekking around Cerro Castillo (G/S)
Title page Lupins along the Mañihuales River in spring (WH); Gaucho crossing a wooden bridge over the Futalefú (G/S); Detail of marble caves at Puerto Río Tranquilo, Lago General Carrera (MVG/S)
Part openers Puerto Varas with Volcán Osorno in the background (page 77; DM/S); Switchbacks on the descent to Cerro Castillo (page 141; HS); Guanaco (*Lama guanicoe*), Valle Chacabuco (page 287; JR/S)

Maps David McCutcheon FBCart.S

Typeset by Ian Spick, Bradt Guides and Geethik Technologies, India
Production managed by Jellyfish Print Solutions; printed in India
Digital conversion by www.dataworks.co.in

Foreword

by Douglas Tompkins

The Carretera Austral is perhaps the most spectacular road in the world. If there is another that provides access to nearly 20 national parks (with as many as five new ones in the making), several national reserves, two of the world's largest private parks with full public access (Pumalín and Patagonia), as well as wild and wide open landscapes, soaring mountains, lakes, glaciers, forests and fjords, then I would like to know where it is. Having travelled to many parts of the world, I have yet to find anything comparable. It is nothing short of a wonder.

So, if you are not yet on this Southern Highway 'Route of Parks', then don't hesitate to make plans for a trip that you will remember forever. The landscapes are unrivalled in their beauty, and the people are friendly and will welcome you with open arms. In short, the Carretera Austral is a trip of a lifetime, and although my wife Kris and I have been living in this fantastic place for the last 25 years, we never tire of travelling up and down this magnificent road. It is a guaranteed adventure of scenic beauty.

What you are about to read in the subsequent pages is a guidebook, but of a different calibre than almost any you will find elsewhere. Besides providing practical information, it considers the 'development model' with which Chile, as a country, evolves its economy. The story along this road is familiar – one of human colonisation that is common throughout history across the world. You see, roads are many-edged swords, and if we start with the old adage that 'it is hard to destroy wilderness without roads', we promptly arrive at the grain of the argument. As beautiful and awesome as the Carretera Austral may be, it has been pivotal in human development. Overgrazing, burned forests, mining, and industrial fish farming are all present as a result of the roads built.

Yet saying all that, we are really bemoaning the state of the world: and Chile is just another country caught up in the 'Myth of Progress'. Yet, no matter where we may be from, we are now united in the challenge to reverse this massive environmental crisis in which we find ourselves and the world embroiled. We are now in what is the 6th Mass Extinction Event, the worst environmental crisis in the last 65 million years. Additionally we have, as a civilisation, had a negative impact on the climate as well – what could be worse than that? So, as we traverse the Carretera Austral, let's pause to reflect about these sobering issues, and when we return home begin the work, as socially responsible citizens of the world, to start paying our rent for living on the planet. There is a place for everyone along the long front of environmental and conservation activism to lend a hand in directing humanity towards harmony with nature.

Douglas Tompkins was co-founder of The North Face among other enterprises, and a major conservationist in Argentina and Chile. He created numerous parks along the Carretera Austral (see box, page 134). He died in December 2015 of hypothermia when his kayak capsized in Lago General Carrera.

AUTHOR'S STORY   *Hugh Sinclair*

It always puzzled me why other children forgot to mention South America in geography classes. For as long as I can remember this was the mysterious continent I had to visit. Straight after university I packed my bags and headed south, and never quite left. During a year-long assignment in Mongolia, my wife and I discovered we were expecting a baby, and for all the joys of life in Ulaanbaatar, raising a family there did not appeal. Instead of endlessly moving to where work dictated, we opened the map to decide where we wanted to go to start a new chapter in life. One place sprung to mind – Patagonia.

I had motorbiked through Patagonia in 2001 as part of a Guinness World Record expedition to establish the fastest passage through the Americas by motorbike, and we had visited the region numerous times since. But it was not until 2011 that I realised I had not actually visited the true gem of this region. I drove down from Bariloche to Cochrane along the Carreterra Austral and discovered a region of verdant jungle, eye-popping glaciers, stunning lakes, and rivers of colours I did not know existed. Thus began my love affair with the Carretera Austral.

I began to receive endless emails from friends, bikers, backpackers, cyclists, etc, asking for information about this mysterious region. Instead of replying to each, perhaps it would be easier to write a summary to send to people? As I thought about the size of such a summary I realised 'book' was a fairer description, and thus I approached Bradt, who leapt at the chance, and supported the project from a crazy idea to the book you now hold in your hands. Patagonia is now open. Enjoy it, and protect it.

AUTHOR'S STORY   *Edward Menard*

The chance to spend a gap year in South America is something no-one should pass up! After finishing school, I headed to Chile, where I was able to learn Spanish, see some of the most spectacular nature in the world, and experience a new culture including staying with a Chilean family in Coyhaique for a month. In a short year, regrettably cut even shorter by the pandemic, I was able to travel the length of the Carretera Austral, and enjoy treks, glacier walks and scenery I couldn't have imagined.

Although new to the region, researching the Carretera Austral with Hugh for this second edition of the Bradt guide has given me a unique insight, which I hope has contributed to Hugh and Warren's work. I feel so lucky I have been able to spend time in this amazing place, and plan on returning many times.

Acknowledgements

More than two-thirds of the land encompassed by the Carretera Austral is protected. The national parks and reserves are truly what makes the region so unique, so untouched, so diverse and full of life. It is all too easy to forget the staff behind the upkeep and protection of these parks, and thus our primary thanks are to them. The 'two Carolinas' at Rewilding Chile were once again a great support, and the fantastic work of Kris Tompkins remains an inspiration – it is with deep regret that we were unable to present Doug with a copy of the first edition, but we strive to reflect his passion for the region in these pages and support the work of Kris.

In many villages we have a core friend who has ventured beyond the call of duty to help us during this second edition, made all the harder due to the pandemic. A special thanks to Carlos and Nela in Cochrane, Marisol in Cisnes, Nicolas and Lotta in Chaitén, Cristian in Cochamó and the 'two Marys' in Cerro Castillo and Bertrand. A third Carolina – of huge help to us during her time at SERNATUR – has now set up her own tour operator business, and has been instrumental in our work around Coyhaique.

Three people really helped us to improve coverage of some of the lesser-known villages: veteran equestrian Eduardo Vas in Murta; intrepid explorer Jorge Parker in Palena; and avid fisherman Claudio Soto in Lago Verde. Although Caleta Tortel has suffered under the strain of tourism, Enrique is a pioneer in the village and helped us enormously throughout the second edition. Likewise with Río Tranquilo, one of the less enjoyable villages from an author's perspective, Enzo showed us a new side to the region, with Cumbre de los Cipreses being one of the most pleasant surprises as we scoured the Carretera for new activities. The wisdom of Daniel Muñoz permeates the Villa O'Higgins chapter and his flights over the ice field remain a highlight of the entire continent. Jonathan Hechenleitner, guru of Raúl Marín in the first edition, has expanded his wisdom to include the ever-tricky topic of ferries and the village of La Junta – invaluable help in both regards.

Following a chance encounter in Cochamó with the production team of a documentary, a certain Claudio became intrigued with our book and has been a guiding light for years now – based beyond the Carretera but always offering us his help. We are grateful.

The inclusion of the more isolated islands and regions previously omitted from the guidebook would not have been possible without the help of Pía Rojo and Hayley Durán – we only regret that time and the restrictions imposed by Covid resulted in this being included as an appendix rather than a dedicated chapter – motivation for the third edition!

Richard and Jennifer at what3words were a great help, and the ability to incorporate full navigation into a guidebook would not have been possible without the work of their company.

The Druett family, once again, have been an invaluable support. From sharing their extensive wisdom of the region to babysitting my daughter, from updating the entire nightlife section of Coyhaique to keeping me informed of the latest developments (and gossip) of the region, they are truly partners in this guidebook. Luisa Ludwig, as ever, revealed the spirit of the region to us, the magic lurking under the surface of the Carretera, as well as offering a roof over our heads in times of need. Eliana Oyarzún helped us at every stage, slogging around Puerto Montt investigating laundries and hounding staff at the ferry companies for updates; she has welcomed us to her house for a decade now, and it is an honour to refer to her as *mi mama chilena*.

SPECIAL THANKS *Hugh Sinclair*
Jessica once again demonstrated astonishing patience and put up with months alone as I pored over Carretera trivia. Vicky put in a sterling effort helping with the *Travelling with kids* section – without her I would have been incapable of assessing the quality of playgrounds in these remote villages! Also a big thanks to Facu and Paola for putting me up during the write-up period, as I commandeered their kitchen table with maps, books and cups of coffee.

SPECIAL THANKS *Edward Menard*
A special thanks to Mike and Dani, who were amazingly generous and fantastic company while I stayed in Bariloche and made my trip possible. Also, to Christian and his family, who I stayed with in Coyhaique, and are the main reason I can speak even a word of Spanish!

KEY TO SYMBOLS

▬▬▪▬▬▸	International boundary	♨	Museum/artgallery
══════	Paved road (regional maps)	✚	Hospital
▬▬▬▬▬	Gravel road (regional maps)	✚	Medical centre/clinic
══════	Poor gravel road (regional maps)	⅄	Campsite
··········	Footpath	♀	Bar
--🚢--	Car ferry	✝	Church/cathedral
--🚢--	Passenger ferry	⊞	Cemetery
⎸5.5km⎸	Distances (between pins)	※	Viewpoint
✈✝	Airport/airstrip	∭	Waterfall
⛽	Petrol station/garage	○	Hot springs
🚐	Bus station etc	▲	Summit (height in metres)
🚗	Car hire	●	Other point of interest
🚲	Cycle hire/maintenance	⤛⤜	Border crossing
P	Car park	🟠	Stadium/sports facility
ℹ	Tourist information office	░░░	National park
$	Bank/ATM	░░░	Urban park
✉	Post office	▓▓▓	Glacier

Contents

HOW TO USE THIS GUIDE

PRICE CODES Throughout this guide we have used price codes to indicate the cost of those places to stay and eat listed in the guide. For a key to these price codes, see page 63 for accommodation and page 65 for restaurants.

AUTHORS' FAVOURITES Finding genuinely characterful accommodation or that unmissable off-the-beaten-track café can be difficult, so the authors have chosen a few of their favourite places throughout the country to point you in the right direction. These 'authors' favourites' are marked with a ✳.

MAPS
Keys and symbols Maps include alphabetical keys covering the locations of those places to stay, eat or drink that are featured in the book. Note that regional maps may not show all hotels and restaurants in the area: other establishments may be located in towns shown on the map.

Grids and grid references Some maps use gridlines to allow easy location of sites. Map grid references are listed in square brackets after the name of the place or site of interest in the text, with page number followed by grid number, eg: [78 C3].

AS THE CONDOR FLIES Throughout the guide we have included boxes to indicate where a town is in relation to the start and end points of the Carretera Austral (by the definition of this guide, Puerto Montt in the north and the border crossing at Villa O'Higgins in the south).

LIST OF MAPS

Most locations in this guidebook contain a physical address (street name and number) and a what3words (W3W) address. This takes the form of ///word1. word2.word3 and is equivalent to a GPS co-ordinate. W3W (w what3words. com) is a UK-based company that developed an ingenious means to identify location using combinations of three words in almost any language.

There are many advantages of using W3W over normal addresses or GPS. First, many places in southern Chile, especially hiking trails, viewpoints, turnings, volcanoes, etc, do not have a traditional address. Even locations that ought to have an address often do not – Chileans are notoriously bad at placing house numbers outside buildings! Second, it is easier to communicate a W3W address than a GPS co-ordinate. And, third, W3W addresses can be instantly scanned for navigation purposes.

The author's favourite bar along the Carretera Austral is Cirus Bar in Puerto Montt (page 90). Its address is Miradores 1177. This is fine if you happen to know where the street Miradores is, how the numbers progress, and assuming the bar displays the house number. The GPS co-ordinates are -41.476377, -72.953386. There is no need for any prior knowledge of the region to use these, but good luck communicating it with friends, and beware if you get a digit incorrect! The W3W address is ///siblings.sweeper.hobbies (///redonda. juro.agrupan in Spanish). With the app downloaded on to your phone, you can scan, dictate or type the W3W address and not only will the destination then appear on your screen, but the app can navigate you to it. Make a small error in this address – entering *sibling* (singular) instead of *siblings* (plural), and the app questions whether it really is a remote plot of desert in Western Australia you wish to visit, or Cirus Bar just a couple of miles away.

Simply go to the Play Store or App Store to download the free what3words app. The box at the top of the screen offers the three means to enter an address: type, scan or dictate. You can use the app without creating an account, but to save or import locations you must sign up, which is quick and also free. For more advanced features, visit w what3words.com.

IMPORT ALL W3W ADDRESSES IN THE GUIDEBOOK TO YOUR PHONE This feature is available only if you have created an account with W3W and must be done on a computer, *not in the app*. This imports over 500 locations, each individually labelled, corresponding to locations in the book, removing the need to manually write/scan/dictate individual addresses from the book into the app:

1. On a *computer*, go to w bradtguides.com/w3w-chile, and click on 'Chile: The Carretera Austral' to download the locations file.
2. Again on your computer, log into w what3words.com and click 'Saved locations'. Then from the 'three dots menu' select: Import lists from CSV > upload CSV > [*select downloaded file*].
3. Log into the W3W app on your phone and the locations will appear momentarily.

Introduction

The 'best road trip in the world' is an oft-heard claim, but in the case of the Carretera Austral it is well and truly justified. This book describes a road trip through one of the most magnificently scenic and diverse regions on earth. From the subtropical jungles south of Puerto Montt to glaciers of dimensions that defy belief, a new vista emerges with almost every bend along the road. Wild rivers connect the Andes with the Pacific Ocean, carving through the narrow strip of land that forms Chile, pausing only to fill lakes with every shade of blue imaginable. Alerce trees have stood guard over the region for thousands of years, towering high above the Carretera Austral. Wild guanacos serve as traffic lights, pumas are considered a pest, Andean condors glide majestically through the valleys in search of carcasses, and beyond the confines of the road itself evidence of mankind's impact is the exception rather than the rule. And yet within this wilderness it is possible to find excellent accommodation, eat fine food, and interrupt the driving with an ever-expanding range of activities. The Carretera is rapidly gaining recognition for being up there with the finest road trips in the Americas, if not worldwide. That being said, it is a challenging region to visit, and even as additional sections of the road are paved each season, it provides access to a mere sliver of southern Chile.

Bruce Chatwin's 1977 book *In Patagonia* and Paul Theroux's 1979 *The Old Patagonian Express* both fired the public's imagination for Patagonia – the end of the earth. However, much of the literature has focused on Argentine Patagonia. Chilean Patagonia's time has surely come. Along the Carretera Austral it is possible to see the vast ice fields that feed the glaciers. Apart from Antarctica and Greenland, which are hugely expensive to visit and offer limited variety in terms of terrain and the range of activities possible, the Carretera Austral is the only place where travellers can see such ice fields.

The variety of flora and fauna along the Carretera Austral warrants its own encyclopaedia, and this book merely scratches the surface of the wildlife encountered. For those interested in nature and conservation, this stretch of Chile competes with some of the flagship regions of the continent, yet it is surrounded by snow-capped mountains, as well as virgin sub-tropical forest.

In addition to its scenic beauty, the Carretera Austral is becoming an adventure activity hub. The trekking and climbing opportunities are already sufficient to keep the most avid hiker busy for multiple seasons. Horseriding, meanwhile, is so commonplace that it is considered a standard form of transport. The kayaking and rafting is world class. Keen to capitalise on the nascent tourism sector, new guides and routes spring up each season. The entire region is essentially in a permanent state of flux.

The history of this region is also fascinating. The first settlers were true pioneers, building villages in places that even a century later could hardly be described as accessible. Some of these settlers and their ancestors live in the same villages to this day. Alas, their tale is not well documented, so you should make the most of any opportunity to hear it from those who lived it while you still can.

No trip to South America is complete without visiting Patagonia, and no trip to Patagonia is complete without traversing the Carretera Austral. Northern Patagonia is a well-established and increasingly developed tourist destination – for better or worse. Southern Patagonia, less so. Regions such as Ushuaia, El Chaltén and Calafate in Argentina, and Torres del Paine and Punta Arenas in Chile, are popular destinations in the extreme south. The Carretera Austral forms a natural bridge between the two, and a route that is far more interesting than a 2-hour flight or a 50-hour bus ride across the arid Argentine steppe.

The main challenge facing visitors to the Carretera Austral is simply the lack of information. Tourism is in its infancy here. Many villages are isolated and lack internet access, while mobile-phone coverage renders communication with the outside world more limited than in other regions of South America. Natural obstacles, most obviously volcanic eruptions, occasional floods, landslides, fallen trees, relentless rain and highly changeable weather require a greater degree of flexibility among residents and visitors alike. Plan ahead as much as possible, especially ferries and accommodation in peak season, and always have a back-up plan.

The Carretera Austral is magical partly as a consequence of its isolation and lack of outside influences. But times are changing, and any trip along this route throws into sharp relief the tensions between the fast-paced, growing tourism industry and the local culture. The original settlers are being rapidly replaced by a younger generation, who have access to airplanes and internet and television. Migration to the region, from abroad and within Chile, is fundamentally altering the social fabric and culture of the area. Whether this will be to the long-term benefit or harm of the region and its local communities remains to be seen.

The region is changing so rapidly that even from one summer to the next the transformation is visible to the untrained eye. Protected by extensive national parks and natural barriers, and indeed its very location at the tip of the continent, the Carretera Austral has thus far been somewhat shielded from the trappings of economic development. Chatwin wrote of Patagonia, 'It is the farthest place to which man walked from his place of origins. It is therefore a symbol of his restlessness.' That restlessness is reflected in the curiosity, the desire for adventure and the eagerness to get off the beaten track of visitors exploring the Carretera Austral. But let's not forget Jan Lundberg's warning: 'It's hard to destroy wilderness without roads.' Visitors to this region have a responsibility to preserve it.

Since the publication of the first edition of this guide, the region has suffered natural disasters, civil unrest and most recently the Covid-19 pandemic, resulting in hundreds of bankruptcies. But Patagonia has suffered such turmoil since mankind first arrived. It is the Wild West – more savage than it initially appears. It is geologically young, still a work in progress – landslides and volcanic eruptions are normal here. In the intervening years between editions, we have witnessed tangible positive impact on the lives of many people thanks to this guide. However, we have also seen the rapid deterioration of villages such as Puerto Río Tranquilo and Caleta Tortel due directly to an influx of tourists. An over-reliance on tourism rendered many families much more vulnerable to the impact of the pandemic lockdowns than their forefathers might have been – further demonstrating the dichotomous impact of tourism. Please think about how your visit to the Carretera may be a genuine net benefit to the region.

JOIN
THE TRAVEL CLUB
THE MEMBERSHIP CLUB FOR SERIOUS TRAVELLERS
FROM BRADT GUIDES
Be inspired
Free books and our monthly e-zine, packed with travel tips and inspiration
Save money
Exclusive offers and special discounts from our favourite travel brands
Plan the trip of a lifetime
Access our exclusive concierge service and have a bespoke itinerary created for you by a Bradt author
Join here:
bradtguides.com/travelclub
Membership levels to suit all budgets
Bradt GUIDES
TRAVEL TAKEN SERIOUSLY

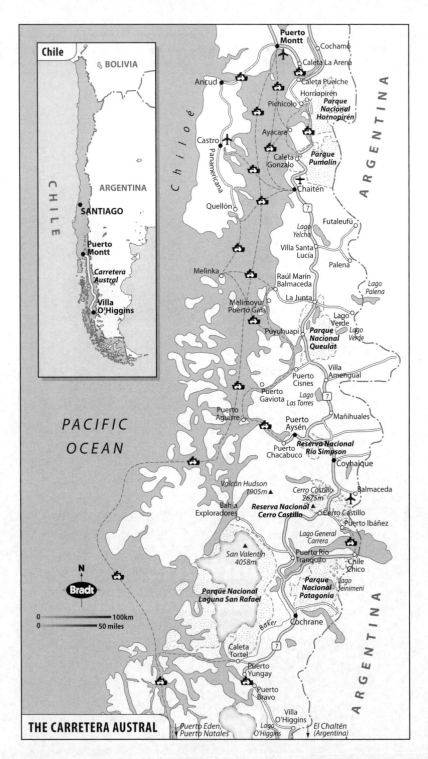

Chile

BOLIVIA

ARGENTINA

SANTIAGO

Puerto Montt

Carretera Austral

Villa O'Higgins

CHILE

ARGENTINA

PACIFIC OCEAN

Chiloé

Panamericana

Puerto Montt

Cochamó
Caleta La Arena
Caleta Puelche
Hornopirén
Parque Nacional Hornopirén

Ancud
Pichicolo

Ayacara
Castro
Caleta Gonzalo
Parque Pumalín

Chaitén
Quellón

Futaleufú
Lago Yelcho
Villa Santa Lucía
Palena

Melinka
Raúl Marín Balmaceda
Lago Palena

Melimoyu/ Puerto Gala
La Junta
Lago Verde
Lago Verde

Puyuhuapi
Parque Nacional Queulat

Villa Amengual
Puerto Cisnes
Puerto Gaviota
Lago Las Torres

Puerto Aguirre
Puerto Aysén
Mañihuales

Puerto Chacabuco
Reserva Nacional Río Simpson
Coyhaique
Balmaceda

Volcán Hudson 1905m
Cerro Castillo 2675m

Bahía Exploradores
Reserva Nacional Cerro Castillo
Cerro Castillo
Puerto Ibáñez

Lago General Carrera

San Valentín 4058m
Puerto Río Tranquilo
Chile Chico

Parque Nacional Laguna San Rafael
Parque Nacional Patagonia
Lago Jeinimeni

N
Bradt

0 ————— 100km
0 ————— 50 miles

Baker
Cochrane

Caleta Tortel
Puerto Yungay
Puerto Bravo

Villa O'Higgins
El Chaltén (Argentina)

Puerto Edén, Puerto Natales
Lago O'Higgins

ARGENTINA

THE CARRETERA AUSTRAL

Part One

GENERAL INFORMATION

Location The Carretera Austral stretches 1,270km through southern Chile, from Puerto Montt in the north to Villa O'Higgins in the south. Chile is located in the southwest of South America.

Size The total area covered by the region, provinces and communes encompassed by the Carretera Austral is 128,000km^2. The total surface area of Chile is 756,000km^2.

Climate Spanning 38° of latitude it is hard to generalise about the climate of Chile. Along the Carretera Austral the climate is mostly temperate oceanic to sub-polar oceanic, with sections of semi-arid Patagonian steppe, along the border with Argentina.

Time Chile Standard Time (GMT −3 hours) – no daylight saving time since 2015

International telephone code +56

Currency Chilean pesos ($), US$/ARG$/£ denotes US dollars/Argentine pesos/pounds sterling where appropriate

Electricity 220–240V (50Hz AC), European two-pin plugs

Exchange rate £1 = $1,096, US$1 = $898, €1 = $916 (August 2022)

Population Within the region encompassed by the Carretera Austral: 125,000; Chile: 18 million (2017 census)

Capital Aysén's capital is Coyhaique; Chile's is Santiago de Chile

Language Spanish

Religion Roman Catholic (45%), Protestant (18%), agnostic/atheist (32%), other (5%) (Encuesta Nacional Bicentenario 2019)

Flag Plain red lower half, upper half has white section to right, white star on blue background to left

Economy Mining (driven largely by copper), agriculture (including salmon, forestry and wine) and services (finance and tourism)

1

Background Information

GEOGRAPHY

The Carretera Austral, Chile's Ruta 7, stretches for more than 1,270km through rural Patagonia in southern Chile, from Puerto Montt in the north to Villa O'Higgins in the south. It encompasses an area of 128,000km^2 – about the size of Greece, or the US state of Mississippi – and covers a wide range of geographical features including vast ice fields, virgin rainforest, lofty snow-capped mountain ranges, hissing volcanoes, arid steppe and pristine rivers and lakes.

Covering a coastal strip between the Pacific Ocean to the west and the southern Andes Mountains to the east, the Valdivian temperate rainforest extends from Villarrica, north of the Carretera Austral, down to Parque Nacional Queulat, Puerto Cisnes and south (and further west) beyond Coyhaique, as far as Caleta Tortel and the Reserva Nacional Katalalixar, where the Magellanic sub-polar forest begins. Further to the west of the Carretera Austral the rainforest spreads from the Reserva Nacional Guaitecas, part of the Chonos archipelago, south of the island of Chiloé, to islands west of the Northern Ice Field in the Parque Nacional Laguna San Rafael. These islands are largely inaccessible and uninhabited.

The region also contains the entire Northern Ice Field, as well as the northernmost 100km or so of the Southern Ice Field. To the east lie the Andes and the border with Argentina. Here, relatively high mountain ranges, with border crossings typically located at historic passes, give way to desert-like areas south of Lago Verde, particularly on the border east of Coyhaique, along the road towards Paso Río Frías-Apeleg, and to the east of Parque Nacional Patagonia (hereafter referred to as Parque Patagonia), which straddles the Patagonian steppe. Chile is divided into **15 regions**. Each region is divided into provinces, and each province into communes. The Carretera Austral traverses Aysén del General Carlos Ibáñez del Campo (abbreviated to Aysén, Region XI), and parts of Los Lagos, Region X. Depending on the precise definition used, the most southern extremity of the Carretera Austral is at the border between Aysén and Magallanes y La Antártica Chilena (known as Magallanes), Region XII. To define the area around the Carretera Austral more precisely, and assuming that Puerto Montt is *not* considered part of the Carretera Austral (see box, page 4), it includes three components: the entire **region of Aysén**, plus the **province of Palena** (one of the four provinces of Los Lagos, consisting of four communes: Chaitén, Futaleufú, Hualaihué and Palena), and the single **commune of Cochamó** (one of two communes in the province of Llanquihue, itself one of the four provinces of the Los Lagos Region).

This latter addition is debatable – the common definition of the Carretera Austral may not include Cochamó, and the official Ruta 7 does not traverse the south of the Reloncaví Estuary but heads directly north to Puerto Montt. However, owing to the importance of Cochamó as a key entry point to the Carretera, the fact that Pinochet

Most documents suggest it is 1,240km from north to south, generally defining the start and end points as Puerto Montt and Villa O'Higgins respectively. However, there is a credible case to suggest that the original Carretera Austral begins at Ensenada and continues south to Hornopirén via Cochamó, Puelo and Caleta Puelche without requiring a crossing of the Reloncaví. A complete journey of the Carretera Austral also continues slightly beyond Villa O'Higgins, further complicating the matter. If you take Ensenada as your starting point the length of the journey is increased by some 55km. If you consider the start as the beginning of Ruta 7 at the southern exit of Puerto Montt, and the end as the centre of Villa O'Higgins and travel directly through the inland route to Hornopirén and follow the gravel road from just south of Mañihuales to Coyhaique, the total distance by road is 1,120km. However, this excludes three ferry crossings: from Caleta La Arena to Caleta Puelche; the longer crossing from Hornopirén to Caleta Gonzalo; and the short hop from Puerto Yungay to Río Bravo. These add up to approximately 80km, thus the total distance is around 1,200km. If one includes the final stretch to the border crossing with Argentina which adds another 70km, the grand total is 1,270km. This distance is approximately the same as Land's End to John O'Groats, Amsterdam to the French/Spanish border, or from New York to Chicago.

began construction of the Carretera in Ralún (just north of Cochamó) in 1976, and with respect to the residents of this commune who refer to their main road as 'the Northern Carretera Austral', it shall be included in our definition of the territory. Prior to the ferry connection between Caleta Puelche and Caleta La Arena, this was the only access point to the Carretera.

Most definitions of Patagonia include the regions of Aysén and Magallanes, as well as the province of Palena. The commune of Cochamó is therefore the only region considered (by the authors) as part of the Carretera Austral to lie outside the formal definition of Patagonia.

The region of Aysén is divided into the following provinces and communes:

- Aysén (capital: Puerto Aysén; communes: Aysén, Guaitecas and Cisnes)
- Capitan Prat (capital: Cochrane; communes: Cochrane, O'Higgins and Tortel)
- Coyhaique (capital: Coyhaique, also regional capital; communes: Coyhaique and Lago Verde)
- General Carrera (capital: Chile Chico; communes: Chile Chico and Río Ibáñez)

The entire **population** of these three combined areas is approximately 125,000 according to the 2017 census. The inhabitants of the Carretera Austral represent a mere 0.7% of the total population of Chile (approximately 18 million), and yet the area covers 17% of the country. Indeed, the population of the Carretera Austral is slightly under one person/km^2, on a par with Alaska (across Chile as a whole, the average population density is 22 people/km^2). In terms of global rankings, only Svalbard, Greenland and the Falkland Islands have lower population densities. Mongolia is approximately twice as densely populated as the Carretera Austral. The region is the size of England, with a population slightly lower than the London borough of Kensington and Chelsea.

Of the 128,000km² encompassing the region, approximately 87,000km² is protected, ie: just over two-thirds. Of the remaining third, much is uninhabitable thanks to its mixed terrain of mountains, swamps, lakes, etc, and large parts of non-protected territory are dedicated to farming. Thus, although this population density appears astonishingly low, the reality is that only a sliver of the Carretera Austral is inhabitable.

According to the definition used in this book the Carretera Austral stretches from 41°30'S at Puerto Montt and Cochamó to 49°00'S at Candelario Mancilla, just south of Villa O'Higgins. The **most easterly point** is Paso Río Frías-Apeleg, which is 71°06'W. The most westerly *accessible* point is either Bahía Exploradores or Caleta Tortel, at 73°30'W. However, the **most westerly point** of mainland Chile is within the province of Aysén, although not easily accessible: the Taitao Peninsula is 75°39'W, at approximately the same latitude as Puerto Río Tranquilo.

CLIMATE

The Carretera Austral has four distinct seasons. The **summer** begins in December and extends into March, although January and February are the most popular months to visit, coinciding with Chilean school holidays. Temperatures exceed 20°C in summer, and very rarely 30°C. The **winter** extends from June to September, and temperatures routinely fall below freezing. The lowest recorded temperature in Coyhaique is –15°C. **Rainfall** is abundant across most of this region, with the wettest months generally being April to August, particularly on the western coast. Puerto Cisnes and Puyuhuapi receive inordinate amounts of rain, contributing in part to the lush vegetation of the region. However, there is no month in the year where a waterproof jacket is not useful. Southern Chile is one of the rainiest regions on the planet. Annual rainfall in Puerto Cisnes, one of the wettest regions, can reach 4,000mm compared with a mere 600mm/year in London. The driest month of the year in Puerto Cisnes, February, typically receives 120mm of rain, raining every other day.

As a general rule, rainfall is lowest in February, and further to the east: Lago Verde receives an average of only 6mm of rain (three days of rain), Coyhaique perhaps double this, and Futaleufú 42mm (five days of rain). Snowfall is actually limited in the region, but it is sometimes possible to ski at the small Fraile ski resort near Coyhaique in winter.

See page 25 for more information.

NATURAL HISTORY AND CONSERVATION

FLORA AND FAUNA ALONG THE CARRETERA AUSTRAL   with James Lowen

Chilean poet Pablo Neruda once argued that 'who doesn't know the Chilean forest, doesn't know the planet'. In traversing a vast swathe of Chile dominated by wooded eco-regions, the Carretera Austral offers visitors the opportunity to gain insights into planet earth.

Much of the region lies in the floristic zone known as **Magellanic rainforest**. This comprises boggy forest dominated by evergreen broadleaf trees. Between Puerto Montt and Ventisquero San Rafael, the evergreen **Siempreverde forest** is common and contains tracts of cypress trees. East of the Carretera towards the national border lie **forests of the Patagonian Andes**. There are broadleaf trees and conifers here too, but also dwarf shrubs at the treeline. In the few areas of **Patagonian steppe**, chilly plains are dominated by grasses and stunted shrubs.

Even without deviating from the Carretera, you should see a modicum of the commoner and larger wildlife, particularly birds. But to respond properly to Neruda's encouragement, detours are advisable, mainly to protected areas scattered off-route. Helpfully for the non-expert, printed materials provided at the reserve entrances generally list the site wildlife.

In Los Lagos (Region X), try Parque Nacional Alerce Andino (a rugged montane, wooded wilderness) and Parque Pumalín (established by conservationist Doug Tompkins, where pristine forests nudge Andean glaciers, the formal name is now Parque Nacional Pumalín Douglas Tompkins). In Aysén (Region XI), key national parks and reserves include: Queulat (montane forest), Río Simpson (evergreen and deciduous forest), Parque Patagonia (Patagonian steppe, deciduous and lakeside forest), Laguna San Rafael (fjords, snowfields and mountains) and Bernardo O'Higgins (fjords, rainforests and glaciers).

Three introductory thoughts about Carretera flora and fauna. First, bear in mind that some species are unique to the region, and one conservation concern is that undiscovered species may be eradicated before they have been documented – a result of deforestation, water contamination and global warming. Second, vast sections of the region have barely been explored. There has been minimal underwater research, and some regions are barely accessible. It is possible that an entirely new species could be discovered at any bend in the road! Third, enjoy. For naturalists, travelling the Carretera Austral is an opportunity to observe wildlife that may be unique to this region, and even if the amateur cannot name the genus of the Andean condor, it is impressive when one flies overhead. Take decent boots, a pair of good binoculars, and plenty of patience. Pablo Neruda would be proud.

Land mammals Native Chilean mammals tend to be difficult to see, a legacy of nocturnal habits, scarcity and hunting-induced timidity. The Carretera's most iconic mammal is **huemul** (*Hippocamelus bisulcus*), a globally threatened Andean deer. Just 2,000 remain overall (some in Argentina), most in the region's protected areas. Your best chance of seeing it is to join a guided trek at Lago Cochrane or Reserva Nacional Tamango. You would need even greater luck to see **pudú** (*Pudu puda*), a dwarf deer that lurks in dense forests. One of South America's four camelids, **guanaco** (*Lama guanicoe*), is a leggy, elegant inhabitant of steppe plains including those at Parque Patagonia or Cerro Castillo national reserves.

Two omnivorous canids occur: **South American grey fox** (*Lycalopex griseus*) and the larger, scarcer **culpeo** (*L. culpaeus*). You could bump into either anywhere, as their habitat preferences range from arid plains to montane forests. Two felines at opposite ends of the size spectrum are only occasionally observed. **Puma** (*Felis concolor*) is widespread but rare, while the tiny, arboreal **kodkod** (*Leopardus guigna*) skulks in bamboo thickets. Two species of **hog-nosed skunk** (*Conepatus* spp.) and **lesser grison** (*Galictis cuja*) – black, white and/or grey relatives of the weasel – inhabit open or lightly wooded terrain.

Rodents scrape into double figures, and come in many forms. The largest and easiest to see is **coypu** (*Myocastor coypus*), a beaver-like animal that munches aquatic vegetation. The most striking rodent is the rabbit-like mountain **viscacha** (*Lagidium viscacia*), which inhabits rocky uplands. Should a bubbling call emanate from under your feet, it will be a **Magellanic tuco-tuco** (*Ctenomys magellanicus*), a toothy burrowing rodent of Patagonian steppes. A clear sign of their presence is holes surrounded by recently excavated soil. Two further subterranean mammals of open grasslands are big hairy **armadillo** (*Chaetophractus villosus*) and its smaller relative, the **pichi** (*Zaedyus pichiy*).

Finally, introduced mammals include **red deer** (*Cervus elaphus*), **American mink** (*Neovison vison*), **European rabbit** (*Oryctolagus cuniculus*), **brown hare** (*Lepus europaeus*) and **wild boar** (*Sus scrofa*).

Marine mammals Only the northernmost section of the Carretera Austral winds around coastal waters, so you will need to maximise opportunities for seeing marine mammals or make a dedicated detour – for example, to Chiloé, where the **blue whale** (*Balaenoptera musculus*) breeds from February to April. Closer to the Carretera, your best chance of seeing cetaceans is to take a boat to the west of Parque Pumalín, where **Peale's dolphin** (*Lagenorhynchus australis*) has been recorded. Often mistaken for a porpoise, the **Chilean dolphin** (*Cephalorhynchus eutropia*) may also be seen in this region. The common **bottlenose dolphin** (*Tursiops truncatus*) and **Risso's dolphin** (*Grampus griseus*) are abundant along the entire coastline.

South American sea lion (*Otaria flavescens*) and **South American fur seal** (*Arctocephalus australis*) both occur in Bernardo O'Higgins, although seeing them probably involves a boat trip along the Canal Baker. To distinguish the superficially similar duo, look for the latter's long pointed snout. Both sea lions and fur seals belong to the Otariidae (eared seals) and are descended from a bear-like animal – as opposed to members of the Phocidae (true seals), whose ancestors were otter-like carnivores. Talking of which… there are **marine otters** (*Lutra felina*) at Bernardo O'Higgins, as well as at Laguna San Rafael (which, along with Queulat, also hosts southern sea lion). Do not assume that every otter swimming in salty water is marine otter, however, as **southern river otter** (*Lontra provocax*) also occurs along rocky coastal shores.

Birds Of all wildlife along and around the Carretera Austral, birds are the easiest to spot. Each habitat – forest, wetland or coast – has its own distinctive suite of species. Fortunately for the novice birdwatcher, there are not too many types to try to recognise. Propitiously for the expert, several are sought-after species whose world range is concentrated on southern South America. So there's something for everyone.

Wetland birds tend to be easy to find – and identify. On freshwater lakes, look for three attractive species of **grebe**: white-tufted (*Rollandia rolland*), silvery (*Podiceps occipitalis*) and great (*P. major*). Common ducks on waterbodies include **speckled teal** (*Anas flavirostris*), **Chiloé wigeon** (*A. sibilatrix*) and **Andean duck** (*Oxyura ferruginea*), the last with its distinctive electric-blue bill and cocked tail. Two species of **steamerduck** occur: flightless (*Tachyeres pteneres*) exclusively on rocky coasts and flying (*T. patachonicus*) on both fresh and marine waters.

Larger, more elegant wildfowl comprise **coscoroba** (*Coscoroba coscoroba*) and **black-necked swans** (*Cygnus melancoryphus*). The former has a rosy, plastic-looking bill, while the latter has knobbly red caruncles adjoining its black bill. On damp fields, **black-faced ibis** (*Theristicus melanopis*) deploys its long decurved bill to rootle for insects in the soil alongside **ashy-headed** (*Chloephaga poliocephala*) and **upland geese** (*C. picta*). Nearby may be **southern lapwings** (*Vanellus chilensis*), a noisy, strikingly patterned and ubiquitous wader that often hangs out in trios during the breeding season. In boggy moorlands in particular, look for two small birds bobbing around: **dark-bellied** (*Cinclodes patagonicus*) and **bar-winged cinclodes** (*C. fuscus*).

Birds of prey vary in size from the tiny **American kestrel** (*Falco sparverius*) to the massive **Andean condor** (*Vultur gryphus*). Both are easy to recognise: the former hovers readily while the condor has enormously long, evenly broad wings that end in 'fingered' tips. Common **raptors** in between these two size extremes are southern caracara (*Caracara plancus*), chimango caracara (*Milvago chimango*), variable hawk (*Buteo polyosoma*) and turkey vulture (*Cathartes aura*), while cinereous harriers (*Circus cinereus*) ghost gracefully over marshy grasslands.

If you visit rocky coastlines, look for four species of **cormorant**, each with distinctively coloured areas of bare facial skin: red-legged (*Phalacrocorax gaimardi*), Magellan (*P. magellanicus*), guanay (*P. bougainvillii*) and imperial (*P. atriceps*). If you see a cormorant away from the coast, it will be a fifth species: Neotropic (*P. brasilianus*). Along the coast look also for **kelp gull** (*Larus dominicanus*) and the attractive **dolphin gull** (*L. scoresbii*). Should your vista include fjords or open sea at any point, perhaps in Bernardo O'Higgins, you may chance upon maritime wanderers such as **black-browed albatross** (*Thalassarche melanophrys*), **Chilean skua** (*Stercorarius chilensis*) or **Magellanic penguin** (*Spheniscus magellanicus*).

Keen birdwatchers may want to spend time tracking down avian specialities in the Magellanic forests. Fine sites include Alerce Andino, Pumalín and San Rafael. Several species are easier to hear than see, so either patience or luck is essential to get views. Tapaculos are particularly notorious for their skulking nature. **Chucao tapaculo** (*Scelorchilus rubecula*) and **black-throated huet-huet** (*Pteroptochos tarnii*) are both ventriloquists with a musical chuckle. When seen well, the former's red face and breast are uncannily reminiscent of a robin! Surprisingly tricky to locate, given its large size and bold coloration, is the **Magellanic woodpecker** (*Campephilus magellanicus*). Once located, however, these can be confiding birds. The same is true of **austral pygmy-owl** (*Glaucidium nanum*), which is usually heard before being spotted.

Forest residents that are somewhat easier to see include **striped woodpecker** (*Picoides lignarius*) and **Patagonian sierra-finch** (*Phrygilus patagonicus*). The **thorn-tailed rayadito** (*Aphrastura spinicauda*) is a smart treecreeper-like bird with a spiky tail, often seen hanging upside-down. Always heading upwards is the **white-throated treerunner** (*Pygarrhichas albogularis*). Other forest residents are the world's southernmost hummingbird, **green-backed firecrown** (*Sephanoides sephanoides*) and parrot, **austral parakeet** (*Enicognathus ferrugineus*).

While woodpeckers are traditionally associated with trees, **Chilean flickers** (*Colaptes pitius*) feed on the ground in sparsely wooded countryside. Other birds of open habitats include **austral thrush** (*Turdus falcklandii*), **southern house wren** (*Troglodytes musculus*), **austral blackbird** (*Curaeus curaeus*), **fire-eyed diucon** (*Xolmis pyrope*) and **black-chinned siskin** (*Carduelis barbatus*). A personal favourite is **tufted tit-tyrant** (*Anairetes parulus*), with its punky crest and staring eye, while one bird that is hard to miss is **rufous-collared sparrow** (*Zonotrichia capensis*).

The **ñandu** (*Rhea pennata*) is a small ostrich commonly found towards the border where the terrain is slightly less green. Ñandus are well camouflaged and prone to panic. The earliest sign of a car will prompt them to run, but often alongside the road, thus affording reasonable viewing of the flightless bird.

Reptiles and amphibians
About 15 species of reptile occur either side of the Carretera. Two-thirds are Neotropical ground **lizards** occupying the genus *Liolaemus*. These are typically 10–15cm long, cryptically patterned and covered in coarse scales. All bar two are terrestrial: painted tree lizard (*L. pictus*) and thin tree lizard (*L. tenuis*) are strikingly coloured tree-climbers that can be seen at Pumalín. The greatest diversity of *Liolaemus* is at Parque Patagonia and Bernardo O'Higgins reserves. The spiny-backed Magellanic lizard (*L. magellanicus*) is the world's most southerly reptile: look for it at Río Simpson, Parque Patagonia and Bernardo O'Higgins. If you spot a lizard with a large, triangular head in any Aysén reserves,

it will be either Darwin's (*Diplolaemus darwinii*) or the similar-looking Bibron's grumbler (*D. bibronii*). The distantly related southern grumbler (*Pristidactylus torquatus*) has a distinctive wrinkled neck-collar; it occurs at Alerce Andino. This site also marks the southernmost location for the region's sole **serpent**, Chilean slender snake (*Tachymenis chilensis*).

Of Chile's 60-odd species of **frogs and toads**, one-quarter reside in the region's damp forests. The star is Darwin's frog (*Rhinoderma darwinii*), named after the great man. Male frogs guard their eggs, then incubate them inside their vocal sac before giving birth through their mouth! Although endangered, you have a fair chance of seeing this frog at Alerce Andino, Laguna San Rafael, Queulat or Río Simpson. The amphibian's scientific name means 'rhinoceros-nosed' and refers to the distinctive, long snout protruding from the forehead. Among other oddities, any frog that appears to have two pairs of eyes will be either Chile four-eyed frog (*Pleurodema thaul*) or grey four-eyed frog (*P. bufoninum*). Look for the former at Alerce Andino and the latter at Aysén's reserves. Bumps on the hips explain the extra set of 'eyes'.

A quartet of wood frogs (*Batrachyla*) occur, none larger than 5cm. Males utter their territorial call during autumn (January–May) from secluded spots in the forest. The similar-sized Chiloé ground frog (*Eupsophus calcaratus*) inhabits wet areas in southern beech forests, including at Pumalín. Emerald forest frog (*Hylorina sylvatica*) – a verdant jewel with a vertical pupil – occurs at Alerce Andino. The five species of spiny-chest frogs (*Alsodes* spp.) favour scrubby ravines with fresh water, and are most readily encountered in Aysén. You need a close view to spot the spiny underside. The sole toad, Patagonian toad (*Chaunus variegatus*), has distinctive pale stripes on its back and flanks. Although rare, it has been recorded at Alerce Andino and Pumalín parks.

Plants The Carretera Austral provides easy access to the great temperate rainforests of southern Chile: Magellanic forest (as at Alerce Andino, Laguna San Rafael and Queulat) and Patagonian Andean forest (Río Simpson and Parque Patagonia).

The boggy Magellanic forest is dominated by the **Magellanic coigüe** (*Nothofagus betuloides*), one of three evergreen species of southern beech trees in Chile. Trees are often covered with lichens, filmy ferns and **mistletoe** (*Misodendrum* spp.). Near the treeline, stunted versions of this species grow alongside ferns, **barberry** (*Berberis* spp.) and **red crowberry** (*Empetrum rubrum*). Along the coast, Magellanic coigüe may grow with **canelo** (*Drimys winterii*). In well-drained soils, companion species include **Magellanic maitén** (*Maytenus magellanica*).

One of Chile's seven deciduous beeches, **lenga** (*Nothofagus pumilio*), predominates in the forests of the Patagonian Andes. This beautiful tree has copper-tinged leaves and can reach 40m in height. It often grows alongside another deciduous beech, **ñirre** (*N. antarctica*), a small tree with crinkled leaves that grows further south than any other tree. The scrubby forest edge can have colourful flowers such as **notro** (*Embothrium coccineum*), **calafate** (*Berberis buxifolia*) and the stately **dog orchid** (*Codonorchis lessonii*).

Two particular trees are worth making the effort to see. The first is **Patagonian cypress** (alerce; *Fitzroya cupressoides*) at Alerce Andino and Pumalín. This is the world's second-oldest living tree species and is protected wherever it grows in Chile as a 'natural monument'. The second is **Guaitecas cypress** (*Pilgerodendron uviferum*), which provides aromatic, gold-coloured timber prized by furniture-makers. It grows at San Rafael and Pumalín.

The Patagonian steppe is the realm of grasses waving in the incessant wind. Occasional bushes manage to grow, and wildflowers lend colour during spring and summer. Their number include the startlingly yellow **sisi iris** (*Sisyrinchium patagonicum*). Plants can of course grow anywhere. By far the most striking plant for many visitors, however, flourishes by the asphalt of the Carretera itself: **giant rhubarb** (*Gunnera tinctoria*). It is well named: leaves stretching more than 2m wide even obscure roadside signposts.

MAIN GLACIERS ALONG THE CARRETERA AUSTRAL While it is hard to traverse the Carretera Austral without seeing a glacier (*ventisquero*), it is a pity to visit the region and not do a specific trip to see these magnificent natural phenomena. The ventisqueros Yelcho and Queulat are two of the most accessible. Caleta Tortel lies between the Campos de Hielo Norte y Sur (the Northern and Southern ice fields), an obvious location for glacier-spotting, but entering the ice fields tends to be a specialised dedicated expedition. Local tour operators can arrange trips to the glaciers. Some are accessible directly from the Carretera Austral, often without a fee. The following list covers only those glaciers that can be readily accessed or seen from the Carretera itself (from north to south):

El Amarillo Parque Pumalín South, El Amarillo; page 132
Yelcho Between El Amarillo & Villa Santa Lucía; page 138

Queulat South of Puyuhuapi; page 185
Chico Visible from the sea by kayak in Puyuhuapi; page 185

THE ALERCE TREE

The legendary alerce tree (*Fitzroya cupressoides*), cut almost to extinction, has attained celebrity status, and can be seen in a number of isolated spots, most easily in Parque Pumalín. It is called larch, or the Patagonian cypress in English, or lahuán in Mapuche. It is the unique species within this genus of tree, and also the largest tree in South America, reaching up to 70m with a diameter of 5m, although Darwin recorded an alerce with a 12.6m diameter. In 1993 a Chilean alerce was found to be 3,622 years old. Alerces have been found in Tasmania, dated to some 35 million years old, demonstrating the connectivity between Australasia and South America. The symbiotic community formed around, and on, the alerce tree is testimony to its ecological value. In addition to its extraordinary girth, the mature alerce is notable for its vertical trunk with the first branches at great height. It grows in cooler regions and in soil of elevated acidity due to ash from volcanic eruptions.

The wood, especially when cut into small tiles, is hard-wearing, waterproof, lightweight and resistant to insects, and is a highly popular building material as a consequence. To the detriment of the survival of the species it thus became unusually valuable and was heavily harvested to the point of becoming a quasi-currency in Chiloé. Logging alerce was banned in 1976 and the tree was elevated to the status of National Monument. It is only possible to extract dead alerce trees, and only with the permission of CONAF. The value of secondhand alerce has risen accordingly, and it is still most clearly visible on Chiloé, and on churches throughout the region. The Alerce trail or Cascadas Escondidas trail in Parque Pumalín (page 136) are two of the best places to observe living alerces, looming over the other trees in the forest.

San Rafael By scheduled boat from Bahía Exploradores, near Puerto Río Tranquilo, page 211; or from Puerto Aysén, page 266
Exploradores Short trek to lookout point along the route to Bahía Exploradores; page 265
Leones Visible across the lake, detour to Lago Leones south of Puerto Río Tranquilo; page 275

Calluqueo Accessible from Cochrane; page 307
Montt & Steffen By charter boat from Caleta Tortel; page 317
O'Higgins By chartered boat from Villa O'Higgins, page 327

PARKS ALONG THE CARRETERA AUSTRAL
Chile has four main types of 'park': national parks, national reserves, national monuments, and private parks. The first three categories are managed by the state-run La Corporación Nacional Forestal (CONAF); private parks, on the other hand, are run by either private companies or, most usually, private foundations. For all practical purposes there is no major difference between these categories. **National parks** (*parques nacionales*) are generally larger, and the flora, fauna and geological formations within them do not require immediate conservation efforts but rather are protected regions. **National reserves** (*reservas nacionales*) are regions requiring special care for their susceptibility to degradation and explicit conservation efforts such as protecting the soil and threatened species are underway. **National monuments** are smaller areas with native species of flora and fauna and used for research, recreational and educational purposes. **Private parks** have their own distinct characteristics depending on the purpose of the park. Entrance fees to parks vary: some are free, including some private parks. No park costs more than US$20 per person (for entrance); camping may incur an additional charge and some incur an additional fee for crossing private land, such as Cerro Castillo.

Forests cover 17.3 million hectares of Chile, approximately 23% of the country. According to the World Bank data on terrestrial protected areas (2018), 18.5% of Chile is protected, compared with only 8.8% in neighbouring Argentina, and slightly below the average for Latin America (23.5%). However, within the region covered by the Carretera Austral this percentage is substantially higher, and most estimates suggest roughly two-thirds of the territory is protected.

The following parks, reserves and monuments are accessible from the Carretera Austral (from north to south).

Note: * indicates no public access; ** indicates that the park is not directly accessible from the Carretera Austral, but requires a boat or trekking.

Reserva Nacional Llanquihue (340km²)
Access point to the Volcán Calbuco (erupted on 22 Apr 2015).
Parque Nacional Alerce Andino (393km²)
Drive & treks to lakes, endangered alerce trees.
Parque Nacional Hornopirén (482km²) Trek to Lago Concha & on to Río Puelo.
Parque Nacional Pumalín Douglas Tompkins (3,250km²) Varied park with a wide range of treks. 2 volcanoes, abundant wildlife, alerce forests, lakes & camping.
Parque Nacional Corcovado* (2,096km²)
Reserva Nacional Futaleufú (121km²)
Endangered wildlife, treks & camping.

Reserva Nacional Lago Palena** (405km²) On Lago Palena, start/end point for Sendero de Chile trek to Lago Verde.
Reserva Nacional Lago Rosselot (127km²)
Main attraction is fishing.
Parque Nacional Queulat (1,541km²) Access point for treks to Ventisquero Queulat viewpoint, various shorter treks.
Parque Nacional Isla Magdalena** (1,576km²) Hot springs.
Parque Nacional Isla Guamblin** (106km²)
Reserva Nacional Lago Carlota** (181km²)
Reserva Nacional Lago Las Torres (165km²)
Main attraction is fishing.

CONSERVATION ISSUES IN THE CARRETERA AUSTRAL

Mankind's inevitable impact on the natural environment is often facilitated by the construction of roads as a principal means of access, and the Carretera Austral is no exception. While pristine untouched nature abounds along the Carretera, the impression of man is equally visible. Obvious examples include roads and buildings, land cleared for farming, electricity pylons, and pollution (limited mostly to Coyhaique in winter). Less obvious threats also exist, often with far-reaching implications.

One such threat is **fish farming**. After Norway, Chile is the second-largest trout and salmon farmer in the world and, from Puerto Montt to the deep south, these farms are prevalent. Aesthetically alone, the floating cages, farming structures and associated debris of the industry disfigure many a view across the region. However, more importantly, the chemicals (pesticides, antibiotics, disinfectants) used in fish farming pollute rivers and lakes, rendering water unfit for consumption and damaging precious aquatic and marine habitats. The government body responsible for regulating the industry, Sernapesca, has been largely ineffective in preventing this contamination over the last three decades. Fines for violating regulations are trivially small and zoning laws have proved ineffective.

The international NGO Oceana (w oceana.org) is active in campaigning against chemical-led industrialised salmon farming, but you can do your bit: if you're eating salmon along the Carretera Austral, be sure to ask if it is natural/river caught or bred artificially before deciding what to order. It is worth tasting both simply to compare the difference.

Reserva Nacional Trapananda (23km²) Small park close to Coyhaique, treks through protected lenga forest.

Reserva Nacional Río Simpson (405km²) Riverside treks & camping, close to Coyhaique.

Parque Aikén (private) (3km²) Small park close to Puerto Aysén, short treks & birdwatching.

Cinco Hermanas National Monument** (2km2) Hot springs.

Reserva Nacional Coyhaique (22km²) Treks of various lengths, close to Coyhaique.

Two Lakes Natural Monument (2km²) A small park containing short treks, lakes & ample birdwatching opportunities, close to Coyhaique.

Reserva Nacional Cerro Castillo (1,797km²) Some of the finest trekking along the Carretera Austral.

Parque Natural Cumbre de Cipreses (private) (13km²) Small park along Exploradores detour, amazing history & view of glacier.

Parque Nacional Laguna San Rafael (17,420km²) A vast park containing the entire Northern Ice Field; main access points are Puerto Río Tranquilo or Puerto Aysén for Ventisquero San Rafael, or further south to Ventisquero Leones.

Reserva Nacional Las Guaitecas** (10,980km²)

Reserva Nacional Lago General Carrera (1,784km²) The main lake along the Carretera Austral, & the largest in Chile.

Parque Nacional Patagonia (3,045km²) Major park formed by the merger of Reserva Nacional Jeinimeni to the south of Chile Chico & Reserva Tamango north of Cochrane with the former Parque Patagonia (also known as Chacabuco Valley) donated to the state by Tompkins Conservation in 2018. Extensive treks, wildlife & birdwatching, spanning forest, mountain, lakes & steppe.

Reserva Nacional Katalalixar** (6,245km²) A large, rarely visited park accessible by boat from Caleta Tortel, evergreen forest & abundant flora & fauna.

Parque Nacional Bernardo O'Higgins (35,259km²) Home of the Ventisquero O'Higgins, challenging treks, entry/exit point to El Chaltén (Argentina).

Forestry is also big business. It has been estimated that two-thirds of native forest in southern Chile has been lost through logging. Deforestation began with the arrival of settlers in the early 19th century, often utilising slash-and-burn policies to clear land for agriculture, the evidence of which can be seen to this day, particularly around Coyhaique. However, the **National Forest Corporation** or **CONAF** (Corporación Nacional Forestal; w conaf.cl) – a Chilean non-profit organisation funded and overseen by the Ministry of Agriculture – has worked hard since 1972 to develop and sustain the country's forest resources. Reforestation initiatives have seen exotic pine species rather than local species planted across the region because they are fast growing and can more quickly protect the land from soil erosion. CONAF is also responsible for Chile's national parks and for fire control within the parks and reserves.

A contentious issue in the region was the proposed **damming of the rivers Baker and Pascua**, which sparked passionate protests and debates from interested parties. The project was eventually dropped in 2017 (see box, page 220).

Beyond CONAF and the work of NGOs, the care of southern Chile's precious ecosystem has so far been left to dedicated individuals such as Doug and Kris Tompkins who have, at times, provoked negative reactions locally, although there is no denying the vast impact of their ambitious conservation projects in the protection of one of the world's last great wildernesses (page 134).

The most basic conservation axiom is applicable to all visitors to the region: take only photos, leave only footprints.

HISTORY OF THE CARRETERA AUSTRAL – AN OVERVIEW

The history of the Carretera Austral can be divided into four distinct periods: prior to the 1973 coup d'état, when the region was isolated, undeveloped and disconnected from mainland Chile; during the Pinochet regime, when the majority of the Carretera Austral was constructed; the years following the dictatorship when work continued (though at a more leisurely pace); and the current day, perhaps the most important and challenging stage in the evolution of the Carretera Austral.

PRE-PINOCHET Previously the most popular theory of the widespread human population of the Americas was that humans crossed the Bering Strait, a land bridge that formed between Russia and Alaska as a result of low sea levels, sometime after 13,000BC. Prior to this, the Cordilleran Glacier would have prevented the crossing. However, in Monte Verde, near Puerto Montt, radiocarbon dating revealed evidence of human settlement from at least 14,500BC, which radically altered scientific opinion. The current theory is that humans sailed from Asia to North America, surviving on marine food alone. The tribes that developed in the Carretera Austral, most notably the Mapuche, lived unmolested by powerful civilisations such as the Incas, who were halted as far north as Santiago, and continued to reside undisturbed in Patagonia. Evidence of other tribes, such as the Tehuelches, Aónikenk and Kawésqar, is abundant in various archaeological sites scattered along the Carretera. These tribes maintained their hunter-gatherer lifestyle until the arrival of the Spanish, when the combination of European diseases and conflict with the invaders led to their eventual demise.

The first record of a European visiting southern Chile was in 1520, when Ferdinand Magellan christened the region Patagonia, referring to the indigenous residents as Patagones (meaning 'large-footed'). The first wave of German settlers to southern Chile (around Lago Llanquihue) arrived in 1848, and monuments to these pioneers are visible in Puerto Montt, Frutillar and Puerto Varas. In 1899 Hans Steffen explored the region of Aysén, documenting the potential opportunities for settlement, as well as naming the Río Baker. He also described the Valle Chacabuco (now Parque Patagonia), a rare east–west valley that had been used by the indigenous population for millennia, and would become a key access point to the region for Argentine settlers, explorers and livestock. William Norris used this corridor in the development of what is now Caleta Tortel (see box, page 312).

In 1927 President Carlos Ibáñez del Campo initiated a formal settling process in Aysén, and throughout the early 20th century a number of concessions and lands were granted to private individuals. However, potential land reforms threatened the ruling elite, eventually leading to a coup d'état.

In the early 1900s, progress on the Carretera Austral occurred at a glacial pace and the region was better connected to Argentina than to Chile. One of the first documented accounts of road construction in the region took place as early as 1904. The SIA (Aysén Industrial Company; page 213) built a road from Puerto Aysén to Coyhaique by hand and required 100,000 coigüe tree-trunks cut in half to traverse the swampy sections. It could take weeks to travel this section, which nowadays takes less than an hour.

As early as the 1940s it was possible to drive from Coyhaique to Balmaceda, and by the 1950s this stretch of road had been extended to Puerto Ibáñez and Villa Cerro Castillo. In the 1960s the section between El Maitén to Cochrane was

ALLENDE AND PINOCHET

Salvador Allende became president in 1970 and was the first ever freely elected Marxist, arousing concerns not only among the Chilean elite but also in the USA. In addition to land reforms, he nationalised a number of companies and re-established communication and trade with Cuba and China. However, by 1972 the economy was in crisis, partly as a result of socialist reforms which had slowed production and frozen prices while increasing wages. The banking sector was gradually nationalised, as was access to natural resources. As the economy stagnated the CIA began inserting secret operatives into Chile, and the Supreme Court denounced Allende for the havoc he had caused. In a failed military coup in June 1973, former army commander Carlos Prats was forced to resign as interior minister, and Allende installed Augusto Pinochet as army commander on 23 August that year.

A month later a successful coup ousted Allende. It is still not known whether Allende killed himself or was murdered, but Pinochet seized power. Henry Kissinger eventually admitted that the USA had assisted the coup. Pinochet changed his title to president in December 1974, and ruled until 1989. In what was likely a rigged election, Pinochet won a plebiscite in 1980 and launched a new constitution. However, the next plebiscite, in 1989, was less successful. According to the Mayor of Puerto Cisnes, Eugenia Pirzio Biroli, this was due to Pinochet selecting a date poorly aligned with the stars. Pinochet was a firm believer in astrology, but failed to consult Eugenia on this occasion (page 186).

completed, and the trail to Argentina through the Valle Chacabuco (now Parque Patagonia, to Paso Roballos) had been used since the early 20th century.

By 1968, the construction of the President Ibáñez Bridge in Puerto Aysén vastly improved travel between Puerto Aysén and Coyhaique. The road north of Coyhaique extended as far as Mañihuales. Puyuhuapi had built sections of what was to become the Carretera Austral to facilitate the transport of animals. A ferry connection between Puerto Ibáñez and Puerto Guadal, close to Cruce El Maitén, facilitated transport across the lake prior to the road around the north of the lake via Puerto Río Tranquilo. Prior to 1973 Chilean governments had made half-hearted attempts to complete sections of the Carretera, but in practice these were isolated sections of road.

PINOCHET (1973–90) Pinochet seized power from Salvador Allende in a military coup on 11 September 1973, and embarked on the project to complete the Carretera Austral three years later. Quite what motivated the president is uncertain. Connecting remote regions of Chile to the 'mainland' was important, and was used as the principal justification for the massive investment. However, concern over encroachments from Argentina in ongoing territorial disputes was also a factor. In 1982 Argentina invaded the Falklands and Pinochet was quick to support the British, and in particular his personal friend Margaret Thatcher, irritating his neighbour enormously. There was a valid reason to construct a road capable of supporting troop deployments in the case of an Argentine invasion, and this no doubt influenced Pinochet.

Over the next decade and a half, employing 10,000 members of the Cuerpo Militar de Trabajo (CMT) (the Military Workforce) and a similar number of civilians, Pinochet embarked on one of the most ambitious infrastructure projects in South America. His critics mocked the idea, suggesting it was of no use to the people, was economically unviable, and that the Aysén Province was bankrupt.

Between 1979 and 1982 the road from Puerto Cisnes to Mañihuales was completed, facilitated in part by the close friendship between Pinochet and the Mayor of Puerto Cisnes, Eugenia Pirzio Biroli (page 186). Futaleufú was finally connected to the Carretera Austral in 1980, up until which point its only terrestrial connection was with Argentina. By 1982 the Carretera extended from Chaitén to Coyhaique, some 420km.

Between 1980 and 1988 the section from Villa Cerro Castillo to Bahía Murta, Puerto Río Tranquilo and to Cruce El Maitén was completed, and by late 1988 it had extended as far south as Cochrane. This was of fundamental strategic importance, reducing dependence upon the ferry between Puerto Ibáñez and Puerto Guadal, and also offering uninterrupted terrestrial access between Chaitén and Cochrane. By some definitions the Carretera Austral, as we know it today, was largely completed by 1988. Meanwhile, further north, from 1982 to 1992 the trunk road from La Junta to Lago Verde was constructed, presumably to provide a connection to Argentina. Chile is still waiting for Argentina to construct a bridge over the Río Pico – until then this border remains largely useless.

Villa Santa Lucía was an important camp, as this junction acted as a hub for construction north towards Chaitén, south towards La Junta, and east towards Futaleufú, Palena and the Argentine border. It was named after Pinochet's wife, Lucía Hiriart. To encourage workers to develop a small village they were entitled to buy land at one Chilean peso per square metre. Some of the original settlers continue to live in the region.

A project of this scale came at a cost. In financial terms, this has been estimated at US$300 million – some 3km of bridges were constructed, over 4 million cubic metres of rubble were removed, and 8 million cubic metres of rock was blasted,

1

using some 500,000kg of explosives. This was a vast sum for a relatively poor nation in the 1970s and 80s; by comparison, this was a third as much as the cost of constructing the Santiago subway. However, there were costs beyond the financial. Conditions for the labourers bordered on slavery: workers were entitled to ten days of rest for every three months worked, camps were primitive with mud floors and no services despite freezing temperatures. Construction was completed with minimal machinery, mostly by hand, and at least 25 lives were lost. In February 1995, five members of the CMT were killed when 60,000m^3 of rock and mud fell on them in the sector Vagabundo just north of Puerto Yungay.

It's perhaps curious to note that despite the widely held belief that the Carretera Austral begins (or ends) in Puerto Montt, Ralún was included in Pinochet's initial plans for the road, supporting the case that this northeastern section of the Carretera, even now referred to as 'the Northern Carretera Austral', should indeed be considered the road's starting point equally alongside Puerto Montt.

Criticism of the Pinochet years is rife, and there is no excusing the brutal actions taken by the military dictatorship (see box, page 18). However, such atrocities were rare in the south, and pro-Pinochet sentiment echoes to this day. Consider the words of one of the founders of Puyuhuapi, Walter Hopperdietzel, with relation to the arrival of the Carretera Austral (*Ercilla* magazine, 11 October 1989, page 28):

> We used to travel by boat to get anywhere. This change has brought tremendous development for agriculture. Then came electricity, allowing us to have refrigerators to store perishable foods. This affects the welfare and health of the population. And now this [referring to the telephone], which has allowed us to speak and with our family in Santiago and Germany. I had not seen any deputy or senator here. However, during this time President Pinochet visited four times. We know each other, and when he comes, he greets me by name. I consider myself as his friend and that's a very nice thing.

The Bishop of Aysén, Monsignor Bernardo Cazzaro, wrote on 5 March 1988:

> Mr. President, I should like to thank you in my capacity as a Chilean for the contribution that you and your Government have given this land. We have seen tangible progress. As a foreign priest we have lived here for many years and seen many hardships, isolation and neglect. We are grateful first to God and then to the instruments that He has used to promote progress in the region.

While the Carretera Austral was largely built by Pinochet, and was initially named after him, only two monuments reflect his accomplishment: one in La Junta and another in Puerto Yungay. Chile may attempt to rewrite its history (and rename the road as the Carretera Austral, or Ruta 7), but to some of the more elderly residents of the region, it will always be Pinochet's Highway. For those interested in learning more, *The Dictator's Highway* by Justin Walker (page 346) is well worth a read.

POST-PINOCHET (1991 TO PRESENT DAY) The road south of Cochrane started in 1990, reaching Puerto Yungay in 1996. Initially it was hoped to connect Villa O'Higgins without recourse to a ferry, but this proved impossible. The last 100km to the current end of the Carretera Austral opened in September 2000, with a 13km ferry connection between Puerto Yungay and Río Bravo (the ferry is named after Father Ronchi; see box, page 161).

The road along the south of Lago General Carrera to Chile Chico was completed in 1991. The following year were completed over the rivers Palena and Rosselot, near La Junta.

The offshoot to Caleta Tortel was finished in 2003, shortly after Prince William completed his voluntary project in the village (page 310). In 2007 the Ministry of Public Works decided to pave Chaitén to Coyhaique, aiming to complete this by 2016, and in early 2022 only a few segments remained unpaved. Raúl Marín Balmaceda was connected to the Carretera Austral in 2009, 120 years after the village was founded, and would provide access from the Pacific to Argentina, were Argentina to complete the crucial bridge required to enter the country at Lago Verde. Perhaps the most important addition to the Carretera Austral is the ferry (pedestrian and vehicular) between Puerto Yungay/Caleta Tortel and Puerto Natales that began operating in late 2016, shortly after the first edition of this guidebook was published. This enables vehicular travel throughout the length of Chile without having to pass through Argentina.

Certainly it was important, and no trivial task, to connect Villa O'Higgins with the Carretera Austral. It is now possible to drive from Puerto Montt to Villa O'Higgins in perhaps three days, requiring the use of three or four ferries, a feat that would have seemed unimaginable prior to Pinochet, and has had a profound impact on the region. Those who were once isolated, who perhaps had stronger ties with Argentina than to their own national capital, are now part of a united country with better access to public services, although some tensions between Aysén and the Metropolitan region do still exist (see box, page 220).

One should not exaggerate the work that Pinochet accomplished – sections of the Carretera were already in place prior to 1973, and his methods were not necessarily in strict accordance with 21st-century health and safety standards. But to deny that progress occurred as a result of Pinochet's bold vision is a myopic view shared by few who actually live in the region.

FUTURE PLANS Perhaps the most important and challenging stage in the evolution of the Carretera Austral lies ahead. Logistically (and literally) two major 'gaps' still require bridging. The first is between Hornopirén and Caleta Gonzalo, where the land in between is largely contained within Parque Pumalín. The 10km road between Fiordo Largo and Leptepú is already complete, as is the 35km section south of Hornopirén, up to Pichanco, just north of Fiordo Quintupeu. The 22km stretches between Leptepú and Huinay, and between Fiordo Largo and Caleta Gonzalo, are feasible but incomplete.

The problem is how to cross the Cahuelmó and Quintupeu fjords between Huinay and Pichanco. As the condor flies, this is only 25km, but completing this section in an environmentally sustainable way will be expensive and complicated. A viable alternative is to improve the ferry service that currently traverses this section, which would be far quicker and cheaper to implement, and have a reduced environmental impact (see box, page 124).

The gravel road from the southern edge of Lago Tagua Tagua (V-725) has now been extended all the way to Segundo Coral, and is within spitting distance of the manned border. A pedestrian-only boat takes visitors across Lago Puelo into Argentina just south of El Bolsón. The main obstacle to completing a vehicular crossing is that the Argentine side is within a national park (see box, page 124). Further south, the Ruta de los Troperos hiking trail between Lago Verde and Villa La Tapera has been converted into a gravel road suitable only for 4x4s in summer. This provides an alternative route around the Queulat Pass, and should be fully

Pinochet was accused of employing a number of oppressive and barbaric tactics during his 16-year rule, perhaps the most notorious of which was the Caravan of Death – a Chilean army death squad that tortured and executed at least 75 people shortly after the coup in September 1973. Precise numbers are unknown, but it is estimated that during the dictatorship, up to 3,000 were executed, 30,000 were tortured and 80,000 were interned.

Pinochet was also a central player in Operation Condor, a campaign carried out by right-wing dictatorships of South America (and backed by the US) for political repression against claimed communists and those willing to oppose governments. Under this operation a number of critics of the Pinochet dictatorship were assassinated, including in Argentina, Italy and the US.

The first attempt to arrest Pinochet for human rights violations came in 1994 by Amnesty International, but this was unsuccessful. In 1998 Pinochet retired from the army, and was arrested in the UK on 16 October while seeking medical treatment. He had been indicted by Spanish magistrate Baltasar Garzón on the grounds of torture of Spanish citizens, the assassination of a Spanish diplomat, and conspiracy to commit torture. The Pope, Margaret Thatcher and the Archbishop of Canterbury leapt to his defence. Pinochet had powerful friends in the UK, having supported the British in the Falklands War: he had allowed British planes to fly under the Chilean flag, and provided military intelligence and radar surveillance to the British, enabling them to anticipate pending attacks from Argentina's military base in Comodoro Rivadavia. Pinochet claimed immunity as a former head of state but this was eventually overturned by the House of Lords on the basis that crimes such as torture were beyond immunity and that Pinochet should be extradited to Spain. Then Home Secretary Jack Straw disagreed, and allowed Pinochet to return to Chile on the grounds of ill-health.

In Chile, Pinochet was initially granted immunity from prosecution, but this was subsequently lifted. He was indicted in late 2000, but evaded prosecution on health grounds. In 2004 he was placed under house arrest and indicted once again, only to see his immunity from prosecution restored by the Supreme Court. He was eventually charged with kidnapping, torture and one murder, but died of heart failure on 10 December 2006 having never faced a conviction. He had also been accused of tax fraud, bribery and illegal arms trades.

Many of the ageing perpetrators of the atrocities are taking their secrets to the grave. It is unlikely that the full magnitude of the murky occurrences of the 1970s will ever come to light, and the extent to which Pinochet ordered specific assassinations may never be known. Many Chileans prefer to consider this a closed chapter, particularly in the south, which was relatively spared the human rights abuses carried out during this period.

accessible to vehicles in a few years. There are rumours of a planned road between Futaleufú and El Amarillo, a route currently only passable by horse.

Perhaps optimistically, it was hoped that the entire Carretera Austral would be paved by 2018, leaving just one gap remaining: there is no means to reach Magallanes Province by land from mainland Chile – the only options were to fly or to travel via Argentina. The three southernmost border crossings around Villa

O'Higgins are impassable by vehicle, thus the only vehicular access was via Paso Roballos close to Cochrane, then heading south to the Don Guillermo crossing just north of Puerto Natales (700km by road). While parts of the Carretera remain unpaved, particularly south of Cerro Castillo, and the long-promised fibre-optic cable has not yet arrived (although internet coverage has improved in recent years), a ferry connecting Puerto Yungay (vehicles) and Caleta Tortel (pedestrians) with Puerto Natales in Magallanes Province now connects Aysén to the extreme south, sparing Chileans the indignity of travelling via Argentina.

The biggest challenge of all is, of course, how to truly complete the Carretera Austral while preserving the unique nature and culture of this region – improved ferry services seem the obvious choice.

GOVERNMENT AND POLITICS

Chile is a representative democratic republic. The president is both head of state and head of government. The two predominant political alliances are Chile Vamos (currently governing, 2022) and the Force of the Majority. The recent and former president Sebastián Piñera is from the centre-right National Renewal Party, and is one of the richest people in Chile. On 20 December 2021 the 35-year-old former student leader Gabriel Boric won the election with a convincing 56% of the vote, defeating his ultra-conservative opponent, José Antonio Kast. He was sworn in on 11 March 2022. This marks a dramatic change for Chile, where right-wing governments have dominated since the 1973 coup d'état. Boric's campaign centred around reducing inequality, a green agenda and promises to tackle the privileges enjoyed by a small minority.

Legislative power is exercised by the government and two chambers of the National Congress: the Senate, with 38 elected members serving eight-year terms; and the Chamber of Deputies, with 120 members serving four-year terms. The judiciary is independent. The Constitution was approved in the 1980 plebiscite under Pinochet, with minor amendments since.

Presidents may not serve consecutive terms, but non-consecutive terms are not limited. The president is selected by direct public vote, with a runoff election if no candidate obtains an absolute majority. Each political party presents one candidate for president.

Universal suffrage was instigated in 1970. From 1949 to 1970 only literate men and women over 21 years of age could vote. From 1934 to 1949 literate women over the age of 25 had been allowed to vote, but only in local elections.

Chile had compulsory voting until 2009. Voter turnout in the 2013 election was approximately half that of previous elections since World War II, and slightly lower in the 2017 election.

ECONOMY

NATIONAL ECONOMY Chile's economy is healthy – its main challenge is a chronic inequality in the distribution of income and wealth. GDP in 2019 was US$294 billion, making it the fifth-largest economy in Latin America after Argentina, Brazil, Colombia and Mexico. GDP growth is currently 4%. In terms of GDP per head Chile competes only with Panama and Uruguay for the number-one slot. Historically Chile has been the 'poor brother' of Argentina, but fortunes reversed in the early 21st century and it appears unlikely that Argentina will overtake Chile anytime soon, fundamentally altering the attitudes between the two nationalities.

1

Inflation is under 3%, while Argentina enjoys one of the highest inflation rates on earth. Unemployment is 7% and fairly stable. According to Transparency International, Chile is ranked 26 in the world, three places behind the USA. Meanwhile its neighbour, Argentina, is ranked 66, one place behind Belarus. In terms of absolute poverty, according to the *CIA Factbook* 14.4% of Chile's population lived below the poverty line in 2013, the lowest in Latin America. However, according to the World Bank the percentage is slightly higher, and Uruguay and Brazil are at similar if not lower levels. The Human Development Index is perhaps a more all-encompassing measure of national welfare, and data for 2019 suggests that Chile is the most developed Latin American nation, on a par with Croatia. Civil unrest in recent years has been fuelled by the inequality of income and wealth in Chile as opposed to the absolute average levels. While Chile does have the highest inequality of any OECD member, according to the World Bank Gini coefficient it is not markedly different from that of Colombia, Panama, Honduras, Costa Rica, Guatemala, Paraguay, Brazil or Venezuela. However, quality of education is a recurring source of discontent, with Chile routinely scoring among the lowest of the OECD countries by any metric.

Copper is by far the largest driver of the economy, accounting for 15% of GDP and 54% of exports. Chile is also the second-largest **salmon farmer** in the world after Norway, producing approximately one-third of world demand, and accounting for 3.7% of national exports (see box, page 12).

In South America, only Brazil and Argentina exceed Chile in visitor numbers, and Chile has consistently been ranked in the top five adventure tourism destinations worldwide (for developing countries) since 2008.

However, not all is rosy in the Chilean economy. Copper production is energy-hungry, and Chile is energy-poor (page 220). This has sparked some of the greatest civil unrest in recent years, as some political and business sectors view the southern region as ripe for hydro-electric development and extractive industries, often with scant regard for the environmental impact or the views of local residents.

REGIONAL ECONOMY The **principal economic activities** in this region are livestock, forestry, mining, fishing, tourism and a small amount of agriculture. Owing to the adverse weather conditions for much of the year only a relatively small share of the region is suitable for growing crops, mainly around Coyhaique, Chile Chico and Puerto Ibáñez. GDP per head is approximately US$14,000, slightly below the Chilean average of US$15,500 but certainly not the poorest region in Chile. However, such statistics are likely to be biased in a region where much production is used for local domestic consumption and not necessarily captured in national statistics. Living costs are also higher along the Carretera Austral compared with better-connected regions of Chile to the north.

According to statistics from the Central Bank of Chile (2013), the largest single contributor to regional GDP was the public sector, at 22.2% of total output. Mining accounted for 16.8%, construction for 14%, and 'education, health and other services' for 12.5%. Fishing accounted for only 8.2% despite accounting for nearly 80% of all salmon produced in Chile, while 'commercial, restaurants and hotels' – a proxy for tourism – accounted for 6.1%. The principal commodities mined include zinc, gold and silver. **Tourism** is growing in importance in Chile, and with the recent improvements to the Carretera Austral this is likely to continue. Tensions run extremely high regarding the exploitation of natural resources in Aysén, and this came to a head in 2012 with the protests over damming the Baker and Pascua rivers (see box, page 220). Tourism is seen as both an alternative source of revenue and an opportunity to persuade the Chilean government not to flood vast sections of this pristine landscape in order to produce electricity.

PEOPLE AND CULTURE

Broadly speaking, the **inhabitants** of Aysén fall into four groups. First, those who have never lived elsewhere, including some that trace their ancestry to the indigenous populations, now largely vanished. Second, well-established families who migrated to the region between the mid 19th century and mid 20th century, including a large number of Germans, but also Belgians (around Chile Chico) and lesser numbers from other European countries. Third, those whose families live on both sides of the Chile–Argentina border, particularly in the south where migration between the countries has blurred the distinction between the two nationalities. There is less animosity here between nationalities and customs are shared, for example, drinking *mate* and the common usage of certain Argentine colloquialisms around the Aysén border regions.

Finally, a number of relatively recent immigrants, both from other parts of Chile and further afield, have arrived in the region around the Carretera Austral – a trend that is likely to increase. Many new hotels and businesses emerge each year largely owned by people not originally from the region seeking to escape the rat race and take advantage of the potential for tourism in this area. In addition, the ongoing economic crisis in Argentina has prompted a number of Argentines to look for employment opportunities across the border.

Chile is generally considered a **conservative** country. Some 45% of the population are Catholic, 18% are Protestant, 32% are atheist or agnostic, and 5% are other. Prior to 2017, Chile's abortion laws were considered some of the most restrictive in the world, with abortion being entirely illegal without exception, including when the mother's life is in danger. Abortion is now permitted under three circumstances: when the mother's life is at risk, when the foetus will not survive the pregnancy, or within the first 12 weeks in the case of rape. Divorce was legalised only in 2004. However, things are changing, and Chile is one of few Latin American countries to permit same-sex marriages (April 2015).

Women were permitted to vote in municipal elections in 1931, and in national elections in 1949. Female participation rates in the workforce are low by Latin American standards. However, according to the 2019 UN Gender Inequality Index Chile is the least unequal country in Latin America, ranked 55 in the world. Chile is one of relatively few countries in the world to have had a female president (Michelle Bachelet, 2006–10 and 2014–18).

Despite Chile blurring the distinction between developed and developing nation, **education** remains a serious weakness within the country, prompting the civil unrest of recent years. Many of the riots in Coyhaique that began with the Patagonia Chilena ¡Sin Represas! movement (page 220) were subsumed by broader social concerns, and in particular education. Chile's education is considered one of the most commoditised in the world and, in terms of purchasing power, the cost of tertiary education in Chile is the highest in the world. Within the OECD, Chile has among the lowest university enrolment rates and proportion of students eventually graduating, as well as one of the smaller shares of GDP invested in education. A negligible number of foreign students attend Chilean universities. Pinochet began to dismantle free universal education in the 1970s, and the trend continued with subsequent governments, and has only been partially reversed by the recent Bachelet and Piñera governments. Less than two-fifths of children attend increasingly impoverished state schools, which accounted for 80% of all education in 1980. Private schools dominate at all levels. In no other country in Latin America do students receive the education their parents can afford, as in Chile. More than two-fifths of students, mainly from poorer areas, do not complete high school. Even public universities charge substantial tuition fees, although accounting for only one-fifth of tertiary education. The best universities in Chile are essentially inaccessible to all but the elite. The Pontificia University, University of Chile, University of Santiago and University of Concepcion consistently score within the top ten best universities in all of Latin America, for those who can afford it.

Chile has, by far and away, the most unequal distribution of income within the OECD. The richest 1% earn 23.7% of the income (compared with 11.7% in the UK). Critics of the education sector claim that this inequality is enshrined in an elitist education system, and suggest former president Bachelet's reforms merely scratched the surface of this societal problem. They call for a complete renationalisation of the education sector. Meanwhile, conservatives are content with the current system, which ensures a smooth transition into top jobs for their children.

Chile has a rich culture, particularly in the **arts**. Famous authors include Pablo Neruda, Gabriela Mistral, Isabel Allende and Luis Sepúlveda. World-class artists include Roberto Matta, Carlos Sotomayor, Claudio Bravo and Camilo Mori. Chilean cinematographer Claudio Miranda was nominated for an Academy Award in 2008 for *The Curious Case of Benjamin Button* and won the award in 2012 for *Life of Pi. Bear Story* rightfully won the Academy Award for best animated short in 2015. It is a moving portrayal of life under the military dictatorship, explaining some of the traits visible in Chilean culture to this day (page 346). *A Fantastic Woman* won best foreign-language film in 2017. The excellent 2001 film *La Fiebre del Loco* is one of the very few movies set not only within the region of the Carretera Austral, but also on the lesser-known island of Puerto Gala (see box, page 337; also page 346).

Chile boasts two Nobel Laureates, both poets and both for literature: Gabriela Mistral (1945) and Pablo Neruda (1971). The award-winning Italian film *Il Postino* (1994) portrays the fictional friendship between Neruda and his local postman on a small Italian island. Co-writer and star Massimo Troisi postponed heart surgery in order to complete the film, and died of a heart attack the day after shooting ended.

Football is taken extremely seriously in Chile, and it is worth having some basic facts to hand. First, avoid discussion of the 2018 World Cup as Chile did not qualify: they were eliminated by Brazil at the knockout stage in the 2014 World Cup. It is generally safer to focus on the regional Copa América, which Chile won in 2015 and 2016. Chile's main football rivals are Argentina (as with most things) and Peru (a legacy of the 1884 War of the Pacific).

After football, the most popular sport is rodeo. To the untrained eye this appears to be a rather repetitive sport involving two gauchos chasing a young cow around in circles and trying to pin it to a large cushion, scoring points for the precise manner in which the bovine is eventually trapped. Rodeos along the Carretera Austral take place in January and February, and are worth watching, if only for the parties that take place afterwards, with elaborate dancing, stamping of feet and drinking.

Chile has never won a medal at the Winter Olympic Games, but has won two Summer Olympic gold medals, both in tennis, both in 2004 (men's singles and doubles).

LANGUAGE

With the exception of a dozen Kawésqar-speakers, Spanish dominates southern Chile. In February 2022 the last living Yagán-speaker, Cristina Calderón, died aged 93. In Puerto Montt and some isolated spots further south such as Puyuhuapi, German is fairly common. English is now mandatory in high school, and thus younger inhabitants are likely to have a basic grasp of English. Otherwise, unless working in upmarket hotels or with tour operators, assume that most people will not speak English. For a description of linguistic etiquette, see page 72. For some unique Chilean words encountered in this region, see box, page 341.

2

Planning

WHEN TO VISIT

The Carretera Austral extends from approximately 41°S to 49°S, and as such suffers cold and extended winters (June–September) and surprisingly warm summers (December–March). Hours of daylight in Coyhaique, approximately midway along the Carretera, range from 9 hours in June to 15 hours in December. Snow is less common on the western side of the Andes, but precipitation is notably higher in winter. However, the coastal region of the Carretera is notoriously wet throughout the year. Puerto Cisnes suffers approximately 4,000mm of annual rainfall.

The **peak summer** season, when most tourists visit, is January and February, when most of the festivals take place. It can be hard to book ferries in these months, and hotels fill up, so it is worth booking in advance. The ideal time to visit is possibly from mid-October until the end of the year, or in March or April when the Chilean school holidays end, as during this time there are fewer tourists, less traffic, lower prices and decent weather. October and April are the earliest and latest times when the Carretera is readily accessible and the majority of businesses are open, although increasing numbers operate year-round. In the low season, transport connections, including ferries, are fewer and some businesses simply close.

HIGHLIGHTS

Spanning more than 1,000km from north to south, the Carretera Austral contains a bewildering array of scenery, from sub-tropical rainforests to glaciers. The range of activities possible is extensive, including rafting, climbing, diving, trekking, cycling, fishing and horseriding, to name but a few. Two-thirds of the territory is protected, thus human interference is negligible most of the time. In addition to being sparsely populated, it is rarely visited (although more so each passing year) and offers a more spectacular alternative route from northern to southern Patagonia than the arid terrain of the Argentine steppe. Highlights include:

COCHAMÓ (Page 101) One of the lesser-known entry points to the Carretera Austral, this delightful village is perched on the edge of the Reloncaví Estuary. Trekking options abound – it is colloquially referred to as 'the Yosemite of Patagonia'. Longer treks extend across the border to the Argentine towns of El Bolsón and Bariloche.

PARQUE PUMALÍN (Page 132) One of the first entirely private initiatives to protect major swathes of forest, pioneered by US conservationist Doug Tompkins (page

	Oct	Nov	Dec	Jan	Feb	Mar	Apr
Chaitén (north)							
Temp (°C min/max)	7/14	9/16	10/18	11/19	11/20	10/18	8/14
Rainfall	96mm	97mm	88mm	72mm	73mm	89mm	107mm
Coyhaique (central)							
Temp (°C min/max)	4/12	6/15	7/16	8/17	8/18	6/15	4/12
Rainfall	48mm	46mm	42mm	38mm	39mm	48mm	59mm
Cochrane (south)							
Temp (°C min/max)	4/12	6/14	7/15	9/17	9/17	7/15	4/12
Rainfall	25mm	20mm	19mm	21mm	22mm	22mm	28mm

134), the park has a number of well-marked treks, campgrounds, two volcanoes, millennial alerce trees and is easily accessed from Chaitén.

FUTALEUFÚ (Page 144) The village of 'Futa' is home to some of the best rafting and kayaking on the planet, as well as boasting a number of other activities for those less interested in watersports. It is also an entry/exit point to the Carretera Austral, being located close to the Argentine border near Esquel and El Bolsón/Bariloche.

RAÚL MARÍN BALMACEDA (Page 167) This sleepy village sits on an island surrounded by a fjord, a river and the Pacific Ocean. It has white sandy beaches, great seafood and fantastic sunsets, and is a paradise for those keen on bird and other wildlife-watching, where penguins, cormorants, dolphins and sea lions vastly outnumber people.

CERRO CASTILLO AND THE BACK ROAD TO IBÁÑEZ (Page 245) The Cerro Castillo mountain range is fast becoming one of the key trekking routes in southern Chile, with options for those seeking a gentle stroll to the most experienced climbers. To the southwest lie some of the most beautiful stretches of road in the region.

VENTISQUEROS SAN RAFAEL AND LEONES (Page 266) It is almost impossible to visit this region and not see a glacier. San Rafael is one of the more impressive and easily accessed, while the more adventurous may enjoy the hike and lake crossing to the Leones glacier. The size and remoteness of the white masses before you are simply breathtaking.

LAGO GENERAL CARRERA (Page 271) From Chile Chico to the Carretera Austral the road hugs South America's second-largest lake – its brilliant turquoise colour defies belief, while the marble caves of Puerto Sánchez are reminiscent of a Salvador Dalí painting.

PARQUE NACIONAL PATAGONIA (Page 294) Following the merger of this park with Tamango and Jeinimeni national reserves, this has become one of South America's leading parks, with abundant wildlife, countless lakes, excellent short and multi-day hikes and stunning scenery.

Planning HIGHLIGHTS

2

COCHRANE (Page 301) A delightful town surrounded by beauty and adventure – snorkel the cleanest river on earth, visit the Calluqueo glacier, access the nearby parks, dodge a few guanacos, check out some waterfalls, visit Caleta Tortel, or simply go fishing.

VILLA O'HIGGINS BORDER CROSSING (Page 319) The end, or beginning, of the Carretera Austral, sandwiched between lakes, glaciers and mountains, the border crossing to El Chaltén in Argentina is one of the lesser-known and yet most iconic crossings on the continent. The O'Higgins glacier is one of the largest in the region.

SUGGESTED ITINERARIES

ALONG THE CARRETERA The optimal itinerary depends on four factors: distance, time available, means of transport and budget. It is important to plan a journey along the Carretera Austral carefully, as there are relatively few entry/exit points, and ferries need to be booked in advance.

Chile is more expensive than neighbouring countries, and more so in the south, and this may be a deciding factor on how thoroughly to explore the region. Visiting the Carretera Austral is often part of a broader circuit around southern South America, particularly as the road connects the popular northern and southern regions of Patagonia. Travelling on public transport is slower than private transport, and hitchhiking is possible although not completely reliable. Below are some suggested one-way journeys along parts, or all, of the Carretera Austral.

The classic route: Futaleufú to Chile Chico (840km; 8 days) This route is something of a 'classic'. It encompasses many of the highlights of the region and uses the easiest entry and exit points. Ignoring all the detours off the Carretera Austral, it can be covered comfortably in eight days, but it can also take up to three weeks. This route encompasses a variety of terrains, from jungle to glaciers, coastline to high mountains, large towns to minuscule villages and stunning lakes, plus fascinating history and endless activities and opportunities to observe wildlife. For those with more time, including the northern and southern extremes of the Carretera Austral is well worth considering.

The route A suggested route (in this case from north to south) may be as follows:

- **Day 1** Arrive at Futaleufú; spend a complete day in the town rafting, kayaking, etc.
- **Day 2** (193km; 1 day; mostly gravel) Travel to Puyuhuapi.
- **Day 3** A day exploring Puyuhuapi and the surrounding area including the Queulat glacier.
- **Day 4** (207km; ½ day; mostly paved) A leisurely drive to Coyhaique over the Queulat Pass, via Villa Amengual and Mañihuales.
- **Day 5** A day in and around Coyhaique visiting Parque Nacional Coyhaique, the Río Simpson or the various lakes in the immediate vicinity. For those willing to get up at 05.00, it is possible to view Andean condors flying from their nests on the cliffs.
- **Day 6** (93km; 1½hrs; paved) A short drive to Villa Cerro Castillo and a half-day hike or horseback ride around the Cerro Castillo mountain.
- **Day 7** (130km; 2hrs; gravel) Travel to Puerto Sánchez to visit the marble caves.

- **Day 8** (217km; ½ day; gravel) Travel to Chile Chico via Puerto Guadal for lunch, along the south side of Lago General Carrera.

Suggested detours A more thorough journey along this 'classic' route would include some detours, and add up to two additional weeks. The following suggestions are listed from north to south:

- **From La Junta to Raúl Marín Balmaceda** (150km round trip; 2 days; gravel) One of the best detours along the Carretera. Enjoy an overnight stay in the village, plus a boat trip to the islands, extensive wildlife, a visit to the hot springs and a short hike.
- **Horseriding from Lago Verde to Villa La Tapera** (59km; 3 days) Become entirely disconnected from the modern world in one of the most remote regions of Patagonia.
- **Puerto Cisnes** (70km round trip from the Carretera Austral; 1 day; paved) This town has a fascinating history and hikes of various lengths, atmospheric hot springs in a national park, and abundant wildlife including dolphins.
- **Puerto Aysén and the surrounding area en route to Coyhaique** (64km from Coyhaique, 58km from Mañihuales; 1 day; paved) Lakes and parks are accessible within an hour of the town, as well as great food in town.
- **Around Coyhaique** (1 day) You can also spend an additional day here exploring the national parks and observing Andean condors.
- **Trekking the glaciers and lakes of Cerro Castillo** (3 days) These are some of the most spectacular and accessible treks along the Carretera Austral.
- **Ventisquero San Rafael or Ventisquero Leones** (1 day; Ventisquero San Rafael 1hr drive/bus each way & 5hrs by boat; Ventisquero Leones 30km south of Puerto Río Tranquilo, 2hr trek & 1hr boat ride each way) Two impressive glaciers accessible from the Carretera Austral.

The northern Carretera Austral (219km; 3 days; mostly paved) The Futaleufú (or Palena) access point joins the Carretera Austral at Villa Santa Lucía, where most visitors head south on the 'classic' route (see opposite). North of this point are three fascinating regions, and this extension to the classic itinerary connects the Carretera Austral to Puerto Montt and Ensenada in mainland Chile. The road extends north to Chaitén, which can be visited in one day, at which point the only northbound connection is via ferry to Hornopirén or a westward ferry to the island of Chiloé. From here, it is possible to reach Puerto Montt in a single day. Budget for at least three days' travel. We have described the route from north to south to correspond with the coverage in *Part Two* (page 77).

The route A suggested route, from Puerto Montt to Villa Santa Lucía (or vice versa if you're joining the road at Futaleufú/Palena and choose to head north):

- **Day 1** (99km paved or 122km gravel) Drive to Hornopirén, ideally via the coastal route and some hot springs, taking the short ferry ride from Caleta La Arena to Caleta Puelche.
- **Day 2** (44km; gravel, last 5km paved) Take the ferry to Caleta Gonzalo and do one or two of the shorter treks in Pumalín before reaching Chaitén.
- **Day 3** (76km paved) Drive to Villa Santa Lucía, witness the brutal destruction caused by the 2017 landslide, visit the El Amarillo hot springs, and explore the southern region of Parque Pumalín.

Suggested detours Those listed below (from north to south) can take as little as three additional days, but it can take as long as two weeks to do this region thoroughly, especially if trekking over to Argentina via Cochamó.

- **Valle Cochamó** Rather than heading from Puerto Montt directly to Hornopirén, head towards Ensenada and then south along the Reloncaví Sound to Cochamó, with some spectacular trekking options ranging from one day to over a week, including the possibility to trek into Argentina.
- **Explore Hornopirén** (at least 2 days) Take time to explore this village and trek in a wonderful national park nearby which includes a volcano hike (return trek to volcano takes 2 days; other shorter treks in the region). Also consider taking the slightly slower coastal route down from Puerto Montt to Hornopirén (1 additional day; around 20km extra; mostly gravel), and visit one of the many hot springs nearby.
- **Parque Pumalín** (at least 2 days) For multiple treks including to the Volcán Chaitén and to see alerce trees.
- **Lago Yelcho and Ventisquero Yelcho Chico** (1 day; en route) The first of the 'great lakes' with ample opportunities for fishing, and the most northern glacier.

The southern Carretera Austral (332km to Villa O'Higgins (inc detour to Caleta Tortel); gravel; 20km hike to Argentina; 40km to El Chaltén; 7 days; gravel)

In some respects this is the most spectacular region of the entire Carretera Austral, but it is often overlooked by those who opt to combine their journey instead with a visit to southern Argentine Patagonia and thus exiting the Carretera Austral at Cruce El Maitén, heading to Chile Chico in order to cross into Argentina. However, there are in fact three border crossings south of Chile Chico and the border crossing at Villa O'Higgins offers foot or bicycle passengers the opportunity to connect directly from the southernmost part of the Carretera Austral with El Chaltén in Argentina, a common destination for southbound travellers. Do keep in mind that this is one of the least travelled parts of the Carretera Austral; it is entirely unpaved, and relies on two ferries, one of which is relatively expensive. Note that for those with a vehicle it is not possible to cross into Argentina from Villa O'Higgins – the most southern vehicular border crossing is at Cochrane, so those with vehicles will either have to return to Cochrane to cross into Argentina, take the ferry from Puerto Yungay (100km northeast of Villa O'Higgins) to Puerto Natales (the springboard for Torres del Paine National Park), or leave the car in Villa O'Higgins and return at a later date.

The route The southern route adds at least six days, but it is safer to assume a week for delays with boat connections. Considering Cruce El Maitén as the beginning point for this section (where the detour to Chile Chico commences), the route may be as follows:

- **Day 1** (62km; gravel) Drive to Cochrane via Puerto Bertrand and the confluence of the rivers Baker and Nef – the road itself is spectacular, and around the town are various lakes and an accessible glacier.
- **Days 2 and 3** (126km; gravel) Drive the spectacular road from Cochrane to Caleta Tortel, weaving alongside the Río Baker, and take a boat trip to the Isla de los Muertos or to one of the glaciers.
- **Days 4 to 6** (144km & 20km hike (Chile); 40km (Argentina); gravel) Depart from Caleta Tortel to Villa O'Higgins, and on to El Chaltén in Argentina – a spectacular journey to the extreme south of the Carretera Austral. The border

crossing is only possible without a vehicle. The nearest vehicular exit is at Cochrane or the ferry from Puerto Yungay.

Suggested detours For a more thorough exploration of the southern region of the Carretera Austral, consider including:

- **Puerto Bertrand and surrounding area** (1 day) For fishing and rafting.
- **Parque Patagonia** (2–5 days) For trekking, including the multi-day trek towards Chile Chico.
- **Around Cochrane** (2 days) Visit lakes, waterfalls and the Calluqueo glacier.
- **Montt or Steffen glaciers from Caleta Tortel** (1 day each, by private boat) Less accessible and more expensive than San Rafael but less visited.
- **Horseriding/trekking from Cochrane to Villa O'Higgins** (at least 1 week) For an alternative means to reach the southernmost point of the Carretera Austral, the old trail used by the pioneers is passable by horse, or on foot. A long, remote and spectacular alternative to driving.
- **Visiting the glaciers and treks around Villa O'Higgins** (at least 1 day) Ranging from short, easy treks to multi-day treks only for qualified professional mountaineers.

NAVIMAG FERRY ROUTE: PUERTO MONTT TO/FROM PUERTO NATALES

In addition to saving the inconvenience of a return trip, this is a spectacular journey surrounded by raw nature and marine/birdlife, with almost no visible sign of human habitation along the entire route. With the notable exception of the Golfo de Penas, a rough stretch of open ocean, the entire trip weaves through the islands and fjords of southern Chile. Accommodation is comfortable and prices include all food. Wine and beer are expensive, but you can bring your own. There is a large deck for sunny days, and a dedicated area inside for children. The shared bathrooms are adequate.

Price per person ranges from US$550 (bunk bed, shared bathroom) to US$900 for a double cabin with private bathroom and window. Cars and motorbikes cost approximately US$500 southbound and US$250 northbound; bicycles are free. Prices fall in low season.

The ferry from Puerto Montt to Puerto Natales departs Saturday at 16.00 (check-in before 13.00), and arrives Tuesday morning at 16.00. The journey from Puerto Natales to Puerto Montt departs Wednesday at 06.00 (check-in before 18.00 Tuesday), and arrives Friday morning. Although Navimag has an office in Coyhaique, the boat does not stop along the Carretera Austral.

The true genius of the Navimag ferry is that it enables a wonderful round trip without having to double back or drive the tedious journey along Argentine highways, while also offering four days to completely disconnect from modernity, read books, count dolphins and sleep.

For further information: e sales@navimag.cl; w navimag.com. It is possible to book online (credit cards accepted), otherwise there are offices at:

Coyhaique Eusebio Lillo 91; ///reunion.client.stores; ☏ 2 2411 2650

Puerto Montt Av Diego Portales 2000; ///paint.fountain.scenes; ☏ 2 2411 2600

TIME REQUIRED TO TRAVEL THE COMPLETE CARRETERA AUSTRAL Omitting most detours (including Caleta Tortel), it is possible to travel the complete length of the Carretera Austral in two weeks; a more thorough trip would take four weeks. A complete trip including all the key detours – Caleta Tortel, Raúl Marín Balmaceda, the glaciers, an extended hike in Cerro Castillo – and a day or two of rest may take approximately six weeks.

AVOIDING BACKTRACKING ON THE CARRETERA AUSTRAL Visitors to the Carretera face a fundamental challenge: if travelling south and then north, how to avoid backtracking along the same routes? And if travelling only one direction, how to decide which route to pick when multiple options are available? One-way car rentals can be expensive, so it is often wise to return the car to the point of origin. The common way to achieve this is to traverse the Carretera Austral in one direction (invariably missing out on a few lovely regions), and then return either via Argentina (generally quicker) or on the Navimag ferry. The suggested itineraries (page 26) describe how to incorporate the Carretera Austral into a broader trip to

ENTRY/EXIT POINTS ALONG THE CARRETERA AUSTRAL

From/to	From/to	Border	Transport
Ralún	Bariloche	Paso Vuriloche	🚶
Puerto Montt	Caleta Gonzalo		🚌🚐🛥️
Ensenada	Caleta Gonzalo		🚌
Quellón (Chiloé)	Chaitén		🛥️
Castro (Chiloé)	Chaitén		🛥️
Puerto Montt	Chaitén		🛥️✈️
Cochamó/Puelo	El Bolsón (Arg)	Paso Río Manso	🚶
Cochamó/Puelo	Lago Puelo (Arg)	Paso Río Puelo	🚶
Futaleufú	Trevelin (Arg)	Paso Futaleufú	🚌🚐
Palena	Corcovado (Arg)	Paso Río Encuentro	🚌
Raúl Marín Balmaceda	Quellón/Melinka (Chiloé)		🛥️
Lago Verde	Las Pampas (Arg)	Paso Las Pampas	🚶
Cisnes Junction	Aldea Apeleg	Paso Río Frías-Apeleg	🚌
Puerto Cisnes	Quellón (Chiloé)		🛥️
Ñirehuao	El Coyte (Arg)	Paso Puesto Viejo	🚌
Coyhaique	Río Mayo (Arg)	Paso Coyhaique/Triana	🚐🚌
Balmaceda	Río Mayo (Arg)	Paso Huemules	🚌
Puerto Ibáñez	Perito Moreno (Arg)	Paso Ibáñez	🚌
Balmaceda	Santiago, Puerto Montt, Punta Arenas		✈️
Chile Chico	Los Antiguos (Arg)	Paso Río Jeinimeni	🚌
Cochrane	Argentina	Paso Roballos	✈️
Caleta Tortel	Puerto Natales		🛥️
Villa O'Higgins	Las Horquetas (Arg)	Paso Mayer	🚶
Villa O'Higgins	El Chaltén (Arg)		🚶

Patagonia. Improved road quality, ferry connections and the sheer beauty of the region make remaining entirely in Chile for your trip an increasingly attractive, and easier, option (albeit at a greater cost).

However, there are multiple options to travel the entire Carretera Austral in both directions without backtracking excessively. This essentially involves using 'loops', or circuits, which can be traversed in different ways in each direction. There are six key loops.

Key loops
Chiloé loop *Map, page 142*
The most obvious means to avoid backtracking is to combine the Carretera Austral with a trip to the island of Chiloé and on to Puerto Montt. There are ferries from Puerto Chacabuco to Quellón on the south of Chiloé, with a number of stops on the route north: Puerto Aguirre, Puerto Gaviota, Puerto Cisnes, Isla Toto, Villa Melimoyu, Puerto Santo Domingo and Raúl Marín Balmaceda all connect with Quellón via Melinka. Puerto Cisnes has a faster ferry to Quellón stopping only in Melinka. Chaitén, towards the north of the Carretera Austral, has direct ferries to both Castro and Quellón on Chiloé. Ferry connections to Chiloé are all from the northern half of the Carretera Austral.

Lago General Carrera loop *Map, page 241*
Just north of Cerro Castillo (93km south of Coyhaique) visitors must decide whether to head southeast towards Puerto Ibáñez, or west towards Río Tranquilo. The two routes converge in Cruce El Maitén (62km north of Cochrane). The western route includes the marble caves of Río Tranquilo or Puerto Sánchez, Cerro Castillo, the San Rafael and Leones glaciers, and about 75km of stunning coastal road around the western extreme of Lago General Carrera.

The eastern route is through Puerto Ibáñez, taking the ferry across the lake to Chile Chico, and then 115km along the southern coast of the lake via Puerto Guadal. There are two routes from Puerto Ibáñez to the Carretera – the main road, highway X-65, connects some 6km north of Cerro Castillo, or the back route via the Levicán Peninsula, which connects about 6km south of Cerro Castillo.

Puerto Aysén loop *Map, page 142*
Residents of Puerto Aysén may claim the true Carretera Austral already passes through their town but, regardless, there are two main routes north of Coyhaique: direct to Mañihuales via Villa Ortega, or northwest to Aysén and then northeast to Mañihuales. Both are worth doing. There are multiple minor roads south of Coyhaique and northwest of Coyhaique following the general direction of the Carretera. The entire section between El Blanco (near the detour to Balmaceda airport) and Camp Grande (just north of Mañihuales) can be done in several ways – there is no need to backtrack on any of this section.

Hualaihué loop *Map, page 76*
This is a 77km alternative (and highly recommended) route from Hornopirén to Contao along the coast rather than the Carretera Austral (54km).

Reloncaví loop *Map, page 76*
From Caleta Puelche, where the ferry shuttles north across the mouth of the Reloncaví Estuary towards Caleta La Arena and on to Puerto Montt, the 'Northern Carretera Austral' continues east along the southern edge of the Reloncaví Estuary

to the stunning trekking regions of Puelo and Cochamó, eventually connecting to highway 225 on the south of Lago Llanquihue with easy connections to Puerto Varas and Puerto Montt, or to the border and on to Bariloche and Villa La Angostura in Argentina.

Huequi loop *Map, page 76*

The ferry between Chaitén and Puerto Montt stops in Ayacara on the Huequi Peninsula. Traverse the Carretera Austral by land between Puerto Montt or Ensenada (the northern gateways to the Carratera) and Chaitén, including Pumalín Park, Hornopirén, Hualaihué, Cochamó, etc, and in the other direction go via Ayacara.

From Hornopirén the only means to connect with the Carretera Austral to the south is via ferry, and most take the bi-modal to Caleta Gonzalo. There are occasional ferries between Pichicolo (15km west of Hornopirén) and Ayacara, and less frequent ferries from Ayacara to Caleta Gonzalo.

Other lesser loops There is a route through the **valleys northeast of La Junta** as an alternative to 12km of the Carretera (page 166).

Another possible route to the west of the Carretera just **north of Cochrane** avoids 23km of backtracking (page 291).

About 7km north of **Mañihuales** take a small bridge to the west and then head north, parallel to the Carretera, until the road rejoins the Carretera half an hour later, avoiding 20km of backtracking.

The main section where backtracking is inevitable is south of Cochrane. However, for those without a vehicle there are a series of additional loops that take alternative trekking routes (Carretera in one direction, trekking the other).

Trekking-only loops Villa O'Higgins to Cochrane via the Ruta de Los Pioneros (instead of Carretera Austral via Caleta Tortel and the ferry across the Mitchell fjord).

Cochrane to Chile Chico through Parque Patagonia (instead of Carretera Austral via Puerto Bertrand and Puerto Guadal).

La Tapera to Lago Verde and on to Palena (instead of Carretera Austral via Amengual, Puyuhuapi, La Junta and Villa Santa Lucía). It is actually possible to trek from Palena to Futaleufú, but this is largely unmarked and only for experienced mountaineers.

Hornopirén north: there is an extensive network of trekking routes to the northeast of Hornopirén connecting with the treks originating in Puelo, Cochamó, Llanada Grande, Primer and Segundo Coral, including two border crossings to Argentina. There is a third border crossing to Argentina (Ruta de los Jesuitos) originating from Ralún at the northeastern extreme of the Carretera Austral.

With careful planning and the wise use of loops, it is possible to traverse the entire Carretera Austral from top to bottom in both directions with relatively little backtracking. It is slightly easier for those without cars or motorbikes.

SUGGESTED ITINERARIES WITHIN PATAGONIA The Carretera Austral is a natural bridge between northern and southern Patagonia. Many visitors to the region also intend to visit San Carlos de Bariloche (Argentina) and the Chilean Lake District north of Puerto Montt. In the far south, popular destinations include, in Argentina, El Chaltén (accessible from Villa O'Higgins), El Calafate (Perito

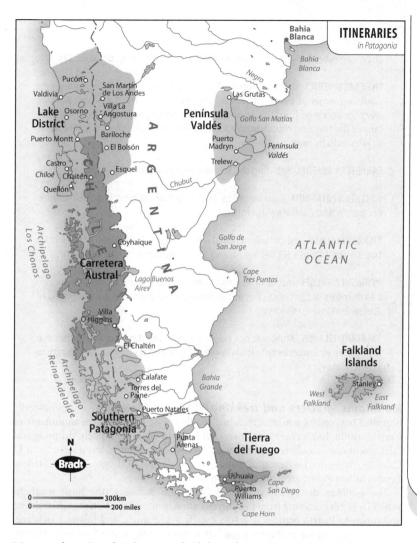

Bahia Blanca

Bahia Blanca

Negro

Pucón

San Martín de Los Andes

Valdivia

Las Grutas

Lake District

Osorno

Villa La Angostura

Península Valdés

Golfo San Matías

Puerto Montt

Bariloche

Puerto Madryn

Península Valdés

El Bolsón

Trelew

Castro

Esquel

Chubut

Chiloé

Chaitén

Quellón

Coyhaique

Golfo de San Jorge

ATLANTIC OCEAN

Archipiélago Los Chonos

Carretera Austral

Lago Buenos Aires

Cape Tres Puntas

Villa O'Higgins

El Chaltén

Falkland Islands

Archipiélago Reina Adelaide

Calafate

Bahía Grande

West Falkland

Stanley

East Falkland

Torres del Paine

Puerto Natales

Southern Patagonia

N

Punta Arenas

Tierra del Fuego

Bradt

Ushuaia

Puerto Williams

Cape San Diego

0 —————— 300km
0 —————— 200 miles

Cape Horn

Moreno glacier) and Ushuaia, and Chilean destinations Puerto Williams and Torres del Paine.

An attractive option, to avoid repeating parts of the journey, is to take the four-day Navimag ferry (see box, page 29) from Puerto Natales (entry point to Torres del Paine) to or from Puerto Montt.

Planning your route The biggest mistake visitors to the Carretera Austral make is poor planning. When including the Carretera Austral as part of a broader tour of Patagonia, be sure to plan your route carefully and consider how to integrate the Carretera with other regions to make the best use of your time.

The obvious thorough tour of Patagonia might appear to be a U-shaped journey along the west of the Andes and the Atlantic coast, connecting in Tierra del Fuego.

However, it is worth thinking about alternative options. To create your 'ultimate Patagonia experience', consider the following information.

There are essentially six main areas of interest (see the map on page 33).

THE LAKE DISTRICT (Pucón, Valdivia, Bariloche, San Martín de Los Andes, etc) spanning Argentina and Chile. This region borders the Carretera Austral, whether accessed from the north (Puerto Montt or Ensenada), from the east (any of the trekking routes from Bariloche/El Bolsón) or entering from Esquel to Futaleufú by road.

CARRETERA AUSTRAL Bridging the Lake District and southern Patagonia.

SOUTHERN PATAGONIA Dominated by Torres del Paine (Chile), but also includes El Chaltén and Calafate (Argentina).

TIERRA DEL FUEGO Ushuaia (Argentina) is rumoured to be the 'end of the world', but Puerto Williams (Chile) lies further south and has fantastic trekking.

PENÍNSULA VALDÉS (Argentina) Famous for whale watching. The (mediocre) beach resort of Las Grutas lies to the north and to the south are the towns of Trelew and Puerto Madryn.

FALKLAND ISLANDS Although not normally considered part of Patagonia, the islands are easily accessible from Punta Arenas, and it's a rare opportunity to visit (cheaply).

Mountains, glaciers and trekking El Chaltén (Argentina) is undoubtedly beautiful but, unless you are intending to climb Fitz Roy, then the mountains of Cerro Castillo, Isla Navarino or Torres del Paine in Chile are equally stunning and offer world-class trekking opportunities. Likewise, the Perito Moreno glacier in El Calafate (Argentina) is beautiful, but any of the glaciers O'Higgins, Montt, Steffen, Leones or San Rafael are at least as impressive.

The 1,200km drive (approx 20hrs) from Paso Roballos (the most southern vehicular border crossing from the Carretera to Argentina) to El Chaltén, El Calafate and down to Puerto Natales is across mostly arid pampa, and misses Cochrane, Caleta Tortel and some stunning glaciers further south on the Carretera Austral. Visit these by taking the (car) ferry to Puerto Natales, the gateway to Torres del Paine, instead. Until 2016 there was no alternative other than to cross from Chile into Argentina in order to continue south, but this ferry service fundamentally challenges the need to enter Argentina at all.

The 'end of the world' Although the town of Ushuaia (54.8°S) is often regarded as the destination for the 'end of the world' photo, in fact Puerto Williams (54.9°S), accessed most easily from Punta Arenas (in Chile, served by DAP Airlines) is not only further south, but boasts the incredible five-day 'Dientes de Navarino' trek. This trek begins *south* of the Beagle Channel and crosses the 55th parallel on the rugged and awe-inspiring terrain of Isla Navarino.

Whale watching It is true that Península Valdés is uniquely positioned for whale watching, particularly the southern right whale, but do not underestimate the whale-watching potential along the Carretera Austral – the best locations to observe blue whale, although rarer than southern right whale, is from Corcovado Bay (northern Carretera Austral) or from Melinka, south of Chiloé.

If whale watching is a priority, do this *early* in the summer season (October) in Península Valdés. Then head west towards the Lake District, perhaps on the trans-Patagonia train from Viedma (just north of Península Valdés) to Bariloche. Visit the Lake Districts of both Chile and Argentina, and begin the Carretera Austral, ideally from Puerto Montt or Ensenada rather than at Futaleufú in order to visit Pumalín Park, Hornopirén and Chaitén. If whale watching is not a priority, head straight to Bariloche, San Martín or Puerto Montt.

Travelling by car, bicycle or motorbike Traverse the Carretera Austral to Caleta Tortel and take the car ferry directly to Puerto Natales. This omits Villa O'Higgins, which is a beautiful region, but the border crossing from there to El Chaltén is not possible with a vehicle. Perhaps if you plan to take a flight over the southern ice shelf (page 327) or have not seen enough glaciers by this point and wish to see Ventisquero O'Higgins, a detour to Villa O'Higgins is worthwhile – but this will inevitably be a round trip.

Pedestrians For those without a vehicle, the advice is the opposite. Continuing beyond Caleta Tortel most probably implies visiting Torres del Paine, in which case we advise negotiating the legendary border crossing to El Chaltén and taking the long journey across arid steppe down to Puerto Natales via Argentina rather than taking the ferry from Caleta Tortel. You can see the O'Higgins glacier as a minor detour on the way to Candelario Mancilla – there is still no reason to visit the Perito Moreno glacier in Calafate after this.

Heading further south
Whatever your mode of transport, Torres del Paine is usually a key destination in Patagonia. But once there, where next? Instead of heading towards Ushuaia, continue south to Punta Arenas and take a short flight to Puerto Williams on DAP Airlines (page 44), or take a slower and more expensive ferry (page 44). The village itself is nondescript, but if the 'end of the world' photo is your goal, this is as far south as you can reasonably go (Cape Horn is very expensive to reach and Antarctica more so). The Dientes de Navarino trek extends even further south and is truly magnificent. There is no reason to take a car to Puerto Williams, as there are almost no roads. Return to Punta Arenas and either fly back to Santiago (pedestrians or those with a one-way car rental) or take the Navimag (car) ferry from Puerto Natales to Puerto Montt.

Falkland Islands The other detour from Punta Arenas (without a vehicle) is to fly to the Falklands (see w bradtguides.com/falklands). Flights from Punta Arenas are weekly, and a fraction of the price of the flights from the UK – a rare opportunity to visit another outlying destination.

The ultimate Patagonia experience
To complete this itinerary, encompassing the entirety of Patagonia on both sides of the border, could easily take a whole season (December to February inclusive). This might be considered the ultimate Patagonia trip, and would run as follows:

- One week in Buenos Aires and Península Valdés (Argentina)
- One week in and around San Martín and Bariloche (Argentina)

- One week in the Chilean Lake District
- Six weeks thoroughly exploring the Carretera Austral, beginning in Puerto Montt or Ensenada and departing by ferry from Caleta Tortel/Puerto Yungay to Puerto Natales
- One week trekking in Torres del Paine
- One week trekking the Dientes de Navarino circuit in Puerto Williams
- One week visiting the Falkland Islands from Punta Arenas
- One week to return to Puerto Montt on the Navimag ferry from Puerto Natales (Chile), or a little longer if driving up the Carretera Austral, perhaps driving through Argentina until the Roballos or Chile Chico crossing and then using loops where possible to avoid backtracking (page 30).

THE ROUTE OF PARKS

The most beautiful scenic route in the world already exists – and it's in Chile.
Route of Parks of Patagonia/Rewilding Chile

The Carretera Austral is only one component of the larger Route of Parks (an initiative of Fundación Rewilding Chile; formerly Tompkins Conservation), a scenic route that covers 115,000km^2 of protected land extending 2,800km from Parque Alerce Andino in the north to Cape Horn. It was conceived as a vision of conservation, since Chilean Patagonia possesses 91% of Chile's protected territory, and the Route of Parks includes some of the largest parks in the Americas. A secondary goal of the Route of Parks is to distribute tourism more evenly across southern Chile. At present the overwhelming focus is upon Torres del Paine.

Along the Carretera Austral Of the 17 parks along the whole route, the Carretera Austral passes by, through or close to 12 of these, ten of which are readily accessible and described in this guide. These are the national parks Alerce Andino (page 99); Hornopirén (page 112); Pumalín (page 132); Queulat (page 185); Isla Magdalena (page 194); Cerro Castillo (page 251); Laguna San Rafael (page 266); and Patagonia (page 282).

The northern sections of Parque Nacional Bernardo O'Higgins and Parque Nacional Kawésqar can be accessed from the Carretera Austral – other access points are further south. Only Corcovado and Melimoyu lack infrastructure for public access, the only public access point to Corcovado, the 3km hike to Yelcho glacier (page 138).

Beyond the Carretera Austral Seven parks lie wholly or partially to the south of the Carretera Austral in the Magallanes region of Chile, most of which, with the obvious exception of Torres del Paine, are largely inaccessible. Since they are outside the geographic scope of the main guide, these are described briefly from the page opposite in north-to-south order.

Our recommended route to explore Patagonia thoroughly (page 35) is to complete the Carretera Austral, visit Torres del Paine, and ultimately reach Puerto Williams to complete the Dientes de Navarino trek. Between Puerto Natales and Punta Arenas the Route of Parks provides at least two interesting detours – Kawésqar and Pali Aike parks. Flying from Punta Arenas to Puerto Williams is the easiest, but the Tabsa ferry provides a relaxing way to at least view the canals of the deep south. The *Australis* cruise ship (from Punta Arenas to Ushuaia) stops in Cape Horn, which is the undisputed southern tip of the continent.

Tour operators and transport

Tour operators

Andes Nativa Cordillera 1060, Puerto Varas; ///outpost.compound.asteroid; ☏65 234 2058, 9 6845 6531; e info@andesnativa.com; w andesnativa.com. 5-day trips to Parque Nacional Kawésqar.

Andes Pure w andespure.com. Tours to Parque Nacional Kawésqar & to Puerto Williams but without the Dientes de Navarino trek.

Australis w australis.com. Cruise from Punta Arenas to Ushuaia (via Cape Horn & passing Parque Nacional Alberto de Agostini & Yendegaia), US$2,500 pp.

Patagonian Fjords w patagonianfjords.com. One of the few tour operators offering multi-day treks, kayak & Montañas fjord within Parque Nacional Kawésqar.

Ruta de los Parques / Route of Parks Klenner 299, Puerto Varas; ///having.clocked.against; ☏65 225 0079; e info@rutadelosparques.org; w rutadelosparques.org/en. Excellent website with all relevant information including a list of approved tour operators.

Turismo 21 de Mayo w turismo21demayo.com. Nautical tours around Torres del Paine including the Balmaceda & Serrano glaciers, US$90/140 pp low/high season.

Companies offering Dientes de Navarino guided treks

Cascada Expediciones US ☏+1 888 232 3813; e reservations@cascada.travel; w cascada.travel/en. Approx US$1,500 (depending on group size, 2–8 people) all included, & option to start/finish in either Punta Arenas or Ushuaia.

Chile Nativo Eberhard 230, Puerto Natales; ///founder.oppress.hacking; ☏61 269 1391, US

+1 800 649 8776; w chilenativo.com. Route of Parks tours along the Carretera, also the Dientes de Navarino trek (6 days, US$2,295 pp), & tailor-made trips to Yendegaia National Park.

Ecotours Chile ☏2 2906 0070, 9 8459 0631; e info@ecotours.cl; w ecotours.cl. Packages include accommodation, flights to/from Punta Arenas, food, tents, cooking equipment, bilingual guide & porter. Prices on request.

Explora Isla Navarino ☏9 9185 0155; e consultas@exploraislanavarino.com; w islanavarino.com. Local tour operator since 2015, good website (Spanish & English) with information on how to get to Isla Navarino, the 5-day Dientes trek (from $840,000 pp, inc satellite communications) & other tours on the island.

Swoop Patagonia (Page 41) US$2,295 pp including flights from/to Punta Arenas, food, accommodation in Puerto Williams, English-speaking guide, 4–8 people.

Turismo Shila ☏9 7897 2005; Puerto Williams, cnr O'Higgins & Prat; ///dinosaurs.foxy.saved; e turismoshila@gmail.com; w turismoshila.cl. Based in Puerto Williams, full Dientes circuit or the Lake Windhond tours starting at $800,000 (min 2 people) including guides, porters, food, tents & GPS.

Transport to Puerto Williams

DAP Airlines w dapairline.com. Flights from Punta Arenas to Puerto Williams 10.00 Mon–Fri, returning same day at 11.30. $80,000 each way. Strict 15kg total luggage allowance.

Transbordadora Austral Broom w tabsa. cl. 6 ferries per month in each direction between Puerto Williams & Punta Arenas. 32hrs each way; food included, regular seat $108,110, reclining seat $151,110.

Parque Nacional Bernardo O'Higgins (35,259km²) This is the largest park in Chile, the second largest in the Americas (after Wood Buffalo National Park, Canada), marginally smaller than Switzerland, and the only park that spans the regions of Aysén and Magallanes. Despite its size, from the Carretera Austral access is limited to the Montt glacier from Caleta Tortel (page 317) or the O'Higgins glacier from Villa O'Higgins (page 328). The 41-hour ferry journey from Caleta Tortel to Puerto Natales passes through the park along the Messier Canal past Puerto Edén. Otherwise, access is by boat from Puerto Natales (frequent tours to the Serrano, Balmaceda or Bernal glaciers, for example).

Parque Nacional Torres del Paine (2,422km²) The most legendary park in the Americas, Torres del Paine boasts multiple trails (including 'W' & 'O'), glaciers,

Some (international) tour operators offer tours along what appears to be the entire Route of Parks. Check the small print. Of the ten parks along the Carretera Austral, two are largely inaccessible. Of the seven parks to the south of the Carretera, Bernardo O'Higgins is easily accessed from Caleta Tortel or Puerto Natales via local operators, and Torres del Paine is probably one of the most accessible parks in Chile – there are more options available if arranged locally. Pali Aike is a day trip from Punta Arenas or Puerto Natales. Kawésqar is accessible but rarely on the itineraries of the large operators, and thus best arranged locally (page 37). Agostini and Yendegaia are inaccessible, and operators that claim to visit these parks generally are merely reselling the *Australis* cruise to Cape Horn that happens to pass them. A 'Route of Parks' tour would not usually include Puerto Williams and the Dientes de Navarino trek, thereby missing one of the best treks in the Americas. We are yet to see a convincing operator offering a genuine 'Route of Parks' trip, and advise using local operators, particularly in the extreme south.

well-developed infrastructure, camping, restaurants, hotels and more. Campsites and cabins need to be reserved in advance. It is one of the most expensive and crowded parks in Chile – 290,000 people visited in 2018, more than double the number of visitors to all parks in Aysén combined.

Parque Nacional Pali Aike (50km²) Northeast of Punta Arenas by the Argentine border, Pali Aike (the name means 'desolate place of evil spirits') is accessible by road. It has three hiking trails including to the Pali Aike cave (of archaeological importance), with evidence of human habitation 11,000 years ago, and traversing incredible basalt structures from recent volcanic activity. Independent visits or tours are possible from Punta Arenas, but there is no lodging within the park – the nearest accommodation, food and services are at Villa Punta Delgada (26km south).

Parque Nacional Kawésqar (24,950km²) The main access to this park with no infrastructure is by boat from Puerto Natales along the Montañas fjord; it is also accessible from Caleta Tortel.

Parque Nacional Alberto de Agostini (14,600km²) The Tabsa boat from Punta Arenas to Puerto Williams passes through this park. There are no trails or infrastructure.

Parque Nacional Yendegaia (1,506km²) There's no road access at the time of writing, but plans are underway to connect the park to existing roads further north.

Parque Nacional Cape Horn (631km²) Cruises from Punta Arenas or private boat/plane from Puerto Williams.

Trekking the true end of the world
The 'photo at the end of the world' is sought after by many visitors to Patagonia. Those who cannot go all the way to the windswept islands of Cape Horn instead settle for Ushuaia, an industrial town in southern Argentina.

Puerto Williams is further south, beautiful, easily accessed and home to the southernmost hike on earth – the stunning five-day Dientes de Navarino trek. A number of tour operators offer this trip (page 37), but it can be done independently as the trail is clearly marked and a guide is not strictly necessary. Beyond the usual trekking/camping kit, consider the following:

- This is extremely remote. There are no helicopters in this region for emergency evacuation. Although not technical, this is for experienced hikers. Do not venture off the trail. Only about 200 people attempt this trail each year.
- Basic navigational skills are required. While the trail is well marked, particularly along the first half, be sure to have physical maps (if only as a back-up), GPS and some form of satellite communication (we use Garmin inReach Mini, page 72), and a USB battery pack.
- Only do the trek in December to March. Take a sturdy tent capable of withstanding brutal winds, and adequate boots and gaiters to deal with mud and snow, even in summer. Do the circuit clockwise (the final descent from Paso Virginia would not be pleasant in reverse).
- Gas cans cannot be taken on the DAP plane, but can be bought in Puerto Williams. Book flights carefully – if the weather deteriorates and you are delayed on the trail, it is a pity not to have a spare day in hand. There is only one flight per day between Punta Arenas and Puerto Williams (US$200 return, 10kg weight limit plus 5kg hand luggage). Accommodation in Puerto Williams starts at about US$25 per person.
- The trail is usually done in four segments, coinciding with suitable campsites. There are very few places to camp outside these designated spaces (with no infrastructure), so think twice about deviating from the standard four-leg route, as you may find yourself sleeping in a swamp or on a 45-degree slope.
- There is an optional detour even further south to Lake Windhond. Again, it's clearly signposted and not technical, and there is a basic hut available (Refugio Charles), as well as camping one day each way from the main trail.
- Hikers are required to register at the police station in Puerto Williams before they trek and to check in after they finish.

✪ AS THE CONDOR FLIES

A Buenos Aires-based condor would face a daunting flight ahead. An initial 1,000km stretch to see the whales at Península Valdés followed by 600km across the arid pampa to Bariloche. A short hop of only 140km over the Andes to Puerto Montt, usually with a head wind, and *Vultur gryphus* would be ready to begin the Carretera Austral. Flying 825km straight south, skirting the eastern edge of the Patagonian Ice Field, west of the Andes, would leave the weary bird in Villa O'Higgins, not even halfway around this Patagonian odyssey. Then, it's just under 500km to Punta Arenas (flying straight over Torres del Paine, of course), and a relaxing 290km glide to Puerto Williams for 'the condor at the end of the world' photo. Relying on wings rather than DAP/Latam flights would enable our feathered friend to save important time flying directly to the Falklands, 740km over the Southern Ocean. And from Thatcher Drive, Stanley, a mere 1,900km straight home to the Buenos Aires nest. A journey of 6,000km in total – equivalent to driving from London to Mongolia. Patagonia is a big place. Even condors need to plan carefully.

3

Practical Information

TOUR OPERATORS

Previously a fringe destination, the Carretera Austral is increasingly attracting the attention of specialist tour operators. Catering to most budgets, tour operators can book hotels, flights, car hire and activities, saving considerable planning time, being particularly useful for visitors who do not speak Spanish, and with the additional benefit of ABTOL/IATA protection. Most tour operators offer standardised tours along well-established routes in a limited number of hotels (most of which are mentioned in this guide), but such trips come at the expense of flexibility. Be careful to check what is and is not included in the price. If time is more limited than budget, a pre-arranged tour might be wise, but the Carretera region has developed over the last decade – independent travel is not as challenging as many believe and English is increasingly spoken. A hybrid alternative is to arrange the main travel itinerary (car hire, flights and ferries) independently, and then book local tour operators for specific regions. This approach will remove much of the minutiae of detailed planning while offering greater local knowledge and flexibility at a reduced price.

CHILE

CicloAustral \9 4015 5577, 9 7766 0416; e info@cicloaustralchile.com; w cicloaustralchile. com. Bicycle rental & guided tours (6–12 people), with service points that also serve as pickup/ drop-off points in Puerto Montt, Coyhaique & Villa O'Higgins. 3 tours specifically along the Carretera: Puerto Varas to Río Puelo & back to Puerto Montt (4 days, $450,000); northern route (Puerto Montt to Coyhaique, 10 days, $930,000) & southern route (Coyhaique to Villa O'Higgins, 12 days, $1,100,000). Tours include support vehicle, guide, mechanic, accommodation (hostels & camping), ferries, food & activities (kayak, hot springs, etc). The tours can be combined, with a rest in between. Slight discount if using own bike, & if the novelty of hauling luggage up steep gravel roads wanes, luggage can go in a support vehicle. Rental service permits additional pickup/ drop-off points in Puyuhuapi, Puerto Río Tranquilo or Cochrane by prior arrangement. Cannondale bikes are provided with Ortileb panniers, rack,

helmet, spare parts, lights, repair kit, phone assistance, & they can help with logistics (ferries, accommodation, etc, for a fee). Prices range from $22,000/day to $480,000/month with 1 free service at one of the service points. English & Spanish spoken.

Dittmar Adventures Puerto Natales; \Chile +56 61 261 4201, US +1 281 213 0115; e info@ dittmaradventures.com; w dittmaradventures. com. Cycling tours including support vehicle, bike & maintenance, food & accommodation. The 10-day northern Carretera Austral trip joins the Carretera in Chaitén & ends in Coyhaique (US$4,770 pp). The 12-day southern Carretera Austral trip extends from Coyhaique to El Chaltén (US$5,304 pp). The 'Lifetime Trip' is 40 days from Bariloche, crossing to the Carretera Austral at Futaleufú, following the Carretera to Villa O'Higgins & crossing over to El Chaltén. The company has been around for a decade & has good local connections/suppliers, etc. Also offers trekking & kayaking in & around Torres del Paine.

UK

Audley Travel ☏01993 838640; w audleytravel. com/chile. Upmarket operator. The 'Aysén Region Uncovered' tour is 13 days, starting at £3,635 pp (inc all flights), covering Lago General Carrera (marble caves, fishing & trekking) & Caleta Tortel, & continues to Villa O'Higgins. Return via Parque Patagonia. Decent accommodation. Also offers a more complete 24-day tour including Torres del Paine, Pumalín, Futaleufú, Puyuhuapi & Coyhaique from £8,625 pp.

Chile Holiday Architects ☏01242 253073; e mail@holidayarchitects.co.uk; w chileholidayarchitects.com. 2-week self-drive trips along the Carretera Austral starting at £4,385 pp (all flights inc). Quality accommodation & San Rafael glacier trip offered as an optional extra. Trips are tailor-made around a broad itinerary, & specialist staff have extensive knowledge of their regions so offer some quirky, off-the-beaten-track ideas.

Cox & Kings ☏020 7873 5000; w coxandkings. co.uk. The 7-day 'Carretera Austral Adventure' tour for £1,095 pp (exc international flights) visits Tranquilo (marble caves), Caleta Tortel (2 nights), Parque Patagonia & Coyhaique.

Journey Latin America ☏020 8747 8315; e groups@journeylatinamerica.co.uk; w journeylatinamerica.co.uk. Offers a 2-week 'Untouched Aisen: Little-known Patagonia' trip, which originates in Buenos Aires & ends in Santiago. The journey enters the Carretera Austral at Futaleufú for some rafting, & goes as far south as Puerto Río Tranquilo, visiting the Exploradores glacier & marble caves; £3,687 pp (exc international flights). 'Self-drive Chile: Off the Beaten Track' encompasses the classic section of the Carretera (Tranquilo, Caleta Tortel & Lake General Carrera) with a couple of days on the Island of Chiloé & the Alerce Andino Park south of Puerto Montt; £3,590 pp (exc international flights). They are also a full travel agency able to arrange international & domestic flights.

Latin Routes ☏020 8546 6222; e enquiry@ latinroutes.co.uk; w latinroutes.co.uk. Good value-for-money self-drive trip for 2 weeks (£3,249 pp inc domestic flights) that covers almost the entire Carretera from Puerto Montt to Caleta Tortel, including Hornopirén, Pumalín, La Junta, Queulat, Tranquilo & Lago General Carrera, including one-way car rental (drop-off in Balmaceda). Gets nicely

off the beaten track & includes some unusual accommodation. Able to tailor most aspects of the journey. Company focuses solely on Latin America & staff almost all speak Spanish & have lived, worked or are from Latin America.

Pura Aventura ☏01273 676712; e info@pura-aventura.com; w pura-aventura.com. Good local knowledge, & since 2000 has tailored trips to most budgets & specific interests (trekking, glaciers, fishing, wildlife, rafting, etc) & visit the more remote regions. The self-drive 'Carretera Uncovered' trip is dedicated to the stretch south of Puyuhuapi as far as Caleta Tortel with guided day excursions & activities for various highlights along the way. Of all the operators, Pura offers the most esoteric trips venturing off the beaten track, including some detours across the border to some unique spots in Argentina, such as the Cueva de los Manos. 2- & 3-week tours cost £4,680/6,485 pp, & a whopping 45-day tour spanning the entire Route of Parks (page 36) is £14,430 pp – international flights not included. Also offered is an innovative 3-week trip combining the 2-week self-drive tour on the Carretera with vehicle drop-off in Balmaceda & then a flight to Punta Arenas & 5 days in Torres del Paine.

Real World Holidays ☏0113 262 5326; e enquiries@realworldholidays.co.uk; w realworldholidays.co.uk. 100% tailor-made trips to South America, so you can book as much, or as little as you like. A truly personal service.

Swoop Patagonia ☏0117 369 0196; e advice@ swooptravel.co.uk; w swoop-patagonia.com. Well-established Patagonia specialists who tailor more unusual road trips down the Carretera Austral, as well as multi-day treks & horse rides in the area. A 7-day self-drive trip starts from £1,400 pp (exc flights) including car hire, mid-range accommodation (B&B), some guided excursions & some meals. They are one of the only operators that can arrange the guided hiking & boat crossing to El Chaltén. They can customise almost any trip, including the Dientes de Navarino & boat tours all the way to Cape Horn.

TravelLocal w travellocal.com. A UK-based website where you can book direct with selected local travel companies, allowing you to communicate with a ground operator without having to go through a 3rd-party travel operator or agent. Your booking with the local company has full financial protection, but note that travel to the destination is not included. Member of ABTA, ASTA.

USA AND CANADA

Renedian Adventures Canada; ☎ +1 778 516 0059; e info@renedian.com; w renedian.com. The definitive motorbike tour of the Southern Cone including the mid section of the Carretera Austral, offered by one of the best-established operators in the region. The tour extends from Mendoza to Ushuaia over 22 days (CAN$16,750, passenger CAN$11,550), including Bariloche, entering the Carretera at Futaleufú, leaving over Paso Roballos & continuing south via Torres del Paine to Ushuaia. The standard bike is a BMW F750, but for a supplement the F850 or R1250 are available. Includes support vehicle, mechanic, all fuel, accommodation, food & great guides. The lead guide is Canadian, married to an Argentine & lives in San Rafael. The company's CEO, Rene Cormier, is author of the legendary biking book *The University of Gravel Roads*.

Ride Adventures US; ☎ +1 458 202 0462; e info@rideadv.com; w rideadv.com. Motorbike tour company specialising in custom & group tours, as well as 4x4 trips, guided & unguided (rental only). The 18-day 'Patagonia, Tierra del Fuego & Ushuaia' tour begins in Osorno & crosses over to Bariloche, Argentina, until entering the Carretera Austral at Futaleufú & leaves 5 days later at Chile Chico, heading down to Ushuaia via Calafate (Argentina), & Torres del Paine Park (Chile), ending in Punta Arenas for a return flight to Santiago. The base price (US$11,475) includes a Honda CB500X with the option to upgrade to a range of larger BMW/Honda/Yamaha/Triumph bikes. Passengers pay US$4,750. There is a budget option for the lone-wolf biker without a support vehicle or pre-booked accommodation. They also offer 4x4 self-drive tours, either accompanying a bike trip, or independently: a 10-day loop beginning & ending in Pucón & passing through Bariloche, Futaleufú & heading north along the Carretera (from US$1,773 pp based on 4 people sharing rooms) or the longer trip extending to Punta Arenas (from US$2,660 pp based on 4 people sharing).

TOURIST INFORMATION

Most towns and villages along the Carretera Austral have a small information booth handing out maps and flyers listing hotels and restaurants. Asking for more specific information is often a fruitless exercise. The biggest challenges for travellers tend to be the lack of information and the apparent impossibility of booking ferries.

Generally speaking, a backpacker hostel will have more information available than a tourist information centre. The police are usually oblivious to such matters, and the border guards tend to rotate between posts quite frequently and have relatively little information about the surrounding area. Even the local tour operators don't know much about regions beyond their immediate vicinity.

RED TAPE

You don't have to jump through many bureaucratic hoops to enter Chile. Tourists can generally stay for up to 90 days, and hopping across the border to Argentina and returning a day or two later is tolerated if not done too often. Visas are required for most Asian nations except Japan, Hong Kong, Mongolia, Macau, Malaysia, Singapore, South Korea and Thailand; and for all African nations except South Africa. Visas are not required for citizens of Russia, Israel, Indonesia, Turkey, Ukraine, UAE or Vietnam.

Chile takes the illegal import of restricted goods very seriously, including various agricultural or food stuffs. Fruit, dairy products, honey, etc, are all prohibited and this is strictly enforced at all airports and to varying extents at land borders. If in doubt, openly ask the border guards – they are generally relaxed if you are honest, and will allow you to eat any apples or sandwiches in their office before entering Chile.

EMBASSIES

There are 72 embassies in Santiago. Of the countries without a full embassy, Bolivia has a Consulate-General, the European Union has a Delegation, the Sahrawi Arab Democratic Republic has a Mission, and Taiwan has a Trade Office. Argentina has a Consulate in Puerto Montt and Punta Arenas. For a full and regularly updated list of embassies and consulates, visit w embassypages.com/chile.

GETTING THERE AND AWAY

BY AIR
International flights Santiago has one international airport – Aeropuerto Internacional Arturo Merino Benítez. International airlines flying to/from Santiago include: Aerolíneas Argentinas, Aeroméxico, Air Canada, Air Europa, Air France, Alitalia, American Airlines, Avianca, British Airways, Copa, Delta, Emirates, Gol, Iberia, JetSmart, KLM, Latam, Quantas, Sky Airline, Taca and United.

From the **UK**, British Airways flies direct to Buenos Aires and Santiago. From the **USA**, there are daily direct flights to Santiago from Atlanta, Dallas, Houston, Los Angeles, New York (JFK) and Miami.

Elsewhere, there are **direct** flights to Santiago from Argentina (Buenos Aires, Mendoza and Cordoba), Australia (Sydney), Bolivia (La Paz and Santa Cruz), Brazil (São Paulo, Brasilia, Iguazu Falls, Florianópolis and Río de Janeiro), Canada (Toronto), Colombia (Bogotá, Cali and Medellin), Costa Rica (San José), Dominican Republic (Punta Cana), Ecuador (Guayaquil and Quito), France (Paris), Mexico (Mexico City and Cancun), New Zealand (Auckland), Panama (Panama City), Paraguay (Asunción), Peru (Lima, Trujillo, Cuzco and Arequipa), Spain (Madrid and Barcelona), Uruguay (Montevideo and Punta del Este) and Venezuela (Caracas). Lufthansa and KLM fly via Argentina. From the Falkland Islands flights go via Punta Arenas, from where it is possible to fly to Balmaceda, Puerto Montt or Santiago.

From **Africa**, the only connections possible are with Ethiopian Airlines (Addis Ababa to São Paulo) and TAAG Angola Airlines (Luanda to São Paulo). From **Asia**, almost all flights go via either the USA or Europe. Emirates flies from Dubai to São Paulo; Turkish Airlines flies from Istanbul to São Paulo, Buenos Aires, Bogota and Panama City; Qatar Airways has flights from Doha to São Paulo. At the time of writing the South African Airways flight between Johannesburg and São Paulo, and the Air Maroc flight between Casablanca and São Paulo were not operating.

Aerolíneas Argentinas, Air New Zealand, Qantas and Latam operate (codeshare) flights between Australasia and Santiago and/or Buenos Aires.

The relevant **Argentine airports for accessing the Carretera Austral** are Bariloche and El Calafate, both of which are served by Latam and Aerolíneas Argentinas from Buenos Aires. Aerolíneas Argentinas also has a flight between Bariloche and El Calafate in high season, and regular flights from Buenos Aires to Esquel. It is a member of Sky Team. Latam is in an alliance with Delta. Flybondi and JetSmart fly between El Palomar (close to Buenos Aires) and Bariloche.

Domestic flights The three principal domestic airlines in Chile are Latam, JetSmart and Sky Airline. Connections with the Carretera Austral are generally via the commercial airports of Puerto Montt, Osorno or Valdivia (to access the northern region of the Carretera); via Castro (the only airport on the island of Chiloé); via Coyhaique/Balmaceda (the only commercial airport on the Carretera Austral); or via the deep south of Chile (Punta Arenas or Puerto Natales).

✈ **DAP Airlines** Ignacio Carrera Pinto 1015, Punta Arenas; ///avocado.cheaply.clock; ☎61 222 9936; Magallanes 131 (Hotel Dreams), Coyhaique; ☎67 221 2898; e ventas@dap.cl; w dapairline. com. DAP operates 2 relevant scheduled flights: Punta Arenas to Coyhaique/Balmaceda 13.30 Tue returning at 14.30 & Punta Arenas to Puerto Williams 10.00 Mon–Sat returning at 11.30. Tickets can be purchased online or at their offices in Coyhaique & Punta Arenas.

✈ **JetSmart** ☎2 2731 8787; w jetsmart.com. Budget airline with domestic & international routes including Coyhaique/Balmaceda to Santiago, Concepción, Puerto Montt & Temuco; Puerto Montt to Santiago & Punta Arenas; Puerto Natales to Santiago; Punta Arenas to Santiago, Concepción, Temuco & Puerto Montt. International flights to Argentina, Brazil, Colombia, Peru & Uruguay.

✈ **Latam** ☎600 526 2000; w latam.com. Flights to Puerto Montt, Osorno, Valdivia, Chiloé (via Puerto Montt), Punta Arenas (direct or via Puerto Montt) & Coyhaique/Balmaceda (direct or via Puerto Montt). Latam has extensive international flights to Europe, the Americas & direct flights to both Auckland (New Zealand) & Sydney (Australia).

✈ **Sky Airline** w skyairline.com. Flights to Puerto Montt, Valdivia, Punta Arenas, Puerto Natales, Coyhaique/Balmaceda (direct or via Puerto Montt), & also to Osorno in high season. They have international flights to Buenos Aires & Mendoza (Argentina); Lima (Peru, with onward domestic connections); & São Paulo, Río de Janeiro, Florianópolis & Salvador de Bahía (Brazil); & codeshare agreements with Avianca (Colombia) & Taca (Peru).

Private airlines A number of smaller airlines with propeller planes fly within the region, and are described in each relevant section. Scheduled flights on these smaller airlines connect Melinka, Ayacara and Chaitén with Puerto Montt, and Villa O'Higgins with Coyhaique. Other destinations are charter only.

BY ROAD The various border crossings are described in more detail in the respective sections – these are critical for planning a successful trip along the Carretera Austral (see box, page 30). The main road border crossings to/from Argentina accessible by a regular private vehicle (in north-to-south order, Chilean town/Argentine town) are: Futaleufú/Trevelin; Palena/Corcovado; Alto Río Cisnes/Aldea Apeleg; Ñirehuao/El Coyte; Coyhaique/Río Mayo (two border crossings); Balmaceda/Río Mayo; Puerto Ibáñez/Perito Moreno; and Chile Chico/Los Antiguos.

The Paso Roballos border crossing is best done in a 4x4 or on foot, but is a challenging border crossing as there is relatively little infrastructure or traffic on the Argentine side. Paso Las Pampas is not possible most of the year due to an incomplete bridge on the Argentine side. Very occasionally trucks and 4x4s can cross this border. The Río Mayer crossing northeast of Villa O'Higgins is not passable by vehicle and is only for hardened backpackers.

BY FERRY The main ferry connections along the Carretera Austral run between Puerto Montt and Chaitén (via Ayacara); Hornopirén and Caleta Gonzalo; Puerto Chacabuco and Quellón (Chiloé, stopping service); and between Chaitén and both Quellón and Castro (Chiloé). The only means to cross from Hornopirén to Caleta Gonzalo is by ferry, and this needs to be booked well in advance (see box, page 61). The five main companies are Naviera Austral, Somarco, Tabsa, Transportes Puelche and Navimag (see box, page 29). Ferries are generally no slower than travelling by land; for example, the direct ferry from Puerto Montt to Puerto Natales takes four days (without delays), and it is a challenge to beat this travelling overland, even via Argentina. Unless opting for a private cabin, prices tend to be reasonable for passengers; cars and motorbikes incur an additional fee, very roughly approximate to the cost of a person.

CHILEAN PATAGONIA

From	To
Coyhaique/Balmaceda	Puerto Montt, Santiago, Concepción, Temuco, Punta Arenas
Osorno	Santiago
Puerto Montt	Santiago, Coyhaique/Balmaceda, Punta Arenas, Puerto Natales
Puerto Natales	Santiago, Concepción, Puerto Montt
Puerto Williams	Punta Arenas
Punta Arenas	Puerto Montt, Santiago, Concepción, Temuco, Puerto Williams, Mount Pleasant (Falklands), Coyhaique/Balmaceda

ARGENTINE PATAGONIA

From	To
Bariloche	Buenos Aires, Calafate, Córdoba, Mendoza, Salta
Calafate	Bariloche, Córdoba, Buenos Aires, Ushuaia
Esquel	Buenos Aires
San Martín de los Andes	Buenos Aires, Córdoba, Rosario
Ushuaia	Córdoba, Buenos Aires, Bahía Blanca, Trelew

FALKLAND ISLANDS

From	To
Mount Pleasant	Punta Arenas (Chile), São Paulo (Brazil), Córdoba (Argentina), Brize Norton (UK)

BY BUS International buses run between Futaleufú (Chile) and Trevelin (Argentina; change bus at border, synchronised), and between Coyhaique (Chile) and Río Mayo (Argentina; the bus continues to Comodoro Rivadavia). There are no direct buses between Bariloche and the Carretera Austral, nor are there buses from Tecka, in Argentina, to Chile, despite this being an obvious route to consider. As of May 2022, all international bus connections remain on hold until the border reopens.

As it is impossible to fly directly from Argentina to any point along the Carretera Austral, it is cheaper and quicker to take a bus between southern Argentina and southern Chile. Within Chile it is certainly convenient to fly to Puerto Montt, and flights are not substantially more expensive than buses if booked in advance. The key decision is whether to fly to/from Balmaceda; although it is quicker, it often means missing a large section of the Carretera Austral. Ultimately this is determined by the chosen itinerary. Overnight buses from Santiago to Puerto Montt save on a hotel night and for those taking larger items such as bicycles it may be easier and cheaper than flying.

Long-distance buses in Chile range in price and comfort. Bus connections between anywhere along the Carretera Austral and Argentina tend to be shorter distances and less comfortable than travelling the same route by air. One common route to the Carretera Austral from Argentina is to fly to Esquel and take the shuttle bus to the border and on to Futaleufú.

BY FOOT Several border crossings are only possible on foot: from Villa O'Higgins to El Chaltén (also by bicycle); from El Bolsón (Argentina) to Cochamó (Chile); from Lago Puelo (Argentina) to Río Puelo (Chile; via Paso Río Puelo); and from Cochamó to Argentina at the more northern Río Manso crossing. A rarely used

3

trail, 'Ruta de los Jesuitos' (page 32), connects Ralún, just north of Cochamó, with Bariloche via the Vuriloche border crossing. Although not recommended, the Río Mayer border crossing northeast of Villa O'Higgins is also only possible on foot.

HEALTH   *with Dr Felicity Nicholson*

Before you travel, check the current Foreign, Commonwealth and Development Office (FCDO) travel advice (w gov.uk/government/organisations/foreign-commonwealth-development-office) as well as the country-specific page, which details any travel restrictions and entry requirements, as well as safety and security advice.

Ensure that any insurance is appropriate for the type of travel that you intend to do; currently this should include cover for Coronavirus-related events such as health problems and travel disruption.

Medical facilities are limited in the Carretera – any serious accident or illness will involve evacuation to Puerto Montt or Santiago. Every village has a *posta de salud*, which is a minimal medical centre for minor problems. Certainly outside of Coyhaique it is unlikely that doctors will speak English.

Tap water is drinkable across Chile, although mineral water is almost always available. To be really safe, stick to mineral water (though this should not be used to make up babies' feeds as the salt content is likely to be too high) or bring water to a rolling boil or use a water filter bottle such as Aquapure to filter any water that you drink. Anyone with a compromised immunity is more susceptible to infections. **Food poisoning and cholera** are not a great problem, but uncooked *ceviche* (shellfish) should be avoided (see opposite). Depletion of the ozone layer, coupled with dry, unpolluted air, has led to increased levels of ultraviolet radiation in southern Chile, causing **sunburn** and increasing the risk of cataracts and **skin cancer**. Be sure to wear good sunglasses and plenty of sunscreen.

While on the road, it is a good idea to carry a personal **first-aid kit**. Contents might include a good drying antiseptic (eg: iodine or potassium permanganate), plasters, suncream, insect repellent, aspirin or paracetamol, antifungal cream (eg: Canesten), ciprofloxacin or norfloxacin (for severe diarrhoea), antibiotic eye drops, tweezers, condoms, a digital thermometer and a needle and thread. Those suffering from allergies should bring the relevant medication or EpiPen with them to the region.

TRAVEL CLINICS AND HEALTH INFORMATION A full list of current travel clinic websites worldwide is available on w istm.org. For other journey preparation information, consult w travelhealthpro.org.uk (UK) or w nc.cdc.gov/travel (USA). Information about various medications may be found on w netdoctor.co.uk/travel. All advice found online should be used in conjunction with expert advice received prior to or during travel.

INOCULATIONS No vaccinations are legally required, but make sure you're up to date with **tetanus** and **diphtheria** – which these days comes with polio as the all-in-one Revaxis – and measles mumps and rubella vaccine (MMR).

Hepatitis A and **typhoid** vaccines may be recommended. These food and waterborne diseases are more likely to occur in travellers who are visiting friends and relatives, long-stay or frequent travellers, or those going to areas where there is poor sanitation. In addition hepatitis A would be also advised for certain occupations, men who have sex with men and intravenous drug users.

Hepatitis B About 2% of the population of Chile carry **hepatitis B** which is classed as an intermediate/high prevalence. Vaccination should be considered for everyone ideally, but especially those who may be at increased risk. Hepatitis B can be spread by having unprotected sex, sharing needles and through working in medical settings and with children. Families who are adopting a child from Chile should also consider vaccination. Three doses of vaccine should be given ideally over a minimum of three weeks for those aged 16 or over. Longer is needed for younger travellers.

Rabies Chile is considered a low-risk rabies country as rabies is only reported in wild animals. Anyone working with animals in Chile should be vaccinated. Most other travellers will be at low risk, but you should consider having a pre-exposure rabies vaccine if you are travelling longer term or are going to be away from good medical care. Ideally three doses of rabies vaccine over about three to four weeks are needed prior to travel. They are relatively painless and in most travellers need to be boosted only following an exposure.

Yellow fever This is not present in Chile and there is no requirement for proof of vaccination even if you are entering the country from yellow fever-infected areas.

LONG-HAUL FLIGHTS, CLOTS AND DVT Any prolonged immobility, including travel by land or air, can result in deep-vein thrombosis (DVT), which can be dangerous if the clot travels to the lungs to cause pulmonary embolus. The risk increases with age, and is higher in obese or pregnant travellers, heavy smokers, those taller than 6ft/1.8m or shorter than 5ft/1.5m, and anybody with a history of DVT or pulmonary embolism, recent major operation or varicose vein surgery, cancer, a stroke or heart disease. If you think you are at increased risk of a clot, ask your doctor if it is safe to travel.

To help prevent DVT, wear loose comfortable clothing, do anti-DVT exercises and move around when possible, drink plenty of fluids during the flight, avoid taking sleeping pills unless you are able to lie flat, avoid excessive tea, coffee and alcohol, and consider wearing flight socks or support stockings, which are widely available from pharmacies.

Symptoms of a pulmonary embolus – which commonly start three to ten days after a long flight – include chest pain, shortness of breath, and sometimes coughing up small amounts of blood. Anyone who thinks that they might have a DVT needs to see a doctor immediately.

ANIMAL/INSECT BITES There are **no venomous snakes**, although the **recluse spider** (*araña de rincón*), found in many homes, has a venomous bite which can kill. There are **biting insects** in summer in the south (and sometimes around Arica) but they don't carry diseases such as dengue, chikungunya or zika. *Tabanos* (horseflies) are prevalent across Patagonia in the summer. They are a nuisance but not life-threatening; they attack humans – particularly short-sleeved-shirt- and shorts-wearing trekkers – often in swarms, and do give a nasty bite. However, they are slow and easily swatted once they have landed on exposed skin. Motorcyclists should keep their visors closed if there is any danger of *tabanos*.

SHELLFISH The Marea Roja or 'Red Tide' is an accumulation of **toxic algae** which concentrate in shellfish and can cause death in humans; it occurs in southern Chile in hot weather. Shellfish is very closely monitored in markets and restaurants, but you should be extremely careful about any you gather yourself.

CHAGAS DISEASE Chagas disease is caused by the parasite *Trypanosoma cruzi*. It is mostly transmitted to humans by contact with the triatomine bug or its faeces. The bug lives in the walls and roof cracks of houses. In the acute phase most people have mild or no symptoms. In the chronic phase it can affect the heart and the gut. It is treatable if caught early. This disease is rare in most travellers.

HANTAVIRUS Andes virus (ANDV) is a type of Hantavirus first found in Chile in 1995. It is a cause of hantavirus cardiopulmonary syndrome (HCPS) which can be fatal. It is predominantly found in southern Chile.

Wild rodents of the family Cricetidae (in particular the long-tailed pygmy rat) carry the virus while looking healthy and can pass it to humans. Transmission occurs by inhaling aerosolised rodent excreta or through touching mucous membranes with contaminated hands. Person-to-person transmission can also occur within households. The incubation period varies from four days to eight weeks and the prodomal illness resembles flu, although sometimes gastrointestinal symptoms of diarrhoea and vomiting are the only early symptoms. Severe complications and death can occur in 35–50% of people with cardiopulmonary symptoms. There is no specific treatment or prophylactic vaccination available.

There is a higher risk in huts and *cabañas* which have been shut up over winter, so ensure they have been thoroughly aired. Cabins and campsites where there is visible evidence of rodent activity should not be used. If camping, ensure that you use a ground sheet, or preferably a camping bed, and ensure good hand hygiene at all times.

TRAVELLERS' DIARRHOEA Travelling in Chile carries a moderate risk of getting a dose of travellers' diarrhoea. It is estimated that around half of all visitors will suffer and the newer you are to exotic travel, the more likely you will be to succumb. By taking precautions against travellers' diarrhoea you will also avoid other infections such as typhoid, etc. Travellers' diarrhoea and the other faecal-oral diseases come from getting other people's faeces in your mouth. This results most often from cooks not washing their hands after a trip to the toilet, but even if the restaurant cook does not understand basic hygiene you will be safe if your food has been properly cooked and arrives piping hot. The most important prevention strategy is to wash your hands before eating anything. The maxim to remind you what you can safely eat is: PEEL IT, BOIL IT, COOK IT OR FORGET IT.

Fruit you have washed and peeled yourself and hot foods should be safe but be careful with raw foods and foods kept lukewarm in hotel buffets, as they can be dangerous. Dairy products such as yoghurt and ice cream are best avoided unless they come in proper packaging. That said, most good hotels and restaurants have good standards of hygiene and travellers should be able to enjoy a variety of foods.

HIV/AIDS The risks of sexually transmitted infection are moderately high in Chile whether you sleep with fellow travellers or locals. In 2020 about 0.6% of the population aged between 15 and 49 were living with HIV. Be safe and use condoms or femidoms, which help reduce the risk of transmission. If you notice any genital ulcers or discharge, get treatment promptly since these increase the risk of acquiring HIV. If you do have unprotected sex, visit a clinic as soon as possible – this should be within 24 hours or no later than 72 hours – for post-exposure prophylaxis.

SAFETY

The entire region of the Carretera Austral is astonishingly safe. The greatest threats are road accidents, or accidents relating to outdoor activities. Consider that communications are often poor, ambulances may have to travel extended distances on poor-quality roads, and medical facilities are limited.

The best means to avoid **road accidents** are: drive slowly; avoid driving at night; always use headlights (even during the day); use a vehicle suitable for the road conditions (page 55); ensure you can see through the rear-view mirror; assume there will be an oncoming truck or horse in the middle of the road on every blind corner and brow of a hill; do not stop on a corner; and pull off to the side of the road when snapping a photograph. For more information on driving in Chile, including rules and regulations, see the box on page 56.

Outdoor activities such as climbing, rafting, diving and horseriding carry inherent risks. Ensure the guide is qualified, has insurance, and participate according to your abilities. Use reputable operators, and if in doubt ask to see the SERNATUR qualification. Companies offering water activities require a licence, although informal and unlicensed companies also operate. Trekking, particularly in mountains, can be lethal for the ill-prepared. Although not as high as other parts of the Andes, weather can deteriorate rapidly.

Glaciers are potentially dangerous. Large chunks of ice fall at random intervals, often emitting small shards of ice in the process. When ice falls into lakes the subsequent wave can be sufficient to topple a boat. Trekking on glaciers should only be done with guides, as crevasses are not always visible.

WOMEN TRAVELLERS

Women travellers are equally safe. Care must be taken in certain rougher areas of Puerto Montt largely due to the prevalence of drunks. Taxis are the best means to travel at night. South of Puerto Montt there are very few safety issues. Around the mining areas it is possible to encounter the occasional drunk miner, but the same common-sense rules apply here as at home. Bars with suspicious red curtains are generally not the safest places in town, as they offer a range of 'services' not found in standard bars, and are perhaps best avoided by women travellers.

LGBTQ+ TRAVELLERS

While **same-sex unions** were legalised in Chile in April 2015, this remains a very conservative country and gay couples would be best advised to avoid public displays of affection. The only gay bar along the Carretera Austral is Club Angels in Puerto Montt (page 91).

TRAVELLING WITH A DISABILITY

The UK's **gov.uk** website (w gov.uk/government/publications/disabled-travellers) provides general advice and practical information for travellers with disabilities preparing for overseas travel. Where possible this guide lists hotels and restaurants with facilities for travellers with disabilities; unfortunately, these are few and far between. For example, it is impossible to drive a car down to Caleta Tortel, let alone a wheelchair, as access is via steep steps made all the more challenging by frequent rain and having to carry luggage. Significant sections of the Carretera Austral are not paved and, although this is slowly changing, the reality is simply that disabilities have not been considered in the construction of the vast majority of towns, buildings, restaurants, hotels, public transport options, roads or tourism facilities, and are the inhabitants of this region accustomed to assisting those with disabilities. It is rare to see people with disabilities, whether visitors or residents, along the Carretera Austral. However, this is changing. Otras Huellas (see box, above) offers a range of programmes enabling those with physical or cognitive disabilities to enjoy Patagonia.

TRAVELLING WITH KIDS

Although the Carretera Austral cannot be compared to Disneyworld, it is a surpassingly child-friendly region. Most villages have a central plaza with a playground. Hitchhiking or travelling by public transport may not be ideal with children, but with a private vehicle, and not travelling extended distances each day, the region offers excellent and unusual activities for children such as horseriding, swimming, moderate trekking, camping, boat trips, cycling some limited routes and visiting hot springs. There are very few museums, however; nor is there a cinema beyond Puerto Montt, meaning that entertaining children on a rainy day can be a challenge.

There are usually child discounts for entry to parks, activities and hotels. Some restaurants have dedicated children's menus, and those that do not will usually rustle up a suitable dish, or serve a smaller portion. However, note that most restaurants do not open before 20.00 for dinner.

For those with very young children, or wishing to do extended treks, a baby-carrier might be a wise purchase. Buggies are not really suitable outside of the towns due to the generally poor road quality. Baby/child seats in cars are obligatory, and the traffic regulations are enforced. It is rare, but not impossible, to find hotels with cots, particularly among the budget options. Sturdy boots and waterproofs are recommended for all outdoor activities.

WHAT TO TAKE

Self-sufficiency is the guiding principle when travelling on the Carretera Austral. Shops are few and far between, and generally overpriced.

GENERAL In addition to the usual items, be sure to take the items listed below. For those travelling by car, a cooler is a welcome treat, and a spare fuel tank may be advisable for some sections.

- Hats: for cold weather and blistering sunshine.
- Suncream and sunglasses: the sunshine can be relentless in this region, particularly on lakes and when trekking on snow or glaciers.
- Torches with plenty of batteries: many campsites do not have electricity.
- USB battery pack: for charging phones, torches, cameras, GPS, etc.
- Basic medical kit (page 46).
- Binoculars: the scenery is spectacular, the distances vast, and the wildlife extensive.
- Walking poles: can be useful.
- Adapter: electricity is 220–240V, standard two-pin European sockets.

<table>
<tr><td>TRAVELLING WITH KIDS – BY A KID</td><td>Victoria Sinclair</td></tr>
</table>

Victoria Sinclair is the author's eldest daughter. She accompanied her father on a research trip for this edition of the guide in December 2019, aged nine. This was her third trip along the Carretera, and these are her notes.

I saw flamingos in a pond and condors in the air. There were also lots of cats and dogs. We saw an armadillo by the border, and bunnies, cows, chickens, horses and geese, and even ñandus [small ostriches] running very quickly. My favourite animal for watching is the guanaco. I chased some in Parque Patagonia, which was naughty. The best playground is in La Tapera, it is very big and I had it all to myself. In Coyhaique there were pedal go-karts which were very fun. Ñirehuao had a huge playground also.

The best trip we did on the Carretera was to the Leones glacier. The boat trip to the glacier was nice, but the zipline across the river was scary. It was exciting going to the marble caves because there was an eclipse at the same time when the sun met the moon. When we saw the two rivers meeting [confluence of the rivers Nef and Baker] I was a bit scared. The museum in Coyhaique was fun for my daddy but it is a bit boring for kids. More fun was playing with a model airplane in the plaza in Coyhaique and seeing daddy climb a tree to rescue the plane. The hot springs in Aysén [Ensenada Pérez] were hot and nice and they gave us good food when we were in the pools and I made friends on the boat ride. It was an adventure to be carried across a river to see a waterfall [Cola de Gallo, Puerto Aysén], but it was really boring going to Lago Verde in the car. I like the ferries as I always made friends and one time I went to the engine room and met the captain of the boat. In Ayacara we had to make a path to cross a cold river, and when we got to the sea it was warm and salty. When we go to Puerto Montt I like to go to Casa de Ideas to buy games.

In the car the best thing to do is to look out of the window for animals. The most important things to take with you is a notebook to write down the animals you see, and colouring stuff. The best hotel in the Carretera is Marisol's hotel with a hot tub in the garden [El Gaucho in Puerto Cisnes], and the best food is fish and chips, and the sandwiches mummy made for the journey to Coyhaique.

Practical Information   WHAT TO TAKE

3

CLOTHES Regardless of the time of year, it rains and is windy in Patagonia. One quip about the changeability of the weather reassures, 'if you don't like the weather, wait five minutes'. A waterproof jacket is essential, and if planning to do extensive or multi-day trekking, consider suitable trousers also. There are a few outdoor clothing shops in Coyhaique, Puerto Aysén, Puerto Natales, Bariloche and Puerto Montt, but along most of the Carretera Austral there is none. Make sure that hiking boots are in good condition – even a simple repair can be hard to arrange and a loose sole could spell the end of some spectacular trekking. Likewise with tents – be prepared for all weather. In Cerro Castillo the weather can change alarmingly quickly; in January 2014 Israeli Noam Rubenstein froze to death on the mountain following a minor accident. If hiking in the high mountains take the required gloves, base layers, thermal socks, gaiters, crampons, etc. Laundry facilities are not always close to hand, so it is useful to have clothes for perhaps a week, and biodegradable soap for the occasional hand wash. Be sure to take swim gear.

CAMPING All standard camping equipment is required, white fuel (*bencina blanca*) is hard to obtain and most Chilean hikers use gas canister stoves, available in most towns. Where possible take repair kits for stoves, inflatable mattresses, tents, etc. Which sleeping bag to take is a tough decision, as temperatures can range dramatically according to the region, altitude and time of year. Down sleeping bags have a better warmth-to-weight ratio compared with synthetic bags, but rapidly lose their insulating properties when even slightly damp, and the Carretera Austral can be very damp. If using a down bag, store it in a dry bag. Stock up on essential food in large towns.

CLIMBERS Stock up on supplies in Puerto Montt, otherwise Coyhaique is the next place with a range of stores. It may be possible to borrow or buy equipment from local guides, but they tend to guard their equipment jealously given the difficulty of replacing it. At the very minimum take your own harness and climbing shoes.

(FREE) DIVERS For those wishing to dive, there is currently only one registered dive centre in the entire region, in Cochrane (page 302). The divers working on the salmon farms are generally unwilling, or not permitted, to fill tanks. Wetsuits and weights are available in Puerto Montt, and Coyhaique sells basic equipment. In practice it is generally easier to take the bare minimum (7mm hooded wetsuit, mask, snorkel, fins, weights, neoprene socks and gloves) and rely on snorkelling and apnea.

CYCLISTS Welding is generally possible at most towns, but there are few specialist cycle shops along the Carretera Austral outside of Coyhaique, and even here spare parts are limited. If buying a bike in Puerto Montt, it may be wise to buy a brand widely available in Chile, such as Trek or Oxford. Be prepared for almost any conceivable repair: spare chain, inner tubes, puncture repair kit, pump, lubricant, basic tools, etc. Also consider wearing a face mask, particularly in January and February when traffic is at its highest and rain is limited. The gravel roads become very dusty and passing cars produce a dust cloud that can linger for minutes. Bicycle helmets are not obligatory, but highly advisable. Cycle racks and panniers should be of high quality and purchased in advance.

MOTORCYCLISTS The simpler the motorbike the better. You will struggle to find BMW parts south of Osorno. On-board computers are a challenge, although

Coyhaique and Futaleufú have fairly well-equipped mechanics. It is useful to have a 12V tyre pump. Off-road or dual-purpose tyres can be bought in Puerto Montt, Osorno or Punta Arenas, and possibly in Coyhaique. The golden rule is simply to know your bike, and to know and anticipate its weaknesses. Essential spares or accessories to carry at all times include a chain link, chain lube, wet-weather clothing and good panniers. It is highly recommended to have a sump guard, engine guard, headlight protector and handlebar protectors (to protect the brake and clutch levers, as well as hands). Optional accessories would include spare levers, cables and possibly tyres. Most motorcyclists carry a spare fuel tank, but this might not be necessary: the longest stretches between petrol stations are detailed on page 58.

MONEY AND BUDGETING

MONEY

Banks and ATMs Only the larger towns have banks or ATMs (Puerto Montt, Hornopirén, Chaitén, Futaleufú, Palena, Puerto Cisnes, Puerto Aysén, Coyhaique, Chile Chico and Cochrane). Coyhaique has the widest range, and it is wise to stock up on pesos, as many places simply do not accept cards. Balmaceda aiport recently introduced an ATM – possibly the last in Chile to do so. Depending on the card, daily withdrawal limits are generally £200, although sometimes it is possible to do multiple withdrawals in a single day from different banks.

Currency The national currency of Chile is the peso ($). The current exchange rate (August 2022) is US$1=$898, £1=$1,096 and €1=$916. Security is generally not a problem along the Carretera Austral, so travelling with substantial sums of cash is not as risky as it would be in other regions. One option is to buy a small car safe that secures around a metal fixture in the car (typically under the seat), and can also be secured inside a hotel room if required.

US dollars can be used fairly extensively, and are worth having as a back-up. Argentine pesos are begrudgingly accepted in some places, but at an ever-deteriorating exchange rate. PayPal is used sporadically, but do not rely on it.

Credit cards Mastercard works at the most prolific bank in the region – Banco del Estado. Other debit/credit cards are more challenging for cash withdrawals, although paying in shops and petrol stations is usually possible with most major cards. Although credit and debit cards are becoming more common, many places are **cash only** – establishments that accept credit cards are listed as such. Also note that some hotels, shops and tour operators will accept foreign credit cards in-store, but not by telephone. Some hotels insist on a deposit to secure a booking, and if they are unable to take a credit card by phone or a written authorisation to charge the card in the case of a no-show, the only alternative is to deposit funds in a local bank account, which is common among Chileans. However, most Chileans working in tourism understand the difficulty this presents to foreigners and are flexible, particularly in the case of Argentines who simply cannot do international transfers. If it is essential to do a bank transfer from overseas, companies such as TransferWise offer favourable rates to Chile. For the benefit of all concerned, do not make reservations that you are not 99% sure to satisfy, as this will merely encourage operators to stop accepting reservations made in good faith. Most report that they have not had problems with taking reservations from foreigners *en confianza* (ie: based on trust), and long may this remain the case. Western Union uses the

3

ChileExpress network for transfers and has offices in Chaitén, Puerto Cisnes, Coyhaique, Chile Chico and Cochrane.

BUDGETING Chile is not the cheapest country in South America, and the Carretera Austral is not the cheapest region within Chile. Petrol is relatively expensive, approaching as much as $1,000 (£1) per litre in the more remote regions. In most places it is possible to sleep for under US$20 per person per night with a simple breakfast, although there are numerous places where wild camping is possible. It is equally possible to eat for under US$10 in most places; buying and cooking food is even cheaper. Public transport is generally quite reasonably priced considering the distances involved, but ferry connections can vary dramatically in cost depending on whether the route is subsidised or not. For example, the ferry from Caleta Gonzalo to Hornopirén is approximately half the price of the ferry from Chaitén to Quellón despite covering a similar distance. The two ferries connecting Villa O'Higgins to El Chaltén are expensive, but one has to consider the alternative cost of heading north, crossing the border at Paso Roballos or Paso Río Jeinimeni and travelling down to El Chaltén. The same applies to the ferry from Caleta Tortel to Puerto Natales. The mode of transport and number of people sharing a vehicle can alter the travel cost substantially. Needless to say, chartering private aircraft is not a budget option, but details of landing strips are covered in the relevant chapters.

Activities range in price dramatically, particularly when visiting Ventisquero San Rafael (US$200 pp) or the glaciers around Caleta Tortel (US$150 pp). The Ventisquero San Rafael is more economically visited from Puerto Río Tranquilo than from Puerto Chacabuco. Some of the more exclusive fishing lodges can be surprisingly expensive.

Car hire can have a big impact on the total cost, and is complex to estimate as the type of car, number of people sharing the cost, and whether it is a one-way rental can impact the overall price per person significantly. It is worth shopping around, but as a very rough estimate, US$50 per day (excluding one-way drop-off fee) should get a reasonable car.

Travelling on a budget A budget traveller should consider US$50 per person per day as the bare minimum, with some flexibility to reduce this slightly by camping, hitching and cooking. A more comfortable budget, including the occasional tour to one of the more expensive locations, could exceed US$100 per person per day, staying in decent accommodation with a private bathroom and generally eating out, slightly less per person if travelling as a couple and splitting accommodation costs. For a couple travelling the Carretera Austral on a tight budget for 20 days it is likely they would spend between US$1,500 and US$2,000 in total, excluding car hire.

Travelling without budget constraints At the other end of the spectrum, there are relatively few accommodation options costing more than US$300 per couple per night, and it is a challenge for a couple to spend more than US$100 per day on food, although fancy wines could stretch this. The few options to fly within the Carretera Austral generally involve missing key sections of the route. For example, to fly from Puerto Montt to Chaitén omits entirely the region around Hornopirén, and then requires renting a car with fewer options. Altogether, a couple travelling the Carretera 'in style' and returning on the finest cabin of the Navimag would be hard-pressed to spend more than US$10,000 for a thorough three-week trip (excluding international flights). Booking this through a tour operator in the UK could easily cost double.

GETTING AROUND

There is public transport to almost every inhabited community, but the frequency and reliability is subject to wide variation. Public transport between Coyhaique and Puerto Aysén is abundant, Puerto Cisnes and Balmaceda airport are well served, while Lago Verde, the Levicán Peninsula and Villa La Tapera are probably the hardest places to reach by public transport. Less frequent are buses to/from Chile Chico and Raúl Marín Balmaceda, and there is currently no public transport to Paso Roballos, Paso Puesto Viejo or Bahía Exploradores.

For a list of the various entry and exit points along the Carretera Austral, see the box on page 30.

BY PRIVATE VEHICLE Private vehicle is by far the most common form of transport. Renting a car is a viable option, and as the road conditions improve it is not necessary to hire a 4x4 to reach most parts of the Carretera Austral. International car-hire companies operate in Puerto Montt, with small concessions in Balmaceda airport affiliated to main offices in Coyhaique and are listed in the relevant sections.

Selecting a vehicle Foreign travellers visiting the Carretera Austral for a month or less are unlikely to bring their own vehicle or motorbike over, as it is too expensive to warrant the cost of shipping. Renting a vehicle or motorbike locally is the obvious alternative. However, an ever-increasing number of travellers ship their vehicles to South America to do an extended tour around the continent, in which case the Carretera Austral is a great option, and unlikely to be the most challenging terrain encountered on such a trip.

Popular choices for extended South American overland trips are long wheelbase 4x4s easily serviced in most regions, such as a Land Rover, Toyota Land Cruiser or Hilux. Any of these vehicles would be more than capable of traversing the Carretera Austral.

Is a 4x4 necessary? This depends on the route followed and the time of year. Certainly for the paved sections a 4x4 is not needed. Roadworks continue along the Carretera Austral as part of the broader road-paving project; ironically in the short term this might actually increase the usefulness of a 4x4, as the road quality generally deteriorates before improving with the arrival of the eventual tarmac. The worst section for roadworks is currently from Cerro Castillo to Río Tranquilo. The longest section of paved road is currently from Puerto Montt to Villa Cerro Castillo or Puerto Ibáñez, from where it is possible to cross the lake to Chile Chico (also paved) and cross into Argentina and join the (paved) Ruta 40 north or south.

There are relatively few places where a 4x4 is absolutely obligatory. Two notable exceptions would be the Argentine side of Paso Roballos when wet, and the westwards back road between Puerto Ibáñez and Cerro Castillo. As a rule, the major advantage of a 4x4 vehicle is the extra traction, the higher clearance and the heavier suspension more suitable for steep, heavily corrugated gravel roads with pot-holes. For the very few people who visit the Carretera Austral in winter, a 4x4 would be advisable.

Outside of winter a high ground clearance (>20cm) car is highly recommended to clear the ridge in the centre of gravel roads formed by tyre ruts and road graders; to cross the occasional river; and for protection from larger rocks and pot-holes.

DRIVING IN CHILE

The only encounter a traveller on the Carretera Austral is likely to have with the authorities is for traffic violations. Traffic regulations are more tightly enforced than in Argentina, but not with the vigour of central and northern Chile. Speed cameras or radar guns are rare and where there are speed limits the road condition itself generally limits maximum speed.

Particularly for those coming from other countries in Latin America it is worth remembering that **Chilean police**, and **border guards**, do not take bribes, and to offer one is a serious offence.

RULES AND REGULATIONS
- Drive on the right-hand side.
- Driving with headlights turned on, day and night, is mandatory.
- Seat belts are obligatory for all – all passengers, including in the back seats, must have seat belts secured, and children must use booster seats when required.
- The alcohol limit is 0.05%. There are heavy fines or possible imprisonment for exceeding the blood alcohol limit.
- The use of a mobile phone while driving without a hands-free kit is prohibited.
- Smoking or listening to a personal music player with headphones while driving is illegal.
- Speed limits: 100–120km/h on two-lane highways, 60km/h in urban areas.
- When changing a tyre by the side of the road, it is obligatory to wear a high-visibility vest, usually provided in rental cars.
- It is illegal to park facing oncoming traffic, ie: always park in the direction of traffic.

SAFE DRIVING PRACTICES
- Care should be exercised when changing lanes or merging as many drivers do not signal lane changes and rarely give way to merging traffic.
- Always drive slowly when approaching a road junction and be prepared to give way even if you have the right of way or the green light (especially relevant for motorbikes and cyclists).
- Give way to pedestrians at all times.
- Take extra care when driving in the mountains because of tight switchbacks without guardrails, and watch out for large pot-holes, rocks and loose gravel.

WHAT TO TAKE
- International driver's licence.
- Adequate road insurance – this is obligatory and often verified at the border upon arrival.
- Passport – in case you get stopped by the police.
- Road map of the area you are driving in (pages 58 and 345).
- If travelling with children, and to avoid the expense of hiring a child booster seat, consider taking your own (eg: the Trunki Boostapak handily doubles as a backpack).

A steel sump guard protector is useful, and all-terrain tyres help to reduce wheel slip and increase traction on gravel roads. Overloading a front-wheel drive reduces traction precisely when it is most needed: ascending steep gravel sections.

We used a standard Renault Duster (1.6-litre petrol, two-wheel drive with 210mm clearance). Such a vehicle will reach all sections of the Carretera Austral in all but extreme cases (snow storms in winter, landslides, floods, etc), and 95% of the detours. Many people living in this region do not have such a car, let alone a fancy 4x4. In the rare cases where such a vehicle cannot reach a certain destination, alternative transport is generally possible for a reasonable fee.

Car hire Most car-hire companies require a minimum age of 22–24 years, a valid driver's licence in the country of origin or a valid international driver's licence, valid passport and a credit-card guarantee of between US$500 and US$1,000. It is important to consider the following factors. First, much of the Carretera Austral south of Coyhaique is unpaved, meaning that a small car with low clearance will not traverse some sections, particularly when wet, and most vehicles have an excess for damages. If considering the more remote sections of the Carretera Austral, get a car that is suitable for the terrain. Second, one-way rentals tend to be expensive, so it is generally wise to plan a loop or round trip, or to return to Puerto Montt on the Navimag (page 29). Third, you will need the vehicle registration to book a ferry ticket; this can be provided at a later date (page 61). Finally, if intending to pass through Argentina ensure the car can be taken out of the country and that you have the required paperwork, including insurance.

Campervan rental A relatively recent phenomenon, campervan rentals are now taking off in Chile. The key differences between the companies, besides the vehicles themselves, are whether they allow one-way rentals, where the pickup/drop-off locations are, if the van can cross the border to Argentina, if insurance is included, sleeping arrangements (internal or roof-top tent), kitchen facilities and whether the daily mileage is limited or not.

Holiday Rent RV \ 2 2745 1988, 9 9822 3896; e reservas@holidayrent.cl; w holidayrent.cl. Offices in Santiago, Puerto Varas, Coyhaique & Punta Arenas. One of the best-established rental companies in Chile, with English-, Spanish- & German-speaking staff & 40 vehicles. Offers a wide selection of 4x4 vehicles, for 2–4 people, ranging from those with basic sleeping/cooking equipment to fully equipped vehicles with bathroom & shower. Authorised to cross borders, 24hr support, limited daily mileage & one-way drop-off charges. €85–300/day (min 15-day rental in high season, includes insurance, cheaper in low season or for longer periods). Rents satellite phones or Garmin satellite communicators.

Kawascars Coyhaique; \ 9 9214 1730; e info@kawascars.com; w kawascars.com. Small 2-person vans starting at $70,000/day (& insurance fee, 250km/day), but can cross into Argentina. Cooler, table & chairs included,

cooking accessories available for a small additional fee. One-way rentals are possible, also for a fee.

Masai Campers \ 2 3202 6365, 9 4211 7790; e info@masaicampers.com; w masaicampers. cl. Keeps things simple: 3 top-quality vehicles to choose from, all with roof tent beds, dramatically increasing living space. Complete camping kitchen, fridge, bedding, full insurance, 24hr support, multi-lingual & able to cross the Argentine border. The game-changer from this company is allowing pickup & drop-off anywhere in the country at no extra cost (min rental 7 days, from US$140/day). This makes it ideal for Carretera Austral trips & is the only company to offer this. Part of Masai Travel empire, who also shoot a popular travel programme – these guys know Chile & help with trip planning along the entire route in both Chile & Argentina, including ferry bookings.

Rolling Patagonia Coyhaique; 9 8527 0691, 9 9462 7844; e info@rollingpatagonia. cl; w rollingpatagonia.cl. 5 types of van, ranging from a 2-person campervan up to a 5-person motorhome, from $105,000 to $245,000/day accordingly (cheaper in low season or for rentals of more than 15 days). Most include bed(s), plates, fridge, sink, solar panel, 220V plugs, table & chairs, & barbecue. The larger motorhomes include bathroom with shower, microwave & full table. Interestingly they include a satellite communicator for emergencies. One-way possible but for a fee; cards accepted.

Soul Vans 9 5417 3743; e mcastro@soulvans. com; w soulvans.com. Pickup/drop-off in Puerto Montt, Santiago & Punta Arenas. Family business, 24/7 support. 3-week trip from Puerto Montt to Punta Arenas including Argentina. 250km/day ranges from $1,500,000 for the basic 2-person van up to $1,950,000 for a 2-person motorhome with shower, full kitchen, etc. Good budget option.

Wicked Campers 9 4207 3790; e info@ wickedsouthamerica.com; w wickedsouthamerica. com. A franchise of the Australian company, with a wide range of vans including some with rooftop tents. Typical one-way rental for 3 weeks is US$2,900. Pick-up/drop-off in Santiago, Puerto Varas or Punta Arenas, insurance added at check-out, low cost, younger audience, 250km daily limit.

Petrol stations
Petrol is available in most towns along the Carretera Austral – where this is the case, it is listed. The dominant petrol companies are COPEC and Petrobras. Informal vendors of petrol do exist, but their availability and the quality of the petrol are uncertain. It is almost unheard of for petrol stations to run out of petrol.

At the time of writing there was no petrol available at the COPEC station in Puyuhuapi (diesel is available). It is not clear if COPEC will install a new tank to store petrol. The nearest petrol station is 47km north at La Junta, 90km south in Puerto Cisnes or Mañihuales. **Note** that it is not permitted to cross the border with a spare fuel tank, in either direction. Towns without a petrol station are:

- Raúl Marín Balmaceda and Lago Verde (150km/156km round trip from La Junta)
- Alto Río Cisnes and the Río Frías Apeleg border (77km/150km to Alto Río Senguer/Gobernador Costa in Argentina; 151km/175km to Mañihuales/ Puerto Cisnes in Chile, ie: maximum distance of 325km from Puerto Cisnes to Gobernador Costa without a petrol station)
- Balmaceda (55km from Coyhaique, 169km from Puerto Río Tranquilo)
- Cerro Castillo (93km from Coyhaique, 125km from Puerto Río Tranquilo) and Puerto Ibáñez (118km from Coyhaique, 157km from Puerto Río Tranquilo)
- The longest single stretch without a formal petrol station is currently Coyhaique to Puerto Río Tranquilo going via Puerto Ibáñez and Puerto Sánchez, which is approximately 330km.

Maps
The easiest map for most travellers on the Carretera Austral to obtain is COPEC's **Chiletur Zona Sur** (w chiletur.cl). This is a small book that is updated annually and includes town and regional maps. It is not the most detailed map on the market, but for most travellers it is sufficient. The COPEC guide can be purchased at any COPEC service station throughout Chile or online as an app. Other maps are available for purchase at kiosks and bookshops throughout the region. **Local tourist information centres** are a great place to pick up a free street map of the town and surrounding areas. Some tourist information centres have an excellent free foldout map of the entire Carretera Austral – it's well worth getting hold of one of these. All national parks and reserves provide maps for the trails within their boundaries.

BY BUS In high season buses fill up quickly (particularly the international bus from Coyhaique to Río Mayo in Argentina), and in low season the frequency diminishes yet further; departure and arrival times are 'flexible'. Some buses deliberately synchronise with connecting boats or buses from other regions, adding an inevitable element of volatility into the timetables. It is wise to arrange public transport in advance wherever possible, arrive early and be prepared to wait – when staying in a village for a few days consider buying your departing bus ticket as soon as you arrive. Often it is possible to make a change for a small fee, or cancel with relatively little penalty if done in advance. However, many routes are served only once per day. Note that a major advantage of travelling by public transport between Chaitén and Hornopirén/Puerto Montt is that the ferry crossing is included in the price, and the bus has an assured place on the ferry. There are buses between Puerto Montt and Hornopirén (direct or via Cochamó/Puelo), with connections to Chaitén. From Chaitén there are frequent buses to La Junta – a relative transport hub in the region – and less frequent buses to both Futaleufú and Palena. La Junta is well connected to Coyhaique, with stops at all main towns and villages along the Carretera Austral. Likewise, Coyhaique is well connected with Cochrane. From Cochrane there are buses to Caleta Tortel and to Villa O'Higgins, but with reduced frequency.

Bus times from Puerto Montt are fairly reliable, but thereafter less so. Scheduled bus times not only change frequently, but even when fixed are subject to the vagaries of weather conditions and traffic.

In this guide, we have given as much information as is available on those companies operating the routes along the various stages of the Carretera Austral within the relevant sections of the book. Note that bus companies, telephone numbers, routes, prices, frequencies and times are subject to constant changes. Most companies do not have a reliable website, so often the only way to confirm a bus time and discover how to buy a ticket is by telephone. Most companies do not accept credit cards so making a reservation can be a challenge, and phone numbers change frequently. Many buses can only be booked locally, in particular those serving the various detours off the Carretera. If travelling by local transport, it is often a case of sticking your thumb out on the side of the road and getting on the first thing that stops.

ON FOOT Hitchhiking is a viable alternative to public transport. Certain stretches are reportedly harder than others, in particular from Chile Chico to the main Carretera and from Puerto Río Tranquilo. Security concerns associated with hitchhiking seem non-existent along the Carretera.

BY SEA The ferry crossings are the single biggest logistical hurdle in the entire region. After long-haul flights this is probably the most important element to arrange in advance. Once organised, be sure to get to the ferry on time, and check the updated time at least one day before departure. A missed ferry can have dire consequences: detours via Argentina can add hundreds of kilometres to the journey and days of additional travel. Chaitén to Puerto Montt takes 9 hours by ferry. Driving south to Futaleufú, crossing into Argentina, crossing back into Chile at Paso Cardenal Samoré and getting to Puerto Montt is an entire day's drive of 830km requiring two border crossings.

Ferry companies

Naviera Austral e contacto@ navieraustral.cl; w navieraustral.cl. Main office,

Puerto Montt, Av Angelmó 1673; \65 227 0430/1/2; Castro; \65 263 5254; Quellón; \65

268 2206/7; Chaitén; ☎65 273 1011/2; Futaleufú; ☎9 7478 2394; Palena; ☎65 274 1319; Puerto Aguirre; ☎67 236 1357; Puerto Cisnes; ☎67 234 6558, 9 8448 2837; Coyhaique; ☎67 221 0638; Puerto Aysén; ☎9 4564 2705; Chacabuco; ☎67 235 1493; Puerto Ibáñez; ☎9 3448 8688; Puerto Gaviota; ☎9 6694 1447; Ayacara; ☎65 280 8431, 9 8593 7221; Melinka; ☎67 243 1510; Raúl Marín Balmaceda; ☎9 7528 8448; Puerto Gala; ☎9 4745 5938. Call centre; ☎600 401 9000.

🚢 **Navimag** e sales@navimag.cl; w navimag.com. Offices in Puerto Montt, Av Diego Portales 2000; ///paint.fountain.scenes; ☎2 2411 2600; Coyhaique, Eusebio Lillo 91; ///reunion.client.stores; ☎2 2411 2650 (page 29).

🚢 **Somarco** Puerto Montt office, Av Angelmó 1673; ///managed.crimson.types; ☎65 229 4855/8; e mmorillo@somarco.cl; Hornopirén office, Ingenieros Militares 450; ///

rousing.autofocus.cucumber; ☎65 221 7413/4; e ymaldonado@somarco.cl; Chaitén office, Juan Todesco 188; ///weeknight.leftover.thereof; ☎65 273 1760/2; e kmillacahuin@somarco.cl; w barcazas.cl (for Chile Chico–Puerto Ibáñez route w barcazas.cl/barcazas/web/lago-general-carrera). Also offices in Coyhaique, Chile Chico & Puerto Ibáñez. Generic e contacto@somarco.cl.

🚢 **Tabsa (Transbordadora Austral Broom)** ☎61 272 8100; w tabsa.cl; Puerto Natales office, Pedro Montt 605; ///unlit.figurines.hyphens; ☎61 241 5966; e reservasnatales@tabsa.cl; Caleta Tortel/Puerto Yungay office; ☎9 6788 6824; e agentetortel@tabsa.cl

🚢 **Transportes Puelche** Av Angelmó 2187; ///smooth.bump.retract; ☎65 247 0101, 65 227 6490; e info@navierapuelche.cl; w transportespuelche.cl

Ferry services

Ferry services The following ferry services are currently in operation across the region. Beware that times are subject to change due to tides/weather.

🚢 **Puerto Montt to Chaitén** (via Ayacara); Naviera Austral; 11.00 Mon, 23.00 Tue–Fri, 22.00 Sat; returns 23.00 Mon, 11.00 Wed–Sat, 23.30 Sun (9hrs; $17,800 pp, $117,000/car (1 passenger travels free with car), $22,000/motorbike, $10,500/bicycle)

🚢 **Caleta La Arena to Caleta Puelche** Transportes del Estuario; 56 return trips per day, day & night, reduces to 40 in low season, prior reservations not necessary (25mins; passengers free, $2,800/bicycle, $7,400/motorbike, $10,300/car)

🚢 **Hornopirén to Caleta Gonzalo** (via Leptepú & Fiordo Largo); Somarco; once daily 10.30, arrives 15.45; return 13.00, arrives 17.15. The journey involves 2 separate ferries, but sold as a single ticket this costs $35,400/car or $8,900/motorbike (1 passenger travels free with car/motorbike, $5,900 each additional passenger). The northern section takes approximately 3½hrs, the southern section only 40mins. The ferries are synchronised with one another, but assume this entire journey will take between 5 & 6hrs. A free bus takes pedestrians from one ferry to the next.

🚢 **Chaitén to Quellón** Naviera Austral; 09.00 Sat, returns 19.00 Sun (4hrs; $17,000 pp, $95,000/car, $18,300/motorbike, $11,500/bicycle)

🚢 **Puerto Cisnes to Quellón** (via Melinka); Naviera Austral; 03.00 Tue, 09.00 Wed, Fri & Sun, returns noon Mon, 18.00 Tue, Thu & Sat (12hrs; $24,490 pp, $49,000/motorbike, $144,120/car)

🚢 **Chaitén to Castro** Naviera Austral; 09.30 Sun, returns 16.30 Sun (5hrs; $17,000 pp, $95,000/car, $18,300/motorbike, $11,500/bicycle)

🚢 **Puerto Ibáñez to Chile Chico** Somarco; 1 or 2 boats/day (2hrs; $2,400 pp, $20,350/car, $4,050/motorbike, $1,550/bicycle); times vary

🚢 **Chacabuco to Quellón** Naviera Austral; 18.00 Mon & noon Fri, returns 01.00 Thu & 23.00 Sat (31hrs; slow indirect service visiting Puerto Aguirre, Puerto Gaviota, Puerto Cisnes, Isla Toto, Melimoyu, Santo Domingo, Raúl Marín Balmaceda & Melinka). Cost for entire journey $37,990 pp, $245,560/car, correspondingly less for segments.

🚢 **Ayacara to Pichicolo** Transportes Puelche; 06.00 Wed & Fri, 10.00 Sun, returns 19.00 same day, 1 ferry less in low season ($2,600 pp, $10,500/car, $3,900/motorbike, $2,600/bicycle)

🚢 **Ayacara to Caleta Gonzalo** Transportes Puelche; 07.00 Mon (also Tue in high season), returns 17.00 same day ($2,500 pp, $6,300/car, $3,800/motorbike, $2,500/bicycle)

🚢 **Chumeldén to Caleta Gonzalo** Transportes Puelche; 08.00 Wed, returns 18.00 same day ($2,100 pp, $6,300/car, $3,200/

FERRY FRUSTRATING – AQUATIC BOTTLENECKS

Booking ferries is one of the most complex, infuriating and urgent stages of planning a trip to the Carretera. The ferry websites range from poor to adequate, and have actually improved dramatically in recent years. Some routes fill up extremely quickly, and there is often no obvious alternative to taking a ferry other than a major driving detour. Pedestrians and those using public transport are spared the worst of the ferry hassles but should still try to book a week in advance in high season. Those with cars should book at least one month in advance. Changes are possible in theory, tricky in practice, always depend on availability of the new date desired and inevitably require an hour or two visiting an office. The main private companies (Navimag and Skorpios) tend to be better run and have far fewer ferries, generally traversing far longer distances. The shorter routes within the Carretera Austral are the main headaches, and three companies dominate these: Naviera Austral, Somarco and Transportes Puelche. The last tends to operate routes less frequently used by visitors. The main routes to be particularly wary of are:

Somarco – the Hornopirén to Caleta Gonzalo route has two ferries per day in high season, the website functions well and accepts most foreign credit cards. If renting a vehicle and you wish to book the ferry before you know the registration number, insert 'RENTxxxx' in the field requesting the registration number, where the xxxx is the last four digits of your ID document. Somarco also operates the ferry across Lago General Carrera, which also fills up in high season. Arriving in January/February and hoping to take a ferry the next day with a car is unwise on any route.

Naviera Austral used to be the nightmare of tourists and locals alike. To be fair, they have improved dramatically. The website now accepts foreign credit cards and if booking a ticket with a rental car but without the registration details, place 'XXXXXX' in the appropriate field and drop them an email, pop into an office, or arrive an extra hour early for the ferry. The daily ferry between Chaitén and Puerto Montt is usually OK if booked a week or so in advance, but the less frequent ferries can pose a problem: Quellón to Chaitén (three per week), Quellón to Cisnes (four per week), Chaitén to Castro (one a week). The stopping service between Quellón and Chacabuco should definitely be booked as early as possible. For those living along the intermediate stops this is their only means to travel.

Tabsa – for the ferry between Caleta Tortel and Puerto Natales, if travelling with a rental car place 'Rentacar' in the online form if you do not have the registration document, and inform them by email when you do.

Ferries often leave early, or late. Delays tend to accumulate, as it is the same boat doing a single route so it's very hard to make up time lost previously. Always confirm a day or so before departure, but do not expect rapid service either by phone or in an office.

motorbike, $2,100/bicycle, only operates the 1st 3 Weds of the month).

🚗 **Chumeldén to Pichicolo** (via Ayacara); Transportes Puelche; 2nd & 4th week of the month, 06.00 Fri, returns 15.00 Sun ($4,700 pp, $16,800/car, $7,100/motorbike, $4,700/bicycle).

🚗 **Puerto Canelo to Puerto Maldonado (Lago Tagua Tagua)** Transportes Puelche; 07.00, 09.00, 13.00 & 18.00 daily, returns 08.00, noon, 17.00 & 19.00 same day (under 1hr; $1,050 pp, $7,000/car, $2,100 motorbike)

🚗 Puerto Yungay (cars)/Caleta Tortel (pedestrians) to Puerto Natales (via Puerto Eden); Tabsa; departs Puerto Yungay weekly 20.00 Sat & Caleta Tortel 22.00 Sat, arrives Puerto Eden noon Sun, arrives Puerto Natales 15.00 Mon; returns weekly on Thu, departs Puerto Natales 05.00, arrives Puerto Eden 07.00 Fri, arrives Caleta Tortel (pedestrians) 22.00 Fri, Puerto Yungay (cars) 01.00 Sat (44hrs; $128,450 pp, $102,760/car, $25,690/motorbike, $10,710/bicycle)

🚗 Puerto Yungay to Puerto Bravo w barcazafiordomitchell.cl; Nov–Mar 10.00, noon, 16.00 & 18.00 daily, returns 11.00, 13.00, 17.00 & 19.00; Apr–Oct noon & 15.00 daily, returns 13.00 & 16.00 (free)

BY AIR Charter flights are expensive, although if travelling with sufficient people to fill the plane the price becomes more accessible. Currently the only scheduled flights within the Carretera Austral are between Villa O'Higgins and Coyhaique, Chaitén and Puerto Montt, Chile Chico and Coyhaique, and Ayacara and Puerto Montt. Commercial flights between Coyhaique/Balmaceda and Puerto Montt/ Santiago/Punta Arenas are reasonably priced.

ACCOMMODATION

Options abound along most sections of the Carretera Austral. Wherever people live there is a hostel or a *casa familiar*, but in peak season these can fill up quickly, particularly in towns such as Lago Verde, Puyuhuapi, Raúl Marín Balmaceda, Puerto Río Tranquilo, Villa Santa Lucía and Caleta Tortel. There is a bewildering range of names for accommodation in Chile, each referring to a specific legal structure. Budget accommodation tends to be referred to as *hostal*, *residencial* or *hospedaje*; *cabañas* (cabins) can range from cheap to positively pricey options; lodges and hotels tend to be mid-price and upwards. Confusingly the term *spa* can refer to a spa (sauna, pool, massages, etc) or to a legal structure of a company in Chile. Camping is possible in every town, and if not, wild camping is usually tolerated.

Since the Covid pandemic there has been a dramatic increase in the supply of informal cabins as residents seek new sources of income. It remains to be seen if these will formalise or phase out over time.

The Carretera Austral lends itself to the adventure traveller, as typified by the younger backpacker armed with a tent and flexible accommodation requirements but comparatively modest budget. Mid-price-range accommodation and food options are increasingly common, but at the higher end of the spectrum those with fewer budget constraints seeking adventurous alternatives to the standard luxury options within South America have a surprising array of options. High-end accommodation along the Carretera Austral was arguably pioneered by the Puyuhuapi Lodge and Spa (page 180), and some upmarket fishing lodges, but there are now a number of positively comfortable, even luxurious, hotels (and to a lesser extent, restaurants) for those not necessarily interested in fishing. Indeed, at the time of writing, the only principal destinations lacking an upper-end place to sleep are Hornopirén, downtown Chaitén, Palena, Puerto Cisnes, Chile Chico and Puerto Ibáñez.

Hot water can generally be taken for granted. Some hostels rely on one central wood stove to heat the building, which is not ideal in winter, but increasingly central heating is becoming an economical and convenient alternative. In all but the most basic accommodation a towel and soap are provided. Wi-Fi is prolific, laundry less so. Off-road parking is abundant, but not strictly necessary as car theft is rare. Motorcyclists typically prefer not to leave their bikes parked on the street if only to enable them to leave non-urgent accessories attached to the bike and avoid kids playing with them.

ACCOMMODATION PRICE CODES

The following accommodation price codes are very approximate and refer to a typical double room with a private bathroom (where a private bathroom is available) in peak season. Many hotels/hostels in this region have a wide range of options within a single property, so we have also included prices within listings to cover anomalies to the double room price.

Some hotels, typically more formally registered companies, are able to offer discounts to foreigners paying in US dollars or on a foreign credit card, with proof that they are non-resident in Chile (passport with stamp suffices). This is because the sale is classified as an 'export' and thus exempt from sales tax (19%).

Luxury	$$$$$	over $150,000	over US$180
Upper range	$$$$	$85,000–150,000	US$100–180
Mid-range	$$$	$40,000–85,000	US$50–100
Budget	$$	$25,000–40,000	US$30–50
Low end	$	up to $25,000	up to US$30

All accommodation listed is open during high season (November to March), but this is extending each year. Places which close during this period, or are open outside of high season, are listed as such.

As a general rule, in early 2022 most villages have basic accommodation with a simple breakfast for under $20,000 per person (US$25). It is rare to find accommodation for under $10,000 per person (or US$12) without camping.

LUXURY ACCOMMODATION For those looking to splash the cash, there are a number of options along the Carretera Austral (all **$$$$–$$$$$**). From north to south, these are:

Hotel Manquehue Puerto Montt. Modern, hip hotel, debatably the finest in town but for surprisingly reasonable rates, & a great restaurant/bar (page 86).

Mítico Puelo Lodge Lake Tagua Tagua. Remote adventure/fishing lodge accessible only by boat, great food & a complete escape from daily life (page 109).

Lodge Caleta Gonzalo Caleta Gonzalo. Delightful, rustic cabins at the edge of Parque Pumalín, with a stunning view over the fjord & the only restaurant for miles (page 133).

Yelcho en la Patagonia 51km south of Chaitén, this upmarket dedicated fishing lodge on the lake is close to the glacier & has a fine restaurant (page 137).

Hotel El Barranco Futaleufú. The finest accommodation in town with pool & quality restaurant (page 148).

Hotel Espacio y Tiempo La Junta. Fine hotel, excellent service & the best restaurant in town (page 162).

Melimoyu Lodge Raúl Marín Balmaceda. Boutique fishing lodge by a volcano with an array of activities & fine food (page 169).

Fundo Los Leones Raúl Marín Balmaceda. Fantastic cabins on the beach with abundant wildlife & fishing (page 168).

El Pangue Lodge Between La Junta & Puyuhuapi. Top-quality adventure lodge (page 181).

Puyuhuapi Lodge & Spa 20km south of Puyuhuapi. Refurbished, classic, top-end lodge with idyllic remote location & hot springs (page 180).

Los Loberías del Sur Puerto Chacabuco. Standard 5-star option, also offering a range of tours including a catamaran trip to Ventisquero San Rafael (page 208).

63

🏠 **Nómades** Coyhaique. A definitive boutique hotel & oasis in the relative hustle of Coyhaique, with fantastic views over the valley, & yet within walking distance of the centre (page 223).

🏠 **Catedral Lodge** Puerto Sánchez. Idyllic cabins on the lake, fine food, catamarans to the marble caves, & utter tranquillity (page 256).

🏠 **Hacienda Tres Lagos &/or Mallín Colorado EcoLodge** 50km south of Puerto Río Tranquilo, close to Puerto Bertrand & the detour towards Chile Chico. Top-end adventure lodges with good restaurants (pages 269 & 270).

🏠 **The Lodge at Chacabuco Valley** 15km north of Cochrane. Magnificent lodge within the spectacular Parque Patagonia, with wildlife visible from almost every window (page 297).

🏠 **Lodge El Mirador de Guadal &/or Patagonia Acres Lodge** Top-end cabins with spectacular views over the lake. On the road from Chile Chico – probably the finest accommodations on Lago General Carrera (page 274).

🏠 **Hotel Ultimo Paraíso** Cochrane. The only upper–mid-range option in Cochrane, a hub of activities, & the owner is a fanatical fishing guide (page 303).

🏠 **Entre Hielos Lodge** Caleta Tortel. The only boutique option in town, with a well-run, homely feel. Can arrange incredible glacial tours (page 315).

🏠 **Rumbo Sur Deep Patagonia Lodge** Villa O'Higgins. Excellent accommodation but no restaurant, first or last stop along the Carretera (page 324).

EATING AND DRINKING

Every village, however small, has a place to eat and a shop. Whether these are open or not is another issue. In smaller villages businesses tend to close around 20.00, or 21.00 if there are no customers, and restaurants may not have formal opening hours. It is wise to eat early. On the other hand, in larger towns restaurants might not open until 20.00. Lunch is generally available from 13.00 to 15.00. In Coyhaique and Puerto Aysén it is possible to find somewhere to eat all day and up to midnight. Coyhaique is the only place with all-night restaurants.

Tips are occasionally included on the bill in a restaurant; if not, they are not expected, and rounding up the amount is appreciated and sufficient.

Chilean fare can become rather repetitive particularly along the Carretera Austral, where culinary creativity seems scarce. Expect to find *merluza* (hake), *congrio* (eel), *mariscos* (shellfish), *puye* (small, whitebait-like fish), a meat dish, perhaps *cazuela* (meat or fish stew), chips, potatoes, a basic salad, deep-fried bread and a range of nondescript puddings. Meat described as *mechada* is shredded, and *milanesa* in thin slices, coated in breadcrumbs; *a lo pobre* contains salad, a fried egg and chips. *Curanto* is a particular delicacy originating in Chiloé, and is certainly worth trying. It generally contains two plates – one of shellfish and fish, and one of meat, a sausage, potatoes and a potato dumpling, all cooked together in the same pot. Strictly speaking a proper curanto should be cooked in a hole in the ground covered with leaves and mud, but this is generally only available on the island of Chiloé. The best place to try curanto along the Carretera Austral is Cocinería Altamar in Chaitén (page 128).

Although limited, there are some variations from Chilean cuisine: Coyhaique has sushi, Italian food and some excellent high-end restaurants. The German settlers of the region in the early 20th century secured an ongoing supply of cakes and savoury snacks (*kuchen*), as well as decent bread. Lamb (*cordero*), where available, is excellent; (*vaca, or ternero*) beef is abundant but rarely cooked to the standard found in Argentina. Seafood is common and vegetarians, even vegans, may actually find this region to be more compatible with their food tastes than Argentina. A number of restaurants offer a vegetarian option.

Many restaurants offer a *menú del día* (set menu with limited choice), which are generally very good value and popular among the locals. Many cabins, and some

The following restaurant price codes refer to a typical meal, per person, excluding drinks.

Luxury	$$$$	over $20,000	over US$25
Upper range	$$$	$13,000–20,000	US$15–25
Mid-range	$$	$8,000–13,000	US$10–15
Budget	$	up to $8,000	up to US$10

hostels or hotels, offer self-catering barbecue facilities (*parrilla/asado*), and often these are included in a separate outhouse, called a *quincho*. Ideal for groups, this is basically a building available for rent with tables, plates, cutlery, etc, where guests can prepare their own food, usually lamb or steak, bought privately or arranged through the hotel/hostel.

Wine is available in mid-range restaurants but tends to be overpriced and offers limited variety; a finer range is available in upper-end restaurants, albeit at a price. Local **beers** are more abundant and cheaper. Chileans debate with Peruvians as to the true inventor of **Pisco**, but it is fair to say that almost anywhere along the Carretera Austral it is possible to find a decent Pisco sour, including flavoured with local berries and fruits. The water is generally fine to drink straight from the tap.

Standard beers available across Chile include Cristal and Escudo, or the now semi-national beers from medium-sized breweries like Kunstmann and Austral. However, a growing passion in the region is the production of fine craft beer (*cerveza artesanal*). What better way to utilise the abundant pure water of southern Chile than to make great beer? Most restaurants and bars will have at least one regional beer (usually bottled, sometimes on tap).

FINE DINING The prevalence of **gourmet** restaurants has not kept up with the number of high-end hotels in the region. Most are within the hotels listed on page 63. South of Coyhaique, upper-end restaurants are few and far between. Nevertheless, the following restaurants (listed below from north to south) are genuinely of a high quality, but even in the most expensive of these restaurants, a couple would be hard-pressed to spend more than US$100 on a single meal excluding wine.

✖ **Fogón Cotelé, Chile Picante & Pa' Mar Adentro** (Page 88) Puerto Montt. Superb quality meat & seafood.

✖ **El Fogón Costero** (Page 111) Hualaihué. Hidden gem of a restaurant on the remote peninsula – superb seafood.

✖ **Cocinería Altamar** (Page 128) Chaitén. The best opportunity to try a traditional curanto along the Carretera.

✖ **Martín Pescador** (Page 150) Futaleufú. Creative flair meets fine ingredients in a lovely space with excellent service.

✖ **El Mesón de la Patiko** (Page 209) Puerto Aysén. Once is not enough – too many exquisite seafood & meat dishes to cope with in a single visit.

✖ **CB Gastronomía Patagonia** (Page 227) Coyhaique. The top gourmet restaurant along the Carretera, equally at home in London or New York.

✖ **Dagus** (Page 227) Coyhaique. Top-notch seafood in an intimate setting. A novel take on standard Chilean dishes.

✖ **Restaurant La Isla** (Page 305) Cochrane. The only contender in the deep south; definitely check out the lamb.

PUBLIC HOLIDAYS

1 January	New Year
late March/early April	Easter
1 May	Labour Day
21 May	Navy Day
29 June	Sts Peter and Paul Day
16 July	Virgen del Carmen
15 August	Assumption of the Virgin Mary
18 September	National Day
19 September	Army Day
12 October	Colombus Day
31 October	Reformation Day
1 November	All Saints' Day
8 December	Immaculate Conception
25 December	Christmas Day

Besides the usual holidays around Christmas and New Year, the main public holidays a visitor to the Carretera Austral is likely to witness are the annual celebrations of individual towns, often based around a rodeo theme, generally in January or February – the exact dates vary from year to year.

SHOPPING

Even the smallest villages have a simple store for basic provisions. If at first they appear closed, knock on the door. However, **supermarkets** (in the normal sense of the word) are found only in the main towns (Chaitén, Hornopirén, Aysén, Coyhaique and Cochrane) and, as a general rule, only the basic necessities are available anywhere outside of Coyhaique. One major benefit of the Carretera Austral is that it is hard to spend money on anything other than food, accommodation and the occasional tour or kayak rental. **Laundries** are less common along the Carretera – those present in villages are listed in the text. As a general rule, wash your clothes when you can.

In terms of **food**, outside Coyhaique there are few shops selling more than basic ingredients. Campers can find the traditional array of tomato paste, tinned products, pasta and occasionally dried soya, but beyond the standard camping fare, options are limited. Stock up on more esoteric ingredients in Puerto Montt or Coyhaique. Local edible products are available; in particular marmalades, bottled shellfish, *nalca* stalks and bread are offered in most towns.

The typical **market** stalls found across most of South America selling brightly coloured handbags and purses (apparently from the region but invariably from Peru) are almost non-existent along the Carretera. Coyhaique has a small trinket market on the central square, and Villa Amengual has an impressive co-operative selling locally made handicrafts at reasonable prices.

ACTIVITIES ALONG THE CARRETERA AUSTRAL

Chile has consistently been voted one of the leading adventure destinations on earth. The range of activities offered along the Carretera Austral does not necessarily involve jumping from an airplane or ice-climbing, but there is something for everyone: adrenaline junkies will be delighted with the climbing and rafting options while more sedentary visitors may be content with a short trek and a spot of fishing. With the obvious exception of beach activities (water temperatures range from solid ice to merely freezing cold), a degree of adventure and exercise can be incorporated into any itinerary.

TREKKING This is possible almost everywhere. Most parks have extensive networks of marked trails. Some people trek the entire Carretera Austral itself. In the northern section, **Cochamó** has extensive marked trails, including over to Argentina, ranging from day treks to treks taking in excess of one week (page 104). The Cochamó trails connect with those of Puelo and further south, as well as those in Argentina reaching Bariloche. **Parque Pumalín** has a number of trails, including to rare alerce trees (see box, page 10). Treks range from half an hour to a full day, and are some of the more accessible treks for young children or for those with reduced mobility. The **Sendero de Chile** between Palena and Lago Verde (see box, page 158) passes the otherwise inaccessible Lago Palena, and also connects to other trails to the east of the Carretera, making multiple-day treks feasible. **Cerro Castillo** is fast becoming one of the key trekking routes in Patagonia. **Parque Patagonia** has relatively few marked trails, but of incredible beauty, including the three-day trek north through the **Jeinimeni sector**. A comparable multi-day trek extends from **Cochrane to Villa O'Higgins** in the extreme south. For the more adventurous it is possible to trek up onto the two ice fields, but generally this requires a guide, and specific experience.

CYCLING The Carretera Austral is considered one of the definitive bike rides on the continent. Mountain bikes can be rented in most towns, but in particular consider Futaleufú, Puyuhuapi, La Junta, around Coyhaique, and Cochrane. As with trekking, the possibilities are almost unlimited.

CLIMBING Cochamó is widely considered to be one of the best climbing spots on the continent, colloquially referred to as 'the Yosemite of Patagonia' (page 104). There are sufficient routes for dedicated climbers to spend an entire season around Cochamó and never climb the same route twice. Watersports may be the principal activity in **Futaleufú** (page 152), but it is also possible to climb. There are also decent climbing routes around **Coyhaique**. **Cerro Castillo** (page 251) offers some challenging routes for experienced climbers, as well as sport-climbing. Needless to say, the ice shelves and glaciers offer ice-climbing options for experienced climbers.

BIRDWATCHING The entire Carretera Austral is an ornithologist's paradise, so this is an almost unavoidable activity. Park maps generally list the most common species. The area around **Coyhaique** is probably the most famous place to see Andean condors (page 233). Thanks to its extensive grasslands and countless lagoons, **Parque Patagonia** has abundant birdlife, including flamingos, owls, condors, ibis and flightless birds such as small native ostriches. The restoration of natural grasslands and native species in Parque Patagonia has resulted in abundant wildlife and ideal nesting grounds for the condor – it is possible to see dozens of Andean condors simultaneously. For sea birds, **Raúl Marín Balmaceda** is worth a visit (page 167). **Villa O'Higgins** offers excellent guided birdwatching treks. Penguins are most easily seen around **Chaitén**. In fact they can be seen along most of the coastline close to the Carretera Austral, but access can be a challenge. They have even been seen in Puyuhuapi.

With special thanks to Randy Clouse, international beer expert, resident of (bars in) Bariloche, Argentina

There are at least ten widely available micro-brews in the region, excluding the many handcrafted beers only available on site or within the village of production. On a well-planned two-week holiday you can try a new beer each day. Adding beer-tasting to your itinerary on the Carretera Austral may come with some risks, but you will come away enriched knowing that you have experienced beer that is only available in remote southern Chile. How many others can say that? As more entrepreneurs add their creative and sometimes exquisite products to the market, the range and quality of craft beers will only increase.

Most craft beers use only four ingredients: water, malted barley, hops and yeast. Generally they are heartier than industrial beers and are not filtered. Don't be surprised if you see a little sediment at the bottom of your bottle; it's just yeast and it's safe to consume. Allow the beer to settle for a minute, pour it slowly in one go so as not to agitate it unnecessarily, and stop pouring before the settled yeast emerges. Newcomers should find they are pouring like a pro within no time.

COYHAIQUE D'Olbek (Baquedano 1899; ☏ 67 223 2947; w dolbek.cl) is the most widely available along the Carretera Austral. Aficionados can tour their facilities, but call ahead to make sure they're open. I went too late one evening and was chased away by some intimidating dogs. The owners guard their elixir at any cost.

Tropera (w tropera.cl) makes a variety of excellent ales available in various bars around Coyhaique, and in bottles across the region. The IPA is their most popular.

Campo D'Hielo (f cerveceria campo d'hielo; ☏ 9 7888 7613) produces three beers made from the same recipe but incorporating water from different sources: glacier, river and spring water. These have a tendency to be murky. You'll be amazed at the impact the water makes, both in flavour and in appearance, depending both on the pH balance and the minerals, nitrates, and salts it contains. Several restaurants in the area, mostly in Coyhaique, carry these beers on their menus.

Pioneros (f Cerveza Pioneros) is also popular, and the varieties include Negra (dark), Roja (red), and Rubia (blond). Many small shops also sell this beer which is recognisable from its label that show black-and-white photos of pioneers in the region. Although not up there with the best, it does the job.

Caiquén (f Cerveza Artesanal Caiquén) is another notable brew. Apparently the brewer started in Villa Cerro Castillo (since that is shown as the origin on the

HOT SPRINGS It is hard to traverse the Carretera without visiting at least one hot spring. They tend to be in the northern half of the Carretera around Río Puelo, Hornopirén and the Fiordo Comau, El Amarillo, Raúl Marín Balmaceda, Puyuhuapi, Puerto Cisnes, Puerto Aysén and a rather modest effort near Bahía Murta.

RAFTING/KAYAKING The thundering rivers around **Palena** and **Futaleufú** are widely considered to offer some of the best white water on earth (page 152), with numerous adrenaline-filled trips possible. Most villages on lakes will have someone, somewhere, willing to rent a kayak, and many hotels will have some for label) but locals informed me that he now produces the beer in Coyhaique. A fine dark or blond ale that goes well either with a sandwich or on its own.

NORTHERN CARRETERA AUSTRAL Leaving the cosmopolitan comforts of Coyhaique doesn't mean giving up on the micro-brews. Elsewhere on the Carretera Austral most towns offer a locally brewed beer.

Hopperdeitzal (w puyuhuapi.com) is brewed just north of Puyuhuapi but has also expanded regionally. Produced with water from Valle Caesar, the three styles are Goldene Jahre Ale, Roter Teppich Ale and Schwarz Ale. The stubby bottles add an old-world charm to this delightful beer.

Puerto Cisnes is home to **Finisterra** (page 192). Their 100% organic beer comes in seven varieties: Rubia (blond), Dorada (golden), Negra (dark), and Rubia con Ají (spicy). The Queulat Mountains are the source of the water. This brewery has been around for a while and has a good reputation. Guided tours of the brewery are a highlight to any visit to Puerto Cisnes.

Futaleufú offers at least three local beers. My personal favourite is **FutaAlhue**, made by Arturo Vivanco Navarete who started brewing back in 2010 at the time of the Chilean bicentennial celebration, and still makes his beer in 20-litre batches giving the beer a special small-batch richness. FutaAlhue means 'Place of Big Souls', and is sold in half-litre bottles in three varieties: Golden, IPA (Blood of the Guide), and Oatmeal Stout (Bosque Nativo, 'Native Forest').

Finally, **Biloche** (cerveza biloche, 9 9271 8367) is brewed along the little-known Hualaihué Peninsula. Porter, amber and golden are brewed, mainly sold in Hornopirén, Ensenada and Puerto Varas, but this peninsula is well worth the detour and combining with a trip to the brewery and a couple of ales could be the determining factor to visit.

SOUTHERN CARRETERA AUSTRAL Micro-breweries in the far south seem to come and go. New breweries have emerged in Cochrane (Tehuelche) and Caleta Tortel (Catedral), while other breweries have vanished in both villages. The most established brewery south of Coyhaique is Cervecería Río Tranquilo (Puerto Río Tranquilo; 9 9895 5577; Cerveza Arisca; page 264) which produces Arisca beer. Arisca in English means 'wild', but this refined beer is most drinkable. In the small factory next door they brew: Baya, a light wheat beer; Alazana, a slightly bitter malty red; and Picasa, a smoky dark with a coffee aroma. Even with 100-litre fermentation tanks, they struggle to meet demand during the high season, so not all styles are always available.

guests. Renting a kayak in **Puyuhuapi** enables a visit to some hot springs (page 185) accessible only by boat at low tide, and also to see a hidden glacier only visible from the far side of the canal. The other rafting destinations are Chaitén, Hornopirén in the north, and **Puerto Bertrand** along the Río Baker (page 289). **Puerto Cisnes** has some interesting lake- and sea-kayaking options. Obviously almost every village around the massive **Lago General Carrera** is suitable for a range of water activities, and most rent kayaks. Instead of taking a guided tour to the marble caves around Puerto Río Tranquilo, consider renting a kayak and spending half a day visiting the caves from **Puerto Sánchez** (page 265). There are countless lakes across the entire region, including around Coyhaique – the options are endless.

The abundant, transparent waters where trout abound, combined with the low number of fishermen, make southern Chile a sport-fishing paradise. From shallow mountain streams to huge rivers, from freshwater lakes to the salty Pacific coast, the variety and range of locations offer a number of options for all experience levels. Most of the common species found in inland waters today were introduced from both North America and Europe over a century ago, dominating the few native species that still exist. Trout species include rainbows, brown and fontalis. Chinook and sakura are the most common salmon species. Salmon farming in the area has increased significantly within the last few decades, especially off the coast, and most of the salmon now found in the area is a by-product of the aquaculture programmes.

Sernapesca (w pescarecreativa.sernapesca.cl) is the government agency that regulates fishing and sells licences both online and in its offices throughout Chile. Some fishing supply stores in Puerto Montt and Coyhaique also sell licences. The main sport-fishing season runs from October to April, with some variation for different types of species and location. A licence for foreigners is around $14,600/$29,100/$43,700 per week/month/year. Catch and release is mandatory in some bodies of water and always strongly recommended. The licence includes a small booklet with more details.

It is advisable to bring equipment with you as it is hard to rent outside of Coyhaique. It will be inspected and disinfected upon entry by border control authorities for a fee and, due to the recent detection of the Didymo algae, the government has started a prevention programme to stop its spread. This invasive algae originated in North America and grows into large slimy clumps in slow-moving rivers; it spreads easily, affecting the visibility and oxygen levels of the water.

To help prevent the spread of Didymo, the Chilean government recommends a thorough cleaning of shoes, waders, gear, lines, and anything else that touches the water. Soak it all in a bucket with detergent for 1–2 minutes, and then dry it all thoroughly. Fortunately many of the larger rivers have not been infected, but it's

HORSERIDING This is deeply embedded in the culture of the entire region. Most villages will have a rodeo, and the gaucho culture is very much alive from north to south. The **Sendero de Chile** route between Palena and Lago Verde is commonly done on horseback (page 156), as is the week-long route between Cochrane and Villa O'Higgins. Horseriding is also common around Cochrane, where inhabitants may tether their horses on the central plaza while they do a spot of shopping. Cerro Castillo also has a number of trails and horses for rent for those preferring to ride rather than hike. The rodeo in Bahía Murta is an insight into the gaucho life, and horse rides in the region are wonderful.

SCUBA/FREE DIVING Although not as common as other activities, Cochrane has an official scuba centre. It is also possible to snorkel on the Río Cochrane, one of the most pleasantly surprising activities along the entire Carretera (page 306). The crystal-clear waters of Lago Cochrane are ideal for diving, and it is even possible to take formal PADI courses there. However, outside Cochrane there is no equipment rental and diving is done entirely with your own equipment at your own risk. Snorkelling and free diving are thus more practical, and it is possible to explore the marble caves in both **Puerto Sánchez** (page 257) and **Puerto Río Tranquilo** (page up to all of us to keep it that way since once Didymo arrives it is nearly impossible to eradicate.

Serious anglers should plan on bringing all their own gear with them. A portable 7ft to 8ft, five- or six-weight rod works well in most situations, and reels and lines that can withstand those 20lb+ trophy fish. A couple of different lines would come in handy: one for floating and one for sinking. Wet flies, dry flies, nymphs and streamers all may work depending on the conditions. Outside Coyhaique finding gear is difficult so bring everything and spares. Only barbless hooks are permitted for catch and release.

Principal destinations are the rivers Baker, Futaleufú, Simpson, Palena, Rosselot, Cochrane and Cisnes, and also Lago General Carrera, Bahía Exploradores and Lago Cochrane. The reality is that almost everywhere on the Carretera Austral is close to some body of water with fish. Some of these waters are so transparent and full of fish that even an amateur can have lots of fun without going too far off the beaten path.

Fishing from the coast is fine, but to hook the big catches you'll need a guide or a boat. Guides and tour operators can be found locally in nearly all villages, but there are a few that stand out for the international fisherman. Prices and services vary. For example Carlos Benes in Cochrane (w hotelultimoparaiso.cl) charges US$400 per day for two people (including lunch). In Puerto Bertrand you can hire a boat and guide by the hour for $25,000 (two people).

A number of great fishing lodges have sprung up in the area as well, including the Yelcho, just south of Chaitén, La Cabaña Fishing 11km east of Villa Santa Lucía, the Coyhaique River Lodge near Coyhaique, and Espacio y Tiempo Hotel in La Junta (see respective chapters for contact details). Most include four- or five-star service, excursions and full board.

Even if you are not an avid fisherman, you will be tempted to try your luck in these legendary waters. You will probably see more fish than people! If you don't catch anything, this outstanding location alone, with breathtaking views, will bring satisfaction and enough material to tell tales about the one that got away.

265) with a decent wetsuit, mask and snorkel. Needless to say, water temperatures are somewhat chilly; a 7mm wetsuit is probably the minimum required. Good opportunities can also be found along the coastal road to Hornopirén; along Fiordo Comau; at many places in Chiloé; at Puerto Cisnes; on the islands around Raúl Marín Balmaceda; and in the endless lakes that stretch along the entire route. There are also options to go out to sea with the traditional fishermen living along the coast to the west of Hornopirén (page 110).

OTHER ACTIVITIES Sports such as canyoning, canopy and dirt-bike rentals are emerging each season. Given the popularity of kite-surfing on the Argentine side of the mountains, inevitably this will begin in Chile also. In winter it is possible to **ski** around Coyhaique (page 233), but this is unlikely to become a major attraction for a number of years.

MEDIA AND COMMUNICATIONS

INTERNET Along the majority of the Carretera Austral there is no internet. However, almost every village with a municipal office or library offers free computers and internet access, and most towns such as La Junta, Futaleufú, Río Puelo, Coyhaique and Cochrane offer free Wi-Fi in the central plazas, and if a village is connected to the internet then even basic hostels will offer this for free.

TELEPHONE Mobile-phone coverage is patchy, to say the least, and none of three main mobile-phone companies (Movistar, Entel and Claro) has universal coverage. In general, Entel seems to have the best coverage at the time of writing, but the ideal solution would be to buy SIMs for all three networks and switch them according to the region (or simply do not rely on a phone!). SIMs are cheap and can be purchased in larger towns (Chile Chico, Puerto Montt, Coyhaique or Aysén) and topped up in most places.

Another option is a satellite phone or, as a cheaper, less bulky and more practical solution, the Garmin inReach Mini satellite communicator. Each message sent from the Garmin includes your precise location. It is sufficient not only for emergencies, but also to alert hotels of a late arrival, change or confirm bookings, seek help from a tour operator or simply to communicate with family. On expeditions, for example on to the ice shelf, this is an essential piece of kit – it is both lightweight and has a long-life battery. It is significantly cheaper to buy and operate than a satellite phone.

Telephone codes in Chile can be complicated. Along the Carretera Austral there are two main fixed line codes: 65 and 67, most of which cannot be dialled on Skype Out. Fixed lines are followed by seven digits, but calling *from* a fixed line is relatively challenging, as there are no public telephones. Mobile phones must use the local dialling code; calling a mobile phone requires a 9 followed by eight digits regardless of the operator or the origin of the call (dial +569 and then the eight-digit code from abroad). Owing to the patchy coverage of all operators, and the mobility of the people, most people (and in particular most companies) have multiple mobile phones, in order to be able to receive calls regardless of their precise location. If the first number does not work as the phone is 'out of coverage area', try the second (or third). Until universal coverage is achieved this is as inconvenient for the recipient as the dialler, but bear in mind that large parts of the Carretera Austral simply have no mobile-phone coverage. Leaving a message is generally a waste of time; it's best to just try again later.

In this guide, telephone numbers are listed in the following order: fixed line first (generally a 65 or 67 prefix, 2 in the case of Santiago phones), followed by the most likely mobile-phone numbers. Mobile phones linked to WhatsApp are included when possible, but internet is not necessarily any more reliable than mobile-phone signals.

CULTURAL ETIQUETTE

Southern Chile is generally fairly laid-back. Although English is not widely spoken, Chileans will generally be delighted to have a chat with foreigners able to converse in even basic Spanish. However, the informality of the Argentine *vos* is not used in Chile, and particularly when speaking to older people or those in authority the *usted* form is more appropriate. Likewise, the Argentine custom of referring to strangers as *che* is not always welcome in Chile. See page 341 for more detail on specific Chilean linguistic idiosyncrasies.

Some topics have to be broached with caution, in part related to 20th-century Chilean history. Southern Chile was generally less adversely impacted by the **Pinochet** military junta (page 15), and indeed some regions positively benefited from Pinochet. Given the constant squabbling with Argentina over the borders separating the two countries, particularly in the south many Chileans believe with some justification that it was Pinochet who protected this region from falling into Argentine hands. However, expressing pro-Pinochet sentiment is often misinterpreted and thus many people, particularly the older generation, are hesitant to discuss this topic. There were also atrocities committed under the military junta in this region, perhaps not to the extent of central and northern Chile, and broaching the topic risks opening old wounds.

The **Falklands War** of 1982 can also raise some lively conversations, but ensure there are no Argentines present. Chile, and in particular Pinochet, supported the UK in 1982, while Chile now officially supports further dialogue and tentatively backs the Argentine claim to the islands. Most locals firmly believe the Falklands are British, but this could equally be discreet national rivalry against their neighbour. Trips to the Carretera Austral inevitably involve border crossings to Argentina, and the topic has a remarkable tendency to crop up, particularly with British citizens. It is best not to enter into a debate on this topic. For anyone under the age of 40 it is usually safer to mention that you were not born at the time and have hardly heard of the dispute. 'What islands?'

Another sensitive topic is **World War II**. A number of German settlers from both sides of the political spectrum arrived both before and after the war, as well as Sudeten Germans (Czechoslovakian German-speakers) and refugees fleeing the war. Tread cautiously when making sweeping generalisations on this topic.

Chile is a **Catholic** country, but the southern region is relatively areligious. This is not as much a delicate topic of conversation as a non-topic of conversation. There are few historic churches in the region; for those interested in exploring fantastic churches that have played – and continue to play – a central role in society, Chiloé may be a more interesting destination.

The issue of installing **hydro-electric dams** in the region stirred huge controversy and plans were eventually scrapped (see box, page 220). '*Patagonia ¡sin represas!*'

DON'T MENTION THE WAR

In October 2014 the team of *Top Gear*, the BBC's popular television series about cars, sparked controversy by driving through Patagonia with a Porsche 928 with the number plate H982 FKL. Argentines assumed this was a discreet reference to the 1982 Falklands War. Whether the choice of number plate was deliberate or coincidental is a matter of some controversy, although the *Top Gear* team and the BBC claim this was a pure chance. All three presenters drove V8 vehicles, and lead presenter Jeremy Clarkson, driver of the offending vehicle, claimed the choice of car was because a Porsche 928 had enabled him to rapidly visit his dying father some years previously. From Bariloche, where the number plate was first spotted, the team drove south and crossed over to the Carretera Austral at Futaleufú (they stayed in the excellent Hotel El Barranco, page 148), and left at Coyhaique. Describing a northern section of the road, Clarkson suggests it appeared like the 'set of *Jurassic Park*, petrified forests, mysterious lakes… this is all very odd… if I go round the next corner and there's a brontosaurus I will not be surprised.'

Upon arriving in Ushuaia (Argentina), where sentiments run high regarding the ownership of the Falkland Islands (Islas Malvinas), angry mobs gathered. The *Top Gear* team decided to flee. Pelted with stones, they eventually sought refuge in Chile.

('Patagonia without dams!') stickers adorn most businesses, cars and shop windows. Unless you have an extremely valid reason to disagree, it is generally safer to go with the mass consensus and broadly frown upon the idea of flooding much of Patagonia in order to provide electricity predominantly for use in Santiago. It is hard to imagine riot police in the region, but emotions ran sufficiently high in Coyhaique as to prompt full civil unrest, and the topic remains a sensitive one to this day.

Related to the anti-hydro-electric dam sentiment, the US philanthropist Doug Tompkins has historically sparked some controversial and critical sentiment, but nowadays he is largely viewed as having been a benevolent contributor to the region, and planet in general (see box, page 134).

There is one topic that sparks serious animosity to this day and is of direct relevance to some travellers along the Carretera Austral – the issue of **Israel**. Strong anti-Israeli sentiment exists, and is increasingly vocal and visible; some hostels even place Palestinian flags in their windows as a discreet means to warn that not all foreigners are welcome. It is not generally anti-Semitism, but anti-Israeli. The local people believe that the Israelis travelling in the region are looking out for new land (given the current situation in Israel), and that they particularly like regions with water. This sentiment is more directed towards groups of young Israeli travellers, particularly those having recently completed their military service. Most hostel owners can recount a story of bad behaviour by an Israeli, mostly unsubstantiated, but sufficient to create a strong feeling across the tourism sector. The national parks often have the park rules specifically printed in Hebrew (and in no other foreign language). This sentiment was not helped by a fire reportedly started by an Israeli backpacker in Torres del Paine in 2011–12 that burned 176km^2 of Chile's most famous national park. A recent and somewhat disturbing trend is for hitchhikers to declare their nationalities either verbally or on small signs (Chileans often carry a flag) specifically to alert drivers that they are not Israeli, aware that many fear stopping for hitchhikers for this reason. The most obvious solution to this problem is that all nationalities, including Israelis, should consider themselves ambassadors for their countries and do their utmost to contribute to the region and create a favourable impression of their country.

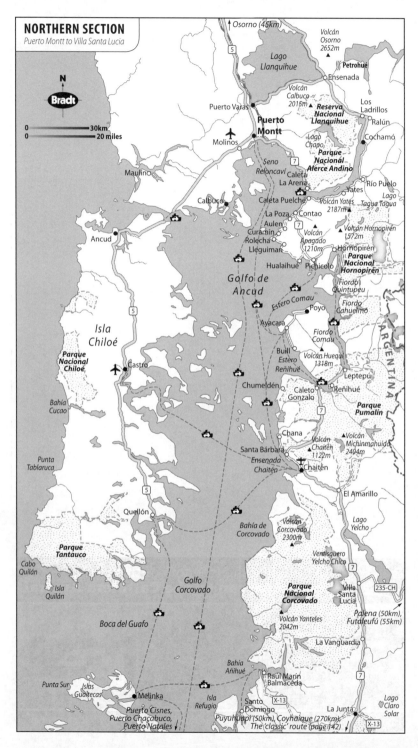

NORTHERN SECTION
Puerto Montt to Villa Santa Lucia

N
Bradt

0 ————————— 30km
0 ————————— 20 miles

↑ Osorno (45km)

Volcán
Osorno
2652m
∭ Petrohué

Lago
Llanquihue

Ensenada

Volcán
Calbuco
2015m

Puerto Varas

**Puerto
Montt**

Molinos

Reserva
Nacional
Llanquihue

Lago
Chapo

Los
Ladrillos

Ralún

Cochamó

Parque
Nacional
Alerce Andino

Maulino

Seno
Reloncaví

Caleta
La Arena

Río Puelo

Yates

Lago
Tagua Tagua

Calbuco

Caleta Puelche

La Poza

Aulen

Curamín

Rolecha

Lleguimán

Contao

Volcán Yates
2187m

Volcán Hornopirén
1572m

Ancud

Volcán
Apagado
1210m

Hornopirén

Parque
Nacional
Hornopirén

Hualaihué

Pichicolo

**Golfo de
Ancud**

Fiordo
Quintupeu

Estero Comau

Poyo

Fiordo
Cahuelmó

Ayacara

Fiordo
Comau

Isla
Chiloé

Parque
Nacional
Chiloé

Castro

Buill

Estero
Reñihué

Volcán Huequi
1318m

Leptepú

ARGENTINA

Chumeldén

Caleto
Gonzalo

Reñihué

Parque
Pumalín

Bahía
Cucao

Chana

Volcán
Chaitén
1122m

Volcán
Michinmahuida
2404m

Punta
Tablaruca

Santa Bárbara

Ensenada
Chaitén

Chaitén

El Amarillo

Lago
Yelcho

Quellón

Bahía de
Corcovado

Volcán
Corcovado
2300m

Parque
Tantauco

Ventisquero
Yelcho Chico

Cabo
Quilán

Isla
Quilán

Golfo
Corcovado

Parque
Nacional
Corcovado

Villa
Santa
Lucía

235-CH

Palena (50km),
Futaleufú (55km)

Volcán Yanteles
2042m

La Vanguardia

Boca del Guafo

Bahía
Anihué

Punta Sur

Islas
Guaitecas

Melinka

Isla
Refugio

Raúl Marín
Balmaceda

Santo
Domingo

X-13

La Junta

Lago
Claro
Solar

Puerto Cisnes,
Puerto Chacabuco,
Puerto Natales

Puyuhuapi (50km), Coyhaique (270km),
The 'classic' route (page 142)

X-13

Part Two

THE NORTHERN CARRETERA AUSTRAL

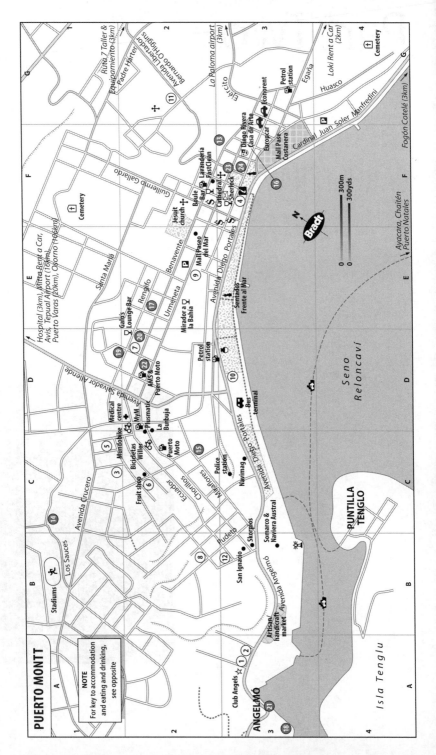

PUERTO MONTT

NOTE
For key to accommodation and eating and drinking, see opposite

Brandt

Puerto Montt

Telephone code: 65

Perched on the Seno Reloncaví (Reloncaví Sound), Puerto Montt is a bustling frontier city driven by commerce and salmon farming and is home to nearly 250,000 inhabitants, approximately double the entire population of the 1,270km region traversed by the Carretera Austral. For those heading south, this is the last bit of modernity for a few weeks – make the most of it. The shopping here is excellent, there are fine restaurants and a thriving nightlife; and the city is the main northern access point to the Carretera Austral and is surrounded by world-class sights such as the island of Chiloé, the Chilean and Argentine lake districts, and the popular tourist town of Puerto Varas to the north.

And yet, perhaps prompted by some scathing reviews in other guidebooks and online, most visitors leave Puerto Montt as soon as possible in search of wonders further north or to join the Carretera proper. Even within Chile, Puerto Montt does not have a great reputation. It does appear to have more than its fair share of drunks, beggars, derelict or burnt-out buildings, monstrous concrete high-rises, overflowing rubbish bins, a bizarre one-way traffic system that does not seem to resolve the endemic traffic problem, E-grade casinos, graffiti, trinket shops selling low-quality Chinese imports, some pretty sleazy neighbourhoods and a McDonald's, but Puerto Montt is authentically Chilean, for better or for worse.

Scratch the surface and you will find an intriguing, upbeat place, which, while not packed with top sightseeing opportunities, does offer those heading south their last chance to eat quality sushi, get a high-speed internet connection, go to the cinema, buy some last-minute gear impossible to find further south, visit a decent mechanic and enjoy some nightlife – all this, as well as stunning views across the Reloncaví Sound and towards the Osorno and Calbuco volcanoes.

A trip along the Carretera Austral is incomplete without a couple of days exploring Puerto Montt.

PUERTO MONTT
For listings, see from page 86

⊜ Where to stay
1	Brisas del Mar	A3
2	Cabañas Refugio Angelmó	A3
3	Casa Perla	C1
4	Gran Hotel Vicente Costanera	F3
5	Hospedaje Corina	C1
6	Hospedaje Vista del Mar	C2
7	Hostal Benavente	D2
8	Hostal Jacob	B2
9	Hotel Gran Pacifico	E2
10	Hotel Ibis	D3
11	Hotel Manquehue	G2
12	Hotel Suizo	B3

⊗ Where to eat and drink
13	Breko Sushi Bar	F3
	Brisas del Mar	(see 1)
14	Chile Picante	C1
15	Cirus Bar	C2
16	Club Aleman	F3
17	El Fogón de Pepe	E2
18	El Mirador de la Irma	A3
	Hotel Manquehue	(see 11)
19	Japón del Lago	D1
	Los Navegantes	(see 9)
20	Nana Bahamonde	D2
21	Pa' Mar Adentro	A3
22	Restaurant Shanghai	D2
23	Rhenania	F3
24	Tablón del Ancla	F3
	Off map	
	Fogón Cotelé	G4

Puerto Montt was founded in 1853 when Germans settled here, and was named after the Chilean president at the time, Manuel Montt, who governed from 1851 to 1861 and was the first civilian president of Chile. Montt himself was of humble origins but he created a presidential dynasty: both his son and nephew went on to become presidents of Chile. Jorge Montt (nephew) was Vice Admiral of the Chilean navy and had served in the War of the Pacific, in which Chile famously denied Bolivia access to the Pacific Ocean, lamented to this day. He was president from 1891 to 1896, during which time he reinstated the gold monetary standard and avoided a skirmish with the Argentines over border disputes by seeking arbitration from the British. He peacefully handed over power to Federico Errázuriz Echaurren in September 1896, and commanded the Chilean navy from 1897 until his retirement

THE 2019–20 CIVIL UPRISING

The collapse of Pinochet's regime in 1990 brought celebration, hope and the promise of change to Chileans up and down the country. Democratic rebirth promised to spread opportunity, prosperity and social justice. Rapid economic development ensued, with Chile's success story a shining example to the rest of South America. GDP increased from US$33 billion in 1990 to US$298 billion in 2018. Poverty declined from 8.1 million in 1990 to 0.7 million in 2017. However, on 19 October 2019 growing social tensions thought to have been resolved 30 years earlier erupted on to the streets of Santiago, resulting in negative global media coverage, destruction, violence and death.

Initially sparked by a $30 (£0.03) increase in metro prices in Santiago, the demonstrations swiftly grew into protests against the severe and widening inequality in Chile. Unrest quickly spread nationwide, with multiple cities under curfew and the military deployed. The benefits of economic growth had not sufficiently accrued to the majority, who felt betrayed and called for president Piñera's resignation.

Initial research for this guidebook coincided with the protests of November 2019. Having just updated information on the Hotel Vicente Costanera (page 86) in Puerto Montt, the authors became entangled in a demonstration, and were tear-gassed shortly afterwards. Although the situation entailed obvious difficulties, the opportunity to talk to protestors provided rare insight into the conflict. The protester demographic was dominated by students, but included 'middle-class' Chileans, and children as young as 14 who seemed neither to understand the reasons nor their ultimate objective in protesting. The authors fled shortly afterwards to update the Hotel Gran Pacifico (page 86), which conveniently has a roof-top bar from where we could observe the chaos below at a safe distance. From the perspective of foreigners monitoring the battle between police and protesters, the provocation seemed to emerge predominantly from the former. Riot shotguns were fired indiscriminately into crowds, tear-gas was launched at every opportunity and water cannons lurked around every corner. Protestors vented much of their anger towards banks and government buildings; however, they vandalised both the recently opened museum and the cathedral (both page 96), which seemed at odds with the stated political aims.

By the end of the year, some 2,840 people had been arrested; 2,500 civilians and more than 2,000 policemen had been injured; and 29 civilians lay dead. Human from the military in 1913. He was Mayor of Valparaiso from 1915 to 1918, and died in 1922. Ventisquero Montt near Caleta Tortel is named after him.

Manuel Montt's son Pedro governed from 1906 to 1910, but has a chequered reputation and nothing of note named after him. He ordered the Santa María School Massacre, in which striking nitrate workers in Iquique were killed by the army on the orders of the president, resulting in approximately 2,200 deaths, including the workers' wives and children. In fact, a more recent massacre also darkened the history of Puerto Montt; in 1969 heavy-handed police killed eight illegal squatters in the city, and the public outcry that ensued contributed to the downfall of the then president, Eduardo Frei, to be replaced by Salvador Allende in 1970. Other key moments in the history of the city include the devastating 1960 Valdivia earthquake, the most violent recorded, reaching 9.5 on the Richter scale and killing up to 6,000 people. The city's cathedral was one of the only buildings to

Rights Watch published evidence detailing severe breaches of human rights by policemen detaining protestors. Accusations of rape, torture, cruel treatment, excessive force, killings and attempted killings were filed against security forces. In that November, the use of rubber pellets in riot shotguns was suspended pending an investigation into the projectiles' composition. Hospital scans of dozens of cases of blinding by the pellets revealed that they were made partially of metal. Many believe that the recent investigations are uncovering ingrained problems with the police lingering from the Pinochet era. The government responded convincingly, assigning 250 human rights police instructors to units engaged in crowd-control operations, and the Attorney General's Office opened preliminary investigations into alleged abuses against 2,278 people.

Prior to the Covid-19 pandemic Piñera was in a difficult position, stuck between appeasing a destructive mob, and preventing looting and violence. He made concessions, including not increasing the Santiago subway fares, setting up a council to change the constitution, and shuffling his cabinet. Many Chileans considered these changes insufficient and demanded Piñera's resignation, yet middle-class Chileans also began to yearn for a return to the previous order and democracy: the health of the Chilean economy was badly shaken by these nationwide riots.

The civil unrest ceased with the arrival of Covid-19 in 2020. Lockdowns enabled the government to remove graffiti and only small demonstrations were held that year. Minor riots continued throughout 2021 but not on the scale of 2019–20.

The April 2020 elections on constitutional reform were postponed until the October. With a turnout of 51%, Chileans voted overwhelmingly to draft a new constitution. Members of the Constitutional Convention were elected in May 2021, and a final vote in September 2022 will accept or reject the new constitution. Although most Chileans want a fairer, more equal society, polls show that there is little desire for a complete economic remodel. Optimistic analysts hope that the core reasons for Chile's success, such as a free market economy with relatively little government interference, will not be dismantled in the proposed constitutional reforms, resulting in no lasting damage to the economy.

The riots had devastating effects for those reliant on tourism along the Carretera Austral, occurring just before peak season when businesses earn the majority of their annual income. Closed tour operators, restaurants and hotels may continue to be evident in the coming years.

survive thanks to its novel construction (page 96). The Historic Museum of Puerto Montt covers the earthquake in detail (page 96).

Although Pedro may have been the last of the Montt dynasty to govern the country, the name resounds in Chilean history to this day. Julio Montt (1861–82) was also a hero in the War of the Pacific. Teresa Wilms Montt (1893–1921) was a writer, poet and anarchist-feminist. Montts have also achieved celebrity status. Cristina Montt (1895–1969) was a movie star, and Marta Montt Balmaceda (1934–2019) is considered Chile's first supermodel. She appeared on the covers of *Life* and *Vogue* magazines, and risked excommunication from the Catholic Church for wearing a risqué white bikini on Zapallar beach in 1967. Andrés Wood Montt (1965–) is an accomplished film director who directed an excellent film about the remote village of Puerto Gala, *La Fiebre del Loco*, in 2001 (see box, page 337); and Rodrigo Montt Swett (1974–), great-great-grandson of the original Manuel Montt whom the city was named after, is a lawyer and politician, but he is based in Santiago rather than in the city that bears his name.

Puerto Montt was impacted by rioting in late 2019. The Plaza de Armas saw windows smashed and the municipal building covered in graffiti; the Latam office was destroyed, the cathedral and museum suffered minor damage and the banks were specifically targeted. The *carabineros* disbursed the crowds with tear-gas. For more about the civil unrest of 2019, see the box on page 80.

GETTING THERE AND AROUND

BY PRIVATE VEHICLE Puerto Montt is 20km south of Puerto Varas (a more manicured tourist base) – see the box on page 30 on the broader access points to the Carretera Austral. This is a public transport hub, but bear in mind that south of Puerto Montt, either in the direction of Hornopirén or via Cochamó and Río Puelo, road quality gradually deteriorates. The Carretera officially starts at the southern exit of Puerto Montt, but there is a valid argument that the entry point via Cochamó is also a key starting point (and avoids one ferry crossing; page 97).

The southern departure from Puerto Montt along the Carretera Austral is the coastal road heading southeast. It is signposted from the city centre, and hard to miss; it's the only road going in this direction. The southwesterly roads from Puerto Montt, in particular Ruta 5, lead to the island of Chiloé. It is possible to join the Carretera Austral from Chiloé via the various ferries from Quellón and Castro (page 44).

Car hire Most of the major car-rental companies have offices in Puerto Montt. Some of the companies listed here also have offices in Coyhaique (city and airport), Puerto Natales and Punta Arenas which is convenient for one-way car rentals. Most car-rental companies require a minimum age of 22–24 years, a valid driver's licence in the country of origin or a valid international driver's licence, valid passport and a credit card guarantee of US$500–1,000. Check the specific requirements of each car-rental company and whether it is possible to cross the border to Argentina. It is often easier and cheaper to book online.

🚗 **Avis** [78 D1] Airport & KM 3 Ruta 226 towards airport; ///directly.paving.files; \2 2795 3982; e puertomontt@avisbudget.cl; w avis.cl/sucursal/puerto-montt. Massive range of cars, one-way rentals possible but no offices south of Puerto Montt.

🚗 **Blue Rent a Car** [78 D1] Airport & bus terminal; \9 4421 7293; e bluerentacar.info@gmail.com; w bluerentacar.cl. Range from small saloons to 4x4s & minivans for up to 8 people. One-way rentals possible for a fee.

Econorent [78 G3] Airport & Antonio Varas 144; ///snaps.rebirth.sheep; 65 248 1264; e reservas@econorent.cl; w econorent.cl. A full range of cars from a small Chevrolet Spark to 4x4s, daily & weekly rentals. Offices in Coyhaique & Punta Arenas.

Europcar [78 G3] Airport & Antonio Varas 162; ///pulled.same.spurned; 65 236 8226; w europcar.cl. A full range of cars from a small Chevrolet Spark to a selection of 4x4s. Offices in Coyhaique, Punta Arenas & Puerto Natales.

Loki Rent a Car [78 G4] Río Maullin 658; ///copy.reveal.glosses; 9 3196 7364; e contacto@lokicars.cl; w lokicars.cl; ⏰ 24hrs. Located slightly out of town, & will deliver/collect cars from hotel/house/airport. Reasonably priced & includes 4x4s.

Mitta Rent a Car Airport & Calle de Servicio 1431; ///cobbled.onto.parts; 65 231 3445; w mitta.cl. Formerly Hertz, boasts one of the widest ranges of vehicles available in the rental car market. Offices in Coyhaique, Balmaceda airport & Punta Arenas.

BY PUBLIC TRANSPORT Countless **buses** serve Santiago and intermediate routes, as well as Chiloé and Bariloche (Argentina). The main bus terminal is located on the waterfront in the city centre [78 D3] (Av Diego Portales 1001; ///spoils.recorder.stags; 65 228 3000), slightly north of the main plaza on the main road through the city. Bear in mind that bus times are highly prone to change; the only means to mitigate this problem is to buy tickets in advance (and be aware that most companies do not accept credit cards or take telephone reservations), check the departure time a day before, and arrive early. Buses to Santiago take approximately 12 hours and cost between US$20 and US$50 depending on comfort, ranging from a basic seat to a 180° reclining seat. Buses to Bariloche take about 6 hours, depending on congestion at the border, and cost around US$20. The main bus companies serving this route are Andesmar (w andesmarchile.cl) and Via Bariloche (w viabariloche.com.ar). The list below focuses on southbound buses only.

Between the nearby towns (such as Puerto Varas), small blue **minivans** can be hailed from any bus stop. Puerto Montt also has a system of **taxis** that follow established routes with multiple passengers, but there is no obvious way to find out which taxi serves which route – ask at your hotel. The system is somewhat confusing.

Buses Estuario 65 284 1200, 9 7916 3162. Puerto Montt to Río Puelo (via Ensenada, Ralún & Cochamó): 15.30 daily, return 05.00; Hornopirén: 10.45, 12.30 & 16.00 daily, return 05.15, 07.30 & 16.00 daily.

Buses Río Puelo 9 7408 9199; e buses.riopuelo@hotmail.com. Puerto Montt to Lago Tagua Tagua (via Puerto Varas, Ensenada, Ralún, Cochamó & Río Puelo): 07.45 Mon–Sat, return 13.30.

Expreso Austral 65 236 9681. Puerto Montt to Hualaihué: 14.00 & 15.00 Mon–Sat, 16.00 & 16.45 Sun, return 05.30 & 06.00 Mon–Sat, 12.30 Sun.

Kemelbus 65 225 3530, 65 225 6450; w kemelbus.cl. Puerto Montt to Chaitén: 07.00 Mon, Wed & Fri, return 11.00 Tue, Thu & Sat; Puerto Montt to Hornopirén: 08.00, 11.00, 14.30 & 17.00 Mon–Fri, return 05.00, 05.30, 07.30 & 13.00; 05.30, 07.00, 13.00 & 17.00 Sat; 08.00, 13.00 & 17.00 Sun.

Los Navegadores 65 225 2926, 9 8773 6977. Puerto Montt to Hornopirén: 08.00 Mon–Sat, return 13.00 same day.

Transhar 65 225 4187. Puerto Montt to Cochamó & Río Puelo: 12.30 Mon–Sat, return 05.30 Mon–Sat.

BY FERRY Both Somarco and Naviera Austral are based at Angelmó 1673, heading slightly out of the city towards the Angelmó district, close to the hostel area. Navimag is just across the road at Diego Portales 2000, 100m south of the bus terminal. Check-in is also here, even if travelling on one of the larger boats that leave from slightly further out of the city – the transfers are free and arranged by the companies.

🚢 **Cruce Andino** Del Salvador 72, Puerto Varas; Mitre 219, Bariloche; e contacto@cruceandino.com; w cruceandino.com. An overpriced daily ferry-bus combination connecting Bariloche (Argentina) with Puerto Varas (Chile, 20km north of Puerto Montt). The route is by bus from Puerto Varas to Petrohué, then by boat across Lago Todos Los Santos to Puella, then a 2nd bus to Puerto Frías (Chilean border control), followed by a 2nd boat across Lago Frías to the Argentine customs. A 3rd bus goes to Puerto Blest, & then a final boat to Puerto Pañuelo, near the Llao Llao hotel, with a final bus to Bariloche. The section from Puerto Pañuelo to Puerto Blest, along an arm of the large Lago Nahuel Huapi, includes an infuriating commentary in multiple languages. 2022 rates (exc food) for adults were US$295 pp (one-way); the return is 50% less; low-season 20% lower. Children under 12 pay half. The route is beautiful on a sunny day, but for those travelling the Carretera Austral it is comparatively mediocre in terms of attractiveness, & extremely expensive. Take the bus instead – it is quicker (6hrs), cheaper ($20), does not include commentary & the route is fairly spectacular, with views over the Volcán Puyehue, which erupted in 2011. Book online (credit card & PayPal accepted) or through a local agent in Puerto Varas or Bariloche.

🚢 **Naviera Austral** [78 B3] ☏65 227 0430/1/2; w navieraustral.cl; ⊕ 09.00–13.00 & 15.00–19.00 Mon–Fri, 10.00–13.00 Sat. Ferries from Puerto Montt to Ayacara & Chaitén 11.00 Mon, 23.00 Tue–Fri, 22.00 Sat (approx 9hrs), return 23.00 Mon, 11.00 Wed–Sat & 23.30 Sun. For advice on other routes not departing from or arriving at Puerto Montt, see page 59. Offices in Chaitén, Raúl Marín Balmaceda, Puerto Gala, Ayacara, Futaleufú, Palena, Quellón, Castro, Chile Chico, Puerto Ibáñez, Melinka, Puerto Gaviota, Puerto Cisnes, Puerto Aguirre, Coyhaique, Puerto Chacabuco & Puerto Aysén.

🚢 **Navimag** [78 C3] ☏2 2411 2600; w navimag.com; ⊕ 09.00–13.00 & 14.30–18.30 Mon–Thu, 09.00–17.00 Fri, 15.00–18.00 Sat. Ferries between Puerto Montt & Puerto Natales, southbound Sat, northbound Wed.

🚢 **Skorpios** [78 B3] Angelmó 1660; /// frosted.cheaply.inhaler; ☏65 227 5643/6; e puertomontt@skorpios.cl; w skorpios.cl. Also has offices in Santiago: ☏2 2477 1900; e skoinfo@skorpios.cl; & Puerto Natales: ☏61 241 2714; e natales@skorpios.cl. These are passenger cruises rather than ferries, no cars onboard, return itineraries only. 2 main routes: from Puerto Montt to Ventisquero San Rafael, stopping in Chiloé, Puerto Aguirre, the nearby Quitralco hot springs & Melinka (summer only; 6 days, 5 nights; approx US$2,500 pp); they also have a ferry service in the deep south visiting the glaciers around Puerto Natales, beyond the southernmost extreme of the Carretera Austral (4 days, 3 nights; approx US$2,000 pp).

🚢 **Somarco** [78 B3] ☏65 229 4855/8; e contacto@somarco.cl; w barcazas.cl; ⊕ 09.00–12.30 & 14.30–18.30 Mon–Fri, 10.00–noon Sat. Ferry from Hornopirén to Caleta Gonzalo 10.30 daily, return 13.00, approx 5hrs.

BY AIR Puerto Montt is served by JetSmart, Sky Airlines and Latam. Despite the airport being formally called El Tepual International Airport [78 E1] (16km west of Puerto Montt; ///mysteries.curtails.bakes), no international flights operate to or from Puerto Montt – destinations include Punta Arenas, Puerto Natales, Balmaceda (Coyhaique), Santiago, Castro (Chiloé) and occasional flights en route to or from Santiago via Valdivia.

The predominant origin or destination of light aircraft travelling between Puerto Montt and the Carretera Austral is Chaitén, arriving and departing from the La Paloma Aerodrome located 5km northeast of Puerto Montt (///gear.slogans.runner).

Airport transfers Taxis to the airport generally charge about $10,000–15,000; if going to the light aircraft airport (La Paloma) be sure to specify this to the taxi driver. Alternatively, various companies operate shuttle buses (approx $2,500 pp) between the main airport and the main bus terminal, synchronised with the flight arrivals and departures.

PUERTO MONTT AIRPORT IN THE MEDIA

At 18.00 on 15 August 1972, an Argentine flight from Comodoro Rivadavia to Buenos Aires made a routine stop in Trelew, on the Atlantic coast. Unbeknown to the pilot a commander from a leftist Argentine guerrilla movement was on the flight, and armed. At 18.30 six guerrillas escaped from Rawson Prison and made it to Trelew airport in a Ford Falcon and boarded the plane, shortly after it landed at 19.20. In the ultimate double-bluff, in order to maintain calm the captain told passengers that this was a simulation of terrorist activity on account of being located so close to Rawson Prison, where a number of famous terrorists were incarcerated. Another 19 guerrillas from various organisations had escaped and were on their way to the airport, but their getaway vehicles had not arrived meaning they had to travel in three taxis. Meanwhile, fearful of the Argentine army and police arriving, the hijackers ordered the captain to take off promptly, to Tepual airport in Puerto Montt, where it refuelled and continued to Santiago. After some hours of negotiation in Santiago the hostages were released and the guerrillas were granted safe passage to Cuba by the Allende government, much to the annoyance of the Argentines. The plane returned to Buenos Aires that same day, and no hostages were hurt. The remaining 19 escapees were trapped in Trelew airport and surrendered on the condition that they would be returned to jail. However, in the early hours of 22 August, 16 of the 19 guerrillas were executed in what is now known as 'The Trelew Massacre'; the official account of the events at the time suggested that there was a second attempted escape which triggered the killings, but the three survivors (and public opinion) severely challenge this version of events, claiming they were led out of their cells, forced to lie face down and then executed. In 2012, three former army officials were sentenced to life imprisonment for crimes against humanity, although in reality this has amounted to mere house arrest.

TOURIST INFORMATION AND TOUR OPERATORS

The **tourist information centre** [78 F3] (San Martín 80; `65 225 6999`) is located just off the main plaza (///small.folds.trainers), offering brochures, leaflets and limited knowledge of the Carretera Austral; its main focus is tours in the region.

It is hardly necessary to use a tour operator for most of the sights and activities in the region; buying a bus ticket and paying an entry fee usually suffices. **Tour operators** simplify logistics, rather than being formally required in order to do a particular tour. However, if time is tight, or your Spanish skills poor, they may be a convenient option. There are also various semi-formal operators in the bus terminal. For tours north of Puerto Montt (ie: in the Lake District region of Chile beyond the limits of the Carretera Austral), Puerto Varas is the tourism hub, and has a greater range of operators serving this region.

Lahuén Andino [78 D3] Calle Ancud 128; `9 6568 0569`; lahuen.aldino. A decent, family-run operator with over 20 years' experience offering all the standard tours around Puerto Montt, including Petrohué (via Volcán Osorno), Chiloé, the Puyehue hot springs (via Frutillar & Puerto Octay), trekking to the refuge on Volcán Calbuco, a penguin colony on Chiloé, the Termas del Sol hot springs (page 108) & along the Carretera Austral as far as Hornopirén. Has private transport & can offer tailor-made tours along the entire length of the Carretera Austral, as well as to Lago Tagua Tagua.

4

85

Turismo San Sebastian ✆65 226 6124, 9 9148 2738; e turismosansebastian12@gmail. com; w turismosansebastian.cl. Another veteran tour operator serving the region around Puerto Montt for over 20 years. All are day trips originating & ending in Puerto Montt, although their tour to Hornopirén can be one way if you wish to continue south. Other tours include to Chiloé, Lago Tagua Tagua, the Puyehue hot springs, Volcán Osorno & to see the penguins. They have their own transport & rent the boats when required.

🏠 WHERE TO STAY

Accommodation in Puerto Montt is more varied than anywhere else along the Carretera Austral. Generally, it is more reasonably priced, and never fills up entirely as some villages further south are prone to do in peak season. The only missing element is camping opportunities, which are almost unheard of (exception: Casa Perla, page 87). The hotels close to Angelmó and the ferry port tend to be cheaper, though this is a slightly rougher neighbourhood (albeit oozing with character). Safety is reasonable in Puerto Montt, but late at night it may be wiser to take a taxi to or from hotels in this area. However, to experience authentic Puerto Montt architecture, this is the place to be, and the houses tend to be raised above the main city with lovely views over the sound and to the volcanoes. This area is also within walking distance of Rengifo, a hive of bars and restaurants. The Hospedaje Vista del Mar (page 87) is a fine example, and very popular. Just down the street is Cirus Bar (page 90), one of the most quintessentially Chilean bars along the entire Carretera. Hotels in the city centre tend to be less pleasant, although perhaps more conveniently located, and the upper-range options in this district are overpriced. The Hotel Manquehue (see below, under new management in 2022), while not as central, is an excellent premium accommodation, and in terms of value for money, one of the best 'treats' in the region. Competition between hotels/hostels is fierce in Puerto Montt, and prices are surprisingly good value compared with further south.

🏠 **Gran Hotel Vicente Costanera** [78 F3] (70 rooms) Av Diego Portales 450; ///decimal.less.dragging; ✆65 243 2900; e reservas@vicentecostanera.cl; w granhotelvicentecostanera.cl. A beautiful building on the main plaza with rooms facing out to sea. However, the interior is dated & the hotel is characterless. Laundry, Wi-Fi, & parking available; credit cards accepted. Most rooms are dbls; US$140 for a junior suite with sea view. Overpriced. **$$$$$**

🏠 **Hotel Gran Pacifico** [78 E2] (48 rooms) Urmenta 719; ///respond.rear.raves; ✆65 248 2100; e reserva@hotelgranpacifico.cl; w hotelgranpacifico.cl. 4-star hotel in a very good, central location, with fantastic views. An upper-end option somewhat less formal than others in this category, only exceeded by the Hotel Manquehue. Has a restaurant on the top floor (Los Navegantes, page 90) boasting 'the best view of Chile Austral', & within Puerto Montt this is probably an accurate description. It's

worth visiting this even if you're not staying here. Although this is certainly not a budget hotel, it is worth splashing out & getting a room with a view. Children under 10 are free if they do not require an additional bed; cots are also free, & they have a babysitter service – ideal for families. B/fast inc. Parking, gym, Wi-Fi, laundry, sauna, jacuzzi & massages. Can book online & credit cards accepted. **$$$$**

🏠 **Hotel Manquehue** [78 G2] (142 rooms) Av Seminario 252; ///contour.swanky.coffee; ✆65 233 1000; e reservas.manquehue@metro-op.com. Superb hotel, the best in Puerto Montt, complete with a small indoor heated swimming pool & gym. Note that it was acquired by the Marriott Group in 2021 & some details remain unknown at the time of going to press. The rooms are spacious, many with good vistas across the sound & city due to its elevated position. Room service, safety deposit box, fully equipped bathrooms (shower only), minibar, & a rapid (overpriced) laundry service. The restaurant & bar area downstairs, where the trendy

& wealthy hang out at w/ends, is positively hip but closes at midnight & is far enough from bedrooms to allow a decent night's sleep. The restaurant is excellent & includes vegetarian options. The b/fast (inc) consists of copious quantities of almost every conceivable item bar eggs. Funky artwork & wooden sculptures adorn the bar, although the range of artisanal beers could be better. It is a short walk from the centre, up a fairly steep hill – location is about the only mildly negative thing to say about it. Surprisingly good value, particularly if booked online. **$$$$**

🏠 **Hostal Benavente** [78 D2] (18 rooms) Manuel Rodríguez 214; ///talent.observe.revolts; ☎ 65 275 6630, 9 7851 6607; e hostalbenavente@ gmail.com; w hostalbenavente.cl. Reasonable accommodation near the restaurant district, not far from the centre, & also walking distance to the ferries & Angelmó district. Rooms are with & without private bathrooms (some with a nice view); parking, Wi-Fi & cable TV. Basic b/fast included, also has a restaurant. A little overpriced, but not a bad option. Credit cards accepted. **$$$**

🏠 **Hotel Ibis** [78 D3] (129 rooms) Diego Portales 1001 (bus terminal); ///declares.cost. stews; ☎ 65 222 7400; e h7491-re@accor.com; w all.accor.com/hotel/7491/index.es.shtml. Bland but highly convenient sgl & dbl en-suite rooms in this recently built hotel, located within the bus terminal. Worth considering if arriving late or departing early by bus. Cable TV, laundry, b/fast available but not included, cards accepted. **$$$**

🏠 **Brisas del Mar** [78 A3] (5 cabins) Angelmó 2186; ///regime.mining.cheesy; ☎ 9 9689 6718; e aguilarrony@hotmail.com. Run by the owners of the restaurant of the same name (page 89). Cabins are not so common in Puerto Montt for some reason, but these sleep 5 or 6 people, fully equipped. Nice garden for kids to play in, & well located near the ferries & Angelmó, but set back from the main road. Parking. $55,000/cabin. **$$–$$$**

✳ 🏠 **Hospedaje Vista del Mar** [78 C2] (6 rooms) Francisco Vivar 1337; ///flushes.sampled.torn; ☎ 65 225 5625, 9 9819 4202; e hospedajevistaalmar@yahoo.es; w hospedajevistaalmar.cl. Located on a quiet street about 10mins' walk (uphill) from the bus terminal, this is the finest budget accommodation in Puerto Montt, & consistently well reviewed by

all who visit. Open all year & lovingly managed by the owner, Eliana Oyarzún. The 2 sgls are small & cheap, possibly a little cramped if you have a lot of luggage; the 2 twins are much more spacious. Upstairs is the only en-suite room (dbl), with splendid views out to the Reloncaví. The final dbl is also very comfortable, but without a view. The shared bathrooms are ample even when the hostel is full (it often is), & spotlessly clean, with good hot water, & the downstairs shower has a great view of Volcán Calbuco. Wi-Fi, a computer & printer available for guests; cable TV in each room, a small communal balcony to enjoy the sunsets with a glass of wine, & a comfortable sitting area. Laundry available, & can use the kitchen. Eliana is from Chiloé originally & knows the region very well, including arranging ferries, tours in the region, good restaurants, etc. The b/fast is excellent – much of which is homemade, with fine bread, marmalades, muffins, unlimited decent coffee, fresh fruit, yoghurt, cereals, etc. Although cheaper options exist in this area, it is worth spending a little extra to stay here. Highly recommended, but do make a reservation as it's extremely popular. **$$–$$$**

🏠 **Cabañas Refugio Angelmó** [78 A3] (6 cabins, 7 dbl rooms) Angelmó 2170; ///sisters. shuffle.pastime; ☎ 9 9059 5416; e refugio. angelmo@gmail.com. Cabins for 3–5 people, basic but fully equipped with fridge, dbl & bunk beds, barbecue in small garden, laundry facilities for all guests & shared kitchen for those in rooms. Decent option for families, & convenient for Angelmó & ferries. Cable TV, Wi-Fi & heating. Cards accepted. **$$**

🏠 **Casa Perla** [78 C1] (4 rooms) Trigal 312; ///bravery.fixed.dollars; ☎ 9 9698 0951; e casaperla@ hotmail.com. Lovely, rustic, traditional hostel in a delightful alerce building over 100 years old. Wi-Fi, laundry, parking for bikes & motorbikes off-road, cars on the road. B/fast inc. Small camping area, free use of kitchen. All rooms have shared bathrooms, 3 dbls & 1 quad. The entire house is wooden, & feels slightly like a museum; the dbl room has a nice view towards the ocean. Reservations by email or phone; no need to make a deposit but call to confirm. Owner speaks English. **$$**

🏠 **Hospedaje Corina** [78 C1] (14 rooms) Los Guindos 329; ///prep.stardom.stutter; ☎ 65 227 3948, 9 8240 3037; e hospedajecorina@gmail.

com; w hospedajecorina.cl. Reasonable option fairly close to the main hostel region & not far from Angelmó & the bus/ferry terminals, in front of the lovely chapel San Alberto de Sicilia. Rooms are pleasant enough at this price range; 12 dbls (both private & shared bathrooms available), 1 sgl & 1 trpl. Nice patio with views of the sea & volcanoes & a grass section for sunny days. English, Spanish & German spoken, parking, cable TV & Wi-Fi. $$

🏠 **Hostal Jacob** [78 B2] (9 rooms) Buenos Aires, cnr with Pudeto 1558; ///renews. standing.qualified; 📞 65 271 1728, 9 7857 5394; e hostaljacob@gmail.com; w hostaljacob. webnode.es. Decent hostel with sgls, dbls & trpls; 2 of the dbls have private bathrooms, the rest are shared. Simple rooms; those overlooking the sea are preferable. Laundry, Wi-Fi, kitchen, parking & cable TV. Good continental b/fast included. Has a small terrace for sunny days. Reasonable budget accommodation if the Hostal Suizo, just around the corner, is unavailable. $$

🏠 **Hotel Suizo** [78 B3] (9 rooms) Independencia 231; ///equality.weekends.

havens; 📞 2 271 6382, 9 9308 5533; e rossyoelckers@yahoo.es; 🕐 Dec–Mar. Located in an amazing house that should be declared a national monument in Puerto Montt, this is a charming, slightly eccentric place to stay. The owners are Swiss & Chilean, & the house has been lovingly built over many years reflecting these 2 architectural styles. The rooms themselves are fine, simple wooden chalet-style. The main house is combination gallery/art studio/museum, with a tower offering views over the city. Some rooms are fairly self-contained mini-cabins, without a kitchen. Has a quincho, parking, Wi-Fi; the only missing item is b/fast, although guests can use the kitchen to prepare their own nibbles, & tea & coffee is freely available. The owner, Rossy Oelckers, is a well-known artist, & her pictures can be seen in the house & occasionally in local restaurants; she also offers painting & Spanish classes. She comes from the family of the Oelckers of Hornopirén who also have a hostel, cabins & a supermarket (page 119). English, German, French & Italian spoken. Good choice. $$

✗ WHERE TO EAT AND DRINK

Puerto Montt has an impressive range of restaurants, and it is worth grabbing a last exotic meal before heading south, where such offerings are largely absent outside of Coyhaique. There is a wide range of cuisines available, from the usual steaks, burgers, fast food and quality pizzas, to sushi, vegetarian restaurants, a huge range of seafood, Chinese and German cuisine.

Particularly towards the centre and along Rengifo, it is possible to grab a decent dinner and then afterwards hop to a bar next door for a drink. Angelmó has a huge range of small restaurants, most of which serve relatively similar good-quality fare, with a focus on seafood.

✗ **Nana Bahamonde** [78 D2] Rengifo 97; ///detained.sheets.revived; 📞 65 225 2552, 9 9005 1936; e nanabahamonde.eventos@gmail. com; 🕐 noon–15.30 & 20.00–23.30 Mon–Sat. Upmarket seafood restaurant in the bar district. Also serve meat dishes but seafood is clearly the focus & it is superb, including some signature dishes involving exotic combinations of salmon, eel, prawns, etc. Limited range of wines & beers. Perhaps not the cosiest place in town, nor competing with the finest restaurants in Puerto Montt, but one of the best along Rengifo street, & easily combined with a trip to a bar afterwards. This is a restaurant with a well-deserved

reputation & it's advisable to reserve a table at w/ends. $$$$

✗ **Pa' Mar Adentro** [78 A3] Pacheco Altamirano 2525, Angelmó; ///images.mondays. verbs; 📞 65 226 4060, 9 7170 0703; e contacto@ pamaradentro.cl; w pamaradentro.cl; 🕐 noon–midnight Mon–Sat, noon–22.00 Sun. One of the top restaurants in Puerto Montt & well worth the lovely stroll to the Angelmó district, although at night it may be wiser to take a taxi. Extensive wine list & wide range of fish, shellfish, meats, pastas & desserts. Does a mean Pisco sour. Interesting décor with lamps made of local algae. Bustling atmosphere, reservations required most of the time, especially at w/ends & in high season. $$$$

✗ Breko Sushi Bar [78 F3] Benavente 260; ///composed.odds.himself; ☎65 229 0099, 9 3626 2259; w brekosushibar.cl; ⏲ 12.30–midnight daily. Sushi restaurants come & go in Puerto Montt, but Breko appears to have generated a loyal following with its membership club for locals. Good-quality sushi with some original takes on standard rolls & tempura (Chilean fusion); also ceviche, & kids' menu. Decent range of beers including artisanal brews, a reasonable wine list & exotic cocktails. Quite possibly the last chance for sushi if heading south. The restaurant is well run, has attentive staff & a good vibe. Top-quality ingredients from the wasabi & soya, to the locally sourced organic fish. $$$

✗ Brisas del Mar [78 A3] Angelmó 2186; ///regime.mining.cheesy; ☎9 9689 6718; ⏲ 13.00–midnight daily. Popular & well-established restaurant approaching the Angelmó district, serving reasonable seafood & meats; the speciality of the house is *cancato* – grilled salmon with melted cheese & tomato, also spicy prawns. Decent, but cheaper & possibly more charming options available in Angelmó, & with a nicer view. Also has cabañas (page 87). $$$

✳ ✗ Chile Picante [78 C1] Vicente Perez Rosales 567; ///turkeys.snooty.guises; ☎9 8454 8923; ⏲ noon–15.00 & 19.00–22.00 Mon–Fri. A quirky gourmet restaurant in an otherwise run-down part of town, housed in a lovely old building with views over the city & out to sea. All ingredients are organic, local & fluctuate with the seasons. The short menu rotates, but always consists of seafood, meat & pasta options. Wine & local beers available. Owner Francisco learned his skills in Santiago but moved south in his youth, & dreamed of opening his own restaurant. This cosy, intimate & surprisingly high-quality restaurant has been open for about a decade & is enjoying a valid surge in attention. A little hard to find, but worth the effort, & particularly convenient if staying in this region of Puerto Montt; families welcome. Only 6 tables, so reservations recommended. $$$

✗ Club Aleman [78 F3] Antonio Varas 264; ///itself.opera.submits; ☎65 229 7000; w clubalemanpuertomontt.cl; ⏲ noon–22.00 Mon–Sat. The private club downstairs is not open to visitors, but the bar is lovely, & the restaurant

offers a range of German foods. The building was founded in 1860, making this the oldest German Club in southern Chile (others exist in Osorno, Frutillar & Puerto Varas). $$$

✳ ✗ Fogón Cotelé [78 G4] Juan Soler Manfredini 1661, Pelluco; ///survey.treble.spines; ☎65 227 8000, 9 8624 5285; e cotele.tools@gmail.com; w cotelerestaurante.cl; ⏲ 13.00–16.00 & 19.30–midnight Mon–Fri, closed Sun & public hols. This is simply a superb restaurant. Beware, it is further from Puerto Montt than maps suggest; ideally drive, take a taxi or jump on the frequent buses from Puerto Montt towards Pelluco. There are 3 meats – sirloin, rib-eye & fillet. The raw meat is brought to your table & you choose the exact cut you want – the price depends on the weight. It is cooked over an open fire by an experienced *parrillero* in the main part of the restaurant with a well-designed chimney to prevent the entire place filling with smoke. There are 2 salads available, & an excellent wine list catering to every budget & taste. 2 things make the restaurant unique. First, the meat is exquisite, probably the best available in Puerto Montt; given the limited menu they go to lengths to buy the very best fresh meat which will not be frozen at any stage, & is basted in a special *chimichuri* sauce (unless requested otherwise). Second, the setting & atmosphere are utterly geared towards relaxing, unwinding, chatting for hours on end, & feeling as though you are in your own home. It's a small restaurant & booking is sensible, particularly considering the distance from town. Technically the restaurant is on the Carretera Austral – a fine eating option for day 1 on the way south. 2 additional branches: Puerto Montt city centre (Rengifo 867; ☎65 225 6249), & Puerto Varas (Imperial 605; ☎65 248 1701). $$$

✗ El Fogón de Pepe [78 E2] Rengifo 845; ///arrives.history.pocket; ☎65 239 6386, 9 7979 7056; ⏲ 13.00–22.00 Tue–Sat. Good steaks in a lovely building that has been in the family for 3 generations. Quality of the meat depends on benchmark – this is neither Argentina nor the Fogon Cotelé, but is good nonetheless. Large portions, great service, & the owner wanders around keeping an eye on everything. Centrally located on trendy Rengifo. Good vibe & wide range of local beers. Not great for vegetarians. Fills up quickly so get there early. $$$

✗ Japón del Lago [78 D1] Rengifo 952; ///nasal.smoker.plan; ☎65 223 1318;

Angelmó opening hours are somewhat random. *Most* restaurants are open *most* days if there are enough people to justify opening, and the owners feel like working that day, but it is not generally possible to make a reservation; Pa' Mar Adentro (page 88) is the exception, with formal opening hours. Saturdays and Sunday afternoons are generally busy and most places are open for lunch, but dinners can be harder to find on Sunday evenings. There are so many restaurants in this district that visitors will not go hungry, but on Sunday evenings outside high season it may be unwise to go to Angelmó.

w japondellago.com; ⏰ 13.00–23.00 Mon–Wed, 13.00–midnight Thu–Sat. Decent Japanese restaurant, & the last chance to have some decent sushi before hitting the Carretera Austral. Perhaps not competing with the finest gourmet sushi found in Santiago or Buenos Aires, but the fish can hardly be any fresher, & a nice vibe. The *trucha de salmon* sashimi is fantastic, as are the nikkei. All standard fare – rolls, cones, soups, vegetarian options & tempura, as well as fixed menus of 18–58 pieces. Lively atmosphere, but fills up quickly so make a reservation. 1 local beer (Colonos, from Llanquihue). $$$

✗ **Los Navegantes** [78 E2] Urmenta 719; ///respond.rear.raves; ☎ 65 248 2152; w hotelgranpacifico.cl/restaurante; ⏰ 12.30–23.00 Mon–Sat, no lunch on Sun in low season. Take the glass elevator up to the top floor of the Hotel Gran Pacifico (page 86) for a surprisingly nice & reasonably priced lunch or dinner with excellent views. Set menus are $7,500 (lunch) or $12,500 (dinner), & offer a choice of 2 or 3 starters & main courses, & a good buffet dessert. A great place to chill out & soak up the view; has decent Wi-Fi to catch up with emails. Reservations usually not necessary. $$$

✳ ✗ **Cirus Bar** [78 C2] Miradores 1177; ///siblings.sweeper.hobbies; ☎ 65 225 2016; ⏰ 10.30–midnight Mon–Fri, until 01.00 Sat. Great, fun bar-restaurant located close to many of the hostels & not far from Angelmó & the bus/ferry terminals. Popular with locals, plus the occasional wandering tourist. Serves a decent ale from Puerto Montt (Trilogía: pale, amber & stout) & good food; seafood features prominently, also *cazuela* (casserole) & ribs. Laid-back atmosphere, & a local musician periodically arrives & sings a few folkloric tunes with his guitar. The bar has been operating for more than 60 years, & the

current owner/manager is the son of the founder. Ocean theme, with flags & boats adorning most of the bar. Hard for a couple to spend over $20,000 without drinking a huge amount of beer. $$

✗ **El Mirador de la Irma** [78 A3] Palafito 46, Angelmó; ///slipping.milder.home; ☎ 9 5532 4224, 9 9977 4405. Possibly the best restaurant within the *palafitos* of Angelmó, with a view along the estuary where sea lions frequently emerge from the water in search of scraps from the fish market downstairs. Decent portions including bread, a Pisco sour & an appetiser. Heavy focus on seafood, but portions are larger in this restaurant than others in this region. Family-run business for over 50 years. $$

✗ **Restaurant Shanghai** [78 D2] Manuel Rodriguez 195; ///jobs.mandates.surveyed; ☎ 65 234 0088; ⏰ noon–20.00 daily. Veteran Chinese restaurant/take-away, over 20 years in Puerto Montt, vegetarian dishes available, quick & decent service, light on atmosphere but satisfies the urge for a last Chinese meal before heading south. $$

✗ **Tablón del Ancla** [78 F3] Antonio Varas 350; ///puddles.downhill.pops; ☎ 65 236 7554/5; w tablondelancla.cl; ⏰ 11.00–01.00 Mon–Sat, 13.00–19.00 Sun. Ideally located on the central plaza close to the main shopping mall, this is a popular place with locals & tourists alike. Constantly full, & doubles as a bar in the evenings with 12 draught beers. Not the quietest venue in town (TVs show sporting events), but a fun & lively place. Serves sandwiches, hamburgers, meat & the house speciality of *pichanga* (a plate of chips covered in an extensive selection of toppings, good for 2 or more people). Good late-night option when other places close. $$

✗ **Rhenania** [78 F3] O'Higgins 167; ///fans.staring.slippers; w rhenania.cl; ⏰ 09.00–22.00

Mon–Fri, 10.00–22.00 Sat, noon–21.00 Sun. Located in the old Latam office that was destroyed in the civil unrest of 2019, this is a nice place for a quick sandwich, slice of (excellent) cake, (reasonable) empanada or a coffee. The original bakery was founded in 1959 in Osorno, & there are also branches in Valdivia & Puerto Varas. $

ENTERTAINMENT AND NIGHTLIFE

Nightlife in Puerto Montt, particularly at weekends, is surprisingly lively; weekdays tend to be low-key. Many restaurants double as bars, in particular Cirus Bar (see opposite), Tablón del Ancla (see opposite), Club Aleman (page 89) and Sherlock. Rengifo has a range of bars, as well as restaurants.

CLUBS AND BARS

☆ **Boule Bar** [78 F2] Benavente 413; ///taster. hydrant.snipped; ☎ 65 234 8973; ⏰ 12.30–15.30 & 18.00–02.30 Mon–Fri, 20.00–02.30 Sat. A good option to relax over a few drinks; the music is not too loud so it is easier to talk. Also serves typical pub food. Boule's has many rooms with tables & candle lighting & a broad range of music from 'Hit the Road, Jack' to hip-hop. Old *Rolling Stone* covers and other musical memorabilia are dotted around the walls. A good bar to carry on late in the evening. Credit cards accepted.

☆ **Club Angels** [78 A3] Av Angelmo 2240; ☎ 65 225 3303, 9 8173 3080; ⓕ Club Angels Puerto Montt; ⏰ 23.00–04.45 Fri–Sat. This is a disco dance club, adult entertainment & gay bar.

☆ **Galo's Lounge Bar** [78 D2] Rengifo 920; ///debating.nimbly.afflict; ☎ 65 231 4493; ⏰ 19.00–03.00 Mon–Sat. Probably the best bar on Rengifo, also serves food but main focus is a place to chill & enjoy an extensive range of drinks. Slightly quieter than the Irish bar across the road (which sometimes charges an entrance fee), better service than the Tex-Mex-style Cactus Bar also across the road, Galo's offers good service before it fills up, & reasonable prices.

☆ **Mirador a la Bahía** [78 E2] Aníbal Pinto 118; ///lorry.soap.definite; ☎ 9 9268 6645; ⏰ 13.00–midnight Mon–Fri. Cool bar with great view, as the name suggests. Serves the Trilogy beer of Puerto Montt (blond, golden & porter), as well as Kuntsmann & D'Olbek, cocktails & pub food.

☆ **Sherlock** [78 F3] Antonio Varas 452; ///drew. writings.pocket; ☎ 65 228 8888; ⏰ noon–04.00 Mon–Sat, noon–midnight Sun. A very versatile café, restaurant & pub, just off the central plaza with outdoor seating for sunny days. The family-run restaurant prepares delicious homemade Chilean dishes. Extensive selection of wines, beers & cocktails; try the highly recommended Pisco sour. One of the best pubs in the city for drinking, dancing & meeting the locals, & often has live music or karaoke downstairs. Credit cards accepted.

CINEMA

🎦 **Hoyts Cinema** [78 F3] Mall Pase Costanera (on the coastal road heading south); w cinehoyts. cl. The only cinema along the entire Carretera Austral. 5 decent screens, AC, popcorn, & while arthouse films are rare, does show the occasional non-Hollywood & Latin one. International films are generally shown with subtitles. Some films shown in 3D.

SHOPPING

This is a large Chilean city with every conceivable shop one might expect. The **Mall Paseo del Mar** [78 E2] (Urmenta; ⏰ 10.00–21.00 daily), close to the Gran Pacifico Hotel, contains an array of shops and a UniMarc supermarket. The department store within this mall is Ripley, selling everything from clothes to camping gear, electronics to make-up. There is a food court on the top floor.

However, this mall pales into insignificance besides the **Mall Pase Costanera** [78 F3] (on the coastal road heading south; ⏰ 10.00–21.00 daily). Visible from miles away thanks to two gigantic white towers containing office space above, this is a truly impressive feat of commercial real estate, a mere 2km from the official starting point of the Carretera Austral. It contains four separate department stores (Falabella, Ripley, Polar and Paris), and the UniMarc supermarket on the ground floor is as big as any in Chile, with a gourmet section where unusual international food may be found (Twinings tea is available, as are some Waitrose products; Marmite, alas, is not). A number of well-known brands have shops, and the food hall upstairs contains all the usual suspects (KFC, McDonald's, Pizza Hut, etc). For those in need of specialised camping equipment, AndesGear (ground floor; ☎65 231 5077; w andesgear.cl; ⏱ closes at 20.00) is a good option, stocking all major brands, as well as GPS devices, sleeping bags, technical climbing equipment, ropes, rucksacks and helmets. Other quality outdoor stores in the mall include Sparta (bicycles and accessories; w sparta.cl), Merrell, CAT, Rockford and Columbia. Two Chilean brands that are not so well known abroad, Doite (w doite.cl) and Lippi also have stores in the mall and offer a decent range of quality equipment often at more reasonable prices than imported products.

Both within the main district of Angelmó and on the main road to Puerto Montt are a number of small **handicraft** shops, mostly selling standard Latin American trinkets found in similar markets across the continent. However, for those needing an additional sweater with the iconic llama images across the front, this is the place to buy such items, and at lower prices than in mainstream stores. One item in particular is often overlooked by visitors: cosy wool slippers are very useful when staying in cabins along the Carretera Austral, and can be picked up for $15,000 in the handicraft market at Angelmó [78 B3]. There are also local handicraft products including food, honey, jams, etc.

OTHER PRACTICALITIES

ATMs, petrol stations and pharmacies are dotted throughout the city. Changing dollars is most easily done in the small money changers southwest of the plaza rather than in the formal banks. The central **post office** [78 D3] is at Rancagua 126 (///mashing.stole.obvious; ⏱ 09.00–19.00 Mon–Fri, 09.30–14.00 Sat). The main **hospital** [78 D1] is on Salvador Allende on the road north out of Puerto Montt (☎65 236 2001).

CAR REPAIRS Car mechanics are abundant in Puerto Montt, including mechanics & dealerships specialising in all major brands.

BIKE AND MOTORBIKE REPAIRS
Austral Motor Sport (AMS) [78 D2] Urmenta 996; ///roving.printers.vertical; ☎9 9059 2071, 9 9512 0266; e ignacio@australmotosport.cl; w australmotosport.cl; ⏱ 09.00–14.00 & 15.00–19.00 Mon–Fri. Probably the best motorbike shop & mechanic in Puerto Montt. Authorised dealer for KTM (motorbikes & bicycles), Suzuki, Yamaha, Royal Enfield, Kymco, Zongshen & Husqvarna. Can fix most problems on most bikes, & has a good stock of parts for these manufacturers, but can obtain parts for most other manufacturers. More complex BMW repairs/parts might not be possible

but MotoAventura in Osorno (see opposite) can work with these. All types of tyres available, including those suitable for the Carretera Austral, as well as all accessories, clothing, helmets, etc. Can also sell spares to take south (filters, etc).
Bicicletas Willer [78 C2] Chorillos 1184; /// spreads.evening.grandson; ☎65 226 8640; e ventas@bicicletaswiller.cl; w bicicletaswiller. cl; ⏱ 09.40–13.00 & 15.00–19.30 Mon–Fri, 09.40–15.30 Sat. Comprehensive bicycle store stocking a decent range of various brands (Shimano, Bianchi, Cannondale, Giant, GT, etc), wheels, lights, tyres, tubes, brakes, chains, pedals, shoes & clothing. Substantially better equipped than any bicycle shop along the entire Carretera, & has basic luggage. However, most cyclists on the Carretera use Ortlieb luggage

systems & these are not readily available in Chile or in this store, & the common advice from cyclists is to bring the luggage system from abroad if possible. Also does repairs & has ample information about the Carretera.

MotoAventura Chile Gregorio Argomedo 739, Osorno; ///thankful.among.door; ✆ 64 224 9123/4/7, 9 9829 8077; e info@motoaventura. cl, motoaventura@telsur.cl; w motoaventura. cl, w motoaventurachile.cl; ⊕ 09.00–18.30 Mon–Fri, 10.00–13.00 Sat. The best-equipped motorbike shop in the region, by a wide margin, including in Argentine Patagonia, is in Osorno, the next large town to the north of Puerto Montt (100km). Predominantly focused on BMWs (authorised dealer, has a scanner), but also services & has parts for KTM, Aprilia & Honda. Sells motorbikes & occasionally used bikes, plus all accessories imaginable (gloves, helmets, jackets, trousers, electronics, GPS, panniers & racks, engine guards, tank bags, boots, body armour, rain gear, sidestands, windscreens, chains & sprockets, etc). Tyres include Bridgestone, Continental, Heidenau, Kenda, MaXXis, Metzeler, Michelin & Pirelli. Also offers motorbike courses & guided tours (including to segments of the Carretera Austral, as well as the rest of Chile, Peru, Bolivia, Argentina & Brazil) in English, German, French, Italian & Spanish; 4x4s can accompany guided tours. Perhaps most interestingly they have an extensive motorbike-rental service with 80 bikes available (BMW 650GS, 700GS, 800GS, 1200GS & Triumph 800XCX). Certainly for BMW enthusiasts this is the best one-stop shop in Patagonia, & non-BMW bikers would be well advised to contact this store. They also have stores in Santiago & Punta Arenas.

MundoBike [78 D1] Vicente Pérez Rosales 297; ///quest.reported.trooper; ✆ 9 6622 6669; 🔲 Mundo-Bike-Puerto-Montt; ⊕ 10.00–18.00 Mon–Fri, 10.00–14.00 Sat. Fully equipped bicycle workshop offering technical service plus Shimano parts, breaks, tyres, etc. Main focus is on repairs rather than sale of bikes or parts, but can obtain

parts to order. Experience with foreigners wishing to visit the Carretera Austral.

MyM [78 D2] Vicente Rerez Rosales 150b; ///trooper.javelin.nipping; ✆ 9 3465 6371; ⊕ 09.00–19.30 Mon–Fri, 10.00–14.30 Sat. Small garage capable of basic repairs of bikes & motorbikes.

Puerto Moto [78 C2] Mechanic: Chorillos 1241, main shop: Urmenta 974; ///over.flasks. firms; ✆ 65 226 6684; ⊕ 10.00–19.30 Mon–Fri, 10.00–14.00 Sat. Motorbikes only, & cheaper brands from India & China, but decent range of accessories. The mechanics are perhaps not as formal as AMS (see opposite) but perfectly decent. Also has a range of tyres – slightly lower budget items than AMS.

Ruta 7 Taller & Equipamiento [78 G2] Volcán Michimavida 358; ///crashing.retina.wacky; ✆ 9 8702 8359, 9 5755 9026; e contacto@r7ciclismo. cl; w r7ciclismo.cl; 🔲 ruta7ciclismo; ⊕ 10.00–18.00 Mon–Fri. Experienced bicycle mechanics with specific experience of Carretera Austral trips, also have limited range of parts & accessories for sale. Able to fix most problems, replace broken parts & offer a full bike overhaul service.

LAUNDRY
La Burbuja [78 D2] Chorillos 1131; ///chef. embarks.jogged; ✆ 9 7750 9468; ⊕ 09.00–18.00 Mon–Fri, 10.00–14.00 Sat. Same-day service available if arrive early.

Lavandería FastClean [78 F2] San Martín 167, stall 6; ✆ 65 225 8643, 9 9353 5275; ⊕ 09.00–17.00 Mon–Fri. Same-day service if drop-off early, 09.30–13.00 Sat.

Lavandería San Ignacio [78 B3] Chorillos 1583; ///receive.spreads.bound; ✆ 9 6835 6795; ⊕ 09.45–18.30 Mon–Sat

Plusmatic [78 D2] Vicente Pérez Rosales 153; ///contact.hatter.reviews; ✆ 65 248 0517; ⊕ 08.00–19.00 Mon–Fri, 08.00–15.00 Sat. Can also do basic repair & wash down items, sleeping bags, etc.

WHAT TO SEE AND DO

Puerto Montt may not be top of any tourist's must-visit list, but it's worth taking a day or two to explore – especially if you like shopping or fancy catching a movie at one of the most southerly cinemas in the world (next stop: Punta Arenas). The city's architecture is varied; the Chilote influence is visible, and colourful alerce tiled woodwork is abundant, ranging from derelict buildings with smashed windows to beautifully restored houses, offering a glimpse of how this city must have looked a century ago.

There is a pleasant pedestrian and cycling path that traces the city's shore, with occasional vendors selling local handicrafts, alongside playgrounds for children, a skateboard park and some old trains. The sunset is truly lovely at the end of a sunny day, best viewed from the restaurant at the top of the Hotel Gran Pacífico, which also serves a decent meal (page 90). Along the coastal path is a gigantic statue called *Sentados Frente al Mar* (*Sitting Facing the Ocean*) of two slightly androgynous figures apparently staring out to sea appearing positively miserable, both with far too much lipstick, and invariably covered in graffiti. Provoking stark opinions, in August 2019 a poll was held to determine whether the statue should remain here or instead be relocated to an island just off Puerto Montt. Arguably one of the strangest statues in Chile, it remains in central Puerto Montt to this day. Another curious statue lies between the coastal path and the Plaza de Armas: a bronze monument to the German settlement that began in the mid 19th century, a teaser to the strong German influence further south along the Carretera Austral.

Although there is no 'tick list' of tourist sites, there's a certain charm to be found here that many are quick to dismiss.

EXTENDING YOUR TRIP – EXCURSIONS FROM PUERTO MONTT

For those leaving the Carretera at Puerto Montt, or for those with more time before they start their journey south, there are some good opportunities for sightseeing close by. These are all beyond the remit of this guide, but here are a few pointers to set you in the right direction.

Endless tour agents (ie: those representing tour operators) litter Puerto Montt, but actual operators are few and far between (Lahuén Andino, page 85, is recommended). The standard tours in the area are the **Saltos de Petrohué (waterfalls)**, the **Volcán Osorno**, the **Termas de Puyehue (hot springs)**, **Lago Tagua Tagua**, trips to the **penguin colonies** near Puerto Montt, and excursions to Chiloé (see below). Most of these can be done independently, particularly with a private vehicle. Renting a car offers increased flexibility and is not necessarily much more expensive than an organised tour. The only standard tours towards the south (ie: to the Carretera Austral) are tours to Hornopirén and to the Parque Nacional Alerce Andino.

Perhaps the biggest natural attraction, however, is the island of **Chiloé**. This is Chile's second-largest island (8,400km², after Chilean Tierra del Fuego), and although it is not technically part of the Carretera Austral, it is possible to travel between Chiloé and villages along the Carretera. It is a wonderful and increasingly popular tourist destination, and visitors can easily spend a few weeks exploring. It is rich in wildlife, including whales in the surrounding ocean, and the entire western side of the island is Valdivian temperate rainforest.

While Latam now serves Castro, Puerto Montt is inevitably a key jumping-off point for visitors to the island with ferries crossing the short Chacao Strait southwest of Puerto Montt. There are also planes and ferries from Chaitén. An indirect ferry from Puerto Chacabuco (near Puerto Aysén, on the Carretera Austral) connects the smaller towns of Puerto Aguirre, Raúl Marín Balmaceda and Puerto Cisnes, eventually crossing the Golfo de Corcovado to Quellón on Chiloé. There are also ferries from Quellón and Castro to Chaitén, and from Quellón to Puerto Cisnes. See page 60 for a full description of all ferry routes.

ANGELMÓ Anyone disillusioned with the relative modernity of Puerto Montt will find Angelmó a tonic for the soul, reminiscent as it is of the *palafitos* of Chiloé. The characterful market [78 B3] is bustling with countless seafood restaurants and shops, all set in a pedestrian area on the coast with fishing boats chugging in and out of the harbour, and kids sitting on the pier with basic fishing tackle periodically plucking their dinner out of the water. Sea lions often emerge from the water in search of scraps of food, much to the annoyance of stray dogs. This is also the last handicraft market for those heading south, and a relaxing place to watch Puerto Montt life go by. On a more practical level, it is close to the main boat ports (Somarco, Skorpios and Naviera Austral) and a 10-minute walk from the central plaza. A trip to Puerto Montt is incomplete without visiting Angelmó (at its best when it's not raining), and both the quality and range of food offerings in this small district will keep even the most fastidious foodie well fed for days.

HERITAGE WALKING TOUR This is the closest thing to a city tour in Puerto Montt. The historic centre is small enough to explore on foot. Maps are available at the tourist information centre on the central plaza, providing a brief explanation of the items of interest, as well as the principal route. The tour starts at the main dock and follows a trail through the central section of the city, visiting the central plaza, the monument to

The east of Chiloé is relatively developed and is where most inhabitants live, and the interior is dominated by large national reserves and private parks, with varying degrees of accessibility. The island has a strong maritime culture stretching back 7,000 years, and is rich in history – the traditional churches of Chiloé are world famous, and many have UNESCO World Heritage status. Its capital, Castro, was founded in 1567, and the island joined the Chilean Republic in 1826. Parque Tantauco, at the southern tip of the island, is owned by business magnate and former President of Chile Sebastián Piñera. Plans to build a bridge across the Chacao Strait were discussed in the 1970s, and although the formal project was cancelled in 2006 due to cost concerns, President Piñera resurrected it in 2012 before leaving his post. The strait is 2km wide at its narrowest point, the current ferries cross a 4km section at the eastern side, so this is indeed a major project. Even before construction began in 2018 the consortium building the bridge requested additional funding due to 'extraordinary works'. One of the main members of the consortium went bankrupt amid the Brazilian Lava Auto fraud scandal, leaving Korean engineering firm Hyundai in total control. No extensions to the budget could be considered until construction began, and although construction commenced in early 2018, a deadline extension and a request for an additional US$200 million in October was rejected by Chile's Ministry of Public Works. Within a year the 36 supporting pilings had been completed, but civil unrest struck the entire country in late 2019 (see box, page 80) and Hyundai again insisted on an extension due to construction difficulties – shortly before Christmas 2019 Hyundai ceased construction of the bridge. Hyundai and the Chilean state accused each other of acting in bad faith, changing the terms of the agreement and failing to meet obligations – and neither side wishes to meet the cost increase. In the meantime opinion about what could approach a $1 billion price tag for a 3km bridge seems divided, although work resumed, sluggishly, in May 2020.

4

the German settlers, the Diego Rivera Casa de Arte, the cathedral and museum. The walking tour takes a couple of hours, and while it is possibly not the most fascinating city tour on the continent owing to the size and relative youth of Puerto Montt, it conveniently encompasses the main points of historic interest.

Diego Rivera Casa de Arte [78 F3] (Quillota 116; ///remotes.install.rising; ↘65 248 2638; w culturapuertomontt.cl) In the 1960 earthquake a small art house in Angelmó was destroyed, and the current building was donated to Puerto Montt by the Mexican government as a replacement, hence the name. Run by the municipal government, it is located in the heart of Puerto Montt and houses a 430-seat auditorium that hosts a variety of cultural events, such as classical and contemporary dance, concerts and theatre, including the Temporales Teatrales (a series of theatre productions from around Latin America, usually held in July). There are four rooms for exhibitions by both local and international artists, the vast majority of which are free. Chilean films that might not make it to the large commercial cinema in the Mall Costanera are often screened here (free or $1,500). The website lists forthcoming events, and there's a decent café upstairs.

Iglesia Catedral (Church Cathedral) [78 F3] (Plaza de Armas; ///angers. owners.smiling) The somewhat confusingly named Iglesia Catedral is of mild architectural interest. Construction began in 1856 and was completed 40 years later; it is built almost entirely of alerce to a design that avoids the use of nails – all the joins are made by dowels, affording the building some mechanical play. Two conflicting stories about the reason for the nail-free design might be heard: that the church could not afford nails during the construction, or that they were frowned upon due to Christ being nailed to the cross. Regardless of the underlying motive, the effectiveness of this design was proven in 1960 when, despite being the oldest building in all of Puerto Montt, the cathedral was unaffected by a major earthquake that destroyed much of the city.

Municipal Historic Museum of Puerto Montt [78 D3] (Av Diego Portales 997; ///sake.dent.confirms; ⏰ 10.00–13.00 & 14.30–18.00 Mon–Fri, free) After some years of indefinite closure the museum is now open, and well worth a visit. Also referred to as the Museum of Pope Juan Pablo II, after his trip to Puerto Montt in 1987, the museum boasts an original bottle of red wine used in the mass he delivered on 4 April. For those heading south, this is an excellent primer for the journey ahead. In a mere two storeys the museum covers the ancient history of the region, from the glacial period and the first-known inhabitants, to the conquest and introduction of Catholicism, and up to the modern era. Of particular interest is the formation of Puerto Montt in 1853, and the catastrophic earthquake of 22 May 1960 ('The Great Chilean Earthquake', which reached 9.5 on the Richter scale – the most powerful earthquake on record). The photographs and description of the earthquake are harrowing, and that the cathedral survived this event is all the more fascinating. There is a summary brochure available in English- and Spanish-speaking guides.

⊕ AS THE CONDOR FLIES

A condor perched on the roof of the Costanera shopping mall, km0 of the Carretera Austral, would face a daunting 825km journey to the southernmost end of the Carretera at the border crossing to El Chaltén.

5

Puerto Montt to Villa Santa Lucía

The Carretera Austral officially begins at the southeastern exit of Puerto Montt. The relative modernity of the city rapidly fades only a short distance from the Costanera shopping mall at the southern exit and, with the exception of a brief interlude at Coyhaique some 560km south, it is wilderness from here onwards. This northern section is often ignored by visitors to the Carretera Austral, who prefer to join the road further south at Futaleufú. However, doing so misses the spectacular scenery around **Cochamó**, with some of the best treks along the entire Carretera. The detour to Lago Tagua Tagua and beyond is equally stunning and the gravel road now reaches almost to El Bolsón in Argentina. The scenic coastal road to **Hornopirén** offers a unique insight into the fishing and boatbuilding traditions of the region, and the ferry from Hornopirén along **Fiordo Comau** that follows the northern section of **Parque Pumalín** is a soothing introduction to the wilderness to the south.

From Hornopirén there are a couple of minor detours, but this is basically the end of this section of road. The only way south is via ferry to **Caleta Gonzalo**, on the edge of Parque Pumalín, from where the Carretera Austral continues towards the town of **Chaitén**, destroyed by a volcanic eruption in 2008. South of this, the road passes the first of many lakes bordering the Carretera, before arriving at the crossroads of **Villa Santa Lucía**, the jumping-off point for Futaleufú and Palena with abundant rafting and trekking options. Alas, Villa Santa Lucía was largely destroyed in a mudslide in December 2017, the damage from which is painfully visible to this day.

Improved ferry connections between Chaitén and Castro/Quellón on the island of Chiloé, and directly to Puerto Montt have significantly improved access to the northern section of the Carretera Austral.

TOWARDS HORNOPIRÉN

There are a number of different route options in this section of the Carretera. The most **direct route** from Puerto Montt involves catching the ferry from Caleta La Arena (///wormhole.pralines.dryly) 45km south of Puerto Montt on the north of the Seno Reloncaví (Reloncaví Sound) to Caleta Puelche (///investigated.crisis. excluder) on the south and then heading along the Carretera to Hornopirén. Along this stretch are the main access points to the Parque Nacional Alerce Andino and the Volcán Calbuco (2,015m), but there is little else of interest. Even with the ferry crossing, this can be done in a single day, although cyclists will need to get up early to do so. The only accommodation along this stretch is in Contao.

There is, however, an **alternative and more scenic** means of reaching Caleta Puelche that avoids both the ferry and Puerto Montt. The departure point for this 'back route' is Ensenada, at the eastern tip of Lago Llanquihue. If heading to the Carretera Austral from Bariloche (Argentina), this is a shorter option, and also more interesting than the developed road through southern Puerto Montt suburbia. From Ensenada a decent paved road heads southeast to Ralún, situated at the head of the Reloncaví Sound, but is of little interest, catering mostly to the salmon farmers in the region. Ralún was where Pinochet began construction of the Carretera Austral in 1976. The road then continues 15km south to the picturesque town of Cochamó, on to the less picturesque town of Río Puelo, and along the southern edge of the sound to Caleta Puelche. Prior to the ferry connection at Caleta Puelche this was the only way to reach Hornopirén, thus the residents of the region have a valid point in claiming that this is in fact the original Carretera Austral.

On arriving in Caleta Puelche, one final decision remains before arriving at the town of Hornopirén. The road continues for 10km (paved) until the town of Contao where it forks. The 'official' Carretera Austral heads directly south through the interior of this peninsula, but there is a lengthier **coastal road** heading southwest from Contao, eventually joining the Carretera Austral approximately 23km from Hornopirén. Indeed, this is one of the few segments of the entire Carretera Austral where the alternative route is more interesting than the 'official' route. The coastal road passes through a number of lovely villages, along stretches of sandy beaches, past some historic churches, and boasts extensive wildlife and lovely views out to the Golfo de Ancud and to some of the islands of Chiloé.

For those with a time constraint, it is possible to travel from Puerto Montt directly to Hornopirén in half a day via the short ferry crossing between Caleta La Arena and Caleta Puelche and by heading directly south through the peninsula on the Carretera (99km driving in total). For those with a little extra spare time, the detour along the coastal route to Hornopirén is worth the effort. However, the more significant detour via Cochamó and Río Puelo is certainly a consideration if time permits, particularly for those connecting with Argentina.

See the map on page 78 for the options.

DIRECT ROUTE FROM PUERTO MONTT TO HORNOPIRÉN (99km; 2hr drive, ½hr ferry crossing; paved) The road is paved to Caleta La Arena (45km; under 1hr), where the ferry departs to Caleta Puelche (page 60). Initially the road heads through southern Puerto Montt suburbia, and then passes through a number of small villages of marginal interest. It is likely that most departing from Puerto Montt will aim to arrive in Hornopirén the same day, which is also possible if travelling by the slightly longer coastal route south of Caleta Puelche. It is 54km to Hornopirén from Caleta Puelche, and takes approximately 1 hour by car. The road is entirely paved, with very few places to stay or eat after Contao.

Getting there by bus Kemelbus and Los Navegadores run frequent daily services between Puerto Montt and Hornopirén (page 83).

Sightseeing and excursions along the route Given the prevalence of spectacular parks along the Carretera Austral, both parks listed here may be of less interest to most visitors who intend to travel further south. Volcán Calbuco erupted in April 2015 and, while the Llanquihue Reserve reopened in 2018, the trail to the volcano is not officially open. However, further south, Parque Pumalín provides extensive opportunities to view towering alerce trees and visit two volcanoes (Chaitén and Michinmahuida).

Reserva Nacional Llanquihue (w conaf.cl/parques/reserva-nacional-llanquihue; free) Located to the east of Puerto Varas and Puerto Montt, and south of Ensenada, the Reserva Nacional Llanquihue is arguably the first point of interest along the Carretera. Its principal highlight is the **Volcán Calbuco** (2,015m), a rarely climbed volcano that erupted in April 2015 with spectacular images of electrical storms and billowing ash clouds reaching the international media. There are two main access points to the volcano: east of Puerto Montt towards Correntoso and Lago Chapo; or north of Puerto Montt close to Ensenada, along the 'back route' to Caleta Puelche (see below). A guide is highly recommended for either route. From Correntoso, at the edge of the Parque Nacional Alerce Andino, the road continues 7km north towards the volcano to a car park. From here the Los Alerces del Río Blanco trek (20km; full day; medium difficulty) heads north for 1½ hours alongside the river to a bridge, before continuing north to a refuge. It then leaves the forest, heading northeast to the summit. There is no park ranger in this reserve, and only one hiking trail (to the volcano).

The easier, northern access to the Volcán Calbuco begins in the village of Ensenada and passes through private property, thus a guide who can secure transit across this land is essential (4½hrs; moderate; see below).

Parque Nacional Alerce Andino (w conaf.cl/parques/parque-nacional-alerce-andino; $5,200/2,600 foreigner/Chilean, but note that there is not always a ranger on duty, so you can pay on exit) This park borders the Reserva Nacional Llanquihue to the north and is the main point of interest between Puerto Montt and the first ferry crossing. There are a number of lakes and well-marked trails within the park. Fauna include pudú, puma, kodkod (the smallest cat in the Americas), and the equally elusive *monito del monte* (no obvious translation in English, a very small marsupial that could be mistaken for a hamster and lives exclusively in this region of Chile and across the border in Argentina). Birds include the condor, the black woodpecker and huet-huet. Trees include larch, coigüe Magallanes and lenga. A number of short to medium-length trails are clearly marked, generally to lakes within the park.

There are three entry points to the park. The first begins some 7km southeast of Puerto Montt at Coihuín/Chamiza. Take the paved V-65 road 20km north to Correntoso. The entrance to the park (///loftily.limb.playable) is just beyond the village of Correntoso, where there is a 2km/1-hour hike to the Huillifotem viewpoint. From Correntoso, it is also possible to continue further north towards Lago Chapo.

The second entry point is a further 13km from Correntoso on the gravel road V-657 towards the Sargazo entrance to the park and lake of the same name. A 2.5km trail (Sendero Laguna Sargazo) reaches the southern shore of the lake. A 9.5km trail skirts the north of the lake and then passes through the forest until reaching Laguna Fría. This is a more challenging trail (medium difficulty).

The third entry point is from Chaica. Head 33km south of Puerto Montt or 12km north of Caleta La Arena to the village of Lenca and then 12km on V-701, a reasonable gravel trail suitable for a car with good clearance, to the park entrance (///unmask.observes.rescuer). A 9km trail extends to Laguna Triángulo, passing the Chaicas waterfall, through an alerce forest, and past Laguna Chaiquenes before reaching the final lake.

THE BACK ROUTE FROM PUERTO MONTT TO CALETA PUELCHE VIA COCHAMÓ

(174km; 3hrs; paved to Cochamó, then gravel) The alternative northern entry point to the Carretera Austral by road is at **Ensenada** (where there is accommodation). Indeed, given that construction of the Carretera Austral began in Ralún this is arguably the original starting point of the Carretera, not Puerto Montt. It is certainly the more scenic option and the recommended route for those with sufficient time. Instead of heading south from Puerto Montt, head north to Puerto Varas (17km; paved) and then east along the southern coast of Lago Llanquihue (47km; paved). This back road also passes through **Cochamó**, an adventure hub colloquially referred to as 'the Yosemite of Patagonia', and the destination point for those trekking from Argentina via Paso Río Manso. Although **Río Puelo** is of less interest, those trekking from Argentina via Paso Río Puelo in the south usually end up here. In fact, these two treks from Argentina to either Río Puelo or Cochamó are connected via a 24km route between Torrentoso (southwest of Paso Río Manso) to the main road towards Llanada Grande and on to Primer and Segundo Coral. Although logistically a little more complex, these two border crossings provide an interesting alternative means for those without a vehicle to begin or end their journey along the Carretera Austral. It is even possible to trek all the way to Hornopirén, but get local information before embarking on this route. Maps are available at the border and also at the destination towns of Río Puelo (the town, as opposed to the river and border of the same name), Cochamó and Hornopirén.

If travelling from (or to) Bariloche or east of Lago Llanquihue, this route is no slower than the direct route via Puerto Montt, particularly in high season, as there is generally less traffic and no need to take the ferry, which often involves a queue.

There is a minor detour to **Petrohué** shortly after Ensenada, which is a popular weekend retreat for Puerto Montt locals, and also the start point of the bus/ferry route to **Bariloche** (w cruceandino.com). For those heading south this is not an important detour, but is a potential (and expensive) means to connect the north of the Carretera with Bariloche.

Getting there by bus There are regular buses from Puerto Montt to Cochamó and Río Puelo offered by **Transhar, Buses Estuario** and **Buses Río Puelo** (page 83).

Towards Cochamó (47km from Ensenada; under 1hr; paved) The winding section prior to arriving in Cochamó is treacherous, narrow and has blind corners, so take care. The road hugs the coast, bordered by sheer rock faces and snow-capped volcanoes, meandering past small livestock and salmon farms. Various campsites and cabins are available along this stretch.

Where to stay and eat

Complejo Montaña – Ensenada (5 rooms, 4 cabins, camping) Ensenada junction; ///traced.resizing.sensations; ＼9 7306 3545; e turismoensenada@gmail.com. Around 44km from Puerto Varas, this hostel/campsite is well located at the junction to the Carretera Austral (via Cochamó), the road to Petrohué (where the boat from Bariloche arrives/departs) & the road north towards Entre Lagos, the Volcán Osorno & on to Argentina. Comfortable rooms each with a dbl bed & bunk bed, with en-suite bathroom, Wi-Fi & cable TV (b/fast inc). The cabins are cosy, wooden, rustic affairs, with fully equipped kitchen, dbl bed & 4 sgls in each; more expensive than the rooms & prices depend on occupancy (b/fast extra). In

Jan & Feb lunch is offered for both residents & public – buffet-style with pork, salmon, lamb & trimmings (◔ 13.00–18.00 Wed–Mon; $9,900). The camping, rather unusually, boasts en-suite bathrooms on the 8 premium sites, & direct access to the lake. **$$–$$$**

Hamilton's Place B&B – Ensenada (9 rooms) 1km before Ensenada junction head south on V-695 about 600m; ///realness.segment.twist; ＼9 9316 7828; e hamiltonsplaceensenada@ gmail.com. Cosy hostel nestled among the trees with garden & deck for hanging out, plus hot tub & a fire pit for asados (barbecues). Sgl & dbl rooms, with en-suite & shared bathrooms. Most rooms have a view of either Volcán Osorno or Volcán

Calbuco. B/fast included (dinner on request), laundry, Wi-Fi & good off-road parking, ideal for bikers. English, Spanish & Portuguese spoken.

Can organise tours in the region including Volcán Calbuco. Credit card & PayPal accepted. **$$–$$$**

What to see and do The main reason for visiting Ensenada is to begin the Carretera Austral. Otherwise visitors push north towards Bariloche or west towards Puerto Varas. However, it is worth pausing in Ensenada – the views over the lake are delightful, it is possible to hike to the crater of Volcán Calbuco, and there is some surprisingly good rafting and kayaking in the region (see page 152 for a description of rafting class levels). Particularly for visitors not intending to take the detour to Futaleufú for undisputed world-class rafting, one operator in Ensenada offers some excellent rafting and kayaking on the Río Petrohué. For those wishing to head south along the Carretera Austral, starting here is a pleasant alternative to Puerto Montt, and for those ending the Carretera Austral at Ensenada, it's the opportunity for one last adventure before emerging into 21st-century Chile!

Ko'Kayak Ruta 225, 3km west of turning towards Cochamó; ///agencies.indicate.thursdays; `\`9 9310 5272; e info@kokayak.cl; w kokayak.cl. Qualified guides from Chile & France, with healthy focus on safety & providing good equipment replaced every 2 years. Local trip is a half-day class III–IV rafting adventure down the Río Petrohué. No prior experience necessary; adrenaline rush without the extremity of sections of the Futa. $35,000 pp including transport from Puerto Varas if required. Also offer sea-kayak trips of 1 or 2 days on the Reloncaví Sound, heading towards Cochamó, as well as multi-day trips down the Comau Canal from Hornopirén, through the northern section of Pumalín Park. English & French spoken.

Cochamó and around Founded in 1979, Cochamó (population 4,000) is a delightful town situated on the Reloncaví Sound. It has a pleasant central square and church, and great views when the sun shines. However, shopping options are limited, and there is neither an ATM nor a petrol station in the town, so come prepared and fill up at Ensenada, Río Puelo or Hornopirén. While there's not a great deal to keep visitors occupied within the town itself, the surrounding region, and in particular the interior mountainous section towards the Argentine border, has been christened 'the Yosemite of Patagonia' by climbers and hikers alike. The Valle Río Cochamó is accessed 5km south of town on a northeastern detour. It may not compete with the parks of Torres del Paine and Cerro Castillo further south, but the region is certainly worth a visit.

Tourist information and tour operators On the main road next to the library is a small tourist information centre (⊕ 08.30–20.00 Mon–Fri, until 17.30 in low season), with maps and information relating to tours in the region. As well as tour operators, there are a few guides offering horse/trekking tours. Also see w municochamo.cl/turismo for extensive information and maps of the region, contacts for local guides, tour operators, hotels, restaurants, etc.

Independent guides

Cristian Igor `\`9 9077 2361. Horseriding including to Leones border post.

Roxanna Rey `\`9 6503 0059. Birdwatching in the region.

Jose Villega `\`9 8453 9755. Horseriding in Cochamó Valley.

Tour operators

Cabalgatas Cochamó Av Cochamó, in front of police station; ///wing.continual.penned; `\`9 9937 2042, 9 7764 5289; e cirovivar@gmail.com; w cabalgatascochamo.wixsite.com/chile. One of the oldest tour operators in Cochamó, specialising in horseriding in the region (9 horses) & offering guides on all the trails around the Cochamó & Río Puelo valleys, including to Valle El León & to both border crossings with Argentina, extending from 1 to 9 days. Can also guide the legendary Ruta de los Jesuitas trail to the lesser-used Vuriloche border crossing (page 106). Also a small hostel (shared bathroom, b/fast included, laundry available; from $20,000 pp; **$**), camping ($5,000 pp; **$**) & cabins (**$$**). Can arrange kayak & climbing trips, via other guides. Ida Delgado is one of the only female guides in the region.

Experiencia Patagonia Juan Jesús Molina 7; ///mentioning.chatters.platypus; \9 9334 9213, 9 8243 9937; e maurok@live.se; **f**. Operating out of the Hostel Maura, Mauricio is a registered guide focusing mainly on horseriding & kayaking trips around Cochamó, but can also advise & guide fly-fishing excursions & other routes (including along the trails to Argentina, to local hot springs & waterfalls). Accepts credit cards.

Patagonia Nativa Av Aerodromo at the northern entrance to Cochamó; ///minutes.recaptured. satisfaction; \9 9316 5635; e cochamo@ patagonianativa.cl; w patagonianativa.cl. Run out of the hostel of the same name, one of the best-established tour operators in Cochamó. All trekking options are available, including those to Argentina. Climbing is available nearby, & kayak tours with certified guides on both the rivers, in the sound & to Termas de Sotomó (hot springs; page 108). Mountain bikes available for rent. For those wishing to hike over to Argentina (although a guide is not strictly necessary as the routes are

well signposted), it might be wise to spend an evening in this hostel & find out more about the trails. English spoken.

Southern Trips Pueblo Hundido, Cochamó; ///asparagus.perpetually.cooperates; \9 8407 2559, 9 9919 8947; e info@southerntrips.co; **f**. 1km west of Carabineros. A range of trekking/ horseriding tours, including all the main routes around the valleys of Cochamó & Río Puelo. Guided treks across either of the 2 main borders to Argentina (Paso Río Manso in the north, Paso Río Puelo in the south), & can also arrange transport between the borders & Bariloche or El Bolsón in either direction – ideal if planning to connect the Carretera Austral with either town. Trips range from 3 to 10 days, & include all food, drinks, etc, & they own their horses. In addition to standard tours listed on the website, experienced guide Favian knows the region well & can give tailor-made tours, including to the El León Valley. For those without a car & disinclined to use public transport, private transfers to/from Puerto Varas or Puerto Montt can be arranged. Operating from the same building as The Coffee House Cochamó – a place to get a decent cup of freshly ground coffee or a fruit juice.

Turismo Aventura Cochamó Moises Morales; ///splurge.fairgrounds.sieving; \9 8411 7029, 9 6559 6684; e sebacochamo@live.com; w turismoaventuracochamo.cl. Run by Sebastian & Victor Contreras, who offer horseriding around the village & to Cochamó Valley, as well as trekking. You can camp on their land for $5,000 pp.

 Where to stay

Hostel Cielo y Tierra (4 rooms) km3.2 sector El Bosque, Av Aeródromo; ///professional.clench. perfects; \9 7311 0845; e hostalcieloytierra@ gmail.com; w hostalcieloytierra.com. Slightly outside town so easier for those with a car, or Andres can arrange a free pickup from Cochamó. Nestled in a region of smallholder farms, with sheep pottering about in the garden, a recently built, well-constructed hostel elevated above the village with fantastic views over the sound & to Volcán Yates. A peaceful option for those not requiring the immediate bustle of Cochamó village & great for families. Great communal seating area with large windows & a well-equipped kitchen for guest use. 3 dbl rooms & 1 quad, with & without private bathroom. Wi-Fi & laundry, no cable TV (but the

view makes up for it). B/fast inc. Will soon take credit card. Can arrange tours in the region. **$$$**

* **Hostel Patagonia Nativa** (6 rooms) Av Aeródromo, at the northern entrance to Cochamó; ///minutes.recaptured.satisfaction; \9 9316 5635; e cochamo@patagonianativa.cl; w patagonianativa.cl. Quality, simple sgl, dbl & trpl rooms, b/fast included; rates slightly higher for a private bathroom. Wi-Fi & parking available, but no laundry. Great view over the sound; perhaps a 5min walk downhill to the coast. The hostel's main attraction is that it is run by one of the most experienced guides in the region, Cristian Cea (page 104). **$$$**

Las Bandurrias Eco Hostal (5 rooms) km3 sector El Bosque, Av Aeródromo;

///absorbs.reverses.restaurant; 📞 9 9672 2590; e info@lasbandurriasecohostal.cl; w lasbandurriasecohostal.cl. A great option slightly out of town (free pickup/drop-off from Cochamó), very high-quality hostel with lovely garden, deck, well-equipped kitchen for guest use, & stunning views over the sound. The Swiss owner, Silvi, also speaks English & French. Ecological design, large solar panels to heat water, water treatment on site, & laundry (extra). Deliberately no Wi-Fi. Full b/fast with fresh coffee (extra). Reservation advisable, cash only. **$$$**

🏠 **Hostel y Cabañas Maura** (9 rooms, 5 cabins) Juan Jesús Molina 77; ///mentioning. chatters.platypus; 📞 9 9334 9213, 9 8243 9937; e maurok@live.se; 📷 hostalmaura. A charming & well-equipped hostel 100m from the church & even closer to the coast – it's one of the best in the town. Sgl, dbl & trpl rooms available without b/fast. Simple rooms, most with shared bathroom; south-facing rooms enjoy a wonderful view over the sound. For larger groups a quincho is also available. In peak season the owner sparks up the sauna in the garden. Laundry service available on site. Ample off-road parking – motorcyclists often stay here. Cabins for 5/10 people, fully equipped but no view towards the water. The hostel was founded by the owner, Nory, in 1996 & her son, Mauricio Mora is the founder of tour operator Experiencia Patagonia (see opposite). Credit cards accepted. **$$**

🏠 **Hostal Edicar** (8 rooms, 4 cabins) Waterfront next to Armada; ///regulate.dossier. pleasantly; 📞 9 7445 9230. Sgl, dbl & trpl rooms, all with shared bathroom, those at the front of the building have fantastic views directly over the sound & a small shared balcony from which to enjoy the sunset. No Wi-Fi, laundry or off-road parking, but location could hardly be better. B/fast inc. Also cabins on Río Cochamó for 4, 7 & 11 people, all with washing machine. Hostel has a well-stocked shop on the ground floor ideal for camping food & a wide range of wines & beers, among usual fare. One of the first hostels in Cochamó, established in 1992 & still run by the original owner, Edita. **$$**

🏠 **Hostel La Ollita** (8 rooms, 1 cabin) Principal; ///plan.akin.heavenly; 📞 9 8807 2716, 9 8166 5225. Part of restaurant of the same name (see below), has comfortable sgl, dbl & trpl rooms accommodating up to 18 people in total. B/fast included, Wi-Fi & laundry. Pleasant communal sitting area & kitchen. Reservations esssential in peak season, deposit normally required. Cabin sleeps 6. Owner has a boat & can arrange trips to the sound. Credit cards accepted. **$$**

🏕 **Camping Cochamó** 0.5km east of Carabineros; ///cluster.validating.humankind; 📞 9 9130 4665. Campsite with hot water & electric lights (solar-powered), showers. Some covered pitches & accepts campervans. Ample parking & benches/tables to eat at. **$**

🍴 Where to eat and drink

🍴 **La Ollita** Main road above church; ///plan. akin.heavenly; 📞 9 8807 2716, 9 8166 5225; 🕐 10.00–02.00 daily in high season, reservation recommended. The largest restaurant in town, lovely views from terrace, great b/fast. Specialities are an impressive range of seafood & ceviche. All food is either homemade or from the region. Offers a rare treat in the region: freshly ground coffee! Doubles as bar in the evenings, sometimes with live music popular with both locals & tourists. **$$$**

✳ 🍴 **El Faro** Waterfront just below church; ///notifies.thickset.unrestricted; 📞 9 8751 2543, 9 5655 4505; 🕐 10.00–23.00 daily. Great restaurant with mesmerising view, get a seat by the window. Offers take-out, but with such a great location this would be sacrilege. Local cuisine on an extensive menu (available in English), including pichanga,

chorrillana, sandwiches, vegetarian options, meat dishes, plenty of seafood options including crab caught daily by the owner, Francisco, & beer brewed on site. Reservation advisable in high season. Highly recommended. **$$**

🍴 **La Cuesta** Pueblo Hundido; ///tempests. undefined.scrapping; 📞 9 3481 5530; 🕐 08.30–21.00 daily. Lovely little restaurant & open late by Cochamó standards. Popular with locals & those passing through, friendly vibe & you inevitably end up chatting with someone. Unexotic range of meat & seafood dishes but well prepared & all local. Fresh ingredients, good portions & reasonably priced. **$$**

🍴 **La Herradura** Pueblo Hundido; ///beakers. overblown.ellipse; 📞 9 9993 4207; 🕐 08.00–midnight daily in high season. Basic restaurant; also has rooms above & cabins in Río Cochamó. Lowest prices in village for food & accommodation. **$$**

✖ **Restaurant del Pueblo** Next to Hostel Maura; `9 8750 0291`. A welcome addition to the culinary offerings of Cochamó, cheap fresh fish dishes, lovely views over the fjord if you can get one of the window seats. Annoying TV blaring but provides a rare opportunity to watch the news. $$

Sightseeing and excursions Cochamó may appear a sleepy town, but there is a huge amount to do in the surrounding region, with excellent trekking, riding and climbing (w cochamo.com/climbing). There are also kayaking options, but given the abundance of alternatives further south it is perhaps not something to prioritise here. There are currently around 160 marked climbing routes, although this is growing, with 100 big-wall routes, including a 1,200m route (Tigres del Norte, 5.12d). Pitches range from 5.6 to 5.13. For kayaking, talk to Cristian Cea at Patagonia Nativa (page 102), who speaks English, offers tours, and knows all the guides in the region.

The trekking options are extensive, and of particular interest to those travelling the length of the Carretera Austral is the option to hike directly to or from Argentina (see below and trail map opposite), from either Cochamó or Río Puelo. The scenery in this region is simply jaw-dropping, and the trekking is some of the best in Patagonia. The treks are generally not technically demanding and are accessible to anyone of reasonable fitness, especially when done partially on horseback. The trails are usually well marked, and a guide is optional for those with basic experience of trekking. In high season it is likely other trekkers will appear periodically along the way. Owing to the array of interconnected treks it is highly advisable to obtain a map, available to download at w turismo.municochamo.cl/mapas.php. Alternatively, you can purchase one from Stanfords (w stanfords.com).

Trekking in Valle Río Cochamó and Valle Río Puelo *Map, opposite*

For those wishing to combine a journey along the Carretera Austral with some trekking, the route between Cochamó and Argentina, which connects with an array of trails extending as far south as Hornopirén, is one of the best options in the region. Although short walks are possible, most people spend at least five days trekking in this area. Leave Cochamó on the main road south, and turn left just before the bridge over the Río Cochamó to the east (about 3km from the southern exit of the village; ///pinstripe.purveyor.intelligence). The gravel road continues for about 6km, accessible by car, but at the park ranger station the road ends, and from this point the route is accessible by horse or on foot only. It is possible to camp here. The main destination is La Junta, often referred to as 'the Yosemite of Patagonia', 13km from the park ranger station, where basic accommodation and food are available. This leg is moderate and takes about 4 hours. La Junta has four campsites. During high season (15 December–15 March) you must book accommodation in advance online (w reservasvallecochamo.org) and register when beginning the trail. La Junta has large granite walls for climbing and various treks of approximately 7 hours, each offering spectacular views of the valley. Camping in La Junta and exploring these trails is highly recommended.

Continuing along the valley beyond La Junta and towards the Argentine border enters significantly more remote terrain, and is more physically demanding. You must carry enough food and camping equipment, bring maps and ideally have GPS (plan on 4 days if crossing to Argentina). From La Junta the trail continues for 10km (5hrs) along Valle Cochamó, involving three river crossings – there are no bridges, so be particularly careful if there has been recent rainfall. There is a large waterfall at the Río El Arco and a shelter on the other side of the river provides an alternative to camping.

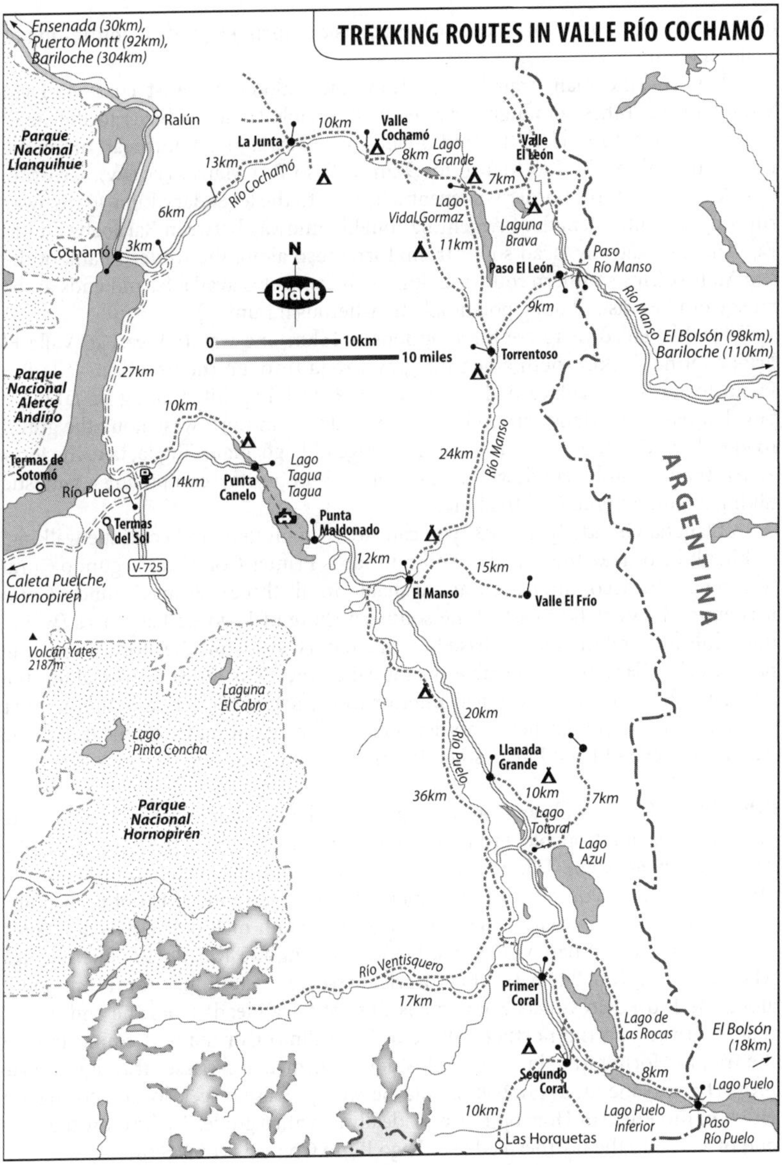
TREKKING ROUTES IN VALLE RÍO COCHAMÓ
Ensenada (30km),
Puerto Montt (92km),
Bariloche (304km)
Ralún
Parque Nacional Llanquihue
La Junta
10km
Valle Cochamó
Lago Grande
8km
Valle El León
7km
13km
Río Cochamó
6km
Lago Vidal Gormaz
Laguna Brava
11km
3km
Cochamó
Paso El León
Paso Río Manso
Río Manso
9km
El Bolsón (98km),
Bariloche (110km)
Torrentoso
0
10km
10 miles
Parque Nacional Alerce Andino
27km
10km
Termas de Sotomó
Río Puelo
14km
Punta Canelo
Lago Tagua Tagua
24km
Río Manso
ARGENTINA
Punta Maldonado
Termas del Sol
V-725
12km
15km
El Manso
Valle El Frío
Caleta Puelche,
Hornopirén
Volcán Yates
2187m
Laguna El Cabro
20km
Río Puelo
Lago Pinto Concha
Llanada Grande
36km
10km
7km
Parque Nacional Hornopirén
Lago Totoral
Lago Azul
Río Ventisquero
17km
Primer Coral
Lago de Las Rocas
El Bolsón
(18km)
8km
Segundo Coral
Lago Puelo
10km
Lago Puelo Inferior
Paso Río Puelo
Las Horquetas

The trail continues from this shelter further east through an alerce forest (less than 1hr, relatively flat), but pay attention in this section not to lose the trail. It then ascends to the southern shore of Lago Grande (campsite) and then to the northern edge of Lago Vidal Gormaz (8km from Río El Arco), with steep sections and passing several small lakes – it's potentially treacherous along this stretch if it is raining. This is a beautiful camping area and it's worth spending a day relaxing here. It might be possible to buy groceries from locals in the region, but don't count on it.

There are trails continuing east towards the Valle El León, but these are technical and potentially dangerous for inexperienced mountaineers. Seek up-to-date information in Cochamó and consider hiring a guide if continuing to Valle El León.

Otherwise, the main trail heads 11km south along the west coast of Lago Vidal Gormaz (4hrs; although for a fee it is possible to take a boat) to the small bridge at Torrentoso. Here the trail divides once again. Head northeast along the northern bank of the Río Manso for 9km to Paso Río Manso (½ day). Crossing into Argentina at this border will eventually lead to the legendary Ruta 40 highway running the entire length of Argentina roughly midway between Bariloche and El Bolsón. Alternatively, head south from Torrentoso along the western bank of the Río Manso. This southern route is 24km, with campsites available, and ends at the village of El Manso (2 days, potentially treacherous if raining).

From El Manso there are three options: a 15km one-way trek east to Valle El Frío; continue 20km south along the gravel road through the beautiful Valle Río Puelo towards the village of Llanada Grande (walking, hitchhiking or taking a bus that passes El Manso around noon); or walk 12km northwest along the gravel road to Punta Maldonado at the southern edge of Lago Tagua Tagua, take the ferry across the lake and head down to Río Puelo (see opposite), completing a fantastic hiking circuit without backtracking.

In Llanada Grande (page 108) you can stock up on food and continue walking, or hitchhike or take the daily bus south towards Primer Coral and Segundo Coral (camping and accommodation are available in all three). From Segundo Coral it is approximately 4km east to the southern shore of Lago de Las Rocas (where the Chilean carabineros are based, a mandatory stop for the border crossing paperwork). Camping is possible on the lakeshore. It is an 8km trek along the northern shore of the Lago Puelo Inferior to the actual border, and 4km further to the Argentine gendarmerie (border police). The exit point from this trail is the Argentine town of Lago Puelo, some 10km south of El Bolsón.

Other trails Other trails exist in this region but these require guides, and the state of the trails is questionable. From Primer Coral it is possible to trek west along the Río Ventisquero some 17km, but crossing the mountains at the end of this trail qualifies as an expedition for professional mountaineers, and it is not clear if any guides can offer this route. Lago Pinto Concha, south of Río Puelo, is accessible from Hornopirén. Road V-725, just before crossing the Río Puelo Chico bridge when entering Río Puelo (///clogs.overlaid.reserves), continues for 11km south along the Río Puelo Chico. Some maps suggest a trail leads from the end of this road southwest to the northern shore of Lago Pinto Concha and connects with the trail to Hornopirén, but this trail is not confirmed and passes through private property. Anyone attempting it should be well prepared, seek local information either in Río Puelo or Hornopirén, and ideally go with a guide. As the crow flies, the end of V-725 to the northern edge of Lago Pinto Concha is only 9km.

A final trek in the region offers an exciting, albeit long trek, to Bariloche: the **Ruta de los Jesuitas**. This is an old trail connecting Ralún in Chile (arguably the starting point of the Carretera Austral, 13km north of Cochamó) to Pampa Linda in Argentina (at the base of the Volcán Tronador close to Bariloche). The trail has been used since pre-Columbian days, and more recently by Jesuit missionaries crossing from the Chilean coast to Argentina. The pass was abandoned in favour of the Pérez Rosales Pass further north (as traversed by the Cruce Andino boat/bus tour to this day, page 84), but in 1998 the Vuriloche Pass was reopened. There is also a well-marked trek from Pampa Linda to the main treks around Bariloche: it is possible to trek from Bariloche to Ralún and connect with the treks originating in

Cochamó and Río Puelo all the way to Hornopirén. While not requiring technically advanced skills, this is a large logistical undertaking and beyond the scope of this guide. Trekking from Ralún to Pampa Linda takes between five and seven days, with a further four days to Bariloche – Cabalgatas Cochamó (page 101) is the only operator offering this journey; Tique (see below) can advise on it.

Río Puelo A further 27km south of the bridge over the Río Cochamó (or 32km south of Cochamó) is the village of Río Puelo, which has grown dramatically since the first edition of this guidebook. Its main virtue is being the start/end point for treks across to Argentina that use the crossing at Paso Río Puelo as opposed to the slightly more northern Paso Río Manso, which is closer to Cochamó. The road to Lago Tagua Tagua begins just north of the village, and the construction of the Termas del Sol hot-springs complex (page 108) just south of the village, have both served to put the village on the map. Although mostly paved, this section can be treacherous. Expect oncoming vehicles often travelling at high speed and drifting towards the centre of the road, often around blind corners. The road narrows to a single track in places, and weaves along steep precipices into the sound. There is a petrol station (///rejoining.bendable.sampled; ⏰ 08.00–21.00) 2km north of the village on the main road, just north of the detour to Lago Tagua Tagua – fill up here as there is no petrol until Ensenada to the north or until Hornopirén to the south, especially if driving towards Lago Tagua Tagua and down towards Segundo Coral, where there is no petrol at all.

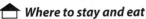

Where to stay and eat
Patagonia Puelo Lodge (4 cabins) Past landing strip, end of coastal road; ///ruffle. leans.erudite; ☎ 9 8157 4618; e reservas@ patagoniapuelolodge.cl; w patagoniapuelolodge. cl. The best accommodation in the village, sumptuous cabins for 3, 4 or 5 people on a broad bend in the Río Puelo. Principally a fishing lodge, but fine for families also. Fine restaurant for guests, lovely garden bordering the river, quincho available, can arrange tours including volcano trips. Decent b/fast included, as are all services except laundry. **$$$$**

❉ **Tique** (1 en-suite dbl, 3 domes, 1 cabin) 2.5km north of Río Puelo; ///subways. droplet.seaweeds; ☎ 9 9549 1069, 9 6802 4275; e victorv@andespatagonia.cl; w andespatagonia. cl. A one-stop shop in Río Puelo – accommodation, healthy restaurant & a shop selling a wide range of local products, honey, marmalades, etc. Can arrange fishing, hiking, kayak & horseriding tours. The entire complex is buried deep in the forest,

including an outdoor hot tub (book in advance as it takes a while to heat up), & the domes are all connected by boardwalks through the trees – a truly unique place, & a great means to disconnect from the relative bustle of the Carretera. Wi-Fi, laundry, hot water & heating (wooden stoves in the domes). The owners, Magdalena & Victor, know the region extremely well & can provide local information on all activities including the lesser-known Ruta de los Jesuitas trek to Argentina. A gem destination for those looking for a rustic retreat, all for a reasonable price. Cards accepted. **$$**

Hospedaje Elsita (3 rooms; 1 trpl, 1 twin, 1 dbl) Pasaje Volcán Yates 10; ///shorthand.ingested. fracas; ☎ 65 235 5530, 9 7607 4142. As authentic as budget Chilean accommodation/restaurants get. A roof over your head, lively conversation with the owners, elderly locals & truckers who frequent this joint, hearty dishes of typical fare, bargain prices & a chance to hear the local village gossip. **$/$**

Sightseeing and excursions
Lago Tagua Tagua The detour to Lago Tagua Tagua is wonderful, if only to enjoy the winding road climbing through the valley up to the edge of the lake. It is the starting point for more trails over to Argentina which connect with the routes from Cochamó. The detour is perhaps 1km north of Río Puelo to the east, and continues

for 12km (gravel) to the ferry port at Punta Canelo (///enables.tenants.nephews; w transportespuelche.cl; 4 Naviera Puelche ferries daily: 07.00, 09.00, 13.00 & 18.00, return 08.00, noon, 17.00 & 19.00; 1 crossing fewer in low season; $7,000 one-way with car, $1,050 for pedestrians), where there is food and camping available. The ferry crosses to Puerto Maldonado (///murky.cost.fuzzily), where the road continues 34km south to Llanada Grande, then 20km further to Primer Coral, and 14km further to Segundo Coral, from which point only travel by horse or on foot is possible.

Hot springs As might be expected along one of the most precarious fault lines on the planet, hot springs litter the Carretera Austral. The natural, rustic springs at **Termas de Sotomó** (☏ 9 9676 3147; e termasdesotomo@gmail.com; w termasdesotomo.cl) are reached by crossing the sound at Yates, a small village just south of Río Puelo. It is important to make a reservation, as access depends on the tides, and also to arrange the boat across the sound. The owner, Edgardo, used to work in the tourist information office (now closed) on the central plaza of Río Puelo and has a wealth of information. Limited accommodation is available fairly close to the springs.

The altogether grander **Termas del Sol** (///tuxedo.easier.dislodge; e contacto@ termasdelsol.com; w termasdelsol.com; ⊕ 11.00–21.00 daily; $28,000/20,000 adult/ child) are at the other end of the hot-springs spectrum. In an exquisite location on the shore of a lake with estuary views, this major construction, with thermal water emerging at 60°C and ten separate pools between 36°C and 45°C has a capacity of 400 people per day. It has a restaurant and changing rooms and is popular with locals from Puerto Montt and often fills up.

Detour: Llanada Grande, Primer and Segúndo Coral *Map, page 105*

By some definitions this might qualify as a detour from a detour, but Lago Tagua Tagua and the cul-de-sac road south to Segundo Coral is a worthy distraction from the important job of traversing the Carretera Austral. It is possible to trek to/from Argentina, but there is no vehicular border in this region. The road runs broadly parallel to the Río Puelo almost to its source in Lago Inferior. Trail maps suggest that there is a hiking trail running roughly parallel to the road south along the western shore of Río Puelo but this trail has been abandoned and is neither marked nor easily traversed. The road is therefore the only means to easily travel this section even if hiking – but it's still a lovely hike with limited traffic.

From Puerto Maldonado at the southern shore of the lake (///murky.cost. fuzzily), the 68km road is good-quality gravel all the way to Segundo Coral, where it ends somewhat abruptly. The journey is simply gorgeous, weaving along the river through the valley, where occasional farms interrupt otherwise untouched forest and snow-capped peaks. Traffic and people are rare – this is one of the most isolated regions of the Carretera Austral and, while it is not bursting with 'things to do', for those with some spare time on their hands it is one of the more interesting detours. In November the community buzzes with excitement over the exotic *morchella* mushroom, a highly prized native fungal fruit that commands high prices on international markets. The end of the harvest is celebrated with a festival, which exhausted the entire beer supply of the only micro-brewery in the region in 2019 (10km south of Maldonado in Mini-market Valle del Puelo). Note that this entire region has very poor phone coverage and often WhatsApp is better.

🏠 ***Where to stay and eat*** The region has a number of informal camping sites and cabins, and at a push, wild camping is unlikely to be a problem. Shops are few and far between beyond Llanada Grande. Phone coverage is patchy, so it's often hard to make reservations. The carabineros in Llanada Grande know most of the accommodation options and have VHF radios to communicate locally. Lore in Cabaña Llanada Grande (see below) seems to know almost everyone and can also help out.

🏠 **Mítico Puelo Lodge** (24 rooms, 2 cabins) Puerto Maldonado; ///adjudicate.conjurer. sending; 📞9 8184 0544; e info@miticopuelo.com; w miticopuelo.com. Stunning, remote lodge, the finest accommodation in the region. For a splurge on the northern Carretera Austral this is a wise choice. Rooms have to be booked in advance, as it is only accessible by a small private boat from the dock at Puerto Maldonado (private transfers from further afield are possible, but note – you cannot walk to the hotel from the port). 2 fully equipped cabins each sleep 6. Rooms in the main lodge are mostly dbl, with some trpl & 1 quad (all with private bathroom). Slightly larger rooms with a view over the lake are more expensive, but all very high quality. Laundry available, Wi-Fi only on the ground floor, no cable TV: nature & water are the attractions here – a chance to disconnect utterly from the outside world, sit on the beach (or in the hot tub) & stare at the stars or across the lake to the mountains. Fishing trips, mountain biking along the Río Ventisquero, a range of treks, horseriding trips & kayaking on the lake & excursions to an impressive waterfall all offered. The top-notch restaurant completes the array of services offered, with local Patagonian cuisine (lamb, steak, seafood, curanto, vegetarian options, etc, & a decent wine list). English/German also spoken. 3km from the lodge the owners have the most southern vineyard in Chile, producing Pinot Noir since 2014, & guests can visit for wine tastings. They also operate a 3,000ha private park dedicated to conservation (w parquetaguatagua. cl). Credit cards accepted. **$$$$$**

🏠 **Cabaña Llanada Grande** (1 cabin, up to 10 people) 1km south of Llanada Grande; /// return.unseeded.absolves; 📞9 5318 1613; e lorec. carabantes@gmail.com. Lovely, cosy, newly built cabin just outside the village, run by delightful Lore, who can help with any information about the region & help set up tours. She is an accomplished chef & operates a restaurant next door called Kultrün, serving food from the region, if not from her garden. Self-catering but b/fast (& other meals) available in the restaurant. Unusually the cabin also has a washing machine. $60,000–120,000, depending on number of people. Cash/transfer. **$–$$**

🏠 **Cayún Family** (1 cabin for 8 people, refuge & camping) Segundo Coral; 📞9 6450 8622, 9 9407 8469; e camilaargelcayun@gmail.com. At the end of the road, informal accommodation with electricity, bathroom & hot water ($15,000 pp). By the lake, traditional Mapuche food available & camping ($4,000/site). Horseriding, trekking & fishing possible; family has a boat. Cash only. **$–$$**

🏠 **Hostería y Camping Río Manso** (5 cabins, camping) 12km south of Puerto Maldonado, 3km northeast up a gravel track; ///amply.dazzles. sorted; 📞9 9136 6448, 9 8332 3719; e gallardo_ oscar@hotmail.com, turismoriomanso@gmail. com; w turismoriomanso.cl. Reasonable cabins for 4–6 people, food. Food, including b/fast, available but not included. Bathrooms & barbecue area available for camping. Has a boat & offers fishing trips & classes. Slow satellite Wi-Fi, cash only. **$–$$**

Trekking routes *Map, page 105*
The trekking routes connect with the main routes from Cochamó and are described on page 104.

Río Puelo to Caleta Puelche (36km; under 1hr; gravel) From Puelo the road continues 36km to Caleta Puelche along the southern shore of the Reloncaví Estuary. Caleta Puelche is where the ferry from Caleta La Arena arrives. This section of road is gravel, with steep cliffs, occasional rocks in the road, blind corners and the occasional oncoming vehicle in the middle of the road. As with this entire stretch of road along the estuary, take care and drive slowly. The views over the estuary are beautiful on a sunny day, but there is relatively little to do along this largely

uninhabited section. Paving of the entire southern side of the Reloncaví Sound is planned for completion in 2022 but as of May 2022 this section remains gravel.

THE COASTAL ROUTE FROM CONTAO TO HORNOPIRÉN (77km; 3hrs; mostly gravel) From Caleta Puelche the road continues 10km (paved) southwest until Contao. From here there are two routes to Hornopirén: the direct route, along the 'official' Carretera Austral (page 98); or the longer coastal route. The latter is recommended for those with time to spare, and is mostly gravel; it adds approximately 30km versus the direct route through the peninsula, but there are numerous places worth visiting, so budget at least 3 hours to get to Hornopirén from Contao via the coast, if not most of a day. A vehicle with high clearance is advisable along this section. Despite its relative proximity to Puerto Montt, this spectacular stretch of road is surprisingly remote and undiscovered. The paving of the more direct route through the peninsula siphoned off the few visitors to this region in the name of expediency. Limited employment opportunities and automation in the fishing industry is creating unemployment and luring inhabitants of the Hualaihué Peninsula to the big cities in search of jobs, leaving the traditional structures and way of life relatively untouched. At the very beginning of the coastal route, some 2km southwest of Contao, is possibly the best accommodation option along the entire coastal section – **Hostal Villa Angélica** (page 116). Other informal options do exist along this section, but of questionable formality and reliability – there are hostels in Aulen, Curamín (see opposite), Lleguimán and Hualaihué port (page 112), camping just south of La Poza (see opposite) and cabins in Punta Poe (page 112).

This coastal region is home to a number of boatbuilders, as well as traditional fishermen who use compressed air and garden hosepipes to dive for shellfish, often staying underwater for hours at a time in 11mm wetsuits. The activity is not particularly safe, and accidents are common. Fortunately decompression chambers are available in Puerto Montt and on Chiloé, but alas those who practise this activity are not always aware of the dangers of extended periods at depth. Anyone diving with the traditional fishermen does so entirely at their own risk; although such fishing methods are generally deemed unsafe, an exemption was made to permit so-called traditional fishing, but this does not extend to tour operators. There are no authorised dive centres or equipment rental stores, so snorkelling or free diving might be safer. Boatbuilders are usually happy to take a break and show interested visitors around their yards, where boats are hand-built with minimal machinery, wood is bent in large metal steam tanks and the smell of sawdust hangs in the air. Most boatbuilders are based along the northern shore of the peninsula.

Getting there by bus Expreso Hualaihué is the only bus company servicing the peninsula to/from Puerto Montt. Buses to Hornopirén will drop off or pick up from the junction north of the estuary, where the coastal road meets the Carretera Austral (page 83).

South from Contao (19km to Nao Peninsula; 1hr; gravel) The first village along the route is **La Poza**, approximately 10km south of Contao. According to locals there is a lake here, but pond might be a fairer description. However, the San Nicolás de Tolentino chapel (///sorted.bustled.hearty) is truly a highlight of the region. Dating back to 1860, this is the oldest chapel in the area, and although in a desperate state of disrepair, it still functions as a working chapel when the priest from Hornopirén comes once a month to deliver mass. It is entirely built of local wood and adorned with alerce tiles. The church bell is Spanish, and apparently one of only five in the country. In 2017 the church was declared a National Monument. To visit the church knock on the doors of neighbours until someone with a key appears – they are usually delighted to receive an inquisitive visitor interested in their village.

At the southern exit of La Poza, just after the bridge, turn left (south) on a dirt track for under 1km to the micro-brewery Biloche (///bitumen.abiding.shallower; \ 9 9271 8367; ◼ cervezabiloche), the only one in the region; the owner, Luis Lagunas, is delighted to receive visitors. Using only natural ingredients Luis makes three beers – porter, amber and golden. The beer is available in Ensenada, Puerto Varas and in Piedra del Lobo in Hornopirén. A further 2km along the main road, in the hamlet of Quildaco, is a small campsite (Camping Don Nacho; \ 9 6469 2111; e proschle.Ignacio@gmail.com; 4 sites, hot water & showers).

A further 2km south is the **San Miguel de Aulen chapel**, built almost a century after the chapel at La Poza (1958) but in a similar style. Of particular interest is the cemetery, visible on the neighbouring island, with colourfully decorated graves. Fishermen can offer a quick shuttle service for those wishing to visit the graveyard, but to some extent viewing it from the mainland is as interesting. The annual festival of San Pedro is held on the island nearby on 29 June.

Curamín
Along the 8km stretch between Aulen and Nao is the surprisingly pleasant village of Curamín, where, on a sunny day, the views out to the Golfo de Ancud are impressive. The village consists of the four key things to warrant an overnight stay: a shop, reasonable accommodation, one of the best restaurants along the Carretera and access to boats. The shop is run by a fishing family (Caty & Adrian, km16.56; \ 9 5050 9101), and has a large sign outside reading 'Mariscos' (shellfish), although it also sells basic food supplies, drinks, local jams and shellfish in jars. The family have a boat and can arrange fishing trips, or visits to the islands. For those with a wetsuit it is conceivably possible to hitch a ride out to sea with the family on a fishing excursion to observe the insanely dangerous hosepipe diving, but be aware that this is entirely at your own risk.

🏠 ***Where to stay and eat*** The family that owns the shop also has a **cabin** available for rent across the road, with spectacular views out to the gulf.

✳ ✗ **El Fogón Costero** Southern exit of Curamín; ///expressed.cards.lockable; \ 9 7656 5121. This is a gem, without a doubt the finest place to eat on the peninsula & one of the best seafood restaurants along the entire Carretera Austral, & apparently the only restaurant in the region to have ever made it into a magazine (the Dec 2014 edition of *Destinos Chile*), which the owner has on proud display. The detour around the Hualaihué Peninsula may be justified by a meal at this restaurant alone. Meat dishes are available, but the focus is seafood, including a seafood buffet, & it's a good opportunity to taste the much-sought-after loco. The restaurant itself is simple, entirely made of wood, with a warm stove & sweeping views over the gulf. This is simply *the* place to eat along the coast, popular with locals & the occasional visitor alike, as well as catering for parties in the region. Excellent & reasonably priced. The owner also has a fully equipped 4-person cabin (**$$**) for rent. **$$**

✗ **El Velerito de Tentelhué** 2.5km south of Curamín, where the road curves inland towards Rolecha; ///objectivity.applicants.reaction; \ 9 9756 5327, 9 7565 3273; ⊕ 10.00–23.00 daily. A small, rustic family-run restaurant serving typical dishes from the region with a focus on seafood. They also serve a decent curanto. Informal hostel, also offers boat trips. **$–$$**

The Nao Peninsula to Hornopirén (58km; 2hrs; gravel) The Nao Peninsula is approximately 8km south of Aulen, and at low tide it is possible to walk over to Nao Island. However, it's all too easy to get stranded on the island, so check tide times locally, and let a local fisherman know your plans prior to departing. The peninsula has a small village, and it is possible to visit boatbuilders here.

Rolecha, approximately 24km south of Contao, is the largest community along the coastal route, and roughly halfway to the junction with the main Carretera to Hornopirén. It is home to a chapel, built in 1940, and also boasts an impressive sandy beach – but beach-lovers are advised to head 14km further south to Lleguimán. **Chauchil**, shortly before Lleguimán, has a school, an impressive yellow church, and free camping. The beach at **Lleguimán** is where the locals go to bathe, and the river is good for fishing.

Approximately 2km south of Lleguimán is an unassuming yet mysterious spot named simply **Camping Punta Poe** (///atoned.preserves.dustbin). This is a gem location to spend a night, either camping or in one of the two simple 2/3-person cabins available just above the beach (65 235 8226, 9 9471 9663; puntapoe; camping $12,000/tent; **$$**). Besides utter tranquillity, at low tide a white sandy beach appears, and the cove offers natural protection for swimming. Some 50m south of the cabins is a series of caves in which human remains were found, and piles of seashells are visible to this day – an important but relatively unknown archaeological site. Don't touch anything, as the archaeologists are still investigating! The caves are not deep or dangerous, and even at high tide the water does not reach them.

The next and final inhabited spot along the coast is Hualaihué. There is a chapel dating from 1930, and a small mountain (Cerro La Silla) that can be easily hiked in a couple of hours; it boasts a small lake at the top, as well as lovely views across the peninsula towards the mountainous interior, across the estuary and fjord, out to the islands of the gulf. On a clear day it is possible to see Volcán Hornopirén. Hualaihué port is home to potentially the first dedicated tour operator along this stretch of coast: Miriam Melipillan (9 8309 1145; e miriam.melipillanwhite@gmail.com). She is based in Hualaihué in the sector Cerro La Silla, and can guide this trek. She also knows of informal accommodation options in the village.

From Hualaihué port the road continues north for approximately 6km, passing through the Hualaihué Estuary, where ample birdlife can be observed. Just 1km before the road meets the Carretera Austral (23km from Hornopirén) is the **final accommodation option** along the route, Residencia Yoanna (page 118), ideal for those seeking an abundance of religious icons and kitsch décor. The more discerning traveller may prefer to push on to Hornopirén. However, tucked behind the hostel is Héctor Bórquez (9 8425 2512), who makes extraordinary honey. Using a process similar to that of ice cream, the honey is churned and becomes aerated – it's definitely worth trying.

HORNOPIRÉN

As with Chaitén and other towns along the Carretera Austral, many visitors use Hornopirén as a quick stopping-off point on their journeys north and south. In fact, Hornopirén is a delightful town with a certain charm, worthy of a day or two, especially for those keen on hot springs, observing the abundant wildlife or simply relaxing by the estuary on a sunny evening. The surrounding area has excellent trekking routes to the lakes and volcanoes. Restaurant options are limited, and it is wise to book accommodation in high season. As with the

Hualaihué Peninsula, it is a mistake to simply push on south or north without spending some time in this underrated village.

HISTORY Although there is evidence of pre-Hispanic visitors to what is now the town of Hornopirén and the surrounding region of Hualaihué, the region was visited by the Spanish during their search for the mythical Ciudad de los Césares (see box, page 116). The village is named by combining two indigenous words: *horno* meaning volcano, and *pirén* meaning snow, or snow-capped. The first settlers arrived around 1890, principally for the abundant alerce wood in the region and to raise animals. Local families often have distinct surnames revealing their origins from the neighbouring island of Chiloé. During the 19th century, such was the value of alerce that planks of the sought-after wood were used as a currency. In the late 1950s, the North American logging company BIMA (a subsidiary of the Simpson Timber Company) established a base in what is now Contao and began deforesting the region, forcing the local inhabitants to seek alternative livelihoods, principally fishing. As a result, the population of Hornopirén swelled from 427 in 1960 to 1,126 a decade later. However, the prohibition of alerce extraction in 1976 and the arrival of Salvador Allende persuaded the Americans to leave the zone, and the Hornopirén population fell to a mere 365 by 1992.

In 1965, a tragic landslide on the volcano bearing the name of the town killed 28 people. The remnants of this landslide can be seen on the hike to Lago Cabrera.

The latest phase of immigration to the area has been fuelled by extensive salmon farming. The name Hualaihué means 'place of aquatic birds', so it is perhaps no surprise that the history of this section of the Carretera Austral is intimately related to the natural resources in the region. The town was formally founded in 1979, and the Carretera Austral reached Hornopirén in 1984; it now has around 5,000 inhabitants.

One intriguing element of Hornopirén's recent past is its lovely church on the central plaza (Parroquia Sagrada Familia; ///bustled.feature.frizz). The priest is a Dutchman named Father Antonio van Kessel who has lived in the region much of his life, after arriving in Hornopirén over 30 years ago. During the Pinochet years, Father Antonio was imprisoned twice, accused of communist tendencies for his support of the poor, and was a personal friend of Father Ronchi (see box, page 161), whose influence extends across much of the Carretera Austral. Father Antonio built the church in 1991, and it was inaugurated on 18 December of that year. He managed to obtain 15 authorised reprints depicting the various stages of the Crucifixion, originally painted by Adolfo Pérez Esquivel, the Argentine Nobel Peace Prize winner, in 1980. In 1993 these reprints were stolen, and have never been recovered; nevertheless, a stubborn Father Antonio obtained a second set of authorised reprints, copies of which can be viewed in the church to this day, and are worth perusing.

GETTING THERE The longer coastal road joins the Carretera Austral 23km north of Hornopirén and the paved road continues uneventfully to the village, passing the lesser-used Pichicolo port and Termas de Pichicolo (hot springs; page 121). There is a cul-de-sac road south of Hornopirén, but for all practical purposes this is the end of road travel for a while – ferry is the only way further south, and there are three options. First, and most commonly used, is the bi-modal ferry to Caleta Gonzalo (technically two synchronised ferries). Missing this, or being unable to book, can have dire consequences. The only alternative route by road, via Argentina, can take days. In high season there is a direct ferry that goes around the Huequi Peninsula directly to Caleta Gonzalo. Third, and least-used by visitors, is a ferry operated by Transportes Puelche (Wed, Fri, Sun) that goes

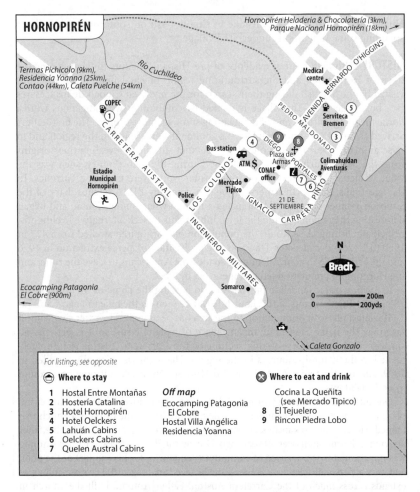

Hornopirén Heladería & Chocolatería (3km),
Parque Nacional Hornopirén (18km)

Termas Pichicolo (9km),
Residencia Yoanna (25km),
Contao (44km), Caleta Puelche (54km)

Río Cuchildeo

Medical
centre

COPEC
1

Serviteca
Bremen
5

PEDRO MALDONADO

AVENIDA BERNARDO O'HIGGINS

CARRETERA AUSTRAL

Bus station
4

DIEGO PORTALES

3

9   8

Plaza de
Armas

ATM $

CONAF
office

Colimahuidan
Aventuras

Estadio
Municipal
Hornopirén

2

Police

Mercado
Tipico

LOS COLONOS

1   6

IGNACIO CARRERA PINTO

21 DE
SEPTIEMBRE

INGENIEROS MILITARES

N

Bradt

Ecocamping Patagonia
El Cobre (900m)

Somarco

0   200m
0   200yds

Caleta Gonzalo

For listings, see opposite

⬤ Where to stay

1 Hostal Entre Montañas
2 Hostería Catalina
3 Hotel Hornopirén
4 Hotel Oelckers
5 Lahuán Cabins
6 Oelckers Cabins
7 Quelen Austral Cabins

Off map
Ecocamping Patagonia
   El Cobre
Hostal Villa Angélica
Residencia Yoanna

✖ Where to eat and drink

   Cocina La Queñita
      (see Mercado Tipico)
8 El Tejuelero
9 Rincon Piedra Lobo

from Pichicolo to Ayacara on the west of the Huequi Peninsula, from where it is possible to take a second ferry to Caleta Gonzalo (Mon) – but as these ferries only go a few times a week and are not synchronised, this is certainly a slower (though cheaper, and arguably more interesting) option. If heading north, the ferry from Caleta Gonzalo to Ayacara departs on Monday and Tuesday, and onward to Pichicolo on Wednesday, Friday and Sunday. Spending a day or two on the Huequi Peninsula (page 130) certainly beats driving via Argentina in order to catch a flight from Puerto Montt.

For ferry tickets, the Somarco office is at Ingenieros Militares 450, just by the ferry port (///rousing.autofocus.cucumber; ☎65 229 4855). The bus terminal is on Los Colonos when entering the town.

TOUR OPERATORS Formal tour operators are scarce in Hornopirén, but not necessarily required to reach most destinations. Individual guides or locals with boats to reach the hot springs are abundant but come and go each season. See w turismohualaihue.cl for a fairly up-to-date list of hotels, restaurants, guides, etc, available, with contact details. Failing that, the tourist information office (☎65 221 7330; e turismohualaihue@gmail.com) on the central plaza is surprisingly good.

Cabalgatas Rupulahual `9 5887 8159;` e cabalgatasrupulahual74@gmail.com; f Rupulahual. Run by Diego Montiel Paillan, a member of the Rupulafken indigenous community, this is an all-inclusive day trip up to Lago Cabrera by horse (2hrs) & then crossing to the north side of the lake in a small boat to some hot springs. While you soak in the warm water, Diego knocks up a lamb roast with salads, etc. The tour also passes the infamous landslide of 1965 that killed 28 people, & Diego is a fount of information on the history & nature of the region. $50,000 pp (min 2, max 10), full day, departs 08.30.

Chinook Adventure Hornopirén `9 9092 7357;` f. Javier Ruiz has a boat for up to 10 people, tours to sea lion colonies, the hot springs & fjords, fishing trips, etc. Also Niko (`9 7122 8038)` & Cristian (`9 8812 1436)` have boats offering similar tours & collaborate with Chinook.

Colimahuidan Aventuras `9 6802 3768, 9 8922 1230;` e ColimahuidanAventuras@gmail. com; f. Boutique tour operator located next to the Oelckers cabins on coastal road (Pinto Concha). Rafting on the rivers Blanco & Hornopirén, a shorter, more relaxed & cheaper alternative to rafting Futaleufú (grade III–IV); for those not doing the Futa detour this is a good alternative along the Northern Carretera. The entire tour takes about 2½hrs with safety talk, transport, etc, for 50mins on the river covering 4km ($30,000 pp, min 3). Also rent kayaks (not guided) to explore the coastal region of Hornopirén, visits to sea lion colonies, etc, suitable for families ($5,000 pp/hr).

Kere-Kere `9 8798 6078, 9 5321 8294;` e kerekereruta7@gmail.com. Valentina & Gabriel offer a leisurely 3hr/4km easy walk beginning at the Río Negro bridge (2km north of centre) towards the estuary. The focus is ornithology & photography: they bring field guides & binoculars & explain the flora, fauna, biodiversity & ecosystems found around the river. Educational, good for families, & it's eye-opening quite how much variety of life there is in this region.

Miriam Melipillan `9 8309 1145;` e miriam. melipillanwhite@gmail.com. Trek up Cerro La Silla in the south of the Hualaihué Peninsula.

Patagonia El Cobre Playa el Cobre; ///abiding. firefight.maxims; `9 8227 5152, 9 7273 2064;` e patagoniaelcobre@gmail.com. Experienced tour operators with a campsite of the same name (page 118). Mountain bikes & kayaks for rent (inc guides). Offers 3–10-day kayak trips in the fjords including multi-day guided trips down the fjord to the Cahuelmó hot springs, plus trips to seal colonies, & penguin- & dolphin spotting.

Turismo Lahuán Cahuelmó 40; ///fanned. bandage.leering; `65 221 7239, 9 8409 0231;` e info@turismolahuan.com; w turismolahuan. com. Owned by those with the cabins of the same name (see below), this company also offers tailor-made tours in the region. These include a tour along the coastal route towards Puerto Montt – often missed by visitors to the region & well worth doing. For those without a private vehicle this is a good means to explore the Hualaihué region, & the company can also pick up or drop off at the ferry port (ie: one-way trips) or Puerto Montt. They also offer ascents of Hornopirén, Yates & Apagado volcanoes; trips to the lakes & hot springs (they have their own boat); kayaking; visits to the sea lion colonies & boat tours along the canal to Cahuelmó & Quintupeu fjords; & trips to Parque Nacional Hornopirén & Lago Cabrera. They have a wealth of information not only on tourist options but also on local history, connections with other parts of the Carretera Austral & Argentina, & the region's surprisingly complex politics. Perhaps more expensive than other operators, but that's expected of private, bespoke tours.

Turismo Trayenco `9 8828 0972;` w turismo-trayenco.negocio.site. Run by a family descended from some of the first settlers to the region, a remote tour operator focused on Lago Cabrera. They guide trips to the lake (inc food) – a pleasant trip & a chance to get out of Hornopirén for a full day – & can also arrange a boat to visit some hot springs on the other side of the lake. Offer camping at the trailhead, 6km from Hornopirén, close to a waterfall.

🏠 WHERE TO STAY   *Map, opposite*

☀ 🏠 **Lahuán Cabins** (3 cabins) Calle Cahuelmó 40, Hornopirén; ///fanned.bandage. leering; `65 221 7239, 9 8409 0231;` e info@

turismolahuan.com; w turismolahuan.com. Walking distance from the centre, top-quality, fully equipped & positively comfortable cabins

The vastness of Patagonia allows legends to abound, and combining its sheer size with the passing of centuries, plus a liberal dose of religious mysticism, the result is the legend of the Ciudad de los Césares, a mythical city of silver and gold. Did some of the Knights Templar escape their coming downfall in Europe in the 14th century, bringing their most famous charge, the Holy Grail, to Patagonia? Is it still buried somewhere beneath the vast and barren Meseta de Somuncura, which spans the provinces of Río Negro and Chubut in Argentina? Or was it built by the Incas, escaping from the Spanish in the north of Argentina, bringing their treasure with them to establish a new colony in the wilds of Patagonia?

In 1515 the Spanish explorer Juan de Solis and his expedition were attacked by local Indians while exploring the area around Buenos Aires. The survivors of his party continued south into Patagonia, and rumours came back that they had discovered a fantastical city inhabited by white men. In 1528, another Spanish explorer, Francisco César, claimed to have discovered a city rich in gold and silver, and he gave it the name Ciudad de los Césares. In 1540 a shipwreck in the Straits of Magellan claimed 200 lives. Twenty-three years later, two of the survivors of the original crew emerged in Chile with stories of a city rich in treasures, silver and gold. Such legends were fanned by two separate flames: firstly, the local indigenous population were more than happy to send colonialist explorers off to the depths of Patagonia in search of mythical cities of gold; secondly, the monarchies of Spain and Britain may have used the idea of a Patagonian El Dorado to motivate their explorers, and give them a reason to establish outposts in remote Patagonia.

In 1783, the explorer Francisco Menendez left from the island of Chiloé together with 16 indigenous people intent on finding the mythical city. He didn't find it, but did discover three large waterfalls, which themselves generated mythical status. In 1961, a group from the 'Centro Andino' of Bariloche in Argentina retraced his trail and discovered the waterfalls at the confluence of the rivers Vodudahue and Vidal Gormaz. They did not, however, find the Ciudad de los Césares.

The only 'evidence' (and this term is used lightly) of the city seems to be the existence of the 'Argentine Fort', situated 15km from the city of San Antonio in the province of Río Negro on the Atlantic coast. While this fort appears to be a natural phenomenon, it would undoubtedly have been a useful strategic fortress were it inhabited. A rather mysterious group of Argentine investigators called the Delphos Foundation claim to have discovered engravings related to the Knights Templar in the fort, including a stone engraved with their cross. A map produced in

---

for 6–8 people; bath, as well as shower, in the largest cabin. Wood-stove heating, sitting area, parking & play area for children; laundry service offered. Views over Fiordo Comau or towards the mountains. The owners, Luis & Betty know the area extremely well & also operate a tour company (page 115), with their own boat & van, & can offer a range of excursions. Credit cards accepted. $$$$

🏠 **Hostal Villa Angélica** (5 rooms) Contao, 45km north of Hornopirén, 10km south of Caleta Puelche; ///arrears.shovels.kites; ↘ 9 9873 0070; e contacto@villangelica.cl; w villangelica.cl. Surprisingly glorious accommodation, finished to a high standard, in an otherwise fairly drab village. Spectacular sea views, lovely deck for sunbathing, pleasant garden & off-road parking. 2 dbls & 1 quad with private bathroom, & 2 dbls with shared bathroom (but can combine into family unit), plus laundry, Wi-Fi, b/fast (inc); dinner & lunch (extra) can be arranged with notice. Can arrange tours to Parque Nacional

1865 by the explorer Juan Antonio Victor Martin de Moussy marks the site of this natural fortress as 'Abandoned Fort', suggesting they had come across something more than just a natural formation. The group carried out a number of expeditions here in the 1990s, but they never found the Holy Grail.

Legend has it that the Knights Templar set up three such fortresses: the 'Argentine Fort' near the Atlantic coast; another at the same latitude on the Pacific coast, near what is now Osorno in Chile; and a third further south in Patagonia, as yet undiscovered. Were these various 'Cities of the Césares' or merely fortresses to protect and serve the one 'City'?

But what were the Knights Templar doing in Patagonia? The Templars were founded in the early 12th century as warrior-monks, primarily to escort pilgrims to the Holy Land. Their role, wealth and importance expanded throughout Europe and the Holy Land.

In the early 1300s Pope Clement V and King Philip IV of France demanded the arrest of all the Knights Templar in order to sequestrate their vast wealth. Some may have escaped from La Rochelle in France with their most important treasures (including the Holy Grail) and subsequently travelled to the American continent.

Rosslyn Chapel in Scotland, long associated with the Knights Templar, has engravings in its stone window arches of maize and aloe vera cactus plants, which did not exist in Europe when it was built in the 15th century. As the chapel was constructed before any Europeans had officially 'discovered' the American continent, this has been presented as evidence, albeit circumstantial, of Knights Templars' travels in the American continent.

A competing theory is that the city was inhabited by Incas fleeing the Spanish after a failed attempt to rescue their leader Pablo Inga in 1535 in the area now known as Santiago del Estero, Argentina. Don Pablo had been working as a guide for the Spanish colonialist Diego de Almagro, but when his posse was forced to flee by the Spanish, they took much of their wealth with them and founded their own city in the remote safety of Patagonia.

Patagonia may well be a vast region, but despite the advent of aviation, GPS, satellite photography and mapping, as well as a large number of expeditions specifically searching for the Ciudad de los Césares, there appears still to be no evidence of its existence. However, if on your travels along the Carretera Austral you wander off the beaten track and happen to stumble upon a fantastical city full of silver and gold, please let us know. *City of the Césares: The Bradt Guide* would be a novel addition to the Bradt list.

5

Alerce Andino, Pichicolo hot springs & the Apagado volcano. **$$$–$$$$**

🏠 **Hostal Entre Montañas** (12 rooms, 2 cabins) Ingenieros Militares, 100m south of COPEC petrol station; ///back.fleshes.planetary; ☎65 221 7352, 9 9439 7505; e entremontanashornopiren@ gmail.com; w entremontanas.cl. Good, basic dbl & quad rooms, all with private bathrooms. Gas heating, Wi-Fi, electric blankets & off-street parking; b/fast included. Cabins are fully equipped & sleep 4. The on-site family-run restaurant

(🕐 14.00–22.00 daily; **$$$**) is one of the best in town, reminiscent of a quincho offering fish & meat dishes, barbecue meat being the speciality of the house. Can also arrange local activities. **$$$**

🏠 **Hostería Catalina** (6 dbl rooms, 2 cabins) Ingenieros Militares, between the police station & the COPEC petrol station, Hornopirén; ///shrivels.perched.impasses; ☎65 221 7359, 9 9086 0912; e hchornopiren@hosteriacatalina.cl; w hosteriacatalina.cl. A short walk to the centre of town, but on the Carretera Austral if arriving from the north. Rooms with private bathrooms available; rates slightly lower in low season or with a shared bathroom. The friendly owner, Vladimir, has lived in Hornopirén for decades & is knowledgeable about the area & history. Rooms are comfortable but simple; central heating & even electric blankets for the cold winters. Large sitting area & quincho; full b/fast included. Wi-Fi, off-street parking, but no laundry service. Can also arrange trekking & horseriding in the area. Decent restaurant for guests offers lunch & dinner. Accepts credit cards. **$$$**

☀ 🏠 **Hotel Hornopirén** (10 rooms) Ignacio Carrera beyond Pedro Maldonado, Hornopirén; ///jeering.tipping.wittiest; ☎ 65 221 7256; e h. hornopiren@gmail.com. One of the few remaining buildings dating back 70 years, this old hotel made almost entirely of alerce was founded by the owner, Oly Bräuning, in 1984. The perpendicular street, Pedro Maldonado, is named after her late husband, & Doug Tompkins stayed in this hotel when he first began exploring the region. For those seeking a modern, plush establishment this might not be the best choice: although a remodelling of the hotel increased the number of rooms with private bathrooms & raised the ceiling a few inches, walls are thin, ceilings remain low, & the wooden floors are rickety – yet it retains the charm of a bygone era & it's undoubtedly one of the most authentic hotels in the region. Sgls & dbls available with private or shared bathroom; try to get a room facing the fjord – the views, & the sunrises & sunsets, are lovely when the town is not shrouded in cloud. Extensive b/fast included, featuring a range of jams, homemade bread & tasty pastries. Wi-Fi & laundry available, private parking, wood-stove heating; deposit usually required. Oly can also offer lunches & dinners for guests, arranged in advance. **$$$**

🏠 **Quelen Austral Cabins, Café and Restaurant** (9 cabins, 6 rooms) Lago Pinto Concha, 50m south of plaza, Hornopirén; ///probability.writers.sandwich; ☎ 9 9099 0281, 41 261 1168. Family-friendly place with attractive garden, in great location a block from the coast & 50m to central plaza. Cosy cabins sleep 2–8 people with price ranging

correspondingly from $38,000 to $75,000, & rooms all with private bathroom. Dogs welcome. Free quadbike & bicycle rentals for guests to explore the village, or if you want to reach more distant places in Hornopirén such as the ice cream shop, or Pichicolo hot springs. Wi-Fi, cable TV, & laundry (for a fee); restaurant open in high season. Cards accepted. Good choice. **$$$**

🏠 **Hotel Oelckers** (18 rooms, 2 cabins) Lago Pinto Concha & Los Colonos; ///unmapped.tickles. particulars; ☎ 65 221 7450; e info@hoteloelckers. cl; w hoteloelckers.cl. Sgl, dbl & trpl rooms available; the **cabins**, located 4 blocks south of the hotel on the coastal road, are more expensive & sleep 2–6 people. A modern & comfortable option; rooms all have private bathrooms, cable TV, Wi-Fi & central heating. Full homemade b/fast included; restaurant for guests only. Off-road parking available, but no laundry service. Accepts credit cards. **$$**

🏠 **Residencia Yoanna** (8 rooms) Hualaihué, 1km south of El Varal junction; ///passion.drearily. aliases; ☎ 9 7655 3182. One of the few options to stay along the coastal road, kitsch to the extreme & laden with religious icons, but cheap & close to the birdwatching region of Hualaihué. Shared bathrooms, b/fast included, Wi-Fi. **$$**

Å **Ecocamping Patagonia El Cobre** (20 sites, some covered) Playa El Cobre; ///abiding. firefight.maxims; ☎ 9 8227 5152, 9 7273 2064; e patagoniaelcobre@gmail.com. Turn left off ferry & head 900m towards the end of the beach. This large waterfront café has accommodation for up to 8 people ($10,000 pp). Camping surrounded by trees, private sites, some with fire pits. Shared bathrooms with hot showers. At high tide, austral dolphins are visible from the café. Organic vegetables available for purchase, or pick mussels at low tide (free). Everything gets recycled here. Kayaks & mountain bikes available to rent. Various high-quality walkways through the bush along nature trails, with trees labelled. Very helpful owner, Robert Catalan, speaks basic English, & can advise on all trekking enquiries in the region (page 115). Check out his impressive waterwheel used prior to the arrival of electricity in Hornopirén. **$–$$**

🍴 **WHERE TO EAT AND DRINK** *Map, page 114*

Hornopirén is light on restaurants; most are either within the hostels and hotels listed from page 115, or are at small, informal stalls dotted around the town or in the market, just west of the plaza. The restaurants Entre Montañas (page 117) and Rincon Piedra Lobo (see below) are probably the best options, but few come to Hornopirén for the food.

X **El Tejuelero** 21 de Septiembre, half a block from plaza; ///rookie.gradients.iodine; 9 5633 5880; ⊕ 11.00–16.00 daily. Slightly informal restaurant, does sometimes open in evenings also, especially if you reserve. Great-value menu of the day, 3 plates available – fish, seafood or meat, all locally sourced. Biloche beer available, as well as soft drinks. Also rents cabañas. Cash only. $$

X **Cocina La Queñita** Local #1 Mercado Tipico; 65 221 7404, 9 6284 8016; ⊕ high season 09.00–22.00 daily, low season 09.00–18.00 Mon–Sat. Bubbly owners offer great typical food (hake, chicken, eel, steak, etc) but also sandwiches & stew (seafood or meat), lamb & seafood soups. Popular with locals, good vibe, accepts credit cards & basic

English spoken. 2-person apts ($–$$) for rent with washing machine – laundry is hard to find in Hornopirén! $–$$

✳ X **Rincon Piedra Lobo** Bernardo O'Higgins, 50m from Central Plaza; ///fatherly.permit.puzzler; 9 9426 8420; ⊕ 09.30–22.30 daily, Tue–Sat in low season. Functions equally as probably the best restaurant in town & also a café with fine coffee. Salads, churrasco, burgers, seafood & local beer Biloche on draught, as well as other artisanal beers, & wines. Sandwiches to eat in or take out. Wi-Fi. Excellent service, a worthy addition to the otherwise limited culinary offerings of Hornopirén. $–$$

OTHER PRACTICALITIES The **tourist information centre** is on the southern corner of the plaza, which can provide maps of the town and some trekking routes, but has uncertain opening hours. The best-stocked **supermarket** in town is on the western corner of the plaza (Oelckers). There is a petrol station at the northern entrance to the town and an ATM just off the central plaza (///sharpening.stutters.icicle). There is no laundry in the village apart from what appears to be an informal **laundry** down an alley just behind Oelckers hotel – it has a 'laundry' sign and the owner hesitantly admits she does wash clothes. A small bicycle shop next door sells a range of parts, rents bikes and can do repairs.

Hornopirén Heladería & Chocolatería (ice cream and chocolate shop) makes for a surprisingly nice outing 3km northeast of downtown Hornopirén (clearly signposted; 9 9087 1411). Opened in 2013, this remains a small outfit, but produces a limited range of surprisingly good ice creams using mostly local ingredients from the region, including gooseberry and some excellent sorbets.

Mechanic
Serviteca Bremen Cnr Cahuelmó & Carretera; ///thickset.shadows.animals; 9 9979 4892; e servitecabremen@gmail.com; ⊕ 09.00–19.00 Mon–Fri, 09.00–14.00 Sat. Basic repairs, tyres, batteries, lubricants, car wash & limited range of outdoor kit (camping, fishing). Does not have tow service but call Grúas M&C (9 9591 5123) if you need a tow. Good service.

PARQUE NACIONAL HORNOPIRÉN

(CONAF park office is on the western side of the plaza; ///lipsticks.graciously. versatility; w conaf.cl/parques/parque-nacional-hornopiren; park entrance & maps free) Containing 482km^2 of rugged Andean mountains and virgin Valdivian temperate rainforests, Parque Nacional Hornopirén borders the northern portion of Parque Pumalín, with Volcán Yates (2,187m) and Volcán Hornopirén (1,572m) at the western boundaries of the park. It is the highlight of the region and includes treks to Lago Pinto Concha (3km from park entrance) and on to the town of Río Puelo, connecting with the treks over the Argentine border (page 104). Hiking Volcán Hornopirén is possible without a guide, but there are many trails and it is easy to get lost. Opinions vary as to whether a guide is required for volcanoes Yates and Apagado, but we would recommend using one, particularly as reaching them involves passing through private land. Most tour operators can arrange this.

GETTING THERE To reach the park from Hornopirén, head for 11km northeast on Avenida Lib Bernardo O'Higgins (paved). A fork in the road directs visitors to the park to veer left for a further 7km on poor-quality, pot-holed gravel. At the end of this section there is parking; and from here, the trek described below begins. There is no public transport to the park, but hitching is an option, or you can get a taxi from Hornopirén.

TREKKING ROUTES Fit trekkers should try the **two- or three-day trek** (depending on whether you climb the summit **of Volcán Yates**), which features three main highlights: the millennial alerce forest; the picturesque Lago Pinto Concha; and the crater of Volcán Yates, from where there are panoramic views.

Day one (10km one-way; 5–6hrs; medium) From the car park, the first day passes initially through private farmland on a well-marked trail crossing multiple swing bridges across crystal-clear rivers. An old lumber trail continues up a steep incline before levelling out at a plateau and then continuing a further 4.5km up a gradual slope to the park boundary. This is the official park entrance, and where the alerce trees start. The track then continues to climb 3km gradually under the cover of mature bush (including some alerce trees) to the shore of Lago Pinto Concha. There is a CONAF ranger shelter on the southwest side of the lake with information for tourists in the summer months and a basic camping area on the western side of the lake, with neither cooking facilities nor drinking water available, although you can drink water from the lake.

Day two (7km round trip; 4–5hrs; medium) The second day reaches the crater of Volcán Yates and is suitable for any experienced trekker with a high level of fitness. From the campsite, the well-marked trail continues uphill through the alerce forest to the base of the volcano, before weaving its way up the southern edge of the crater passing over volcanic rock and scoria. Spectacular panoramic views from the top make it all worthwhile. It is possible to see into the crater of Volcán Yates, as well as across the entire park with views of Lago Pinto Concha and Fiordo Hornopirén. You can return to Hornopirén on the third day.

AROUND HORNOPIRÉN

LAGO CABRERA This is a beautiful and accessible lake involving a light trek. Head northeast from Hornopirén on the Carretera Austral along the Río Negro. Just before the bridge (1km), veer left (north). This road continues for 6km, but depending on the type of vehicle and the state of the road you might not reach the end. As the crow flies the lake is only 2km from the end of the road. With a car this is a short, pleasant hike; without a car it might be a 4-hour round trip. The terrain is easy, but best walked in boots capable of sludging through muddy sections. Take water. There are actually hot springs on the other side of the lake, but these are privately owned and access requires a boat and a guide. Any of the tour operators can arrange these, in particular Colimahuidan Aventuras (page 115).

HOT SPRINGS There are at least five hot springs around Hornopirén, and also geysers. With the exception of Termas de Pichicolo, a boat is needed to reach them. The boat ride itself is an experience, with ample opportunities to spot wildlife: if you are particularly lucky, you may see a whale, but dolphins, penguins, sea lions and a wide range of birds such as shags, petrels, pelicans and kingfishers are abundant; migratory birds such as flamingos and swans can also be seen. Most of the hot springs are accessed from Fiordo Comau (page 122), south of Hornopirén. This is the fjord traversed by the main ferry south connecting to the Carretera Austral. Along Fiordo Comau are two additional fjords that cut eastward into the continent: Quintupeu and Calhuelmó (see below; the latter has hot springs).

The Termas de Llancahué (w termasdellancahue.cl) on the island of Llancahué, at the north of Fiordo Comau, some 10km south of Hornopirén, require a boat ride. The Porcelana hot springs and geysers (two distinct destinations, mistakenly assumed to be in the same location) are on the Huequi Peninsula south of Hornopirén and north of Caleta Gonzalo – technically connected to the continent, but accessible only by boat.

Termas de Pichicolo (9km north/west of Hornopirén; ☏ 9 5637 8303, 9 5416 4588; e termaspichicolo@gmail.com; w termasdepichicolo.cl; ⊕ Jan–Feb 11.00–15.00 & 16.00–21.00 daily, Mar noon–20.00 Tue–Sun, Apr–Nov 10.00–18.00 Sat–Sun & public hols, Dec 11.30–19.00 Tue–Sun; $16,000/12,000 high/low season, children slightly less) When in Hornopirén one must visit at least one hot spring and Pichicolo is the most accessible (not requiring a boat). Nestled in verdant forest, seven pools are connected by wooden boardwalks through the trees (10mins to the furthest tub). These are natural, open-air springs laden with minerals and boasting various health benefits, relaxation being the most obvious.

FIORDO QUINTUPEU AND FIORDO CAHUELMÓ Fiordo Quintupeu does not boast any hot springs but is often visited on boat trips in this region en route to other hot springs. It is of historic interest: with 600m towering and inaccessible walls, a narrow entrance, but a clear line of sight across Fiordo Comau and to Golfo de Ancud it was the ideal hideout for the SMS *Dresden*, the only German battleship to have survived the 1915 Battle of the Falklands, after fleeing the British fleet. Quintupeu is home to alerce trees up to 3,600 years old, has spectacular waterfalls cascading down the walls (Quintupeu means 'Place of Five Waterfalls'), and is technically part of Parque Pumalín, albeit in one of the most remote and inaccessible areas. **Fiordo Cahuelmó** is approximately 10km further south, and has hot springs.

Neither Fiordo Quintupeu nor Fiordo Cahuelmó can be accessed by land, nor do scheduled ferries visit: private boat is the only means of access. A cursory glance at both fjords demonstrates the enormous challenge of continuing the coastal road from Hornopirén any further south. The Carretera Austral reaches Pichanco, some 34km beyond Hornopirén, and a mere 3km from the mouth of Fiordo Quintupeu – but all options for traversing the fjord – tunnel, bridge or a road around it, seem daunting. Expect the ferry to be the only means of traversing this section for some years yet.

VOLCANO TREKS Hornopirén boasts three local volcanoes: Hornopirén itself, Yates and Apagado. The latter two require guides. They are possibly not as frequently climbed as the well-marked trails in Parque Pumalín a little further south – Chaitén (page 122) and Michinmahuida (page 132) – but for more adventurous trekkers this is yet another reason to explore this region.

⊕ AS THE CONDOR FLIES

Hornopirén is 65km from Puerto Montt and 780km from the end point of the Carretera Austral at the border crossing to El Chaltén.

TOWARDS CHAITÉN

The ferry ride through Fiordo Comau – which separates the majority of the Carretera Austral from the main road network of Chile – is a dramatic introduction to what lies in store further south. It arrives at Caleta Gonzalo on the edge of Parque Pumalín (page 132), one of the most important private conservation projects on earth. From here, the Carretera continues south to Chaitén, El Amarillo and Villa Santa Lucía.

FIORDO COMAU Bordering the northern section of Parque Pumalín, this fjord runs directly south of Hornopirén to Leptepú on the Huequi Peninsula. Ferries to Caleta Gonzalo traverse the length of it, at which point a 10km gravel road connects to the other side of the peninsula at Fiordo Largo, where a second ferry crosses the short stretch to Caleta Gonzalo, entry point to Parque Pumalín and on to Chaitén. The openings to Quintupeu and Cahuelmó fjords can be seen from the ferry. Between Caleta Gonzalo and Chaitén the main attraction is the northern section of Pumalín Park (page 132).

CHAITÉN

The town itself is of mild interest beyond witnessing the aftermath of a major volcanic eruption. All basic services are now available, but most visitors spend their time in Parque Pumalín or depart Chaitén after a meal, refuelling and perhaps doing some laundry. For those heading north without a ferry ticket, the first port of call might be the Somarco or Naviera Austral office to secure a ticket. The lesser-used ferries operated by Transportes Puelche can only be booked online or by telephone (page 60) – they do not have a physical office in Chaitén. Be careful to distinguish between ferries that leave from Chaitén (town) and Caleta Gonzalo (44km north of Chaitén), and also those that go to/from Hornopirén (town) and Pichicolo (village 10km west of Hornopirén). Those heading northbound without a vehicle can simply buy a bus ticket which includes the ferry crossing, removing one potentially serious headache. Chaitén is also a useful base from which to access Parque Pumalín – both the northern section (between Chaitén and Caleta Gonzalo) and the southern section (accessed from El Amarillo). In addition to the ferries, passenger boats visiting the sea lions and whales depart from Chaitén.

HISTORY The earliest record of permanent habitation in Chaitén suggests there were three houses in 1933. However, the town began to grow as boats wishing to access Lago Yelcho needed to traverse the Río Yelcho which connects the lake to the Golfo Corcovado at Chaitén. However, Chaitén's history is dominated by the eruption of Volcán Chaitén in May 2008, evidence of which is still visible. As a result of the eruption, Chaitén temporarily lost its status as capital of the province of Palena, when most governmental activities moved temporarily to Futaleufú.

The first visible signs of the eruption are the various channels of debris left from the volcanic ash and trees destroyed by the volcano, passing under bridges on the Carretera Austral between Caleta Gonzalo and Chaitén. Within the town most of the debris has been removed, and gradually the downtown section of Chaitén returned to normality. However, as a result of the accumulation of debris along the shore, Chaitén's coastline actually shifted about 1km out to sea. The coastal road now seems somewhat out of place, offering views out to what appears to be a gigantic rubbish dump. It is a pity to pass so many volcanoes along the Carretera and not climb one, and the Volcan Chaitén is one of the easier and more accessible such treks.

One of the less fortunate impacts of the volcanic eruption was that the Río Blanco changed course as a result of this excess of water and debris, and the new path runs straight through the middle of Chaitén. The town was evacuated, and many suggested it would not be reconstructed given the significant danger to residents. Chaitén's fate seemed sealed when Chile's interior minister, Edmundo Pérez Yoma, announced in January the following year, 'We are not going to invest public funds in a city that ought not to be located here'. However, residents did return, and slowly but surely the town literally emerged from the ashes. The town currently has approximately 3,500 residents.

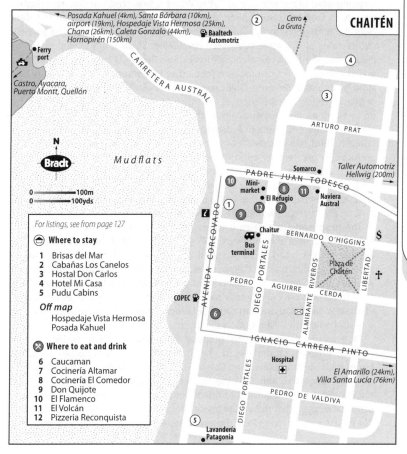

5

However, the reconstruction of Chaitén is far from complete and most visitors find it a slightly depressing and drab town with little to offer. Surrounded by the marvels of Parque Pumalín to the north and south, and onwards to Futaleufú and La Junta, there is little reason to stay in Chaitén for more than a day or two other than to use it as a base to explore the surroundings.

GETTING THERE
About the route
Caleta Gonzalo to Chaitén (44km; 1hr; first 24km gravel, last 20km paved)
The road surface is reasonable-quality gravel passable in any vehicle, but beware of pot-holes, particularly at the ends of bridges. Undulating hills will exercise the legs of cyclists. The road passes a number of bridges where the debris from the volcanic eruption of 2008 is clearly visible. The two main lakes to the west of the road are Lago Río Negro and Lago Río Blanco, both with hiking trails and camping options.

A BRIDGE TOO FAR?

The 'gap' in the Carretera Austral between Hornopirén and Caleta Gonzalo is more political than it initially appears. Two rival proposals are on the table. First, the **ongoing plan** of the Ministry of Public Works is to extend the Carretera Austral entirely by land from Hornopirén along the east of the Fiordo Comau to Caleta Gonzalo, through territory which is mostly within Parque Pumalín. So far only two sections of this route have been completed: 35km south of Hornopirén to Pichanco, and a 10km stretch across the Huequi Peninsula between Fiordo Largo and Leptepú. Five major problems jeopardise this proposal. First, there are two large fjords along the route (Quintupeu and Cahuelmó). Going around the fjords, or building bridges across them, is expensive. Some estimates suggest it could be up to 50 times more expensive than the proposed alternative. Second, this will involve further environmental damage to the region, including within Parque Pumalín. Third, this so-called 'interior route' would be more expensive to maintain and involve greater fuel consumption for those that use it. Fourth, the route would traverse very steep mountainous coastline subject to torrential rains and landslides (periodically they cause road closures along the comparable stretch south of Puyuhuapi), thus this road is unlikely to be a reliable alternative to ferries. And, finally, this route would take 20 years to build!

The **proposed alternative** is to operate an *efficient* ferry from Hualaihué or Pichicolo (just west of Hornopirén) to Poyo, on the north of the Huequi Peninsula. There is already a road from Poyo south to Ayacara and on to Buill, from where a second ferry would head initially to Caleta Gonzalo. The road from Chumildén, just west of Caleta Gonzalo, to Chaitén is not yet finished. Once this is completed, the ferry could go from Buill directly to Chumildén, passing the villages of Refugio, Chana and Santa Bárbara. This could be launched almost immediately, and would actually benefit the villages along the route.

One argument against the proposal requiring ferry connections is that southern Chile has a mixed record when it comes to running a reliable service. The ferries between Hornopirén and Caleta Gonzalo aren't known for their efficiency (see box, page 61), although the service offered by Somarco has improved; but those from the mainland to Chiloé function well. Other critics of the ferry proposal suggest that this would imply ongoing subsidies, at a cost to the state. But constructing a road would be vastly more expensive so this also involves a

Most of this section passes through Parque Pumalín, with numerous trails of varying lengths (page 134) and also spectacular views of Volcán Chaitén. The only village along this route is Santa Barbara, with relatively little of interest, although the coastal road towards Chana (via the airport) begins here.

By bus Kemelbus operate a thrice-weekly service to Puerto Montt (page 83). **Los Navegadores** runs a daily bus. Buses Chaitén leave daily from both Palena and Futaleufú to Chaitén (depart 06.00 & 11.00, return to each village at noon & 16.30). Becker Buses (\67 223 2167, 65 273 1429; w busesbecker.com) go to Coyhaique (depart 11.00 Wed & Sun, return 08.00 Tue & Sat). **Buses Entre Verdes** go to Puyuhuapi (depart 16.30 Mon, Wed & Fri, return same day & time different bus!). At least two companies operate a shuttle service between Chaitén and Caleta Gonzalo, including Chaitur. There is a weekday-only bus from Chana to Chaitén (depart 08.30, return 13.00).

massive implicit subsidy. Or would this be a toll road, in which case many of the inhabitants probably could not afford the fee to use it? Either route will involve a subsidy, one way or the other. Indeed, there already is a thrice-weekly ferry from Pichicolo to Ayacara, and a twice-weekly ferry from Ayacara to Caleta Gonzalo (not synchronised). This is a genuine service to the people of the Huequi Peninsula, but it can hardly be described as an efficient alternative to the longer daily ferry between Hornopirén and Caleta Gonzalo (page 60).

One of the myths surrounding Parque Pumalín was Doug Tompkins's apparent refusal to allow a road through 'his' park in a deliberate attempt to thwart development in the region and to divide Chile geographically. This is simply untrue. The Chilean government can requisition terrain from any private individual, and the possibility of a road through Pumalín was incorporated into a memorandum of understanding (MoU) between Pumalín and the Chilean government 20 years ago. It is even considered in the COPEC Road Atlas! Furthermore, Doug Tompkins never *owned* Parque Pumalín; it was a foundation managed by a board of seven directors (five Chileans, plus Doug and his wife Kris), that has subsequently been donated to the Chilean state. It is true that Pumalín were generally in favour of the ferry alternative, but not because they refused to allow a road through the park – a road would attract additional visitors. Rather, they believed it was an unnecessarily expensive and environmentally damaging proposal with a viable alternative solution.

But here lay the political motivation. The terrestrial route would traverse precisely the same route that the proposed electricity pylons from the halted HidroAysén dam project would use (see box, page 220). Building a road along this route would facilitate the subsequent construction of electricity transmission enormously, serving the economic interests of the powerful mining sector. Fortunately the HidroAysén dam project was abandoned.

A well-run ferry service across this section would be cheaper, more environmentally friendly, of greater service to the local communities, quicker to implement, and easier to maintain. And yet the road construction project has not yet been abandoned, possibly for political and economic reasons. In the meantime connectivity will remain a problem for all those living in this region or wishing to visit it.

Airport transfers, synchronised with arrivals and departures and picking up/ dropping off anywhere in Chaitén, are available by shuttle bus (↖9 5726 2794), or from Chaitur (see below).

Bus routes and times are notoriously flexible. Many depend on connecting ferries or synchronise with other buses. However, bus connections from Chaitén are generally quite reliable, and all buses depart from the central bus station run by the main tour operator, Chaitur (see below). The advantage of going via Chaitur is that there is no need to deal with the individual bus companies. If only such a service existed in all towns along the Carretera Austral!

By ferry Naviera Austral offer services from Puerto Montt to Chaitén (6 times a week; 9hrs, via Ayacara), between Chaitén and Quellón (weekly; Chiloé, 5hrs) and between Chaitén and Castro (twice weekly; Chiloé, 5hrs) See page 60 for times and prices. Less frequent ferries (used mostly by locals rather than visitors) connect Ayacara and Pichicolo; Ayacara and Caleta Gonzalo; Chumeldén and Pichicolo; and Chumeldén and Caleta Gonzalo. For details of how to use these lesser-known ferries to circumvent the usual Hornopirén–Caleta Gonzalo route, see page 61. But note – ferries are notoriously unreliable in this region; even the timetables published on websites and printed on flyers cannot be completely trusted.

By air Chaitén is one of the few places along the Carretera Austral with scheduled flights. Most other regions are reached by charter flights only, which are substantially more expensive. Flights to Puerto Montt, the only scheduled destination, cost approximately $50,000 one-way (45mins). The airport is 20km north of Chaitén, where light aircraft fly to and from the La Paloma airstrip in Puerto Montt, not the main commercial airport. Purchase tickets at Chaitur (see below) or directly from the airlines.

For those with a vehicle, including bicycle, flying is not an option. However, foot passengers may find this convenient – it saves substantial time for a reasonable cost, but does mean missing Hornopirén. It also removes the necessity to take the ferry from Caleta Gonzalo – although this is a beautiful ferry ride through the Fiordo Comau, it is often hard to secure a seat. The flight is equally spectacular on a clear day.

✈ **Aerocord** ↖65 226 2300, 9 7669 4515; e aperez@aerocord.cl; ▪ aerocord.cl. Puerto Montt to Chaitén: 09.30 Mon–Sat, return 10.30 (also flies from Puerto Montt to Melinka).

✈ **Pewen Air Services** ↖65 222 4000, 9 9734 1413; e ventas@pewenchile.com; w pewenchile. com. Puerto Montt to Chaitén: 09.30 & 11.30 Mon–Fri, return 10.30 & 12.30; only the first flight on Sat & Sun.

TOUR OPERATORS

Chaitur Excursions O'Higgins 67; ///drummers. solos.maritime; ↖65 273 1429, 9 7468 5608; e nchaitur@hotmail.com; w chaitur.com. This is the best-established operator in town. In addition to selling bus tickets & running the bus terminal, Chaitur can book ferry tickets, arrange flights & airport transfers, & excursions in the region. Tours include trips to the Palena & Pumalín parks, Volcán Chaitén, the Yelcho & Michinmahuida glaciers, hot springs; mountain biking, rafting & boat trips

to the sea lion colonies, visits to the caves near Santa Barbara, etc, & tailor-made tours of any description. English spoken.

Kahuel Tours 4km north of Chaitén; ///flick. reusing.sparring; ↖9 5629 2694; e reservas@ kahuel.cl; w posadakahuel.cl. Operated out of the hostel of the same name (see opposite), Kahuel offers guided kayak tours & treks in the region (inc Michinmahuida), & boat trips. They have a 7m open boat for up to 6 passengers to visit the sea lion colonies, watch dolphins & potentially see whales. Also astronomical viewings & birdwatching trips.

Natour Santa Barbara beach; 📞 9 4234 2803, 9 4234 2799; e hola@natour.cl; w natour.cl; f. Located in Santa Barbara village, some 10km north of Chaitén. Easily identified as based in a converted bus that also doubles as a rather fine b/fast restaurant. Rent bicycles, have some

camping sites & can arrange almost any tour in the region, including to Pumalín, the El Amarillo hot springs, boat & sea kayak trips to see the sea lion colonies, penguins, pelicans & cormorants. If seeking some more strenuous exercise, climb the Volcán Chaitén. Some tours require a minimum of 2 or 4 people. Private transport provided. English & German spoken. Open all year & accepts credit cards.

WHERE TO STAY *Map, page 123*

Brisas del Mar (9 cabins) Av Corcovado 278; ///payroll.sparky.magic; 📞65 273 1284, 9 9515 8808; e cababrisas@hotmail.com. Clean, slightly dated cabins on the coastal road. Central heating, Wi-Fi, cable TV, off-road parking, laundry, fairly complete kitchen (no microwave) with seating area, plenty of natural light thanks to large windows. Sgl beds double as sofas. Larger cabins for up to 7 people are better value. No deposit necessary, but call a day or 2 before arriving to confirm. A short walk to the plaza, by the sea. **$$$$**

Hotel Mi Casa (16 rooms) Av Norte 206; ///wrestlers.divider.woodworker; 📞65 273 1285, 9 7608 4895; e hotelmicasachaitenchile@ gmail.com. Founded in 1980, this magnificent hotel suffered severely in the volcanic eruption in 2008. Refurbishment has restored much of its former glory. Located slightly out of town up a hill, it is one of the few options with a fine view over Chaitén & out to sea. All rooms with private bathroom & b/fast. A sauna, hot tub & gym are available for an additional fee. Wi-Fi available, full central heating, no laundry services (but available in town), has a large garden & TV room, as well as a small bar. The owner, Maria Angelica, can put visitors in contact with known tour operators if required, & her son offers rafting trips on the Río Michinmahuida. The restaurant closed after the eruption & has not reopened other than for b/fast & for preparing sandwiches or packed lunches. **$$$$**

Cabañas Los Canelos (4 cabins) Av Norte, 200m past junction; ///murmur.manifold.mills; 📞65 273 1417, 9 8188 2423; e migonzat54@ gmail.com. Decent accommodation slightly out of town, lovely cabins, some with ocean views. All with private bathrooms, hot water, heating (wood-stove & gas), Wi-Fi & cable TV. Laundry not possible, but available in town. 10mins' walk

to the central plaza, so perhaps easier for those with a private vehicle. Ample off-road parking. Extensive b/fast available ($7,000). Guests cannot use the kitchen. **$$$**

Hostal Don Carlos (22 rooms) Almirante Riveros 53; ///reduced.dimness.gentlemen; 📞65 273 1287; e doncarlos.palena@gmail.com. Distinctive for its kitsch décor, a good choice for downtown Chaitén at reasonable prices. All the standard features: Wi-Fi, hot water, large off-road parking, cable TV, basic b/fast (inc); plus a comfortable sitting area downstairs. Most room types are available, & are clean, with wooden fixtures, & decent bathrooms (en-suite or shared); but the walls are thin & some of the interior rooms lack windows. There is neither restaurant nor laundry, but both are within walking distance of the hostel. Endless china trinkets adorn the common area; be careful with kids, it is extremely easy to smash a porcelain duck in this place. For bikers or cyclists not requiring a cabin this is a good option. **$$$**

Pudu Cabins (7 cabins) Av Corcovado 668; ///vitality.scariest.fatalist; 📞65 273 1336, 9 8227 9602; e puduchaiten@hotmail.com. Established in 1997, this is a great budget option & a favourite among motorcyclists. The smallest cabin sleeps 3, & is fairly basic, with paper-thin walls & is dated. The larger cabins, for 4–7 people, are notably superior & positively comfortable. Wi-Fi, full heating. Quincho available for larger groups. Extensive off-road parking. The owners, Anita & Juan, were some of the first people to return to Chaitén after the eruption, & can provide extensive information on the region. Book ahead as fills up in the summer season; deposit not required but call to confirm. Open 24/7. **$$$**

Posada Kahuel (7 rooms, 1 cabin, 1 tiny house) 4km north of Chaitén towards Santa Bárbara; ///flick.reusing.sparring; 📞9 5629 2694;

e reservas@kahuel.cl; w posadakahuel.cl. A great option for those wishing to stay slightly outside Chaitén (ideally with a vehicle), with direct access to the beach. Tastefully decorated, with comfortable rooms for up to 4 people, all with central heating, cable TV, lovely wooden floors & views out to the forest. Cabin sleeps 8. Basic b/fast included, also has a restaurant (mainly but not exclusively for guests) offering pizzas & a range of local foods rotating every 3 days. Wi-Fi available &, unusually for Chaitén, laundry service also offered. The icing on the cake, however, is the on-site micro-brewery, producing a modest supply of blonde, amber & red ales, EsPumalín, Traka & Trapananda. Also offers tours (page 126). Accepts credit cards. Price depends on number of people. $–$$$

🏠 **Hospedaje Vista Hermosa – Chana** (3 rooms) Costanera Puerto, 5km north of airport;

///tread.thrushes.infringed; 📞 9 5195 2659, 9 6313 4124; e vivianacarolinmayorga@gmail. com. Fantastic rural retreat from Chaitén, along the lovely coastal route past Santa Barbara. Has Wi-Fi despite remote location, can do laundry, has wood stoves for heating, b/fast included. The owners are charming, & delighted to show you the region, almost doubling as tour operators in this fairly secluded spot. Can arrange any of the usual tours, visits to the caves, birdwatching or a leisurely stroll along the beach to search for seafood to eat that evening (they can prepare a full curanto). Homemade food for guests, using ingredients from the region. Guests can also use the kitchen. Close by are ancient pools (only visible at low tide, used to catch fish) – a recently discovered archaeological site. Private transport for collection/drop-off at Chaitén or further afield. $$

✖ WHERE TO EAT AND DRINK   *Map, page 123*

✳ ✖ **El Volcán** Juan Todesco 153; ///homily. arachnid.realism; 📞 65 272 1136, 9 8186 9558; ⏰ 11.00–midnight daily, all year. Great restaurant, all the usual meat & seafood options covered within a large cosy space, roaring wood stove in the middle of the room, also space to chill & have a beer. Decent range of beers & wines, good service. The salmon is excellent, as is the crab stew & the ceviche. Wise to make a reservation in high season. $$–$$$

✖ **Caucaman Restaurante** Corvocado 455; ///clinician.outsmart.trustful; 📞 9 6496 0824; ⏰ 08.00–midnight daily. Competes head-on with Cocinería Altamar to be the best restaurant in Chaitén. Great location on the coastal road. Offers a kids' menu & has the local beers from Chaitén. Meat available, but the focus is seafood, & the *paila marina* (seafood broth) is not only excellent, but the recipe is a closely guarded secret, passed down from the owner's grandmother. Warm fire for chilly evenings, intimate space with only 7 tables, good atmosphere – definitely worth a visit, great value. Reservation recommended in high season. $$

✳ ✖ **Cocinería Altamar** Portales 258; ///imply.skydiver.apple; 📞 9 8170 8983; ⏰ 08.00–23.00 daily in high season, 08.30–17.00 Mon–Sat rest of year. The best-value meals in Chaitén, if not along the entire Carretera Austral. The restaurant was originally started as a co-operative following

the eruption in 2008 & has become a favourite among locals. The portions are gigantic, & reasonably priced. The speciality of the house, the Chilote curanto, could feed a small family. A trip to Chile is incomplete without trying a curanto, & this is *the* place to do so along the Carretera. The first bowl contains fresh mussels & clams in abundance. Then arrives the 2nd plate, cooked in the same pot, with a sausage, chunk of pork, a decent chicken portion, a homegrown potato & some less identifiable potato-/wheat-based items. The *paila* is equally filling, more like a seafood soup, & delicious. They've got standard dishes too, such as *merluza* (hake), & in very generous portions. Wine & beer available also. The most expensive dish on the menu is $8,000. Open for b/fast. $$

✖ **Don Quijote** O'Higgins, opposite bus terminal; ///noon.outdone.manlike. Very laid-back budget restaurant that becomes an informal bar in the evenings. The owner, Javier, was one of the first back to Chaitén after the eruption, & his knowledge of the region is phenomenal. The menu is limited, cheap, rapid but reasonable quality. The *congrio* (eel) with homemade chips is worth trying. Also a hostel, but not recommended. $$

✖ **El Flamenco** Av Corcovado 218; ///doorbell. cabins.emitter; 📞 65 273 1301, 9 6678 9718; ⏰ 10.00–midnight daily. On the coast at entrance to Chaitén from the north. Massive sandwiches,

reasonably priced, local beers available, some on tap. Slightly drab atmosphere, blaring TV but good place to catch a football game or the news. Wi-Fi. Accepts credit cards. $$
✗ Pizzeria Reconquista Portales 269; ///economy.felines.sprees; ✆ 9 6186 8859; ⊕ 10.00–23.00 Mon–Sat. A good selection of pizzas to eat in or take away for about $10,000. Also offers b/fasts, cheap beer, sandwiches & lemon pie. $$

✗ Cocinería El Comedor Portales 218; ///mistresses.locally.dollars; ✆ 9 8966 9916; ⊕ 08.00–23.00 daily, closes at 21.00 in low season. Great little restaurant & small bakery, local fare including seafood stew, *bistec a lo pobre* (full meat extravaganza with a fried egg), hake/salmon/eel, hot dogs, no alcohol licence. The owner, Eudalia, has been running the restaurant for a decade, one of the vintage locations. No need to reserve; accepts credit cards. $

OTHER PRACTICALITIES There is a **tourist information centre** at the northern entrance to the village on the main coastal road, but the office is minuscule; Chaitur is probably more helpful (page 126). The **Somarco** office is at Juan Todesco 188 (///weeknight.leftover.thereof; ✆ 65 221 7413). The **Naviera Austral** office is on Almirante Riveros 188 (///getaway.shopkeepers.comfort; ✆ 65 273 1011). There is a well-stocked **mini-market** on the corner of Diego Portales and Juan Todesco (///stash.spurring.untold), and next door is El Refugio, which sells a range of products including meat and gas cans for cooking. Chaitén has an ATM on the northeast side of the plaza.

Mechanics
Baaltech Automotriz Avenida Norte 70; ///informal.nationality.implicitly; ✆ 65 273 1058, 9 9832 3886; e baaltech@gmail.com; ⊕ 08.30–13.00 & 14.30–18.00 Mon–Fri, 09.00–13.00 Sat. The best mechanic in Chaitén & can certainly look at most problems for most vehicles & motorbikes, including basic electric work. The main problem is obtaining spare parts, but given the proximity to Puerto Montt this can potentially be resolved. A range of tyres & batteries, wheel alignment & emergency pick-up service (24hrs).
Taller Automotriz Hellwig Ercilla 353; ///lynched.husbands.float; ✆ 9 6879 7033;

e hugo_hellwig@hotmail.com; ⊕ 09.00–13.00 & 15.00–17.00 Mon–Sat. General mechanic including rescue & basic motorbike repairs.

Laundry
Lavandería Patagonia Lautaro 62; ///though. racing.reverb; ✆ 9 8396 9280; ⊕ 09.00–22.00 daily. After the closure of the former laundry, Chaitén's tourists faced a chronic clothing crisis, resolved by an entrepreneurial family at the southern edge of town. They have dryers, so if you leave clothes in the morning they will be washed & dried by the evening. Knock on the window if no-one appears in, or pop back an hour later.

WHAT TO SEE AND DO This section of the Carretera Austral is dominated by Parque Pumalín. Chaitén itself is not a cultural centre, often used as a mere laundry stop on the way north or south, or as a base for exploring Pumalín, which has a wide range of well-maintained trails for all tastes and difficulty levels. However, there are **sea lion colonies** accessible by boat from Chaitén and **hot springs** in the area. As a government-designated Nature Conservancy, **fishing** is not permitted in Pumalín, but is permitted south of the park, particularly around Lago Yelcho. Just south of Puerto Cárdenas is a short trek to **Ventisquero Yelcho**, taking about 1–2 hours to reach the ice wall, a little less if only trekking the marked trail. There is no need for a guide, but one can be arranged at Yelcho en la Patagonia (page 137) if desired. As well as hiking and fishing, the main activity is exploring the **marine life** in the region, including the potential prize of spotting blue whales and penguins. Incredible birdwatching opportunities are available, particularly near Chana. Kahuel (page 126) and Chaitur (page 126) can arrange such trips. Pumalín has two of the most accessible **volcano** trails, and if you are only visiting one volcano along the entire

5

Carretera, Volcán Chaitén is a rare chance to see not only the damage a volcano can cause, but also to climb the culprit and peer into its crater. The debris along the coastline is testimony to the sheer mass erupted and dislodged over a decade ago, and a prelude to the December 2017 mudslide visible in **Villa Santa Lucía** a mere 76km south. There is a small detour to Chaitén Viejo 7km south of Chaitén. It is rarely visited, perhaps because there is very little to see beyond a cemetery and horses grazing on wetland grasses, but the view out to sea at the mouth of the Río Yelcho is fantastic at sunset.

HUEQUI PENINSULA – A DETOUR One of the least-known regions of all the Carretera Austral is the peninsula between Caleta Gonzalo and Hornopirén. Despite its relative proximity to Puerto Montt, less than 100km to the north as the condor flies, the peninsula is remarkably isolated, sparsely populated and with minimal infrastructure. However, it is stunningly beautiful, particularly on the interior section that can be accessed by road, and the southern section around **Buill**. To the east of the peninsula is the Fiordo Comau; the Gulfo de Ancud and Chiloé are to the west. The Porcelana hot springs and geysers are on the eastern side of the peninsula and accessed by boat from Hornopirén, but there is no means to cross the peninsula itself. Although **Ayacara**, the main village on the west of the peninsula, is the closest the peninsula has to a capital (the municipal building and ferry terminal are here), Buill in the south is the most interesting place to visit: both guides are based there, the coastline and scenery is most breathtaking, and there are better accommodation and eating options.

Visiting the peninsula is logistically convenient for those wishing to traverse the Carretera Austral as a round trip but preferring not to cover the same section twice: traverse the main Carretera in one direction, and on the return journey visit Ayacara as an alternative route between Chaitén and Puerto Montt.

Getting there Although flights are occasionally possible for non-residents, the main connection to the peninsula is by ferry, either to/from Pichicolo (west of Hornopirén, 3 times a week; page 113), to/from Caleta Gonzalo (twice a week; page 113), or more likely by taking the Naviera Austral ferry (6 times a week) between Chaitén and Puerto Montt which stops in Ayacara (page 126).

✈ **Archipiélagos** 9 9920 8308; e reservas@ archipielagos.cl; w archipielagos.cl. Daily flight from La Paloma (Puerto Montt) to Ayacara (09.20, return 11.00; 30mins; $30,000 pp with up to 15kg of luggage). Fills up quickly as also serves the salmon farms on the peninsula. 9 passengers & pilot.

Getting around It is hard to get lost on the Huequi Peninsula, as there are only three roads. The main road, W-813, extends from Buill in the south up to Ayacara in the middle, and to Huequi and Poyo in the north (45km in total, gravel). The second gravel road also goes from Ayacara to Huequi but around the coast. The third road, or rather a gravel track detour, is approximately 4.5km north of Ayacara on the road towards Huequi and branches east through a series of gates towards Laguna Ayacara (also known as Laguna Huequi).

Tour operators Jonathan Mancilla (9 9627 6516) is a useful contact who knows the region well and can connect with guides. His wife runs the **Naviera Austral** office next to the ferry terminal just south of the church in Ayacara (which also sells tickets for **Transportes Puelche**), so she is an equally helpful contact.

Comau Expediciones ☎9 4514 3178, 9 5808 5750; e ecomaucesar@gmail.com; **f**. Cesar & Ricardo are the only formal guides on the entire peninsula, leading the effort to develop tourism in this isolated region. Lack of infrastructure limits potential, but they can arrange 4 key trips: boat trips or kayaking to the Ica Island (penguin & sea lion colonies, potentially dolphin spotting, $20,000 pp); visiting & kayaking on Laguna Ayacara/Huequi ($15,000 pp); multi-day trips to the Fiordo Comau visiting the Termas de Cahuelmó, Porcelana (geysers & hot springs; $150,000 pp); & hiking Volcán Huequi. The last is a 3–4-day, medium-difficulty climb for 2–4 people ($180,000–145,000 pp accordingly), including all transport, food, camping gear, packhorse for 1st day & English-speaking guide.

🏠 **Where to stay and eat** Although there are other accommodation options available, some are booked up by the salmon companies, so the two listed here are the only confirmed tourist-friendly options available. There is only one standalone restaurant on the peninsula, so either bring your own food or rely on one of these two hostels.

🏠 **Hospedaje Familiar Micho's** (3 dbl & 1 sgl room, 1 cabaña, 1 apt) Buill Norte; ///attainment.recipe.aspiring; ☎9 8309 1589, 9 6839 0584; e larivera_heise@hotmail.com; w hospedajemichos.webnode.es. A delightful house on the beach with a deck from which to observe sunset & sunrise, $30,000 pp with all meals included (inc asados & curanto, limited food options available on the peninsula), or $20,000 pp with b/fast only. Restaurant for guests only. Self-contained cabin for 4, or apt for 3 with b/fast included, both with views out to sea. The owners, Ralph & Paola (the hospedaje is named after a cat) are delightful & know the region extremely well, & have become the de facto tour operator in the region, able to arrange all tours & knowing most of the population, available activities, logistics, etc. Can also arrange private boat transfers to regions not served by the main ferries, including to the hot springs south of Hornopirén. No Wi-Fi but other amenities include laundry. Cash only. **$$**

🏠 **Pension Santa Gemita** Main beach of Buill Norte; ///removals.batches.helicopter; ☎9 3504 0844; e montoyacarol87@gmail.com. In low season used mainly by salmon farm employees, but usually empty in the tourist high season. The rooms are poky, but the communal area has a great view over the bay. $20,000 pp with b/fast included, & full board available. The restaurant is available to non-guests if arranged a day in advance. Shared bathrooms, no Wi-Fi, laundry available, cash only. Difficult to contact as does not use WhatsApp. **$$**

✗ **Terrazas Restaurant** Eastern end of Ayacara bridge, 1km north of ferry; ☎9 6160 5453; ⏱ Mon–Sat. Basic food & decent sandwiches. Wise to call in advance as not always open, seems to open only when asked. Convenient for grabbing a sandwich for the boat or upon arrival. **$**

Other practicalities There is no petrol or ATM on the peninsula, but there is a shop and a church in Ayacara. Note that phone reception is appalling; Movistar works best, and WhatsApp is more reliable than regular calls.

What to see and do Laguna Ayacara (also known as Laguna Huequi) is definitely worth a visit but unless you have your own kayak it might be better to go with a kayak tour. Fishing also possible.

Hiking Volcán Huequi (1,318m) is located roughly in the middle of the peninsula. It can be hiked in four days, starting at Laguna Huequi/Ayacara. The first 2 hours are relatively flat, passing two waterfalls of about 50m and 20m height. The ascent is of modest difficulty and passes many alerce trees. It is possible to see the footsteps of pudú, and on rare occasions spot one. Cries of pumas can be heard, and this is a great region for birdwatching. The view from the summit extends to the Comau and Cahuelmó fjords to the east and over to the Andes. To the west it is possible to see to Chiloé and the Gulfo de Ancud. Volcán Michinmahuida can be seen to the south, as well as the entire Huequi Peninsula itself.

PARQUE NACIONAL PUMALÍN DOUGLAS TOMPKINS

(Information centres at Caleta Gonzalo & El Amarillo; w conaf.cl/parques/parque-nacional-pumalin-douglas-tompkins; free; ⏚ all year) If ever there was a reason to visit the northern section of the Carretera Austral, it is Parque Pumalín. US conservationist Doug Tompkins acquired the Reñihué farm in 1991 and over the following years the US foundation The Conservation Land Trust added substantial land to create the park. In 2005 the park was declared a nature sanctuary and was managed by the Chilean Fundación Pumalín, until 2017, when it was donated in its entirety to the Chilean state and converted to a national park, affording it the highest level of environmental protection in Chile. As a result, it is entirely prohibited to fish, even with a permit. The park is now under the management of CONAF, and covers an area of approximately 300,000ha.

Many visitors to the Carretera miss this section in favour of entering or leaving via Futaleufú. This may save the minor inconvenience of having to take two or three ferries to eventually connect with Puerto Montt, but visiting the northern section of the Carretera is worth the effort. If using the Futaleufú border, do consider the 76km (mostly paved) detour to Chaitén and on to Parque Pumalín.

There are two main sections to the park. **Pumalín Norte** is actually the more difficult to access, as visitors need to hire a boat from Hornopirén. Information on this section of the park is available at the Puerto Varas information centre. **Pumalín Sur** is more accessible. This part of the park is broadly divided into **two sub-regions**: the various trails and campsites located between Caleta Gonzalo and Chaitén; and those accessed from the extreme south of the park at El Amarillo – there are CONAF offices in all three locations.

The first park ranger station is located just north of the (old) landing strip approximately 10km north of Chaitén. South of Chaitén the Carretera is paved, and touches the park once more, at the southern extremity of Pumalín. This southern entrance is called 'El Amarillo', and located in the village of the same name, 24km south of Chaitén. The village of El Amarillo has undergone a major urban beautification scheme, sponsored by Conservacíon Patagónica (CP).

Where the Carretera Austral buckles south towards Lago Yelcho at the exit of El Amarillo, continue straight ahead into the park. The second park ranger and tourist information kiosk is on the right-hand side, and can provide maps and local information (✆ 65 220 3107). The road continues straight to the El Amarillo hot springs, or left into the park and to the trails and four campsites (Puente Carlos Cuevas, Vuelta del Río, Grande and Ventisquero El Amarillo). The Ventisquero campground, at the foot of Volcán Michinmahuida, is considered one of the most dramatic and spectacular settings for camping in Chilean Patagonia.

Hot springs are dotted along the length of the Carretera Austral, with perhaps the most famous being the Puyuhuapi Lodge and Spa (page 180). The **El Amarillo hot springs** (ask in El Amarillo for opening times; $7,000 pp/day), about 5km northeast of the park's southern entrance, are worth visiting. There are various pools filled with thermal water originating from Volcán Michinmahuida, said to possess healing properties, and undoubtedly containing sulphur. The springs are located among lush vegetation, well beyond the reach of mobile-phone coverage, and with ample picnic areas, a quincho and five barbecues. On 16 May 2020 a landslide destroyed the neighbouring lodge, and the springs were closed for some months.

The village of **El Amarillo** underwent a 'beautification' project supported by Tompkins Conservation shortly after the eruption in 2008. Almost all the local residents participated in upgrading both the public use areas, and private residences in the village, and constructing new facilities such as a supermarket. Pumalín's landscape architects and builders painted houses, planted trees and flowers, and transformed the village in a very visible manner.

WHERE TO STAY AND EAT There are five campsites between Caleta Gonzalo and Chaitén. From north to south, they are as follows: Caleta Gonzalo, convenient for connecting with the ferry to/from Hornopirén (///matter.forecasters.splintered); Cascadas Escondidas, 14km south of Caleta Gonzalo (///duke.hurt.bracelets); Lago Negro (///forts.spellings.astronauts) and Lago Blanco (///motivations. assessed.found) are 20km and 25km south of Caleta Gonzalo respectively; and El Volcán, close to the trail to Volcán Chaitén and the closest campground to Chaitén (approximately 30km from both Chaitén and Caleta Gonzalo; ///jilted. dicey.happy). The Vodudahue campsite near Leptepú is located north of Caleta Gonzalo in the Valle Vodudahue.

All campsites have dedicated pitches for campers, as well as communal sites. Bathrooms (with cold showers) are available, as are basic washing facilities for clothes. Rules are simple: no campfires, camp only in designated areas (and leave no trace), you must use only authorised bathroom facilities, and must not destroy the habitat. Parks may post additional rules specific to the region.

In the El Amarillo region of the park there are three main campgrounds: the Carlos Cuevas campground (2km north of Pumalín South park entrance; ///tweeting. fundraiser.stupider), with views of Mount Tabique, a camping shelter and bathrooms; the Vuelta del Río campground (///unheroic.inkwell.cradle) with similar facilities, around half a kilometre further; and the Ventisquero campground (///insanity.parks. bettered), around an hour further, with stunning views of the valley and glaciers of Volcán Michinmahuida – this is one of the most magnificent campsites along the entire Carretera Austral.

In addition to the campsites within the park, accommodation options are limited to Caleta Gonzalo and Santa Barbara/Chaitén.

☀ **Lodge Caleta Gonzalo** (9 cabins) ///velvet.disdain.bakes; e reservas@ lodgecaletagonzalo.cl; w lodgecaletagonzalo. cl; ⊕ all year. 7 excellent cabins accommodating 2–5 people (without kitchen); 2 smaller cabins for 2–4 people (with kitchen). All with well-equipped bathrooms & comfortable beds. Electricity for heating is generated by a mini-turbine located along the nearby Cascadas trail. The cabins are entirely made of wood, with open timber ceilings & extensive windows, in a unique setting, surrounded by park on 3 sides & a fjord on the 4th. The neighbouring restaurant (⊕ 07.30–10.30, noon–16.00 & 18.00–22.00 daily; $$$$) is the only option between Caleta Gonzalo & Santa Barbara/Chaitén. Food is mostly locally produced, & organic wine is available. A fine & full b/fast. The cabins & restaurant were owned & operated by Tompkins Conservation but passed to a new concession-holder in late 2021. Information on local trails & campsites available. A convenient location for ferry connections, situated under 100m from the pier. Walk-ins accepted, but the cabins fill up promptly, & it is highly advisable to book in advance, particularly in high season. Bookings can be done entirely on their website, which has chat feature for questions. Although accommodation may be more expensive than in Chaitén, these are top-quality cabins – a good night's sleep is guaranteed. In this remote region, Wi-Fi, mobile-phone coverage & laundry facilities are not available. Cards accepted. $$$$

Perhaps no contemporary couple have so divided opinions in Chile as Douglas and Kristine Tompkins. Pioneering conservationists, or evil destroyers of Chilean culture? Supporters claim they have demonstrated a practical means to save the delicate ecosystem of the planet from imminent collapse. Detractors suggest they were part of a plot to seize control of Chile's water supply, breed pumas to kill the sheep of local farmers, and obstruct the development of southern Chile by preventing passage through their land stretching from the ocean to the Argentine border.

Such criticisms do not stand up to even the mildest scrutiny. Most of the land acquired has been donated to the state. The only breeding programme they operated was to raise Great Pyrenees dogs to protect the sheep belonging to local farmers from predators. The difficulty (and corresponding expense) of constructing a road through Pumalín is largely due to two fjords, and their only requirement was that such a road had a minimal impact upon the environment – hardly an unreasonable request in a state-designated national park.

Doug Tompkins was an avid skier, climber, kayaker, pilot and explorer. He set up The North Face in 1964 initially as a retail store selling camping and climbing equipment, and sold it in 1969 for a modest profit. He made most of his money with the Esprit clothing company. By the late 70s Esprit had annual sales surpassing US$100 million. Disillusioned with the environmental impact of the fashion industry he sold his shares in 1990 and become a professional conservationist. He invented the first tents that did not require a central pole.

He established the Foundation for Deep Ecology in 1990, which went far beyond standard 'green' issues and campaigned for a fundamental realignment of core values to prevent ecological disaster. His profound belief of the planet as a harmonious system stems from the work of Norwegian philosopher Arne Næss, and suggests that economic growth is not a panacea for global problems, but a cause of these same problems.

Putting such beliefs into action, Doug began acquiring land in what subsequently became Parque Pumalín in 1991, with the purchase of Reñihué farm. In 1992 he founded the Conservation Land Trust (CLT; w rewildingchile.org), the main way by which land for parks was acquired. CLT purchased land around Reñihué farm, often from absentee landowners. The park was converted to a Nature Conservancy in August 2005 and was donated to Fundación Pumalín the same year, managed by a board of five Chileans, along with Doug and Kris.

The land between Hornopirén and Chaitén is almost entirely within Parque Pumalín. One exception is the 340km^2 owned by the San Ignacio del Huinay Foundation towards the southern end of the Fiordo Comau. In 1994 CLT and US philanthropist Peter Buckley acquired 840km^2 of forest destined for logging, adjacent to land owned by various governmental agencies including the Chilean Armed Forces. On the basis that the combined territory be converted to a national park, CLT offered the property to the Chilean state. In 2005 President Lagos accepted the offer, forming the 2,940km^2 Parque Nacional Corcovado. Doug Tompkins was also an active supporter of Patagonia Chilena ¡Sin Represas! (see box, page 220).

WALKING TRAILS There are eight trails in the park between Caleta Gonzalo and Chaitén. Seek up-to-date information from the park rangers or information centres at entrances to the park, as new trails may open and existing trails may close, or

Kris Tompkins kept a lower profile than her husband, but has had an equally profound impact in southern Patagonia. She was former CEO of the Patagonia clothes brand, married Doug in 1993, and set up Conservación Patagónica (CP, merged into Tompkins Conservation and subsequently into Rewilding Chile) 'to create national parks in Patagonia that save and restore wildlands and wildlife, inspire care for the natural world, and generate healthy economic opportunities for local communities'. Her first project was to create Parque Nacional Monte Leon in southern Patagonia, the first coastal national park in Argentina. She then embarked on a more ambitious project between Cochrane and Lago General Carrera, to restore the overgrazed Estancia Valle Chacabuco to its former glory and merge it with Tamango and Jeinimeni national reserves. She realised her dream in 2017.

To the greatest extent possible, Kris seeks to revert land to its original state, with minimal intervention once the damage has been corrected. CP arranged school trips for local children to learn about conservation and has awarded 50 scholarships for children to continue their education beyond the secondary school offered in Cochrane. In Patagonia National Park, Rewilding Chile is actively rewilding threatened and endangered species (such as huemul deer and potentially the Andean condor) and has the only native species reintroduction centre in a Chilean national park, focused on Darwin's rhea (ñandu).

Philanthropic conservation is a relatively new phenomenon in Chile, and was initially greeted with suspicion, particularly when large areas were purchased by non-Chileans. Removing livestock, the main source of income, sparked animosity. However, as local communities see the transformation of these regions, and as tourism plays a growing role in the local economy, fears about foreigners covertly plotting to control Chile's water supply are fading.

The trajectory of Estancia Chacabuco, as well as many other large-scale sheep farms in Patagonia, was very clear – bankruptcy. Having resurrected this land, a world-class park complete with trails and facilities now remains protected for future generations. The fragile ecosystem has been restored after a century of exploitation. And this has been accomplished by two successful 'ecobarons' determined to correct the unbalanced development of the 20th century. A tangential goal of the Tompkins is to demonstrate a model for sustainable conservation. In 2005 President Piñera founded Parque Tantauco in southern Chiloé along similar lines to Pumalín, and others have replicated this model. In Chile and Argentina, Tompkins Conservation conserved over 14 million acres by helping to create 11 national parks and two marine parks. With help from donors, the non-profit continues to work in conservation in the Southern Cone.

Perhaps ecopioneer is a better description? Doug and Kris assisted in the writing of the first edition of this book. Doug wrote the foreword to the first edition and it was with great regret that he died shortly before we were able to present him with the final printed version. In this second edition we strive to promote the Carretera Austral with the spirit and passion of Doug, and to support Kris's ongoing work.

be undergoing temporary maintenance. Although maps are available from the tourist information kiosk, the trails are very well marked and it is easy to do them independently. The main ones along this section (listed from north to south) include:

Caleta Gonzalo–Cascadas trail 6km round trip; 2–3hrs; easy. A loop following a river to the waterfalls. Well-maintained path with frequent boardwalks spanning wet sections.

Tronador trail (check if trail open) 5km; round trip; 4hrs; difficult. An initial ascent along a gorge, views over snow-capped Volcán Michinmahuida, arriving at the amphitheatre Lago Tronador.

Alerce trail (///wedged.ranking.took) Under 1hr loop; easy. A short trail through a section of forest housing a number of impressive alerce trees approaching 3,000 years of age. The alerce has been cut to near extinction over the previous 2 centuries for its valuable wood. The path is well maintained & contains occasional explanatory boards.

Cascadas Escondidas trail (///duke.hurt. bracelets) 4km round trip; 2hrs; medium. A fantastic trail alongside a river, to a series of increasingly impressive waterfalls. Wooden boardwalks are well maintained, but take care when climbing the wooden ladders which may be slippery. A small detour on the way down goes via approximately half a dozen alerce trees of impressive size.

Volcán Michinmahuida trail (/// accumulation.snippet.composts) 24km round trip; 10hrs; difficult. Probably the most physically demanding of all the trails in this section of the park, traversing forest, volcanic basalt & an unnamed glacier.

Volcán Chaitén trail (///overwhelmed.perk. fake) 4km round trip; 3hrs; medium. This trail heads to the edge of the Chaitén crater, where steam emerges from the ground on the far side. One of the most accessible volcano hikes on the entire Carretera Austral, & well worth the effort. Having lain dormant for nearly 10,000 years, in May 2008 this volcano erupted, causing massive devastation to the nearby town.

Darwin's Frog trail (4km north of entrance to Pumalín Park South) 2.5km round trip; easy. An informative loop explaining how forests grow following logging or fire. Pick up the interpretive guide in the tourist information centre at the entrance to the park. Darwin's frog is endangered & rather small, but can be seen along this trail, although perhaps only by those with a trained eye.

Ventisquero El Amarillo trail (Pumalín Park South; ///insanity.parks.bettered) 20km round trip; 6hrs; easy. An excellent trail to the base of a glacier protruding from the south side of Volcán Michinmahuida.

EL AMARILLO TO VILLA SANTA LUCÍA

The road running south of El Amarillo passes two points of interest before reaching Villa Santa Lucía: the impressive **Yelcho en la Patagonia** (see opposite) situated on the beautiful Lago Yelcho – an excellent hotel with great fishing; and the **Ventisquero Yelcho Chico** – the most northerly accessible glacier along the Carretera Austral.

Villa Santa Lucía, located 76km south of Chaitén and 68km north of La Junta, exists as a crossroads. The scenic 30km road up to Puerto Ramírez and on to Futaleufú (an additional 48km) and Palena (an additional 43km) begins here, as well as the first two vehicular border crossings to Argentina. The village was named after Pinochet's wife during the construction of the Carretera Austral. There is no petrol, and little reason to stay in the village other than to pop into a shop to grab some supplies. As a key junction along the Carretera Austral, Villa Santa Lucía's principal function is as a bus stop (located at the junction of the Carretera Austral and the eastward road towards Futaleufú and Palena) where hitchhikers also await a ride.

No public transport exclusively serves this stretch, but southbound buses from Chaitén and northbound buses from La Junta will stop at Puerto Cárdenas and Villa Santa Lucía if required. Villa Santa Lucía was abruptly put on the map in December 2017 when a colossal landslide destroyed most of the village, killing 22 people. As with Chaitén a little further north, this is a violent and graphic reminder of the power of nature in this region.

GETTING THERE
About the route
Chaitén to Villa Santa Lucía (76km; 1hr; paved) A decent 24km paved road connects Chaitén to El Amarillo. The further 19km on to Puerto Cárdenas at the northern end of Lago Yelcho is fairly nondescript until it reaches the lake, passing through agricultural regions with mountains to the east. The road winds around the northwest corner of Lago Yelcho to Yelcho en la Patagonia before heading south. The access route to the Yelcho glacier trek (page 138) is 6km past Yelcho, and then the road continues to Villa Santa Lucía. The entry to the village is memorable for the destruction caused by the landslide, clearly visible now and undoubtedly for the next few decades.

WHERE TO STAY AND EAT

La Cabaña Fishing Lodge (5 rooms, 2 cabins) 11km east of Villa Santa Lucía towards Puerto Ramírez; ///fluorine.occupier.tools; 9 9802 3112; e reservas@yelchoflyfishing.com; w yelchoflyfishing.com; ☺ Oct–Apr. Awesome wooden lodge set back from the road with a gorgeous view over the valley to the lake, all rooms with a view & private bathroom. The rooms are warm in all senses of the word, the communal sitting area is extensive & has a deck for warm days & evenings with a delightful hot tub overlooking the valley & lake, as well as an extensive garden. Lunch & dinner can be provided for a fee & with due notice. Established in 2016 principally attending to the fishing crowd, they also can arrange other tours in the area: fishing dominates in Nov–Dec, 'normal' tourism the rest of the season. Linked with Patagonia Elements in Futaleufú (page 147) to arrange rafting trips. Wi-Fi & laundry available. English spoken. **$$$$**

☀ **Yelcho en la Patagonia** (8 rooms, 6 cabins, camping) Northern end of Lago Yelcho, 27km south of El Amarillo & 25km north of Villa Santa Lucía; ///lied.mopes.ribbing; 65 257 6005/8; e reservas@yelcho.cl; w yelcho.cl; ☺ Oct–Apr. An excellent option for those keen on fishing, otherwise a good base for visiting the Yelcho glacier & enjoying the property. A top-quality, full-service hotel at a reasonable price. The rooms boast all the usual features of such an establishment, with central heating, full b/fast included, safety deposit box, laundry service, full private bathroom, etc. Every room & cabin has a lake view. Fishing is firmly the focus, & the hotel arranges half- & full-day fishing trips. The lake is unusual for containing all species of trout & landlocked salmon. Fishing lessons for beginners

are also available, as are trips to the local glacier & guided horse rides within the grounds. There is a small farm on the property that can also be visited, a short walk to a viewpoint, & a sandy beach for swimming. The restaurant sources most ingredients locally, many vegetables are grown on site, & the ice cream, bread, desserts & pastas are all homemade. Local beers also available, & a decent wine list. Spectacular views over the lake from the upper-floor sitting area, with a small library & a shop laden with fishing accessories. The 15 campsites are along the sandy beach & have a covered barbecue area, hot water, bathrooms & electricity. B/fast not included in the cabins or camping, but available for $5,000. English spoken, accepts cards, & has an official Patagonia (clothing) store on site & a hot tub by the lake. Camping **$$**, main lodge **$$$$**, restaurant **$$$$**

Hostería La Cumbre (5 rooms, 1 sgl, 1 trpl, 3 dbl) 8km north of Villa Santa Lucía; ///peppercorns.archery.improve; 65 286 8897, 9 9778 2704; e fernando.sanhueza@hotmail.com. Small, rustic B&B with views down the valley, north of Villa Santa Lucía. The owner built the bridge over the Río Yelcho at Puerto Cárdenas, the longest bridge of its kind in Patagonia (cable-stayed). Has a 1km path on the property through a forest packed with birds. Lovely sitting area, & wood-stove heating. B/fast included, can provide dinner (additional fee) & a great kitchen that guests can use. Wi-Fi. Accepts cards. **$$$**

Caviahue Cabins (3 cabins) 1.5km west of El Amarillo; ///rewrites.competitive.tints; 65 226 4422, 9 5672 6422. Fully equipped cabins for 3, 4 & 6 people, b/fast available (for a fee), off-road parking, Wi-Fi, cable TV, wood-stove heating & laundry available. Very good value for money. Restaurant (open to public). **$$–$$$**

At 09.03 on 16 December 2017 a landslide almost entirely wiped Villa Santa Lucía off the map. The total volume of debris was 7.2 million cubic metres, 2 million of which flowed straight into the village. To this day, the site is reminiscent of images of Hiroshima. Fortunately the destruction occurred on a Saturday when the school was not in use; the building completely vanished.

Villa Santa Lucía was founded on 24 February 1982 when the Chaitén to Puerto Aysén stretch of the Carretera Austral was inaugurated by Pinochet. The village is named after his wife. Villa Santa Lucía is no stranger to natural disasters – in May 2008 Volcán Chaitén erupted. The entire population of the village of Chaitén was evacuated, with many of those displaced housed in Villa Santa Lucía.

In the first hours after the disaster five casualties were discovered and 15 people were missing. Over the next few days, spanning Christmas, ten more bodies were found. The last body was not recovered until 16 March the following year, and one victim has never been found. In total 22 people died, including four children.

Substantial rain had fallen during the preceding 24 hours. Although the precise reason for the landslide is still disputed, it seems that this excess rain had weakened the soil on one of the higher slopes of a valley just north of Villa Santa Lucía and caused an initial landslide which dislodged part of the glacier beneath. This mass of sediment began to flow down the valley, gathering momentum and destroying everything in its path. Worst of all, it gained additional mass as it scooped up rocks, trees and mud from the Río Burritos as it slid ominously down the valley and began to accumulate in a huge natural bowl. The only exit from this bowl, clearly visible to this day, is a narrow canal leading straight to Villa Santa Lucía. The sediment eventually flowed down this valley at speed and fanned out across the plain beneath, with Villa Santa Lucía, alas, perched at the northern edge.

In all likelihood it was the confluence of various factors, possibly some due to global warming, that led to the disaster, but the end result was clear: the

🏠 **Comida Donde la Betty** (1 room) Los Cipreses; ///lace.darns.massage; 📞 9 8396 5058. Located at the southern end of the street, this is a convenient one-stop shop. Only has 1 room, for 2 people, with bathroom. Restaurant serves homemade food (🕐 07.00–23.00 in high season, often the only place open in the village; roughly $6,000 pp; $). Manuel is also a fly-fishing guide (📞 9 7240 2137; **e** fly_fishing@outlook.cl), mainly on Lago Yelcho but also knows some more less-visited spots in the region. Plus if you run out of petrol he might know where you can find some in an emergency. **$$**

🏠 **El Mate Hospedaje, Los Coihues** (8 rooms) ///tuxedo.surer.unamused; 📞 9 6148 1578, 9 6564 0360. Options are limited in Villa Santa Lucía following the landslide. This building was empty the day the mudslide hit & suffered almost no damage. The cabins next door were destroyed. Incredible views over ground zero of the mudslide destruction. All dbl rooms with private bathroom for a very reasonable price (b/fast inc). Wood-stove heating & laundry. Wi-Fi tentatively available, reservation & deposit not required, just make a quick phone call. **$$**

SIGHTSEEING AND EXCURSIONS A short **hike** to **Ventisquero Yelcho Chico**, just south of Puerto Cárdenas, is a pleasant detour (8km round trip; 3hrs; easy) and an introduction to the abundant glaciers further south. Guides are available northern half of the village ceased to exist. Mario Inostroza, who operated the former Illampu guesthouse in Villa Santa Lucía, which filled with ice and debris, has turned the building into a small museum about the landslide, called La Casa de Bandera, and it is well worth a visit. It is easy to find – it is the only building standing in the north of the village (see below).

SERNAGEOMIN (the National Service of Geology and Mining, a Chilean governmental institution) had published a report in June 2008 warning specifically of the dangers that Villa Santa Lucía faced. The report was prompted by the need to relocate those displaced by the Chaitén eruption in May 2008, and Villa Santa Lucía was a potential location. The report suggested that Villa Santa Lucía itself could be adversely impacted by volcanic or seismic activity, and that any form of landslide would inevitably reach the plain upon which Villa Santa Lucía precariously sits. Although the report focused more on the potential effects of volcanic or seismic activity, rather than the events that actually took place, the fact remains that it clearly documented how vast quantities of sediment, however agitated, would directly flow straight into the village.

La Casa de Bandera ///reversal. durations.form; ☏ 9 8144 1927, 9 9173 7459; e contacto@museolacasadelabandera. com; w museolacasadelabandera.com; ⊕ Jan–mid-Mar 10.00–20.00 Mon–Sat, mid-Mar–Dec 10.00–14.00 & 16.00–18.00 Mon–Sat; $1,500 (children over 5, $1,000). A simple & yet superb museum explaining the events of that fateful day. At the very least, watch the video on the website featuring a moving series of interviews & astonishing footage of how Mario pulled his 4-year-old granddaughter from the mud. He also offers a guided tour to the location of the landslide, explaining how & why the landslide occurred & its impact on the village ($8,000, light trek to first lookout; $12,000 more challenging trek to close to the glacier that collapsed). He moved to the region that is now Villa Santa Lucía in 1979, before the village was inaugurated, while working with the Cuerpo Militar del Trabajo on the construction of the Carretera Austral. Like a phoenix rising from the mud, Mario rebuilt his house, which includes accommodation for 4 people.

at Yelcho en la Patagonia, but aren't essential. The route starts at the Puente Ventisquero (bridge) 6km south of Yelcho Lodge, and parking is available (///economically.pearl.cliffs). The shorter hike only to waypoint #7 (the final viewpoint is at #24) is a mere 15 minutes from the parking and has a spectacular view of the glacier. There are also **fishing** opportunities on and around Lago Yelcho. South of the glacier there is relatively little of interest until the junction of Villa Santa Lucía (17km), where the road to Futaleufú and Palena begins. To the west of the road lies the **Parque Nacional Corcovado** (w conaf.cl/parques/parque-nacional-corcovado), also originally acquired by Doug Tompkins/Conservation Land Trust, but unlike Parque Pumalín to the north and Parque Patagonia much further south, Corcovado is largely inaccessible. The Ventisquero Yelcho Chico offers about the only glimpse of the park possible. The park contains two volcanoes, Corcovado (2,300m) and Nevado (or Yanteles, 2,042m) and extends south to the border between Los Lagos and Aysén regions.

While most people are simply passing through, it is worth spending a little time in Villa Santa Lucía. Without wishing to promote 'disaster tourism', and always showing respect for those remaining in the village (it's a small village and inevitably most people you speak to will have lost a relative or friend), it is worth pausing to understand the sheer forces unleashed that fateful morning. There is a small museum in the former hostel Illampu, now named 'La Casa de Bandera' (see box, page 139).

⊕ AS THE CONDOR FLIES

Villa Santa Lucía is 220km from Puerto Montt and 620km from the final end point of the Carretera Austral at the border crossing to El Chaltén. A southbound condor would be almost exactly one-third of the way.

Part Three

THE CLASSIC ROUTE

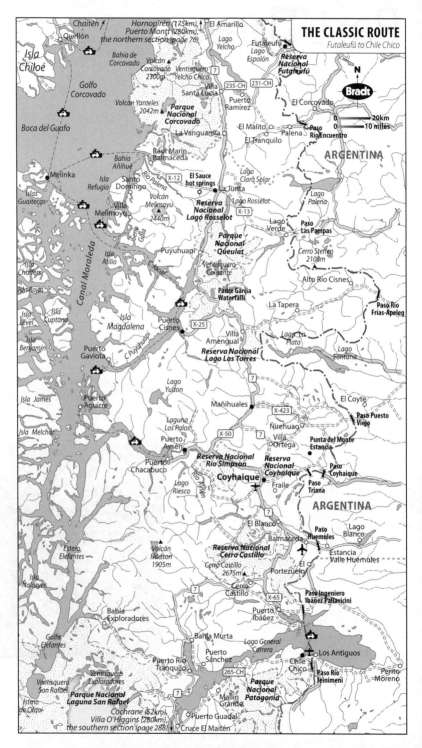

THE CLASSIC ROUTE
Futaleufú to Chile Chico

Isla Chiloé

Chaitén
Quellón
Hornopirén (175km),
Puerto Montt (280km),
the northern section (page 76)
El Amarillo
Lago Yelcho
Futaleufú
Lago Espolón
Reserva Nacional Futaleufú

N
Bradt

Golfo Corcovado
Bahía de Corcovado
Volcán Corcovado 2300m
Ventisquero Yelcho Chico
Villa Santa Lucía
7
235-CH
231-CH
El Corcovado
Paso Río Encuentro

0   20km
0   10 miles

Boca del Guafo
Volcán Yanteles 2042m
Parque Nacional Corcovado
Puerto Ramírez
El Málito
El Tranquilo
Palena
ARGENTINA

La Vanguardia

Bahía Añihué
Raúl Marín Balmaceda

Melinka
Isla Refugio
Santo Domingo
Río Palena
X-12
El Sauce hot springs
La Junta
Lago Claro Solar
Lago Palena

Islas Guaitecas
Villa Melimoyu
Volcán Melimoyu 2440m
Reserva Nacional Lago Rosselot
Lago Rosselot
X-13
Lago Verde
Paso Las Pampas

Isla Chaffers
Isla Rojas
Seno Gala
Isla Atilio
C Uchar
Puyuhuapi
Parque Nacional Queulat
Cerro Steffen 2108m

Isla Level
Isla Cuptana
Isla Magdalena
Ventisquero Colgante
Alto Río Cisnes

Isla Benjamín
C Puyuhuapi
Puerto Gaviota
Puerto Cisnes
X-25
Padre García Waterfalls
Villa Amengual
La Tapera
Lago La Plata
Lago Fontana
Paso Río Frías-Apeleg

Isla James
Reserva Nacional Lago Las Torres
7

Lago Yulton
Puerto Aguirre
Mañihuales
El Coyte
Paso Puesto Viejo

Isla Melchor
Laguna Los Palos
X-50
Ñirehuao
Villa Ortega
7
Punta del Monte Estancia

Puerto Aysén
Reserva Nacional Río Simpson
X-423
Reserva Nacional Coyhaique
Paso Coyhaique

Puerto Chacabuco
Lago Riesco
Río Aysén
Coyhaique
Fraile
Paso Triana

ARGENTINA

Estero Elefantes
Volcán Hudson 1905m
El Blanco
Balmaceda
Paso Huemules
Lago Blanco

Isla Malcayec
Reserva Nacional Cerro Castillo
Cerro Castillo 2675m
El Portezuelo
Estancia Valle Huemules

Bahía Exploradores
Cerro Castillo
X-65
Puerto Ibáñez
Paso Ingeniero Ibáñez Pallavicini

Golfo Elefantes
Bahía Murta
Lago General Carrera
Los Antiguos

Ventisquero Exploradores
Puerto Río Tranquilo
Puerto Sánchez
Chile Chico
Paso Río Jeinimeni
Perito Moreno

Ventisquero San Rafael
Istmo de Ofqui
Parque Nacional Laguna San Rafael
265-CH
Parque Nacional Patagonia

Cochrane (52km),
Villa O'Higgins (280km),
the southern section (page 288)
7
Mallín Grande
Puerto Guadal
Cruce El Maitén

142

6

Futaleufú to
La Junta

Located some 80km east of the Carretera Austral by the Argentine border, **Futaleufú** is the start (or end) of the 'classic' route. Many visitors to the region enter or leave via Futaleufú to/from Argentina, in particular from Bariloche, skipping the northern section of the Carretera altogether. This beautiful, mountainous region is home to some of the best rafting and kayaking on the planet, with huge forests, lakes and rivers. **Palena**, a 91km drive south, is also a pleasant town with a lesser-used border crossing to Argentina. It competes with Hornopirén for the prize of least-known gem of the Carretera.

While this region is of particular interest to those keen on white-water rafting, there are a number of good treks of varying lengths, lush national parks, excellent horseriding opportunities, exciting mountain-biking routes, fly-fishing possibilities, and fine accommodation and food.

The road west of Futaleufú and Palena is spectacular, weaving along thundering rivers, past isolated lakes, beneath steep cliffs, traversing the southern edge of Lago Yelcho (the first of the 'great lakes' of the region), before finally arriving at Villa Santa Lucía on the Carretera Austral. Heading south, you come to **La Junta**, the crossroads to two of the most spectacular detours from the Carretera Austral. To the east, **Lago Verde** is the central point for the horseriding route between Palena and La Tapera, and a fantastic (albeit somewhat rough) drive through one of the more isolated sections of the region. To the west lies **Raúl Marín Balmaceda**, one of the most recommended detours in this guide, with abundant marine wildlife, spectacular views of Volcán Melimoyu, and hot springs.

If entering at Futaleufú and heading south along the Carretera Austral, do consider the short, paved detour north at least to Chaitén and Parque Pumalín, if not all the way to Hornopirén. For those heading north towards Bariloche but wishing to do some world-class rafting, Futaleufú is certainly worth visiting, but consider returning to the Carretera and completing the northern section. Bariloche can be easily reached from Puerto Montt, or by trekking across any of the three non-vehicular borders around Cochamó – far more interesting than the bus ride north through Argentina.

IF YOU'RE COMING FROM VILLA SANTA LUCÍA...

For those not joining the Carretera at Futaleufú, but instead making this town a detour from Villa Santa Lucía, leave Villa Santa Lucía on the Ruta 235 heading 30km east towards Puerto Ramírez where the road splits and becomes the 231 (towards Futaleufú) and the 235 (towards Palena). Further details of this route are given on page 145.

Upon arrival it becomes pretty apparent what the main draw to 'Futa' is. There are as many kayaks as cars in the town, and every other business is somehow related to kayaking or rafting. The town is surrounded by mountains and retains a frontier feel reminiscent of towns in Alaska. The inhabitants are generally pretty laid-back and, when not in the water, the central plaza is a good place to relax and have a fruit juice. Fly-fishing and trekking are also possible, but the Río Futaleufú is considered one of the top rivers worldwide for rafting, and most visitors come here to dip their toes in the water.

HISTORY Futaleufú was not connected to the Carretera Austral until 1980. Until then, the primary contact with the outside world was with Argentina, and to this day the town has a strong Argentine ambience. It temporarily became the provincial capital following the Chaitén volcanic eruption in 2008.

As with many towns in this region of Chile, the history of Futaleufú is poorly documented and interspersed with legend. The first settler was Don Ceferino Moraga, originally from Chiloé. He and his family arrived in 1912 via Argentina. What is now called Futaleufú, meaning 'Great River' or 'Great Waters' in the native language, was an inhospitable dense forest at this time. Slowly the family cleared enough land to raise cattle, sheep and oxen. Moraga jealously guarded his territory, and resisted the arrival of other settlers who wished to exploit

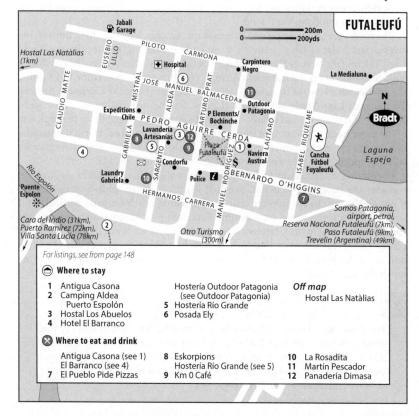

For listings, see from page 148

Where to stay
1 Antigua Casona
2 Camping Aldea Puerto Espolón
3 Hostal Los Abuelos
4 Hotel El Barranco
   Hostería Outdoor Patagonia (see Outdoor Patagonia)
5 Hostería Río Grande
6 Posada Ely

Off map
Hostal Las Natàlias

Where to eat and drink
Antigua Casona (see 1)
El Barranco (see 4)
7 El Pueblo Pide Pizzas
8 Eskorpions
   Hostería Río Grande (see 5)
9 Km 0 Café
10 La Rosadita
11 Martín Pescador
12 Panadería Dimasa

the fertile land. According to legend, all the men in the Moraga family were thus slain between 1919 and 1920 by Chilean pioneers who wished to populate the region and, given the lack of any authorities in the area, the crime went unpunished. However, this cavalier approach to law and order came to a halt in 1929 when Police Chief José Felmer Patof and a group of surveyors arrived and subsequently founded the village on 1 April that year. A single house from this period remains on Lago Espolón, and to this day serves as a warehouse. Settlers continued to arrive and slowly inhabited the regions of El Espolón, Las Escalas, Río Azul and Loncanao. Since the arrival of this single pioneering family the population of Futaleufú has swelled to an impressive 2,600 according to the 2017 census.

⊕ AS THE CONDOR FLIES

Futaleufú is 210km from Puerto Montt and 645km from the border south of Villa O'Higgins to El Chaltén. Palena is 600km from this border, and 255km from Puerto Montt. From either town it is approximately a 950km drive to Villa O'Higgins including one ferry crossing.

GETTING THERE
About the route
Villa Santa Lucía to Futaleufú (78km; 2hrs; reasonable quality gravel) For those making a detour from Villa Santa Lucía on the Carretera Austral, the road ascends 30km to Puerto Ramírez. Futaleufú is a further 48km (1hr) from Puerto Ramírez along Ruta 231 (northeasterly from the junction at Puerto Ramírez). The road is of reasonable quality, although there are sections of exposed rock. Be prepared for surprising, unmarked hairpin bends, and the occasional cow in the road. There are steep ascents and descents which might be frustrating for cyclists. Initially the route climbs through a steep gorge, and then skirts around Lago Yelcho, with mountains crashing vertically into the lake. Evidence of violent landslides is visible: deforested, scarred sections of mountainside are exposed, some presumably quite recently judging from the lack of new vegetation. You will pass snow-capped peaks along the way. This is a well-traversed section and traffic is comparatively common. After Lago Yelcho the road winds around the Río Futaleufú, crossing a number of bridges (including over the Río Azul, another rafting river). The final section runs along the shores of Lago Lonconao and then along the Río Espolón: this sparsely populated area has spectacular mountain scenery, with snow-capped peaks, and virgin bush running down to river valleys and lakes.

Trevelin (Argentina) to Futaleufú (49km; 1hr plus time at border; paved in Chile, gravel in Argentina) As the start (or end) of the 'classic' route, many travellers enter (or leave) Futaleufú from Argentina, as it is approximately 9km to the Chilean/Argentine border (wonderfully paved). From here, it's 40km to Trevelin in Argentina on treacherous loose gravel and then 23km (on a paved road) to Esquel on Ruta 40 and with connections to Bariloche, Tecka, the deep south, and to the Atlantic coast.

At the crossing of Paso Futaleufú (9km from town; ⊕ 08.00–20.00) the usual formalities apply. As there is very rarely snow in the region, even in midwinter this border is passable without chains or snow tyres. The Chilean customs and immigration are efficient and housed in a modern building. It is approximately 200m across the actual border to the Argentine customs and immigration, passing a signpost reminding travellers that the Falkland Islands are, were, and will always be, Argentine. The road quality deteriorates rapidly to gravel.

By bus When the border with Argentina is open buses travel directly to Osorno and Puerto Montt without having to use the ferries, but at the time of going to press these services had paused. To get to **Argentina**, Hostal Los Abuelos (page 150) offers a daily minivan to the border, which synchronises with an Argentine bus that continues to Esquel. To reach Futaleufú from Esquel, see w transportejacobsen.com.ar. There is a bus to Chaitén (06.00 & 11.00 daily with onward connections, return noon & 16.30). **Transportes Jerry** (✆65 274 1319) goes from Palena to Futaleufú (08.00 Mon & Fri, return 13.30; 05.30 & 13.30 Wed, return 08.30 & 16.30).

If direct buses to more distant locations are not available, or the routes are not served in low season, it is always possible to get to Chaitén (north) or La Junta (south) where onward connections are possible. Naviera Austral have an agency at Pedro Aguirre Cerda 640 (///marina.fallback.gravel; ✆9 7478 2394).

TOUR OPERATORS

Bio-Bio Expeditions ✆2 196 4258, US +1 800 246 7238; w bbxrafting.com/product/futaleufu-rafting-multi-sport. US-based adventure tour operator mainly providing package trips for dedicated kayakers. Not geared towards walk-ins. All-inclusive 9-day packages cost US$4,500 pp.

Bochinche Expediciones Pedro Aguirre Cerda 545; ///tofu.buttered.taxation; ✆9 3392 0745; e info@bochinchex.com; w bochinchex.com. All the standard tours: bridge to bridge ($60,000 pp), bridge to Macal ($75,000 pp), Azul to Macal ($105,000 pp), the gentler Espolón family trip ($25,000 pp) & the Azul river ($50,000 pp, more intense than Espolón, but not quite the Futa). Also offers kayak courses & trips for experienced kayakers; river safety courses; multi-day packages, including a 10-day tour to other Chilean rivers; & fishing trips.

Cara del Indio 34km south of Futaleufú, 14km north of Puerto Ramírez; ///plights.feigning. booths; ✆9 7468 1573; e caradelindiofutaleufu@ gmail.com; w caradelindio.cl. Located along the river between the 2 key bridges over the Futa, this truly local company is one of the few not based in town. Overlooking their land is a famous rock formation that resembles the face of an Indian – hence the name. This was the first rafting centre along the river & they host the annual FutaXL competition. The usual rafting trips are available & it's the focal point for

kayaking. Camping for $5,000 & cabins of various sizes starting at $30,000 for 2 people (total capacity 100) on a large estate, with fishing, hiking trails & lovely beaches. Sauna, hot tub & asados available. Location might be better suited to those more interested in rafting/kayaking rather than the other services offered in town. Can be booked in town through Carpintero Negro (see below).

Carpintero Negro Manuel Rodriguez 10; ///replay.classroom.acrobat; ✆9 5825 4073; e info@carpinteronegro. com; w carpinteronegro.com. Finally, a tour operator offering something unrelated to rafting & kayaking. Treks to the local gems, including Pozon de Los Reyes, Lago Las Rosas, Piedra del Aguila, Montaña de los Cóndores, & evening sunset trails (3–12hrs, min 2 people). Manuel grew up in Patagonia & his ancestors settled in Patagonia in 1900. He also offers birdwatching at Laguna Espejo (native marsh & forest birds including Pitio & Chucao). The popular rural tourism trip consists of a 2hr hike along the Río Espolón to the 'Devil's Throat' waterfall, culminating at Lago Espolón where visitors enjoy a traditional lamb asado & learn about rural culture at a local farm; also offers a 2hr night trek through valleys & along rivers to observe the stars. Ideal for families who might not want to spend all day rafting, & those who wish to enjoy the stunning nature in the region that is often

above

Ventisquero Colgante — Queulat's 'hanging glacier' — protrudes from the Northern Ice Field, where occasional chunks of ice crash onto the rocks below (AL/S) page 185

right

Puyuhuapi, with its many traditional houses, is one of the best-preserved historic villages in all of Aysén (SS) page 174

below

The southern road along Lago General Carrera, Chile's second-largest lake, offers magnificent vistas of the distant ice fields (HS) page 271

above The Valle del Rio Ibañez in the region around Cerro Castillo — a hidden gem (JLC/S) page 253

left The thundering rivers around Futaleufú are home to some of the greatest white-water rafting in the world (HS) page 152

below The descent towards Cerro Castillo, with a series of hair-raising switchbacks, is one of the most dramatic sections of the whole route (DM/S) page 245

above left A rare monument to Pinochet in La Junta, who was responsible for connecting some of Chile's remotest regions with the Carretera Austral (HS) page 15

above right The Carretera Austral is one of the world's definitive motorbike tours (HS)

below The marble caves at Puerto Río Tranquilo (pictured) and Puerto Sánchez are a unique highlight of the region, particularly on a sunny day (G/S) page 265

bottom Crossing rivers was one of the major challenges in the construction of the Carretera Austral – pictured here, the beautiful Puente General Carrera just north of Cruce el Maitén (LQ/S) page 269

above Approaching the Argentine steppe in Parque Patagonia, where mud-flats and open plains replace the lush vegetation and fjords (HS) page 294

left A *huaso* (Chilean gaucho) by the El Salto waterfall (WH) page 307

below Lago Bertrand is one of the most photogenic spots along the whole route (HS) page 289

above left   Llamas on the back route from Puerto Ibáñez (WH) page 239

above right   The globally threatened huemul (*Hippocamelus bisulcus*) is the Carretera Austral's most iconic mammal, pictured here beside the ice floes of Ventisquero Montt (HS) page 6

left   Andean fox, or culpeo (*Lycalopex culpaeus*) (r/S) page 6

below   The rocky shores of Raúl Marín Balmaceda are bursting with marine mammals and birds; such as pelicans and South American sea lions (*Otaria flavescens*) (HS) page 167

right   Chilean flicker (*Colaptes pitius*) (e/S) page 8

below left   Andean condors (*Vultur gryphus*) are prolific in the region, particularly around Coyhaique where the Punta del Monte Estancia presents a rare opportunity to get up-close with these massive creatures (AJ/S) page 233

below right   Austral parakeets (*Enicognathus ferrugineus*) are common forest-dwellers (RL/S) page 298

bottom   The guanaco (*Lama guanicoe*) is one of South America's four remaining camelids (JR/S) page 6

above   **Reloncaví Sound** (IBH/S) page 79

left   **Puerto Montt is the last major city before heading south on the Carretera Austral — and it is certainly worth exploring. Pictured here, craft markets** (TG/S) page 91

below   **Puerto Varas, in the shadow of Volcán Osorno, is a popular tourist town** (TG/S) page 85 overshadowed by the focus on the Futa. Manuel is also the Futaleufú contact person for Cara del Indio rafting, located some 30km south of the village (see opposite). Recommended.

Condorfu O'Higgins, ½ block west of plaza; ///foods.logos.wavelets; ☎ 9 4213 9636; e vanessa@condorfu.cl; w condorfu.cl; ⊕ Nov– Mar. Range of trips & activities including light rafting on the Río Espolón ($20,000 pp, good with kids), a 2-day all-inclusive rafting trip along the entire Futa ($200,000 pp), & a 3-day all-inclusive rafting/kayaking/canyoning combination trip ($300,000 pp). Also the standard ½-/full-day Futa descent ($50,000 or $90,000 pp), & a novel 2-day women-only trip that includes the standard ½-day tour plus the Macal section, camping overnight at a remote beach only reached by river. The canyoning that other tour operators sell is actually owned & operated by Condorfu.

Earth River ☎ US +1 800 643 2784; +1 845 626 2165; e info@earthriver.com; w earthriver.com; ⊕ Dec–Mar. One of the companies that pioneered commercial rafting on the Futa. The founder, Eric Hertz, was the first person to raft the entire river in 1991. His 2 sons now run the business & guide the tours. 9-day full river tours staying in upmarket lodges along the river (US$4,950 exc flights) including transport to/from Puerto Varas. Rafting trips can be customised to almost any wishes, including calmer sections suitable for families with children.

Expeditions Chile Gabriela Mistral 296; ☎ 65 256 2639, US +1 208 629 5032; e rosi@exchile. com; w exchile.com. Founded by Chris Spelius, US Olympic kayaker, who sometimes guides the trips. Originally kayak & rafting tours, & now also offers mountain biking, trekking, horseriding & canyoning too. Multi-day & multi-sport packages, as well as an unusual 5-day descent of the Futa from Macal to Lago Yelcho & then down the Yelcho river to the ocean in sea kayaks, wild camping en route. Can do 'all-inclusive' tours, with a focus on specific skill development, & everything in between, catering to all skill levels.

Otro Turismo Lautaro 386; ///fitted.freeway. blasts; ☎ 9 8250 6170; e otroturismofutaleufu@ gmail.com; ▯ otroturismofutaleufu. Unusual tour operator offering an array of activities. Guided mountain biking & rappel (suitable for beginners) are the most 'normal'. Marco also offers a range of treks in the region (½ to 2-day)

but with a major emphasis on nature – 'trekking with your head up', thoroughly exploring the nature rather than stomping past it. He proudly claims he does a 4hr trek in 8hrs! He runs birdwatching trips with the aid of audio recordings of all the birds in Chile, combined with his knowledge of where the birds are likely to be, attracting individual species. But perhaps the most interesting tour is *fungi-turismo* – a trek with a very specific focus on the mushrooms, edible & otherwise, in the area. Educational, unusual, & delivered with passion by someone utterly enamoured with the region in which he lives.

Outdoor Patagonia Manuel Rodriguez 129; ///aromas.depicted.fixate; ☎ 9 8570 2407, 9 7132 7512; e raftingoutdoor@gmail.com; w outdoorpatagonia.cl. Well-respected family-run operator in town with local & international guides. All the standard tours including Puente-Macal ($70,000 pp) & Azul-Macal ($99,000 pp), as well as full-day trips down the lesser-traversed upper section of the Futa to their basecamp, El Guapito, for an asado & hot tub ($90,000 pp), & the complete river (less Zeta rapid) for $130,000 pp. Personalised kayak lessons (3hrs on water, $50,000 pp) & the calmer rivers (good for families) are also available. Also 4- & 7-day packages with pickup/drop-off at Puerto Montt or Esquel (Argentina) using their bases both in the village & at the lodge along the river, blending full & ½ day's rafting with horseriding & trekking, great food, sauna, hot tub & massages (fee). A great one-stop shop with B&B, restaurant & riverside lodge (page 149).

Patagonia Elements North side of plaza; ///hallmarks.sways.milkshake; ☎ 9 7499 0296, 9 9261 9441; e info@patagoniaelements.com; w patagoniaelements.com. A well-respected operator with Chilean staff, many of whom live in the region & have years of experience with the company. All standard trips on the Futa plus family trips on the Espolón & kayak courses. They have a basecamp in the Loncanos section (downstream from the village) with restaurant, changing rooms, area for kids to play, etc. Great for families. Also offer fly-fishing by cataraft on the upper sections of the Futa, horseriding through forests & to Lago Espolón (good for families), trekking, guided mountain-bike trips & bicycle hire.

A trip along the Carretera is incomplete without some river action, and Futa offers both the 'extreme' adrenaline rides, as well as more sedentary, child-friendly trips. For those that wish to combine a visit to Futa with the Carretera Austral, two great options exist.

First, for experienced kayakers or novices seeking a serious adrenaline burst, one operator offers a truly exceptional Futa experience: the Serrasolses brothers are in town! (Serrasolses Brothers River Co; \+34 623 181 066; e info@sbriverco. com; w sbriverco.com). Born in Catalunya, Gerd and Aniol first came to Futaleufú in 2006–07 and fell in love with the river. Gerd took his younger brother kayaking when Aniol was only 12 years old, and they have worked their way up the kayak world rankings to the highest possible levels ever since, securing sponsorship from Red Bull and Go-Pro among others. With a long list of titles and awards between them, including various world championships, these brothers are two of the best kayakers ever.

In 2017 they established the **Serrasolses Brothers Program** (SBP) to promote local participation in kayaking and broader conservation of rivers, as well as free training clinics for young kids with talent and motivation but limited resources to progress.

For the ultimate baptism by white water Gerd and Aniol offer a truly unique option for the relative newbie to kayaking – the **Bridge-to-Bridge section in a tandem kayak**, with the brothers at the helm. No prior experience is necessary, but participants must weigh under 80kg and be under 180cm tall. If rafting the Futa is a white-knuckle experience, kayaking it is a new dimension in adrenaline and fear. Rafts are wide, heavy (with 6+ people) and stable. A tandem kayak feels more like sitting on a cork. Pounding through wave after wave, often with limited visibility due to permanent bombardment of water from every conceivable angle, Gerd and Aniol control the kayaks with absolute precision. While the participant must paddle, at times with force, the brothers navigate rapids they have traversed hundreds of times previously. Looming rocks, waves and holes might appear terrifying to the uninitiated, but their utter command of the kayak

WHERE TO STAY *Map, page 144*

Hotel El Barranco (10 rooms) Av Bernado O'Higgins 172; ///pods.tasers.stormed; \65 272 1314, 9 7697 7574; e hotel@elbarrancochile. cl; w elbarrancochile.cl; ⊕ Sep–Apr. A gem of a hotel with a hidden swimming pool for sunny afternoons. This is where the *Top Gear* team stayed when visiting Futaleufú (see box, page 73). A few blocks' walk from the centre, views fluctuate between mountains & forest. The hotel itself is entirely made of wood, all rooms with private bathrooms & fantastic, large beds, security box & central heating. Wi-Fi available, including on the deckchairs by the pool, but no TV – this is a place to unwind. Finnish sauna & massages available. Complete buffet b/fast (inc), with yoghurt, cereals, cheeses, meats, jams, juice, etc; also a restaurant (page 150). Parking for 5 cars, & space for motorbikes. Wheelchair accessible. English & Spanish spoken. The owner is very knowledgeable about all local activities, & can arrange guided fly-fishing trips, rafting, kayaking, trekking, canyoning, mountain biking & horseriding in the region. An upper-end option, but well worth splashing out. Free for kids under 12. **$$$$$**

✳ **Antigua Casona** (5 rooms) Manuel Rodriguez 215; ///locking.primes.rosemary; \65 272 1311, 9 8476 4480; e antiguacasona.futa@ gmail.com; w antiguacasona.cl. In a magnificent, historic building on the central plaza, this small boutique hotel (& restaurant) is a good mid-price option. Rooms (2 trpl & 3 dbl) all with private bathrooms, Wi-Fi, laundry & excellent b/fast (inc).

is most reassuring. Rafting versus kayaking the Futa might be compared to flying in a plane versus skydiving – this is a unique opportunity to safely do something that very few people will ever experience, guided by World Champions. Highly recommended for expending more adrenaline than almost any other activity along the Carretera Austral.

For intermediate/advanced kayakers, Gerd and Aniol offer kayak trips and clinics in both Pucón and Futaleufú. These are intense courses for up to six participants at a time, spending 6 hours per day on the river perfecting skills, with food/accommodation/transport and world-class equipment. Participants must be confident in class III–IV rapids. One-on-one sessions are also available, as are premium-quality kayak rentals.

Whether an experienced kayaker wishing to reach the next skill level, or a beginner wishing to safely dip the proverbial toe into the water of hardcore kayaking, receiving genuinely world-class instruction and guiding is rare. Gerd and Aniol have a fascinating story, and despite stiff competition from some excellent tour operators based in and around Futaleufú, these extreme kayakers offer the ultimate Futa experience.

For a slightly gentler experience, look to **Outdoor Patagonia** (page 147), currently the only operator that can offer a one-stop shop in Futa. Their office, just off the plaza, has decent accommodation for a range of budgets, a restaurant, a great terrace bar for sunny evenings (the only one in the village), and all the standard rafting options, including Puente-Macal and family trips on the calmer rivers. They offer multi-day programmes and have their own river lodge, as well as the main office/hostel. The owner, Peter, was born in Pucón but has lived in Futa since 1995, also working in Peru, Argentina, Ecuador and Bolivia, and has extensive experience in rescue and safety. A great outfit, offering personalised attention, and above all, it takes the headache out of arranging a trip to Futaleufú – including food, accommodation, rafting and pickup/drop-off in Puerto Montt or Esquel (Argentina) if required – all with one phone call. Recommended.

Ultra-cosy wooden construction, great furniture, the owners have attended to the finer details of the building with a loving touch, right down to comfortable beds & central heating instead of wood stoves. The craft beer is made by Helmut Hopperdietzel in Puyuhuapi – one of the best along the Carretera. A fishing theme permeates the building, with a fly shop in the corner, revealing their true motivation for moving from Italy to Futaleufú. English, Portuguese, Italian & Polish spoken. This upper-end option is very good value for money. **$$$$**

🏠 **Hostería Río Grande** (16 rooms & 1 apt) Bernado O'Higgins 397; ///unprotected.probably. spine; ☎65 272 1320, 9 9756 0818; e renzo@ pachile.com; w pachile.com. Reasonable, mid-range accommodation, centrally located 1 block

from the plaza, with off-street parking. All rooms with private bathrooms, Wi-Fi, full b/fast (inc). Decent but overpriced at US$80 (sgl), US$110 (dbl), US$130 (trpl), US$150 (6-person apt). A reasonable restaurant (page 151). Staff speak French, Italian, Spanish & English. Credit cards accepted. **$$$$**

🏠 **Hostería Outdoor Patagonia** (7 rooms) Manuel Rodriguez 129; ///aromas.depicted.fixate; ☎9 8570 2407, 9 7132 7512; e raftingoutdoor@ gmail.com; w outdoorpatagonia.cl. Run by & from the same building as the rafting outfitter. Pleasant spacious rooms (3 dbl with private bathroom, 4 dbl/twin with shared bathrooms), good beds, & also has a great sitting area & outdoor terrace from which to enjoy the sunset. The small restaurant serves meat, pork chops, chicken, salmon, sandwiches, pizzas, tablas & pichangas. Wi-Fi & laundry available. Offers packages with kayaking/rafting (page 147). Cards accepted. **$$$**

🏠 **Hostal Las Natàlias** (9 rooms) 1km along northwest exit of Futaleufú; ///darns.being.surgery; 📞 9 9882 4637, 9 9631 1330; e hostallasnatalias@gmail.com; w hostallasnatalias.cl. Wonderful, rural setting with mountain & river views, yet within walking distance of the town. Ideal for trekkers wishing to visit Cero Teta, Lago Espolón, Las Rosas & Noreste lakes & the Garganta del Diablo. The owner, Nathanial, is a very experienced kayak guide & instructor. He can arrange fly-fishing trips, treks, any variety of watersports, & rents bicycles. Dorm with bunk beds for 8 people, 6 private rooms with dbl beds for 2–6 people (5 with private bathrooms), 1 sgl & 1 dbl with shared bathroom. B/fast ($2,000), but guests have full use of a well-equipped kitchen. Off-road parking & Wi-Fi. English & Spanish spoken. Cash, card or PayPal accepted. **$$**

🏠 **Posada Ely** (6 rooms & 1 apt) Balmaceda 409; ///interns.gnome.disposable; 📞 65 272 1205, 9 7656 7591; e posada.ely.futaleufu@gmail.com. Cosy budget accommodation 2 blocks from the centre run by Betty, who prepares an excellent b/fast (inc) with fruit juice, real milk & homemade jams. All rooms with private bathroom, heating & hot water; apt has a stove & fridge. No English spoken, but familiar with hand signals for most requirements. **$$**

🏠 **Hostal Los Abuelos** (dorm, 1 cabin) Pedro Aguirre Cerda 436; ///ghosted.coveted.hooked; 📞 65 272 1424, 9 9444 8196; e centro-tel@hotmail.com; 📘 LosabuelosHostel. Best budget option in an otherwise expensive town. The hostel has room for 30 people in various dormitories, & a 5-person cabin, all with shared bathroom & shared kitchen. The hostel serves as the only money-changing outfit in town. They can organise tours in the region & also operate a shuttle service between Futa & Esquel/Trevelin (Mon/Wed/Fri in high season, Mon/Fri in low season, $3,000 one-way, tickets only available in hostel or in the Esquel bus terminal, when the Arg/Chile border is open). Wi-Fi but no laundry facility, but there is a laundry just around the corner. Simple restaurant serving basic food. One of the longest-established hostels in the town, & a favourite budget option. Reservations not usually required. Accepts cards. **$**

⛺ **Camping Aldea Puerto Espolón** Southern entrance to Futaleufú; ///anklet.servicing.unused; 📞 9 9122 8192, 9 5324 0305; e puertoespolon@gmail.com; w aldeapuertoespolon.cl. Pleasant campsite a short walk from the centre, dome tents for rent ($40,000 for 4 people), camping ($8,000 pp, kids under 5 free, age 5–10 or over 65, $5,000) with hot water, bathrooms, quincho with gas for cooking, electricity, facilities for handwashing clothes & access to the Río Espolón (return catch). Arturo Vivanco, the owner, is also the creator of the Futalhué beer. **$**

✗ **WHERE TO EAT AND DRINK** *Map, page 144*

✗ **El Barranco** Av Bernado O'Higgins 172; ⊕ Sep–Apr 13.00–5.30, 19.00–22.00 daily. One of the best restaurants in town, part of the hotel (page 148) & not necessarily for budget travellers. Includes local delicacies such as wild boar, hare, roast lamb & the usual salmon dishes. It's a pity not to try hare while visiting Futa as it's rarely on the menu elsewhere, & Barranco has a fine offering. Excellent service in a lovely building. **$$$$**

✳ ✗ **Martín Pescador** Balmaceda 603; ///paratrooper.spreading.regrouped; 📞 65 272 1279, 9 9558 2561; e restaurantemartinpescador@gmail.com; 📘 martín pescador – restaurante; ⊕ noon–22.00 daily. Founded in 2003, this is a fine restaurant that doubles as a bar later in the

evenings. Has the look of a formal establishment built in the style of a fishing lodge, with tablecloths, nice wine glasses & very good service – not typical along the Carretera. But it also has a laid-back atmosphere, with sofas & wacky art, bar & fireplace all housed in a large space of wooden construction with wide windows to watch Futa life go by. You can also sit out on the deck on a warm evening. The US/Chilean owners are very knowledgeable about the region, activities, rafting options, etc. Mitch is a fishing guide & Tatiana is the chef. All food is organic &, where possible, sourced within 200km of the restaurant. Serves beef, wild boar, hare & all seafood is caught by local fishermen. Respectable selection of reasonably priced wines (inc organic), beer on tap, & local cheeses. The tasting menu is excellent. Not large portions, so if you're ravenous, it might not be the best-value meal in town. It's wise to reserve a table in high season. Offers take-out & accepts credit cards. $$$$

Antigua Casona Manuel Rodriguez 215; 65 272 1311, 9 8476 4480; Sep–Apr 12.30–15.30 & 19.30–22.30 daily. A good opportunity to try something slightly different from the usual Chilean offerings in a lovely building on the central plaza (also hotel, page 148) with outdoor seating. Genuine Italian food made by Italians, & even has the history of ravioli on the placemats. Serves the best pasta on the Carretera – homemade ravioli, gnocchi, lasagne, an exceptional seafood tagliatelle, & seasonal dishes with the sought-after morcella mushroom. The very good craft beer is made by Hopperdietzel. A little expensive, but a nice atmosphere. $$$

El Pueblo Pide Pizzas Cnr O'Higgins & Isabel Requelme; ///voters.arrival.goody; 9 6485 1412; noon–15.00 & 18.00–23.00 Tue–Sun. A highly qualified Argentine chef with international experience, Fabio decided to simplify his range of dishes to one: the Italian pizza. The outcome? The best pizzas on the Carretera Austral, bar none. Thin crust, a wide range of toppings or simply choose your own ingredients. Everything is carefully selected by Fabio, fresh, organic, mostly from the immediate region & cooked to perfection. $10,000–15,000 per pizza. A couple would probably not share, as the pizzas are not huge. Very friendly, speaks English, offers take-out, has a range of local ales & some wine. Small, simple, no reservation required. $$$

Hostería Río Grande Bernardo O'Higgins 397; noon–22.00 daily. Reasonable food in the hotel of the same name (page 149), with dishes including great locally caught salmon, good pork, but mediocre wines. Also serves as one of the town's main bars. $$$

La Rosadita Sargento Aldea 348; ///toddling. retro.interval; 10.00–14.30 & 18.00–23.00

Mon–Sat. If anyone was going to compete with Fabio (see left) for the prestigious 'best pizza of the Carretera Austral' award it would be fellow Argentine pizza rival (& fishing guide) Franco, of La Rosadita in Palena. Upping the stakes, Franco has opened this branch in Futa, bringing the battle to an intense face-to-face dash to victory. As in Palena, also has mouthwatering waffles & great sandwiches. Given the scarcity & mediocrity of most pizzas along the rest of the Carretera Austral, why not visit both? $$$

Km 0 Café Arturo Prat 262-B, west side of the Plaza; 9 7176 2468; 09.30–21.00 daily. A conveniently located café/fast-food restaurant selling hotdogs, burgers, milanesas, sandwiches, fruit juices, salads, beef steak or salmon with chips. Rustic décor with old wooden floors painted green, rough sawn timber half walls & a sack-like cloth ceiling (likely covering a multitude of amateur carpentry & electrical sins). A bit dark if you choose a table away from the main window, but don't worry, the food is good. $

Panadería Dimasa Pedro Aguirre Cerda 458; ///grouchy.marina.recognition; 07.00–22.00 daily. This bakery half a block from the plaza makes pizzas, sandwiches & hamburgers to eat in or take away, plus a good selection of fresh hot bread. The mouth-watering meat empanadas are not to be missed, with decent chunks of hand-cut meat & whole olives specially prepared by the owner. $

Eskorpions Gabriela Mistral 265; ///essays. fixate.nuisance; until late. Nightlife in Futaleufú is mostly limited to the hotels, but this bar offers a slightly wilder alternative. Beware of women dressed in attire more suited for the beach sitting at your table without any formal invitation & asking for drinks at suspiciously elevated prices. But this is often the only place in town for a beer.

OTHER PRACTICALITIES The **tourist information centre** is on the south side of the plaza (O'Higgins 565; ///system.division.proofed), but better information is available in the hostels/hotels. The rafting outfits are clustered around the central blocks of the town, and it is worth shopping around for a suitable deal, depending on the duration and difficulty level. Equipment hire is generally included in a guided package, but some will rent gear for use on the more peaceful rivers and lakes. The **petrol station** (///anew.swaddles.salary) is located approximately 1km east of town on the main road (Ruta 231) towards the Argentine border.

Mechanic

Jabali Garage Cnr of Piloto Carmona & Eusebio Lillo; ///turnover.goatees.outgrowth; ✆ 9 7497 5920. Owned by English-speaking Leonardo, who is a very competent mechanic with a range of equipment. The only thing he does not do is tyres, but there are 3 tyre specialists in town. He works with most cars & motorbikes, as well as bicycles, although the latter are not his speciality. Spare parts are the main bottleneck (some sourced in Esquel, Argentina if necessary), but he will attempt to fix most things. He also has a tow truck for emergencies. As a side business Leonardo also hunts the hares that appear on the plates in some restaurants.

Laundry

Laundry Gabriela Mistral 393, at the corner with Hermanos Carrera; ✆ 65 272 1469; ⊕ 09.00–21.00 Mon–Sat. Same-day service available if drop off clothes early.

Lavandería Artesanías Sargento Aldea, just around corner from Hostal Los Abuelos; ✆ 9 9424 5210; ⊕ 09.30–13.00 & 15.00–20.00 Mon–Sat

SIGHTSEEING, ACTIVITIES AND EXCURSIONS The main attraction in the region is world-class **rafting** and **kayaking**. Professionals from across the world visit this town specifically to raft the river, so if you have never rafted before but were always curious, this is possibly the finest place in Latin America to do so. Up to class V+ rapids offer even the most experienced kayakers a serious challenge, and the **Río Futaleufú** is notably safe as the main white-water sections are invariably followed by more tranquil waters which makes rescue operations easier. The **Río Espolón** has class III rapids suitable for less experienced rafters, and is offered by most of the operators listed.

At the northeast corner of town lies the all-important rodeo, **La Medialuna**. Horse-related activities are taken very seriously both here and in Palena, a consequence of the gaucho legacy. Next to the rodeo is a small lake, **Laguna Espejo**, and a short trail around the north shore of the lake leads up to a viewing platform, Torre de Agua, with sweeping views over the town and valley.

UNDERSTANDING THE RIVERS AND CLASSES OF RAFTING/KAYAKING IN THE REGION

The rafting/kayaking community has devised a class system to gauge the difficulty of a rapid. However, the volume and depth of water varies, so local knowledge is also required to assess the safety of a rapid – use a recognised tour operator. Class I and II rapids are basically ripples and small waves with limited obstacles to negotiate, suitable for kids. Class III is where the adrenaline begins to flow: larger waves, faster currents, and fairly easily avoided obstructions. Class IV rapids are faster, longer, and may involve narrow sections, unavoidable waves and holes – this is when the guide is essential and the fear begins. Class V is when you may wish to bring a spare change of swimming trunks: extended, fast, complicated rapids with unavoidable waves, drops, holes and narrow sections. Beyond class V – madness.

RÍO FUTALEUFÚ (five main sections, downstream in order): **Cañón del Infierno**, five rapids, class IV–V (there are actually two additional rapids downstream (Zeta and Trono) which are class V+ and only for very experienced kayakers); **Milla Salvaje**, four rapids, class III–IV (after the last of these rapids the Río Azul enters the Futaleufú); **Terminator**, six rapids, class III–V+ (the V+ rapid is called Terminator and is the highest class of rapid most people will do; there are no more class V+ rapids downstream from here); **Puente to Puente**, 13 rapids, class III–IV+ (given

A number of **horse**, **hiking** and **mountain-biking** trails surround Futaleufú for those less interested in rafting, generally following the main rivers. To the northwest of the town are a number of lakes and trails, as well as fishing options. Day treks include Lago Azul, Lago los Cedros and Piedra del Águila – Las Cascadas del Lago Espolón. Multi-day treks are possible around Espolón. There are also rock-climbing routes in the region – ask at Las Natàlias (page 150). Patagonia Elements (page 147) offer some non-river trips, but only two tour operators focus on non-river activities: Carpintero Negro (page 146) and Otro Turismo (page 147). Indeed, Futaleufú is almost a victim of its own success – rafting and kayaking have so dominated tourism in the region that other activities seem to have been squeezed out. These two operators are noteworthy for trying to promote the other (often amazing) activities the village offers.

For something completely different, **Somos Patagonia** (east of Futa on the road towards the border; ///trunks.reimpose.froze; 📞 9 9953 3160; e contacto@somospatagonia.cl; w somospatagonia.cl) offers canopy tours suitable for anyone over five years old (under nine with guide). This is a short half-hour trek up, followed by six descents covering 800m; $20,000 pp).

The 12,000ha **Reserva Nacional Futaleufú** (w conaf.cl/parques/reserva-nacional-futaleufu) lies to the south of the town and has three trails and a couple of miradores, easily accessed by car. For the more adventurous, and with the advice of the CONAF guard, it is possible to hike through the reserve and on to Palena. There is a road heading south through the valley towards Cerro Cónico, but then an unmarked trail begins – this is for experienced hikers only.

PALENA – A DETOUR

Palena is a hidden gem. Tourists flock to Futaleufú for rafting and easy connections to Argentina, while the sleepy town of Palena is slightly harder to get to, borders a

the number of rapids and lack of any class V rapids, this is the most popular stretch of the river); the final section is **El Macal**, six rapids, class III–V.

The standard tour is **Puente to Puente** (maximum class IV+). Some operators offer the **Macal** extension for some extra adrenaline if they think the team is ready for it (two class V rapids). The **Azul to Puente/Macal** begins upstream of Puente to Puente on the Río Azul and includes the Terminator section of the Futa before covering the Puente to Puente section and possibly continuing to Macal (sometimes called full-day, as opposed to full-river). The **full-river** trips usually avoid the Zeta and Trono rapids (class V+) between the end of Cañón del Infierno and the beginning of Milla Salvaje – it is possible to walk this section. Not all operators offer full-river and some do not offer the Macal section.

RÍO ESPOLÓN Class I–III: this tends to be where family tours or kayak courses take place. However, remember to get out of the river before it joins the Futa, as this is the usual entrance to the Cañón del Infierno section (class V)!

RÍO AZUL Class II–III+: rapids inducing some adrenaline but not to the extent of the Futa. However, tours labelled 'Azul to Puente/Macal' begin in the Río Azul in order to enter the Futa at the Terminator section (class V or V+), not to be taken lightly.

relatively nondescript part of Argentina far from the Ruta 40, and apparently has little to offer tourists. Dig a little deeper and this is a wonderful place to explore, with or without a car thanks to surprisingly good local bus services. Trekking and fishing are particular highlights, combined with some decent food and a very laid-back vibe.

The rodeo is taken extremely seriously in Palena. The town, correctly named Alto Palena, maintains a strongly Argentine feel, and the gaucho culture more typically found on the east of the Andes is dominant here, at least in part due to the historic confusion over the precise border. The rodeo stadium seems disproportionately large for such a small, sleepy town, and the Rodeo de Palena, held over the last weekend of January, is a spectacle to be seen by anyone remotely interested in horses. Palena attracts fewer tourists than neighbouring Futaleufú, and its border is less frequently traversed. Agriculture and animal husbandry are the main economic activities of the region, although tourism is growing. It is the southernmost town in the X Region (Los Lagos) and has a population of 1,800.

Palena was originally inhabited by Tehuelche Indians and was named by Nicolás Mascardi, a Jesuit explorer. It was founded in 1929, the same year as Futaleufú. The main attraction is the hike/horse ride south to connect with the Sendero de Chile (see box, page 158) to Lago Verde and on to La Tapera, and good fishing.

GETTING THERE
About the route
Puerto Ramírez to Palena (43km; 1hr; gravel) Palena is situated 10km (paved) west of the Paso Río Encuentro (Argentine border; ⊕ 08.00–20.00 high season, 08.00–19.00 low season), and 43km southeast of Puerto Ramírez. From Puerto Ramírez it is either 30km west to the Carretera Austral, or 48km northwest to Futaleufú. The road quality from Puerto Ramírez to Palena fluctuates violently, from pleasant gravel to rough, loose gravel, often with corrugation. At times the road is two lanes wide, at others a single track. There are also some major ascents and descents, which must make this one of the most challenging sections for cyclists, with descents as difficult as ascents given the corrugations and blind corners. The road is also home to a number of cows and dogs, so additional care is required.

By bus
Buses Becker (67 223 2167, 65 273 1429; w busesbecker.com) Offers a twice-weekly bus between Chaitén & Coyhaique, but this is complicated to arrange as it is a combination service with another company (page 125).

Buses Expresos Patagonia (9 9871 3646) Has 2 buses per day to Chaitén (06.00 & 11.00, return noon & 17.00). They go to El Diablo (08.00 & 16.00 Tue & Fri, return 10.30 & 17.30), & to Valle

California (08.00 & 16.00 Mon & Thu, return 09.30 & 17.30).

Buses Río Palena (65 274 1319, 9 8822 1150) Runs buses to Futaleufú (08.00 Mon & Fri, return 13.30, & 2 buses 05.30 & 13.30 Wed, return 08.30 & 16.30). They go to El Tranquilo (08.30 Mon, return 11.00, & 11.00 Wed & Fri, return 13.30). The bus to Puerto Montt (06.00 Wed & Sun, return 06.00 Tue & Fri) is temporarily suspended until the Argentine border reopens.

WHERE TO STAY AND EAT
Hostal Torres Castaño (7 rooms, 2 cabins) Pedro Montt 820; 9 7499 1796; e claluzcarde@gmail.com. A more modern offering for accommodation a mere 100m from the central plaza. Large, simple but stylish rooms & a small communal b/fast area, shared & private

bathrooms. $32,000 per couple with self-service b/fast (inc). Wi-Fi & laundry. Cash only, no cards. **$$$**

Residencial El Paso (12 rooms) Pudeto 661; 65 274 1226; e frutospalena@gmail. com. This building burned down in 2011 & took

The Paso Río Encuentro at Palena has an unusual history, as possibly one of the most hotly contested borders in the area. The Chileans and Argentines have squabbled over the precise border for centuries. In 1893 both countries agreed to determine the line of the border according to an apparently simple geographic principle: Argentina would 'hold in perpetuity all territory to the east of the line of the highest peaks which divide the waters while Chile was to hold in perpetuity all territory to the west of that line'. As sensible as this might sound, the ridge connecting the highest peaks does not always coincide with the water divide line, thus opening up the potential for continued bickering. The King of the United Kingdom was to arbitrate in the case of disputes, and in 1902 formally declared the lie of the border. However, the demarcation posts were placed too far apart, in particular around Palena. Residents of both countries began entering this nebulous no-man's-land for agriculture and grazing, and eventually agreed to resubmit the case to the Queen rather than risk an all-out war over such an obscure plot of land. And so in 1966 the border was redefined, with 21 intermediate posts designed to avoid any subsequent dispute. 'The boundary shall cross the Palena to the mouth of the River Encuentro.'

Another border dispute was eventually settled in 1994, awarding the Laguna del Desierto to Argentina. Travelling from Villa O'Higgins to El Chaltén in Argentina requires a boat trip across this lake – now the newest official region of Argentine territory. To this day a border section within the southern Patagonian ice field of some 80km remains undefined. In 2006 Argentine president Néstor Kirchner invited Chile's president Michelle Bachelet to define the border, but the Chileans declined. However, perhaps the greatest source of border tension lies not on the South American continent at all, but rather in Antarctica. The claims of Argentina, Chile and the UK overlap almost entirely, and such claims are of the utmost strategic importance, as the region encompasses the entire Antarctic Peninsula, the main access point to the frozen continent.

2 years to rebuild. Pleasant rooms, 6 with private bathroom. Also has a restaurant, with a focus on fish & lamb. Wi-Fi & laundry, cash only. $$$

🏠 **Hospedaje Horzas** (6 rooms) Pedro Montt 1024; 📞65 274 1380; e horzas_palena@ hotmail.com; ⏲ Dec–May. New option in town for reasonable prices. Wi-Fi available. Also has a restaurant. $

✘ **Dulce Patagonia** PedroMontt 828; ///renovating.flaming.drank; 📞9 7655 5634; e dulcepatagonia.palena@gmail.com; ⏲ 09.30–13.00 & 15.00–20.00 Mon–Fri. Café & bakery serving traditional kuchen, sandwiches, cakes, tea, coffee, hot chocolate. Accepts cards. $$

✳ ✘ **La Rosadita Restotur** Luis Risopatrón 621; ///harness.shopkeepers.paraded; 📞9 8380 6526, 9 6295 5200; e francoguia005@hotmail. com; ⏲ 08.30–14.00 & 18.00–22.00 Mon–Sat.

This highly recommended one-stop shop is very conveniently located on the main road entering the village from the south, by the plaza. An excellent restaurant serving sandwiches & some of the best pizzas found anywhere along the Carretera (competing with El Pueblo Pide Pizza in Futa), as well as mouth-watering waffles with fresh fruits doused in chocolate or dulce de leche. Local ingredients used where possible, & stocks the local ale – Moro de Palena. An extremely popular restaurant, so it's wise to reserve in high season. Also 2 rooms available for rent ($24,000 for 1 person, $34,000 for 2; private bathroom; $$$). The Argentine owner, Franco, is a well-known fishing guide, with boats & equipment, who offers tours in the region, including to some remote locations that few know of. Wi-Fi available & English spoken. Accepts cards. $$

OTHER PRACTICALITIES There is a petrol station (///backlogs.brace.friendship) one block south of the plaza and an ATM (///explode.afar.coupon) on the northwestern corner of the plaza.

Mechanic

Gemma Taller Mecanico Hurtado de Mendoza 860; ☎ 9 6230 3558; e jmovando@hotmail.com. Offers basic repairs, fixes punctures, has a scanner, can do oil changes, etc. Basically the only option in town, just beyond the COPEC petrol station.

SIGHTSEEING AND EXCURSIONS While Palena can't be described as a 'must-see' of the Carretera Austral, there are endless **horse-related activities** for those with equine interests. **Kayaking** is also an option on the Río Palena although enthusiasts are better advised to get their fix in Futaleufú. Palena is the access point to the **Sendero de Chile** (see box, page 158) with excellent **horseriding and trekking trails** traversing mountains and lakes to Lago Verde and then on to La Tapera.

Hiking and trekking The valleys around Palena are well worth exploring. Tourism in this region is undeveloped, there are no formal trekking outfitters, and the best way to find a guide is by asking around the village. These trails are not well maintained and particularly those that venture beyond El Tranquilo, or south of El Azul, are only recommended for competent hikers with adequate equipment, and ideally with a guide. Websites such as w wikiloc.com or w wikiexplora.com provide more detailed maps and GPS waypoints, but locals have the most up-to-date information. Although not technically difficult, these are little-used trails far off the beaten track. However, even the gravel roads that connect the villages within the valleys are barely used by vehicles and offer wonderful hikes through virgin forests. These can either be walked as loops, or with some mild planning can be hiked in one direction and then return to Palena via the sporadic public transport serving the valleys.

Valle California (8km on the paved road east towards the border followed by 5km south on gravel) This is probably the least interesting of the valleys, passing predominantly through farmland. The gravel road continues for 10km south of Valle California where a hiking trail connects with El Azul (and the Sendero de Chile), enabling a circuit.

El Azul Approximately 20km south of Palena on the way to Lago Palena, and the first part of the Sendero de Chile trail all the way to La Tapera (see box, page 158). Head south on W-969 (past the COPEC petrol station) and after 5km veer left (south) on W-971 for 9km until arriving at the trailhead to El Azul (4x4 access only) and towards **Lago Palena**.

El Tigre Accessible by road. Exit Palena as though going to El Azul, but do not veer south on W-971. Continuing beyond El Tigre is only possible in a light 4x4. It is possible to walk this section and continue all the way to El Tranquilo or take the small ferry (*balsa*) towards El Malito, which is on the main road between Palena and Puerto Ramírez and the Carretera Austral.

El Malito This is a small, fairly nondescript village 22km from Palena on the main road to Puerto Ramírez (and on towards the Carretera Austral or up to Futaleufú). There are some hot tubs by the Río Palena available to rent along this stretch of road at Tranquera Negra (☎ 9 6809 5638). At the eastern entrance to the village is a detour south (W-961) which heads 3km to the Río Palena and the balsa across the river. On the south side of the river it is possible to head east, along a treacherous stretch of road only suitable for 4x4s (or hiking) to El Tigre. However, the road heading west from the balsa towards **El Tranquilo** is marvellous. It runs parallel to the Río Palena, with some astonishing views over the river and valley, on reasonable gravel. There are occasional steep sections, and horses on the road, so caution is required. A small bridge crosses a tributary of the Río Palena which seems an incredible investment for so scarce a population. Some 17km after the balsa is the village of El Tranquilo. It appears there is only one family living here, who conveniently offer accommodation and food at **Hospedaje Buena Vista** (3 rooms, 2 beds each; ///rebuking.dodgy.woof) – a fantastic, authentic opportunity to experience the quintessential gaucho Patagonian life. It is almost impossible to make a reservation as Benedicto rarely leaves the village and there is no mobile-phone reception. Susana Fernández (◊ 9 7555 1824) may be able to make a reservation via radio, but this hospedaje is rarely full, and you can always camp freely anywhere in this region. There are endless trekking opportunities from this base, as well as horse rides.

Benedicto's neighbours, located 2km beyond his house at the end of the road (///compact.swiftest.poke), are Nicolas and Aurora. Their house, Los Alamos, is next to a small footbridge over the Río Tranquilo which connects to a trail along the south of the Río Palena to Lago Yungue (15km; 7hrs; medium). From the lake to the Carretera Austral is a 2hr, 7km hike parallel to the Carretera Austral but on the east side of the Río Palena. There is no need to cross the river as the Carretera crosses the river at El Carneraso, 20km north of La Junta. This trail is strategically interesting – an alternative means to connect the Carretera Austral with Palena.

One final detour in these valleys is worth mentioning. At the northern entrance to El Malito the main highway (235) towards Puerto Ramírez heads northeast. There is a gravel track to the left (west, the W-957 signposted to **El Diablo**) that continues through virgin forest towards El Diablo (no population as far as we could discern), and then buckles south for a further 14km. The road deteriorates in quality and we were unable to reach the end of the road, but en route are two spectacular lakes: Golondrina and Negra. It is possible to camp at Golondrina, which is a known fishing destination. At the end of this road (or where your car can no longer pass) it is possible to trek along the north shore of the Río Palena and arrive at La Vanguardia on the Carretera Austral. It is possible to do this trek without river crossings, as there is a bridge just south of La Vanguardia across the Río Palena.

Trail guides The two key routes from Palena are the multi-day trek to Lago Palena and on to Lago Verde and La Tapera; and from El Tranquilo or El Diablo to the Carretera Austral. Both of these treks are stunning, but also of strategic importance, particularly to those without private transport: it is possible to continue along the Carretera Austral via some of the most stunning and remote treks without using public transport or even a road. Experienced hikers can do both these trails unguided, but a guide not only improves safety and reduces the chances of getting lost, but can also provide horses, and most importantly, enable visitors to understand the history, flora and fauna of the region.

It is difficult to communicate with people in the region, as most of this area is not covered by the mobile-phone providers. The guides listed here *might* be able to provide more information or guide the routes. You may be able to find other informal guides in El Tranquilo, El Diablo, El Malito and Valle California.

Arturo Cassanova El Azul; ✎ 9 8186 4942, 9 7647 5025; e rincondelanieve@gmail.com; 🅕 Rincón De La Nieve Turismo Rural Palena. Provides agro-tourism in the El Azul sector & can arrange horses for the last hour of the journey to reach his house for those without a 4x4. Accommodation for up to 5 people, or camping with bathrooms & hot water, in a homestay on a functioning farm, milking cows, making cheese & exploring the region on horseback. He has a short trek to the Escondido waterfalls on the property. Food available, including traditional *cordero al palo*. Can also do the trek/horse ride to Valle California, but Arturo does not go further south towards Lago Palena.

Franco Duarte ✎ 9 6295 5200; e francoguia005@hotmail.com. Fishing guide who runs the excellent La Rosadita restaurant & cabins. Very knowledgeable of the area but does not guide treks.

Mauricio Gracia Palena; ✎ 9 7604 4002. Fishing guide with inflatable boats offering trips to Río Palena & Laguna Golondrina. Can also guide the trek from Palena to Lago Palena, but not onwards to Lago Verde.

Jorge Parker Palena/El Azul; ✎ 9 9322 9903; e reservalagopalena@gmail.com. Veteran explorer, with the CONAF concession to manage cabins on Lago Palena, but at the time of going to print these were still being repaired. An accomplished guide

SENDERO DE CHILE   (w senderodechile.cl)

This was an ambitious plan to create the longest trek in the world: 8,500km of trails connecting the entirety of Chile, from the Atacama Desert to the remote regions of Tierra del Fuego/Magallanes. Within this area, the full trail spans from Lago Palena to Lago Verde (55km; 4 days one-way), with an onward trail to La Tapera (page 197); there's also a section of the *sendero* in Cerro Castillo (page 250). As it is not yet a tourist attraction in its own right, organised tours along the route are not readily available, so treks must be arranged ad hoc in La Tapera, Lago Verde or Palena. Camping is possible along most of the route, and there are occasional refuges; it is wise to go on horseback and with a guide. Maps are available locally, or GPS waypoints can be downloaded from most trekking websites. There are no permits or fees, but do visit the tourist information centre (on the plaza) or CONAF in advance to advise who is going, and to request permission to stay at the refuge at the end of day one.

The original name for this part of the Sendero de Chile is 'La Huella de los Troperos' (literally 'footprint of the cattle ranchers'), and the journey falls into four sections. The first (5km) departs from Lago Palena, and is the most challenging section, ideally done with horses, or with light rucksacks. It ends at the Sánchez Pobre refuge, where there are places to camp. The second leg (15km) is an easy walk to the shore of Lago Quinto where it is also possible to camp. The third leg (15km) is slightly more strenuous due to steep inclines, with mud and branches slowing travel by horse, ending at the Río Quinto refuge. The final stretch is an easy hike (20km) to Lago Verde along the Río Quinto. The entire trail is clearly marked with 35 guideposts. It passes glaciers and mountains (some of which are un-named), crosses rivers, carves through virgin forest, skirts around pristine lakes, and is a good opportunity to see pumas and condors among other animals, and countless waterfalls. This is the most northern of the top four treks along the Carretera, the others being the four-day Cerro Castillo circuit (page 251), the four-day trek through Parque Patagonia (page 294), and the seven-day trek from Cochrane to Villa O'Higgins (page 319). Hikers would be well advised to do at least one of these.

with many years of experience in Torres del Paine, & knows the region very well. He can guide the Palena to Lago Verde route & on to La Tapera, as well as shorter treks in the region, eg: to Laguna Témpanos. **Hugo Rosas** El Tigre; 📞9 6232 6157. Independent guide born & raised in the region, offering various routes, including the trail to Lago Palena (trekking or on horseback), & on to Lago Verde (trekking only due to a landslide) & the trek from El Azul to Valle California. Most uniquely, he can guide the trail from El Tranquilo to the Carretera Austral along the southern shore of the Río Palena to Lago Yungue & south to the Carretera (trekking only), as well as the northern route from El Diablo to La Vanguardia along the northern shore of the Río Palena.

PUERTO RAMÍREZ

Heading back towards the Carretera Austral, this village is located 6km west of the junction to Villa Santa Lucía, and is usually skipped by most. Even the locals are surprised when someone stops, especially if not related to a flat tyre. However, those en route from Futaleufú or Palena may find this a useful stop, and westbound cyclists who can't make it all the way to Villa Santa Lucía 30km away may sleep here. There are a number of mostly unmarked trails in the region, opportunities to go fishing, a waterfall, and accommodation. Note that the village has terrible mobile-phone coverage.

For route details connecting Puerto Ramírez to Villa Santa Lucía, see page 145.

 WHERE TO STAY AND EAT

🏠 **Cabañas Cumbres Nevadas** (1 cabin, 2 rooms) ///craftily.versatile.toolbars; 📞65 224 1926, 9 7213 1877, 9 6133 8206; e cumbres. nevadas@hotmail.com. 1 decent equipped cabin for up to 5 people, with Wi-Fi, hot tub & quincho, $50,000/day regardless of number of guests. Close to Lago Yelcho, offering full-day fly-fishing trips on the Futaleufú & Palena rivers, Lago Yelcho & other lakes in the region, with food & accommodation for $260,000/2 people. **$$$**

🏠 **Hospedaje El Valle** (4 cabins, 2 apts) ///housekeeping.tutorial.proofed; 📞65 224 1925, 9 8395 3785; e adelinasaid@hotmail.com. The cabins (sleeping 2–6) are comfortable & well equipped with full kitchen, washing machine, sitting area, wooden bar, cable TV & Wi-Fi. $60,000/night regardless of number of people. Apts (2 people) are adequate but not up to the standard of the cabins. $35,000/night. Can also provide lunch/dinner, including roast lamb (with notice), & have a quincho. **$$**

🏠 **El Cruce** (6 rooms) ///dwell.livelihoods. bamboozled; 📞65 224 1931; e aliciajaramillosaid@ gmail.com. A little gloomy on the inside, but lovely building from the outside. The owner, Alicia, has lived here all her life. Dbl & trpl rooms, 2 with bathroom, 4 shared, b/fast included. Lunch/dinner available or guests can use the kitchen. Also camping with use of hot showers & bathrooms. Popular with backpackers & cyclists. **$**

LA JUNTA AND AROUND

Having joined the Carretera Austral at Villa Santa Lucía from Futaleufú/Palena, or arriving from the north, the paved road continues 68km southwards to La Junta. Although set within an impressive valley, the transport hub of La Junta is little more than a large **petrol station** (situated at the southern exit of the town, and boasting an ATM) and stopping-off point en route to other places. La Junta is at the confluence of two rivers (Figueroa/Rosselot and Palena), as well as two roads and, as such, much is made of the 'joining' concept (the Spanish verb *juntar* means to meet or join together), but do not forget that *junta* is also a name for the military dictatorship, although the town was named prior to Pinochet's arrival. La Junta boasts a rare monument to Pinochet revealing the favourable sentiment to the former dictator and is a good base from which to explore the area.

HISTORY The original name of La Junta was Medio Palena (Middle Palena), as it lies a little over halfway between Alto Palena (High Palena, the full name for the town now referred to simply as Palena) and Raúl Marín Balmaceda, which was originally called Bajo Palena (Low Palena). It is no coincidence that the Río Palena runs through all three towns. Throughout the 19th century La Junta was a strategic hub for those in the region wishing to bring animals for sale in Puerto Montt, using the ports of Raúl Marín Balmaceda or Puyuhuapi. The town was not formally founded until 1963, and opened its first school in 1970; Fernando Sotomayor was its first teacher. Father Ronchi (see box, opposite) also taught here. The logistical benefits of being situated at an important junction, the development of the Carretera Austral (connecting La Junta in 1986), and fertile agricultural and grazing land around the confluence of two rivers eventually established La Junta as the main hub in the region.

GETTING THERE
About the route
Villa Santa Lucía to La Junta (68km; 1hr; paved) The road from Villa Santa Lucía to La Junta is pleasant. There are lovely views of snow-capped mountains on both sides of the road and occasional views of the river, but there are no lakes along this section. Halfway along this stretch, just past La Vanguardia, is the border between Region X (Los Lagos) and Region XI (Aysén). The only decent accommodation and restaurant along this stretch is close to La Vanguardia – Funda Violeta (page 164) – of strategic interest to cyclists who may not make it to the next accommodation. The entire region to the west of this stretch of road is Parque Nacional Corcovado, without access points.

By bus La Junta is a transport hub, with buses to/from **Coyhaique** and **Chaitén** passing through here (page 125). Buses Entre Verdes (📞 9 9510 3196) has three services a week to **Cisnes** via Puyuhuapi (07.00 Mon, Wed & Fri, return 16.00). Terraustral (📞 67 234 6757, 9 8241 5526; has a daily service to Coyhaique (05.30 Mon–Sat, 07.00 Sun, return 15.00), and also to Chaitén (07.00 Mon, Wed & Fri, return 16.00). **Lago Verde** is hard to reach by public transport: Buses Entre Verdes go from Coyhaique to Lago Verde (15.00 Mon & Fri, 08.00 Tue, return 08.00 Wed & Thu, noon Sun). All these buses go via La Junta, although the precise time is nebulous. Otherwise hitchhiking is the only option. **Raúl Marín Balmaceda** is slightly easier to reach by public transport, Mauricio Pacheco (📞 9 9312 5244) goes from La Junta to Raúl Marín (08.00 Mon, Wed & Fri, return 15.00, 09.00 Sun & public holidays, return noon). A second service (with no formal name; 📞 9 9473 8219) departs from Coyhaique for Raúl Marín Balmaceda (via La Junta) (09.00 Tue & Fri, return 08.00 Wed & 10.00 Sun). Buses Entre Verdes also go three or four times a week from/to La Junta; see 🆚 buses.entreverdes for up-to-date times, and have one bus a week from Raúl Marín to Coyhaique (08.00 Sun, return 09.00 Fri).

TOUR OPERATORS
Entre Aguas Patagonia Carretera, in front of Espacio y Tiempo; ///slurs.inflecting.inflict; 📞 9 8438 8285; e entreaguaspatagonia@gmail. com; w entreaguaspatagonia.cl. Good rafting outfit for those skipping Futaleufú or seeking a slightly calmer river. Experienced guides know the area & visit regions usually only accessed from

upper-end fishing lodges. Their signature trip is 4 days rafting/kayaking down the Río Palena from Lago Rosselot to Raúl Marín Balmaceda. Also trips on the rivers Figueroa, Quinto or Rosselot (class III–III+ rapids), for 4–14 people, with safety raft, & all transport & snacks included. Children must be over 14 (Río Palena also possible with younger children). Fishing on lakes & rivers in the area, for trout & chinook among others, is also offered, with kit provided.

Yagan Expeditions 5 de abril 350; ///unofficial. photographic.erasable; 67 231 4352, 9 6697 6138; e info@yaganexpeditions.com; . The premier operator in town, run by knowledgeable Bruno who has lived in La Junta since the late 1990s. A range of tours on offer, including rafting on the Río Figueroa for the more adventurous, or kayaking on Lago Rosselot or the Río Palena for those seeking a more relaxed afternoon. Also horseback rides from Lago Claro Solar towards the Sendero de Chile (full day), trips to the El Sauce hot springs, & to Puyuhuapi & the Ventisquero Queulat, & fishing on the Rosselot River/lake or Río Palena.

THE LEGEND OF FATHER RONCHI

Father Ronchi, the self-proclaimed 'rascal priest', came from a small village in Italy in 1960 to remote Chilean Patagonia with the sole goal of transforming the region. Three decades of total devotion forever changed the destiny of more than 50 towns in the regions of Aysén and Chiloé with his influence extending the entire length of the Carretera Austral. He founded three new villages, created an extensive network of radio and television stations, built dozens of chapels, schools, lodges, boats and workshops, and developed a number of projects that nowadays might well be described as 'social enterprises'. He had many loyal followers and friends within Aysén, but he also had critics. Many of his peers did not agree with his focus on the poorest and most isolated communities of the region, while others did not approve of his methods. For his life's work parliament granted him Chilean nationality. Today he is adored in all corners of southern Patagonia.

Ronchi was sent to Chile in 1960, to work in a shelter in the city of Rancagua with the Mother of the Divine Providence Mission. The following year he moved to the Shelter San Luis of Puerto Cisnes in the Region XI of Chile – his official arrival in Patagonia. In addition to his pastoral services he proactively worked closely with several local authorities and businesses to encourage them to help the local inhabitants progress in their spiritual, personal, social and economic development. In 1967 he moved back to Rancagua to become the local parish priest but lasted only five years until he was sent back to his beloved Puerto Cisnes. He worked in the Parish of Nuestra Señora del Trabajo (Our Lady of Work) and for more than 20 years he worked predominantly in the most remote towns in the region. Many such villages had neither roads nor communications and were surrounded by dense forests, mountains and fjords. Thus one of Ronchi's first accomplishments was to install FM radio antennas and television transmitters. Such was the impact of connecting such villages to the outside world that to this day the FM transmitter remains a Historic Monument and is marked on maps. Ronchi established various social projects with food supplies he managed to get from the Catholic Church in Europe. He built chapels and lodges, workshops for handicrafts, boats, small docks and infrastructure necessary to develop the local community. He did all this inspired by the belief that God wanted the people to lead dignified lives and for them to be happy.

Father Ronchi died on 17 December 1997 in Santiago, aged 67. He was buried in the cemetery of Puerto Aysén. Today he has a foundation named after him, the Fundacion Obra Padre Antonio Ronchi (Foundation for the Works of Father Antonio Ronchi) that seeks to keep his legacy alive and continue the works that he started.

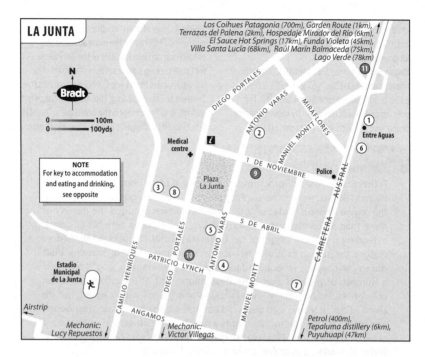

They can organise tailor-made expeditions across the Futaleufú–Palena–Lago Verde–Puyuhuapi region, & arrange the full 4-day kayak trip from Palena to Raúl Marín Balmaceda, run once a year (Feb) for around 200 kayakers & rafters. They have their own transport for tours in Raúl Marín Balmaceda accordingly, including visits to the penguin & sea lion colonies. They also provide accommodation (page 164).

 WHERE TO STAY *Map, above*

🏠 Alto Melimoyu Bed & Breakfast
(11 rooms) Carretera Austral, km375; ///infinite. fidelity.kites; 📞 67 231 4320, 9 9930 6483; e info@ altomelimoyu.cl; w altomelimoyu.cl. Along the Carretera Austral, just south of the northern entrance to the town. The building is constructed entirely from wood. Sgl, dbl or twin rooms, a little overpriced, but the beds are top quality, all rooms have cable TV, & there is central heating, laundry service, Wi-Fi & off-road parking. Can also arrange bicycle tours, treks & kayak rental, as well as trips to Raúl Marín Balmaceda for those without private transport. Credit cards accepted. **$$$$**

✳ 🏠 Hotel Espacio y Tiempo (9 rooms, 1 chalet) Carretera Austral 399; ///milkmaid. craved.timely; 📞 67 231 4141, 9 9222 9220; e info@espacioytiempo.cl; w espacioytiempo.cl. Probably the finest accommodation in town, with a very good restaurant (page 164) & a gorgeous manicured garden. All rooms with central heating,

cable TV, a safe, private bathrooms, wooden finish & garden views. Wi-Fi, laundry service & superb b/fast. Patios for outdoor eating, & large cosy communal seating areas with a roaring log fire & a bar. Chalet has 1 dbl, 2 sgl & 1 sofa bed, self-contained & set apart from the hotel it has a kitchen but b/fast is available in the restaurant (additional fee). While the hotel does not offer tours, they have all information & contacts. This is a positively pleasant hotel with a corresponding price tag, but worth the splurge if feeling like a treat. If accommodation breaks the budget, consider dining here. Accepts credit cards. **$$$$**

🏠 Los Coihues Patagonia (4 cabins) Southern side of bridge to north of village; ///firefighters.serves.dozes; 📞 9 8230 0380; e ealbertz@enalco.cl. Decent fully equipped cabins with terraces & space to park motorbikes out of the rain. A decent quincho with restaurant service, & extensive gardens to soak up the rays when it's not

LA JUNTA
For listings, see opposite

raining. Laundry available. Multi-talented owner Enrique is also a helicopter pilot, with a heliport on the plot, an accomplished cook & knows the region extremely well. Cards accepted. **$$$$**

Cabañas Mi Ruca (4 cabins) Libertad 220; ///thanksgiving.foldable.tiff; ✆ 9 8209 0455; e lisveth_hellriegel@hotmail.com. A good-value option with 4 new & tidy mid-range cabins in well-maintained grounds. Cabins are fully equipped, sleep 4 (1 dbl room & a 1 bunk-bed room), with cable TV & Wi-Fi. Kitchen/dining room with a cosy wood-fired heater. Laundry service provided. Secure parking on a quiet street. Credit cards accepted. **$$$**

El Colono Cabins (5 cabins) 5 de April, cnr Camillo Henriquez; ///impossibly.ratifies.blotting; ✆ 67 231 4166, 9 8502 2830; e elcolonoltda@ gmail.com; ⓕ DeptosElColono. These simple cabins (sleeping 2–5 people) with basic kitchen, wood-stove heating, cable TV, Wi-Fi & off-road parking are a great option, especially for families. Laundry & b/fast available (additional cost) & pet friendly. Lovely garden tucked away from the village, & small open-air quincho for barbecues. They know all the guides (Yagan is next door) so it's easy to arrange tours in the region & also sell local artisan products, marmalades, etc. Call ahead & they will spark up your stoves to ensure a toasty arrival. Cash only, can reserve without deposit but call a couple of days ahead to confirm. **$$$**

Hospedaje Tia Lety (7 rooms) Antonio Varas 596; ///thriving.elapses.inhabited; ✆ 9 7885 5822; e samogama@hotmail.com; ⏰ all year. A charming family-run hostel. All rooms share 2 bathrooms, & the ceiling in 2 of the upstairs rooms is a mere 1m from the floor – fine for kids, less so for adults wishing to sit up in bed. Towels provided, off-road parking, laundry & Wi-Fi. Guests cannot use the kitchen, but there is a superb b/fast with homemade jams & bread, local cheeses & scrambled eggs. Better value in low season. Legendary 'Aunt Lety' alas died in 2020 but her niece has taken over the business. **$$$**

Mi Casita de Té (4 apts) Carretera Austral, cnr Patricio Lynch; ///costing.traction.sneakily; ✆ 67 231 4206, 9 7802 0488; e elypaz.cortes@ gmail.com. Quality accommodation, although upper floors are a little cramped. Apts each 1 dbl & 2 sgl, with Wi-Fi, cable TV & central heating. Offers laundry but no kitchen. B/fast (inc) in restaurant of the same name next door (page 165). Off-road parking, excellent for bikers. Reservation advisable in high season, no deposit required but call a couple of days before to confirm or you will lose the room. Also has camping for 20 tents (6 covered sites) with hot water, Wi-Fi & bathrooms/shower included, b/fast not. **$$$**

Terrazas del Palena (3 cabins) Carretera Austral km345, La Junta; ///opposites.joyful. sandpit; ✆ 9 8549 3679; e terrazasdelpalena@ gmail.com; ⓕ; ⏰ all year. Fully equipped cabins 2km north of La Junta. Nicely furnished wooden cabins with excellent views, & big, comfy beds. Each cabin sleeps 4 (1 dbl bed & 2 sgls). Kitchen, cable TV, Wi-Fi, laundry, parking & wood-stove heating. Restaurant in the same building, so no trip to La Junta necessary for food. B/fast available ($5,000). Reservation & deposit required. **$$$**

Hospedaje Mirador del Río (2 cabins) 6km west of La Junta junction; ///admirals. guzzled.intake; ✆ 9 6177 6894; e contacto@ miradordelrio.cl; w miradordelrio.cl. Good option along the road to Raúl Marín Balmaceda, 11km before the El Sauce hot springs. Beautiful old wooden construction but, despite the name, the river view is from the large garden only. Well-equipped spacious cabins ($60,000 for up to 6 people) with fridge & Aga-style oven. Laundry available (for fee), Wi-Fi limited, solar energy for electricity, wood-stove heating but good hot water. Lunch & dinner available (extra cost). Good for families – there is a trail within the property to an unnamed lake (2hrs). Wise choice if wish to stay outside La Junta & intend to visit hot springs or Raúl Marín, as there are limited options along this stretch. Conveniently run by the family who operate Entre Aguas tour operator (page 160). Cash only. $$–$$$

🏠 **Hostería Valdera** (13 rooms) Antonio Varas; ///oppose.hilarious.mimed; 📞67 231 4105, 9 9123 8299; e hosteriavaldera@gmail. com. Sprawling hostel located ½ block south of the plaza with rooms of various capacities, both with or without private bathroom. Decent parking area, laundry, cable TV, Wi-Fi & basic b/fast (inc). $$–$$$

🏠 **Yagan Expeditions** (7 apts) 5 de abril 350; ///unofficial.photographic.erasable; 📞67 231 4352, 9 8459 9708; e info@yaganexpeditions. com; f. A good option, particularly if doing tours with Yagan – the main operator in La Junta (page 161). Decent apts (3 twin, 2 dbl, 2 trpl), all with quality beds, Wi-Fi, cable TV & private bathrooms are either 'standard' (slightly older, shared kitchen, wood-stove heating) or 'superior' (own kitchen, central heating). Laundry service available, & bed linen/towels provided. Nice garden by the standard cabins (if not filled with cars). $$–$$$

✳ 🏠 **Funda Violeta** (8 rooms) Valle Frío Carretera Austral, 23km south of Villa Santa Lucía just north of La Vanguardia, 45km north of La Junta; ///riddle.futures.slanders; 📞9 6463 4874; e violetavmonjes@gmail.com. There are few accommodation or food options along this stretch of the Carretera, & this is a pleasantly quirky surprise. On entering this rambling farmhouse, with its bull skulls at the entrance, one might be excused for mistaking the restaurant/hostel for the set of a western movie – this is no normal residence. The interior is tastefully decorated with a gaucho cowboy horse theme, complete with rustic rough sawn timber finish & log roof structure. The friendly & talkative hostess, Violeta, will ensure a pleasant stay, & speaks basic English. The simple accommodation has 4 dbls & 4 sgls all with shared bathroom. A decent b/fast (inc) with farm-cooked eggs, homemade jam & fresh baked bread, fruit juice & coffee. There is access to the Río Frío below the road for good trout fishing. Camping also possible for $7,000 pp with bathrooms. This doubles as a roadside café with a large deck & beautiful mountain views, offering basic meals ($$). Very popular location with cyclists. $$

✘ WHERE TO EAT AND DRINK   *Map, page 162*

✘ **Hotel Espacio y Tiempo** Carretera Austral 399; ///milkmaid.craved.timely; 📞67 231 4141, 9 9222 9220; e info@espacioytiempo. cl; w espacioytiempo.cl; 🕓 12.30–14.30 &19.00–21.30 Mon–Sat. A fine choice – excellent food, decent-sized dishes & good service. Range of local beers & wines, good salads & puddings. Cosy atmosphere with views out to the garden. Top choice in town. $$$$

✳ ✘ **La Junta Delivery** Northern entrance to village; ///gutsy.certificate.vaguest; 📞9 8131 9151; 🕓 11.00–22.00 daily. Awesome new restaurant run by Jonathan Hechenleitner from Raúl Marín, clearly benefiting from the great seafood dishes at his restaurant there (page 169). Slow food concept with strong Patagonian/German influence. Usual fare but also some surprisingly good meat options, sandwiches & burgers, pizzas, kuchen, & the true speciality of the house, a highlight of southern Chile but hard to find, is the puye. Do not leave the Carretera without trying these at least once! Vegan dishes, & chorrillanas/ pichangas (a veritable feast of various ingredients draped over a mass of chips, for 2, 4 or 6 people). Good wine list, & serves bottled Hopperdietzel, D'Olbek & Finisterra beer, as well as their own strong ales (pale, IPA, calafate & porter on tap). Decent cocktails including Tepaluma (see box, opposite) & flavoured Pisco sours. Lovely building, cosy fireplace for winter, outdoor area for summer evenings & table football. To top it all, Jonathan is a superb source of information on the region & speaks basic English. $$$

✘ **Terrazas del Palena** Carretera Austral km345, La Junta; ///opposites.joyful.sandpit; 📞9 8549 3679; e terrazasdelpalena@gmail. com; f terrazasdelpalena; 🕓 13.00–22.30 daily. Great view, simple menu: 3 starters, 3 main dishes (fish, meat & vegetarian), 3 homemade pizzas, plus some good puddings. Local ales & Tepaluma gin. Member of Austral Garden Route (see box, page 167). $$$

✘ **Barros Arana** Half a block east of the plaza; ///curves.tangy.soaped; 📞9 8189 8386; 🕓 09.00–

21.30 daily. Food options are fairly limited in La Junta, & even those that exist are often closed, so this place is a welcome addition to the culinary options. Gigantic sandwiches that can easily feed 2 adults, *salchipapas* for the kids (diced sausages on bed of French fries, not the healthiest option but goes down well). Also doubles as a small shop & sells beers, doughnuts, cakes, bread, chocolates & marmalades from the region, including nalca jam (hard to find). The main focus is take-away but there is 1 table to eat in. $$
✕ **Kofketun** Lynch 662; ///whichever.disputing. degradation; ☎ 9 9870 7802; ⊕ 13.00–midnight

daily. The name means 'eat bread' in the Mapuche language. This restobar serves bar food (sandwiches, pizzas, quesadillas, kebabs & tablas). Open late, providing the only nightlife in the town, & a great vibe when fills up. Hopperdietzel, D'Olbek & a local beer (Sendas) on tap. Surprising range of cocktails including some esoteric gin-based cocktails using Tepaluma gin from the village (see box below) & Pisco sours, often using local ingredients such as calafate & nalca. $$
✕ **Mi Casita de Té** Carretera Austral, cnr Patricio Lynch; ///costing.traction.sneakily; ☎ 67 231 4206, 9 7802 0488; e elypaz.cortes@gmail.com; ⊕ all

TEPALUMA – PATAGONIA IN A BOTTLE

///frill.sitter.fleshly; e contact@tepaluma.com; w tepaluma.com

Some 6km south of La Junta lies Tepaluma, one of the most southerly gin distilleries in the world, in what might appear at first glance to be an unusual location. After a decade dabbling in hobby distillation, it was cunning logic that led Englishman Mark Abernethy and his **Belgian-Chilean** wife Andrea Zavala to locate this extraordinary distillery precisely here. Look across the valley and at the glacial waters tumbling from the mountains that provide the main raw ingredient, sniff around in the forests for the various trees and berries that provide the distinct flavour and aroma of their gin, and one fact becomes patently obvious: this is not simply a gin made *in* Patagonia, but *by* Patagonia.

This is no novelty gin, rather a labour of love. The unusual aroma arises from the use of three local ingredients from the Austral forests. First, the tepa leaf (*Laureliopsis philippiana*) – snap a leaf in your fingers and the smell is aromatic but hard to define – there are elements of mint and lime, and yet something else lingers.

The 'luma' comes from the berries of two trees: *Amomyrtus luma* berries produce a citric edge, but might spark fear in the hearts of Chileans for the association with the extremely hard wood historically used to make police truncheons (colloquially referred to as *lumas* to this day); and *Luma apiculata* berries, which have been used medicinally for centuries by the Mapuche, and have a sweet spicy tang.

These various ingredients are placed in a traditional copper gin still (imported from Spain) producing batches of 500 litres, and up to four batches per month. The final product is a distinct and yet subtle London gin, unusual even to the gin connoisseur, and yet by no means overpowering. Bitters are not usually added, although Mark and Andrea use slightly more exotic tonics than those found on supermarket shelves. Labelled by hand, and with some slick marketing, Tepaluma is already being exported to Europe. Bottles are in high demand (usually stocked in Kofketun in La Junta, see above, and Mi Sur in Puyuhuapi, page 182), and it's a worthy tipple for visitors to take back home and savour. Guided tours of the distillery are possible by arrangement. Thoroughly recommended.

day. Popular with locals & travellers, this cosy restaurant comes highly recommended for the reasonable prices & local food, & is more than a tea & kuchen house. Serves b/fast, lunch & dinner. Personal service from the owner herself, who cooks up fresh home-cooked Chilean specialities such as stew or chicken. Nice salads & good espresso too. The best-value option in La Junta for a sit-down meal. Rotating dish of the day usually around $9,000. Accepts cards. $$

OTHER PRACTICALITIES There is a petrol station and an ATM in La Junta.

Mechanics

Lucy Repuestos Henriquez, cnr Esmeralda; ☎9 7557 3734; ◪; ◷ 09.00–13.00 & 15.00–20.00 Mon–Fri, 09.00–14.00 Sat. Sells tyres, vehicle accessories & batteries.
Victor Villegas mechanic Diego Portales, cnr Magallanes; ☎9 7660 6612; ◷ 09.00–13.00 &

15.00–20.00 Mon–Sat. Victor is about the only reliable option for car/motorbike/bicycle repairs in La Junta, although other places are available to repair tyres. He has limited parts, but can fix most basic problems one way or another. Prices are reasonable.

SIGHTSEEING AND EXCURSIONS La Junta is the key access point to the 12,725ha Reserva Nacional Lago Rosselot (w conaf.cl/parques/reserva-nacional-lago-rosselot). The Río Figueroa flows into Lago Rosselot, within the park, and the Río Rosselot flows from the lake towards the Pacific, joining the Río Palena west of La Junta. Besides the beautiful lake itself, surrounded by mountains, the national reserve provides ample fishing opportunities and has trails accessed from the La Junta entry point. It is possible to see the rivers and Volcán Melimoyu in the distance.

Some 18km north of La Junta is a small turning to the east towards **Lago Claro Solar**, with wildlife, fishing and trekking options. These trails eventually connect to the trails heading north up through the **Valle El Quinto**, ultimately forming part of the Sendero de Chile trail heading up to Palena (see box, page 158). Despite some maps suggesting otherwise, it is possible to drive around Lago Claro Solar and reach the road from Lago Verde to La Junta, some 15km east of the junction. This section is best done in a 4x4 or at least in a high-clearance vehicle – road quality is poor, there are exposed rocks and high ridges along the centre of the gravel road. It's also rarely transited.

La Ruta de Palena is a four-day organised descent of the Río Palena in late January, from La Junta to Raúl Marín Balmaceda by kayak or canoe. The first three days are spent on the river, camping en route to Raúl Marín. On the final day various events are arranged in Raúl Marín, including treks, and then return to La Junta on the fourth day. The event changes each year; for more information contact **Entre Aguas Patagonia** (page 160).

Parques las Bardas is a group of trails opposite Mi Casita de Té (page 163). The Sendero Queulat has three viewpoints across the valley; however, after the second of these the path is overgrown and impossible to pass. The Cueva Árbol Mapuche is a 10-minute walk from the entrance to the park. This cave was used by the Mapuche, although the exact reason why is unclear.

La Junta is the latest place to develop **climbing** routes, although not on the scale of Cochamó and the region to the north. Currently there are eight routes (10a–12c, 15m), aimed mainly at experienced climbers with their own kit, although kit can be scrounged locally. There are no formal guides in the village, but for more information ask in Mi Casita de Té, or Yagan.

Paul Coleman and Konomi Kikuchi (just north of the village; ///yearns. seminal.quacking; ☎9 3442 5514; e australgardenroute@gmail.com) give tours of their garden, as well as running vinegar and kimchi, sushi, and wool-spinning

THE AUSTRAL GARDEN ROUTE

The Austral Garden Route (📞 9 3442 5514; e australgardenroute@gmail.com; w australgardenroute.com) was founded by Paul Coleman and Konomi Kikuchi (see opposite) out of a common desire to grow their own food, protect the forests and preserve the traditional way of life. They decided to create a route that would offer this experience for visitors and locals alike. There are now ten members of the Austral Garden Route, stretching almost 300km along the Carretera, from Chana, a remote coastal village near Chaitén (page 125), to Villa Amengual. Fantastic workshops (such as distillation of essential oils, sourdough bread, permaculture gardening, vegan cooking, basket weaving and mushroom hunting) with no more than ten participants have been very well received by locals long starved by a lack of information on their culture and contact with the outside world. In addition, the route has garden and forest tours, accommodation and restaurants.

Accommodation on the route ranges from refugios and campsites in the forests surrounding Parque Nacional Queulat and on the banks of the Río Cisnes, to the three-star Terrazas del Palena hotel.

For the more adventurous, the Austral Garden Route offers a unique three-day tour, beginning with a river crossing on horseback, up the remote Quinto Valley into a densely forested wilderness, where the life of the pioneers who settled this region can be experienced during a farm stay.

To encourage local participation, all workshops and garden tours have been set at the reasonable price of $15,000 (reduced price for children).

workshops. They are the founders of the **Austral Garden Route** (see box, above), and are focused on educating tourists and locals alike on sustainable, self-sufficient life on the Carretera. They transformed a barren hillside into an organic farm and food forest, featured on Chilean TV, and soon had tourists climbing over their garden fence hoping for an insight into their lifestyle. By opening up to the public, they aim to generate a local economy based on products not destructive to the natural environment of Patagonia, and preserve local culture and the traditional way of life. All tours and workshops are $15,000, with English, Spanish and Japanese spoken.

The **La Junta Rodeo** takes place on the second weekend of February.

RAÚL MARÍN BALMACEDA – A DETOUR

If a visitor to the Carretera Austral has time for only one of the various detours off the main road, this is possibly the most interesting. Founded in 1889, Raúl Marín is the oldest inhabited place in the entire province of Aysén, in part for being an obvious access point for the early settlers from Chiloé. It is situated at the confluence of ocean, river and fjord, barely populated (under 500 inhabitants), and boasts spectacular wildlife and vistas. Accessible from La Junta (75km) via a short ferry ride, or by boat from Chiloé twice a week, and sandwiched between Volcán Melimoyu to the south and Parque Nacional Corcovado to the north, it is hard to find somewhere quite as remote as this even elsewhere along the Carretera Austral. With the possible exception of thriving nightlife, there is something for everyone in this small village – from birdwatching to sailing, sitting on sandy beaches to eating fine seafood, and from hot springs to kayak trips.

GETTING THERE
About the route
La Junta to Raúl Marín Balmaceda (75km; 2hrs inc boat crossing; gravel) This road was completed in 2009, some 120 years after its founding, and is truly spectacular, one of the highlights of the region. Depending on traffic, the short boat ride (⏰ 08.30–13.30 & 16.30–21.00 daily; free) across the Río Palena takes only 5 minutes, but the boat can take only six vehicles. This is where the jungle canopy to the north meets the forest canopy to the south. The initial section of the road is flat, easy gravel until the El Sauce hot springs (page 170). Thereafter the road becomes more treacherous and narrow, with occasional steep sections and tight curves. The river widens as the road approaches Raúl Marín, and is periodically visible in its turquoise splendour. Beware of oncoming vehicles, particularly trucks that often travel in the middle of the road at high speed. There are extended sections of loose gravel. The forest encroaches on the road at times, creating a tunnel effect. The few signposts that exist, invariably warning of dangerous curves ahead, are barely visible as the forest covers them. Huge nalca plants (oversized rhubarb) can be seen along the way. Towards Raúl Marín the road passes a swamp area. The final section after the boat crossing is increasingly sandy, so it is particularly difficult for cyclists and motorcyclists.

By bus See page 160 for details.

By ferry Raúl Marín Balmaceda is connected to Quellón on Chiloé by a twice-weekly service (page 60), and to Puerto Chacabuco (via intermediate villages) to the south also twice a week. To book tickets in Raúl Marín Balmaceda speak to Vanessa Hechenleitner at Hostería Isla del Palena (📞 9 7528 8448; e agencianavierarmb@gmail.com; see opposite), or ideally book tickets as far in advance as possible at any Naviera Austral office.

TOUR OPERATORS
Chungungo Expediciones Av Costanera; ///freely.strums.roadshow; 📞 9 9999 2797; e luis_bohle@hotmail.com. Born & bred on the island, Luis is the grandson of one of the first pioneers to inhabit Raúl Marín & has a wealth of information regarding the history & politics of the region. He offers tours to the Las Hermanas islands & the Pitipalena Estuary, & does special trips upon request to more remote locations: Anihue (private), Tic Toc, Santo Domingo, Melimoyu, etc. He has 2 8-person boats, partially covered to protect from the elements. Although not a formal fishing guide, he can provide transport for fishing trips & has single & double kayaks for rent or for guided trips in the fjord.
Turismo del Palena Las Hermanas; ///news. against.soundman; 📞 9 6608 9536/7. In addition to a decent hostel, small shop, marmalade business

& a fine restaurant (see opposite), this family business is also a tour operator. They can arrange any tour in the region including kayaking to the lesser-known hot springs on Fiordo Pitipalena or up the estuary. English-speaking Jonathan's evening boat trips to the Las Hermanas islands are divine, a highlight of the region, & he knows the behaviour of the numerous animals so well, it's a surprise he hasn't named them all. His boat is ideal for the trip, accommodating 10 people but with a covered section in case of rain. He has useful knowledge & contacts & can arrange or advise on almost any conceivable tour in Raúl Marín. The fact that his family also run the best hostel & restaurant in the village & they are the authorised Naviera Austral agent truly makes this a one-stop shop, all at reasonable prices.

WHERE TO STAY AND EAT
Fundo Los Leones (4 cabins) 1km before Raúl Marín Balmaceda; ///delivering.spits.exactly; 📞 9 3257 1145/6; e info@fundolosleones.com; w fundolosleones.com. A truly unique destination,

in an old organic farm previously owned by Doug Tompkins, & the new owners still retain a strong conservation objective. It is located shortly before the entrance to Raúl Marín from La Junta (at km72), & the landing strip is at the northern end of the property. Outside the village & far from the road, the only sounds are the water lapping the shore, birds & the occasional boat pottering past. The property has direct access to an extensive beach, where sea lions & dolphins can be seen, as well as abundant bird species – lovely for an evening stroll or a morning swim. The cabins vary in size & décor, all with private bathroom, decent furniture, comfortable beds, full b/fast included, & a deck (with seats) overlooking the Fiordo Pitipalena & mountains. There is a lovely quincho. Wi-Fi is available only in the main house, but this is a place to unwind, boxed-in by nature. Prices vary depending on the number of visitors, from approx US$150 for a sgl to US$250 for a trpl (less in low season). Lunch or dinner can be arranged, consisting of principally organic food sourced locally (vegetables, steak, fish & lamb). They can arrange tours in the region, particularly for fishing, & kayaks & stand-ups are available for exploring the fjord. An excellent, if not the only upper-end choice in the village. **$$$$$**

🏠 **Melimoyu Lodge** (4 rooms) Halfway between La Junta & Raúl Marín Balmaceda; ///interpreted.triumphant.change; ☎ 9 3392 6956; e contact@melimoyulodge.com; w melimoyulodge.com; ◷ Nov–Apr. Sumptuous boutique lodge with unique views towards the Melimoyu volcano. Popular region for fishing, with resident guides available, but also offer birdwatching, horseriding, mountain-bike & trekking trips in the immediate vicinity (which is at the edge of Melimoyu National Park), & kayaking on the Palena River. Also arrange trips to Queulat & Raúl Marín to see the glaciers & wildlife, & helifishing to reach the remotest of locations & fly over the Melimoyu volcano or the glaciers. Offers massages & a hot tub. Private hot springs are a short boat trip away, & there is a superb restaurant (including an obligatory roast lamb in one of the finest quinchos in southern

Chile). All-inclusive packages (all activities, food, premium open bar, airport pickup/drop-off, fishing lessons for the uninitiated) start at about US$1,640 for a couple per night, or US$5,800 for the entire lodge. Considering the activities & all food & fine wines included, as well as the sheer quality of this superb lodge, this is good value for money. A trip to the Carretera is incomplete without the Raúl Marín Balmaceda detour – what better way to explore the area than from such an exquisite base? **$$$$$**

🏠 **Hostería Isla del Palena** (5 rooms, 4 cabins) Las Hermanas; ///news.against.soundman; ☎ 9 6608 9536; e isladelpalena@gmail.com. Surprisingly good accommodation for such a remote village. All rooms with private bathroom, cosy wooden effect, heating & hot water. The friendly owners seem to know everything & everyone in the village, run a shop across from the hotel & can arrange most tours. Laundry available, Wi-Fi. Credit cards accepted. The superb restaurant Isla del Palena ✳ (beneath the hostería; ◷ lunch & dinner; **$$$**) is the best place to eat in town; lively atmosphere, doubles as a bar in the evening. Excellent seafood, reasonable selection of wines & some local ales. Serves an excellent puye dish & occasionally has crab or king crab. Family business, with a mini-library of fascinating books about the village & further afield, all centred around a novel wood stove made out of 2 truck wheels, radiating warmth in the winter. **$$**

🏠 **Residencial y Cabañas El Viajero** (7 rooms, 5 cabins) Av Costanera; ///restarts. gloriously.buns; ☎ 9 6608 4858, 9 8420 6181; e mauriciokleinrmb@hotmail.com. Reasonable rooms, b/fast included, shared bathroom. Fully equipped cabins for 4–6 people. Wi-Fi in hostel & 1 cabin, & laundry. **$$**

✕ **Restaurant El Faro** Las Hermanas; ///poetic.wafers.remand; ☎ 9 7600 2860. Local, simple dishes, plenty of seafood, in what appears to be the main sitting room of someone's house. No alcohol available – only tap water when we visited. Pleasant enough. Also has 7 rooms (3 sgl, 4 dbl; **$$**), with laundry but no Wi-Fi, $25,000/couple. **$$**

OTHER PRACTICALITIES There is no petrol station, garage or laundry in Raúl Marín, so fill up in La Junta and take clean clothes. There is an ATM. The **tourist information office** is on the central plaza (☎ 9 7963 6241; e informacionturistica.raulmarin@gmail.com).

SIGHTSEEING AND EXCURSIONS

El Sauce hot springs (///fattens.rooks.drainage; ☏ 9 9454 2711; e alejvc@
hotmail.com; ⊕ Dec–Feb/Mar 09.30–20.00; $10,000/8,000 adult/child) Hot
springs of varying quality litter the Carretera Austral, but El Sauce, some 17km
from La Junta on the road to Raúl Marín, is one of the finest and cheapest. Run
by Claudio Berger, the springs are lovingly maintained in lush vegetation, and
there is one large communal pool and two smaller private pools. The water
emerges from the spring at 84°C and is mixed with cold water from the river to
reach 40°C. Claudio can arrange private transport, or visitors can combine with
the bus to/from Raúl Marín, but this requires walking 3km to/from the main
road. There's no food available, but the property has a lovely garden ideal for
picnics. Electricity is generated by solar panels, and tepid showers are available.
Claudio also offers local fishing excursions; call ahead to ensure the water level
is high enough.

Other hot springs are found at the estuary of the Río Rodriguez, upstream of the
Fiordo Pitipalena, accessible only by boat from Raúl Marín Balmaceda.

Wildlife watching The village is technically an island, with the sea to the west
(the Golfo Corcovado and Bahía Añihue), the estuary of the Río Palena to the
southwest, and the Fiordo Pitipalena to the east. As a result of this confluence
of water, and a lack of major human interference, marine life flourishes. Whales,
otters, penguins, sea lions, pelicans, cormorants, oystercatchers, geese, austral
gulls, vultures and dolphins are frequently observed. It is possible to see the rare
Magellanic flightless steamer duck on the islands, a duck of such great proportion
that its wings no longer serve for aviation and are used merely as paddles. The Las
Hermanas islands (30mins by boat from Raúl Marín) have permanent sea lion and
penguin colonies – every hotel and restaurant in the village can arrange a boat trip
here. Trips further out to sea to spot whales, or to visit Tic Toc (access to Parque
Nacional Corcovado) have to be arranged especially and prices depend mostly on
distance and the interest of the fisherman himself in visiting that area. The Golfo
Corcovado is one of the best places in the entire southern hemisphere to observe
blue whales, but the national park is not readily accessible (page 139).

Trekking For a leisurely stroll, the **Sendero Chucao** trailhead is at the northern
end of the village, a short trail that takes approximately 20 minutes through a
small but dense forest of ferns, coigües and old man's beard, up to the sand dunes
facing the open sea. From here walk down the sand dunes and head around the
sandy peninsula back to town. Check if it is possible to reach the beach, as often
the undergrowth is very dense. The slightly longer but equally easy **Sendero Los
Arrayanes** (3hrs) begins at the entrance to the town just past the landing strip
(///coffeepot.superiors.suave). It circumnavigates the north of the island with
several viewing platforms. At the fifth marker, descend to the beach, and walk the
last half of the route along white sand.

LAGO VERDE – A DETOUR

A frontier town without a frontier. Alas, the Argentine side of the border has not
been completed, and while in theory it is possible (and permitted) to cross the
border, the absence of a critical bridge across the Río Pico makes this a treacherous
crossing. Generally the water level of the Río Pico is low enough to cross safely
only a few days per year so, in all likelihood, this is a 160km spectacular round-trip

drive beginning and ending in La Junta. Those intrigued by isolated communities perched in the middle of nowhere will find it interesting, but make sure the fuel tank is full and the spare tyre is inflated before departing.

The region was originally inhabited by Tehuelche Indians, and the first known permanent inhabitants were the family of Don Antonio Solís Martínez, of Chile. Owing to the proximity to Argentina, and the lack of a road connection (the road connecting Lago Verde to the Carretera Austral was completed in 1992), many of the subsequent immigrants were from Argentina. Indeed, the village was entirely dependent on Argentina until the landing strip was constructed in 1945. Although founded in 1936, this village didn't have its own municipality until 1979.

Given the lack of through traffic, to describe Lago Verde with its population of just 900 souls as 'sleepy' risks understatement. There is minimal tourist infrastructure, very poor mobile-phone coverage and almost no services. Consequently, it is easier to arrive in the village and go straight to the de facto tourist information centre at El Mirador (page 172) rather than attempt to arrange trips in advance. Many residents have no telephone.

The main highlights, beyond the journey itself, are centred on **trekking and horseriding**: a stroll down to the spectacular lake takes just 30 minutes from the centre of the village and there's a short trek to see local **cave paintings** (4hrs; 12km). Horseriding opportunities range from a few hours to over a week. **Boat trips** and **fishing** around the lake are also options.

GETTING THERE
About the route
La Junta to Lago Verde (78km; 2hrs; gravel) As with the Raúl Marín Balmaceda detour, this is one of the most beautiful roads of the region. It is initially flat, passing the northern edge of Lago Rosselot. Shortly after, the road enters a valley which increasingly narrows to a gorge, winding alongside the Río Figueroa. The road is single track and barely visited, but take care of oncoming vehicles and do not stop on curves however tempting the photo opportunity might be. There are steep inclines, hairpin bends and loose gravel, with sheer drops down to the river. Approaching Lago Verde the road emerges from the gorge on to a plain, with a final section of straight road that ends in the village of Lago Verde. Before this connecting road was constructed in 1992, the route took up to a fortnight to traverse. Note the border is not passable for most vehicles most of the year.

EDUARDO SIMON

A person of great influence in the village of Lago Verde was Eduardo Simon, a young Frenchman who arrived here in 1950 and bought substantial lands which formed the Estancia Cacique Blanco. He developed the region quickly, installing drinking water and electricity, and perhaps most heroically, he bought an airplane from the USA which finally connected Lago Verde to Coyhaique. The plane was used for the *estancia*, but also to transport pregnant women and people with medical emergencies to Coyhaique. He also used the plane to take children to (boarding) schools in the nearby towns, avoiding the need to make a substantial trek. He originally served in the French army as a parachutist in occupied France, and in 2011 was awarded Chilean nationality for his services to the country. He died in 2016 aged 93.

By bus It's possible, albeit difficult, to reach Lago Verde by bus – see page 160 for details.

TOUR GUIDES Estepa Expediciones (✆ 9 5744 5784, 9 9358 5528; e claudiosotosolis83@gmail.com) Claudio Soto is probably the most easily contacted guide in the region. He offers the southern Sendero de Chile tour to La Tapera (see box, page 158), as well as fishing and trekking trips, but also knows all the other guides in the village. He can advise on the northern route to Palena, but does not offer it as a standard tour. There are **horseback** guides, two guides offering **lake tours**, and two guides offering **trekking** and **fishing** trips. Claudio or Herman (see below) can arrange these, possibly with the assistance of a VHF radio. Claudio and Browlio Barriga (✆ 9 6901 4490) have boats on Lago Verde for fishing or for tours around the lake.

🏠 **WHERE TO STAY AND EAT** There are relatively few places to stay in Lago Verde, two of which house the only restaurants in the village. There's also an option across the lake.

🏠 **Cabañas Entre Coihues** (2 cabins) 5mins' walk from town towards lake; ✆ 9 9415 2216; e yauff1972@hotmail.com; 🇫 . 2 fully equipped 4-person cabins just outside the village for those wishing to escape the hustle & bustle of Lago Verde. Fairly simple, with wood-stove heating, gas oven & hot water. **$$**

🏠 **Residencial Nina** (12 rooms) Trapananda 214; ///newscasts.solely.dinky; ✆ 9 8900 5120; ⏱ all year. Dbls & sgls with & without private bathrooms. Central heating, hot water, use of washing machine, parking, (sketchy) Wi-Fi, & food available (**$$**). Located in the village, so more convenient for those without transport. **$$**

🏠 **Hostal El Mirador** (7 rooms, 1 cabin, camping) Camino a la Frontera; ///narrowest. stargazing.denial; ✆ 9 8476 9191, 9 7383 1473; e hostalelmirador@yahoo.com; ⏱ all year. Located 200m past the Chilean border post, up the hill. If you are stopped by the border police

clarify your intention to go to the hostel rather than into Argentina. 1 dbl & 6 sgls, shared bathroom, Wi-Fi, laundry & full b/fast included. Basic English spoken. The restaurant has simple meals available (**$$**). The cabin is suitable for up to 4 people ($40,000). Camping has 4 covered sites, as well as various exposed sites & a quincho, with electricity & bathrooms with cold showers ($4,000 pp). Herman is the de facto tour operator of the village & can arrange tours, fishing trips & kayaking. Great views. **$-$$**

🏠 **Lafkentrayenko** Reached by crossing Lago Verde, 1hr, book directly; ✆ 9 5695 8218 WhatsApp; e Leamagda.3@hotmail.cl, or via Claudio (see above). A family-run business with cabins available to rent, utterly disconnected from the 21st century. Lovely beaches, dense vegetation, fishing, & they can arrange fantastic food including a traditional Patagonian asado.

OTHER PRACTICALITIES There is no **petrol** in Lago Verde, so be sure to refuel in La Junta, nor is there an ATM. **Bus tickets** to La Junta or Coyhaique can be purchased at the Santa Teresita store on Los Baguales 247 between Caique Blanco and Los Maitenes (Lago Verde to La Junta 08.00 Tue, return 15.00; Lago Verde to Coyhaique 08.00 Wed, return 09.00 Fri). Other shops include: Minimarket Nina, next to Residencial Nina (see above), which also has a public telephone (Trapanada 221); Minimarket and bakery San Daniel (Pioneros 294; camping also possible); Supermarket Eca on the plaza; a hardware store at the exit of the village towards the lake; Camilo Alvarez (✆ 9 9618 2525) can fix a puncture; and Ruta Verde (✆ 9 7602 3550; e loncochinocarolina@gmail.com) rents bicycles and arranges cycling trips in the area.

There are isolated farmsteads both north and south of Lago Verde, and it is a short drive to the lake itself. The road to the north (high-clearance car a minimum,

4x4 advisable) crosses a small rickety *pasarela* (///coursed.soups.hiking) over the Río Pico from where it continues either east or west to some isolated farms. There are no activities or facilities – this is purely to go for a spin in the countryside.

7

La Junta to Puyuhuapi and Cisnes

The Comuna de Cisnes stretches from Raúl Marín Balmaceda and La Junta in the north to Puerto Cisnes and Villa Amengual in the south. It is home to some 6,500 people, and covers 16,100km². Within this region lie two of the most historically fascinating villages along the entire Carretera Austral – **Puyuhuapi** and **Puerto Cisnes**. This is a stunning section of the Carretera, passing through the sub-tropical rainforest of the **Parque Nacional Queulat**, skirting glaciers, enchanted forests, beautiful lakes and jaw-dropping scenery. There are ample treks in the region, kayak and rafting opportunities, fly-fishing, and remote islands to explore by boat. However, the most intriguing aspect of this section is the history – Mussolini, Hitler and Pinochet; World War II refugees; vanishing submarines and Sudeten German settlers make up the rich history of the region, with a healthy dose of magic, astrology and mythology added for good measure.

This chapter begins where the previous chapter finished: at La Junta. It includes Puyuhuapi and Puerto Cisnes, as well as the smaller village of **Villa Amengual**, notable only for lying on the Carretera Austral close to an important but little-known detour to the Argentine border at Río Frías, but with surprisingly fine accommodation.

For those in a rush Puyuhuapi may be little more than a petrol and lunch stop. Puerto Cisnes is a detour from the Carretera Austral, although it is also an increasingly important entry/exit point with ferries to the remote islands as well as direct connections to Quellón on Chiloé. The Parque Nacional Queulat has become one of the must-see places to visit along the entire Carretera and is well worth the short hike or boat trip to the glacier.

PUYUHUAPI

On a sunny day there are few places more beautiful than Puyuhuapi along the entire Carretera Austral. Although it might not compete with the likes of Futaleufú for adventure activities, or with Cerro Castillo for trekking options, it boasts great food, lovely accommodation, a pioneering history, and a superb place to unwind overlooking the canal of the same name. The nearby Parque Nacional Queulat is one of the finest parks in this region of Chile, competing with Parque Pumalín in the north and Parque Patagonia in the south, and is home to one of the more accessible glaciers. Many visitors pass through Puyuhuapi without stopping. For those that pause, discover a little of the history, and perhaps rent a kayak to visit the hot springs in the bay from where another glacier becomes visible, this is truly a highlight of the entire Carretera.

There is perhaps no better place along the entire Carretera Austral to appreciate the pioneering spirit of the region than Puyuhuapi. Fortunately the history of the village is well documented in an excellent book published in 2011 by Luisa Ludwig (page 344, published in English in 2017), daughter of one of the original settlers who still lives in Puyuhuapi. Luisa's former house, Casa Ludwig, is a Historic Monument of Chile and a fine hotel (temporarily closed due to change of management, page 178). A close competitor is the equally magnificent and historic Hostería Alemana (page 181), run by the Flack family, also direct descendants of the original settlers.

HISTORY Puyuhuapi all started with a book. A group of young Sudeten Germans had enthusiastically read Hans Steffen's book about the region of Aysén. Steffen was an avid explorer, and the glacier north of Caleta Tortel is named after him. So enthused were these impressionable adventurers with this book that they visited Hans in Switzerland in 1932. As tensions were rising in the inter-war years, Walter Hopperdietzel and a group of friends were considering emigration, including to Australia or Canada. They lived in the small town of Rossbach in Czechoslovakia, close to the border with Germany. The combination of Steffen's book and the offer of free land to settlers persuaded these hardy pioneers to select southern Chile. It even had the same damp climate as Czechoslovakia!

Sudeten Germans were Czechoslovakians by nationality, but ethnically German. Indeed, prior to World War I they had been Austrian. In the annexation of the Sudetenland during World War II the nationality of most Sudeten Germans was

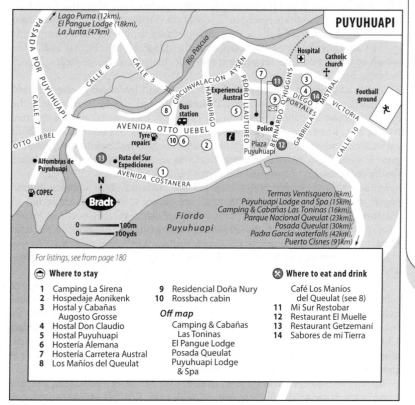

For listings, see from page 180

Where to stay

1 Camping La Sirena
2 Hospedaje Aonikenk
3 Hostal y Cabañas
  Augosto Grosse
4 Hostal Don Claudio
5 Hostal Puyuhuapi
6 Hostería Alemana
7 Hostería Carretera Austral
8 Los Mañíos del Queulat
9 Residencial Doña Nury
10 Rossbach cabin

Off map
  Camping & Cabañas
  Las Toninas
  El Pangue Lodge
  Posada Queulat
  Puyuhuapi Lodge
  & Spa

Where to eat and drink

  Café Los Maníos
  del Queulat (see 8)
11 Mi Sur Restobar
12 Restaurant El Muelle
13 Restaurant Getzemaní
14 Sabores de mi Tierra

7

changed to German. In the case of the settlers of Puyuhuapi, this placed them in a bind: renounce their German citizenship and become Chileans, or lose any right to free land. In a bold act of bridge-burning, they opted for the former.

A wealthy businessman called Robert Uebel financed the emigration in an effort to create a form of colony, or outpost, as war loomed. The idea was to establish a base and then bring over new settlers, but the war dampened the feasibility of others joining them. Robert was a sympathiser of Konrad Henlein, founder of the German Sudeten Party, which supported the annexation of Sudeten Germany, albeit subsequently aligning members with Nazi Germany following the annexation in 1938.

Carlos Ludwig and Otto Uebel arrived in Chile in 1933 and 1934, and began scouting out suitable locations. They first looked around the region of Llanada Grande (between Cochamó and Río Puelo), but eventually settled on a plot at the northern end of a canal (now called Canal Puyuhuapi) some 45km north of Puerto Cisnes. Puerto Cisnes was uninhabited at this point. So isolated was this spot that those leaving Puyuhuapi would speak of 'returning to Chile'. Steffen and fellow explorer Augusto Grosse had previously, albeit independently, explored this channel, and had discovered one abandoned (and extremely basic) house, and piles of seashells typical of prior visits from Chono canoeists (likely centuries old).

Thus in 1935 Puyuhuapi was founded. Walter Hopperdietzel arrived in June, and Ernesto Ludwig in August. Along with Carlos and Otto, these were the four founders of Puyuhuapi. Although Augusto Grosse was part of the initial group, he left shortly afterwards and is consequently not considered one of the true founders. In fact, in 1941 Grosse was placed in charge of the construction of the Ofqui Canal (page 267), and purchased all the timber required for the project from Puyuhuapi.

The Canal Puyuhuapi was named prior to the village, after the Poye islands at the mouth of the Fiordo Queulat where it joins the main canal. *Huapi* means 'island' in Mapuche.

Utterly unprepared, these sprightly settlers had to learn everything the hard way, building a village from scratch, clearing land and cutting trees to build the first basic accommodations. Pipes used to transport water were hollowed-out tree trunks. They knew very little about farming in Patagonia, a modest amount about agriculture, and almost nothing about fishing. They learned how to raise pigs, but grew fond of them, and slaughtering them was always a problem. (It seems their fondness of sausages outweighed this minor obstacle.)

Initially they depended entirely on passing boats travelling between Puerto Montt and Puerto Aysén for equipment and supplies. They would row out to Patience Island (not visible from the Carretera Austral, directly north of Puerto Cisnes at the mouth of the Canal Puyuhuapi where boats would traverse the Jacaf Canal) and hail a boat, sometimes having to wait for days in pouring rain.

Their first two houses flooded, having been built a little too close to the shore. The third burned down during a warm summer due to a fault in the chimney.

The Chilean government had initially offered 5,000ha to each settler, but following the outbreak of World War II, Chile severed ties with Germany and ceased granting land to any foreigners, by which point the settlers had inadvertently become German following the annexation of the Sudetenland. By becoming Chilean they could claim only 600ha. However, by assuming a public sector duty, albeit unpaid, this was extended to 1,000ha, and thus they all assumed nominal public sector duties in order to obtain more land.

Initially the settlers relied on food from Puerto Montt, before starting to grow basic crops in 1936. The first experiment with cattle was not entirely successful, as their food was sufficiently coarse to grind down their teeth, and half starved to death in the winter of 1937. The next herd of cattle was even less successful – they suffocated in an inadequate container on their way to Puerto Montt for sale. The health authorities were unimpressed by this cavalier attitude to farming. However, by 1940 the settlers worked out, with some advice from farmers in the region, how to raise cattle, and established a dairy which subsequently supplied cheese and butter to the village and Puerto Montt.

Summer labourers from Chiloé were initially hired, but it was not until 1938 that Chilote families moved to and stayed in the village. In 1942 the first hydro-electric plant was constructed. This provided electricity first to the dairy, and subsequently to the houses. Around this time the sawmill was upgraded with more suitable equipment obtained in Osorno, and timber soon became an important source of income for the village.

All finances were initially managed in Germany, until the outbreak of war, and subsequently from Puerto Montt where Carlos spent most of the time. Employees' salaries were invariably spent on buying provisions from the small store run on a cost-covering basis. Money was used only occasionally. In practice the settlers had created something akin to a co-operative, but over the years this was gradually replaced with more usual commercial relationships. Otto was the de facto leader of the commune; he came from a rich family that owned carpet factories – experience that would come in handy in subsequent years.

In 1943 Walter built some basic looms based on sketches he had copied in Germany. Initially they produced tweed and plaid, but in 1948 the factory began producing carpets, initially to provide employment to the women, with wool purchased in Lago Verde. The carpets were of high quality and readily sold in Puerto Montt and subsequently in Santiago. Over the following decades wool production became less profitable and the wool factory eventually closed. Imported carpets were cheaper than those produced in Puyuhuapi, and the factory gradually slowed production until ceasing operations altogether in 2018. Given the infrastructure and logistics of the mid 20th century it is impressive that such a quality cottage industry was so successful in Puyuhuapi.

In 1943 a key event took place, engraved on the minds of residents to this day: the ironically named 'taking of Puyuhuapi'. A boat arrived in the village bringing English soldiers searching for spies. The settlers were Nazi sympathisers, and Otto and Carlos were on a blacklist. But their Nazi sentiment was divorced from the realities of Germany, and was more concerned with supporting the reunification of ethnic Germans in the Sudetenland with Germany. However, the settlers were suspected of supporting German submarines, and when it became clear there were neither submarines nor German soldiers in the village, they were questioned about the radio communications. When the soldiers asked some of the locals what the Germans did in their free time and discovered they would climb mountains, they believed this was where the radio must be hidden, so the soldiers demanded to be taken up the mountain – but they were unfit to make the climb. Embarrassed and apologetic, the naval officer in charge of the inquisition compensated the settlers with a dinner aboard the frigate – an act which cost him his job.

After all Germans were expelled from Czechoslovakia in 1947, Helmut Hopperdietzel and Ernesto's family moved to Puyuhuapi. In 1949 the settlers built the first decent boat belonging to the village, the *Paloma*. In 1951, Helmut set up the first public radio. In 1954 the first major calamity struck the village: typhus, likely brought from Chiloé. The disease was transmitted by lice bites and spread rapidly due to unsafe funeral practices; the Germans were unaffected as they did not attend these funerals. Walter secured antibiotics from Aysén and the disease was stopped immediately, albeit having claimed 15 lives in two months.

The following years saw a stream of disasters. In 1958 an electrical short-circuit caused a fire in the carpet factory, which was largely destroyed. The factory was rebuilt thanks to a loan. An earthquake struck the village in 1960 (no casualties). And in 1964, the village was infested with rats – an event firmly fixed in the memories of the inhabitants. So abundant were the rats that wild cats, usually hard to spot, were clearly visible in trees ready to pounce. For some inexplicable reason one day the rats all ran into the water and drowned, in a rare case of 'rat mass suicide'.

Construction of the village continued unabated. Formal education started between 1955 and 1956, and the first school was established in 1958. In 1966 the first Catholic church was built, in traditional Chilote style. Up until the early 1970s Puyuhuapi was not a 'village' in the traditional sense. The region was privately owned and those living there were first and foremost employees rather than residents. This changed in 1971, when the Chilean state formally recognised Puyuhuapi. Two years later, in the coup, Pinochet's troops arrived, suspicious of this unusual German-run collective, and one person was reportedly killed for having left-leaning tendencies (although not one of the original settlers). By the mid 1970s Father Ronchi (see box, page 161) began playing an increasing role in the village, building a small chapel at the cemetery, and subsequently installing an additional radio antenna and television. However, TV stations had begun to encrypt their signals, and the only channel freely available in the village was from Mexico. According to Walter Hopperdietzel this led to the children picking up Mexican slang!

The year 1982 was pivotal for the residents of Puyuhuapi – many signs of which are visible to this day. Firstly, Pinochet inaugurated the Carretera Austral, passing through the centre of the village. In fact the Carretera Austral was inevitably to pass through Puyuhuapi, as the village had already built significant sections of the road north and south in order to facilitate the movement of cattle. However, due to the difficulty and cost of crossing the Fiordo Queulat the Carretera veered westward, over the Queulat Pass, rather than continuing south along the coast, much to the annoyance of Eugenia Pirzio Biroli, Mayor of Puerto Cisnes. The first regular bus service connected Puyuhuapi to Coyhaique (run by Becker Buses, still operating to this day). Ursula, the wife of Helmut, opened Hostería Alemana which is still one of the finest accommodation options in the village (now managed by her daughter, Hildegard). Walter installed the first petrol station (now replaced by a COPEC station, currently selling only diesel, next to the carpet factory).

Telephones arrived in 1988; state-operated electricity the following year; mobile phones in 2007 and internet in 2008. The Parque Nacional Queulat was formed in 1983, but the first trails were not opened until 1994, which resulted in a notable increase in tourism to Puyuhuapi. In 2011, Casa Ludwig was the first private residence in Aysén to be declared a Historic Monument. Alas it is temporarily closed to the public but should open shortly. In this same year Luisa Ludwig, former owner of Casa Ludwig, published her historical account of the village, *Curanto y Kuchen* (see box, opposite, and page 344). The landing strip was paved in 2012. Perhaps the last major historical event was the launch of Hopperdietzel beer in 2013.

Ernesto Ludwig died in 1969, aged 57. Otto Uebel died in 1975, aged 69. Helmut Hopperdietzel died in 1979, aged 58, and Carlos Ludwig died in 1996, aged 90. The last of the original settlers, Walter Hopperdietzel, died in 1996, aged 85. While many of the descendants of the 'original four' have left Puyuhuapi, some have remained.

The history of Puyuhuapi is perhaps no more remarkable than that of many villages along the Carretera Austral, but two key factors make the village unique from a historical perspective. Firstly, many of the buildings and people, or rather, their descendants, remain integral parts of the village. Secondly, the history is written down. Puyuhuapi *knows* where it comes from. Many villages, even larger towns along the Carretera Austral, display a cavalier attitude to history. And, as migration from other parts of Chile continues, this is likely to deteriorate further. Coyhaique opened its museum as recently as 2018. Eugenia Biroli's house lies abandoned in Puerto Cisnes. The museum of Father Antonio Ronchi in Villa O'Higgins is a modest affair, to put it mildly. Oral history passed down through the generations is fine for as long as the custom is maintained, but in the 21st century, with increased migration, urbanisation, mobility of residents, and expanding university attendance inevitably drawing the youth to other parts of Chile, can Chile rely on oral records to record its own origins?

Luisa Ludwig's wonderful book *Curanto y Kuchen* contains an insightful and charming personal account of the lives of the early settlers and the sheer magnitude of forming a village in so remote a location. The book is packed with colourful anecdotes from various perspectives. The name is not easily translated to English – *curanto* is a traditional dish originating in Chiloé, prepared in a hole in the ground, while *kuchen* is the name of German pastries and cakes common across southern Chile where German settlers played such a significant role in the development of the region. Thus the title of the book reflects these two vital cultural influences upon southern Chile.

The Carretera Austral is unique, and not simply for its otherworldly glaciers and pristine rainforests. It emerged in relative isolation from the outside world, and its history is both fascinating and under threat. The early residents are ageing – the time to write the history of the Carretera Austral is now. Let Luisa's work be an example to other villages. The book is published in English, Spanish and German, and is available to buy in Puyuhuapi or via e curantoykuchen@gmail.com.

GETTING THERE
About the route
La Junta to Puyuhuapi (47km; 1hr; paved) Finally this notorious section of gravel has been paved. The road is fairly uneventful until reaching El Pangue Lodge (page 181) at the northern edge of Lago Risopatrón, and from there skirts the edge of the lake almost until Puyuhuapi. A truly spectacular section begins south of the village, leading to a challenging stretch of the Carretera that is still largely unpaved.

By bus All buses from Coyhaique to La Junta (and further) pass through, as do all southbound buses heading towards Coyhaique. **Buses Entre Verdes** go to Chaitén (via La Junta 16.30 Mon, Wed & Fri, return same day & time) and to Puerto Cisnes (08.00 Mon, Wed & Fri, return at 16.00 same day).

TOUR OPERATOR
Experiencia Austral Av Otto Uebel 36; ///lighters.sari.insolvent; ✆ 9 8744 8755, 9   7766 1524; e contacto@experienciaustral.com; w experienciaustral.com. The finest operator in

town. Rents kayaks (dbl $6,000/hr; sgl $4,000/hr), & also offers kayak tours along the fjord. Bicycle rental ($8,000/half-day or $15,000/day) – useful for a day trip by bike to the Queulat glacier (it's possible to do this one-way & they will carry your rucksack). Treks in the region include to Ventisquero Queulat & Laguna de los Pumas. They also offer multi-day trips including airport pickup (to/from Balmaceda airport). The owner, Adonis Acuña, has a boat available for longer trips along the fjord (prices vary according to length of trip). This is the same company that operates the boat to the Queulat glacier within the park ($10,000 pp).

🏠 WHERE TO STAY *Map, page 175*

🏠 **Posada Queulat** (6 cabins) halfway between Puyuhuapi & Cisnes Junction; ///emptied. tiebreaker.retrace; 📞9 9319 0297; e rosario1@ aisen.cl; w posadaqueulat.cl; ⊕ Sep–Apr. One of very few options between Puyuhuapi & Puerto Cisnes/Villa Amengual, offering far more than good-value top-notch accommodation – these fantastic cabins are a great base from which to explore the region. Set within 130ha of forest, rivers & waterfalls, with convenient access to the Queulat glacier, & 2.5km of both the Queulat River & the estuary, Posada also owns the island Poyeguapi. Particularly good for families, & there are ample activities within the grounds – including kayak trips, a 3hr hike up to a waterfall, boat trips to the island – & a small hot spring & a hot tub. All electricity comes from renewable sources as the Posada is entirely self-sufficient with solar & hydro power. Cabins (sleep 2–7) are private & spaced far apart from one another, fully furnished (but without kitchen), & well heated with wood stoves. All include both b/fast & dinner – ideal given the proximity to the nearest restaurant. Only slow Wi-Fi, but laundry available. Reservation required, cards accepted. $$$$$

🏠 **Puyuhuapi Lodge & Spa** (30 rooms) Bahía Dorita, 15km south of Puyuhuapi; 📞2 2225 6489; e info@puyuhuapilodge.com; w puyuhuapilodge.com. Something of a legend in the region, this is one of the better-established upper-end options along the Carretera Austral, with good reason. If budget constraints limit stays in such locations to a single splurge, this would be a serious contender. The location is unique: accessed by boat from a dedicated pier approximately 15km south of Puyuhuapi (///hayrides.coffeemaker.repented) or 8km north of the entrance to the Parque Nacional Queulat (arranged with accommodation). Indoor swimming pool, & an impressive spa housed in a magnificent high-ceilinged wooden complex with stunning views over the Puyuhuapi Canal – ideal for a relaxing massage! There are 3 thermal pools of varying temperatures, ranging from moderate to positively hot, one of which is close enough to the canal to enjoy a quick dip in the cold water after an invigorating soak at 35°C. Dense vegetation encroaches on all sides. The rooms are of excellent quality, spacious & tastefully decorated, each with fully equipped private bathroom (hot water comes from the hot springs; leave the tap running a while as the pipes are long). Construction began in 1982, but it was not converted into a hotel until 1989. Considering the logistical hurdles of operating with 50 staff in so isolated a spot, the price tag is actually quite reasonable for a truly fantastic location – these are the best hot springs in this region of Chile. The decks are raised above the beach at low tide, & at high tide the water laps underfoot. The view on a sunny evening over the canal towards snow-capped mountains is simply world-class. The communal areas are a pleasure to sit in & enjoy a cold beer, with impressive wooden beams & wood/stone finish. The bar stocks the local Hopperdietzel beer, as well as a decent wine list & quality cocktails. The b/fast is excellent (probably the only place on the Carretera Austral serving boiled eggs in proper egg cups), & the restaurant serves an impressive array of seafood & lamb, among other options, with most ingredients sourced locally or from their own gardens. Kayaks available, as are guides, & there are 2 nature trails. The lodge can arrange tours in the region, although there are sufficient activities on site to keep one busy for a couple of days, including with children. The all-inclusive packages with tours in the region are perhaps best for those without private transport. The half-board option (with access to the hot springs, b/fast & either lunch or dinner) is ideal for most visitors to the Carretera. B&B rates are available, but they include neither hot springs nor lunch/dinner – & this lodge deserves at least a full day. Discounts for longer stays & for children. All services provided except Wi-Fi, & there is no mobile-phone coverage. In all senses this is a getaway, a place to disconnect from everything, even from the Carretera Austral. $$$$$

El Pangue Lodge (8 rooms & cabins) Carretera Austral, 18km north of Puyuhuapi, 30km south of La Junta; ///pelts.strangest.surrounds; ☏ 67 252 6906, 9 9799 5394; e reservas@elpangue. com; w elpangue.cl. At the upper end of the accommodation spectrum in the region, this lodge (founded in 1987), perched on the northern end of Lago Risopatrón, is a pleasant surprise & a wonderful place to unwind from the Carretera Austral. Located in a 16ha park with trekking trails, & entirely surrounded by native forest, with immaculate gardens. Many of the rooms & cabins overlook the fjord & surrounding mountains. Cabins (sleep 4–7, b/fast excluded, but full kitchen provided) with spacious sitting areas & en-suite bathrooms, plus 8 rooms in the main lodge (b/fast inc). All centrally heated with basic services (patchy Wi-Fi, laundry, English/German spoken), & also heated swimming pool, sauna, hot tubs, a bar & pool table, & a large quincho. They also offer guided kayak tours, fly-fishing (inc classes), boat trips, & it is possible to swim in the lake. Restaurant in the main lodge serves b/fast, quick lunches (or lunch boxes for those doing an excursion) & full dinners, including venison, as well as the usual Chilean seafood & meat dishes ($$$$). If not staying, be sure to book ahead to dine. $$$$

Hospedaje Aonikenk (10 rooms, 4 bungalows) Hamburgo 16; ///incidentally. spire.shuttered; ☏ 67 232 5208, 9 8200 1354; e aonikenkturismo@yahoo.com; ⊕ all year. Clean, spacious rooms with big windows & rustic beds, electric heating & hot water, private bathrooms & b/fast included for all rooms & bungalows. Ask for upstairs rooms if possible, some have a balcony. Pleasant upstairs sitting area with books in the main building. The bungalows do not have kitchens. No laundry service on site, but it can be arranged. Parking available, Wi-Fi, basic English spoken, & has a hot tub. The charming owner, Veronica Gallardo, can also arrange tours in the region. Reservations without a deposit are possible if reconfirmed a week prior to arrival. Fills up in Jan & Feb. Accepts credit cards. $$$

Hostal y Cabañas Augosto Grosse (3 rooms, 2 cabins) Camilo Henriquez 34;

///coins.splurge.pollens; ☏ 9 8826 0638; e hostalaugostogrosse@gmail.com; ◪ hostalaugostogrosse; ⊕ all year. Cramped rooms with shared & private bathrooms, all set off a communal seating area. The cabins, however, are lovely, with a wooden interior & fully equipped kitchen. Wi-Fi, laundry, parking, cable TV, b/fast included. There is a shop selling artisanal products in the hostal. Accepts credit cards. $$$

✳ **Hostería Alemana** (7 rooms) Otto Uebel 450; ///shunning.doctoral.redefining; ☏ 67 232 5118, 9 9881 3164; e aflackk@gmail. com; w hosteriaalemana.cl. This hostería is still run by the family of some of the earliest German settlers & is a serious contender for the top accommodation in Puyuhuapi. Beautifully designed, tastefully decorated, large rooms with large beds & private bathrooms. Heating is via gas or wood stoves. An outstanding b/fast true to German cuisine. It is popular with motorcycle groups, & reservations are required. English & German spoken. Accepts credit cards. $$$

Hostería Carretera Austral (5 rooms) Otto Uebel s/n; ///cutie.blame.wavelengths; ☏ 67 232 5119, 9 6643 2425; e hosteriacarreteraustral@ gmail.com; ◪; ⊕ all year. Big, simple accommodation, good for families. Large communal room for b/fast with views of the port. Private & shared bathrooms. Wi-Fi, parking, cable TV & b/fast (included with the dbl rooms with private bathroom, but also available for other guests). Also offers transport to Parque Queulat in transit vans & can arrange transport to Chaitén & Futaleufú. Reservation required, accepts credit cards. $$$

Los Mañíos del Queulat (6 rooms) Circunvalación s/n; ///flustered.chafed. hushing; ☏ 9 7664 9866, 9 9491 1920; e losmaniosdelqueulat@gmail.com; ◪ losmanios.delqueulat. Recently constructed good-quality hostel run by the entrepreneurial & efficient owner of the restaurant of the same name (page 182). 3 dbl & 3 trpl rooms (4 with private bathroom). Off-road parking, Wi-Fi (but not in restaurant), good b/fast (inc), can arrange laundry, wood-stove heating but gas for hot water. The 2 best rooms are those with a view & sound of the river. Popular in high season. Accepts cards. $$$

Residencial Doña Nury (14 rooms, 2 cabins, 1 apt) O'Higgins 40; ///thundering. unswerving.imperative; ☏ 67 232 5109, 9 9081

3232; e marciavidalgomez@gmail.com; ⊕ all year. A wide range of room sizes for almost any combination of guests, all with private bathrooms & basic b/fast included. Great for larger groups & particularly good for families. 4 rooms on the ground floor suitable for people with limited mobility. There is heating & hot water, & visitors can use the kitchen. Decent cabins for 5 or 6 people, apt for 8 people (no kitchen). Off-road parking. The owner's pet peeve is wet rucksacks that dirty the rooms! Reservations without deposit accepted. **$$$**

🏠 **Rossbach cabin** (1 cabin, 4 apts) Otto Uebel next to Hostería Alemana; ///foot.fruits. unhooks; 📞9 6599 0317; e marisolpuyuhuapi@ gmail.com.Delightful cabin in a central location with obvious German influence. Dbl room downstairs, 4 sgls upstairs, 1 bathroom, great sitting area, full kitchen, area to leave wet boots & jackets. The apts are by the COPEC garage, of similar quality & reasonably priced. Also has a boat & offers trips in the area, including to Isla Magdalena or Gala. **$$$**

🏠 **Hostal Don Claudio** (5 rooms) Diego Portales 15; ///spotlight.translating.samplers; 📞9 3881 3900, 9 7880 5039. Best-value accommodation in Puyuhuapi. 2 dbls, 2 twin, 1 sgl, all clean, with fast Wi-Fi, large b/fast (inc), laundry service (extra), parking, wood-stove heating & guests can use the kitchen. All for $15,000 pp – a hostal at camping prices. **$$**

🏠 **Hostal Puyuhuapi** (6 rooms, 1 cabin) Llautureo 27; ///predicament.says.workroom; 📞9 8185 7814; e juliacuevas31@gmail.com; 📘; Reasonable budget accommodation 1 block from plaza. Rooms (4 dbl, 1 trpl & 1 sgl) with shared & private bathrooms. Decent b/fast (inc), Wi-Fi, laundry service. Cabin for 7 people ($90,000/night) is well equipped, with a washing machine. Accepts cards. **$$**

🏠 **Camping & Cabañas Las Toninas** (3 cabins, camping) 16km south of Puyuhuapi; ///unimpeded.kindly.intolerance; 📞9 9522 0390; e lastoninas.camping@gmail.com; 📘 camping. lastoninas.puyuhuapi. Many campgrounds are popping up around Queulat but this wonderful campground on the water is the oldest – Elva Fuentes has been here for over 40 years. 10 sites with roof ($10,000 pp), shared bathrooms with hot water, all electricity from turbines in a stream. No need to reserve, as there is always space (even if without a roof). Cabins (for 2, 6 or up to 10 people) all reasonably priced & well equipped. Large quincho. Good vibe, with wonderful views on a sunny day. **$–$$**

⛺ **Camping La Sirena** Costanera 148; /// eternal.metallic.northward; 📞67 232 5100, 9 7880 6251; e lasirenapuyuhuapi@gmail.com. 24 tent sites with a roof overhead (for the incessant Puyuhuapi rain) hot water, & a communal wood-fired stove doubling as a means to dry clothes. Right by the fjord. Wi-Fi available. $5,000 pp. **$**

✕ WHERE TO EAT AND DRINK *Map, page 175*

✕ **Café Los Maníos del Queulat** Circunvalación s/n; ///flustered.chafed.hushing; 📞9 7664 9866, 9 9491 1920; 📘 losmanios. delqueulat; ⊕ 19.00–21.00 daily. A convincing range of homemade cakes & pies in the kuchen capital of Chile, as well as a full restaurant serving hamburgers, pizzas, salmon, steaks & salads. Seating for 20 people, a little overpriced, but high-quality food & local ales. Wi-Fi unavailable as the owner (wisely) thinks visitors should speak to one another while eating. Accepts credit cards & it's wise to reserve. **$$$**

✕ **Mi Sur Restobar** On plaza; ///glittered. regally.universities; 📞9 7550 7656; ⊕ 13.00–23.30 daily. Finally, some nightlife in sleepy Puyuhuapi, with a kicking atmosphere in high season. Rustic wooden effect outside & in, tree-trunk stools, cool wood/glass/seashell tables,

seating outside to watch life meander by. Pretty good food – bar food & the usual suspects plus soups, salads, lasagne, ceviche, pizzas (including the elusive seafood pizza) & some novel seasonal dishes. Hopperdietzel, draught beer, Pisco sours, cocktails, Tepaluma gin from La Junta (see box, page 165), reasonable wine list. Fast becoming the place to go in the village, deservedly & at long last. Accepts cards. **$$$**

☀ ✕ **Restaurant El Muelle** Av Otto Uebel, towards southern exit of Puyuhuapi; ///slamming.feisty.deserved; 📞9 7654 3598; e elmuellepuyuhuapi@gmail.com; ⊕ Sep–Apr noon–16.00 & 18.00–22.00 daily. Finest place in town, with spectacular views along the fjord – indeed the only restaurant with a view of the canal. Decent service, cosy atmosphere & a deck for those rare occasions when the sun shines.

Wide range of dishes, local beers (including Hopperdietzel from Puyuhuapi, D'Olbek & Finisterra). Specialities of the house are merluza, pork, certified organic steak & a number of German dishes, including a potato purée dish blending German & Chilean influences from an original recipe of Snra Ursula, the wife of one of the first pioneers (page 179). Vegetarian dishes available. Can also knock up a decent Pisco sour, including with local flavours – try cauchao & calafate. They also rent kayaks. Wi-Fi available & credit cards accepted. $$$

✳ ✕ **Restaurant Getzemaní** Costanera 172; ///speeches.atoned.smoked; \9 7600 0083; ⏱ Nov–Mar, informal hours but stays open until midnight in high season. Madame Tussauds with merluza. One of few late-night options in Puyuhuapi is little more than a small heated hut next to a very basic campground. The restaurant has become something of a legend in the region, with its crooked, rickety walls, hosting an otter skin, what appears to be the stuffed torso of a cat with a wooden moose head attached, a large dried trout peering ominously at visitors, a semi-snake, an obviously fake octopus, some Barbie dolls nailed to the walls, a martín pescador that died prematurely, & an orca made of eel skin. Cleanliness could be improved (the floor, tables, walls & ceiling are mostly clean; however, the plates & cutlery are spotless) but if not put off by first impressions it is an exceptionally nice restaurant for bargain prices. The owner, Sarealla Salidaz, is lovely, & an accomplished cook. She grows many of the ingredients in her garden behind the restaurant. The merluza is simply excellent, & portions are large, the chips are hand-cut, the bread is freshly baked, & her rhubarb jam is delicious. She used to work in the Puyuhuapi Carpet Factory, of historic importance in the region. Most meals cost $8,000. Also has a campsite ($4,000 pp) – the cheapest in town, but also the most basic. $$

✕ **Sabores de mi Tierra** Diego Portales 20; ///giraffe.moderates.baggy; \9 8732 6573; e acarolinapuyu@gmail.com; ⏱ noon–22.00 daily. Surprisingly good restaurant set back a little from the main road, with outdoor seating. The usual seafood & meat dishes (including a lo pobre), hamburgers, salads, vegetarian dishes & a children's menu. Rotating daily dessert & ice creams, but the forte is kuchen (also for take-away). Silvia has won the regional kuchen competition twice, quite some feat given how seriously it is taken in the region. Decent freshly ground coffee, Hopperdietzel on tap & bottled D'Olbek, wines & fresh fruit juices. Silvia's grandparents arrived shortly after the German pioneers & are featured in Luisa Ludwig's book (page 344). Her parents were both local fishermen, possibly explaining her skills in preparing seafood dishes – a true Puyuhuapina. Recommended. $$

OTHER PRACTICALITIES Along the main street, within a block of the plaza, lie a number of shops, a bakery, the bus stops, police, fire station, the sole tour operator, and the rather useful **tourist information office**. The *gomería* (tyre repairs) is at the northern entrance to the village before reaching the plaza, but there is no mechanic. The COPEC **petrol station** is on Aysén Street just off the northern side of the bridge at the north of the village (///wiggles.crikey.astounds), but a dispute regarding the storage tank resulted in no petrol, only diesel being available in early 2022. There is neither a laundry nor an ATM.

SIGHTSEEING AND EXCURSIONS Quintessentially quaint, Puyuhuapi is the 'historical heartland' of the Carretera Austral. For those interested in the early settlements and history of the construction of the route, this is a fascinating village to explore. The walking tour covers the main places of interest, but ultimately it is by conversing with the residents that one can truly understand the history. In terms of attractions in the region, the Ventisquero Queulat dominates most itineraries, closely followed by the hot springs for those with a more flexible budget.

Puyuhuapi village tour (2hrs) For those interested in history, this is a pleasant way to explore the village on a sunny day. Pick up a map at the tourism office on the plaza. The tour starts at the southern entrance to the village and ends at a lovely viewing platform overlooking the canal, mountains and village, traversing much of the lower section of the Río Pascua. Points of interest along the route include: various original German houses and the German graveyard with a monument naming the original founders of Puyuhuapi; the old path to Lago Risopatrón; the original school built in 1958 and the Catholic church built in 1966 (the first priest was the legendary Father Antonio Ronchi; see box, page 161); the old boat yard; some wetlands with various birds; the old hydro-electric water wheel; the distinctive architecture of Puyuhuapi homes. There is an optional hike up to a viewing platform, but alas the famous carpet factory has now closed and cannot be visited. The trail then returns to the main dock by the plaza, ideal for popping into El Muelle (page 182) or Mi Sur (page 182) for a drink or meal.

Termas Ventisquero (6km south of Puyuhuapi; ///purport.yell.settlers; 9 7966 6862, 9 6860 3454; e termasvp@gmail.com; f; ⊕ 10.00–20.00 daily) Following a total remodelling, these hot springs are now thoroughly recommended. Right on the beach, with a great view of the fjord, they are cheaper and more accessible than Puyuhuapi Lodge, and a notch above El Sauce near La Junta. There is one main pool, pleasantly warm, and three smaller pools (one with a roof), decent decks, and it's pleasant even in the rain. Rather than taking a cold shower, you can simply jump straight into the canal for an utterly refreshing temperature shift ($25,000 pp includes a towel & locker). There is also a decent restaurant (serving lunch, ravioli, pastas, pizzas & kuchen; $$$) where you can buy a drink to take to the springs. It's ideal after a day of hiking in Queulat.

Boat along the Fiordo Puyuhuapi As it is perched at the head of a fjord, it is little surprise that many activities around Puyuhuapi, besides visiting the Queulat glacier, revolve around water. Kayak rental is prolific, but for greater distances a boat might be a wise option, particularly for a group. There are sea lion colonies, dolphins frolicking around, hot springs, and it's an opportunity to view the Queulat glacier from a different angle. Two operators have decent boats:

Nautica Queulat 9 9670 4075, 9 8426 0072; e claudio26oyarzo@gmail.com

Ruta del Sur Expediciones Costanera, next to Getzemaní; ///flattened.fellowships.clashing; 9 9298 2424; e turismo.rutadelsur@gmail.com

Ventisquero Colgante/Parque Nacional Queulat (w conaf.cl/parques/parque-nacional-queulat; $8,200/4,100 foreign adult/child, $4,100/2,100 Chilean adult/child; 10 camping sites within the national park: $6,000 pp plus the cost of entrance to the park; bathrooms inc hot water & showers on site) This is the main park along the central route of the Carretera Austral, located 21km south of Puyuhuapi or 35km north of Cisnes Junction on the Carretera Austral (turning to park at ///consolation.hardening.lodgings). Although treks in the park are limited to Lago Témpanos and the famous Ventisquero Colgante (hanging glacier), it is well worth a visit.

The glacier protrudes from a high valley, with occasional chunks crashing down on to the rocks beneath and eventually melting into the lake. The park is 1,541km^2 and contains extensive evergreen forests, prolific flora and fauna, snow-capped mountains and has easy access to Ventisquero Colgante. Both trails start at the car park (///carnivorous.stutters.hooter) and cross an impressive hanging bridge over a mesmerising and violent section of river. Over the bridge the 3-hour trek to the viewpoint of the hanging glacier veers to the left, for the 'postcard' photo of the region. There are limited views on the way up to the viewing platform. It can be quite muddy so take hiking boots if possible. The trail to the right after the bridge goes to the edge of the lake (15mins), from where small boats ferry visitors towards the glacier. Although the boat trip is often shunned in favour of the legendary hike, in fact the views from the lake are possibly more spectacular, as the entire valley is visible rather than one narrow angle from the viewing platform above and there are some waterfalls visible only from the boat, not from the main trail. For those with limited mobility this is a great way to see the glacier.

Termas de Goñoti (Free entry) These hot springs are situated on the west side of the canal and are accessible by kayak or boat from Puyuhuapi. From here one can see Ventisquero Chico, not visible from either the Carretera Austral or Puyuhuapi itself. Check with locals regarding the best times to visit the hot springs, as they are submerged at high tide.

Padre Garcia waterfalls (14km north of Cisnes Junction; ///recurrent.pushy. exchanges) A mere 200m from the Carretera are some interesting waterfalls named after a Jesuit priest who was searching for the mystical lost City of the Césares (see box, page 116) and instead stumbled across these waterfalls. Beautiful, verdant green, and worth the half-hour round trip on a clearly marked, short trail. There is no formal parking, so leave the car by the road, but not on the bend where the path begins. There are some other waterfalls (Salto El Cóndor; ///addition.texts.several) further south, also worth a photo stop.

Lago Puma (12km north of Puyuhuapi; ///spoil.identifies.repaving; 10km round trip; 4hrs; medium but steep ascent) This is a lovely, well-marked hike to a little-visited lake through dense virgin rainforest ending on an open grassland with views of the surrounding mountains.

PUERTO CISNES – A DETOUR

When it's not bucketing down with rain, this is a delightful village. Located at the foot of towering mountains at the widest point of the Puyuhuapi Channel, it is the main access point to the remote communities of Puerto Gaviota, Puerto Gala and Melimoyu. Puerto Cisnes is accessed via a paved 32km detour from the Carretera Austral (the 'Cisnes Junction'), weaving along the Río Cisnes through a dramatic evergreen valley with lofty cliffs and the occasional waterfall.

The usual array of activities are available: kayaking, fly-fishing, trekking, relaxing on beaches (in between showers), mountain biking, visiting hot springs, admiring the stunning scenery and wildlife spotting. It is also a functioning fishing village and port, with local boats to nearby communities and longer-distance ferries connecting this central region of the Carretera directly with Chiloé. There are reasonable accommodation and eating options and some pleasant treks in the surrounding area, but Puerto Cisnes is worth visiting for one reason above all others: the history. Its sleepy appearance belies a turbulent political past.

HISTORY The history of Puerto Cisnes, and the life of its enigmatic mayor, Eugenia Pirzio Biroli, are inseparable.

Eugenia Pirzio Biroli was born on 15 May 1906 in Turin, Italy. She was a keen sportswoman, tennis player, sprinter and discus thrower, winning various European championships. She established the first ever women's rowing club in Rome.

Her father was a commanding officer in the Italian army, and spent from 1921 to 1927 in Ecuador, likely sowing the seeds of curiosity for Latin America in the mind of the young Eugenia. In 1941 Biroli was promoted to General, and served as Governor of Montenegro from 1941 to 1943, crushing an uprising in 1941. In 1942 he ordered the execution of 50 hostages for every Italian soldier killed, but only ten for a wounded soldier. He told his troops: 'I have heard that you are good family fathers. That is good at home, but not here. Here, you can't steal, murder and rape enough.' He was declared a war criminal in the United Nations War Crimes Commission, but was never tried and lived out his old age in Rome.

This somewhat heavy-handed administrative style may partially explain the authoritarian leadership approach of Eugenia.

While attending Spanish classes at the Spanish Academy in Ecuador she met her future husband Genaro Godoy Arriaza, from Chile. They married in 1932. In addition to Spanish and Italian, Eugenia studied Greek and Latin, and spoke good English.

Eugenia and Genaro moved to Chile after World War II. Genaro was an opera singer and a philologist, but it is not entirely clear what Eugenia did until she began working with some local charities in Santiago, and quickly developed a passion for working with abandoned children. In 1952 the Chilean government donated some land in a remote spot in the region of Aysén to a charity called Obra Don Guanella, which then built a dedicated school and safe environment for abandoned children from Santiago. Eugenia visited the spot in 1957, and never quite left. According to her account of her arrival there were only four houses in the village.

Puerto Cisnes had been founded, as a nascent village, in February 1955. Thus Eugenia lived in Puerto Cisnes almost from inception, and was a key player in the formation of the village. The first mayor was David Solis, a retired policeman, and Eugenia was one of the four councillors. Through her friendship with then-president Jorge Alessandri, Eugenia was able to secure some surprising public-sector works in Puerto Cisnes despite its minuscule size. Alessandri, for example, ordered the construction of the municipality, an agricultural school and a landing strip, and installed electricity. Eugenia also built the first church (in 1959, in an astonishing 42 days – the current church is the third to sit on this spot), and subsequently the library. In fact she spent her entire inheritance developing the village. She was renowned for being stubborn, frequently travelling to Santiago and sitting for hours, knitting, outside the offices of national ministries until government officials agreed to hear her requests. She would lobby government and companies on behalf of Puerto Cisnes, and secured the village's first ambulance from Fiat. Her refusal to take no for an answer is evidenced in the disproportionate development of Puerto Cisnes compared with other towns in the region. Even today it is possible to observe a greater role of the state in the day-to-day activities of Puerto Cisnes compared with other communities such as Puyuhuapi, which was always somewhat sceptical of public-sector intervention and far preferred to 'go it alone'.

While Eugenia secured astonishing developments for the village, she lived modestly and never accumulated personal wealth. Genaro never moved to Puerto Cisnes, and apparently visited only rarely. It took at least four days to reach Santiago. Despite this slightly unorthodox marriage Eugenia and Genaro had two children, one of whom died. Their son Estanislao became a geologist and professor at the University of Chile, and still visits Cisnes sporadically. Genaro died in 1979, and Eugenia continued listening to cassettes of his operas for the rest of her life.

In 1960 Father Antonio Ronchi came to Chile, and the following year to Puerto Cisnes. Ronchi soon became the self-named 'rascal priest' (see box, page 161). He contributed immensely to the economic and spiritual welfare of Puerto Cisnes and the surrounding region, as far afield as Villa O'Higgins in the south and north to La Junta, while Eugenia had only one interest above all others – the development of Puerto Cisnes. Ronchi's style was more collaborative, and he appears to have made fewer enemies. The two never got on.

Puerto Cisnes was upgraded to a formal commune in May 1965 under the Frei presidency, with authority over La Junta and Puyuhuapi (which is resented to this day). In 1971 a new mayor was elected and Eugenia continued working as councillor, until the coup d'état on 11 September 1973. Eugenia was appointed mayor by Pinochet in November that year, and held this position for 17 years, narrowly losing an election in 1989 shortly before Pinochet was replaced by Patricio Aylwin. Her friendship with Pinochet is subject to much speculation, and critics refer to her as 'Pinochet's Witch' on account of her uncanny astrological readings. Pinochet fiercely believed in astrology, and visited Eugenia in Puerto Cisnes to consult with her on numerous occasions. Relations between the two soured when Eugenia failed to predict an unsuccessful attack by the Frente Patriotico on Pinochet's convoy as it made its way to his weekend retreat in 1986.

Perhaps one of Eugenia's greatest regrets was that the Carretera Austral did not pass through Puerto Cisnes, but did pass through the rival village of Puyuhuapi. Indeed, the Carretera Austral could conceivably have traversed a more coastal route through Puerto Cisnes, or even a more easterly trajectory through La Tapera. Eugenia had to make do with a 35km connecting road to the Carretera Austral, which was completed in 1982, but resulted in Puerto Cisnes being a detour. It is in fact possible to trek from Cisnes along the eastern shore of the Puyuhuapi Canal and connect with the Carretera Austral near Posada Queulat (page 180), but this trail passes through private properties and must be arranged locally, likely only with a guide.

Eugenia is a divisive character in Puerto Cisnes to this day. Her authoritarian style was perhaps necessary to achieve the development she desired, but it isolated parts of the community. Her close association with the Pinochet regime may have served her and the village during that era, but nowadays pro-Pinochet sentiment is not so openly stated. Similarly, some older residents are hesitant to speak too openly about Eugenia. Some supporters of Eugenia speak of her with almost religious fanaticism, believing her contribution to the village, and astrological prowess, was little short of divine. While her accomplishments were impressive, in neighbouring villages she is less popular, accused of putting the interests of Puerto Cisnes before broader regional development.

Eugenia died in Coyhaique on 22 February 2003 aged 96. She had moved to a home for the elderly run by the charity Obra Don Guanella, the same charity that had first persuaded her to head south nearly half a century previously. She is buried in the Cisnes Cemetery, which she also built, and she wrote her own epitaph: 'Here rests her body, but her spirit remains vigilant in the skies over Cisnes' (2km south of village; ///lids.this.warble). Tragically there is no museum dedicated to Eugenia's work, her house lies abandoned in the centre of the village and her grave is rarely attended to. Padre Ronchi's legacy is that of a national hero, yet Eugenia's contributions, albeit more locally focused, were no less profound. The view of Pinochet in 21st-century Chilean culture is complex, and perhaps Eugenia's friendship with Pinochet places her too firmly in a chapter of Chilean history that many wish to forget.

The only book about Eugenia is the Italian/Spanish *La Italiana de Patagonia*, written by her niece Idanna Pucci, which contains marvellous photographs of Eugenia from infancy to late in life, as well as testimonies from various people impacted by her works. Idanna Pucci also made a documentary, *Eugenia of Patagonia*, featuring extensive video footage and interviews with Eugenia; it won the Audience Award at the Turin Film Festival in 2005. Although not currently available in Puerto Cisnes, these can both be purchased directly from Idanna Pucci (e idannapucci@gmail.com). They offer a fascinating glimpse into the life of one of the most charismatic and influential mayors of (southern) Chile.

GETTING THERE
About the route
Puyuhuapi to Puerto Cisnes (91km; 3–4hrs; partly paved, partly poor gravel) This section has some of the worst road quality on the Carretera Austral. Paving has begun south of Puyuhuapi, and the gravel section along the canal is reasonable. Expect roadworks along this stretch, and check to see if there are any planned road closures. When major work is required the road is closed for certain hours of the day to enable the use of explosives and heavy machinery. These hours change weekly or monthly – signposts north and south usually highlight the current situation, or ask locally. This can have a major impact on planning journeys through this section. Along the coastal gravel section, where landslides are common, thick wire meshes can be seen along the cliff faces in an effort to prevent rocks from falling.

The most challenging section is the Queulat Pass – where the Carretera veers away from the canal and crosses over the mountain range at the southern end of the Parque Nacional Queulat. This is entirely gravel, around hairpin bends, often with limited visibility, and dust from the traffic hangs in the air. The Padre

Garcia waterfalls are on this uphill section (page 185). Over the pass, and heading downhill once again, there are other waterfalls (Salto el Condor) before the road eventually reaches the Cisnes Junction (///outgoing.anticipated.chug), where paved bliss returns. The road to Puerto Cisnes is paved, as is the Carretera from here until Cerro Castillo, south of Coyhaique.

By bus Buses Terraustral (Piloto Pardo 368; ⟍67 234 6757, 9 8249 1655; go to Coyhaique (06.00 Mon–Sat, 10.00 Sun, return 16.00). **Buses Sao Paulo** (Carlos Condell 150; ⟍67 225 5726, 9 7759 6088; w busessaopaulo.cl) also go to Coyhaique (06.00 Mon–Sat, return 16.00). **Buses Entre Verdes** (⟍ 9 9510 3196) depart to Puyuhuapi and Cisnes (16.00 Mon, Wed & Fri).

By ferry As well as the service four times a week to Quellón, there is also a slow ferry twice a week that serves the route Chacabuco–Puerto Aguirre–Puerto Gaviota–Puerto Cisnes–Isla Toto–Melimoyu–Santo Domingo–Raúl Marín Balmaceda–Melinka–Quellón (page 60).

TOUR OPERATORS

Drakkar Tours Latorre with Arturo Prat; ///butting.sashimi.straining; ⟍9 8742 8544, 9 5017 7033. Marcelo, an experienced fisherman who has lived in Puerto Cisnes since 1971, offers 2 main tours in his well-maintained boat which has a small covered section in case of bad weather. The first tour is spotting wildlife & hopefully dolphins ($20,000 pp, 2hrs) in the Puyuhuapi Canal & inlets. The second is to the Isla Magdalena thermal springs ($40,000 pp, 4hrs). On the way to the springs, Marcelo catches fish using only a spool of line, & grills it with tomato & bread for visitors to eat while bathing in the hot springs. The springs themselves don't live up to the standards of others in the region in terms of infrastructure, but the authenticity & spectacular setting provide a fantastic experience. Marcelo is a fount of information on the history, culture & politics of the region.

Kike Aventuras Juan Jose Latorre 225; ⟍9 8723 7657; e augusto.oyarzo@gmail.com. Augusto spent 15 years scuba diving & his entire life in or around Cisnes, for the last 4 years running boat tours in the region – so he knows the waters. He has a 14-person covered boat & offers tours to the Isla Magdalena (hot springs), & dolphin-spotting trips. He's a keen fisherman, providing fishing trips along the Puyuhuapi Canal or on the Río Cisnes (sport fishing & also traditional fishing, using a line with 50 hooks attached, as practised in the area), as well to Lago Escondido. Tailor-made trips are also possible, including to Puertos Gaviota & Gala.

Tours Bellavista Séptimo de Linea with Gabriela Mistral; ///cutie.erudite.berries; ⟍67 234 6408, 9 6590 9244; e tourbellavista18@gmail.com; w tourbellavista.cl; ⊕ all year. Operating out of the hostel of the same name (page 191), offers a range of standard & tailor-made tours in & around Cisnes, such as fishing & boat trips in the bay, including to Isla Magdalena, visits to hot springs, & to the sea lion colonies & to spot dolphins. Accepts credit cards.

Turismo Cahuelche Séptimo de Linea 130; ///largest.disgruntled.reloaded; ⟍9 8272 5999, 9 8828 1423; e turismocahuelche@gmail.com. Tours in Spanish, English & Portuguese, run by the grandson of one of the original settlers in Puerto Cisnes. Celestino has a 15m boat (up to 12 people) & his tours centre around Isla Magdalena & the Puyuhuapi fjord. He has been working in tourism for over a decade & has a sixth sense for where the dolphins are likely to be frolicking. There are sea lion & penguin colonies along the fjord, as well as hot springs on the main island, from where it is possible to see the Queulat glacier on a clear day. He can also provide tailor-made tours including to Puerto Gaviota, where whales are often seen.

Viva La Lluvia Av Arturo Prat, at southern exit of village; ///mascara.wickets.green; ⟍9 8742 6545, 9 9001 2143; e vivalalluviapatagonia@gmail.com; w vivalalluvia.cl. Competent tour operator with a decade of experience in Cisnes & well-qualified guides, focused on conservation. Tours include a full-day trip to Parque Nacional Queulat ($45,000 pp), kayaking on the Río Cisnes, & fly-fishing, as well as the 2-day ascent of Cerro Gilberto, with tents & food included ($80,000 pp, min 2). This is a challenging climb not offered by most operators, but the views over the fjord & towards various volcanoes are spectacular, with fairly sheltered camping (page 193). They also have access to hot springs in Parque Nacional Queulat. All guides have satellite phones, 1 guide speaks English & a snack is always included. Bike, kayak & paddleboard rent available. There is a café in the office, serving coffee, tea, fresh fruit juices, cakes, sandwiches, pizzas & local beers – ideal while mulling over which tour to do.

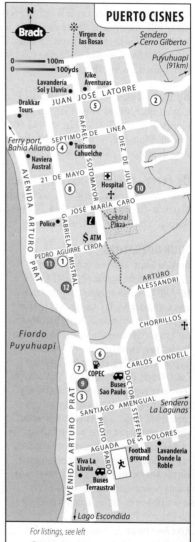

WHERE TO STAY *Map, right*

Hostal Patagonia Home (7 rooms, 3 cabins) Juan José Latorre 136; ///clout. resisted.capped; 9 9997 6364, 9 7750 2067; e hostalpatagoniahome@gmail.com. Surprisingly good refurbished hostal with 1 trpl & 3 sgl rooms (shared bathroom), 1 trpl with private bathroom, & 2 stellar dbl rooms with private bathrooms – the gem of the hostal. Reasonably priced ($20,000 pp for sgl, $60,000 for the king suite for 2 people). The cabins offer spacious accommodation for 4 or 5 people ($55,000/65,000). B/fast included in hostal (not cabins), & Wi-Fi & parking available. **$$–$$$$**

Cabañas y Quincho Gilberto (3 cabins) Cnr Gabriela Mistral & Aguirre Cerda; ///workplaces.bathrobes.untimed; 67 234 6440, 9 7744 3118; e roloriffo@hotmail.com; ⏰ all year. Reasonable cabins (2 & 3 bedrooms) at a reasonable price, a little dated, but centrally located. Wi-Fi, hot water, gas heating, single-glazed windows, TV, full kitchen (no microwave) & off-road parking. B/fast not included. Excellent quincho for larger groups. Good bread shop/mini-supermarket next door. Owners have lived in Puerto Cisnes for 65 years, & Gueseita founded the first school in the village. Their son now manages day-to-day operations. **$$$**

✳ **Hostería El Gaucho** (7 rooms) Augusto Holmburg, halfway up block; ///competitors. afar.tension; 9 4428 0927; e marisolgabriela@ hotmail.com. A beautiful historic building, probably the best accommodation in Cisnes. The original owners arrived in 1946 & from 1955 the building served as the first school in the village; in 1963 it was converted to become the first hostel in the town. Totally refurbished in 2018 by Marisol (of

PUERTO CISNES

Virgen de las Rosas
Sendero Cerro Gilberto
Puyuhuapi (91km)

0 ——— 100m
0 ——— 100yds

Kike Aventuras
Lavandería Sol y Lluvia
Drakkar Tours
JUAN JOSÉ LATORRE
RAFAEL DE
SEPTIMO DE LINEA
DIEZ DE JULIO
SOTOMAYOR
Ferry port, Bahía Allanao
Naviera Austral
Turismo Cahuelche
21 DE MAYO
Hospital
JOSÉ MARIA CARO
AVENIDA ARTURO PRAT
GABRIELA MISTRAL
Police
Central Plaza
$ ATM
ARTURO ALESSANDRI
PEDRO AGUIRRE CERDA
CHORRILLOS
Fiordo Puyuhuapi
CARLOS CONDELL
COPEC
Buses Sao Paulo
DOCTOR STEFFENS
Sendero La Lagunas
SANTIAGO AMENGUAL
PILOTO PARDO
DE DOLORES
AGUADA
AVENIDA ARTURO PRAT
Viva La Lluvia
Football ground
Lavandería Donde la Roble
Buses Terraustral
Lago Escondida

For listings, see left

🛏 **Where to stay**

1 Cabañas y Quincho Gilberto
2 Camping Señora Anita
3 Hospedaje La Panchita
4 Hostal Bellavista
5 Hostal Patagonia Home
6 Hostería El Gaucho
7 Lafquén Antú Hostería
8 Portal del Mar

✕ **Where to eat and drink**

9 Carretera Austral
10 Finisterra
   La Panchita (see 3)
   Lafquén Antú Hostería (see 7)
11 Panadería Coty
12 Pimienta Canelo

Lafquén Antú hostel & restaurant). Set slightly above 'downtown' Cisnes, it has sweeping views across the bay & a fantastic semi-covered deck with comfortable chairs from which to enjoy the view. There is a good-sized garden with a hot tub (unique in the village – takes a couple of hours to warm up so advise Marisol in advance). 1 twin, 3 dbls & 1 sgl, all with private bathroom & cable TV, & 2 sgls with shared bathroom. Cosy sitting room with wood stove, small bar & a table for b/fast (inc), also with a lovely view over the village. Wi-Fi & laundry available. **$$$**

🏠 **Lafquén Antú Hostería** (5 rooms) A rturo Prat 213, cnr with Carlos Condell; ///forces.edit.inflecting; ☎ 67 234 6382, 9 4428 0927; e marisolgabriela@hotmail.com; ⊕ all year. A relatively new hostel in a lovely location overlooking the Puyuhuapi Canal towards Isla Magdalena. Dbl, twin & sgl rooms with full b/fast included. Shared bathrooms with hot water, 1 dbl room with private bathroom. Large communal areas with a computer & video games, & restaurant/bar downstairs (see below). Good meeting place for travellers. Reservations do not require a deposit but do confirm the day before. No English spoken. **$$$**

🏠 **Hospedaje La Panchita** (9 rooms) Arturo Prat 805; ///pollens.blazers.beautifully; ☎ 9 3439 1139; e lapanchitarestorant@gmail.com; ⊕ all year. Pleasant budget option a short walk from the centre, but with lovely views on the few days of sunshine in Cisnes. Sgl, dbl, trpl & quad rooms, some overlooking the bay towards the mountains. All bathrooms are shared, & rooms towards the back are a little gloomy. Wi-Fi, central heating, laundry service & some off-road parking. Very good b/fast with a decent serving of scrambled eggs. The menu of the day is very good value (page 192), & they have a quincho available. Accepts credit cards. **$$**

🏠 **Hostal Bellavista** (8 rooms) Séptimo de Linea with Gabriela Mistral; ///cutie. erudite.berries; ☎ 67 234 6408, 9 6590 9244; e tourbellavista18@gmail.com; w tourbellavista. cl; ⊕ all year. Recommended budget accommodation in Cisnes. Rooms are tastefully decorated, comfortable & spacious, & many have views over the bay. Decent restaurant (**$$**), shared bathrooms, Wi-Fi & cable TV. B/fast included & coffee available all day – guests cannot use the kitchen but microwave, fridge & oven available. Wood-stove heating & good insulation for the winter (which also means you don't hear the neighbours). Off-road parking & laundry service. The owner has run the hostel since 1992, & since 2005 has also run a tour company (page 189). Also offers left-luggage service & showers for non-guests awaiting the late-night ferries. Deposits are required, & can be taken by credit card. **$$**

🏠 **Portal del Mar** (4 cabins) 21 de Mayo & Gabriela Mistral; ☎ 9 8268 0616, 9 9222 2522; e teresa.montiel@gmail.com; w portaldelmar. cl. Probably the best cabins in Cisnes. Note the reception is a block away at Sotomayor 855 (///mummies.swoon.possible) in the Ferreteria El Rayo shop. Good-quality wooden cabins, 1 with glimpses of the sea, sleeping 4–6 people for $50,000 to $70,000. There is a small garden & a fence around the property, which is reassuring for those with children. Wi-Fi, laundry (by arrangement), dedicated parking, wood-stove heating & gas for the hot water. Fully equipped & good sitting area. Well located for visiting the rest of the village. Reservation advisable in high season. Cards accepted. **$$**

🏠 **Camping Señora Anita** Northern entrance to Cisnes; ///satchels.force.audiences; ☎ 9 9890 2552. When entering the village from the northern entrance (Juan Jose Latorre), cross the bridge & the camping is located at the end of a small cul-de-sac immediately on the left. Cheap, basic camping ($5,000 pp on synthetic grass without roof, $6,000 pp with roof), also has 4 refugios upstairs, which are basically 4 walls, a roof & rough carpet to place sleeping mat & bag without the need to erect a tent ($7,000 pp). Hot showers & bathrooms. Drying room for wet clothes (inevitable in Cisnes) and for cooking. Wi-Fi available. One of the cheapest imaginable ways to escape the rain, check emails & wash, but it does the job well. There is a strict ban on alcohol on the premises. No need to reserve, accepts cards. **$**

✕ **WHERE TO EAT AND DRINK** *Map, opposite*

✕ **Lafquén Antú Hostería** Arturo Prat 213; ///forces.edit.inflecting; ☎ 67 234 6382, 9 4428 0927; e lafquenantucomidas@gmail.com; ⊕ 12.30–23.00 Mon–Sat, 13.00–18.00 Sun. Part of the hostel of the same name (see above), this restaurant is a delightful place on a sunny evening. Good for a quick beer or cup of tea while admiring Isla Magdalena in the distance. Service can be a little slow when crowded, but scores highly for location & ambience. Wooden interior, local beers, friendly owners & occasional live music & events. Specialities include a wide range of seafood, ceviche, a great fried hake with spicy roast potatoes, & it's one of the few places offering *puyes pil pil*. Try to get a window seat if possible. $$$

✕ Carretera Austral Arturo Prat with Condell; ///clammed.conductors.chicken; ☎ 67 234 6868, 9 8158 0083; ⏲ all day. Popular restaurant with a great location overlooking the canal, but excels in neither food, drinks nor service. Bright lights & blaring TV might appeal to some, & it is the only place in Cisnes where someone once had their ear bitten off in a brawl. The menu appears quite extensive, ranging from ceviche to hot dogs, with vegan & vegetarian options, b/fast & sandwiches. Has a slightly strange vibe. Better options are available. $$

✳ ✕ Finisterra Restaurant Diez de Julio & José María Caro; ///accentuate.enrichment.gruffly; ☎ 67 234 6407, 9 6310 4187; ⏲ 16.30–01.00 Mon–Sat. Located next to the legendary brewery, this restaurant offers typical Chilean bar – pizzas, pichanga, salchipapas, etc – but it's good quality & reasonably priced. Serves all the Finisterra beers, including some on tap, as well as micheladas. Note this is a licensed restaurant, so beer can only be sold with food. For those not wishing to consume endless beers there are also fruit juices,

coffee & soft drinks. Arrive early in high season to get a table. If staff are available, it might be possible to combine with a tour of the brewery, & beers can be bought to take away (from 10.00). Recommended. $$

✕ La Panchita Arturo Prat 805; ///pollens.blazers.beautifully; ☎ 9 3439 1139; e lapanchitarestorant@gmail.com. A simple, family-run restaurant serving good-sized portions. Seafood is the main speciality, with meat dishes also available. Menu of the day with 2 or 3 options & a vegetarian plate. Cosy atmosphere, with good service as long as the restaurant doesn't fill up, & a hotel upstairs (page 191). Good budget option – be sure to grab a window seat for lovely views. $$

✕ Panadería Coty Pedro Aguirre Cerda, just above coastal road; ///occults.affronts.rainbows. Excellent homemade empanadas, savoury & sweet pastries, & a small shop. $

⌸ Pimienta Canelo Gabriela Mistral, just north of port; ///themes.restarts.celebrities; ☎ 9 9312 6327; ⏲ 16.00–23.00 daily. Cool coffee shop offering a range of pastries/cakes, sandwiches, pizzas, quesadillas, salads, juices, teas, ice creams & vegan options to eat in or take away. The owners try to use only organic & locally sourced ingredients, & also sell products made by local artisans. No Wi-Fi or TV – talk or read a book instead. A pleasant place to chill & have a coffee or bite to eat to escape the rain. Recently started producing their own beer. $$

OTHER PRACTICALITIES The **tourist information centre** is on the central plaza, as is the municipality building, the library (with free use of computers with internet) and the bust of Eugenia Biroli. **Naviera Austral** have an office on the Costanera not far from the dock (///distortion.pigtails.elapses). The COPEC **petrol station** is on the corner of Piloto Pardo and Carlos Condell. There is an ATM on Pedro Aguirre Cerda (half a block from the plaza).

Laundry

Lavanderia Donde la Roble Aguda de Dolores 8; ///undermines.visages.sneezed; ☎ 9 7808 6341; ⏲ 09.00–21.00 daily; small rucksack $6,000. Same-day service if get there early.

Lavandería Sol y Lluvia Cnr Sotomayor & Juan José Latorre; ///correspond.obstacle.freebie; ☎ 9 8439 8859; $2,500/kg. Same-day service if drop off clothes to Pilar early.

SIGHTSEEING AND EXCURSIONS On a sunny day, there are plenty of options for visitors to Puerto Cisnes. Perched as the village is on the edge of the Puyuhuapi Canal and close to the Río Cisnes, there are mountains and lakes within walking distance of the centre. Isla Magdalena is visible across the bay, and the village's rich history is simply fascinating. However, incessant rain can dampen enthusiasm.

A good starting point, and a useful way to get to grips with some of the history of the region, is a trip to the **central plaza**, home to the tourist information centre with a map of an **interpretive trail** around the village. The trail covers all the main sights, including the coast and viewpoints, with occasional opportunities to stop for a coffee or local ale – it takes at least 2 hours, but you could easily spend a day pottering along. The library on the plaza is a surprisingly beautiful building, resembling a small wooded Greek temple, and well equipped with information on the region. It is next to the municipal building of Puerto Cisnes, with a statue of Eugenia Pirzio Biroli on the plaza in front.

It is a pity to traverse the Carretera Austral without trying the local ales along the route and, of the micro-breweries open to the public, the **Finisterra microbrewery** (José María Caro 297; ///accentuate.enrichment.gruffly; ⟍67 234 6407, 9 6310 4187; **e** cervezafinisterra@gmail.com; **w** cervezafinisterra.cl) is the one to visit. While other breweries come and go, Finisterra has stood the test of time, tracing its first production back to the 1990s. It is one of the largest in the region, producing approximately 9,000 litres per month. Tours are free, and operated by the master brewer Camilo, son of the founder. He explains the process and ingredients used, the differences between the various beers they produce, and is usually preparing a batch during the tour, so don't be surprised if he has to pause to alter temperatures or add ingredients. The main beers are blonde, golden and an award-winning porter. The blond beer is also mixed with seasonal fruits, honey and chillies to produce four other beers. The spicy beer is an unusual, acquired taste that some people love, others detest, with chillies imported from Mexico. The beer is fairly widely available along the Carretera, and the tour around this family-run business is delightful – a very good use of an hour or so, particularly if it's raining. They also offer a 'menu of the day' lunch in high season.

The cove to the south of Puerto Cisnes boasts a beach fit for **swimming**, Balnearios; it's not particularly impressive, but it has the advantage of a lifeguard in high season. If you're looking to swim the open sea there are finer places than this, albeit without the benefits of a lifeguard. Beyond the beach, it is possible to continue by foot, car or bicycle alongside the Río Cisnes and return to the village via the **Sendero Las Lagunas**, a 1-hour hike along the main road towards the eastern end of Santiago Amengual Street, taking in two small lakes with plenty of opportunity for wildlife spotting.

To see the village and bay from up high, follow the **Sendero Virgen de las Rosas** (1km round trip; 1hr; easy) – a short trek up through dense vegetation (but decent path/stairs) to a lookout with a lovely view over the village and towards the beach area, nicely lit at night, beginning at the end of Rafael Sotomayor Street (///howling.sourced.hoods).

The **Sendero Cerro Gilberto** (2 days; difficult) is a substantial hike to the summit of the mountain that looms over Puerto Cisnes. It is a hard climb over two days and if you're attempting the summit, you're advised to take a guide (ask at the tourist information centre or tour operator Viva La Lluvia, page 189). The view from the summit is spectacular, extending across the canal to the islands, and mountains to the east. **Fishing** on the Río Cisnes (which originates 160km upstream at the Argentine border) is possible; tour operators and the tourist information centre can arrange a guide. However, providing you have a fishing licence, a guide isn't necessary. Tours Bellavista (page 189) can arrange a boat if you intend to fish the less accessible parts of the river by the estuary, including combining such trips with visits to the sea lion colonies or Isla Magdalena.

7

Kayaking is another option, either on a guided tour or independently. It's 4 hours upstream to **Lago Escondida**. Other options include kayaking to the sea lion colonies or visiting the waterfalls north of Puerto Cisnes along the canal.

To the north, heading along the Puyuhuapi Canal, lies the **Allanao beach**, with short hikes to the estuary of the Río Anita and also to a small lake (Laguna Cipress). This can be visited by boat or kayak. It is then possible to cross the canal over to the hot springs at **Parque Nacional Isla Magdalena** (w conaf.cl/parques/parque-nacional-isla-magdalena-2), accessible by boat only, due to distance, currents and tides.

Sometime between late January and mid-February thousands of people descend upon the village for the three-day **Fried Fish Festival**. They come to enjoy music, local customs and delicious fried merluza, a staple fish in the southern fjords. Each year before the festival, the community selects a local family in need of a new house, which is constructed with municipal funds, and then placed on a trailer and manually towed through the village to its designated site. This is also the period when Puerto Cisnes elects the village queen. It's a wonderful celebration of tradition and community spirit.

VILLA AMENGUAL AND A DETOUR TO PASO RÍO FRÍAS-APELEG

Few people stop at Villa Amengual. It is one of the less interesting villages along the Carretera Austral, and without even a petrol station there is little reason to pause here. It was founded in 1983 during the construction of the Carretera Austral. Its main claim to fame is that it is the nearest village to the turning towards Villa La Tapera and on to the rarely used Argentine border crossing at Paso Río Frías-Apeleg. However, before dismissing this village entirely, note that there are three surprisingly **good accommodation** options (camping/hostel/cabin) nearby, excellent food, a lovely lake, an impressive church built by the original Chilote immigrants, and a small market selling local handicrafts. The road to the border is magnificent, but rough, and best done in a car with decent clearance if not a 4x4. Villa Amengual lies on a sparsely populated stretch of the Carretera Austral, some 60km north of Mañihuales and 90km south of Puyuhuapi, and is thus a useful break for weary cyclists.

The village, and its fine accommodation, serves as a useful base to explore the region. By car it is 1 hour to Puerto Cisnes; 1½ hours to Puyuhuapi (less to the hot springs or Queulat National Park) or to the Argentine border; and only 2 hours to Coyhaique.

GETTING THERE
About the route
Cisnes Junction to Villa Amengual (34km; 30mins; paved) A beautiful stretch of paved road sandwiched between towering cliffs and the Río Cisnes. There is an impressive viaduct at Piedra del Gato running alongside the mountain. The old road is still visible, precariously hugging the side of the cliff. The road zigzags up to magnificent views over the Valle Río Cisnes and continues to Villa Amengual.

Villa Amengual to Paso Río Frías-Apeleg (106km one-way; 2½hrs; 2km paved to junction, 104km of tough gravel) This offshoot is spectacular, weaving along the Río Cisnes with almost no traffic – the border receives only 400 crossings per year. There are countless hairpin bends, and a challenging section for cyclists, as well as dramatic canyons, verdant lush grass (suitable for camping), cows, goats, sheep and hares at every turn, plus plenty of birdlife. Minuscule **Villa La Tapera** is approximately halfway from Villa Amengual to the border (page 197), one of the more isolated places on the entire Carretera Austral. There is little reason to stop here unless you need somewhere to stay when travelling to or from Puerto Cisnes or the border, if beginning or ending the trek to Lago Verde/Palena, or if you're planning on doing some fishing in the region. It is 4 hours from the border to Coyhaique.

In general, this border crossing is only convenient for those travelling directly to Puerto Cisnes from Argentina; most will use the more northerly border at Palena (page 153), or the more southerly Paso Puesto Viejo (page 200), which is a better-quality and a more direct route to Coyhaique.

Most of the road is rough and accessible only with a 4x4 or a high-clearance 2WD travelling with caution, although in good weather and with sufficient patience it could qualify as a 'regular gravel road' in many places. However, the road quality deteriorates notably in Argentina. Expect slow travel, hairpin bends, steep ascents and descents and a narrow road. The road is slightly flatter and straighter from Villa La Tapera to the border, so less arduous for cyclists than the first section.

Paso Río Frías-Apeleg (⊕ 08.00–20.00 all year) The Chilean border post (❧ 67 256 7096) is manned all year, but may close in June and July if the road becomes impassable (chains are obligatory in winter). It is 20km on reasonable gravel to the actual border, opening and closing seven gates as the road passes through working farms. The Argentine border post (❧+54 2945 496074) is located in Aldea Apeleg, approximately 28km southeast of the actual border on poor-quality, deep gravel. From Aldea Apeleg the nearest petrol to the north is at Gobernador Costa (122km) or to the south at Alto Río Senguer (49km). If taking the most common north–south route using this border between Gobernador Costa (Argentina) and Mañihuales (the first/last petrol station in Chile), have sufficient petrol for 350km mostly on gravel. Officially it is not permitted to take fuel in a container across the border, so top up the tank from any such container before crossing.

Given the uncertainty of using this border in winter it is wiser to use the Palena/Futaleufú crossings to the north (pages 153 and 144), or the Puesto Viejo crossing further south (page 200).

By bus Buses heading north and south along the Carretera inevitably pass through Villa Amengual and stop. **Buses Aranda** (❧ 9 9764 2062) offers the only public transport to the border: Coyhaique–Amengual–La Tapera–Río Alto Cisnes (noon Sun & Wed, return 07.00 Mon & Thu); Amengual to La Tapera (noon Mon, return 16.30); Coyhaique to Amengual (17.00 Mon, 16.00 Tue, return 07.00 & 19.00 Tue).

WHERE TO STAY AND EAT

✳ 🏠 **Fundo Lago Las Torres** (5 rooms, 7 cabins, 1 house) 5km south of Villa Amengual on west side of Carretera Austral; ///bottleneck. remnants.amplifies; ❧ 9 8176 0709, 9 9822 2685; e jlgalvez@lagolastorres.cl; w lagolastorres.cl; ⊕ all year. A gem of a location offering a wide range of accommodation options within 2,800ha of land, which includes a lake. The main building feels like stepping back a century in time to gain a glimpse of true Patagonian life before the

advent of smartphones. The property has been in the family for over 80 years & is one of the most authentic, rustic Patagonian accommodations along the entire Carretera Austral, & surprisingly good value for money. Energy is generated from a small hydro-electric plant on site (with lights occasionally dimming according to the water level), there are some solar panels, & heating is via wood stoves. Good hot water once the stoves are fired up. Laundry available, but no Wi-Fi, &

internet coverage is only via Claro. Most visitors are self-catering, but food can be prepared if arranged in advance, including a mouth-watering cordero asado (roast lamb). The owners are true locals & can arrange airport transfers & any tour imaginable. They also offer fly-fishing on the lake & in the nearby rivers, including Río Cisnes, with classes for beginners if required. There are ample trekking & horseriding opportunities within the estancia. The property has a boat, & can reach remote & unknown spots, including a hidden lake that involves hauling the boat 500m over land. Nature-lovers might be a little put off by the puma skins, but these were presumably killed many decades ago! The Ventisquero El Elefante is visible from the property, which also doubles as a working farm. It's all too easy to drive past this highly recommended establishment. **$$$**

★ 🏠 **Hostería Casona del Bosque** (7 rooms, 1 cabin) 700m south of Villa Amengual, on the east side of Carretera Austral; ///skid. fooling.hugger; 📞 9 5353 7484, 9 9227 5430; e contacto@hosteriacasonadelbosque.cl; w hosteriacasonadelbosque.cl; 🖪; A lovely, family-run business offering top-notch food. This delightful hostel is run by Anita & Victor Hugo, both highly accomplished chefs. The rooms are simple but pleasant; dbl & twin rooms with either shared bathroom or en suite, 2 trpl with shared or en-suite bathroom, & the cabin sleeps up to 5 people & has a dishwasher. Gas heating, Wi-Fi, off-road parking, superb b/fast (included with rooms, not with cabin) & a comfortable sitting area to relax by the fire. The excellent restaurant serves homemade local food, kuchen, lemon pie, ice cream, biscuits, local beers, & some surprisingly good cocktails (**$$$**). Can also arrange trekking & horseriding tours in the region. **$$$**

★ 🏠 **Refugio Río Cisnes** (30 camping sites, 1 cabin) 24km south of Cisnes Junction, 7km north of Villa Amengual; ///impressions.transplants. vegans; 📞 9 7154 8068, 9 7468 6725; e info@ refugioriocisnes.com. Excellent campground on the Río Cisnes for $7,000 pp (b/fast extra). 10 covered sites, hot water, lovely garden with beach, & a decent restaurant (🕐 08.00–21.00) serving b/fast, sandwiches, pizza, kuchen, teas, great coffee & 'cake of the day' – useful given the scarcity

of shops or restaurants nearby. Great for kids & also has a small indoor play area, & sheep. Electricity is generated by a turbine with water from the river. They also have a quasi-hostel, essentially a fantastic large cabin that sleeps 9 ($23,000 pp in dorms, 1 dbl for $50,000 b/fast inc), but can also be rented in its entirety ($200,000 b/fast inc). Laundry available (for a fee), & it is possible to fish in the river below. The entire plot is 12ha & there are 2 hiking trails (20mins & 1hr, both along river). English spoken. This is the most southerly member of the Austral Garden Route (see box, page 167). Recommended. **$–$$$**

🏠 **El Indio** (5 rooms) Carmen Arias 10, Villa Amengual; ///humbles.prefer.anguished; 📞 67 221 5434, 9 8507 8137. Basic accommodation (4 dbls & 1 sgl), with shared bathrooms, b/fast (inc). Guests can use kitchen, & laundry & Wi-Fi available. Dinner or lunch can be provided (**$**), & can prepare an asado for groups if booked in advance. **$$**

🏠 **El Paso** (6 rooms) Carmen Arias 12, Villa Amengual; ///tuxedo.isolator.flute; 📞 9 7420 9990; 🕐 all year. Basic dbl & trpl rooms with shared bathrooms, good for families with 1 child, $15,000 pp. Wi-Fi, parking, cable TV & basic b/fast with eggs available for $4,000. Restaurant (🕐 all day every day; **$$**) downstairs with typical Chilean fare. **$$**

🏠 **Hospedaje Doña Virma** (4 rooms, 1 cabin) Domingo Bilbao, Villa La Tapera (51km east of Amengual junction); ///seeded.bagful. bridesmaids; 📞 9 8147 7497; 🕐 all year. Located 1 block from the plaza, good-value, simple dbl rooms with 2 shared bathrooms, hot water & heating. B/fast $5,000 extra. Sporadic Wi-Fi in hostel, but the village does have internet (Claro also works). No English spoken. Laundry service available. Restaurant also serves dinner ($7,000) – there is nowhere else to eat. Virma knows everyone in the village, will advise on the region & fuss over your stay; her husband, Hannibal, is a fishing guide & can organise local fishing trips or horseriding, although he does not provide these himself. While it's rarely full, it is worth reserving in Jan & Feb because this is currently the only option in the village, & there is little else until well over the Argentine border, or in Puerto Cisnes, Puyuhuapi or Villa Amengual. **$$**

SIGHTSEEING AND EXCURSIONS There are limited options in Villa Amengual – a church built by Father Ronchi (see box, page 161), and a small handicraft store selling local woollen products from the region at reasonable prices (cash only). Historically this was a huge wool producing region, with women working for private farms or for the state. However, with the overgrazing of the estancias and the global competition of cheaper wool from overseas, wool production has declined dramatically and is now a niche activity employing very few people, and destined principally for handicraft markets rather than mass production. Without even a petrol station, few people stop in the village.

Villa La Tapera Some 50km east of Villa Amengual, there is a valid reason why Villa La Tapera appears so rarely in guidebooks. With a population of approximately 400 people, it must be one of the remotest inhabited spots in the entire region accessible by road. It was founded in 1970, and has grown slowly ever since. The border crossing to Argentina is rarely used (page 195) and there are very basic services including a police station, four mini-supermarkets, a medical centre, a school and one hostel (see opposite). In 2015 there was a plan to open a pub in the village, but alas it never materialised. There is a mechanic, Eveder Candia (\ 9 2052 9091), who can do basic repairs on cars, motorbikes and bicycles as well as fix tyres. He is a deer hunter by night.

The main activities around La Tapera involve fishing, hiking or horseriding. Two guides are based in the village. **Gerardo Carillo** (\ 9 3499 3368; e gerardo. caflo@gmail.com) offers fishing and horseriding tours including the trek to Lago Verde and on to Palena. His fishing trips include remote and unknown places with abundant fish, and he has regular clients visiting from abroad for over a decade. His multi-day trips inevitably end with a lamb roast. He has five horses but can rent more if required, he can arrange any necessary transport (eg: pickup/drop-off at the Carretera Austral or Villa Amengual), and he speaks basic English. He does not have tents or sleeping bags for rent, so for the multi-day trips bring your own. Horses carry much of the load, as well as the food.

The small mini-market El Huasito (\ 9 7281 7803, 9 6818 0608; e Yoyi_ montecinos_31@hotmail.com) has operated for over 35 years, and was the first store in the village (basic food and alcohol, accessories for riding and fishing, camping gas, ice creams, toothpaste, etc). It is owned by **Wolfgang Neserke**, who is also a guide. His ranch, Los Corales, is located 1km north of the village. He has an incredible range of riding saddles collected over the years (huaso, English, jumping, Mexican, with/without spurs, etc) which he confidently claims can precisely meet the needs of any rider. He can arrange multi-day tours and has all cooking equipment, tents and mattresses. The mounts for attaching luggage to the horses are all handmade; Wolfgang tries to use almost no factory-manufactured or imported products in the entire ranch (except for the more exotic saddles). Tours

CONNECTING WITH THE SENDERO DE CHILE

It is possible to connect with the Sendero de Chile (see box, page 158) from La Tapera by heading north to Lago Verde (59km; 3 days, 2 nights; horse & guide advisable). This section follows the same trail taken by the traditional gauchos centuries earlier and is utterly disconnected from the outside world, passing lakes, crossing rivers, and entering thick, barely visited forest. A good local guide is **Claudio Soto** (page 172). The trail is not technically difficult, and passes two high-altitude points with impressive views of mountains and glaciers: the Portezeulo Los Contrabandistas and Golondrinas.

include Lago Solis, day tours in the vicinity of La Tapera, and as far afield as Lago Verde, often combined with fishing if desired. He also has private transport and can pickup/drop-off at the Carretera Austral or Villa Amengual.

Estancia Alto Río Cisnes Just before the Argentine border, as the terrain flattens out to Patagonian steppe, a vast shearing shed with the name 'Río Cisnes' written in huge letters across a bright red roof looms ominously. Besides this building is a landing strip. This is a 130,000ha functioning sheep farm called Alto Río Cisnes, dating back to 1904. There were three major concessions granted to mega-estancias in the early 20th century: The Industrial Society of Aysén (SIA, land predominantly around Coyhaique); the series of companies that managed the land between Valle Chacabuco and the Baker Delta (page 213); and Alto Río Cisnes.

The ranch at Alto Río Cisnes was formed in 1904 as the Anglo-Chilean Pastoral Company, consisting of land granted to Joaquín Rodríguez Bravo and Antonio Allende. By 1924 the ranch converted to a new legal structure, renamed the 'Río Cisnes Ranch Cattle Company'. Many of the residents of La Tapera work on the ranch. Some of the buildings were declared National Historic Monuments in 2009, and it is sometimes possible to tour the facilities by prior arrangement – call or visit their office in Coyhaique (Baquedano 776; 67 223 3055, or 2 196 4513 for satellite phone, expensive to call). This remains a working farm to this day, with 40,000 sheep and some cattle.

⊕ AS THE CONDOR FLIES

Villa Amengual is 368km south of Puerto Montt, and 470km north of the border crossing at Villa O'Higgins to El Chaltén in Argentina.

8

Puerto Aysén and Chacabuco

As the Queulat sub-tropical rainforest fades away, the road continues south beyond the rather obscure detour to La Tapera towards Puerto Aysén and Coyhaique. The Carretera initially continues south from Villa Amengual to a small town often overlooked by visitors – **Mañihuales**, where a landslide in 1966 altered the entire province of Aysén.

Besides a few minor roads to the east, the main points of interest between Mañihuales and Coyhaique are the ports of **Aysén** and **Chacabuco**. Strictly speaking a trip along the Carretera Austral bypasses both these towns and heads directly south to Coyhaique on a gravel road (page 217), so this could be considered a detour. Puerto Aysén's former glory faded thanks to massive deforestation beginning in the 1940s, causing excess sedimentation in the region to clog the port for all but small vessels. The port subsequently moved 14km southwest, and Coyhaique soon took over as the principal city of the region, both economically and culturally. Today, the landscape is characterised by newly planted pine forests and agricultural land, interspersed with lush meadows of brightly coloured lupins and the occasional farm, and the town itself retains a certain charm.

Puerto Chacabuco remains important for local commerce and as an entry/exit point for some visitors, and is also an access point to the **Ventisquero San Rafael** further south. There are some lovely parks in the region, including the **Reserva Nacional Río Simpson**, some decent accommodation and food, and a surprising number of activities.

MAÑIHUALES AND AROUND

Founded in 1962, **Mañihuales** seems to attract only those in search of petrol, with relatively little of interest in the vicinity – Puente Piedra is the emerging exception. It is the closest town for access to the unattractive Toqui mine (although this is not open for visitors and can hardly be described as a highlight) and is consequently home to a number of miners. Mining operations began in 1983, and in 2011 Belgian mining conglomerate Nyrstar acquired the mine and expanded production, but sold to Melbourne-based Laguna Gold Ltd in 2016. The mine produces zinc, lead, silver and gold, and has employed over 400 people in the past. In January 2019 it filed for bankruptcy. The region surrounding Mañihuales was routinely destroyed by slash-and-burn timber practices for much of the early 19th century, evidence of which can be seen to this day. Large sections along the Carretera Austral appear nothing more than tree graveyards, and the mountainsides are scarred with the impact of relentless logging and the subsequent erosion this produces. There is actually a **national reserve** by the town, but it is rarely visited and the tourist information centre closed some years ago. For those genuinely interested in the history of the region it may be worth spending a day in the town. Besides the petrol station there are limited services – there's no ATM or laundry and few shops. However, a boutique tour operator is already placing the village on the tourist map. The main event of historic importance was the landslide of 1966 which destroyed a large part of the town and had major repercussions across the region, yet is largely forgotten in the annals of history (see box, page 203). The current population is approximately 3,000.

Some 12km **south of Mañihuales**, the Carretera Austral splits (confusingly) into two roads both marked 'Carretera Austral': the gravel route southeast to Coyhaique (page 217) and the paved road southwest towards Puerto Aysén and Puerto Chacabuco (page 204). Note that the roads around the Toqui mine tend to be in poor condition, periodically destroyed by heavy trucks. Branching off from the direct route to Coyhaique, there is a pleasant detour to **Ñirehuao** and on to the Argentine border along reasonable gravel and undulating hills. The village has a shop, a police station and an emergency medical post. The only other inhabited village in this region is **El Gato**, slightly north of **Ñirehuao**, which offers camping and accommodation (see opposite) – it might be worth a stop for cyclists, or for those crossing the border late at night or early in the morning. Small ostriches (ñandu), flamingos and armadillos frequent the region, and the road passes various lakes. It also involves a number of minor river crossings, so a high-clearance car would be a wise choice.

The short road connecting the borders of **Paso Puesto Viejo** and **Paso Coyhaique** is beautiful. It traverses the border with Argentina, and rarely is the contrast between the two countries so visible: barren wasteland steppe to the east; to the west, increasingly green and undulating sections, populated mostly by animals. However, this stretch is on rough gravel and involves minor river crossings; it is therefore only suitable for a high-clearance vehicle.

However, unless actually intending to pass into Argentina, or visit one of the parks in this region, there is little to see and do.

GETTING THERE
About the route
Villa Amengual to Mañihuales (45km; under 1hr; paved) This pleasant paved road with relatively few detours or activities en route passes the excellent **Casona del Bosque** (page 196) and goes on to Lago Las Torres and the **Fundo Lago Las Torres** (page 195) to the west, with nice places to picnic. The region is a large valley with flat pastured farmland on either side, flanked by mountains. The scars of deforestation are still visible.

Towards Ñirehuao and Paso Puesto Viejo (30km from Villa Ortega to Ñirehuao & a further 32km to border; 1hr; gravel) The few roads to the east of the Carretera in this region are gravel and a high-clearance vehicle capable of minor river crossings is required. The roads to the north head towards the Toqui mine and some minuscule villages along the Argentine border, but it is not possible to cross into Argentina here. The most southern roads in this region are the two main border crossings closest to Coyhaique (Paso Triana and Paso Coyhaique), and in between lies the largest village in the region – Ñirehuao, 30km east of Villa Ortega. It is a further 32km to the Argentine border – probably the best border crossing to use if heading between Coyhaique and Esquel or further north in Argentina. Very limited services are available in this entire region, and mobile-phone coverage has not reached most of this section.

By bus Mañihuales benefits from its relative proximity to Coyhaique and Aysén and abundant buses pass through the town both south- and northbound. Some traverse the longer but paved route via Puerto Aysén, others the direct gravel route to Coyhaique – the time difference is marginal. Mañihuales does not have its own dedicated bus company. There is no formal bus company serving Ñirehuao or to the border.

TOUR OPERATOR

Bajando Ríos y Montañas 2 streets east of Calle Mañihuales; ///costumed.homily.flagging; 📞 9 9877 9579; e bajandoriosymontanas@ gmail.com; ⓕ. Highly recommended, reasonably priced, well-run tours put together by a passionate team who have (finally) put Mañihuales on the map. The main tour ($30,000 pp, min 4; 6–7hrs) is a trek to a mysterious rock formation known as 'Puente Piedra' carved by the Río Picacho. The river has carved bizarre formations & pools into the rocks forming a narrow canal, but with translucent water enabling breathtaking visibility into deep green pools where the rocks have formed shapes comparable to giant melted candles. Along the way Luis Ojeda explains the history of the Picaflor region, well off the Carretera Austral, pointing out the unusual plants along the trail, & a chance to spot chucaos & martín pescadores. The tour passes through private land & an authorised guide is obligatory. It includes transport, lunch & wetsuits. Take a towel & warm clothes – the sun penetrates through the trees but the water is freezing. A great trip, excellent value & fun for kids. For those seeking something more strenuous, the full-day hike up Cerro Colmillo (to the summit, weather permitting) is a good workout with the possibility of seeing the rare huemul & condors, among other wildlife treats. Transport, guides & lunch are included ($45,000 pp, min 3). Rappelling, including down waterfalls, is also on offer.

WHERE TO STAY, EAT AND DRINK

🏠 **Hospedaje/Cabin/Camping Campo Lindo** (2 rooms, 1 cabin, 6 camping sites) 4km east of El Gato, 18km west of Ñirehuao; ///plum.postponing.subtitle; 📞 9 8253 9328, 9 9155 5376. This is a good base from which to explore this region, ideal for pottering about back roads & enjoying the spectacular views, & a pleasant alternative to returning to Coyhaique or feeling obliged to continue along the Carretera. 2 dbl rooms with shared bathroom, 1 cabin for 4 people ($55,000 per cabin, no b/fast, well equipped, inc towels), & 6 camping sites with hot water ($6,000 pp). No Wi-Fi or cable TV, all heating via wood stoves. The owner, Rosa, has lived in El Gato all her life & can explain all the minor back roads, as well as the history of the region. Nearby there is a local restaurant, Sabores del Bosque, selling artisanal products and local food. **$–$$$**

🏠 **Pancita Feliz** (3 cabins) Villa Ortega; 📞 9 9718 2086. Sandwiched between Puerto Aysén, the Argentine border, Mañihuales & Coyhaique, it is little surprise that there are few sleeping options in the region, & besides Campo Lindo this is the only accommodation outside of Mañihuales. The owner, Idis Bilbao, offers simple, surprisingly good-value cabins ($35,000, up to 5 people). Reduced prices for couples can be negotiated. No Wi-Fi or laundry, but Idis can cook upon request – 'I just love cooking' – she's the ideal neighbour for weary travellers in a self-catering cabin. Reservations not required. Cash only. **$$**

☀ 🏠 **Ruta 7** (5 rooms, 2 cabins) General Marchant 155, Mañihuales; ///modifies.allow. albatrosses; 📞 9 7637 7969. Excellent, cosy & reasonably priced rooms on the eastern side of the plaza, 2 blocks from the Carretera. Good option for those wishing to avoid Coyhaique, to get an early start heading north or for pottering around Mañihuales. 2 trpl & 3 dbl rooms, all (decent) shared bathrooms & laundry available. B/fast $2,500 extra. 2 fully equipped cabins for up to 6 people ($45,000/night). Wood-stove heating, Wi-Fi, & parking on the street just outside or off-road for bikers. Friendly owners & a small restaurant downstairs (🕐 until 22.30, empanadas, chicken, seafood, $). Quintessentially rustic décor including a papier mâché lamb on a spit. No beer/ wine served, but you can bring your own. Accepts cards. **$$**

These two towns are often considered a single location connected by a 14km paved road. Puerto Aysén is the second most populated town in the entire region spanned by the Carretera Austral, but often overlooked by visitors. Some guidebooks fail to mention it entirely! It is true that the town itself is not particularly impressive, but the road towards Laguna Los Palos is a highlight in the region, with some great, reasonably priced accommodation options and tours, excellent if travelling with kids owing to the variety of family activities available, and only a 10-minute drive to town, where there is an ever-expanding range of good restaurants. It's debatable whether Puerto Aysén lies on the Carretera Austral, but even as a detour it is worth spending a couple of days here. Chacabuco, however, is a port and little else. Unless taking a boat north or south, there is very little reason to visit. The road to Mañihuales, to the northeast, is pleasant but relatively nondescript, although the road to Coyhaique carves straight through the Reserva Nacional Río Simpson. The regions to the immediate north and south of Aysén are worth a visit.

HISTORY What is now Puerto Aysén has been populated since the mid 19th century, predominantly by Chilotes, German settlers and Argentines, attracted by farming opportunities and cypress extraction. In the early 20th century the Chilean government began awarding concessions, and most importantly to the SIA (Sociedad Industrial de Aysén; page 213). Puerto Aysén was founded in 1913, mainly as the location for shipping products out of the region for the SIA. It was the principal population centre of the region and in 1927 was declared the capital, and upgraded to a 'city' in 1928. It soon became the main transport hub between Puerto Montt and Punta Arenas, driven primarily by timber and agricultural products. The Ibáñez Bridge over the Río Aysén was inaugurated in 1968, and is the longest suspension bridge in Chile. It was declared a National Monument in 2002, and was the scene of riots in 2012.

Sedimentation began to clog the port of Aysén in the 1960s, accelerated by the Mañihuales landslide (see box, opposite) and eventually Puerto Chacabuco replaced Puerto Aysén as the principal port in the region. The population of Coyhaique had surpassed that of Puerto Aysén by the late 1950s, and in 1975 Puerto Aysén lost its status as capital of the Aysén region to Coyhaique. Pinochet's valid concerns of an Argentine invasion may have also provided justification to move the capital closer to the border. The Carretera Austral served to transport the military in the case of an invasion.

Between January and April 2007 a series of earthquakes struck the Aysén Sound (Fiordo Aysén). The largest of these was on 21 April (magnitude 6.2) and caused landslides on the surrounding mountains which in turn created waves of up to 6m. Eleven people died, and a number of salmon farms were damaged. The earthquake was felt as far away as Santiago. Aysén's mayor at the time, Óscar Catalán, complained bitterly that the region had not received sufficient help from the government, and when President Bachelet visited the region she was met with protests and inhabitants waving black flags. Catalán was briefly arrested, according to police for a minor traffic offence. The event raised awareness of the danger of tsunamis in the region, and in particular in narrow fjords where they can occur almost spontaneously from landslides and travel quickly. This event prompted the government to install tsunami warning signs and evacuation routes, which are visible along most coastal regions.

Mañihuales was officially founded in November 1962, and yet knowledge of the great Mañihuales landslide of May 1966 is scarce. In the 1940s substantial deforestation of the region fundamentally altered the soils and ecosystem, fuelled by a desire to build houses rapidly and to export timber. Juana Carrillo had arrived from Llanquihue with her parents in 1953 in search of land, and settled in Mañihuales. They planted potatoes, wheat and peas and had various fruit trees including cherries and apples. Life was simple in those days, but particularly heavy rains in 1966 clogged the bare soil. The deforestation, visible to this day, had limited the extent to which the steep slopes around the village could support the weight of such immense quantities of water-clogged earth.

On the night of the landslide, 21 May, the residents of Mañihuales were celebrating a Chilean national holiday in style at the rodeo. On Juana's side of town were only four or five houses, a school and a winery. At 03.00 the landslide struck. The absence of casualties was presumably due to the party proceeding on the other side of the village. Juana, a responsible mother with six children and a 40-day-old baby, had retired from the party some hours earlier, and in the wee hours heard an ominous rumbling.

She looked out of the window and realised her options were limited. She shouted to all the children, gathered her baby in her arms, and fled the house, only to see her entire worldly possessions obliterated in front of her eyes. Other family members took care of Juana and her children, although she pointedly mentioned that they received no help from the government – a message more recently echoed by the victims of both the El Chaitén volcano and the Villa Santa Lucía landslide.

The sediment from this landslide (and others to the south) entered the Mañihuales and Simpson rivers, eventually flowing into, and clogging, the port of Aysén. The port had been suffering economically for some years, but this sediment was the final nail in the coffin for Aysén: it was simply not deep enough to offer safe harbour to larger vessels. This prompted the construction of Chacabuco port, on the Aysén Fjord and a safe distance from the estuaries of these rivers. Chacabuco gradually took over as the principal port of the province. Today the town of Aysén bears few signs of its former glory as the main trading hub of the province.

When asked if she ever considered leaving Mañihuales after this event, Juana categorically declared that the idea did not even occur to her, nor after the 1971 eruption of Volcán Hudson that showered the village with ash. What will the ongoing development of the Carretera Austral mean for the village of Mañihuales? Juana believes increased traffic will be good for the village, as they will be able to sell things to people passing through, but some aspects of modernity concern her. 'Before families used to have many children, but no television. Now we have television, but very few children.'

In 2012, Puerto Aysén was the epicentre of a series of protests led by the Movimiento Social por Aysén. The movement was prompted by an ever-increasing cost of living, reduced fishing quotas for local inhabitants, and was also related to the Patagonia Chilena ¡Sin Represas! movement (see box, page 220). On 7 February a group of fishermen seized the Ibáñez Bridge. A week later they took over the airport in Melinka. On 14 February 300 people blocked access to Puerto Aysén and Chacabuco, for the first time directly confronting the police. The following day saw protests escalate, with access to Balmaceda airport and the landing strip at Puerto Aysén prevented and various barricades established in Coyhaique. On 16 February, Coyhaique suffered electricity cuts, a few shops were looted and large parts of the city were blockaded. The following day the road to Mañihuales was blocked, as was the Cruce El Maitén, restricting access to Chile Chico or further south. Gradually media attention shifted towards Coyhaique, where the main police brutalities occurred. Meanwhile the movement reached as far as Villa O'Higgins, at the extreme south of the Carretera Austral, where protesters took over the landing strip.

On 22 February, armed police and Special Forces attempted to retake the Ibáñez Bridge, with full body armour, helmets and shields, riot shotguns and tear gas. Nine people were wounded and five arrested, but the citizens of Puerto Aysén were able to drive back the police by the early hours. The police attempted again to secure the bridge, attacking three groups of journalists from Radio Santa María, Chilevisión and Canal 13. Two people lost their eyesight in the fighting that ensued. The director of the National Institute of Human Rights declared: 'there was a disproportionate use of riot shotguns, used as a deterrent, but it seems according to all the data and testimonies gathered – that guns were aimed not pointing upwards (the correct procedure), but directly at the people.' This description seems unnervingly similar to reports of the 2019–20 civil unrest.

Civil unrest has largely ceased since the demise of the HidroAysén project (see box, page 220). Meanwhile a lesser-known hydro project to be run by Energía Austral (a joint venture between Swiss Glencore and Australian Origin Energy) is located a mere 45km from Puerto Aysén, damming the Río Cuervo. This 640MW plant was approved by the state in 2013. Environmental activists submitted a plea to the Supreme Court, but on 21 August the court granted the environmental permits for construction to begin. Subsequent concerns relating to building a hydro-electric plant on the unstable Liquiñe–Ofqui tectonic fault line close to active volcanoes eventually prevailed, and the project was abandoned in 2017.

GETTING THERE
About the route
Mañihuales to Puerto Aysén (58km; under 1hr; paved) Excellent paved road for the first 12km, where the road forks. The western fork continues to Puerto Aysén, the eastern fork to Coyhaique. Somewhat confusingly both are referred to as the Carretera Austral. In fact, the direct, gravel route to Coyhaique is the original Ruta 7, and the road to Puerto Aysén is Highway 50.

Beyond the junction the paved road is reasonable quality all the way to Puerto Aysén, weaving alongside the Río Mañihuales through lush fields of purple, pink and white lupins. Some 10km past the junction heading south, the road crosses the river at Puente Mañihuales – a spectacular bridge worth a photo stop. Note the deforestation still visible along this section of road – the dead tree trunks are vestiges from the timber industry stretching back to the 1940s. Smallholder farmland with horses, cattle and sheep dominates this region: from here until Lago General Carrera agriculture and livestock farming is a major industry. This is a pleasant road with plenty of sweeping views over the valley, and endless hairpin bends – great fun on a fast motorbike but be careful when the road is wet.

Aysén to Chacabuco (14km; 15mins; paved) This section passes Parque Aiken del Sur (page 212), but is otherwise nondescript.

Aysén to Coyhaique There are two connections between these towns, the paved road (page 216) and the scenic back route involving a minor ferry crossing (page 217).

By bus Frequent buses travel between Puerto Aysén/Chacabuco and Coyhaique (such as the hourly service with **Buses Suray**). Some northbound buses from Coyhaique do not go via Puerto Aysén, but head directly north along the gravel section of the Carretera towards Mañihuales, so it is often necessary to travel to Coyhaique first for connections.

By ferry A twice-weekly service operates between Chacabuco and Quellón (Chiloé), but this is quite slow (31hrs) with multiple intermediate stops (page 60).

TOUR OPERATORS

Atex Patagonia km3.4, Camino Lago Riesco, Puerto Aysén; ☏ 9 8945 4078; e atexpatagonia@ gmail.com; ⬛ Atex Patagonia Operadores. Note this is not along the access road to Lago Riesco from Chacabuco but along the south side of Río Aysén. Bilingual guides (English, German & French) offering a range of trips & assistance with logistics in the region. Kayaking, floating, trekking & fishing along Río Blanco & Río Simpson, including ascents of the rivers by motorboat. Also tours to further locations, including to the Campo de Hielo Norte (Northern Ice Field). Guided tours within the Reserva Nacional Río Simpson. Can arrange multi-day treks to the spectacular mountain range beyond Lago de los Palos into Campo El Tabo. Kayaking courses & rafting tours. 3 *domos* (circular, temporary tent structures) available for rent with a hydro-massage spa within an arrayan forest at their Río Aysén base.

Eclipse Patagonia Tour Av Municipal 565, Puerto Aysén; ///precursors.diverse.globes; ☏ 9 7747 9376, 9 9152 8472; e contacto@ eclipsepatagoniatour.cl; w eclipsepatagoniatour. cl. Something of a one-stop tour operator in the region, & an excellent alternative to arranging tours individually. Able to book almost any tour, including those run by Los Loberías del Sur (San Rafael glacier & Ensenada Pérez hot springs), & as far south as Puerto Río Tranquilo (marble caves). They also offer their own activities & tours, as well as those of many other independent guides in the area including horseriding, fishing trips, mountain biking, birdwatching, & tours of the city of Puerto Aysén, along the road to Lago de los Palos & in the Simpson Reserve. English-speaking guides & private transport. Accepts credit card.

Los Loberías del Sur José Miguel Carrera 50, Puerto Chacabuco; ///sneakily.tripling.prodigy; ☏ 67 235 1112; e info@loberiasdelsur.cl; w loberiasdelsur.cl. Luxury tours operated by the Loberías del Sur Hotel (page 208). Trips to the San Rafael glacier on a comfortable catamaran, tours to the Marble Caves & Parque Nacional Queulat, visits to their private Parque Aikén del Sur, the only hot springs in the region at Ensenada Pérez, & to Caleta Tortel. These can be booked independently, or as part of a package operated by Loberías. Classic & special tours from 3 to 9 nights offered, which include accommodation in the Loberías del Sur Hotel. Loberías can be relied upon to provide detailed local information, excellent customer service & vigilant attention to detail. Experienced guides with a range of languages including English, French, German & Hebrew.

Teuber Excursions ☏ 9 8456 5733, e g.teuber@outlook.es. Gerhard offers 2 main tours. The first is a trek up Cerro Cordon (1,350m) to the most magnificent viewpoint over Puerto Aysén, the mouth of the Río Aysén, various lakes & the fjord. The mountain is close to Puerto Aysén but is a challenging full-day trek of some difficulty ($80,000 pp). The 2nd tour is canyoneering, scaling down waterfalls armed with little more than suitable clothes, a helmet & a rope ($55,000 pp).

Trapananda Austral ☏ 9 9129 5875, 9 4813 1479; e hola@trapanandaaustral.cl; ⬛ Trapananda Austral. Owner Jose Molina has very stable inflatable mini catarafts ideal for fishing & gently pottering down rivers. He offers tours down 5 rivers: Blanco, Aysén, Pangal, Mañihuales & Simpson. All but the last are relatively easy, require limited prior experience

& are suitable for families (children over 12 years old) – a relaxing way to enjoy the river, learn the history of the region & observe the flora & fauna. Incredibly, sea lions occasionally venture up to 20km upriver & can be spotted frolicking & hunting salmon. Prices range from $35,000 pp for 2hrs to $48,000 pp for 4hrs (min 2 people), with discounts for larger groups. Mountain-bike tours in the region, including to Bahía Acantilada (page 210) & from Lago de los Palos to Fogón de Tabo. He also offers the trek to Cola de Gallo either as an independent tour, or combined with the bike trip to Fogón de Tabo. Jose is an experienced fisherman & offers fishing trips along the Aysén & Mañihuales rivers, or to Los Palos/Portales lakes, fishing from the shore, motorboat or cataraft.
Turismo el Pionero \ 9 9088 5898;
e elpioneroaysen@hotmail.com; ◼ El Pionero Aisén. Although pioneer might be a generous

term, what Peter Flores offers is a great, simple product: boat trips in the region. In a small covered boat capable of taking 7 or 8 people, Peter guides tailor-made fishing trips, & tours to hot springs, down the fjord, & exploring the 3 main islands outside Puerto Aysén (Carmen/Ciervo, Partida & Transito). In particular, he is authorised to trek on the privately owned Carmen Island, including night-treks, when the dense forest takes on a life of its own. Throw in some juicy local politics, history, mythology & astute knowledge of the local flora & fauna, & Peter can offer a delightful tour, more flexibly than the larger operators. Tours often involve viewing dolphins & extend as far as to the Cinco Hermanas Monument. His shortest tour is simply to explore the Aysén River around the town itself & cross beneath the longest suspension bridge in Chile, offering a slightly different viewpoint from

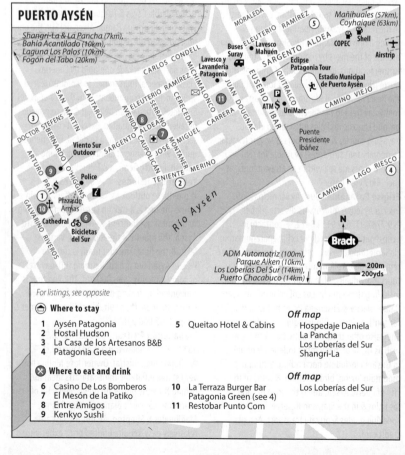

For listings, see opposite

🛏 **Where to stay**

1	Aysén Patagonia
2	Hostal Hudson
3	La Casa de los Artesanos B&B
4	Patagonia Green

5   Queitao Hotel & Cabins

Off map
Hospedaje Daniela
La Pancha
Los Loberías del Sur
Shangri-La

✖ **Where to eat and drink**

6	Casino De Los Bomberos
7	El Mesón de la Patiko
8	Entre Amigos
9	Kenkyo Sushi

10	La Terraza Burger Bar
	Patagonia Green (see 4)
11	Restobar Punto Com

Off map
Los Loberías del Sur

the town. Even more so than with other tours in this region, much depends on the weather. With a larger group prices are reasonable & Peter periodically offers free trips for people with disabilities or for underprivileged children who rarely get the chance to explore the region.

WHERE TO STAY
Puerto Aysén *Map, opposite*

Aysén Patagonia (9 sgls, 5 dbls) Sargento Aldea 560; ///restarting.vintage.alteration; ✆67 233 0928, 9 9789 6938; e recepcion@hotel-aysenpatagonia.cl; w hotel-aysenpatagonia.cl; ⊕ all year. The most upmarket hotel in town. A convenient, well-located & well-maintained upper-end option boasting all the facilities a weary traveller from the Carretera might require. Located 1 block from the plaza, & despite catering principally to business clientele, it retains a Patagonian feeling. All standard facilities provided, including off-road parking, laundry & central heating. Good-quality service, b/fast included. The hotel has a decent restaurant (⊕ 07.00–23.00 daily; $$$) & a reasonably priced menu of the day. Late check-outs possible. Reservations do not require a deposit, & foreigners do not pay VAT, reducing the price by approximately 20%. Credit cards accepted. $$$$

Patagonia Green (6 rooms, 4 cabins) Lago Riesco 350; ///crackles.tastefully.pretzel; ✆67 233 6796, 9 9841 2509; e patagoniagreen@gmail.com; w patagoniagreen.cl; ⊕ all year. An exceptional place to stay – probably the best accommodation option in Puerto Aysén. Located across the Río Aysén approximately 15mins' walk from the city centre, so more suited for those with private transport, although the hotel has a private van & taxis are easily arranged. The entire facility has been built gradually over a 15-year period to a very high standard. The 'green' refers both to the lush vegetation that surrounds the entire hotel & cabins, & also to the focus on environmental sustainability (recycling where possible, low-energy lighting, central heating without burning wood, & certified by the Responsible Tourism Institute). Particularly child-friendly, with a large lawn & playground (without direct access to the river). The cabins (for 2–5 people) are centrally heated & offer Wi-Fi, full kitchen & comfortable seating area, but don't include b/fast. There are 3 dbl & 3 twin rooms, each with balconies & b/fast included. Staff are friendly & knowledgeable, & speak Italian, English, Spanish & German. A variety of tours

are offered, the main one is to the Ventisquero San Rafael, as well as Parque Aikén & Ensenada Pérez hot springs. Most visitors stay for 2 or 3 days to combine with these day trips. Bike rental also available, but only for residents. Credit cards accepted. $$$$

Queitao Hotel & Cabins (2 rooms, 5 cabins, 1 apt) General Marchant 640; ///restricting.plasma.airlock; ✆67 233 6635, 9 8899 9202; e info@queitaopatagonia.cl. An ocean theme runs through the main building, with a bar that looks like a boat & old scuba kit on display. Not the best value in town – only 2 rooms of average quality but overpriced, cabins (up to 7 people) are better value, well equipped & with good sitting area. The apt for 3 people has a kitchen & sits on top of the hotel. Caters to companies mainly. Wi-Fi & parking available. Accepts credit cards. $$$$

La Pancha Camino Laguna Los Palos km 7; ///prepay.disapprove.braces; ✆9 9827 8106, 9 9887 8572; e info@ecoturismolapancha.cl; w ecoturismolapancha.cl. Camping, cabins & tour operator in one, this is a great place along the road to Lago de los Palos, nestled on the edge of the Río Pangal. Kayaks & a range of tours available, including the San Rafael glacier & the Ensenada Pérez hot springs with Loberías del Sur. Private transportation for those arriving in Puerto Aysén without a car. With both the kayak & horseriding trips, they either offer their own tours on the river & to the lake, or co-operate with other guides in the region venturing further afield. It's 2hrs to kayak from the lake downstream along the river to La Pancha, & suitable for children (16 people max). The horse ride is also a couple of hours along the valley (max 5 people). They can also arrange guided tours up the Cerro Cordon, mountain-biking trips & rock climbing. The campsite has space for 10 tents, some with electricity & most with a roof, all with a firepit, solar-heated hot showers & 2 quinchos to relax, cook & eat in ($8,000 pp). They have 2 high-quality, fully equipped A-frame cabins for up to 6 people with wood-pellet heating ($60,000–80,000 depending on number of people). Wi-Fi is patchy, but fairly reliable in the reception area. Laundry & b/fast available for an additional cost. Like Shangri-La next door, this is a great base for families to explore the area. **$–$$$$**

🏠 **Hostal Hudson** (10 dbls) Teniente Merino 1080; ///swats.biographies.powering; 📞9 9439 1571; e administracion@hostalhudson.cl; w hostalhudson.cl; ⏰ all year. A basic, good-value hostel by the river, 3 blocks from central square. Rooms with large, comfortable beds & shared or private bathrooms, b/fast included. Wi-Fi available, off-road parking, & laundry ($5,000). Large homely communal area & use of kitchen. Can arrange tours. **$$$**

✳ 🏠 **Shangri-La** (10 cabins) km7; Camino al Lago los Palos; ///radiated.shins.heartthrob; 📞9 7738 1405, 9 9159 0401; e complejoshangri.la@ gmail.com; w shangrilapatagonia.com; ⏰ all year. Another great option on the road to Lago de los Palos. Set in a large pasture with access to the river, this is certainly a peaceful option away from the relative chaos of Puerto Aysén. It's a good place to base yourself for a few days & explore the region while feeling you are in the middle of nowhere. 3 smaller cabins (4 people) & 7 large cabins (up to 7 people), including sofa-beds. The larger cabins have 2 bathrooms. Well equipped with full kitchen, good hot water, wood-stove heating with plenty of wood available. Comfortable beds & spacious, cosy communal area. Excellent place for kids to play, including a small playground. Loreto, the owner, can arrange tours in the region, including those in the immediate vicinity towards Lago de los Palos (kayaking, horseriding, boat trips, fishing, etc), as well as to the hot springs, rafting & treks further afield. Has mobile-phone coverage & Wi-Fi. Although the cabins are self-catering, a neighbour runs the 'Donde Yiya' food service. Also has a wonderful quincho for larger groups or for private events. Accepts credit card. **$$$**

✳ 🏠 **La Casa de los Artesanos B&B** (5 rooms) O'Higgins 830; ///thrill.chafing.blushes; 📞9 9802 1744; e reservascasadelosartesanos@ gmail.com; w casadelosartesanosbb.cl. Located on the road towards Lago de los Palos, this is the place to stay for those interested in the culture & history of the region. The highlight of this B&B is speaking to the owners. Claudio is an established author, both his books explaining the mythology & magic of Patagonia rather than strictly the history are widely read at schools in the region – English, Italian & German editions available for a fascinating, alternative glimpse of life in Aysén. His wife, Martha, produces a range of knitted products including *boinas* (the traditional beret-like cap worn in the region), souvenirs & excellent jams (blueberry, the lesser-known white raspberry, & gooseberry). For those able to speak Spanish, the option to spend half an hour chatting with the owners about the regional politics, history & mythology is priceless. Regardless, this is a charming, rustic, familial option far cosier & more intimate than most others in the town. 1 trpl, 3 dbls, 1 sgl, all shared bathroom, full b/fast included, reservation required in high season. Wi-Fi, can use laundry, wood-stove heating, basic English & German spoken. **$$**

Chacabuco

🏠 **Los Loberías del Sur Hotel** (60 rooms) José Miguel Carrera 50, Puerto Chacabuco; ///sneakily.tripling.prodigy; 📞67 235 1112; e info@loberiasdelsur.cl; w loberiasdelsur.cl. The only official 4-star hotel in the province of Aysén, & the largest hotel in the entire region. This is a fully fledged luxury hotel with all the trimmings – sauna, gym, events room, laundry, Wi-Fi, decent restaurant (**$$$$**), bar, small business centre, & b/fast included. The only thing they don't offer is massages. Lovely views out to the Aysén Sound, & the port itself is visible from the hotel. The company also owns the nearby Parque Aiken for hikes & water activities, & a catamaran that services the Ventisquero San Rafael & the hot springs at Ensenada Pérez. Packages combining such tours are available. The rack price is punchy, but most guests combine with a package trip to the glacier. A very comfortable & convenient option for those wishing to visit the glacier (page 211). English spoken. Credit cards accepted. **$$$$$**

🏠 **Hospedaje Daniela** (6 rooms) Diego Portales 314, Puerto Chacabuco; ///codifies.surely. checked; 📞9 8282 3157; e marimgloria26@ gmail.com; 🄵 hospedajedaniela. A good cheap alternative in Puerto Chacabuco. Sgl or dbl rooms all with a shared bathroom. Big comfy beds, & some rooms have a view over the port. Wi-Fi, cable TV, central heating & parking. Cash only. **$$**

🍴 WHERE TO EAT AND DRINK *Map, page 206*

The following entries are in Puerto Aysén – for eating options in Chacabuco, Los Loberías del Sur Hotel (see opposite) has a very good restaurant, mainly used by guests.

🍴 **Patagonia Green** Lago Riesco 350; ///crackles.tastefully.pretzel; 📞 67 233 6796, 9 984 12509; e infogreen@patagoniachile.cl; w patagoniagreen.cl; ⏰ 19.00–22.00 Mon–Sat. Excellent restaurant, gourmet but informal – can wear shorts & flip-flops & not feel awkward. Wide range of seafood dishes, but the speciality is the conger eel. Short walk over the bridge from downtown Aysén, but worth the effort. Also offers accommodation & tours (page 207). $$$$

✳ 🍴 **El Mesón de la Patiko** Serrano Montaner 550; ///sparks.accumulates.scrounge; 📞 9 7977 8371; ⏰ 13.00–16.00 daily, 19.00–22.00 Mon–Sat. A worthy member of the new wave of high-quality restaurants in the region, but without a corresponding price tag. This relatively new restaurant has displaced other contenders from the #1 spot in Puerto Aysén by a wide margin & is highly recommended. The menu is so extensive that one visit is simply not enough. Decent wine list & local ales including Tropera on tap, but the food steals the show. On the seafood side of the menu, ceviche with a kick, crab & octopus dishes (not so common in the region), & all the usual Chilean fare, but unusually they also have a fish tabla (selection of fish for sharing), fish stew, spicy shrimps & crab chowder. Meat lovers will also be delighted, with deer options, steaks (including entraña, popular in Argentina but less so in Chile), & British diners will appreciate the lamb curry. There are risottos, carpaccio, a wide range of excellent desserts, & multi-flavoured Pisco sours including nalca. Chilled atmosphere, & terrace available when not raining. Reservations advisable, especially at weekends. English spoken. Accepts credit cards. $$$–$$$$

🍴 **Entre Amigos** Sargento Aldea 1077; ///suffers.calmly.sways; 📞 67 233 3433; ⏰ 10.00–21.00 Mon–Sat. The place to go in town for a good parrilla – piles of various meats & a generous helping of potatoes for up to 6 people. The menu also has all the Chilean classics & standard dishes you could hope for: sandwiches, various options a lo pobre, a whole slew of pizzas, salmon, merluza, congrio & also D'Olbek beer. Locals say the place is of higher quality than other dining options in Aysén, though the price remains reasonable. $$$

🍴 **Kenkyo Sushi** Sargento Aldea 633-B; ///dislocation.fellows.people; 📞 67 252 4039, 9 4098 3457; f Kenkyosushi; ⏰ 14.00–22.30 Mon–Sat, 13.00–22.00 Sun & holidays. This gem of a restaurant is a rare opportunity to deviate from standard Chilean fare. Run by Valeska, an entrepreneurial woman with big ambitions to create Aysén's finest Asian restaurant. Ingredients are locally sourced when available, from fresh salmon from the fjord to local boutique regional beers. Standard sushi options available, but with some interesting local adaptations. The Aysén roll, for example, contains avocado, asparagus, meat & cheese – a combination rarely found in Japan. There is also a range of exotic Pisco sours made from local fruits & berries, such as the calafate Pisco sour, well known in town, & other variations include blueberry, rhubarb, rose mosqueta, ginger & cardamom. The food itself is surprisingly good & reasonably priced. The local community was slow to adopt sushi & the restaurant catered mainly to tourists, but within a year Valeska had convinced them of the merits of raw fish, & the restaurant now has a thriving take-away business. Cash only. $$$

🍴 **La Terraza Burger Bar** Carrera 540; ///loafing.placated.sidebar; 📞 9 8596 1502; ⏰ noon–15.00 & 17.00–23.00 Mon–Fri; 17.00–23.00 Sat. A gourmet burger bar that also serves milanesas, sandwiches, tablas, salads, ceviche. Children's menu & a limited range of deserts. Indoor & heated outdoor section, wide range of local beers, fruit juices, some wines, & freshly ground coffee. A rare opportunity to relax in the evenings over a brew. Popular with locals. $$–$$$

🍴 **Casino De Los Bomberos** Teniente Merino 600; ///fuels.poach.decorated; 📞 9 4971 9707; ⏰ noon–16.00 Wed–Sun. A local favourite with excellent-value tasty food & large portions. The service is good, with friendly staff, & the food arrives quickly. The blackboard menu of the day includes an entrée, main, dessert, fruit juice & tea or coffee, though you need to arrive early. The main is usually salmon, merluza, turkey or beef with the choice of a salad, mashed potatoes or chips. An adequate selection of beer & wine. It is also a café between main mealtimes, serving a selection of cakes. The atmosphere leaves something to be desired; all the walls are painted with lime green paint & there is no further attempt to refurbish the restaurant. $$

✗ **Restobar Punto Com** Calle Sargento Aldea 1356; ///sealer.headsets.gleefully; ☏ 9 7380 3172; ⓕ Puntocomrestobar; ⊕ noon–midnight daily. Typical Chilean fare such as lomo & salmon a lo pobre & sandwiches. Serves b/fast, & becomes a bar in the evenings. A decent range of imported beers, as well as artisanal beers from D'Olbek. Wi-Fi available. Accepts credit cards. $$

OTHER PRACTICALITIES There is **petrol** available in both Puerto Aysén (COPEC and Shell) and Chacabuco (COPEC). **Patagonia Rent a Car** (Gabriela Tisi ☏ 9 7490 2696; e gabrielatisi@gmail.com; w patagoniarentacar.cl) operates out of the Shell petrol station in Puerto Aysén. There are multiple **ATMs**, and the **tourist information centre** is on Jose Miguel Carrera on the eastern side of the plaza just past Banco Estado. For **shops**, options are limited in Chacabuco, but you'll find a couple along Aysén's main street (Sargento Aldea). **Viento Sur Outdoor** (Sargento Aldea 685; ///shared.infancy.concealing; ☏ 67 233 0354; w vientosuroutdoor.cl; ⊕ 10.15–13.00 & 15.30–19.30 Mon–Sat) is an outdoor shop with leading brands such as Marmot, Patagonia, Icebreaker, Outdoor Research, Ortlieb and Arc'teryx. Visit **Bicicletas del Sur** (Teniente Merino 602; ///proposes.tardy.exceed; ☏ 9 9967 5646; w bicicletasdelsur.cl; ⊕ 10.00–19.00 Mon–Sat) to buy bicycles, and for rental and repairs.

Mechanics
ADM Automotriz Lago Portales 200; ///frustration.condors.scalp; ☏ 9 6237 8564; ⊕ 09.00–19.00 Mon–Sat. Basic car repairs, suspension, accessories, tyres, etc.
Carlos Mohr Eleuterio Ramirez 502; ///milder. rounds.thoughtless; ☏ 67 233 0900; ⊕ 09.00–13.00 & 14.30–18.00 Mon–Fri, 09.00–14.00 Sat. Tyres, lubricants, batteries & other repairs.

Laundry
Lavanderia Mahuén Eleuterio Ramirez 1550, Puerto Aysén; ///sealer.headsets.gleefully; ☏ 67 233 2828; e lavaseco.mahuen@outlook.cl; ⊕ 10.00–13.00 & 15.00–19.00 Mon–Fri, 10.00–13.00 Sat. Laundry, dry-cleaning & ironing.
Lavaseco y Lavanderia Patagonia Sargento Aldea 1385, Puerto Aysén; ☏ 9 7890 9442; ⊕ 09.30–14.00 & 15.30–20.00 daily. Laundry & dry-cleaning service.

WHAT TO SEE AND DO For those not intending to head further south or with less time, Puerto Aysén offers the opportunity to visit one of the Carretera's undisputed highlights, the spectacular **Ventisquero San Rafael**, as well as various nearby lakes and parks. Puerto Aysén is also used as a base from which to visit the **Reserva Nacional Río Simpson** (page 212).

Bahía Acantilada A modest beach great for taking advantage of a rare sunny day in Aysén. Quinchos, kayaks and boats are available to rent, although it is worth noting that no alcohol is allowed in the quinchos. It is, as the name suggests, next to a cliff. There is a small café serving tea, coffee and ice creams.

Laguna Los Palos A lovely detour on a sunny day, through verdant forestation of arrayan trees and up to Laguna los Palos surrounded by snow-capped mountains. Head north out of Puerto Aysén on Eusebio Ibar Street, until leaving the main inhabited area, and turn left along Pangal towards a small, scenic bridge with some fishing boats (Puerto Palos). After the bridge turn right (ie: north) towards Lago de los Palos, or continue straight on towards Bahía Acantilada. Reaching the beach is possible in any vehicle, but head north towards Lago de los Palos only with a car capable of traversing moderate gravel. Beyond the end of the lake, a 4x4 is recommended. The road weaves through spectacular mountains, with snow-capped peaks visible, some farmland, and then a few cabins. Various outfits along the road offer a range of activities, from treks to horseriding, kayaking, boat trips, fishing excursions and cycling trips. It is possible to continue beyond the lake to Fogón El Tabo, but this is private property and has to be arranged through a tour operator. **Atex Patagonia** (page 205) offer multi-day treks in this region.

SIGHTSEEING AND EXCURSIONS

Ventisquero San Rafael (Loberías del Sur, page 205; prices from US$245 to US$350 pp, under-5s pay half, discounts for over-55s, packages combining accommodation plus glacier trip available) Despite being located some 200km north of the Ventisquero San Rafael, Puerto Aysén is one of only two main access points (the other being from Bahía Exploradores, accessed from Puerto Río Tranquilo – page 260) for those wishing to visit the glacier. And, although tours from Puerto Aysén travel a substantially greater distance, the experience is five-star, compared with the more arduous trip available in the south. All tour operators and hostels offering this tour are ultimately selling the same service, provided by the same company that owns Los Loberías del Sur Hotel and Parque Aiken. The round trip takes a full day, travelling by fast, comfortable catamaran. The frequency of boats depends on the time of year: there are between 11 and 15 trips per month from October to April, and weekends only the rest of the year (except July), and the price includes all food and drink, plus the zodiac trip to the glacier through the icebergs. The glacier is spectacular and undoubtedly a highlight of the entire Carretera Austral (page 267).

Ensenada Pérez Hot Springs (Loberías del Sur, page 205; $55,000–65,000 pp, discounts for children & over-55s) The newest addition to the tours operated by Loberias in the region of Puerto Aysén; on Sundays and Thursdays, departing at both 09.00 and 16.00 (arrive 1hr early to check in). The catamaran used for San Rafael visits these hot springs, perched on the edge of the fjord with almost-vertical tree-covered cliffs behind. The three pools connected by wooden walkways are slightly different temperatures. Once in the water the view looks to the fjord, forest and the boat. Staff shuttle back and forth bringing drinks and canapés as you wallow in the water. Two permanently flowing cold showers from a waterfall above offer an invigorating break between pools. These are the closest hot springs to Coyhaique, and the entire tour is well run, with towels, crocs, a dressing gown and surprisingly good food provided. The later tour doesn't get back until around 22.00, so it's wise to have accommodation arranged. On the way back the boat passes by the Cinco Hermanas Natural Monument. Visiting hot springs is *de rigueur* for any trip to the Carretera, but springs are scarce further south, and unless visiting Puyuhuapi or Cisnes, these are the best option in the region. It's not the cheapest, but this is Loberías del Sur: high-quality, great-service tours with good attention to detail.

Fogón del Tabo (end of road towards Lago de los Palos; ///eloped.mindset. committing; ✆ 9 9290 2477; e fogondeltabo@gmail.com) Approximately 20km north of Aysén along the delightful road towards Laguna Los Palos, Mauricio offers a range of treks on land owned by his family for three generations. A high-clearance car is advisable to reach the trailheads. There is a basic quincho with rustic beds if sleeping here is absolutely necessary, but the highlight is the 6km trail to the Cola del Gallo waterfall ($3,000 self-guided, or $5,000 with a guide), which takes approximately an hour in each direction, with multiple river crossings and a leisurely walk through virgin evergreen forest (tepa, coihue, arrayanes, etc). This is the waterfall that Teuber Excursiones rappel down (page 205). On the way to the waterfall is the unusual sight of two distinct trees, a coihue and a tepa, wrapped around one another – aptly named 'Los Enamorados' (the lovers). This is one of those quirky but worthwhile tours that are so easily overlooked. A slightly longer trail following a different route back from the waterfall is also available.

Parque Aiken to Lago Riesco (\ 67 235 1112) The park is owned by Loberías del Sur and accessed via a short gravel road of approximately 4km before arriving at Chacabuco. The 250ha park has four trails, and contains a simple visitor centre that provides information and maps. The **River Trail** (2km one-way) follows the El Salto Creek from the visitor centre to a waterfall, and the **Waterfall Trail** (1km round trip) connects the road to the waterfall. The longest trail is the **Arrayanes Trail** (2.5km one-way), which can be extended to the quincho by the lake by walking a further 600m (technically the **Lake Trail**). Bilingual guides are available. Vegetation includes cafayate, michay and chilcos shrubs, plus the common maqui shrub which is able to grow in burnt and eroded soils, producing a small fruit that is used as a colorant. The park has various ferns, lichens and mosses, including the *Lophosoria quadripinnata*, which is apparently unique to the region around the waterfall at the end of the River Trail. Trees include the arrayan, notros, tepa and myrtaceous, as well as a 300-year-old Chilean myrtle (*Luma apiculata*). Animal species include pudús and pumas (apparently), huet-huet, kingfishers, foxes, woodpeckers and Chucaos. The large bandurria (*Theristicus caudatus*) is common across the park and the region as a whole, clearly visible prodding the ground or marsh searching for small insects, spiders and frogs. The park also includes a small botanic garden located approximately halfway along the road through the park, with 32 native trees and bushes. Alas the view over the lake has been spoilt somewhat by an ugly salmon farm. From November to April it is possible to fish in the lake (with a licence; brown trout are common).

Other lakes south of Puerto Aysén It is possible to drive along the south side of the Río Aysén and then along the Río Blanco to **Lago Portales**, or continue along the Río Riesco towards **Lago Riesco** (the southeastern side of the lake, as opposed to access from Parque Aiken which reaches the northern extreme of the lake). The road continues to the smaller **Laguna Alta** and **Laguna Baja**.

RESERVA NACIONAL RÍO SIMPSON

(e fernando.mansilla@conaf.cl; w conaf.cl/parques/reserva-nacional-rio-simpson; entry foreign adult/child $8,200/4,100, Chilean adult/child $4,100/2,100) Situated on the main road between Puerto Aysén and Coyhaique, the Reserva Nacional Río Simpson is a small (41,620ha) reserve that covers the mountains and valleys to the west and northwest of Coyhaique. It was established to restore the delicate ecosystem following environmental damage caused by deforestation in the early 20th century. The Río Simpson is the main watercourse in this region. There is a small native forest and environmental education centre at the park headquarters, where a description of the fauna and flora of the El Pescador Trail is available in English or Spanish. There is a **CONAF campsite** ($7,000 pp; booking not essential) on the river 2km towards Coyhaique from the park headquarters. There are ten camping sites that consist of a covered hut suitable for wet weather, with a concrete floor, table and bench seat and a built-in barbecue area. There is also a large quincho for 30 people. The park can also be accessed from Coyhaique via the Área de Protección del Huemul Río Claro (a protected area within the national reserve where huemules reside) along a 16km trail passable only in a 4x4.

One of the first explorers in this region was Captain Enrique Simpson whose name was bestowed upon the river. At the beginning of the 20th century the first settlers opened up this route to provide access from the port of Aysén to Coyhaique. In 1904 the livestock company SIA (Sociedad Industrial de Aysén) hired people to build this notorious road. It is said that to complete this route the forest lumberjacks had to cut in half 100,000 4m-long coigüe poles, to cover 20km of swamp land. In 1920 and 1948 extensive fires ripped through this valley due to slash-and-burn agriculture practices used in this period to clear bush land for farming purposes. The subsequent land erosion in the Valle Río Simpson from the 1966 floods (see box, page 203) was catastrophic and is partly responsible for the closure of the port at Puerto Aysén due to river sedimentation blocking the river from larger boats. As a result of this manmade disaster, the Chile Tax Authority acquired private land in the valley to form the Reserva Nacional Río Simpson to protect this fragile ecosystem.

Today the Río Simpson is renowned for its great **fly-fishing** and is considered one of the top four fly-fishing rivers on the planet. There is also a new, well-maintained **trail** that follows the northern riverbank and is suitable for children. There are plans to build a bridge across the Río Simpson, and to extend trails further.

GETTING THERE
About the route
Puerto Aysén to Reserva Nacional Río Simpson (31km; 30mins; paved) Follow the main road (Ruta 240) between Puerto Aysén and Coyhaique, driving through the main 'T' intersection at km17 where the Carretera Austral heads north towards Villa Mañihuales. Follow the Río Simpson into the river valley for a further 14km. The entrance for the reserve and the trail is directly across from the shrine of San Sebastián (///snacked.gardening.already). After leaving the reserve, the **road to Coyhaique** continues through temperate rainforest with stunning views of the river to rolling grassland within a few kilometres. Coyhaique is 27km south of the reserve entrance.

By bus Buses **Suray** run hourly between Puerto Aysén and Coyhaique – ask the driver to drop you at the park's entrance (but be vigilant in case he forgets). To continue from the park to Coyhaique, simply flag down a passing bus. **Buses Ali** offer a comparable service at an elevated price.

THE RUTA DE LOS PIONEROS TRAIL (The Pioneers' Trail; 3km; 1½hrs one-way; easy) is part of the original trail used by the early explorers and settlers and winds through beautiful native forest with stunning river views. The trailhead is 27km north of Coyhaique towards Aysén or 37km east of Aysén. The changing landscape from Coyhaique evolves from rolling grassland to temperate rainforest within a few kilometres. The entrance for the reserve and to the trail is directly across from the shrine of San Sebastián. The hike starts in a pine forest which is part of a reforestation initiative but soon enters the native forests of the temperate rainforest ecosystem. It follows the Río Simpson for the entire trek, from sections of relative

8

calm to roaring white-water rapids. Keep your eyes peeled for a variety of wildlife and plant species. The native vegetation is mainly the mixed forest of common coigüe and lenga with some nire in the humid sectors. There is also a mix of exotic shrub species introduced to try to control the erosion after the deforestation. The chilco (*Fuchsia magellanica*), native to this area of South America and which grows prolifically in many gardens in subtropical climates, will be easily recognisable to many as the common fuchsia, with its distinctive bright red-and-purple flowers. Chilco is abundant and has adapted very well to this environment.

A moss-covered stone house, easily missed, is a restored shelter built by the Pioneros. Inside is information on their lives, including diary entries and historical accounts. Then comes a section with challenging rapids popular with local kayakers. Thereafter the trail leaves the forest and emerges into a section predominantly covered with the giant leaves of the nalca plant – a rhubarb plant on steroids – and an impressive display of the colourful red flowers from the Chilco bush.

⊕ AS THE CONDOR FLIES

Puerto Aysén is 435km from Puerto Montt and 395km from the border crossing south of Villa O'Higgins at the extreme southern end of the Carretera Austral. Southbound condors are a little over halfway to their final destination.

9

Coyhaique

Coyhaique is the only city of notable size along the Carretera Austral. Previously visitors would rarely stop here for anything more than a change of clothes, a bite to eat, to pick up provisions, repair vehicles or to catch a bus. However, this situation is starting to change. The shopping possibilities have grown substantially, to include camping gear, clothing of all qualities, bicycle accessories, well-stocked pharmacies and most of the essentials one might expect, albeit at elevated prices. There are even bookshops! The city boasts an ever-increasing array of restaurants, including sushi and vegetarian cuisine (there is not yet an Indian restaurant). There are garages, roadside cafés, ATMs, tour operators, hotels of every conceivable price range, and a fine micro-brewery, La Taberna D'Olbek. It is the logistical hub for the entire region – book ferry tickets and flights here. Nightlife is reasonable in high season, but there is no cinema. The weather is pleasant in the summer, occasionally reaching the high 20s (Celsius), but a raincoat is required all year. The central plaza is a popular spot to enjoy an ice cream on a sunny afternoon. Ironically for so remote a city in such a pristine environment, pollution is a problem in winter, mainly due to wood-burning stoves. The city is safe, laid-back, surrounded by forests, mountains and rivers, and increasingly bohemian.

However, the architecture is fairly drab and beyond the few blocks comprising downtown Coyhaique there is relatively little to do. Public transport is chaotic, confusing and frustrating to arrange. The entire city is built around a pentagram which destroys any natural sense of direction. It is likely that within a few days the call of the Carretera Austral will lure visitors away from the city and back into the stunning region of which Coyhaique is the capital.

HISTORY

Prior to the arrival of the settlers, mainly of Spanish descent, this region was occupied by the various nomadic tribes of the Tehuelche (also called Aonikenk), Kawésqar (Alacalufes) and Chonos. Most had been driven away, killed or died of disease by the mid 19th century. The first documented record of what is now the city of Coyhaique was by Rear Admiral Enrique Simpson Baeza, who visited the area in December 1872 while studying the lakes and rivers of the region. Permanent inhabitants began arriving in the late 19th century, followed shortly thereafter by large cattle herders.

Settlement was facilitated by the state awarding large tracts of land to private individuals, as in other parts of the province. In 1903 Luis Aguirre, originally from Punta Arenas, was awarded a 22-year concession over the valleys of Coyhaique, Mañihuales and Ñirehuao. These were subsequently ceded to the wealthy industrialist Mauricio Braun, who formed the Sociedad Industrial de Aysén (SIA – Aysén Industrial Society; page 213). Braun was the industrialist behind the failed development around Caleta Tortel which resulted in the mysterious deaths of approximately 80 people in the winter of 1906 (see box, page 312). SIA established its main facilities at the confluence of the Coyhaique and Simpson rivers, and began mass deforestation in order to create space for cattle grazing. This involved cutting and burning large tracts of native forest (some estimates suggest as much as 3 million hectares), the damage of which is still visible to this day.

SIA failed to comply with the terms of the concession, namely in building roads, the government began to intervene more forcefully in the 1920s, and in 1927 created the Territory of Aysén, with its capital in Puerto Aysén. The following year Luis Gonzalez Marchant established the village of Baquedano, which was formally incorporated on 12 October 1929.

Naming the village in honour of the Chilean military commander Manuel Baquedano González turned out to be unwise, as post invariably was sent to the better-known town of Baquedano in northern Chile. Thus, in January 1934 the state decided to change the name of the town to Coyhaique. The origin of the name is the subject of some dispute. In Mapudungun, the language of the Mapuche people of the region, *koi* means 'water', or 'lagoon'. However, in the language of the Tehuelches, *coi* means *coihue* (the tree). Given that the region has abundant trees and water both explanations seem reasonable. *Áiken* in Mapudungun means 'camp', while *aike* in Tehuelche means 'place' – comparable meanings. Thus the name Coyhaique broadly means 'place of water or trees'.

The population grew as more settlers were attracted to the region for its rich logging opportunities. The town also became the hub for livestock trading. By 1940 there were over 4,000 inhabitants in the town, but it was still eclipsed by Puerto Aysén, with nearly 6,000, and the dominant port of the region. The slightly confusing pentagonal plaza in downtown Coyhaique was built in 1945, but it was not until July 1947 that Coyhaique became a formal municipality, and built the town hall the following year. By 1959 the town's population had overtaken that of Puerto Aysén and Coyhaique was upgraded to a department. In part this was likely due to Coyhaique's location serving as a trade hub for the region, being closer to the Argentine border, and also for the relative demise of the port at Puerto Aysén in the 1960s.

A livestock crisis in the 1970s left the region heavily dependent on public investment, and following the overthrow of Salvador Allende in 1973, Pinochet decided to move the regional capital from Puerto Aysén to Coyhaique. The following year work resumed on building road connections in the region in what subsequently became the Carretera Austral.

According to the 2020 census Coyhaique has just under 60,000 inhabitants.

GETTING THERE

ABOUT THE ROUTE Puerto Aysén to Coyhaique (64km; 1hr; paved) The road is initially flat and opens out into a wide valley, leaving the snow-capped mountains of Puerto Aysén in the distance. Road quality is good and there is reasonable traffic along this route, connecting two of the most populated towns of the entire Carretera Austral. However, take care of unexpected pot-holes and subsidence when approaching Coyhaique. The road follows the Río Simpson and passes through the centre of the Reserva Nacional Río Simpson, with the valley gradually narrowing to offer some fantastic views down to the river, and passing through the only tunnel along the entire Carretera Austral (Túnel Farelló). According to local superstition, if you stop to look at Cascada La Virgen (30km from Puerto Aysén;

///mystify.bras.neater) the ghost of a boy, completely dry, emerges from the waterfall and gets into your car. Various waterfalls can be seen along the route, and plenty of farmland and fields bursting with purple and white lupins, with dramatic cliffs in the background. At times the cliffs are not so distant, as the road weaves along the gorge, so take care particularly when the road is wet. There is a wind farm on the approach to Coyhaique.

There is an alternative route between Coyhaique and Puerto Aysén. Travelling from Coyhaique take the X-608 travelling south from the town. The road passes the north of Lago Atravesado, and continues, following the Río Quetro to Lago Portales. The road then skirts around the north of Lago Portales, and joins with the X-606, which crosses the Río Blanco by *balsa*. (No prior booking is necessary, and the boat operates daily.) After the boat, take the X-550 north to Puerto Aysén. The road is gravel, and passable by most cars, but a 4x4 is recommended. Watch out for gauchos speeding round blind corners herding cattle. The valley is spectacular, and in the spring the air is thick with the smell of blossom. Untouched forest flanks the valley, while farmland and streams lie in the centre. It's a fantastic route on a sunny day, when time is not a priority.

Mañihuales to Coyhaique (72km, under 2hrs; mostly gravel) Aysén is a pleasant town, but purists may prefer to take the original Carretera Austral directly south to Coyhaique avoiding Puerto Aysén and Chacabuco. The road is paved from Mañihuales until the junction 12km south of the town, but Ruta 7 is gravel from this point onwards (approximately 50km) until the final 10km into Coyhaique. The route passes through some lovely valleys resplendent with colours that seem almost unnaturally bright (in summer, when sunny). There is a modest amount of traffic along this route, so take care, particularly at night. The road initially tracks the Río Emperador, with stunning views over the valley. This is also an agricultural and farming region, and it is not inconceivable to find cattle or sheep on the road. The gravel quality is generally fine, but there are some steep ascents and descents which might challenge a tired cyclist. Some heavy trucks servicing the farms use this road, adding to the degradation of the gravel surface and creating occasional ruts, particularly if wet. Villa Ortega is a minuscule village with a shop, restaurant and cabins for rent, but it is connected to the mobile-phone network, so this is an opportunity to confirm a hotel reservation in Coyhaique. For the various detours east, see page 199.

BY BUS Informal buses leave from the UniMarc supermarket, but with unscheduled times and routes liable to change. Buses departing from the central bus station are marginally more reliable, although it may be wise to confirm times and book tickets in advance, particularly in January and February. It is possible to take direct buses from Coyhaique to most destinations, including as far north as Osorno and Puerto Montt, and to Argentina.

Direct buses from Coyhaique do not generally go further **north** along the Carretera Austral than La Junta, at the northern edge of the Aysén region, but La Junta is a hub for buses further north into the region of Los Lagos (Futaleufú, Chaitén, etc). An exception to this is the weekly **Queilén Bus** services (w queilenbus. cl) to Puerto Montt, Ancud, Santiago and Castro via Argentina (subject to the border being open).

Southbound buses from Coyhaique generally go no further than Cochrane, but likewise, connecting buses to Caleta Tortel and Villa O'Higgins depart from Cochrane. There are occasional direct buses to Puerto Cisnes, but failing that, take

9

any northbound bus to the Cisnes Junction and then take a local bus. There are direct buses to Chile Chico (via Puerto Ibáñez and crossing the lake), and Buses Transaustral Patagonia previously offered a twice-weekly service to Comodoro Rivadavia (Argentina). Visit w transaustralbus.com to check the current status of this service.

Buses to Puerto Aysén are available daily with **Buses Suray** (w suray.cl) from their office [224 C4]. **Buses Ali** offers a similar service, but at an elevated price (f buses.ali.5)

Despite Coyhaique serving as a natural hub for public transport along the Carretera Austral, many destinations off the main road are not served and must be arranged locally. Given the broader unreliability of buses in the region, such connections incur an element of risk, thus building spare time into your itinerary is essential.

BY AIR Balmaceda airport is 55km to the southeast (page 237). **Sky Airlines** (w skyairline.cl) and **Latam** (w latam.com) offer flights to Puerto Montt and Santiago. **JetSmart** (w jetsmart.com) is a budget airline with flights between Coyhaique/Balmaceda and Santiago, Puerto Montt, Concepción and Temuco. Two other airlines offer **charter flights** to Cochrane, Chile Chico, Melinka, Chaitén, Laguna San Rafael, Puyuhuapi, Palena, Futaleufú, La Tapera, Puerto Montt, etc. **Aerocord** (\ 67 224 6300; w aerocord.cl) offers a scheduled flight to Villa O'Higgins for $36,000 per person one-way on Monday and Thursday. Note this is subsidised by the state and non-residents can only fly (at this same price) if there is a spare seat available. Charter flights elsewhere are available. **Aero Taxis Del Sur** (\ 65 225 2523, 9 9583 8374; e administracion@aerotaxisdelsur.com; w aerotaxisdelsur.com) offers only charter flights. **DAP** (scheduled flights \ 61 222 9936; e ventas@dap.cl, charter flights \ 61 261 6100; e agencia@dap.cl; w dapairline.com) offers a flight to Punta Arenas on Tuesdays, as well as charter flights.

SUFFOCATING IN PATAGONIA

Surrounded by mountains and with relatively little wind, when the residents of Coyhaique spark up their fires to keep warm through the winter the consequences are surprising. A 2018 study by the World Health Organisation (WHO) of over 4,000 cities worldwide discovered that Coyhaique had the worst air quality of any city in the Americas. To breathe worse air one must go to China, India or Mongolia. The WHO suggests fine particulate levels should not exceed $25\mu g/m^3$. Coyhaique averaged 67 – more than five times that of London. In part this is due to the high moisture content of the wood being burned – such is the demand that there is insufficient time to adequately dry the wood before selling it. Low clouds prevent the smoke from escaping the natural bowl that is Coyhaique – on bad days all sports activities are prohibited. The government has tried to persuade residents to switch to less polluting energy sources, but the roaring log-burning stove heating the house is part of life in Coyhaique. Cleaner pellet-burning stoves are available, and government subsidies encourage residents to switch, but many stubbornly prefer to burn cheap, poorly dried wood, particularly as the pellets are often in short supply. Electricity prices are already relatively high, and supply of electricity in winter is also not historically reliable, dissuading residents to switch to any electric-based heating system. Another reason to visit the Carretera Austral in summer.

Coyhaique is littered with people and agencies claiming to be tour guides. In fact they're usually just agents representing operators situated local to the sights themselves. Hotels earn a small commission for recommending particular operators. For those travelling the Carretera Austral, many of whom will have their own vehicle, many of these activities do not require additional transport and are as easily, and often more cheaply, arranged locally. Also, there are very few travel agencies with their own offices, meaning that everything is done by phone, which adds an extra element of complication. The agencies that have a physical presence and are able to offer impartial advice, as well as tours off the beaten track, are listed below.

The 'standard' tours offered by most agencies generally consist of the following: **marble caves** (easily arranged in Puerto Río Tranquilo through a variety of operators); **Ventisquero Queulat** (accessible from the main Carretera, small entrance fee); **Ventisquero San Rafael** (requires a tour operator); **Caleta Tortel glaciers** (can be arranged locally, but less hassle and more reliable through an agent); and **viewing the Andean condors** waking up in the morning from their nests on cliff edges (guide required).

100% Patagonia Slow Travel km6 towards Coyhaique Alto; ///curtain.inked.audacious; \9 7765 3570, 9 9486 4989; e carolina@100patagonia.cl; w 100patagonia.cl. A company run by 2 tour operators with decades of experience working in tourism, including 15 years on the Aysén Tourism Board. They focus on tailor-made trips for those interested in getting off the beaten track, offering exposure to the local culture & travel outside the normal high season, explicitly avoiding the classic trap of cramming in too many places to visit in too short a time. The usual trips are possible (San Rafael/Queulat glacier, Tranquilo caves, etc), but also excursions to the lesser-visited northern sector of Parque Patagonia around Chile Chico (as well as the rest of the park), & the more interesting regions of Lago General Carrera – Puerto Sánchez, Cristal, etc. They offer unusual kayaking/cycling/horseriding options, ornithological trips, exploring the 'back route' between Ibáñez & Cerro Castillo (page 246), as well as fishing & trekking. A novel angle is the option for visitors with specific skills (musicians, scientists, artists, etc) to engage with the local community for a more symbiotic experience. They provide fully guided trips, or help arrange self-drive tours (logistics/reservations only), including assistance with car rental. They prepare fine picnics, accommodating all eating preferences, & are environmentally responsible. English-speaking guides available. A good alternative to arranging things independently, recommended & reliable managers, & an informative website.

Aysén Patagonia Tour [224 B5] 12 de Octubre 417; ///remit.prosper.curve; \67 223 5797, 9 8132 3080; e rodrigo@aysenpatagoniatour.cl; f. A wide variety of both standard & tailored tours along the entire Carretera Austral provided by owners with over 20 years' experience in tourism in the area. Specialises in group travel, with buses for groups of up to 30 to travel the Carretera Austral from Bariloche, & offer tailored tours for biking, cycling, trekking & sailing. Experienced English- & Spanish-speaking guides. Accepts credit cards & payment online or in the Coyhaique office.

Buen Viaje [224 C4] Oficina 1, Bilbao 260 Interior; \9 8133 2944; e operador.regional@gmail.com; f Buen Viaje. One of the longest-established tour operators in Coyhaique. Tours to Lago Frío, Puerto Aysén, Laguna San Rafael, Chile Chico & 6 Lagunas. Prices range from $55,000 pp (horseriding) to $100,000 pp (Lagiuna San Rafael). All guides are local gauchos (1 English-speaking), who offer a unique insight into the area. All tours include transport & food, if needed. It is possible to pay online or in the shop in Coyhaique. Accepts credit cards, & open all year round.

Tim Druett \9 8418 7304; e timdruett2@gmail.com. Tim first set foot in Chile over 25 years ago with Raleigh International, & since then has become a goldmine of information for those looking to learn about Coyhaique. His knowledge of both the flora & fauna of the area provides fascinating insight. Tim offers custom

Chile needs energy, and lots of it. Sustained economic development over two decades and a huge mining sector have increased energy consumption dramatically. Despite being one of the most prosperous countries in Latin America, it is energy-poor: it produces virtually no oil or gas of its own, and neither Argentina nor Bolivia will sell their gas to Chile.

Chile's mining industry is expected to nearly double its electricity consumption within a decade. It produces about a third of the world's copper (with China as a major consumer), and approximately 27% of the cost of copper production is attributed to energy costs. In 2014 the industry's regulator published a report warning that the copper-mining sector needs to increase its power capacity by 18,000 gigawatts in order to meet future demand.

In 2004, Endesa Chile, the largest private electric utility company in Chile, commenced a plan to develop five hydro-electric dams on the Río Baker (near Cochrane) and the Río Pascua (near Villa O'Higgins). The annual energy production from such dams is estimated to be 18,430 gigawatts.

And so began the 'HidroAysén' project.

Endesa (a subsidiary of the Italian conglomerate ENEL) held a 51% share in the project. The remaining 49% was owned by Colbun, a Chilean private electricity supplier. HidroAysén's proposal was to deliver energy to Chile, and development to the region of Aysén. This development would come largely in the form of jobs, 20% of which would be employed locally, and promises of even more local employees once HidroAysén started local training initiatives. This in an area of comparatively low wages compared with the cost of living, and relatively high unemployment.

As well as jobs, HidroAysén offered to improve 187km of the Carretera Austral; construct a 100m jetty in Puerto Yungay; build a meat processing plant and a waste disposal dump in Cochrane; install cultural and tourist information centres in Cochrane, Caleta Tortel, Villa O'Higgins, and Puerto Bertrand; and to donate hospital equipment to Cochrane's hospital and the health centres in Caleta Tortel and Villa O'Higgins. They would provide VHF radio coverage for 95% of the project's area, various scholarships, training courses, school equipment, teacher training, charitable donations, as well as construct community spaces, and develop 14km of trekking trails in a conservation area for tourists. This led to accusations of trying to win favours by 'taking the place of the state', as many suspected that the company proposed engaging in functions that are usually performed by government.

Naturally HidroAysén also expressed its utmost commitment to environmental conservation. Their Environmental Impact Survey included a host of measures to mitigate the impact of the project on the local environment, and to preserve the local forests, water supplies, flora and fauna, despite flooding nearly 6,000ha of pristine wilderness and constructing 2,300km of electricity transmission cables up to Santiago.

Not everyone was convinced by HidroAysén's environmental claims. Local and international environmentalists began to challenge the project, and in 2007 the Patagonia Chilena ¡Sin Represas! (Chilean Patagonia Without Dams) campaign was born. The Foundation for Deep Ecology, Pumalín Foundation and Conservación Patagónica, all established by US conservationist Doug Tompkins (see box, page 134), supported the campaign.

Using one of Chile's most emblematic landmarks, the campaign began with an image of Torres del Paine being crossed by electricity pylons. However, since the project was located hundreds of kilometres further north, they were criticised of misinforming the public and so they countered with a clever campaign showing the famous stone figures of Easter Island being criss-crossed by pylons, with the slogan: 'It wouldn't be acceptable here. Neither in Aysén.'

Patagonia Chilena ¡Sin Represas! gained national attention. Polls suggested that 58% of Chileans were hostile to the project. Some 14 national services, among them the Forestry Service, the Ministry of Public Works, and the National Geology and Mining Service, also opposed the project.

An open letter was written to the then president Michelle Bachelet, requesting her not to approve the HidroAysén project. Fearing a nationwide movement against them, HidroAysén contracted three different PR companies to improve their national image and stress the positive impact the project would bring to the country and to the region of Aysén. One of these PR companies was Burson-Marsteller, who had previously represented some rather dubious companies, including Babcock and Wilcox, the owners of the Three-Mile Island nuclear reactor, which caused the world's second biggest nuclear disaster after Chernobyl, and Union Carbide, after 2,000 people were killed by a gas leak in Bhopal, India. MSNBC's anchorwoman Rachel Maddow quipped: 'when evil needs public relations, evil has Burson-Marsteller on speed dial.'

However, in May 2011, the Chilean government (now under Sebastian Piñera) approved the HidroAysén project with 11 votes in favour and one abstention, sparking demonstrations in Puerto Aysén and Coyhaique. In June 200,000 people protested in Santiago, partly about the approval of the project, but also about the growing inequalities between private and public education. Teachers, students and unions joined the protests. Polls suggested 78% of Chileans were against the HidroAysén project.

In January 2012, Chile's Human Rights Commission of the House of Representatives presented a 416-page report showing irregularities and illegalities in the approval process of 2011. Among the other issues, one of the ministers who had approved the project was found to have owned 109,804 shares in Endesa.

Other grievances, both regional and national, had merged into the growing opposition to the project, and this came to a head in Aysén in February 2012, when a group of 20 organisations including Patagonia Chilena ¡Sin Represas!, students, workers' unions and fishermen all came together under the banner of the 'Social Movement of Aysén'.

Their list of demands was extensive: subsidies for gas, petrol, paraffin, wood, electricity and water; health-care improvements; increasing the minimum wage; a university based in Aysén; regionalisation of water and mining resources; increased rights and benefits for fishermen; increased pensions for senior citizens and the disabled; and perhaps least surprisingly, greater decision-making in the construction of hydro-electric dams.

This joint movement channelled the anger and frustration in the region into protests focused mainly in Puerto Aysén and Coyhaique, which in turn led to riots in March, when the Chilean police used tear gas, batons and water cannon to control the protesters. The protests continued for more than a month. Transport in and out of the region was paralysed for two weeks. Many protestors were injured, including one shot by the police, and Coyhaique made it to the international news.

After the worst of the protests had died down, on 4 April, the report which had questioned HidroAysén's approval process in 2011 was rejected by the Supreme Court of Chile. On 2 January 2013 the Senate's Mining and Energy Commission legalised the project's Electrical Transmission Highway, slipping through the legislation just as most Chileans were starting their national holidays. Chile's president Sebastian Piñera had been an advocate of the HidroAysén project, but on 11 March 2014 Michelle Bachelet won the presidency for a second time. Within a month her Environment Minister Pablo Badenier led a committee to review 35 legal cases brought against the project, mainly by local communities which would be affected. According to Badenier, there were insufficient plans for relocating communities displaced by the proposed flooding caused by the dams.

On 10 June 2014, the government officially repealed the approval of the HidroAysén dam project, causing celebration among environmentalists and opposers of the project, and concern among its supporters. Endesa and Colbun had pointed out that just 0.05% of Aysén's surface area would be flooded – a small sacrifice for the vast amount of power it would supply – up to 20% of the country's energy needs within a decade. Bachelet's own Energy Minister, Maximo Pacheco, who voted against the project, expressed his concern about Chile's growing energy requirements, insufficient infrastructure, and rising costs.

Endesa's website stated in a notice dated 29 January 2015:

There is uncertainty about the recovery of the investment, due to the fact that it depends on both judicial decisions and the Energy Agenda's definitions that the company's currently unable to predict. At the same time, HidroAysén is not in the company's immediate projects portfolio.

On 17 November 2017, ENEL and Colbun confirmed the end of the project. Their reasons were, according to Francesco Starace, CEO of ENEL, the delay of more than three years, the absence of international supply deals needed for economic viability and the rejection of the project by the local community. Support for the Patagonia Chilena ¡Sin Represas! movement is still visible across southern Chile.

tours – each one unique – around Coyhaique; contact him by phone to arrange. He is able to organise last-minute tours, but it is best to book in advance. **Fundo Don Gerardo** [225 B8] Road X-608 approx 5km south of Coyhaique; 9 9718 5777; e fundodongerardo@gmail.com; f. An authentic Patagonian farmer 'day-in-the-life' experience. Run by the entrepreneurial Alicia Haro Mardones, who has broken the mould & opened up her farm to tourism (winning a 'Tourist Businesswoman of the Year' award in 2018). A day at the farm includes b/fast, asado, sheep shearing & other farm-based activities. Features a sheep pen in an innovative heart shape, & you can take part in Alicia's ecotourism project, where visitors can plant trees. Eventually, these trees will spell out 'PATAGONIA', & be visible from planes flying to Balmaceda airport. Costs $55,000 pp (min 2 people, max 50), with transport from Coyhaique. A fantastic way to experience local Patagonian culture & traditions first hand. **Gran Patagonia Tour** [225 D6] Eusebio Lillo 377; ///seats.reported.weaned; e info@ granpatagonia.cl; w granpatagonia.cl. A decade of experience, with a reputation as one of the best tour companies in Coyhaique. Specialises in high-quality tours for all the locations on the Carretera Austral & further south. Offers all tailored & standard tours in the local area, & a 13-day tour of the Route of Parks. Can organise the whole Carretera Austral trip. Tickets available for the ferry from Caleta Tortel to Puerto Natales directly from their office in Coyhaique. Purchase tours online or over the phone only. Accepts credit cards, open all year round.

WHERE TO STAY

🏠 **Coyhaique River Lodge** [225 G5] (8 rooms) Km8.5 Camino Coyhaique Alto; ///dared.apprehended.efficient; 📞67 221 9710, 9 4221 9688; e info@coyhaiqueriverlodge.com; w coyhaiqueriverlodge.com. A 10km drive from the centre of Coyhaique, this fishing lodge set in a valley with beautiful views over the Coyhaique River is an ideal place to stay for families & keen fishermen alike. The spacious & comfortable rooms all have 2 queen-sized beds & en-suite bathroom. B/fast included, with fresh eggs available. Restaurant seats 50. The bar, communal area, sauna & outdoor jacuzzi all look over the valley. Fly-fishing opportunities are at a premium here, with a dedicated team of guides. Trekking, biking, riding & boat trips down the river are also on offer. Central heating & Wi-Fi throughout the building, parking & laundry service also available. Reservation required. Open from Oct to the end of Apr. **$$$$$**

🏠 **Hotel Dreams Patagonia** [224 B4] (38 rooms, 2 suites) Magallanes 131; ///strategy.climate.collide; 📞67 226 4700; e reservas@mundodreams.com; w mundodreams.com. The only 5-star chain hotel in Coyhaique, complete with casino, frequent live music, heated swimming pool, sauna, gym, conference hall, a bar & restaurant. A characterless & rather generic chain hotel. Takes credit cards. **$$$$$**

🏠 **Nómades Hotel Boutique** [224 E1] (8 rooms) Baquedano 84; ///proofs.diamond.steeped; 📞67 223 7777; e reservas@hotelnomades.com; w hotelnomades.com. The leading boutique hotel in Coyhaique & one of the finest on the entire Carretera Austral. If you feel like treating yourself to one decadent treat in Coyhaique, this is a contender. Rooms face the mountains & the only sound audible is the rushing river below, & yet the hotel is a mere 5min walk to the central plaza. The rooms are spacious & bright thanks to large windows overlooking the gorge, with a balcony or chimney, large TV, room service, safety deposit box, Wi-Fi, etc. A spare bed can be added to any room. The restaurant offers b/fast (guests only) & dinner. The bar stays open until midnight. The interior is of wood & stone with a gaucho feel – rustic, quality materials, ample animal hides & antlers, etc, creating a certain Patagonian lodge ambience despite being in a city. In peak season, prices range from US$180 to US$350; in low season they are approximately US$60 cheaper, but they also have special offers when prices can fall further. The managers will go to lengths to

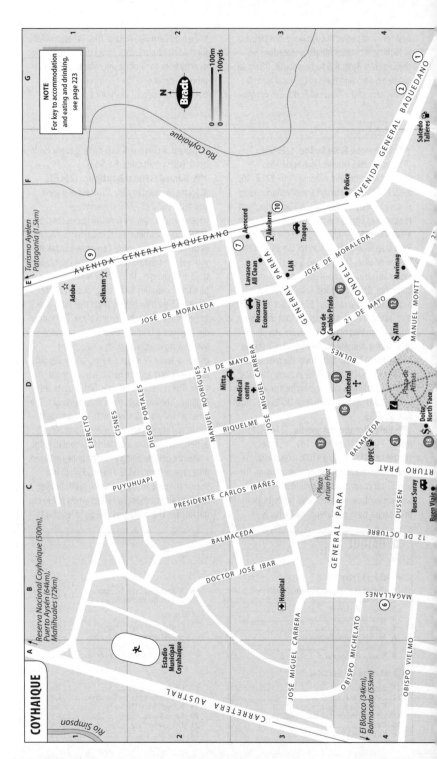

COYHAIQUE

NOTE
For key to accommodation
and eating and drinking,
see page 223

Río Coyhaique

N
Bradt

0   100m
0   100yds

Reserva Nacional Coyhaique (500m),
Puerto Aysén (64km),
Manihuales (72km)

Río Simpson

CARRETERA AUSTRAL

Estadio
Municipal
Coyhaique

El Blanco (34km),
Balmaceda (55km)

Turismo Ayelen
Patagonia (1.5km)

AVENIDA GENERAL BAQUEDANO

Adobe ☆

Selknam ☆

JOSÉ DE MORALEDA

EJERCITO

CISNES

DIEGO PORTALES

MANUEL RODRIGUES

PUYUHUAPI

PRESIDENTE CARLOS IBÁÑES

21 DE MAYO

Mitta

Medical
centre

RIQUELME

JOSÉ MIGUEL CARRERA

Plaza
Arturo Prat

GENERAL PARA

BALMACEDA

DOCTOR JOSÉ IBAR

JOSÉ MIGUEL CARRERA

OBISPO MICHELATO

OBISPO VIELMO

MAGALLANES

Hospital

12 DE OCTUBRE

DUSSEN

RTURO PRAT

BALMACEDA

COPEC

Buses Suray

Buen Viaje

Aerocord

Akelarre

Traeger

Lavaseco
All Clean

LAN

Recasur/
Econorent

GENERAL PARA

JOSÉ DE MORALEDA

Casa de
Cambio Prado

BULNES

19

21 DE MAYO

Cathedral

11

16

13

21

Dotre
North Face

ATM

Plaza de
Armas

MANUEL MONTT

Navimag

21

18

12

ATM

JOSÉ DE MORALEDA

CONDELL

Police

AVENIDA GENERAL BAQUEDANO

Salcedo
Talleres

9

7

10

6

1

2

224

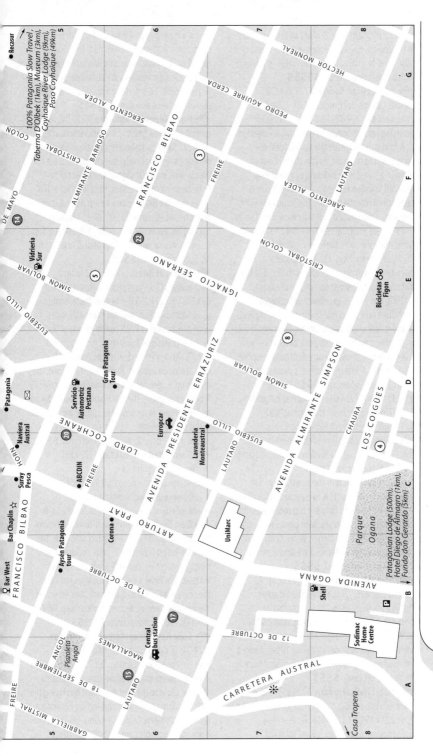

● Recasur

100% Patagonia Slow Travel ,
Taberna D'Olbek (1km), Museum (3km),
Coyhaique River Lodge (9km),
Paso Coyhaique (49km)

DE MAYO
CRISTÓBAL COLÓN
⑭
Vidriería
Sur
SIMÓN BOLÍVAR
⑤
EUSEBIO LILLO

ALMIRANTE BARROSO
SERGENTO ALDEA
FRANCISCO BILBAO
IGNACIO SERRANO
⑳
FREIRE
③
SERGENTO ALDEA
PEDRO AGUIRRE CERDA
HÉCTOR MONREAL
CRISTÓBAL COLÓN
LAUTARO

Bicicletas
Figón

Patagonia ⊠

Servicio
Automotriz
Pestana
Gran Patagonia
Tour

LORD COCHRANE

HORN
Naviera
Austral
Suray
Pesca
● ABCDIN

Bar West   Bar Chaplin ☆
FRANCISCO BILBAO
● Aysén Patagonia
tour
● Corona
ARTURO PRAT
12 DE OCTUBRE

AVENIDA PRESIDENTE ERRÁZURIZ

Europcar
Lavandería
Monteaustral
EUSEBIO LILLO
LAUTARO

AVENIDA ALMIRANTE SIMPSON

SIMÓN BOLÍVAR

⑧

④
LOS COIGÜES
CHAURA

UniMarc

Parque
Ogana

Patagonian Lodge (500m),
Hotel Diego de Almagro (1km),
Fundo don Gerardo (5km)

Shell
AVENIDA OGANA

12 DE OCTUBRE

Sodimac
Home
Centre

P

⑰
Central
bus station
MAGALLANES

CARRETERA AUSTRAL

⑮
LAUTARO
18 DE SEPTIEMBRE
ANGOL
Plazoleta
Angol

FREIRE
GABRIELLA MISTRAL

Casa Tropera

ensure a pleasant stay, & also can arrange tours in the region. English spoken. Accepts credit cards (also used to guarantee a reservation in advance, which is recommended). **$$$$$**

🏠 **Patagonian Lodge** [225 B8] (20 rooms) Camino del Bosque 1170; ///widest. asleep.bidder; 📞 9 8293 8049; 📧 reservas@ thepatagonianlodge.cl; 🌐 thepatagonianlodge. cl. A fantastic lodge ideally suited for those with private transport, as it is slightly out of town in a forest. The building is a rambling restored wooden farmhouse oozing charm & tastefully decorated inside. The rooms are very spacious, some with a fantastic view over the forest to the mountains, very comfortable beds & excellent en-suite bathrooms. Wood stoves, Wi-Fi, secure parking, etc. The restaurant, also open to non-residents, is one of the best in town, although certainly not one of the cheapest, & the b/fast (inc) is excellent, unlimited & contains every conceivable item, including eggs to order. Not great value for money compared with other options in this price category – you can get better service/rooms for the same price elsewhere – & internet access is patchy. Staff speak English & Spanish. **$$$$$**

🏠 **El Reloj** [224 G4] (19 rooms) Baquedano 828; ///purple.pleasing.manliness; 📞 67 223 1108; 📧 reservas@elrelojhotel.com; 🌐 elrelojhotel.com. One of the finest hotels in this price range, with excellent service. A 10min walk from the centre of town, but still gives a feeling of immersion in the forest. There are fantastic views from this cosy, wooden family-friendly lodge. Sgls, dbls & a trpl room, all with private bathrooms. Restaurant opens for b/fast (buffet, inc), lunch & dinner. Wi-Fi, cable TV & laundry. Parking available. Excellent service. Open all year, except Jul. **$$$$**

🏠 **Hostal Patagonia Live** [225 C8] (7 rooms) Lillo 826; ///dubbing.asteroid.payer; 📞 67 223 0892, 9 9886 7982; 📧 contacto@ hostalpatagonialive.cl; 🌐 hostalpatagonialive. cl. Well run, clean, reasonable-sized rooms, well-equipped bathrooms, decent b/fast, limited off-road parking, cable TV, Wi-Fi & central heating. Accepts credit cards. **$$$$**

🏠 **Hotel Belisario Jara** [225 E5] (8 rooms) Francisco Bilbao 662; ///wings.nickname.swinging; 📞 67 223 4150, 67 223 4155; 📧 reservas@ belisariojara.cl. Spacious & light sgl & dbl

rooms, simple but well equipped & with private bathrooms. Buffet b/fast included. There is a room for eating & socialising with a fireplace next to the bar, ideal for families. Wi-Fi, laundry, central heating, cable TV & parking available. Reservation required, as well as a deposit. **$$$$**

🏠 **Hotel Diego de Almagro** [225 B8] (87 rooms) Av Ogana 1320; ///lockets.sample.actor; 📞 67 221 5200; 🌐 dahotelescoyhaique.com. A generic chain hotel with little character, & the 20min walk makes it slightly too far out of town to be convenient for restaurants. However, it has views over the Río Simpson Valley, helpful staff & restaurant (🕐 until 23.00). Wi-Fi, laundry, parking (when available), cable TV & buffet b/fast included. Also a sauna, indoor pool & small gym. Accepts credit cards. **$$$$**

🏠 **Hotel Los Ñires** [224 E3] (22 rooms) Baquedano 315; ///toys.pickles.comical; 📞 67 223 2261, 67 221 7563; 📧 ventas@hotellosnires. cl; 🌐 hotellosnires.cl. A 3-star, centrally located hotel constructed in 1970, making it one of the oldest in Coyhaique. Fairly small rooms (sgl, dbl & trpl), although very clean & comfortable, & all with private bathrooms. Buffet b/fast included. The restaurant is open for lunch & dinner. Wi-Fi, cable TV & parking available. There is a laundry service for an additional cost. More luxurious options are available at this price elsewhere. Reservation is required, as well as a 50% deposit. Accepts credit cards. **$$$$**

🏠 **Raices Bed & Breakfast** [224 F3] (6 rooms) Baquedano 444; ///marriage.aged.famous; 📞 9 9619 5672; 📧 info@raicesbedandbreakfast.com; 🌐 raicesbedandbreakfast.com. Located a 5min walk from the town centre, well-furnished rooms with private bathrooms & comfortable beds. The included b/fast is excellent, with a wide range of fruits, jams, coffee, cereal & yoghurt. However, make sure to book a room which does not face the noisy road. Rooms at the back have views over the garden, & ensure a quiet night's sleep. Wi-Fi & cable TV. Credit cards accepted. **$$$$**

🏠 **Cabañas y Departamentos Mirador** [224 G4] (5 cabins, 2 rooms) Baquedano 848; ///renew.supplied.sing; 📞 67 223 3191; 📧 miradorbaquedano@gmail.com; 📘 Cabañas Mirador. Close to the centre of town but facing the river & mountain – a peaceful setting ensuring a good night's sleep. Cabins or rooms. Wi-Fi, private bathrooms, friendly owner, secure off-street parking. No b/fast. The bay window in the end cabin has truly spectacular views. **$$$**

🏠 **Hostal Español** [225 F6] (10 rooms, 6 cabins) Sargento Aldea 343; ///evolving. watching.tenses; 📞 67 224 2580, 9 8669 9365; e reservas@hostalcoyhaique.cl; 🔲 Hostal Español en Coyhaique. A good mid-range family-run hostel about 10mins' walk from the centre in a quiet neighbourhood. Clean & friendly, with a Spanish theme throughout. Sgl or dbl rooms all with central heating, Wi-Fi, cable TV, & private bathroom. The rooms are large & tastefully decorated with great attention to detail to give a homely Spanish feel, down to the tiled bathrooms. There is a shared TV/lounge & 24hr reception. A hearty continental b/fast (inc with rooms, extra for cabins) includes cereals, fruit, yoghurt, ham, cheese & eggs. Lockable off-street parking provided. The cabins on the opposite side of the road are fully equipped with microwave & wood-fired heater, etc, & are very spacious for 4 people. Bookings can be made online. **$$$**

🏠 **Turismo Ayelen Patagonia** [224 E1] (camping for approx 20 people, 10 cabins) Av Baquedano 75; ///unit.sulked.deprive; 📞 9 5679 5015; e turismoayelen71@gmail.com; 🔲; ⏰ campground: Nov–May, cabins: all year. A basic campground by the road including a simple outhouse with 2 shared bathrooms, kitchen with a fridge & communal seating area. Outdoor & indoor BBQ facilities. This is the closest campsite to Coyhaique, a 15min walk from the central square. The cabins are surprisingly pleasant, relatively new, spacious & with views over the river. All have satellite TV, full kitchen, Wi-Fi & a seating/dining area. Sizes range from 3 to 7 people, & the 2 largest cabins have washing machines. No English spoken, ample parking. Good value. Reservations by email. Campground **$**, cabins **$$$**

🏠 **Huella Patagonica** [225 D7] (6 rooms, 3 dorms) Ignacio Serrano 621 cnr Lautaro; ///repeats.royally.gear; 📞 67 223 0002, 9 4410 1571; e contacto@huellapatagonica.cl; w huellapatagonica.cl. Dbl, trpl & quad rooms with private bathrooms, & dormitories (6 beds), very popular with backpackers. Big bunk beds with charging ports & individual lockers. Good, clean shared bathrooms. A big b/fast is included for all guests & served in the café below the hotel (⏰ 07.30–noon). Fantastic service & English spoken. Small library with a computer for guests. Wi-Fi, laundry service, kitchen, storage space, parking & bike shed with electric bike charger all available. Also has private transport. Accepts credit cards. **$–$$$**

✖ WHERE TO EAT AND DRINK

✳ ✖ **CB Gastronomía Patagonia** [225 F5] 21 Mayo 655; ///wake.wardrobe.drain; 📞 9 5657 4181; e cbgastronomiapatagonia@gmail.com; ⏰ 13.00–14.30 & 19.00–22.00 Mon–Fri, 13.00–15.00 & 19.00–23.00 Sat. Serious competitor for best restaurant along the entire Carretera Austral, so book a table in advance. Not only is the food extraordinary but the building is a work of art – originally a factory, it has been tastefully remodelled into an intimate, cosy restaurant – enjoy a cocktail in front of the fireplace & admire the fish tank (rare in southern Chile for some reason). Chef-owner Christian's bold attitude is not to simply repeat the 'old recipes' but to constantly push the boundaries, using novel ingredients & methods which result in entirely new flavours & combinations. Almost all ingredients are local & include some, such as hare, octopus & alpaca, that are far beyond the 'traditional Chilean fare' that permeates much of Aysén. Christian's main passions are berries & mushrooms, & he has spent years finding specific people in Aysén who can supply him with the most exotic species. Prices vary widely depending on the wine & specific dishes, but expect to pay anything from $50,000 to $100,000 pp; the set-menu lunch ($12,000 pp) is excellent value. True gourmet food of international quality. **$$$$**

✳ ✖ **Dagus** [225 A6] Lautaro 82; ///sensual. graver.pills; 📞 9 7498 4204; ⏰ 13.00–midnight Tue–Sat, 13.00–20.00 Sun. One of the best restaurants in Coyhaique & probably the best-value option within this price category, especially for the daily menu ($7,500). The chef is formerly of Mama Gaucha, one of the best-established restaurants in Coyhaique. The menu goes well beyond typical Chilean fare, offering terrific *tablas* (assortment of food on a board) & sublime seafood including crab, eel, salmon, etc. The only place in town offering both duck confit & rabbit, & also serves

9

hare (rare in this region). Succulent slow-cooked meat options, vegetarian dishes available & good desserts. Portions are generous, unlike in some upper-end restaurants, especially if combined with a first course. Relatively new, but also quite small, so it's wise to reserve in high season. The building itself is homely. Accepts cards. **$$$$**

✗ **Casino de Bomberos** [224 C3] General Parra 365; ///leotard.patrol.roving; 📞 67 223 1437; ⏰ 12.15–16.00 & 19.15–22.00 daily. Something of a classic in Coyhaique, popular with the locals for both lunch & dinner. Very good value for money & large portions. Wide range of standard Chilean dishes. The restaurant is hard to find – it is at the back of the fire station & poorly signposted. Ask a local if in doubt. **$$$**

✗ **Lito's Restaurant** [225 B6] Lautaro 147; ///thick.highways.ruled; 📞 9 8415 4989; ⏰ 11.00–23.00 Mon–Sat. Another favourite among locals, with fantastic seafood. The meat dishes are excellent & plentiful. Good, buzzing atmosphere & a wide range of local boutique beers & a reasonable wine list. Friendly staff & positively good service. **$$$**

✗ **Rosselot Sur Delivery** [226 E4] Condell 193; ///kitten.universally.debater; 📞 9 6461 0496; w rosselotsurdelivery.cl; ⏰ 10.30–23.45 daily. Good for a quick lunch while waiting for a bus or a quick dinner after a long day. Burgers, pichangas, sandwiches, fries & pizzas. Good value, large portions, & has its own range of beer. Take-away or delivery. Accepts credit cards. **$$$**

✗ **La Esquina Tropera** [224 D4] General Para 302; ///decency.magazine.sailors; 📞 9 3250 4693; ⏰ noon–01.00 Mon–Sat. The best burgers on the entire Carretera Austral, as well as the full selection of beers from the La Tropera brewery. Vegetarian & vegan options in their 'poke' bowls, which have some resemblance to a salad. Very busy & no reservations, so arrive early for a guaranteed seat. **$$**

✗ **Restaurant Mama Gaucha** [224 C4] Paseo Horn 47-D; ///assorted.dizzy.ranches; 📞 9 221 0721; ⏰ all day Mon–Sat. The best pizza in town, & former home of the local La Tropera beer. Good-value, quality food – the artichoke starter

is delicious. Great atmosphere, popular with foreigners & locals alike. Doubles as a sports bar during important football games. It may be cliché to recommend this restaurant, so well known in the city, but this reputation has been earned for valid reasons. Conveniently located 50m from the central plaza & very close to the Naviera Austral offices. Extensive range of pizzas. Fills up fast so get there early or reserve. **$$**

✗ **Sabo Sushi** [225 C5] Cochrane 345; ///grows.sprays.farmer; 📞 9 6848 5049; ⏰ 13.00–20.30 Mon–Fri. Good-quality sushi restaurant offering delivery service, limited range depending on fish available, no local beers, but a pleasant change to standard fare found elsewhere on the Carretera. Cash only. **$$**

✗ **Uruz** [225 E6] Bilbao 715; ///blessing.cool.honey; 📞 67 227 2080; w uruzsushibar.cl; ⏰ 13.00–15.00 & 18.00–23.00 Tue–Sun. Sushi, Thai & Chinese lunch, dinner & take-away. A good option for those wishing to broaden their diet from the standard Chilean cuisine. A range of local beers. Good value, & excellent service. **$$**

✗ **Basilic Bistrot** [224 D4] General Para 220; ///tribe.freshen.rinse; 📞 67 227 2197, 9 7994 4780; ⏰ 08.30–18.00 Mon–Fri, 10.00–16.30 Sat, may close later in summer. A rare chance to eat at a vegetarian restaurant on the Carretera Austral. Very focused on local & environmentally sustainable produce. Vegan options also available. Sandwiches, natural juices & other dishes on offer. Wi-Fi available, & has an intimate outdoor seating area. **$–$$**

☕ **Café de Mayo** [224 E4] 21 de Mayo 543; ///crisps.flat.boring; 📞 67 227 3020; ⏰ 08.00–21.00 Mon–Fri, 09.00–21.00 Sat. A large selection of coffees, cakes & sandwiches. Wi-Fi available, although not in the outdoor area. **$–$$**

☕ **Te Quiero Café** [224 C4] Dussen 360; ///pines.debt.kings; 📞 67 221 0050; ⏰ 09.30–21.00 Mon–Fri, 17.00–21.00 Sat. Located just off the main plaza with variety of good coffee, hot chocolate, tea, juices, cakes, sandwiches, & ice cream. Patchy Wi-Fi & a nice atmosphere with friendly staff. Good place to catch up with emails. **$–$$**

ENTERTAINMENT AND NIGHTLIFE

Coyhaique is the Carretera Austral's nightlife capital, although perhaps that's not saying much. Some restaurants double as bars once everyone has finished eating,

Mama Gaucha (see opposite) and Esquina Tropera (see opposite) being fine examples. Coyhaique actually has a few dedicated bars, particularly around the Central Plaza and on General Parra. Nightclubs seem to come and go so it's worth asking at the tourist information office on the central plaza.

☆ **Adobe** [224 E1] Baquedano 9; ///output. annoys.stick; ☏9 4276 0745; ❢ Casa Adobe coyhaique; ⊕ 12.45–02.00 Mon–Sat. A rustic restobar a short walk from the town centre. Good burgers, sandwiches & other pub food, as well as a wide range of beers.

☆ **Akelarre** [224 E3] General Parra 26; ///expert.ticking.lifted; ⊕ 16.00–21.30 Tue–Sat. A large bar & the best place in the city to see live music. If there's not a band playing, join in for karaoke. Stays open late on w/ends.

☆ **Bar Chaplin** [225 C5] Francisco Bilbao 260; ///comments.blushed.lofts; ☏67 239 1187; w chaplin.cl; ⊕ 18.00–01.45 Mon–Thu, 18.00–02.45 Fri & Sat. Cool bar with a wide range of beers including multiple artisanal ales, decent pub food, pizzas, salads & sandwiches at reasonable prices. Central location, friendly staff, happy hour, occasional live music & karaoke. Delivery available.

☆ **Bar West** [225 B5] Bilbao 110, cnr Magallanes; ///seats.usual.destined; ☏9 8219 6434; ❢ viejobarwest. An old western-themed bar that claims to be the longest-running bar in Coyhaique. Large selection of beer & spirits, with karaoke on Thu & live music some nights. Popular with locals, good atmosphere.

☆ **La Taberna D'Olbek** [225 G5] Baquedano 1895; ☏9 7381 2369; ⊕ 17.00–midnight Mon–Sat. Lovely inside/outside areas for a family lunch/dinner, serves a wide range of their craft beers, some of which are unavailable elsewhere, & a large variety of reasonably priced sandwiches & pizzas, as well as vegetarian options. 20mins' walk from plaza, parking available.

☆ **Selknam** [224 E1] Baquedano 93; ///decency.clash.trace; ☏9 2067 4624; ⊕ 17.00–00.30 Tue–Thu, 17.00–01.45 Fri & Sat, 13.30–21.00 Sun. Open-air resto-bar serving a large selection of local themed drinks, with local liquor brands. Perfect for social meetings, local college nightlife & occasional live music.

SHOPPING

Coyhaique is the main supply hub for the Carretera Austral outside of Puerto Montt. The range of products available is constantly increasing as Coyhaique catches up with the rest of Chile's cities. There are boutique climbing/outdoor stores, electronic shops and most main banks. This is the first and possibly last chance to stock up on supplies at a reasonable price. Condell is home to most banks, with ATMs, and it is worth stocking up on cash here as there are few ATMs north or south.

BOOKSHOP

La Librería Arturo Prat 162; ⊕ 10.00–13.30 & 15.00–19.00 Mon, Tue, Thu & Fri, 10.00–19.00 Wed, 11.00–14.00 & 16.00–19.00 Sat. Local literature as well books on Patagonia, among various other genres.

CAMPING AND OTHER EQUIPMENT

ABCDIN [225 C5] Arturo Prat 380; ///egging. counts.rugs; w abcdin.cl; ⊕ daily. A department store with a full range of computers, electronics & telephones.

Corona [224 C6] Arturo Prat 429; ///smashes. shield.pylon; w corona.cl; ⊕ daily. Probably the largest range of low- to mid-quality clothing at the cheapest prices. For high-end sporting & climbing clothes, go to one of the specialist camping & climbing stores.

Doite [224 D4] Horn 47; ///tile.nickname. barmaid; w doite.cl; ⊕ 10.00–20.00 daily. Chilean company offering good-quality clothing & camping equipment at reasonable prices.

North Face [224 D4] Horn 47; ///tile.nickname. barmaid; ☏67 225 2096; ⊕ 10.00–19.30 daily. Premium clothing & camping gear.

Patagonia [225 D5] Calle de Plaza 485; ///elated.storm.tubes; ☏67 258 3232; ⊕ 10.00–20.00 Mon–Sat, 10.00–19.00 Sun. Premium clothing & limited camping equipment.

9

Recasur [225 G5] Av Baquedano 909; ///punks. foiled.rails; ☎67 245 0228; w recasur.cl; ⊕ 09.30– 12.45 & 15.00–19.00 Mon–Fri, 09.45–13.00 & 15.00–18.00 Sat. Spare parts & accessories for cars, roof racks, headlights, tyres, batteries, etc.
Sodimac Home Centre [225 B8] Av Ogana 869; ///retina.match.books; w sodimac.cl; ⊕ 08.30– 20.30 Mon–Sat, 09.00–20.30 Sun. A large chain hardware store. Ideal for stocking up on tools or any other hardware items. They have a camping section & also sell low- to mid-range boots & rainwear. Also useful for buying white gasoline for camp stoves (*bencina blanca*).
Suray [225 C5] Pesca Prat 269; ///revision.lentil. charted; ☎67 223 4088; w suraymontana.cl; ⊕ 09.00–21.00 Mon–Sat. Fishing supplies & some camping gear.

FOOD

UniMarc Supermarket [225 B/C7] Lautaro 331; ///humans.stocky.displays; w unimarc.cl; ⊕ 09.00–18.00 Mon, 08.30–19.30 Tue–Sun. A large supermarket chain.

HANDICRAFTS

Artisan market Central Plaza; ⊕ daily, but more limited on Sun. Last chance to stock up on knitted gloves & local handmade trinkets, as well as the usual 'artisan' supplies found in most markets in South America all apparently made locally but appearing remarkably similar. However, renowned stone artist Oscar Ziehlmann has a stall in the market where his artwork can be admired.

OTHER PRACTICALITIES

Coyhaique is, for all practical purposes, the last opportunity on the Carretera Austral to make any repairs. All major car makes can be serviced in town, and parts are generally available or can be found quite quickly. Bicycle and motorbike mechanics are few and far between beyond the confines of the city.

REPAIRS

Bicicletas Figon [225 E8] Simpson 805; ///lodge.topples.dissolve; ☎67 223 4616, 9 5398 7600; e bicecleteriafigon@gmail.com; ⊕ 10.00– 13.00 & 15.00–19.00 Mon–Fri, 10.00–13.00 & 15.00–18.00 Sat. Bicycle repairs & sales (Norko & Scott), spare parts including tyres, helmets & riding gear.
COPEC petrol station [224 C4] Balmaceda 455, off central plaza; ///detained.happen.loses. Chipped windscreens are a common problem on gravel roads, surprisingly hard to repair, & if not repaired promptly a small chip will spread & require a full windscreen replacement. This petrol station in the centre of town has a quasi-employee who has the kit to repair such chips (☎9 9570 0801). Costs approx $25,000/chip – far cheaper than replacing a windscreen.
Servicio Automotriz Pestana [225 D5] Bilbao 457; ///pebble.nuns.stared; ☎67 221 4546; ⊕ 09.00–13.00 & 15.00–19.00 Mon–Fri, 10.00– 14.00 Sat. Service & parts for Honda, Yamaha, Keeway, Suzuki & Zongshen, although will help with other manufacturers if possible. Also has a reasonable range of accessories.
Vidrieria Sur [225 E5] Simon Bolivar 180, beside the telephone tower; ///topped.petted.sweeter;

☎67 221 9029; e vidreriasur.coyhaique@gmail. com. Reasonable stock of the most common car windscreens that are replaced in the city. Other windscreens are ordered in.

LAUNDRY

Lavanderia Monteaustral [225 D7] Lillo 555; ///skip.decades.tutored; ☎67 224 7009; e lavanderia@monteaustral.cl; f Lavanderia Monte Austral; ⊕ 09.00–13.00 & 15.00–17.00 Mon–Fri, 10.00–13.30 & 15.00–18.00 Sat. Laundry & dry-cleaning service. Laundry service is $2,000/kg for 1-day service. Express service is $3,500/kg.
Lavaseco All Clean [224 E3] General Parra 55; ///outlines.ruby.allow; ☎67 221 9635; e all-clean@123mail.cl. Laundry & dry-cleaning service. $2,600/kg. Credit cards accepted.

MONEY EXCHANGE

The following places will exchange euros, US dollars & possibly Argentine pesos, but are closed on Sun.

Casa de Cambio Austral [224 D4] Horn 40
Casa de Cambio Prado [224 D4] 21 de Mayo 417

CAR HIRE
See page 238; most Balmaceda car-rental agencies have offices in Coyhaique.

FERRY COMPANIES
Navimag [224 E4] & **Naviera Austral** [225 C5]; both have offices in Coyhaique.

NOT ANOTHER VOLCANO

It is almost impossible to visit Chile without seeing a volcano, and seeing one erupt is not as hard as one might imagine. Depending on the precise definition used, there are approximately 500 volcanoes in Chile, of which a little over 100 are active. **Chaitén** is possibly the best known within the region of the Carretera Austral, erupting in both 2008 and 2011 – the damage is still very visible. **Villarrica** made it to the international headlines in 2015 with some spectacular photos of night-time lava fireworks by the lake. **Puyehue**, just north of the Carretera Austral, closed airports as far afield as Australia in 2011. However, the **Volcán Hudson** is possibly the most feared – the 1991 eruption was one of the largest of the 20th century, and it is not far from Coyhaique.

Hudson is, fortunately, extremely remote. For this reason no-one actually died in the 1991 eruption. It is approximately 80km southwest of Coyhaique, or 65km south of Puerto Aysén, but can only readily be seen by air. Where the road to Lago Caro ends, Hudson is a mere 40km away, but not visible from this vantage point. The 4750BC eruption may have been responsible for wiping out what limited human population existed in this region at that time. The volcano was barely known until 1971, when a minor eruption caused lahars (mudflows) that killed five people. However, the 1991 eruption was big news in the region. Some 4.3km³ of ash was ejected from the volcano covering an area of approximately 150,000km² and reaching as far as the Falklands. At the time, news of the eruption was overshadowed by the double whammy of the eruption of Mount Pinatubo and Typhoon Yunya striking the Philippines at the same time, killing 847 people. The combination of these two eruptions led to global cooling over the following years and the Antarctic ozone hole grew to its largest size ever recorded. Hudson was placed on red alert in October 2011, but the subsequent eruption was minor.

The **Volcán Lautaro** is notable for being sub-glacial. Despite an altitude of nearly 3.5km, only the final 1km is visible above the ice of the Southern Ice Field. The only practical means to see the volcano is by plane from Villa O'Higgins (90km). From the airfield near Candelario Mancilla it is only 50km.

The following list focuses mainly on volcanoes both within reach of the Carretera Austral and easy to climb, or at least visit (altitude and any recent eruption in parentheses):

Ayacara Huequi (1,318m, 1920)
Hornopirén Yates (2,187m), Hornopirén (1,572m, 1835) & Apagado (1,210m)
Parque Pumalín Chaitén (1,122m, 2008 & 2011) & Michinmahuida (2,404m, 1835)

Puerto Montt Calbuco (2,015m, 2015) & Osorno (2,652m, 1869)
Raúl Marín Balmaceda Melimoyu (2,440m)
Villa O'Higgins Lautaro (3,623m, 1979)

SIGHTSEEING AND EXCURSIONS

Coyhaique serves mainly as a hub for transport and tour operators, but it's worth pausing here, if only to recharge one's batteries from the relative isolation of the Carretera. The region around the town also has a number of attractions, including one of the finest condor-spotting locations in all of Patagonia, accessible parks and a modest ski resort.

MIRADOR RÍO SIMPSON (RÍO SIMPSON LOOKOUT) This lookout is located on the bypass behind the casino (///lucky.dabbing.postcard), an easy 15-minute walk from the central plaza. It is often referred to by the locals as the 'Costanera'. Walk west on the street Jose M Carrera until you reach the bypass, where there are spectacular views over the Río Simpson, the Río Claro and the greater Valle Río Simpson. Below the viewing point are the remaining buildings of Coyhaique's first milk plant. In the distance are large wind turbines harnessing the power of the perpetual Patagonian wind. An eroded rock formation vaguely resembles the profile of a human head, reportedly that of an Indian, hence the name Cabeza del Indio. There is a picnic area with benches and a playground, but due to the lookout being right next to a busy road it is not a pleasant place to loiter.

RESERVA NACIONAL COYHAIQUE (w conaf.cl/parques/reserva-nacional-coyhaique; foreign adult/child $6,200/$3,100, Chilean adult/child $3,100/$1,600) This national reserve covers 22km² and is conveniently located only 5km north of Coyhaique, making it an accessible detour and a chance to explore the native forests and birds of the region. It is also a good option with children and older people because of its accessibility by car and the relatively easy circuits within the reserve.

Take the paved road from Coyhaique to Puerto Aysén. Cross the first bridge and then turn right on to the gravel road which is signposted to the reserve. This access road and the roads inside the park are open to cars in the summer, but 4x4s are needed in the winter. The **CONAF staff** are helpful and provide a good **map** of the park with distances and altitudes. All trails are well marked. Take food, suntan lotion and water – especially if you are planning on trekking. The climate of the reserve is relatively dry and hot in summer, while rain and snow are frequent in winter. The 7-hour trek up **Cerro Cinchao** (1,361m) offers a panoramic view of Coyhaique and its surrounding mountains. The summit is barren, and there can be strong winds and snow at the top, even when the weather is fair at the base. There is a 9km circuit which you can **drive** round. Sheltered barbecue areas (*fogons*) overlook Laguna Verde and the hills in the background. There is also a sealed path suitable for **wheelchairs** to a lookout over Coyhaique. A well-maintained **campsite** set among the trees at Casa Bruja is the only campsite in the reserve. There are 5km of tracks dedicated to **mountain bikers**.

The **two main treks** are the 10km (approximately) half-day, medium-difficulty circuit to Laguna Verde and the 15km full-day, medium-difficulty circuit leading to the top of Cerro Cinchao – an extension of the half-day circuit.

The first 3.5km of the walk to Laguna Verde has two main highlights. **Casa Bruja**, at km2 (the witch's house) is an early settlers' house in the area which provides an insight into living conditions in the region. The **viewpoint** just before Laguna Verde offers spectacular views of the farmland in the valley and Coyhaique city with the mountain backdrop behind. Besides these two notable highlights, however, the walk is disappointing due to the abundance of artificially planted pines. The slash-and-burn agricultural practices of the 1950s resulted in deforestation in this area and so, in an effort to minimise erosion, CONAF developed a strategy to plant fast-growing species. It is worth pushing on to **Laguna Verde** – the clear waters, abundant fish and birdlife, and beautiful views across the forest and of the mountains that soar up to high peaks behind the lagoon are worth the effort.

From here on this circuit is full of mature native bush and plentiful birdlife and there are another three lagoons. Some 500m past Laguna Verde on the right-hand side is the 6.7km **detour to Cerro Cinchao**. This is a 600m ascent of medium difficulty, rewarded with spectacular views of the reserve and panorama of the city. A good sunhat, sunblock, sunglasses and plenty of water are recommended for this section.

The trail descends to the forest to rejoin the half-day 10km circuit. From here, there is a gradual descent through the native bush and then a further 4km to return to the start point at the reserve entrance.

FRAILE SKI RESORT (67 221 3187; Centro de Ski El Fraile) Situated 29km southeast of Coyhaique, Fraile is one of the more modest ski resorts in Latin America. It has five pistes serviced by two lifts, and a café and rental shop. In theory it operates from May to September: it barely opened in 2015 owing to the lack of snow, but had a decent season in 2019. You would be better advised to stick to the ski resorts around Bariloche or Las Leñas in Argentina, the resorts around Santiago or even Cerro Castor in Ushuaia.

CONDOR'S AWAKENING (Punta del Monte Estancia; 9 9884 4950; e condores@ puntadelmonte.cl; w puntadelmonte.cl) This is a truly unique opportunity to observe the legendary Andean condor up close, as they awake in the morning, stretch their wings and finally launch themselves from their nests on the cliff edges into the thermal updrafts. Condors are large beasts, reaching up to 15kg and with a wingspan of up to 3m. They can weigh as much as a three-to-four-year-old child, and reach 1m in height. They take advantage of up-currents of warm air to launch off the cliffs, and rely on thermal currents to remain aloft with the minimum effort possible.

The Punta del Monte Estancia is a functioning farm, with 9,000 sheep, 200 Hereford cows and 200 alpacas, but it is also uniquely located at a natural nesting area for the condors, with access from above. It is possible to observe their awaking, morning preparations and eventual launch from a matter of metres away.

Tours can be arranged from Coyhaique through an operator, including all transport, but for those with private transport it is possible to book directly with the estancia itself (see above). Either way, arrive at the entrance to the estancia by 06.30, approximately an hour's drive from Coyhaique towards the Argentine border (43km to Coyhaique Alto, a further 6km to Paso Coyhaique; mostly gravel). From here a 4x4 takes you the final 17km to the lookout point. The standard tour includes all transport (to/from Coyhaique), breakfast either in the forest or close to the ledges where the condors nest, a full roast lamb lunch either in the main house or in the quincho (depending on the weather) with wine, soft drinks, coffee, etc. Prices depend on the number of visitors, ranging from US$159 pp for large groups (over 20 people) to US$399 pp (for one or two people). For those with their own vehicle and able to reach the estancia by 06.30, the cost is reduced by US$100 pp, but note that you'll miss out on some background explanation of the estancia provided on the journey. It is possible to stay overnight in the estancia, which reduces the need for such an early start, for an additional US$150 pp (maximum four people). Multi-day packages include horseriding tours and fishing trips among other activities, as well as the celebrated condor-watching excursion. Alejandro Galilea, one of the owners of the estancia, provides a fascinating explanation of the lives of condors. Having studied their behaviour for decades he can interpret the subtlest of changes, understands the means by which they communicate in the air, and knows their flight paths based on where food sources are likely to be. His knowledge also covers the history and pre-history of the region (archaeological remains can be seen in the estancia), the settlement of Patagonia and the impact of climate change. Highly recommended.

REGIONAL MUSEUM OF AYSÉN [225 G5] (Km3, Coyhaique Alto; ///trotted.nerve. whacking; ✆67 257 6800; ⊕ 11.00–19.00 Tue–Fri, 14.00–19.00 Sat & Sun – check before you visit; free entry) The museum is built on the site of the first houses of the original English settlers of Coyhaique who arrived in 1904, and provides an enjoyable and comprehensive tour of the dramatic geological, animal and human history of the region. There are numerous interactive exhibits, including an impressive life-size reproduction of a Chilote boat, a replica mountain hut and shearing shed made by one of Chile's leading carpenters, a model of the lakes and terrain of Aysén, and recorded messages from some of the original pioneers of Chile. Although focused mainly on the culture and possessions of the natives and settlers, along with the history of production, trade and exports in the region, there is a section dedicated to the pre-Ice Age and Ice Age history of Chile, including footage of the alarming retreat of many glaciers in Aysén. All exhibits are in Spanish and a visit takes approximately 2 hours. In 2021 the museum was the Latin American nomination in the 'Leading Culture Destinations' awards. It's certainly worth a visit to fully appreciate the southern Carretera Austral.

⊕ **AS THE CONDOR FLIES**

Coyhaique is 460km from Puerto Montt and 380km from the border south of Villa O'Higgins to El Chaltén.

10

South of Coyhaique: to Cruce El Maitén via Lago General Carrera

The region south of Coyhaique perhaps contains the highest density of spectacular sights, glaciers and trekking opportunities along the entire Carretera Austral.

Lago General Carrera is gigantic, beautiful, and possesses some of the finest views of Aysén, with various adventures departing from this section of the road. The lake straddles Chile and Argentina (where it is known as Lago Buenos Aires), and is the second largest in South America (1,850km² – Lake Titicaca is 8,372km²). Strictly speaking the southern coastal road is not part of the Carretera Austral, but it is important for two reasons: it is truly spectacular, and is a common entry/exit point for visitors to the Carretera. As a branch off the Carretera, this section invariably involves doubling back on oneself if wishing to continue on the Carretera north or south. It is not an easy section to traverse, mainly for logistical reasons, but is worth the effort.

A principal destination for those heading south is the tourist hub of **Puerto Río Tranquilo**, from where boats shuttle to the marble caves and tours to the **Ventisquero San Rafael** originate – this is one of the more accessible glaciers along the Carretera. For those wishing to combine a trip to a glacier with a moderate hike, albeit with marginally more planning required, the **Ventisquero Leones** is highly recommended. En route, **Cerro Castillo** offers some of the best, and most accessible, hiking along the Carretera Austral, varying from leisurely strolls requiring no prior experience, to some challenging technical climbs. The weather is volatile, at times turning an apparently easy hike into a dangerous adventure.

The only commercial airport along the Carretera Austral is just south of Coyhaique in Balmaceda (not to be confused with the village Raúl Marín Balmaceda further north). South of the airport lie the fantastic roads around Puerto Ibáñez, including the little-known Levicán Peninsula. From Puerto Ibáñez it is possible to take a ferry directly to Chile Chico and enjoy the southern side of the lake, but this involves either missing the marble caves and the surrounding glaciers, or doubling back later. Ideally visitors should visit both sides of the lake.

The marble caves are worth checking out, but if possible visit those around Puerto Sánchez rather than around Puerto Río Tranquilo – they are closer to the village, less crowded, cheaper and deeper. However, there is limited public transport to Puerto Sánchez and the road, although utterly spectacular, is one of the most hazardous in the region, with cliff edges merely centimetres from the road.

Cruce El Maitén is both the southern limit of the 'classic route', and the beginning of the more remote southern Carretera Austral. The dramatic scenery and abundance of activities covered in this chapter is a mere introduction to what lies in store further south.

LAKES SOUTH OF COYHAIQUE

There is no need to travel far from Coyhaique to discover stunning beauty. The village of **El Blanco** lies 34km south of Coyhaique on the Carretera Austral, 6km before the only fork in the road for approximately 200km. The road heads southeast towards **Balmaceda** (village and airport) and on to the **Paso Huemules** to Argentina, or southwest towards **Cerro Castillo** on the Carretera Austral. Although this stretch to El Blanco is not particularly interesting, is paved and suffers relative traffic congestion (by Aysén standards), a number of small detours to the lakes are worth the effort.

To the east lie three main **lakes**: Frío, Castor and Pollux. To the west are lakes Atravesado, Elizalde, Desierto, La Paloma and Monreal. The road to Atravesado actually continues all the way to Lago Portales and on to Puerto Aysén. The largest and most visited lake in this region is **Elizalde**, where accommodation is available. The road to Elizalde continues to **Lago Claro** – a stunning drive, but without any services or accommodation. Some of the lakes to the southwest of Coyhaique border, or are within, the **Reserva Nacional Cerro Castillo**.

The **roads** in this region are generally gravel, but of reasonable quality. The road extending towards Lago Caro deteriorates and is perhaps best suited to a high-clearance vehicle or a 4x4. However, between Villa Frei and Coyhaique the road is now paved. The roads extending east towards Lago Pollux and Lago Castor actually connect to the main road from Coyhaique to the border (Paso Triana crossing), so for those wishing to enter or leave Chile without passing Coyhaique this is a short cut between Argentina and the southern Carretera. Signposting in this region is good.

Public transport only traverses the main road, heading to and from Balmaceda airport, Puerto Ibáñez, Cerro Castillo and further south. This section is relatively

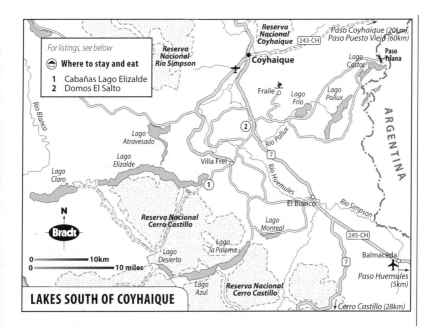

For listings, see below

🛏 **Where to stay and eat**
1 Cabañas Lago Elizalde
2 Domos El Salto

Reserva Nacional Río Simpson

Reserva Nacional Coyhaique [243-CH]

Paso Coyhaique (20km), Paso Puesto Viejo (60km)

Coyhaique

Paso Triana

Lago Castor

Fraile

Lago Frio

Lago Pollux

ARGENTINA

Río Blanco

Lago Atravesado

Lago Elizalde

Villa Frei

②

Río Pollux

Lago Claro

①

[7]

Río Huemules

El Blanco

Río Simpson

[245-CH]

N

Bradt

Reserva Nacional Cerro Castillo

Lago Monreal

Lago Desierto

Lago la Paloma

0 ——— 10km
0 ——— 10 miles

Balmaceda

[7]

Paso Huemules (5km)

Lago Azul

Reserva Nacional Cerro Castillo

LAKES SOUTH OF COYHAIQUE

Cerro Castillo (28km)

well travelled, so hitching is easy. See page 217 for information about public transport. To visit the lakes in this region, a private vehicle is required.

🏠 **WHERE TO STAY AND EAT** *Map, above*

🛏 **Cabañas Lago Elizalde** (7 cabins) 33km from Coyhaique, next to Lago Elizalde; ///eruptions. shareholders.pearl; ☎ 2 231 1902, 67 235 1112; e info@loberiasdelsur.cl. An excellent & peaceful option close to Coyhaique, with cabins overlooking the lake. All cabins sleep up to 4 people with a mix of twin & dbl beds, fully equipped with private bathroom & balcony. No Wi-Fi but sat TV, restaurant, 24hr electricity (220V). When not fishing, the surrounding forest is ideal for short walks to enjoy the beauty & silence in the shade of the native coihue & lenga trees or for longer walks to several

scenic viewpoints. There are no shops nearby. Credit cards accepted (reservations are made via Hotel Loberías del Sur; page 208). **$$$**

🛏 **Domos El Salto** (2 domes) 5km south of Coyhaique; ///reshoot.crucial.safety; ☎ 9 7648 3665. 4-man domes with great views up the Valle Simpson & over the El Salto waterfall. Small kitchen with a deck, barbecue, heating & hot water, no Wi-Fi or television. A pleasant escape from Coyhaique without having to travel too far. $60,000–70,000, depending on number of people. **$$$**

BALMACEDA – EXITING THE CARRETERA AUSTRAL

There's no real reason to spend any time here other than to make use of the **airport**. The village boasts a fast-food restaurant, a couple of shops, and one reasonable place to eat/sleep – **El Rincon de Mirna** (Mackena 832; ///floodlights. mammoth.silvers; ☎ 9 8341 3528; e mirnanivia@gmail.com; $$), but given that flights to and from Balmaceda do not generally leave or depart very early in the morning or very late at night, there is no obvious reason why a tourist would ever need to stay. Note that there is **no petrol station** in Balmaceda – the nearest are in Coyhaique (55km north), Puerto Río Tranquilo (193km southwest), or Chile Chico (93km south combined with a ferry across the lake). Balmaceda airport was recently catapulted into the 21st century with the long-awaited arrival of an

ATM. A tourist information centre is yet to materialise. There was a museum, but it is now closed.

GETTING THERE
About the route
Coyhaique to Balmaceda (55km; 1hr; paved) The road between Coyhaique and Balmaceda is paved, and the first half of this stretch south of Coyhaique can be quite busy at times. Unless taking the detour to the lakes (page 236), there is little to see or do along this section. At 6km southeast of El Blanco, the road (becoming the 245-CH) forks towards Balmaceda airport (a further 15km; ///foamed.spenders. exfoliating) or along the main Carretera Austral towards Villa' Cerro Castillo (a further 53km). Regular shuttle buses, including Buses Suray, synchronise with flight arrivals and departures between the airport and Coyhaique.

Balmaceda to Paso Huemules (5km; 5mins; paved) A further 5km east of Balmaceda and the airport is the Paso Huemules border crossing. Paperwork is done at the southern exit of Balmaceda. The road in Argentina is 106km of gravel to the Ruta 40, with petrol available in the village of Lago Blanco 33km east of the border. For those travelling north in Argentina, or coming from more northern Argentina, it is probably easier to use one of the Coyhaique border crossings (page 200). For those travelling south in Argentina, or coming from southern Argentina, it is probably easier to use the Chile Chico border crossing and take the ferry across the lake (page 279).

Car-hire companies The following companies are represented at the airport; each has a main office in Coyhaique. Most of the companies have a full range of vehicles.

Econorent ☎67 223 8990; e reservas@econorent.cl; w econorent.cl. Daily & weekly rentals.

Europcar ☎9 7806 3025, 67 267 8640; w europcar.cl

Mitta ☎9 7749 3315; e cchiguay@mitta.cl; w mitta.cl. Daily, weekly & monthly rentals. Offers buses for up to 9 people. One-way rental as far south as Punta Arenas.

Recasur ☎67 223 8990, 9 9015 8550; e reservas@recasur-rac.com; w recasur-rac.com

Traeger ☎67 223 1648, 9 9640 6412; e contacto@traeger.cl; w traeger.cl. A local company with 28 years' experience in the region. Daily, weekly & monthly rentals.

Varona ☎67 221 6674, 9 8929 1802; e ventas.aeropuerto@rentacarvarona.cl; w rentacarvarona.cl

By air Latam (☎600 526 2000; w latamairlines.com) has two or three flights a day to Puerto Montt and Santiago. Sky Airline (w skyairline.com) has one or two daily flights to both Puerto Montt and Santiago. JetSmart (☎600 600 1311, 2 2731 8787; w jetsmart.com) has two or three flights a week to Concepcíon, Puerto Montt and Temuco, and four flights a week to Santiago. DAP (office in Hotel Dreams, page 223; ☎61 222 9936; e ventas@dap.cl; w dapairline.com) has one return flight a week to Punta Arenas on Tuesdays. There are currently no international flights to/from Balmaceda.

Airport transfers As well as the standard bus companies working this route, private transfers to and from the airport can be organised with three companies. Prices in a shared van are approximately $5,000 per person ($8,000 to Puerto Aysén), while a private taxi service is more expensive. Arrange with 24 hours' notice.

Transfer T & T Balmaceda airport, by car-hire stands; ☏67 225 6000, 9 9312 3939; e tranytur@gmail.com; w transfertyt.com
Transfer Valencia Lautaro 828, Coyhaique; ☏67 223 3030; e transfervalencia@hotmail.com; f transfer.valencia.coyhaique

Transfer Velasquez ☏67 225 0414, 9 8906 4578; e transfer.velasquez@gmail.com; f transfervelasquezcoyhaique

PUERTO IBÁÑEZ AND THE LEVICÁN PENINSULA – A DETOUR

PUERTO IBÁÑEZ South of the Carretera Austral, at the junction 6km before Cerro Castillo, Puerto Ibáñez is a modest town visited principally en route to/from Argentina or for the Chile Chico ferry. The traditional pottery of the region is the cultural highlight, utilising a reddish clay partially covered with stretched leather, often painted with images from the archaeological cave paintings in the region. Around the town is some beautiful countryside, but it is rare for visitors to spend more than a day in the town itself. The central square is disproportionately large for a town this size, but in proportion to the looming mountains in the background. Wide avenues and long roads create the impression that Puerto Ibáñez is larger than it really is. It does not even have a petrol station, and the few restaurants seem to open randomly, if at all. However, it is logistically important as a main ferry route to Chile Chico, which may necessitate spending a night here.

History The commune of Río Ibáñez was founded in 1921, but the town was not founded until 1924. Both are named after a Chilean miner, Cornelio Ibáñez. The commune also includes the localities of Cerro Castillo to the north, Chile Chico to the south, and Bahía Murta, Puerto Río Tranquilo and Puerto Sánchez to the west. The commune is part of the province of General Carrera, within the region of Aysén.

Various **cave paintings** demonstrate clearly that this region was inhabited at least 6,000 to 7,000 years ago. The main murals can be found in the Valle Ibáñez and consist of handprints which, archaeologists assume, represent the people that lived in the area during this period. There are also basic paintings of guanacos and ñandú (a small native ostrich) being hunted which shows how this population lived. In winter, these animals would seek shelter and food from the snow-capped mountains and bitterly cold windswept estepa (arid native grassland) in this valley, making them an easy target for the hunters as they could be easily hunted within the confinements of the valley. The most famous of these archaeological sites open to the public is the 'Parédon de los Manos' ('Hands Mural'), with paintings thought to be 3,000 years old. It can be accessed from the Museo Escuela in Cerro Castillo (page 250). Other samples can be found on the northern shores of Lago General Carrera and in the cave of the Río Pedregoso close to Chile Chico.

The region was inhabited by the Aónikek (also referred to as Tehuleches, or Patagones), who arrived in southern Chile approximately 12,000 years ago. They were nomadic hunter-gatherers, and the first documented encounter with Europeans was in 1520 with Hernando de Magallanes, one of South America's key explorers. They lived in patriarchal societies, where wives were purchased with guanaco skins, ñandú feathers, or by offering the family a certain amount of hunting days. Guanacos were the main source of food and the skins were used as clothing and to make boots. Despite the abundance of water in the region, they barely ate fish, and needless to say fruit and vegetables were scarce at these latitudes.

Today the town has a population of approximately 800, and survives mainly from agriculture and tourism.

Getting there
About the route
Balmaceda junction to Puerto Ibáñez (78km; 1hr; paved) South of El Blanco and the junction to Balmaceda, the Carretera Austral continues southwest on a fine paved road for 47km to a second junction. It continues west a further 6km to Cerro Castillo, or detours 31km south to Puerto Ibáñez. There are impressive views of the Lago General Carrera at the approach to Puerto Ibáñez.

Puerto Ibáñez to the Argentine border (20km; 30mins; gravel) Some 20km east of Puerto Ibáñez lies the border with Argentina (Paso Ingeniero Ibáñez Pallavicini). Paperwork is completed at the eastern exit of Puerto Ibáñez. The road quality towards the border is reasonable gravel, and even in winter the road is passable without the use of chains. However, reports are mixed as to the road quality on the Argentine side of the border, and it is approximately 100km further to Perito Moreno in Argentina, on gravel. This is not a common border crossing, and for those heading north (or arriving from the north), it may be wiser to use Paso Huemules (Balmaceda; page 237) or one of the various Coyhaique borders (page 200). For those heading south (or arriving from the south), the Chile Chico/Los Antiguos border is far easier and paved (page 279). Indeed, it appears that the

---

CHOOSING THE BEST ROUTE

There is little reason to visit Puerto Ibáñez in its own right, other than to take the **ferry** from here to Chile Chico. Taking the ferry to Chile Chico and continuing south involves either missing the spectacular section of the Carretera Austral between Villa Cerro Castillo and Puerto Río Tranquilo, or doubling back on oneself at El Maitén (ie: heading north to come back south).

However, skipping Puerto Ibáñez in favour of driving through Villa Cerro Castillo and Puerto Río Tranquilo implies either missing the stunning lakeside road along the south of Lago General Carrera east of Cruce El Maitén in the direction of Chile Chico, or doubling back on oneself at Chile Chico to rejoin the Carretera Austral at Cruce El Maitén. This can be done as one long day trip.

For those intending to **cross into Argentina at Chile Chico**, it is perhaps wisest to avoid the ferry and take the longer terrestrial route north of the lake and drive along the south of the lake to the border. Both these routes are worth doing if time allows it.

Our recommendation, for those with sufficient time, is to do a round-trip visit to Chile Chico in one or two days if the weather is acceptable. We would also highly recommend taking the back road from (close to) Cerro Castillo to the Levicán Peninsula (page 244), although this cannot be done in reverse in anything other than a sturdy 4x4. Thus our recommended tour excludes only one section in this region: the ferry.

If time constraints are an issue, a good alternative for those with their own vehicle is to miss the southern coastal road to Chile Chico, and instead visit Puerto Sánchez (page 254), which offers comparable views over the lake. This would allow a visit to the marble caves (page 257) from Puerto Sánchez rather than from Puerto Río Tranquilo, which would also be our preference.

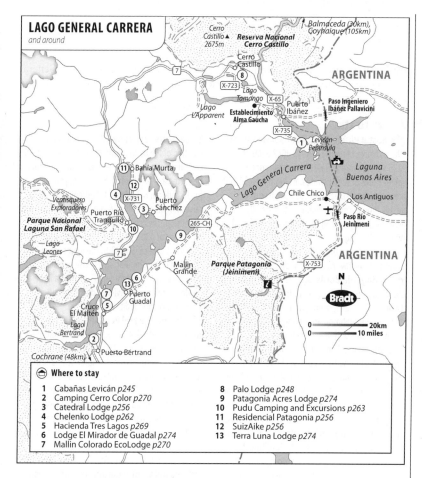

LAGO GENERAL CARRERA
and around

Where to stay

1 Cabañas Levicán *p245*
2 Camping Cerro Color *p270*
3 Catedral Lodge *p256*
4 Chelenko Lodge *p262*
5 Hacienda Tres Lagos *p269*
6 Lodge El Mirador de Guadal *p274*
7 Mallin Colorado EcoLodge *p270*
8 Palo Lodge *p248*
9 Patagonia Acres Lodge *p274*
10 Pudu Camping and Excursions *p263*
11 Residencial Patagonia *p256*
12 SuizAike *p256*
13 Terra Luna Lodge *p274*

Ibáñez border is principally used by people in a hurry who are unable to obtain a ticket on the ferry and prefer to drive from Chile Chico to Puerto Ibáñez via Argentina, which is quicker than going around the entire Lago General Carrera.

By bus Various shuttle vans operate between Coyhaique and Puerto Ibáñez to synchronise with ferries to Chile Chico (page 60). This is a well-transited route, and hitchhiking is also possible. For those wishing to go towards Cerro Castillo or further down the Carretera Austral, take any shuttle up to the Carretera Austral and await a southbound bus or hitchhike. **Transportes Iturra** (\9 8218 9251) runs a bus from Cerro Castillo to Puerto Ibáñez (depart 09.00 Mon, Wed, Thu & Fri, return at 16.00 same days). There is a bus connecting the Solar region with Ibáñez, but the concession frequently changes. Ask locally for updated prices.

Three shuttle buses operate between Coyhaique and Puerto Ibáñez – **Buses Carolina** (\67 221 9009, 9 8952 1529; e buscarolina@hotmail.com), **Buses Lino** (\9 8858 3149) and **Transportes Lukas** (\9 8354 1503) – synchronise with the ferries. **Freddy Morales** (\9 9506 2906) serves Puerto Ibáñez to Balmaceda airport (depart 11.15 daily, return 17.00, $10,000 pp); and to El Claro (depart 08.00 Mon & Fri, return 09.00, $700 pp). **Transportes Iturra** (\9 8218 9251) has a shuttle from

Cerro Castillo to Puerto Ibáñez (depart 09.00 Mon, Wed, Thu & Fri, return 16.00 same days).

By ferry Puerto Ibáñez is the northern terminal for ferries across Lago General Carrera (page 60). Ferries permit bicycles, as well as foot passengers, and have limited space for cars and motorbikes.

🏠 Where to stay

🏠 **Hostal Pirámide** (3 rooms) Diego Portales 298; ///heaven.fogging.rift; ☎ 9 4042 2900, 9 9295 9299. A surprisingly nice hostel & good value. 3 dbls (1 with private bathroom for a $2,500 premium), good b/fast included (with eggs & freshly ground coffee). Veronica, the friendly owner, can help with information, how to fix a flat tyre, etc. Parking available, Wi-Fi but no laundry. Guests cannot use the kitchen but there is a communal microwave. $20,000 pp. **$$$**

🏠 **Patagonia Bordelago** (5 cabins, 6 rooms) Luis Risopatron 55; ///giver.puts.halo; ☎ 67 242 3284, 9 6847 2273; e info@patagoniabordelago. cl; w patagoniabordelago.cl. High-quality cabin complex with a well-maintained garden & parking. A good option for a larger family or group. 2 cabins with dbl or twin beds, 3 cabins with dbl bedroom & a 2nd bedroom with 2 bunk beds. The largest cabin sleeps up to 7 people. The cabins are fully equipped with sat TV, microwave, refrigerator, Wi-Fi & wood-fired heaters. Rooms are dbl, twin & trpl with private bathroom. Native wood is used extensively for the furniture. Has a quincho, sauna, children's playroom, table tennis, & board games in each cabin. Laundry service available. Home-cooked local meals & b/fast can be arranged. They offer horseriding, fishing trips & 4x4 tours of the region. Mountain bike rental available. Reservations via their website. **$$$**

✳ 🏠 **Cabañas Doña Leo Main** (3 cabins, 2 rooms) road 1km north of Puerto Ibáñez; ///laughable.laundry.doubly; ☎ 9 5657 8392, 9 8832 3728; e parceladonaleo@gmail. com; 🔲 parceladonaleo. The best accommodation

in Puerto Ibáñez, slightly outside town, at the junction of the main road & the detour towards the Levicán Peninsula. The land was a working farm for the extensive family of Doña Leo. Her youngest son (of 11 children & 3 adopted children) continues to raise animals, grow fruit & run the cabins & a good restaurant. The cabins are top-notch, each with a terrace, for 4 to 7 people & reasonably priced (4-person cabin is $60,000). The rooms (en suite) are $25,000 pp. Popular, so it's wise to reserve in high season. Great for families as has a large garden with animals. Wi-Fi, cable TV, wood-stove heating. Accepts credit card. **$$**

🏠 **Hospedaje and Restaurant El Cata** (7 rooms) Av Padre Antonio Ronchi 30; ///helicopters. destroyer.divines; ☎ 67 242 3283, 9 8383 6888; e lethi.cq@hotmail.com. The longest established accommodation in the village. A backpacker option with small rooms & shared bathrooms, Wi-Fi, central heating & a basic b/fast (inc) consisting of homemade marmalade & fruit juice. The hostel runs a reasonably sized restaurant, serving milanesa, chicken & chips, salad, menu of the day & cakes ($). $15,000 pp. **$$**

🏠 **Hostal Vientos del Sur** (5 rooms, 2 cabins) Av Padre Antonio Ronchi 282; ///cuff.hoedown. tune; ☎ 9 7512 2813; e vientosdelsurptoibanez@ gmail.com. Comfortable rooms, 1 dbl with private bathroom, 4 dbls with shared bathrooms, $23,000 pp, b/fast (inc). Small café-style area at the front of the hostel. A decent option for couples, but not geared towards families. Cabins for 3 or 4 people, $55,000, b/fast extra cost. Has restaurant & Wi-Fi. Good value. **$$**

🍴 Where to eat and drink

There is rumoured to be a bar on the central plaza called the Hudson, but little evidence of it ever opening. (If anyone manages to visit this bar, please send us feedback!) Restaurants are notoriously unreliable in the village, so take opening times with a pinch of salt.

🍴 **Doña Leo** Main road 1km north of Puerto Ibáñez; ///laughable.laundry.doubly; ☎ 9 5657 8392, 9 8832 3728; e parceladonaleo@gmail.

com; 🕐 08.00–22.00 daily. Easily the best restaurant in the village, with most food grown on site or in the region; also sells homemade marmalades & liquors. Good range of cakes, & doubles as a café during the day. Semi-formal, with tablecloths (rare in the region), but also cosy & family-friendly. Excellent quality food, including all a lo pobre varieties, salmon, vegetarian dishes, salads, a children's menu, lamb dishes & a 3-course menu of the day for $8,000. Fresh coffee & local beers available, & can do a full lamb roast for groups of families if booked in advance. Very good service from the friendly owners, who also run the cabins. $$–$$$

✗ **Restaurante Portal de la Patagonia** Paseo Comerical #1; ///mitigates.improvised.collage; 📞9 8825 3189, 9 9065 0513. Open when it opens, this is the only place for hundreds of miles to find a decent pizza made entirely with local ingredients (except the flour, the owner is quick to point out). $7,500 per pizza. If open, this might be one of the best choices in a town with extremely limited culinary options. $$

✗ **Restaurante Vabu** Av Padre Antonio Ronchi 192; ///patrols.finder.copying; 📞9 5632 6235. Both a restaurant (🕐 08.30–15.00 daily) serving homemade regional fare & a simple bar in the evenings, when a few locals may gather over cans of Cristal & Escudo or a glass of the limited stock of spirits. Fri may witness karaoke or live music. Very flexible opening hours & days. $$

✗ **Servicio de Comida Ximena** Av Padre Antonio Ronchi 415 & cnr of Carlos Soza; ///sphinxes.sizes.squabbles; 🕐 10.30–21.30 daily. A small café that will stay open until past midnight at w/ends if enough people turn up. Simple food & drinks with vibrant Chilean dance music, the décor is hauso (the Chilean gaucho) themed. The only real late-night option in town, & the dancing starts well after midnight. $$

🍽 **Bakery Muffy** Av Antonio Ronchi 257; ///yell.backyard.magazine. Freshly baked bread Mon–Fri. $

Other practicalities There is **no petrol station** in Puerto Ibáñez – be sure to fill up in Coyhaique (115km north of here), Chile Chico (across the lake), or Puerto Río Tranquilo (162km southwest). It is usually possible to buy petrol from unofficial vendors at elevated prices, but it's best not to rely on this (also in Villa Cerro Castillo). Tyres can be repaired at the 'Vulcanizacion' sign at the northern entrance to the village. There is no ATM.

Sightseeing and excursions If you're in Puerto Ibáñez, make time to visit a pottery workshop. While there is little else to see and do within the town itself, it makes a good base for excursions in the area, including trips to Chile Chico or into Argentina.

Pottery workshops The characteristic pottery of the region is made from the clay from the Río Ibáñez and is, broadly speaking, terracotta-coloured. Most workshops are on the plaza or a block away. The painting of the pottery is based around local prehistoric paintings found in the region. The classic symbol is of a long-necked guanaco (that to the untrained eye might appear like a giraffe) feeding its baby (*guanaca con cría*), taken from one of the prehistoric cave paintings.

Pottery is a relatively new arrival in Puerto Ibáñez. Father Antonio Ronchi (see box, page 161) launched training programmes in 1967 and into the 1970s for the female residents to develop an income-generating skill. A subsequent modification was to stretch thin sheets of leather around parts of the pottery, hand-stitched, typically around the bases of jugs. There are a variety of objects available for sale (cups, plates, bowls, jugs for example), and also two standard sets consisting of six or seven items, and available in different sizes. A tour of a workshop is interesting for Spanish-speakers, and generally free if you buy something. The pots are one of the few truly distinctive souvenirs of the entire Carretera Austral region and, while quality ranges widely, they are unique items not found elsewhere in Latin America. Many items are sturdy and not overly ornate, so can be fairly safely packed into a rucksack. Opening hours are informal.

The **Taller Artesanal Marina workshop** (Carlos Soza 246; ///tortoises.charcoal. falafel; ☏9 8172 8708; e artesanias_eva61@yahoo.es) is owned by Eva Carrillo who was one of Ronchi's first students. Her workshop is on the north of the central plaza, and she offers a quick tour explaining the process, from preparing the clay and the moulds to the firing process, polishing and painting the finished product, and the use of leather.

Establecimiento Alma Gaucha (15km west of Puerto Ibáñez on X-723; ///cheer.recites.scrapping; ☏9 9167 0089, 9 9612 7002; e almagauchaturismo@ gmail.com; w almagaucha.cl) is part of a new wave of rural tourism, with less focus on activities and more on the culture, music, food, history, flora, fauna and people of the region. They can arrange a traditional goat/lamb asado and offer one- or two-day visits to immerse yourself in the gaucho way of life, beyond simply horses and eating meat. One of the founders is descended from the original pioneers to this region, and the purpose of Alma Gaucha is to inform visitors of the way of life that still exists in some of these more distant parts of the Carretera.

THE LEVICÁN PENINSULA Quite why there is a road to Levicán is unclear. It is barely inhabited. There are no services. At the isthmus connecting Levicán to the mainland there are a few houses, some small farms, a campsite and two cabins for rent. The road continues on to the peninsula and ends abruptly at a beach. However, if only for the sole purpose of admiring the region's stunning beauty, particularly on the return journey north, with incredible views of Cerro Castillo in the distance, travelling the road to Levicán is an opportunity not to be missed. Along this section, depending on the weather, views of Puerto Ibáñez, with the mountains in the background, reveal the true scale of the southeastern extreme of the Reserva Nacional Cerro Castillo. Periodic views of Cerro Castillo in the distance emerge through lesser mountains in the foreground. It is 23km from the dead end of this road to the junction. Continue straight to return to Puerto Ibáñez, or veer left (in a 4x4 only) on the 'back route' to Cerro Castillo (page 246). With good weather the roads immediately to the north and south of the lake are some of the most beautiful in the whole of Aysén, as is the road to the Levicán Peninsula.

Getting there
About the route Head 3km north out of Puerto Ibáñez on the main road and take the simple detour west towards the dramatic **Río Ibáñez waterfall** (///coldness. carloads.unthinkable). This is worth a quick stop. Clambering on the rocks to get a closer view is exciting and dangerous in equal measure – take care as there are no marked trails nor handrails. Thereafter continue for approximately 1km across two bridges and up a very steep gravel road to a junction. To the left lies the Levicán Peninsula; to the right the road continues up to the Carretera Austral close to Cerro Castillo. It is possible that a high-clearance non-4x4 can reach Levicán, but do not attempt the northward section of this road towards the Cerro Castillo in a regular vehicle, due to a brutal gravel incline (for more on this road, see opposite).

By bus The only public transport to/from the peninsula (Puerto Rey, 2km before the end of the road) is a state-subsidised bus operated by **Freddy Morales** (Lautaro 592; ☏9 9506 2906). This departs Puerto Ibáñez 08.00 and 17.00, and Puerto Rey 09.00 and 18.00 (Mon & Fri, 1hr, $900 pp). The bus leaves/enters the village to the north on the X-723, very close to the Cabañas Doña Leo (page 242). It is possible to embark/disembark the bus here, but call Freddy to warn him.

Where to stay and eat

🏠 **Cabañas Levicán** [map, page 241] (2 cabins) Puerto Rey, 2km before end of the road, opposite church; ///persuade.retouch.exiled; 📞 9 5606 8986. The only accommodation on the peninsula. The larger cabin (5 people, $50,000) is gloomy & has no communal sitting area; the smaller cabin (3 people, $40,000) is far nicer. Wood-stove heating, modest kitchen, TV, no internet, minimal mobile-phone connection (only Claro) & no laundry. B/fast included, other meals with notice &, given the lack of any restaurant on the entire peninsula, this is worth considering. Can do a lamb roast & asado. Large quincho for self-catering. Offers sport fishing tours from the coast of the lake. $

▲ **Camping Levicán Peninsula** ///practical. sprinter.brags. 1km west of Puerto Rey, just past the cemetery, a gravel road heads south off the main road. Follow for 1km to a lunar beach, suitable for camping if the wind is not too ferocious – there is limited shelter among bushes. Absolutely no services whatsoever, but a small creek provides drinking water (perhaps worth boiling first). Lovely views across a relatively sheltered bay on the south side of the peninsula. No charge.

CERRO CASTILLO

The dramatic approach to the village of Cerro Castillo offers vast panoramic vistas of the entire valley, with the snow-capped mountain range of the same name glistening to the west. A dozen hairpin bends later, the village itself is fairly drab, serving as a mere springboard to the mountain that deservedly features on most itineraries along the Carretera Austral. Besides the beauty of the valley, Cerro Castillo offers some of the most accessible trekking and horseriding opportunities along the Carretera. The jagged basalt peaks are the crown jewel of the national reserve, named for the resemblance to the battlements of medieval castles, and reach an altitude of 2,675m. The reserve covers 1,380km² of rugged mountains and roaring trout-filled rivers, waterfalls, hanging glaciers, lagoons and native bush. Indeed, Cerro Castillo, along with Parque Pumalín to the north and Parque Patagonia further south, are fast becoming as iconic a Patagonian trekking destination as the more established treks around Torres del Paine and El Chaltén.

GETTING THERE Note that the nearest petrol station is Coyhaique or Puerto Río Tranquilo, but see also the mini market (page 249). The paved road from Coyhaique (93km) terminates at the southern end of the town, where glorious gravel begins. The Carretera Austral is almost entirely paved from Cerro Castillo to Puerto Montt. From Cerro Castillo south it is mostly unpaved. As a popular tourist destination, **hitchhiking** around here involves some fierce competition and long waits.

About the route

Puerto Ibáñez to Cerro Castillo (37km; under 1hr; paved) The quickest and easiest route between Puerto Ibáñez and Cerro Castillo is on the paved X-65. The road is of modest interest until the junction (31km) with the main Carretera Austral. Cerro Castillo lies 6km west of this junction and 97km southwest of Coyhaique. However, the final section of road to Cerro Castillo is spectacular. The road ascends through a series of hairpin bends to a **viewpoint** over the entire valley, where the mountain range of Cerro Castillo is visible in all its splendour, with the minuscule town of Cerro Castillo beneath. There is a parking area where budding photographers can safely snap one of the definitive shots of the entire Carretera Austral. The road snakes down into the valley and enters Cerro Castillo.

The 'back road' from Puerto Ibáñez (36km; 1hr; gravel) This spectacular stretch of gravel road of 36km (which connects the Carretera Austral, 5km west of Cerro Castillo, and the X-65 3km north of Puerto Ibáñez) is a highlight of the region, but of poor-quality, steep gravel, and even when dry this is barely passable in anything other than a 4x4. If done from north to south (ie: from Cerro Castillo), it is possible in a high-clearance car, but the hill towards the junction down through a gorge is so steep that it is not possible to do this section without a 4x4.

The road weaves through stunning forest, with views of Cerro Castillo and the panoramic horizon of the Reserva Nacional Cerro Castillo. In the foreground are a series of lakes, some of which are unnamed. This single section of road competes seriously as one of the most picturesque in the entire region of Aysén. There are no services to be found along this relatively isolated stretch, and the only available accommodation is Palo Lodge (page 248). If travelling along this route, it is worth taking the short 23km detour to the Lévican Peninsula before heading to Puerto Ibáñez (page 244).

By public transport No official buses begin or terminate in Cerro Castillo, but almost all buses heading south from Coyhaique, or north from Cochrane, pass through the town. **Transportes Iturra** (◌9 8218 9251) have a shuttle between Cerro Castillo and Puerto Ibáñez (page 241).

Several private drivers offer a direct morning (depart around 07.30, return around 17.00, $5,000 one-way) trip to Coyhaique; ask the receptionist at any hotel to call and arrange since they don't have a bus stop. In Coyhaique they leave from in front of the UniMarc supermarket (Lautaro 331). Look for the white vans that have 'Villa Cerro Castillo' written on them. There is no public transport from Cerro Castillo to the Levicán Peninsula.

TOUR OPERATORS

Senderos Patagonia Southern exit of town on Carretera Austral; ///reason.unbreakable. droid; ◌9 6224 4725; e senderospatagonia@ gmail.com; w aysensenderospatagonia.com. Offer a wide range of horse treks in the region, including some more off-the-beaten-track options, ranging from short day treks to multi-day adventures. The shorter trips can combine trekking & horseriding, & visiting the lakes of the national park. They guide the main 4-day Cerro Castillo trek (page 251) & the Jeinimeni trek through Parque Patagonia (page 282). Their longer horseriding trips are spectacular, unique, & hard to do independently: riding from Cerro Castillo to the abandoned town of Puerto Cristal on the northern shore of Lake General Carrera (8 days), or a shorter trip through the Las Ardillas region & Lago Tamango (which the back-route to Levicán passes through, page 244). This trek was featured in *National Geographic UK* (Mar 2017). Finally, they also offer the legendary 'Ruta de los Pioneros' ride from Cochrane to

Villa O'Higgins (page 213). The owner, Christian Vidal, is a recognised horse trainer, & practises 'Natural Horsemanship' – think of the horse whisperer. It is possible to observe him training wild Patagonian horses, which are very strong & sure-footed in this rough terrain where they were born & raised – riders will be amazed where these Patagonian-bred horses will go. For those interested in horseriding, this is possibly the single best operator along the entire Carretera Austral & based in an ideal location. Senderos Patagonia also run a campsite/hostel (page 249).

Villa Cerro Castillo (Servicios Turísticos) Bernardo O'Higgins 428; ///tipping. manfully.sunk; ◌9 6902 1632; e contacto@ villacerrocastillo.com; w villacerrocastillo.com. A one-stop shop for visitors to the region. Run by Clara & Federico, a charming Argentine couple who have lived in the region for years, they can arrange almost anything anyone might need in & around Cerro Castillo up to expedition logistics: hotels, tours, guides & transport (including

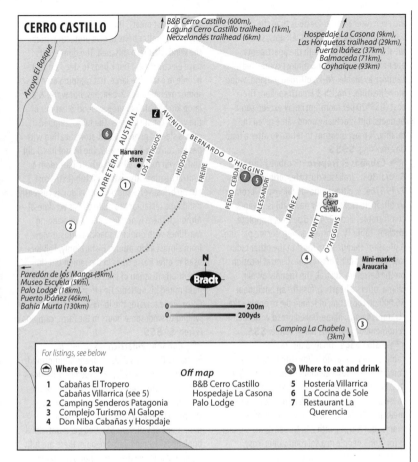

CERRO CASTILLO

B&B Cerro Castillo (600m),
Laguna Cerro Castillo trailhead (1km),
Neozelandés trailhead (6km)

Hospedaje La Casona (9km),
Las Horquetas trailhead (29km),
Puerto Ibáñez (37km),
Balmaceda (71km),
Coyhaique (93km)

Arroyo El Bosque

CARRETERA AUSTRAL

AVENIDA BERNARDO O'HIGGINS

Harware store

LOS ANTIGUOS

HUDSON

FREIRE

PEDRO CERDA

ALESSANDRI

IBAÑEZ

MONTT

O'HIGGINS

Plaza Cerro Castillo

Mini-market Araucaria

Paredón de los Manos (5km),
Museo Escuela (5km),
Palo Lodge (18km),
Puerto Ibáñez (46km),
Bahía Murta (130km)

N

Bradt

0 ———— 200m
0 ———— 200yds

Camping La Chabela
(3km)

For listings, see below

🛏 **Where to stay**
1 Cabañas El Tropero
  Cabañas Villarrica (see 5)
2 Camping Senderos Patagonia
3 Complejo Turismo Al Galope
4 Don Niba Cabañas y Hospdaje

Off map
B&B Cerro Castillo
Hospedaje La Casona
Palo Lodge

✖ **Where to eat and drink**
5 Hostería Villarrica
6 La Cocina de Sole
7 Restaurant La
  Querencia

transfers to the trailheads, Balmaceda, Lago Tamango, etc) & operate essentially as a tourist information hub, particularly with advice on treks of different difficulty levels (English spoken). However, they also have their own range of tours & services, extending beyond the 'standard' offers available elsewhere. They offer a great 4x4 tour meandering the back roads to Puerto Ibáñez, through the lesser-known Ardillas sector, or a city tour around the immediate vicinity of Cerro Castillo (including the Museo Escuela; page 250). There are approximately 20 marked routes for

beginners/intermediate climbers, & they offer full-day trips to the rock with kit, transport & instructors. In addition to climbing equipment, it is possible to rent sleeping bags & fishing equipment, & they sell gas canisters for portable stoves. They can arrange (guided) fishing trips. They can provide hot showers & bathrooms for clients, & have a small shop, El Arbolito, with tea, coffee, hot chocolate, kuchen, bread, eggs, marmalades, local ales, locally made soaps & cosmetics. Credit cards accepted.

WHERE TO STAY *Map, above, unless otherwise stated*

🏠 **B&B Cerro Castillo** (4 rooms, 2 apts) Camino El Bosque km1; ///received.monk. snuggles; ☎ 9 8248 6928; e consultasrcc@gmail. com; w refugiocerrocastillo.cl. At last, top-quality accommodation in Cerro Castillo. Slightly

outside of town, the rooms all have wonderful views towards the mountains & along the valley, excellent-quality construction & furnishings, full bathrooms with rain showers, large, comfortable beds, & full b/fast included. The apartments

10

are even nicer & more spacious than the rooms, with terraces & kitchenettes. All dbls, so not ideal for families (although the apartments are next to one another & almost connected). Laundry available, Wi-Fi, off-road parking, wood-stove heating, English & French spoken. The cost (US$120 per room/apt) may exceed some budgets, but is actually good value given the quality, & most pleasant to return to after a hard day trekking. **$$$$**

🏠 **Cabañas El Tropero** (3 cabins) Carretera Austral 305; ///aliases.dusty.featuring; 📞 9 7759 5766; e eltroperohospedaje@gmail.com; w eltropero.cl. Relatively new cabins, clean & comfortable, sleep 2, 4 or 6 people, complete kitchen, cable TV, central heating, secure parking. A pleasant change from most of the other older low-quality cabins in the area. Central location on the Carretera Austral. The friendly owner, Eliana, offers a hearty b/fast for an additional $6,000 pp consisting of lemon pie or apple cake, scrambled eggs, home-baked bread with cheese & homemade jam, plus tea or coffee. **$$$**

🏠 **Palo Lodge** [map, page 241] (2 cabins) Lago Tamango; ///distributed.second. converter; e info@palolodge.com; 🅵; 🕓 Nov–Apr. Perched on the southern shore of the lake, these 2 cabins are isolated & romantic in equal measure. The larger cabin sleeps 5 people in 2 rooms (dbl & trpl), with 2 bathrooms; the smaller is for 2 or 3 people in a sgl room. Uber-cosy, wood-stove heating, terrace, compact kitchen fine for self-sufficiency, lovely bathrooms with good hot water, but electricity is in short supply (no internet/mobile coverage or laundry). Can arrange activities in the region (fishing, biking, trekking, kayaking), or prepare a roast lamb in their own quincho, but ultimately this is a place to escape contact with the outside world & enjoy the utter peace & remoteness of this hidden corner of the Carretera. High-season prices $120,000/90,000, lower off-season, min 2-night reservation, drop-off/pickup from Balmaceda airport possible for a fee. **$$$**

🏠 **Complejo Turismo Al Galope** (4 cabins, camping, 3 domes, 5 rooms) Los Pioneros 962; ///bodes.cupful.wiggly; 📞 9 5632 1978, 9 9076 9801; e turismoalgalope@gmail.com; w turismoalgalope.cl. A family-run rural tourism outfit with a farm, various accommodation options & offering excellent parillas & asados

al palo (roast meat). The huge campground has good tree shelter belts to give protection from the winds that lash this area. The dome tents have electricity & 4 bunk beds to sleep up to 8 people in each. The large, flat camping area has some covered tables & benches, hot water & a large kitchen area to prepare food & eat out of the wind, & hot showers. The fully equipped cabins sleep 4 people, wood-stove heating with gas for cooking & hot water. The hostel has 3 dbl and 2 twin rooms, all with private bathroom & central heating. Also has a hot tub (extra cost), but no b/fast yet – the owner, Felidor, is currently building a restaurant to address this weakness! Although there is no Wi-Fi, there are vending machines with drinks & snacks. Fantastic view from almost all locations. Disturbingly, Felidor used to offer horse treks in the region but the recent privatisation of land around Cerro Castillo has limited his options. He offers a 3hr trek to Cerro Moñe towards the Ibáñez Valley. For those willing to work some hours in the farm, camping is free. **$–$$$**

🏠 **Cabañas Villarrica** (5 cabins) Av Bernardo O'Higgins 592; ///cleanser.unfinished. goofing; 📞 9 6656 0173; e hospedaje.villarrica@ gmail.com. The main office operates out of the restaurant but the actual cabins are just off the main Carretera, alas with no view of the mountains or valley. At $50,000 per night, dbl & bunk beds sleeping 3 or 4 people, these are fully equipped & somewhat basic, but good value. Wood-stove heating with a decent supply of wood, off-road parking & a small mini market located next door. **$$**

🏠 **Don Niba Cabañas y Hospedaje** (4 rooms, 1 cabin) Los Pioneros 872; /// investigation.washed.detours; 📞 9 9474 0408; e donniba19@gmail.com. A popular, clean, comfortable hostel, all with private bathrooms & decent hot water. However, the highlight of this place is the owner, Nibaldo Calderon, who has spent over 40 years exploring the region, was the first person to promote Cerro Castillo for its archaeological treasures & has appeared on countless TV programmes including the Discovery Channel. He knows more than 80 sites, most of which are almost entirely unknown, & he can arrange tours for those specifically interested in truly understanding the prehistory of the zone. Cabin sleeps 4 people. **$$**

🏠 **Hospedaje La Casona** (4 rooms, 1 cabin) Ruta X-65; ///homerun.orangey.nicer; ☎ 9 9138 9084, 9 7106 3591. Great little place easily missed to the untrained eye, being in an unusual location. 8km north of Cerro Castillo begins the road (X-65) to Puerto Ibáñez, & 1.5km along this road lies the hospedaje – in the middle of nowhere with views towards Cerro Castillo, but with no shop or restaurant for miles. The village of Cerro Castillo is nearby which is certainly convenient for getting to or from the Ibáñez ferries. One of the first hospedajes in the region, operating for 20 years, it has all the usual services (Wi-Fi, laundry, TV, wood-stove heating). 1 trpl, 1 dbl, 2 sgls, all shared bathroom. Try to get a room with a view over the mountains if possible. Mary, the owner, knows almost everything about the region, & if not, she knows someone who knows. Extremely peaceful, nice areas for sitting outside, awesome b/fast (inc with rooms, extra cost for cabin), & vintage building with creaky floors & low ceilings. Cash only. **$$**

⚓ **Camping Senderos Patagonia** (10 campsites, 1 dorm, 1 room, 2 apts) Southern exit of town on Carretera Austral; ///reason.unbreakable.droid; ☎ 9 6224 4725; **e** senderospatagonia@gmail.com; **w** aysensenderospatagonia.com. A family-run campground with good shelter from trees & spectacular views of Cerro Castillo. The campsites are neatly terraced out of the side of a bush-clad hill providing privacy between sites. There is hot water & a separate kitchen. The hostel has 5 bunk beds & 1 dbl room, all shared bathrooms with hot water. $12,000 pp, $10,000 with your own sleeping bag. Spacious sitting area & decent-sized kitchen for cooking & eating, but sketchy Wi-Fi. Besides the stunning views, the owners, Cristian & Mary, are professional mountain guides & also offer horse trekking. Their company, Senderos Patagonia (page 246), specialises in riding and trekking in Patagonia. Mary knows everything & everyone in the region, so very helpful for planning trips. Apts are self-contained, with private bathroom & own entrance. A great place to meet fellow travellers. **$–$$$**

🍴 **WHERE TO EAT AND DRINK** *Map, page 247*

🍴 **Hostería Villarrica** O'Higgins; ///theatrics. swishes.avenge. The restaurant of this hostel offers a wide range of churascos (sandwiches that resemble a large hamburger), a lo pobre dishes, & salad & vegetarian options. There is beer on tap, as well as a small selection of wines & regional beers such as Caiquén. Friendly staff & good service in a relaxed family atmosphere. **$$**

🍴 **Restaurant La Querencia** O'Higgins 522; ///basements.slouches.magistrates; ☎ 9 6636 5424; 🕐 13.00–22.00 daily. A favourite with locals. Tour buses use this restaurant as their lunch stop. Sandwiches, salmon, a lo pobre; the churasco is possibly large enough for 2. Limited selection of beers & wines. Good service. **$$**

✴ 🍴 **La Cocina de Sole** Carretera Austral 7; ///migrations.questions.socked. An excellent place for a quick sandwich or a simple meal with drinks, located in 2 decommissioned Coyhaique buses joined together & converted into a roadside diner at the base of Cerro Castillo. The owner, Soledad, started this business in the back of a van which survives to this day as a drinks stall. These buses have nostalgic significance for the people of the region, particularly those who met their partners while riding on them! Open till late, this is a great place to meet other travellers while sitting outside on the small deck watching the stars on a warm summer's evening. Great value and fun with kids ($7,000 for meal & drink). **$**

OTHER PRACTICALITIES The **tourist office** is located beside the radio masts as you enter the village from the north (cnr Av Bernado O'Higgins & Carretera Austral), and is worth visiting if planning to hike in the region. There are very few shops in Cerro Castillo, and no petrol station, ATM, or dedicated car mechanic. The small **mini market** (Araucaria Herminio Vargas 297) has a wide assortment of essentials such as meat, fruit, dry foods, and possibly fuel for your car in five-litre bottles. The **hardware store** on Los Antiguos might be able to help with mechanical problems. **Fernando Rivas** has a taxi service (☎ 9 6204 1342; **e** sandovalrivasfernando@gmail. com). There is one **laundry:** Lavandería Sandra (Ramón Freire; ☎ 9 5234 5201).

SIGHTSEEING AND EXCURSIONS Those who stop in Cerro Castillo for anything other than a sandwich generally come for the **trekking and horseriding**. The paved road from the north ends at the town limit and many simply push on south towards Puerto Río Tranquilo, yet the climbing and trekking on Cerro Castillo are probably the most accessible along the entire Carretera Austral.

Horseriding

This is a wonderful area for horseriding with many breathtaking views of snow-capped mountains, roaring rivers and picturesque lakes and it is a lot easier (and quicker) to ride a horse along this steep, bush-clad, mountainous terrain than it is to attempt it on foot. Cerro Castillo has a strong gaucho history as the horse was the main form of transport until recent times when the road was fully developed. Many of the old cattle trails used by the farmers to transport their cattle to market are now being rediscovered through horse trekking in the region, and tourists can now get off the beaten track and experience the true gaucho culture – Senderos Patagonia (page 246) offer treks, including one to the lagoon at the top of Cerro Castillo.

Museo Escuela

(School Museum; Carlos Soza 161, Puerto Ingeniero Ibáñez; \67 242 3216; e info@museoescuela-cerrocastillo.cl; w museoescuela-cerrocastillo. cl; ◷ 10.00–17.00 Tue–Sun; entry $2,000/1,000 adult/child) Follow the Carretera Austral south for approximately 1km and then take the first left turn after the bridge over the Río Ibáñez. Drive or walk for approximately 2km to the site of Villa Cerro Castillo's first school.

After years of neglect, the old Cerro Castillo School has been restored – it was recognised as a national monument in 2008 and inaugurated in January 2014 as a museum. This impressive two-storey school was built by settlers in 1955 and operated for 16 years. Its original construction used traditional materials and building techniques. Its outer walls are brick, the floor and rafters were hand-cut from enormous tree trunks, and the spectacular roof was constructed with hand-carved *tejuela* wood shingles. This beautiful building now serves to educate visitors about the settlers of Valle Ibáñez and the first inhabitants of the area. These were groups of hunter-gatherers who occupied these lands more than 9,200 years ago. The focus of the museum is on the historic problems of education in an isolated region, forcing parents to send their children far away to boarding schools, and the impact that had on families.

There is a large viewing platform to admire the landscape of the Río Ibáñez and Cerro Castillo. Below is a central investigation centre where archaeologists investigate more than 80 recorded sites of the original inhabitants of the area. Geologists and volcanologists also use the on-site laboratory to study the active and sometimes destructive nearby Volcán Hudson (page 231).

Paredón de los Manos archaeological site

This site is located only 200m before the Museo Escuela and is an excellent opportunity to explore ancient Patagonian culture and see the traces left by the Tehuelches. The Valle Ibáñez is one of the most important archaeological regions in central Patagonia. The Paredón de los Manos is a rock wall protected under an overhang with handprints of adults and children dating back approximately 3,000 years. The Tehuelche artistic style was constantly evolving with some of the earlier paintings depicting hunting scenes of guanacos. Later they began to portray hands as positive and negative images. They painted with a mixture of dyes, including blood and mineral oxides blown through a hollowed-out guanaco bone. Fortunately most of these paintings are protected from the elements. The guides are informative and give a brief description of the hunting that took place in the valley below. Some speak basic English.

Reserva Nacional Cerro Castillo (w conaf.cl/parques/reserva-nacional-cerro-castillo; entry foreigners $8,200/4,100, Chileans $4,100/2,100 adult/child) This 18,000ha national reserve is located 75km south of Coyhaique, and its main attraction is the impressive south face of Cerro Castillo (2,675m). The basalt spires are the crowning centrepiece and from a distance this mountain looks like a medieval castle. The upper slopes are covered with large névés and hanging glaciers, and below the formidable mountain peaks are beautiful valleys with roaring rivers and southern beech forests. The reserve headquarters are located at the southern point of Laguna Chiguay on the Carretera Austral, 60km south of Coyhaique and 35km north of Cerro Castillo. A great website for more information, including maps (also in .kmz format), camping areas, park fees, etc, is w parquenacionalcerrocastillo.cl.

TREKKING CERRO CASTILLO (45–62.5km, depending on detours; four days, but can be shortened to three; medium to demanding – requires a high level of fitness (highest pass is 1,600m); $27,000/29,000 Chileans/foreigners) The best time to trek Cerro Castillo is between mid-November and late March, subject to weather conditions – be aware that extreme weather and snow storms with gale-force winds can occur even in January. There are no refuges and mountain guides recommend a four-season tent, a three-season sleeping bag, layered thermal clothing and rainwear to cover all possible weather conditions. Trekking poles and hiking boots with ankle support are recommended, especially to assist with river crossings, steeper descents and rocky scree. For river crossings a pair of sandals are a useful accessory. A mountain stove and food for an extra couple of days are prudent accessories in case you have to wait out a storm. Do not forget a brimmed hat, woollen hat, sunglasses and sunscreen. Be prepared for strong winds on the higher mountain passes. There are abundant water sources throughout the trek, apart from when crossing mountain passes. Wild camping and fires are not permitted, but there are campsites with bathrooms. The Chilean phone service provider Entel has a reasonable signal on the mountain passes.

It is not obligatory to register at the Reserva Nacional Cerro Castillo headquarters, but it is highly advisable, for safety reasons, to obtain up-to-date information (about the trek, the status of the river crossings, weather forecasts, etc), and also to pick up a free map. For more information, go to w parquenacionalcerrocastillo.cl. Ask the park ranger to clearly mark on the map where the 'emergency exit' is, as it is not marked on the standard CONAF map. There is a CONAF **campsite** directly in front of the reserve headquarters which allows trekkers to get an early start the next day. For those starting at the reserve headquarters, the first stage of the trek is to walk or hitchhike 7.5km south along the paved Carretera Austral section to the trailhead at **Las Horquetas Grandes** (68km south of Coyhaique and 27km north of Villa Cerro Castillo). Those starting from Villa Cerro Castillo will need to arrange transport to this point (the tourist information centre or a hostel can arrange

> **NOTE**
>
> This four-day trek can be shortened to three days either by exiting at the 'emergency exit' on day three, or by combining days three and four into one 18km, 8–10-hour day.

this; alternatively, hitchhike or take a northbound bus and ask to be dropped off at the trailhead). Las Horquetas Grandes is no more than a sharp bend in the road where two streams meet. If arriving from Coyhaique, any bus to Cerro Castillo will pass the trailhead and will stop there when asked.

Day one: Las Horquetas to the Río Turbio campsite (15.4km; 5–6hrs) The

trek starts on an old logging road that is now used by local gauchos to herd cattle into the valleys for summer grazing. The road veers left past an old house and continues through vibrant lenga forest and farmed pastures. It follows a beautiful clear stream that must be crossed three times – take care particularly after heavy snow melt or rain. Water levels are usually higher in spring and can be chest-high. Consider wearing sandals for river crossings in order to keep trekking boots dry, and trekking poles will assist with balance. The trek continues for roughly 15km to the **CONAF hut** where the entry fee is paid at registration. After 4–5 hours there is a small **campsite** with toilet, fireplace, table and benches. However, most continue for another hour to the **Río Turbio campsite**. Pass the roaring Río Turbio and follow the track south, taking in the spectacular views of glacier-fed waterfalls over huge vertical cliffs, until it re-enters the lenga forest. The campsite sits at the head of the alpine Valle Río Turbio, where the rare huemul deer occasionally graze. There are simple tables and a dry toilet.

Day two: Río Turbio campsite to Bosque campsite (9.5km; 6hrs) An early

start is recommended, as winds pick up at around 13.00–14.00 on Paso Peñon, the first mountain pass. The trail continues upstream along the Río Turbio, which is fed by the **Ventisquero Peñon** (not visible from the main trek). The glacier and lagoon can be accessed via a **small detour** that starts 1km west of the Río Turbio campsite. For this, follow the river's south bank for about half an hour until you arrive at the muddy meltwater pool below the glacier. Back on the main trail, continue uphill through the forest and along a steep scree section to cross the El Peñon saddle (1,460m). This scree section is treacherous and may be covered in snow in spring, further complicating the pass. However, the views from the pass are spectacular, particularly for the relative proximity to a glacier emerging from Cerro Peñon and a full view of Cerro Castillo. Andean condors are often spotted here gracefully gliding between the mountain peaks with their huge wingspans. This is the halfway point of the day. Once trekkers have descended from the El Peñon Pass on the steep and unstable scree-covered slopes, the trail borders a small stream fed from the icy outcrops that hang off Cerro Peñon stream. This is where the jagged peaks of the Cerro Castillo become visible. The track continues downstream until it arrives at the **Estero del Bosque junction** with the somewhat larger western branch of the stream descending from the Estero. The track veers right into the Valle Estero del Bosque and ascends moderately to the El Bosque campsite set within a sheltered valley among the thick lenga forest. There is a toilet, a fireplace, table and benches. In the event of bad weather this is a safe refuge to pause before the high pass the next day. From the camp there is an optional detour (2km round trip; 1hr) to a glacial lagoon with floating icebergs.

Day three: Bosque campsite to Porteadores campsite (8.8km; 6–7hrs)

CONAF recommend an 08.00 start to comfortably arrive at Laguna Cerro Castillo with enough time to traverse the mountain pass before midday, as after this the wind picks up making the crossing more dangerous. The trail begins with a steep initial **climb** of 740m along the banks of the stream cascading down from the Cerro

Castillo glacier lagoon, until reaching a small plateau at the base of the Castillo. The view from the plateau is worthy of a short break and photograph opportunity. The track then ascends moraine to a vantage point. This is arguably the most spectacular vista in the entire reserve, overlooking the Valle Ibáñez and the turquoise lagoon. On a fine day the view extends to Lago General Carrera and beyond to Argentina. To the other side, the mountain and glacier provide a stark contrast to the lake, interrupted with the sound of ice cracking and tumbling into the lagoon below. Despite the scenic location this could equally be one of the most dangerous places on the mountain if the weather takes a turn for the worse – gale-force winds are not uncommon here. In the event of a storm lie low as there is no shelter in this section, and advance between gusts. This ridge has a clearly marked **emergency exit** (*salida de emergencia*). The track then crosses the Cerro Castillo saddle (1,600m) before descending to the forest and on to the **Porteadores campsite**. There are impressive views of Cerro Palo and there is an optional extension (3.4km) on day three to camp at **Campo Neozelandés campsite**. This allows for the ascent of Laguna Duff (2.6km) on day four, as well as the return to Villa Cerro Castillo.

Day four: Porteadores campsite to Villa Cerro Castillo (10km; 3–4hrs) This is potentially the shortest day of trekking due to the flat nature of the landscape – a far cry from the mountainous terrain of previous days. The trail descends 4km through the **Parada Canyon** with views towards the Río Ibáñez to the CONAF tent, where registering your hike is required. From here the trek continues 6km to Villa Cerro Castillo. The trail leaves the reserve through a traditional Patagonian sheep and beef ranch, out of the park and along a country road. Hitchhiking is possible here, but cars are rare.

TREK TO THE NEOZELANDÉS CAMPSITE If the four-day marathon trek of Cerro Castillo is a little too long, consider the excellent day hike to Campo Neozelandés. The trailhead and park entrance is 6km west of Cerro Castillo (///heckler.navels. spoonfuls) – to reach it, hitch, trek or drive. The entrance is clearly marked, and is actually the exit point for those doing the four-day trek. The trek roughly parallels the Estero Parada (river), passes through forest most of the time, and only the final leg up to Laguna Duff is exposed. It is a fairly easy trek to the Campo Neozelandés; the trek to Duff is a little more challenging and involves some scrambling over rocks, but is certainly worthwhile and possibly the highlight of the day. There is abundant water along the way.

The fee for a single day is $18,000 for foreigners, $14,000 for Chileans, which is more than most other park entrance fees, but $6,000 of this goes to private landowners whose land you must cross – the remainder is the CONAF fee (all private landowners and concession holders make local donations to the village). The first leg of the trail is 4.3km and takes under 2 hours, with magnificent views of the valley, as well as the lower section of the river. The first camp reached is Campamento Porteadores, with bathrooms and water. The trail heading eastwards is the last stage of the four-day trek – do not take this trail but head through the Porteadores camp and continue towards the Neozelandés camp (water and bathroom available). This second leg is 3.6km, easy and takes a little over an hour. The final leg to Laguna Duff is 2.6km and takes at least an hour each way across large rocks. The lake is not visible until the last few metres and is absolutely spectacular, with turquoise water and the occasional mini iceberg. The river starts in this lake, but looking down the valley other pools can be seen, as well as spectacular views of the top of Cerro Castillo from close up.

Climbing There are an ever-increasing number of climbing routes around Cerro Castillo and it is fast becoming a climbing Mecca. Facilities are limited currently so this is mainly suitable for experienced climbers with their own kit (see Villa Cerro Castillo (Servicios Turísticos) who rent kit and have guides, page 246). The main hub is **Camping La Chabela**, located 3km east of the village (↘9 9210 1649). With 47 routes, graded intermediate to advanced 5.9–5.13d (UK system: 5a-7a), the rocks are fairly clean, but do take a helmet. A 70m rope with 15 quick draws will suffice for all routes. Camping is possible for $2,000 per person, and all rubbish should be removed.

BAHÍA MURTA AND PUERTO SÁNCHEZ – A DETOUR

Bahía Murta was originally located at the mouth of the Engaño River, but a flood/landslide in 1954 destroyed much of the village, and only the graveyard remains on the original location. Periodic eruptions of the Hudson volcano prompted more people to leave the village, which to this day depends heavily on livestock. Bahía Murta is only recently emerging as a tourist destination, in part as an overflow for Puerto Río Tranquilo when there are simply no beds left, or as a waypoint on the journey to Puerto Sánchez. However, the village does have a character of its own, perhaps in part because it is so heavily focused on horses, cattle and sheep and less so on tourism. The rodeo of Murta is one of the most important in the region and takes place around the second week of January.

The road to Murta continues 25km on to **Puerto Sánchez**, a delightful village and previously an important mine. Public transport to and from Puerto Sánchez is sporadic – hitching or private vehicle may be the only option, otherwise it's a long and steep walk. The road to Puerto Sánchez is both one of the most spectacular and dangerous along the entire Carretera Austral. It is rarely traversed, but worth the effort, and visiting the marble caves from Puerto Sánchez is notably more pleasant than doing so from Puerto Río Tranquilo. Puerto Sánchez has recently developed several accommodation options – previously camping on the central plaza was the only option. In addition to visiting the caves, a number of tours are available and food can be purchased. Note that phone coverage is sketchy in both villages, and the existence of street names appears debatable – no-one seems to use them.

GETTING THERE
About the route
From Cerro Castillo to Bahía Murta and Puerto Sánchez (130km; 4hrs; gravel) The Carretera Austral continues for 101km west and then south from Cerro Castillo. The road quality is acceptable but the paved road ends at Cerro Castillo, and from this point onwards a high-clearance vehicle is recommended. There are no villages, towns or services along this section, possibly due to being comparatively close to Volcán Hudson (page 231) – dead trees and ash along the way serve as reminders of previous eruptions. The road passes some small lakes and weaves along two rivers (Río Ibáñez and then Río Murta), but while scenic, there is little reason to pause until the road finally reaches Lago General Carrera.

Bahía Murta is a minor (4km) detour from the Carretera Austral, some 24km north of Puerto Río Tranquilo. The road to Puerto Sánchez from Bahía Murta was completed in 2000, until which point access was exclusively by boat, usually from Puerto Río Tranquilo. Traversing the road is an adventure in itself: it's hard to imagine how anyone could cram in more hairpin bends into so short a road. Take extreme caution. One sign warns of 'danger for 12km' – this is no understatement.

There are no safety barriers; the road winds around some perilously high cliffs with landslides both above and below, and in many places there is barely sufficient room for even a single vehicle to pass, let alone two. Although only 25km, allow for an hour for this section. The ascent from Bahía Murta is simply brutal; cyclists beware. Over the pass, the road meanders less steeply down to Puerto Sánchez. Views over the lake are stunning – this is one of the only locations from which to enjoy a bird's-eye view of the turquoise Lago General Carrera. The road further south towards Chile Chico also offers stunning views of the lake, but from a lower altitude. Attempting this road at night or when wet is unwise.

By public transport Bahía Murta is 4km from the Carretera Austral, but by far the easiest option is to take any bus travelling between Cerro Castillo and Puerto Río Tranquilo and ask to get off at the junction to Bahía Murta and walk or hitchhike to or from the village. Travelling the final 25km to **Puerto Sánchez** is even harder. **Buses Pacifico Sur** (♦9 5712 1453) run from Coyhaique to Puerto Sánchez via Bahía Murta (depart 14.00 Tue, return 09.00 Wed, & depart 16.00 Fri, return noon Sun).

TOUR OPERATORS Bahía Murta and Puerto Sánchez are worth visiting for two principal reasons: visiting the marble caves in a more relaxed setting than across the lake at Puerto Tranquilo; and riding horses. Otherwise these villages are minuscule and boast very limited infrastructure.

Alto Murta Bahía Murta; ♦9 5782 5886, 9 4266 3504; e altomurta@gmail.com; ⬛. Family business run by equestrian veteran Eduardo Vas, who used to work on cattle & sheep farms in California & Utah & speaks English. Eduardo is originally from Murta & offers 3 routes originating in the village, ranging from 4–6hrs ($45,000–55,000 pp), including one that visits hot springs. He has 5 horses, but can obtain more if required. The tour is for groups of 3–10 people, & Eduardo can also pick up tourists at the junction with the Carretera Austral or in Tranquilo if without a car for a small fee. In addition to simply riding horses, Eduardo knows the history of the trails & why they were used by the pioneers – an authentic gaucho insight adding depth to simply trotting around the region. Indeed, he featured on the front cover of the Mexican edition of *Travel + Leisure* magazine in an article entitled 'The secret trails of Patagonia' – instant celebrity status in the sleepy village

of Bahía Murta. Some prior riding experience is useful but not essential. Eduardo can also arrange longer, multi-day rides, but does not provide tents, sleeping bags, etc.
Cabalgatas los Troperos Puerto Sánchez; ♦9 9352 3406, 9 5631 6049; ⬛. 4 tours in & around Puerto Sánchez. The first is around the village (1hr; $5,000 pp), the second goes up to a viewpoint above the village (1½hrs; $15,000 pp), the third goes all the way to the mine (4hrs; $28,000 inc snack) & the fourth an all-day tour including lunch to the Miller Valley & glacier (7hrs; $40,000 pp). 6 horses available, but can rustle up more if needed.
Patagonia Amada Puerto Sánchez; ♦9 6749 8730; ⬛ Patagonia_Amada_Turismo. Tours to the marble caves ($10,000 pp min 4, $23,000 pp with Capilla & Catedral, page 257), but also goes to the abandoned mine explaining the history of the region, and to the Miller Valley & glacier.

WHERE TO STAY AND EAT These villages are only just waking up to tourism, contributing both to the charm and frustration of visiting them. Formal accommodation in both Bahía Murta and Puerto Sánchez is sparse, with the likelihood of nothing at all being available – around the rodeo (second week of January) it might be worth booking something in Bahía Murta. Most accommodation is basic and cheap, with SuizAike and Catedral Lodge the only exceptions; cabins seem to pop up and vanish periodically. If the options listed here are full, try Cabañas Aitue (main road at northern entrance to village; ♦9 3212 0340,

10

9 8228 2782; e josvarmu@hotmail.com) or Cabaña Valle Hermoso (18 Septiembre 215; ↘9 9515 9420), which has a cabin sleeping four, a two-person apartment and claims to have a laundry service, both in Bahía Murta; or Urzula Alfaro (↘9 7659 5275; $45,000), offering a four-person fully equipped cabin, Alfita (2 rooms; ↘9 9316 8369) or Fabián Venegas (↘9 8757 1166), a basic campground with showers, bathrooms and covered cooking area, in Puerto Sánchez. Worst-case scenario, you can put a tent almost anywhere and no-one will mind.

There are small, informal shops in both villages, but limited restaurant options. Wi-Fi and laundry are rare.

✻ 🏠 **Catedral Lodge** [map, page 241] (6 cabins) 2km before Puerto Sánchez; /// guaranteeing.removing.ages; ↘9 6919 8094, 9 9887 9998; e reservas.catedrallodge@gmail.com; w catedrallodge.cl. Fantastic cabins & restaurant situated just outside the village on a private beach. Each cabin has 2 rooms, with a large dbl facing the lake. The 2 larger cabins ($160,000) have a twin room towards the back with a 2nd bathroom (no shower) & a 5th bed can be added if required. The 4 remaining cabins sleep 3 ($140,000). All cabins come equipped with a kettle for making tea/coffee/mate. A sumptuous b/fast (inc) is served in the restaurant, with free-range eggs, marmalades, freshly baked bread, etc. Lunch & dinner are available upon request & include the full range of options, from lamb roast by the lake, parrilla in the quincho, to the usual array of Chilean huaso fare, seafood, merluza, etc – all with a spectacular view & a fine choice of wines & beers. For more information & on excursions offered, see the box on page 258. **$$$$$**

✻ 🏠 **SuizAike** [map, page 241] (1 room, 1 cabin) 5km south of Bahía Murta towards Puerto Sánchez; ↘9 9597 5454; e ninoska_540@ hotmail.com. Fantastic log cabin perched on the edge of the lake, run by an eccentric Swiss-Chilean couple who have created more than mere accommodation since arriving 3 decades ago. Take the road towards Puerto Sánchez; there is a gate with a small sign on the right-hand side (///scoop. incursions.preparations), park the car just beyond the gate & walk down the path for about 15mins. At a large meadow peppered with alpacas, veer left towards what initially appears to be a cliff. There is a trail down the slope, with some stairs at the steepest section, & the log cabin in front. Forget wheelie bags, take the minimum possible as it is a mini expedition just to reach this place, especially with kids. The cabin is quintessentially Swiss, plucked straight from a postcard, complete with lake & mountain view. One of the most remote places to stay, & yet has Wi-Fi & mobile phone coverage thanks to its proximity to Bahía Murta. The property has a beach, treks (half or full-day), kayaks & is a working farm – sheep, goats, chickens, horses & the occasional prowling puma. B/fast included & can arrange other meals upon request, of superb quality & almost entirely from the property, including Swiss dishes, cheese, etc. 1 twin room in the main house ($70,000), or a separate 3-person self-contained cabin ($100,000). Unforgettable experience, one of the most unusual & delightful places to stay along the entire Carretera. **$$$$**

🏠 **Residencial Patagonia** [map, page 241] (13 rooms, 2 cabins, camping) Bahía Murta, junction with Carretera Austral; ///queens. prescribe.optimally; ↘9 8725 9186; e cotimama@ gmail.com. On the Carretera 24km north of Puerto Tranquilo, a decent plan-B if Tranquilo is full in high season, & a good springboard for a day trip to Murta & Sánchez. Rooms of most varieties – sgl, dbl, twin, trpl, quad, most with shared bathrooms. Rooms facing the garden are preferable to those facing the Carretera. Has a feeling a little like a sprawling rustic English farmhouse, but in fine condition with good private bathrooms. Open all year, but rarely full, reasonably priced & includes full b/fast. The house has a nice garden, offers basic camping (5 covered sites or camp under cherry trees, on grass or towards the Río Murta), bathroom with hot shower, & ample parking space. There is a small restaurant offering menu of the day for $8,500, or dinner arranged in advance. Also has a small museum (for guests only), with relics from the region & further afield, collected by the family over a few decades. The collection is slightly eclectic – from women's side-saddles, yokes, old farming equipment, 2m-long saws, sheep-shearing tools & ageing kitchen utensils, all the way to animal horns & snakeskins from the USA.

The tales behind the items are possibly of more interest than the items themselves. Final addition to the property is a short 1km trail leading to a view over the Río Murta. Laundry service for a fee, Wi-Fi, take credit cards. **$$$**

🏠 **Cabañas La Cascada** (3 cabins) 52 La Cascada, Bahía Murta; ///junkets.takers. disapprove; 📞 9 7568 7443; e asandovalr30@ gmail.com. 3 cabins for 3/6/7 people ($45,000–$65,000). The smallest cabin has a dbl & sgl bed, otherwise 3 dbls and 2 or 3 sgls. Well equipped, with towels, etc – they might do laundry if asked nicely! Take credit card, Wi-Fi available. The owner, Sylvia, keeps the cabins spotless, provides good service & as she has lived almost all her life in the village, can advise on the local attractions, including the waterfall that the cabins are named after. **$–$$$**

🏠 **Residencial Marianela** (8 rooms, 3 cabins) Av 18 de Septiembre 476, Bahía Murta (opposite church by plaza); ///zipper.respectful.trooping; 📞 9

8228 2782; e angelica1373@gmail.com. A basic but clean option for backpackers consisting of 8 twin rooms ($20,000 pp), 5 with shared, 3 with private bathrooms, including a basic b/fast, & 3 cabins for 4–6 people ($60,000–80,000). Wi-Fi, sat TV, ample off-street parking & a free laundry service. There is also a restaurant next door 📞 9 8896 8996; $). Reservations are taken by phone or email. This hostel is often full in Jan & Feb so book in advance. **$**

🍴 **Flor de Murta** 21 de Mayo 663, Bahía Murta; ///empowering.aliases.domain; 📞 9 6692 6031; e flordemurta@hotmail.com; ⏰ 11.00–22.00 daily. Charming little family-run restaurant, best in village, all food from the region if not from the garden, salmon & steak. Reservation not required, but wise to call ahead to ensure if it is open at all. Friendly owner also able to help with questions about the region, & a rare place in Murta with an internet connection. **$$**

EXCURSIONS AND SIGHTSEEING For many, a trip to the marble caves at Puerto Sánchez is preferable to the more touristy caves in Puerto Río Tranquilo. Firstly, they are far closer to the town – with a decent pair of binoculars the caves are visible from the shore. The boat trips are therefore shorter, and thus cheaper ($15,000 pp, min 4 people), and less exposed to the prevailing winds. Secondly, the caves are not heaving with hundreds of camera-toting tourists – it is quite likely there will be no more than a couple of boats per day. Finally, the caves are at least as spectacular as those at Puerto Río Tranquilo. It is also possible to swim in the caves without the worry of endless boats zipping around. Take a wetsuit (7mm minimum), mask and snorkel, fins and weights, as these are unavailable locally. Diving in the caves is great fun, and it is possible to enter the caves far further than by boat. Water transparency is not great – this is a glacial lake. However, deep cracks within the caves offer free divers some fun exploring. Some caves are sufficiently deep to warrant taking a waterproof torch.

Although there might not be quite so many adrenaline-fuelled activities in this region, for those seeking peace and quiet, both Bahía Murta and Puerto Sánchez are idyllic, sleepy villages. Visits to abandoned mines might not appeal to all tastes, but the entire northern shore of Lago General Carrera was once an important mining region. Horseriding, particularly in Murta, is so engrained in the culture, and combined with a trip to the rodeo this is a truly authentic snapshot of untouched gaucho culture. For those wishing to get even further off the beaten track, the Miller Valley has only just become accessible to tourism.

For a **spectacular panoramic view** of the village, the Lago General Carrera and the rugged Andean mountain backdrop, walk for 10 minutes or drive up the hill behind the old mine to a viewing platform.

The standard **tours** to the caves in Puerto Sánchez are at least as impressive as those of Puerto Río Tranquilo, but omit the famous Marble Chapel and Cathedral. However, a slightly longer tour from Sánchez will actually cross the lake and visit these two monuments also – it is approximately 12 minutes to cross the lake on

The joy of visiting Puerto Sánchez was in part due to its isolation. Few realised there were marble caves at least as impressive as those of Puerto Río Tranquilo located only a few hundred metres from the coast of Puerto Sánchez. But this came at a price: zero infrastructure. Camping on the plaza was the only accommodation on offer (with no bathrooms), there was no restaurant and only one person with a boat offered tours to the caves.

At last, fine accommodation has arrived in Puerto Sánchez. The cabins at **Catedral Lodge** (see also page 256) compete with the best of the entire Carretera Austral. From the outside they appear like six metal cubes plonked along the beach, but under closer scrutiny these are tastefully decorated, comfortable cabins, each with large windows and a deck overlooking the turquoise lake. The attention to detail is impeccable – especially when one considers the sheer distance of getting even a bar of soap to this remote village. Two of the cabins also have a roof terrace (complete with swinging chair and table) from which to enjoy the sunset with a glass of wine. The only sound is the lapping of water beneath the deck, the occasional sound of the wind, a bird, or a boat heading back from the caves. At night the view of the stars is stunning as there is no light contamination for hundreds of miles.

Catedral Lodge also boasts a restaurant – a welcome addition given the absence of almost any other restaurant for miles – with outside dining, weather permitting.

The main activity in the region is a visit to the marble caves, and the lodge has opted for a slightly larger catamaran over the usual narrowboats, for up to 12 people. This is notably more comfortable and has a removable roof for either rain or relentless sun. The other major advantage is that at full throttle it is possible to cross the lake to the famous Cathedral and Chapel marble structures otherwise accessed from Puerto Río Tranquilo. The slight disadvantage is that the extra width means the boat cannot enter the caves to the extent that a

the faster catamaran offered at Catedral Lodge. Tour operators in Puerto Sánchez are semi-formal and seem to come and go between seasons. The tours they offer also seem to fluctuate, and the following information is indicative only. Generally there is no need to book well in advance (with the exception of the Catedral Lodge perhaps), and certainly the cave tours can be arranged upon arrival and operate from early in the morning to last light.

For cave tours by boat, contact **Raquel Garrido** (9 4280 3757), **Jose Diaz** (9 3253 8991), or **Karen Márquez** (9 8723 0861). For a more thorough tour to the caves, the private island where the caves are mostly located, and with the possibility not only to visit the working farm on the island but also to spend the night in a dome tent, contact **Paola Herrera** (9 9670 5493), **Francisco Leiva** (9 8414 5331) or **Valeria Leiva** (9 3371 1904), all of the same family (f isla los arrayanes). Besides the caves visible from the lake, the island has natural marble tunnels of approximately 60m in length that can be visited (helmets and torches provided). The farm has sheep, goats and horses and offers a trek taking approximately 2 hours, visiting arrayan forests, potentially seeing condors and visiting some viewpoints over the lake. The visit can be done by boat or kayak, and if going by boat it is possible to combine with the Catedral and Capilla formations on the other side of the lake. The most basic tour of the shipwrecks and the Sánchez caves is $15,000 per person (min 5 people), with the most extensive tour (including the Cathedral and Chapel formations across the lake, trekking on the narrower boat might. Lago General Carrera can whip up waves in an instant, and the catamaran is more stable than the narrower, single-hull boats, meaning you don't get quite as wet when the wind picks up. The tour visits the carcasses of two historic boats – the *Don Jorge* tugboat was an Argentine boat owned by the main mining company and used to transfer people between the ports and mining villages, particularly for medical emergencies, mining accidents, etc. The boat was decommissioned in 2001 once the road between Puerto Sánchez and Bahía Murta was built. The 50-ton-capacity *Don Cote* was used to transport minerals from the mines to Puerto Ibáñez, and return with fuel, food and passengers. It operated until 1993, when the last mine closed. The boat trips are generally best done in the mornings, when the sun shines into the caves creating unusual reflections, or in the later afternoon with the long shadows. The guide explains the relevant history of the region, and the erosion process that created the caves. Trips cost $150,000 for up to 12 people, taking 1½ hours for the basic tour to the nearby caves and the boats. It is worth spending $30,000 extra for an additional hour to see the Cathedral and Chapel structures on the other side of the lake.

To complete the array of services, the lodge also offers mountain bike rental ($6,000/hr, $25,000/day), kayak rental ($10,000/15,000/hr sgl/dbl, guide available) and fishing trips ($50,000/hr), and can arrange any of the standard tours in the region, such as visiting the mines, the nearby Lago Negro or trekking and riding in the Miller Valley.

In a nutshell – fantastic accommodation, excellent food, a range of activities along a beautiful and remote stretch of the lake, and a welcome alternative means to visit marble caves without hordes of other tourists or having to negotiate the melee of Puerto Río Tranquilo. Credit card payments will be available soon.

island and entering the interior caves) $35,000 per person. The kayaking option ($40,000) only extends to the region closest to the village. Sleeping on the island is arranged separately.

Tourist information (west side of plaza; ///reorder.freed.milky) is (usually) open November–March 10.00–20.00 daily. There is a small **museum** (200m south of plaza; ///bingo.humble.liquidation) which opens whenever someone wishes to visit it, by calling ↘9 7603 2179. A modest building of mild interest, the historic section consists of a dozen old photos and a few old sewing machines, typewriters, lamps and various boat paraphernalia. The most interesting section focuses on the mine, with a few pieces of old mining equipment and samples of the minerals extracted from the mine in their various stages of processing – the lead samples from various stages of the refining process are particularly interesting.

PUERTO RÍO TRANQUILO

Thanks to some extensive marketing Puerto Río Tranquilo has emerged as a tourist hub. The town is not particularly attractive, but is located close to some **marble caves** which draw tourists by the thousand meaning that, during peak times, finding accommodation and transport can be problematic; be sure to make advance reservations. The sheer volume of tourists also makes hitchhiking tricky – in fact, Tranquilo and the road to Chile Chico are the most difficult sections for hitchhiking on the Carretera Austral – and public transport is scarce. However, while the town itself may be underwhelming, it is well located. Just across the lake (or, more likely, 53km driving) is the lovely village of **Puerto Sánchez**, with caves at least as impressive as those of Puerto Río Tranquilo. Some 28km south is the entry point to the **Ventisquero Leones**. From Puerto Río Tranquilo, it is only 49km to the junction at **Cruce El Maitén**, where the Carretera Austral continues south towards Cochrane and east on one of the most important subsidiary roads along the spectacular south side of Lago General Carrera towards Chile Chico and into Argentina (page 271).

Perhaps the biggest draw to Tranquilo is the detour to **Bahía Exploradores**, and on to the embarkation point for boats towards **Ventisquero San Rafael**. Although this is a stunning glacier, the lesser-known Ventisquero Leones (28km south of Tranquilo) is a cheaper alternative involving a healthy trek through a forest rather than the relatively sedentary bus/boat trip to San Rafael. The uncontrolled growth of the town, and the sheer lack of infrastructure for the hordes of tourists that flood in daily, is a warning to the entire region. A tour operator in a nearby village begged us, 'please do not speak badly of Puerto Tranquilo, the last thing we want is those tourists coming to our village instead'.

GETTING THERE
About the route
Cerro Castillo to Puerto Río Tranquilo (125km; 2–3hrs; gravel) A diverse section of the Carretera Austral with reasonable quality gravel passable in most vehicles, but be aware that dust clouds when passing other vehicles reduce visibility considerably. There are corrugations on steeper sections and pot-holes on flatter sections, especially around valleys with swampy ground. There are no imminent plans to pave this section so get used to gravel from this point onwards.

The road initially follows the canyon formed by the Río Ibáñez. The first turning to the left leads to the **Museo Escuela** (page 250). The road then zigzags up a rocky outcrop devoid of any vegetation, but offering spectacular views of Cerro Castillo and the Valle Ibáñez below. At km7 there is another turn-off to the left towards **Lago Tamango** (the 'back road' to Puerto Ibáñez, page 246, ideally by 4x4). The Carretera continues along a ridge before descending to **Laguna Verde** on the left at km18, and then winds its way along the valley following Río Ibáñez to cross the low Cofré Pass. Laguna Cofré is on the left. Dropping down into the **Valle Río Murta**, dead trees and ash from the 1991 eruption of Volcán Hudson (page 231) can be seen. At km70 there is a lookout over the dead forest (*bosque muerta*) and the opaque turquoise-green Río Cajon fed from the glacier melt. The road continues along the Valle Río Murta to the turn-off on the left to Bahía Murta and Puerto Sánchez (km100). Shortly thereafter Lago General Carrera finally comes into view, and the Patagonian steppe begins. The road then circumnavigates the lake until Puerto Río Tranquilo.

By bus All buses travelling between Cochrane and Coyhaique pass through Puerto Río Tranquilo. There are also regular buses to Puerto Guadal. **Transportes Costa Carrera** (◊9 8738 8886) goes to Balmaceda airport and on to Coyhaique daily in high season (depart 07.00, return 14.30).

TOUR OPERATORS The focus in Puerto Río Tranquilo is heavily skewed towards the San Rafael glacier and the marble caves, both of which are crowded. The discerning traveller may prefer to visit an alternative glacier, or visit the caves from Puerto Sánchez. Two exceptions stand out – visiting the Isthmus of Ofqui (via the San Rafael glacier –

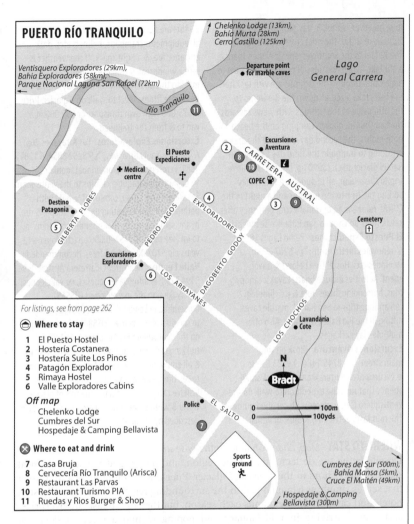

PUERTO RÍO TRANQUILO

Chelenko Lodge (13km),
Bahía Murta (28km),
Cerro Castillo (125km)

Lago General Carrera

Ventisquero Exploradores (29km),
Bahía Exploradores (58km),
Parque Nacional Laguna San Rafael (72km)

Departure point
● for marble caves

Río Tranquilo ⑪

Excursiones
● Aventura

El Puesto
Expediciones ② ⑧ CARRETERA AUSTRAL *i*

✚ Medical
centre ⑩

† COPEC ☎

Destino
Patagonia ④ EXPLORADORES ③ ⑨

GILBERTA FLORES PEDRO LAGOS

⑤ Cemetery 🕇

DAGOBERTO GODOY

Excursiones
Exploradores

① ⑥ LOS ARRAYANES

LOS CHOCHOS Lavandaría
● Cote

For listings, see from page 262

N

Brad[t]

🛏 **Where to stay**

1 El Puesto Hostel
2 Hostería Costanera
3 Hostería Suite Los Pinos
4 Patagón Explorador
5 Rimaya Hostel
6 Valle Exploradores Cabins

Off map
Chelenko Lodge
Cumbres del Sur
Hospedaje & Camping Bellavista

Police ● EL SALTO

⑦

0 ━━━━━ 100m
0 ━━━━━ 100yds

Cumbres del Sur (500m),
Bahía Mansa (5km),
Cruce El Maitén (49km)

Sports
ground
🕴

✖ **Where to eat and drink**

7 Casa Bruja
8 Cervecería Río Tranquilo (Arisca)
9 Restaurant Las Parvas
10 Restaurant Turismo PIA
11 Ruedas y Rios Burger & Shop

Hospedaje & Camping
Bellavista (300m)

only Destino Patagonia offer this excellent tour, see below), or the Cumbre de Cipreses (fascinating trek, astonishing view, page 268).

Bahía Mansa 5km south of Puerto Río Tranquilo; ///chiming.juiced.avoided; ☎ 9 8262 4040; e pedrocmarmol@hotmail.com. For those with a car it is better to visit the caves from here rather than from Puerto Tranquilo. The road down is sketchy, but you can just about do it without a 4x4. Being physically closer to the caves has 3 advantages: you can do it in a kayak (guided), by boat it involves less time getting there and back, & it is less crowded ($15,000 by boat, $30,000 by kayak or $50,000 double kayak). English guides & take credit cards.

Destino Patagonia Gilberta Flores 208; ///tumbling.armfuls.sheepish; ☎ 9 8822 9491, 9 9158 6044; e contacto@destinopatagonia. cl; w destinopatagonia.cl; ⊕ Aug–Apr 10.00–20.00 daily. Best tour operator in town with 2 high-quality boats (for 12 or 13 people with bathroom). The basic San Rafael glacier trip includes a short trek & visit to the ruins of the Ofqui hotel, US$250 pp. A 2-day version includes a night in a CONAF refuge with the national park & a longer trek to a viewpoint overlooking the glacier (US$375 pp). The supreme San Rafael tour, however, is their 3-day tour crossing the Isthmus of Ofqui. The boat crosses the Laguna San Rafael to the southwestern side, then there is a 2hr hike, where vestiges of previous attempts to dig a canal through the isthmus are visible. After the hike, take a zodiak down the Río Negro to the other side of the isthmus with views towards the San Quintin glacier, camping on the beach both nights, the second day exploring the area, returning to Tranquilo the third day via the San Rafael glacier itself ($590 pp, but the definitive trip to the region, all included). A fourth day adding the trek to the mirador and a night in the CONAF refuge is an optional extra, plus they offer kayak tours on Laguna San Rafael – see website.

El Puesto Expediciones Pedro Lagos 18; ///renovates.metro.misfit; ☏ 9 6207 3794; w elpuesto.cl. Hostel (see below) & travel agent. Activities include boats, kayaks, canopy trips, horseriding, hikes, rock & ice climbing, & can arrange trips to San Rafael, marble caves, rafting in the Río Baker, & fishing. Also offer multiple-day packages.

Excursiones Aventura Kiosk on the main street; ☏ 9 8745 1486, 9 9383 8523; e excursionesaventura@gmail.com. A small agency that runs the expedition to walk on the Ventisquero Exploradores with certified guides. The tour lasts between 6 & 8hrs, of which

2–4hrs are actually on the ice. They provide all equipment (crampons, helmet, etc), park entrance fee, & a light snack. If the weather is nice a windbreaker & fleece should be enough, making this an easy way for anybody with a moderate fitness level to walk on a glacier. Price is $75,000 with own transport or $80,000 in a van to & from the trailhead.

Excursiones Exploradores Los Arrayanes 205; ///nappies.spots.driveway; ☏ 9 8252 8854, 6 1261 4681; e recepcion@explorandopatagonia.cl; w explorandopatagonia.cl. Trips to the Ventisquero San Rafael on a larger, comfortable boat with bathroom on board seating up to 22 people & run by the same company that offer decent cabins in town (see opposite). $140,000 pp (children 6–12 years old $70,000, under 5 free). Recommended.

Valle Leones Beachfront, Carretera Austral; ☏ 9 3394 2298; e info@valleleones.cl; w valleleones. cl. Kayaking to the marble caves (US$65), horseriding in Leones Valley (US$75), trekking to see the Leones glacier (US$80) & ice trekking on the Ventisquero Exploradores (US$120). Ice trekking includes transport to the glacier, a snack & all equipment provided. A fantastic opportunity to see the glacier from a different perspective. Visit ice caves, drink from the streams of glacial water & witness the startling regression of the ice described by the guide.

WHERE TO STAY   *Map, page 261, unless otherwise stated*

Despite being the de facto hub of the region, and bursting at the seams in peak season with visitors to the caves and glacier, Puerto Río Tranquilo is a drab town that serves simply as a launch pad to the surrounding region. The range of hostels, hotels and campgrounds expands each season, but they fill up fast, are overpriced and simply arriving in mid-January and hoping to find a place to sleep can be a grave disappointment – book in advance. If the marble caves are the main attraction, they are better visited from Puerto Sánchez (closer to Murta) than from Tranquilo. If glaciers are the focus, they can equally be visited from Cruce el Maitén or Puerto Guadal.

Chelenko Lodge [map, page 241] (10 cabins) 13km north of Puerto Tranquilo; ///landowners.sunken.restates; ☏ 9 4734 2558, 9 5629 2538; e info@chelenko.com; w chelenko. com. Easy to miss as the sign is barely visible from the road, but worth finding. Tiny cabins perched on the lake with stunning views, often accompanied by the relentless sound of the howling wind. One almost feels as though out at sea. The cabins are compact, 36m², have a small kitchen, dbl bed & a

bunk bed. Great chance to disconnect & far more peaceful than staying in the village. No Wi-Fi or TV, pets welcome. The icing on the cake is a hot tub on the terrace of each cabin ($25,000 extra). Cabins are $110,000 for a couple, $130,000 for 3 or 4 people. **$$$$**

El Puesto Hostel (10 rooms) Pedro Lagos 258; ///charities.troll.sluggish; ☏ 9 6207 3794; e contacto@elpuesto.cl; w elpuesto.cl. Touted as the premier accommodation in Puerto Río

Tranquilo, but more likely the best of a mediocre bunch. Typical of the new breed of 'boutique' hostels – pleasantly designed but overpriced. Includes a decent b/fast & a laundry service for an extra charge. The design of the building is great (Francisco, the co-owner, is an architect), & guests must remove shoes & wear the slippers provided indoors. The rooms themselves are certainly a cut above the typical hostel, with comfortable beds, a cosy atmosphere, large windows, fully equipped bathrooms & a fine wooden finish. There is a decent restaurant (for guests only, vegetarian options, all local produce, river-caught salmon & trout, ethical treatment of animals), a lovely spacious sitting area, & ample parking. They arrange tours in the region (see opposite), & own one of the access points to the Ventisquero Exploradores. Popular with tour operators so reservations essential. A good-quality hostel, but not necessarily the best value for money. **$$$$**

🏠 **Valle Exploradores Cabins** (6 cabins, 15 rooms) Los Arrayanes 205; ///nappies. spots.driveway; 📞 9 8252 8854, 9 1261 4681; e recepcion@explorandopatagonia. cl; w valleexploradores.cl; 📘. Reasonable cabins in a town historically known for limited accommodation. Each cabin has 2 rooms, either twin or dbl, each with its own private bathroom. A simple kitchen is adequate, particularly considering that few will spend more than a couple of days in town. Reliable hot water supply, & the internet connection is surprisingly high speed. Decent sitting area, although the tables are a little small for a full dinner. Cable TV, & a dedicated parking spot next to each cabin to avoid lugging bags far. The rooms (all dbl & trpl) include a basic kitchen with a mini fridge, good private bathrooms, but thin walls. Includes a common area to prepare your own b/fast which doubles as a sitting area. Already overpriced before they charge an additional $5,000 for b/fast. The same company also operates one of the boats to the Ventisquero San Rafael (see opposite). **$$$$**

🏠 **Cumbres del Sur** (2 domes, 1 tiny cabin) 0.5km south of Puerto Tranquilo; ///molten.perms. parity; 📞 9 8886 6708. A pleasant & peaceful alternative to staying in the village, but walking distance to eat. Set among trees with a view over the lake. All sleep 2, $60,000, basic kitchen & wood stove for heating. **$$$**

🏠 **Hostería Costanera** (12 rooms & 2 cabins) Cnr of Pedro Lagos & Carretera Austral; ///darts.responders.overgrowth; 📞 9 5743 2175; e ipinuerhostal@gmail.com; w hosteriacostanera. com; 🕐 all year. The largest & most upscale hotel in town, with all front rooms having great views overlooking the lake. 5 dbls, 5 twins, 1 trpl, 1 quintuple & 2 cabins for 6 & 7 people. Includes a basic b/fast with the rooms, free internet in the dining area, & parking. The owner is the daughter of some of the original settlers in town, who arrived in 1937. Accepts all major credit cards & major currencies. **$$$**

🏠 **Hostería Suite Los Pinos** (8 rooms) Dagoberto Godoy 51 (in front of COPEC petrol station); ///instinct.forge.griddled; 📞 67 241 1572, 9 7399 0240; e reservalospinoshosteria@gmail. com; 🕐 all year. All rooms (3 dbls, 5 sgls) en suite, with thick mattresses, central heating, Wi-Fi & basic b/fast included, making this hostel popular with motorcyclists. There's a café/restaurant (🕐 08.00–22.00; $). B/fast for $5,000. Better quality than many alternatives, for a slightly higher price. A 50% deposit is required to make a reservation. Credit cards accepted. **$$$**

🏠 **Patagón Explorador** (5 cabins) Exploradores 238; ///outfitters.unregulated. cyclists; 📞 9 9911 8124, 9 6649 0508; e toya_ jara@yahoo.es; 🕐 all year. Rustic, spacious cabañas close to the centre of town. The owners have a store just next to the cabins where travellers can stock up on supplies. The cabañas have Wi-Fi, cable TV, wood stoves, refrigerators, kitchens & hot water. Laundry available for $4,000/load. 50% reservation policy. **$$$**

🏠 **Pudu Camping and Excursions** [map, page 241] (camping, 1 cabin) Carretera Austral, 1km south of Puerto Río Tranquilo; ///storytelling.timed.swallowing; 📞 9 8920 5085; e campingpudu@gmail.com. An upmarket campground on the shore of Lago General Carrera. The campsite is set in a valley with good natural shelter & a rock cliff face to the west. The 14 pitches have a rustic table & benches, with BBQ areas & wind breaks (but no electricity). Fires strictly prohibited. New bathrooms with hot water. The cabin is an accommodation highlight in Tranquilo, with double-glazed windows, for 4 people set on the hillside with amazing views of the lake, is also now available year-round, with a dbl bedroom & a 2nd room with twin beds.

There is a couch in the lounge that can sleep an extra person if needed. The beautiful pebbled beach, with spectacular lake & mountain views, is suitable for swimming. A laundry service, massage bed & electric sauna are also offered. The access road is suitable for all types of vehicles including buses & trucks. Excursions can be booked from the campsite including fishing trips, horseriding, glacier treks & the (almost obligatory) marble caves. Reservations can be made online or by phone, 50% deposit required; confirm 3 days before arriving. Cabin **$$$**, camping **$**

🏠 **Rimaya Hostel** (5 rooms) Gilberta flores 260; ///consist.renewable.grace; 📞 9 4273 3470; e rimayahostel@gmail.com; 📘. A backpacker hostel with 1 dbl room with private bathroom. Otherwise 4 male/female dorms of 4 people with big bunk beds. The shared bathrooms are decent, & there is a communal living area with a selection of books & a table for eating or planning trips. There is a policy of no shoes, but slippers are provided. Fully equipped kitchen, Wi-Fi, parking & stove heating. Nicely furnished, & one of the better options in the village. **$$$**

🏠 **Hospedaje & Camping Bellavista** (15 rooms, camping) Población Estadio; ///explores. naturals.storefronts; 📞 9 8152 8505. Located conveniently close to Casa Bruja, this is the best budget option in town with good service & decent beds. Dbl & trpl rooms ($15,000 pp), all with shared bathrooms & basic b/fast available ($5,000). Camping for 30 tents ($5,000 pp). Good hot water, shared kitchen & communal eating/ sitting area, Wi-Fi, laundry service (extra) & grill for BBQ. **$–$$**

✕ WHERE TO EAT AND DRINK *Map, page 261*

✕ **Restaurant Las Parvas** Main road just south of COPEC; ///displays.constituted.guidebooks; 📞 9 8760 7609; w lasparvas.cl; ⏱ 13.00–22.00 Mon–Sat, 13.00–17.00 Sun. Undoubtedly good food but cripplingly expensive. Lamb & steaks, but speciality is seafood, including risotto, crab, hake & congrio. Great location & quirky décor, good wines & beers including Pioneros on draught. Excellent service & English spoken. A very good restaurant for those with little concerns for price. **$$$$**

✳ ✕ **Casa Bruja** Los Chochos 332; ///walkouts. unsuccessful.overstating; 📞 9 8929 4785, 9 7814 5854; ⏱ 13.00–21.00 daily. Unpretentious & the best restaurant in town, serving local ales. Great view from the upper floor, & the witch-scene is underplayed – it refers to the speed with which the building was constructed rather than magical qualities. Kick off with a decent calafate sour or mojito, then choose from ribs, lamb, beef or seafood dishes, served promptly & politely. Homely atmosphere, also have ceviche, crème brûlée, lasagne, etc. Pleasantly off the main drag but fills up so reserve in high season. Like most things in Tranquilo, it's not cheap. But unlike most places in Tranquilo, this place is worth it. Closest thing to a gourmet restaurant for miles. **$$$**

✕ **Cervecería Río Tranquilo (Arisca)** Carretera Austral; ///perplexed.lifts.cavern; 📞 9 8425 8466; 📘; ⏱ lunch & dinner until midnight, kitchen closes at 23.00. Excellent & popular brewpub directly on the Carretera Austral. Great food, albeit a bit pricey, with 4 quality beers that are brewed next door. Menu includes selection of meats, pizzas, salads & lasagne. Friendly service & a full bar for non-beer drinkers. **$$$**

✕ **Ruedas y Rios Burger & Shop** Main road; ///refused.treadmills.clued; 📞 9 6232 9042. Only place serving until 02.00, meat, lamb & veggie burgers, fries, excellent local beer (Ofqui) & a range of cocktails. Lively, buzzing vibe. **$$$**

✕ **Restaurant Turismo PIA** Carretera Austral 257; ///illegally.reissued.gloom; 📞 9 6609 6573, 9 5239 9212; e mmooch2012@hotmail. com; ⏱ 11.00–21.00 daily. A popular fast-food restaurant that serves sandwiches & soft drinks, with a midday menu. Credit cards accepted. Sit down **$$**, take-away **$**

OTHER PRACTICALITIES There is a COPEC **petrol station** in Puerto Río Tranquilo that has an **ATM. Lavandaría Cote** (Los Chochos, between Exploradores & Los Arrayanes; 📞 9 9612 9509) offers same-day **laundry** service at $3,500 a kilo if dropped off early. **Shopping** is limited to a couple of small supermarkets. For repairs, try calling at **Residencial Darka** (Arrayanes 330), and ask for Victor (Don Vicho) who is rumoured to provide mechanical repairs.

EXCURSIONS AND SIGHTSEEING The main reason people find themselves in Puerto Río Tranquilo is to visit the Ventisquero San Rafael and the marble caves. Other activities in or around town include rock climbing, fishing and horseriding, all of which can be organised through the tour operators listed on page 260.

The **Ventisquero Leones** some 28km south of Puerto Río Tranquilo also deserves a mention (see box, page 275, for a full description). The main guides offering this service are based out of Puerto Guadal (page 271) but offers transport to and from the trailhead, including with pickup or drop-off at Guadal, Puerto Río Tranquilo or Cochrane, for an additional fee. Leones has the advantage of fewer tourists and a lower cost than the better-established tours to San Rafael, although accessing the glacier does involve a bit of trekking and, with no village close by, it also requires marginally more organisation to arrange a trip. In terms of sheer size, the snout of Leones is certainly smaller than that of San Rafael, but is still an impressive sight. Tours from Puerto Guadal offer two novel twists to the glacier-gig: Pascual Diaz's trek to Leones (page 273) has the option to sleep at the glacier, and Philippe's jet boat to the glacier is an adrenaline rush.

Marble caves The original attraction in Puerto Río Tranquilo is the network of marble caves. The glacial waters of Lago General Carrera have eroded the limestone walls surrounding this section of the lake over centuries to form unusual, Salvador Dali-esque caves. These structures appear almost to have melted into the water, supported by frozen-in-time lava-like columns which disappear into the watery base of the caves. Some of the caves are large enough for small boats to enter. On sunny days the light reflects off the cave walls and from the relatively shallow pools at the bottom of the caves creating surreal ripple-like patterns along the walls while the water itself reflects in myriad shades of turquoise.

Countless operators offer trips to the caves and there is no need to book in advance. The journey typically takes around 2 hours including the ride to and from the caves, and boats leave from the shore of the lake next to the Carretera in the middle of the town; it can be rough and cold so be sure to take a windproof jacket. It is possible to **kayak** to the caves (the same vendors of the boat trips also rent kayaks), but do consider the strength of the wind, particularly when attempting to return in the evening. The standard boats take approximately five to seven people and cost $15,000 per person.

For those with their own boat or kayak, there is no need to use a tour operator as the caves are not privately owned, but expect some unwelcoming glances from the operators. It is unwise to swim in the caves due to the sheer volume of boats – go to Puerto Sánchez for cave-swimming. Note that the water is extremely cold all year: a wetsuit is essential, and not available for hire.

The marble caves are certainly worth a visit, but in peak season the sheer number of tourists can be off-putting. Far more recommended is to visit the caves in Puerto Sánchez (page 254), which is a more pleasant village – the tours can also cross the lake to visit the Catedral and Capilla formations accessed from Tranquilo.

Ventisquero Exploradores The second key attraction around Puerto Río Tranquilo is the relatively accessible glacier approximately halfway along the 51km road to Bahía Exploradores. A short trek up to a viewing platform permits views over the Ventisquero Exploradores, and tours are available to hike down to, and on to, the glacier itself. The hike to the viewing platform is well marked and not technical. However, people with limited mobility and young children may find it exhausting, and slippery. There is no public transport along this road, and few people live along it so hitchhiking is difficult. However, it is a standard tour offered by various operators (page 260), including transport. For those with a vehicle the road is poor-quality gravel, meaning that a high-clearance vehicle is recommended but 4x4 is not essential. Although only 51km, budget for 2 hours one-way to reach the end of the road at Bahía Exploradores, or 1 hour if only going to the glacier itself. There are some pretty waterfalls along the way that are worth pausing for. The road connects with the Carretera Austral at the northern exit of the town.

The glacier emerges from the Northern Ice Field, and as such is part of the Parque Nacional Laguna San Rafael, and thus accessible to all. A nominal fee was charged to those wishing to traverse the private property that leads to the viewing platform (belonging to the owners of the El Puesto hostel). However, in March 2015 Victor Osorio, the Minister of Bienes Nacionales, announced that they had restored free public access to the glacier. 'We have realised an act of justice, to re-establish public access to an asset that belongs to all Chileans.' The entry point is now managed by CONAF, who charge the same price as for the rest of Parque Nacional Laguna San Rafael.

The view of the glacier from the viewing platform is not to be compared with trips to glaciers in the region such as Montt, Steffen, San Rafael, O'Higgins, Leones or Queulat. However, for those with limited time, this is one of the most accessible glaciers in the region, and also one of the cheapest to visit. All the main tour operators offer this trip, and it is also possible to arrive by private vehicle, pay the entry fee and do the trek independently. However, a guide is required if trekking on to the actual glacier.

Parque Nacional Laguna San Rafael (w conaf.cl/parques/parque-nacional-laguna-san-rafael; $4,100/2,100/8,200/4,100 Chilean national adult/child/foreign adult/child) This park is fast becoming a key tourist attraction for the entire Carretera Austral region, facilitated in part by the road connection from Puerto Río Tranquilo. Previously access was possible only from Puerto Chacabuco or Puerto Montt on more expensive boats travelling far greater distances or by charter plane (which is still an impressive means to view the glacier!). The national park extends as far south as Caleta Tortel but in practice the main access points are to Ventisquero San Rafael (by boat), Ventisquero Leones (trekking and boat), or Ventisquero Steffen near Caleta Tortel (trekking and boat). Experienced trekkers can enter the park independently at other locations, and guides are available in Puerto Bertrand and Cochrane for multi-day hikes towards the ice field, but these are non-standard treks for experienced hikers and mountaineers. There are no formal, marked trails in the park authorised by CONAF.

The park itself is approximately 17,400km² and encompasses the entire Northern Ice Field. Within the park are a number of mountains, including San Valentin (4,058m) and Nyades (3,078m). A number of glaciers emerging from the ice field are accessible without huge effort: San Rafael; Leones, just south of Puerto Río Tranquilo; Soler, reached from Puerto Bertrand; Steffen to the south, accessed from Caleta Tortel; and with some additional effort the Ventisquero San Quintin (hiking beyond San Rafael). However, San Rafael, and the lake named after it, are the main attraction, with a number of companies offering tours to the glacier's snout.

Laguna San Rafael is incorrectly named, as it is connected to the open ocean to the north and is therefore not a lake at all, but due to the formation of mountains around the lake it appears to be an enclosed body of water. Indeed, the southern edge of the lake borders the Isthmus of Ofqui. In 1937 the Chilean government embarked on a project to connect the Laguna San Rafael to the Río Negro, enabling a direct channel to the Golfo San Esteban to the south of the isthmus. The project was abandoned in 1943 due to lack of funding. This would have enabled boats to traverse through the inner passages of the region from Puerto Montt to Puerto Natales without having to pass the dreaded Golfo de Penas. The Navimag route between these two cities passes through the Messier Canal, but at approximately the same latitude as Caleta Tortel the boats must circumnavigate the Taitao Peninsula into open ocean, causing many a Navimag passenger to suffer seasickness.

Ventisquero San Rafael The most common reason to enter the park is to visit the Ventisquero San Rafael, and this is only possible with a guided tour as a boat is required (see page 260 for operators), and the park fee is included in the tour price. Flights over the glacier can be arranged (at a cost!) by charter, with Patagonia Helitours (page 272) or with Aires del Sur (page 322).

The first documented visits to the glacier date back to 1675. Darwin visited the glacier on the *Beagle* in 1834. John Byron, grandfather of Lord Byron, was shipwrecked on Wager Island in 1742, and has an island named after him at the southern side of the gulf. He was eventually rescued by members of the Kawésqar tribe who lived in this region at the time. It is not clear if Byron actually visited the Ventisquero San Rafael.

The Ventisquero San Rafael is in retreat. Historical accounts clearly record the extent to which the glacier protruded into the lake – early witnesses claimed that most of the lake was covered by the glacier. This protrusion has now vanished and the glacier is firmly confined to the valley. It is estimated to have retreated 12km over the last 150 years. Although this may seem dramatic, the Ventisquero Jorge Montt is perhaps the fastest retreating glacier in the region, shrinking almost 1km from February 2010 to January 2011 and a further 2.7km over the following seven years.

Intriguing history and worrying evidence of global warming aside, the glacier is an impressive sight by any standards. A number of boats regularly visit the glacier (those owned by the tour operators in Puerto Río Tranquilo, and the catamaran from Los Loberías in Puerto Aysén; page 208). Occasional airplanes and helicopters may interrupt the silence momentarily as they fly overhead, providing an astonishing point of reference to the sheer size of the glacier. At places it looms over 60m high from the water level, and is over two miles wide. Boats keep a suitable distance from the face of the glacier for fear of icebergs (*témpanos*) breaking off and generating waves large enough to overturn a boat.

The boats travel down the Elefantes Canal and then through a relatively narrow channel into the laguna itself, at which point the glacier becomes visible. Initially it appears to be of modest size, until you realise the size of the laguna; from this distance it is possible to see up on to the ice field behind the glacier and appreciate the sheer magnitude of ice. The Northern Ice Field is the smaller of the two, covering 4,200km² and extending 120km from north to south. As the boat approaches the snout of the glacier the icebergs become larger, and it is probable that you will see chunks of ice calving off the glacier. The pressure caused by the sheer volume of ice squeezes the air bubbles out of the snow as it is subsumed into the glacier, and because compacted ice better absorbs light at the red end of the spectrum, the light reflected from the glacier appears surprisingly blue. Particularly on a sunny day the contrast of the bluish glacier, the ice field behind, the lake, icebergs and sky are

10

simply mesmerising. The only sounds are the occasional bird and the groaning of the glacier as it inches forward, sometimes interrupted by the thunderous roar of chunks breaking off.

A trip to the Carretera Austral is incomplete without a visit to a glacier, where you can watch in real time the mechanism that shaped much of our planet, and the Ventisquero San Rafael is one of the more accessible glaciers in the region. Well worth a visit, or consider the Leones glacier slightly further south for a more isolated and strenuous trip (see box, page 275).

Cumbre de Cipreses – Parque de Conservación (9 9251 4821, 9 6591 8501; e ci.cumbredecipreses@gmail.com) Amid the array of tours on offer in Tranquilo and the furore of street vendors touting the marble caves and glacier trips, it is easy to miss this quirky, informative, charming, but understated tour which will imprint a lasting memory on any visitor. So unique, it is hard to define what it actually is. Based loosely around the life of a hermit called Orlando, who lived in this evergreen forest for about 35 years, occasionally going for over half a year at a time without any human contact, it is an educational trek through his dense 1,300ha forest. The vegetation is simply intense, the old-man's-beard creates a green glow over almost everything and the sun tries to penetrate through the foliage, but most of the time only occasionally rays reach the forest floor. It's damp, everywhere; wellington boots would be useful but hiking boots will suffice.

The guides are perhaps the most passionate we have met, intrigued by the hermit's life story and recounting his tales, observations and views of the changing culture, climate and way of life that he witnessed from this very forest. They intersperse the story of the hermit (who lives to this day, but no longer in the forest) with descriptions of medicinal (and in one case, hallucinogenic) plants, fungi, all the main trees including the Ciprés de las Guaitecas (*Pilgerodendron uviferum*), and pluck edible plants and berries for tasting. The forest is home to the Tepa tree (*Laureliopsis philippiana*), with its uniquely fragrant leaf, and the Luma tree (*Amomyrtus luma*), with its extremely hard wood. Given the tense political situation in Chile in 2020 it was poignant that this same wood was used to make the truncheons of the Carabineros, used so vociferously against the protesters and colloquially referred to as 'lumas'. (The leaves and berries from the Tepa and Luma trees are key ingredients in the exotic gin made in La Junta by Tepaluma – see box, page 165.)

Flora aside, the tour has a dark undercurrent. The hermit began to notice that things were changing, in the forest, in the society, with the weather, and with the glacier. Challenging without confronting, the guides ask the visitors what their impact on society is. What could we do individually to lessen our impact? Are the hermit's observations simply incorrect, despite the clear evidence of change? And while these thoughts are meandering through one's mind, the tour reaches its climax. In a rare moment without dense vegetation, and somewhat disoriented from being in a dense forest for a couple of hours, the Exploradores glacier and Mount San Valentin appear. Not a mere glimpse, but the definitive panoramic view of the mountain and its glacier, in all its majesty, and from such a distance as to see the full size and appreciate the magnitude of the ice field behind it.

This tour is excellent, and a pleasant (and cheaper) alternative to the standard 'trekking on glacier' tour that hundreds of people do daily in high season. As with many tours in Tranquilo – the initial offering to which the crowds flock is no longer pleasant, and alternatives are emerging. An easily overlooked but highly recommended tour.

CRUCE EL MAITÉN

There is little here except an important junction towards Chile Chico, packed with hopeful hitchhikers, and a couple of very decent lodges. Note that the nearest shops or restaurants are Puerto Guadal (10km to the east), Puerto Río Tranquilo (49km to the north), or Puerto Bertrand (15km to the south). The only food options are the restaurants in the only two hotels. Mallín Colorado (page 270) operates a boutique tour operator (**w** aysenjourneys.com) that can design tailor-made packages using the hotel as a base and removing the headache of planning trips in the region – Parque Patagonia, Confluencia, the marble caves, rafting on the Baker, visiting the San Rafael glacier, and as far south as Caleta Tortel.

GETTING THERE
About the route
Puerto Río Tranquilo to Cruce El Maitén (49km; 1hr; gravel) This section includes some of the most spectacular vantage points of Lago General Carrera – there are some great photo opportunities, particularly in the morning and evening. The road quality is reasonable quality gravel with a number of steep hills and tight curves, passable in any vehicle.

At km5 on the left is the entrance to **Puerto Mansa**. The road then ascends to the top of a hill offering one of the best panoramic views of the lake. At km32 the road crosses the **Río Leones** (the entry point to the Ventisquero Leones trek) – with views of the snow-capped peaks of the Northern Ice Field. Lago General Carrera drains into **Lago Bertrand** under the bridge at km43. **Lago Negro** is on the right at km49 and the **Cruce El Maitén** is at km50.

 WHERE TO STAY AND EAT *Map, page 241*

Hacienda Tres Lagos (14 dbl/twins, 3 suites, 3 bungalows, 2 floating cabins) 1km north of Cruce El Maitén; ///collection. spherical.eyepatch; ****67 233 0027; **e** ventas@ haciendatreslagos.cl; **w** haciendatreslagos.cl; ☺ Sep–Apr. More comparable to a resort than a hotel or lodge, this upmarket complex is perched on the northern shore of Lago Negro, not far from the road to Chile Chico, 50km south of Puerto Río Tranquilo, & close to Puerto Bertrand. This ideal location permits the hacienda to offer just about every conceivable tour in the region from the Ventisquero San Rafael & the marble caves in the north to fishing on the Río Baker to the south, trekking & horseriding in the region & some excursions towards Guadal. The Ventisquero Leones is the only obvious current omission, but can be arranged independently. The main building is built in the style of a lodge, rustic with plenty of wooden finish, where the principal restaurant & suites are located. The bungalows are ideal for families, sleeping up to 4 & located

A CRUCIAL JUNCTION

The Cruce El Maitén (///censored.biking.merry) is one of the most important junctions on the entire Carretera Austral. Those doing the 'classic' route north to south will depart the Carretera Austral here and head east along Lago General Carrera towards Chile Chico and then Argentina. Those planning the 'classic' route from south to north, entering from Chile Chico, will head north at the Cruce El Maitén. For those not wishing to leave Chile and continue either north or south along the Carretera, the Cruce El Maitén raises a difficult question: go to Chile Chico along the spectacular coastal road, or leave this section out? See page 240 for more on this.

South of Coyhaique: to Cruce El Maitén via Lago General Carrera   CRUCE EL MAITÉN   **10**

269

to the south of the main building facing the lake. 4 dbl/twin rooms are each housed in 3 separate buildings to the other side of the main lodge. All standard features included, including access to a games room, hot tubs & sauna; laundry, massage & transfers from almost anywhere are available for a (fairly hefty) fee. The latest edition is 2 extraordinary floating cabins on the lake, fully equipped & connected via a small boardwalk – novel, complete with terrace, dbls only. B/fast included, dinner/lunch is available ($$$$). There is also a full quincho for lamb roasts, an art gallery & a cafeteria. Every room overlooks the lake & has a balcony. Private beach with kayaks, & a 10-person covered boat for tours on lakes General Carrera, Negro & Bertrand or the Río Baker. The tours are somewhat overpriced compared with arranging them independently, but this lodge is about relaxing & not having to deal with such administration – ideal for couples/families, & probably for multiple-day stays. Full-board multi-day packages are also available including transfers & excursion – see their (decent) website. This was the first officially certified luxury hacienda in Patagonia. A decent one-stop shop, accommodation is approximately US$300/couple, a little higher in the suites, lower in the bungalows. Credit cards accepted. $$$$$

☀ 🏠 **Mallín Colorado EcoLodge** (6 rooms, 4 cabins) 2.5km north of Cruce El Maitén; ///clips.worries.programmers; 📞 9 7137 6242, 9 7137 6242; e paulach@mallincolorado.cl; w mallincolorado.cl; ⏰ Sep–May. Rustic cabins with superb interiors overlooking Lago General Carrera set in a 500ha estate. One of the best established upper-end lodges in the region, along one of the most picturesque sections of the entire Carretera Austral. The rooms are located in a separate building all with stunning views over Catalina Bay & across the lake from a private terrace, with a communal sitting area. Also lovely beds, bed linen, slippers, fluffy towels & top-notch bathrooms. Minibar, wooden floors, central heating for 2 or 3 people (2 dbl rooms & 2 twin rooms for US$180/night, & 2 trpl rooms for US$190/night). More suitable & economical than the cabins for couples or those with only 1 child. Also, 4 independent cabins sleep between 2 & 7 people, with viewing points & trails connecting the rest of the complex, including trails over the back of the ridge with views over the glaciers

at the edge of the Northern Ice Field. Excellent bathrooms in all cabins depending on the size of the cabin – the 6-person cabin has 3 bathrooms. All cabins have a sitting area overlooking the lake with comfortable armchairs & plenty of space & light, & quality beds with duvets. Full b/fast included. Only the largest cabin has a full kitchen, otherwise guests use the restaurant ($$$$). Laundry service, decent mobile phone coverage but no Wi-Fi. Most people choose to spend 3 or 4 nights here enjoying the range of activities on offer. Treks within the property access the Laguna Mallín & a waterfall. Also offer tours through subcontracted, trusted guides to the marble caves, fishing trips, treks to the glaciers & rafting on the Río Baker, as well as horseriding on their private land. The owners are Danish–Chilean, & the décor reflects the European–Latin influence. The restaurant is something of a fusion of Danish & Patagonian cuisine. Prices are comparatively high depending on the number of guests & choice of cabin, ranging from US$250/night for 2 people to US$600/night for 7 people. Cheaper & comparatively comfortable accommodation is available elsewhere, but Mallín Colorado is a well-established, fully fledged luxury lodge in a truly unique region, & offers a viable alternative to the limited accommodation options in Puerto Río Tranquilo. An excellent option for those travelling with a family. Accepts credit cards. $$$$–$$$$$

🏕 **Camping Cerro Color** (8 sites) 2km south of Cruce el Maitén, 12km north of Puerto Bertrand; ///unavailable.sobered.corks; 📞 9 5663 1830; e campingcerrocolor@hotmail.com; ⏰ Oct–Mar. Fantastic location sandwiched between Lago Negro to the north & an inlet of Lago Bertrand to the south, run by a charming couple who have lived here all their lives. Hot showers, surprisingly large well-equipped kitchen/quincho to prepare food, on-site vegetable garden with organic produce & eggs for sale, fresh bread baked each morning & can use BBQ otherwise camping stoves only. A lamb roast can be prepared if arranged in advance. B/fast available for $5,000 extra, laundry also available for $5,000/load. Small boat available for tours of the lake. One of the best campsites along the Carretera Austral in an idyllic setting, combined with excellent, healthy food available, & a chance to utterly unwind without distractions of cars, music or internet. $8,000 pp. $

CRUCE EL MAITÉN TO CHILE CHICO – A DETOUR

Chile Chico is the start or end point for those doing the 'classic' route along the Carretera Austral. Across the border lies Los Antiguos and Perito Moreno, with transport to the rest of Argentina and the road between Chile Chico and Cruce El Maitén offering some of the most stunning scenery of Lago General Carrera. For those wishing to complete the entire Carretera Austral this may involve doubling back on oneself, but on a sunny day it is a mild hardship to have to repeat such a stunning 115km road. The more pressing decision for those with a vehicle is whether to do the three-day (each way) hike between Chile Chico and Parque Patagonia (page 283) – who returns to get the car?

THE ROAD SOUTH OF LAGO GENERAL CARRERA From Cruce El Maitén, a 115km gravel road connects the Carretera Austral to Chile Chico and Argentina, passing through the villages of Puerto Guadal and Mallín Grande. On a sunny day the views of the lake are breathtaking, as the coastal road winds around headlands and through sections of forest until the Patagonian steppe emerges closer to the border. It is possible to reach the Argentine border in under 3 hours.

At first sight **Puerto Guadal** appears to be little more than a sleepy village (population approximately 600), en route to elsewhere, but it is a hub for adventure activities, and Terra Luna Lodge (page 274) is an excellent base from which to explore the region.

The first settler arrived here in 1926 on the boat *Andes* – the only form of transport in the region before any roads were built. Some of the early settlers were of Lebanese or Arab descent, and set up the first trading companies focused on wool and leather. In the 1950s zinc and lead were mined from the La Escondida site, 12km from the village. French investors wishing to exploit the mineral reserves in the region boosted the local economy in the 1970s precisely when agricultural prices were in decline. Following the construction of the Carretera Austral and the subsequent road connecting the Carretera to Guadal which was completed in 1986, the village has increasingly focused on tourism – to the extent that the mobile phone companies installed an antenna in the town in 2012.

Mallín Grande, some 28km from Puerto Guadal, is extremely small (despite its name). The central plaza is home to a number of chickens and turkeys. The church and medical post are the only buildings of note. A small footbridge unites the main village with the back of the gardens of three houses perched on the other side of a creek.

Puerto Guadal
Getting there
About the route
Cruce El Maitén to Mallín Grande (via Puerto Guadal) (44km; 1hr; rough gravel) The road suddenly opens up here with towering mountains in front and dramatic 180° vistas over glaciers. The lake is only periodically visible. More hairpin bends and precipices are encountered, but west of the El Maitén Bridge the road flattens.

10

The initial 10km to Puerto Guadal is smooth, relatively flat gravel. The next 34km to Mallín Grande is rough gravel with frequent inclines, hairpin bends and precipices, and caution is required. There are occasional cars and buses, often in the centre of the road and travelling fast.

By bus Buses ECA (///blearily.babbled.spuds) go twice a week from Puerto Guadal to Coyhaique (depart 07.30 Mon & Thu, return 13.00 Tue & Fri).

Practical information Guadal has a **petrol station**, but no ATM or laundry. Located on Las Araucarias just by the gate to the east of Guadal (///shard.linger. detachment), car mechanic **Claudio Soto** (✆ 9 8278 5601) is the person to visit with any mechanical problems. He sells and can fix tyres in a jiffy, has a scanner, can solder and patch damaged exhaust systems, and can order parts from Coyhaique quickly. He can also do basic work on motorbikes and bicycles (eg: tyres, soldering), and takes credit cards.

ONCE IN A LIFETIME OPPORTUNITY?

Before rejecting the rather extravagant idea of a **helicopter flight**, consider one simple factor: if you don't do this here, the only alternatives are Antarctica or Greenland at ten times the price. Obviously this is not a cheap form of transport, but this is a rare opportunity to see one of the most truly unique regions of our planet from an optimal viewpoint. Every destination can be experienced via some (often extensive) trekking over rough terrain – the ability to do so in an hour, and from above, is a luxury… But if willing to indulge on one exotic treat, might this be it? Along with Aires del Sur's flights from Villa O'Higgins over the Southern Ice Field (page 322), these are two of the most memorable and awe-inspiring trips in all of Patagonia, if not on earth.

   Patagonia Helitours (Puerto Guadal; ✆ 9 8449 1092, 9 9883 6285; e info@ terraluna.cl; w patagoniahelitours.com) offers flights ranging in time from 12 minutes to 1½ hours, and ranging in price from US$150 to US$810 per person (min 2, max 4 people; for <30min flights, min 4 people). Destinations include the Escondido, Meliquina, San Valentin, Leones, San Rafael, Soler and Nef glaciers. Flights only visit the Northern Ice Field, with San Rafael being the furthest destination, some 90km from Puerto Guadal as the condor would fly.

   For most people this is a stupendous extravagance. But this is not purely a matter of convenience or luxury. This is an opportunity to see how our planet was formed; to understand why the valleys we trek in are shaped as they are; to appreciate how vast the ice fields are, and how the glaciers we observe from the land/boat are actually the proverbial tip of the iceberg (or the snout of the ice field). Above all, combining the majesty of the ice field and a cursory understanding of how the glaciers are retreating may put the issue of global warming and climate change into perspective. This might be beyond some budgets, and that is ultimately a consequence of the laws of physics. But our advice is to seriously consider this as a rare opportunity that you have already invested in extensively simply to arrive at the Carretera Austral…but on one condition…think laterally about your role on this beautiful planet in all its splendour, and allow this experience to alter your behaviour in order to protect it.

Excursions and sightseeing Involving a short drive from Guadal and a hike of approximately 8km it is possible to see a broad range of **marine fossils** offering a glimpse of the geological and climatic changes that have occurred over the last 20 million years. The trek passes through a beech forest, either trekking or on horseback up the hills behind Puerto Guadal until reaching the fossil bed. Fossils aside, the views towards the Northern Ice Field and the lake below are majestic. Some of the fossils here originated in the Atlantic Ocean. Do this trek only with an authorised guide, as otherwise erosion and reckless visitors will eventually limit access for all.

Other tours accessed from Guadal include visiting the wonderful Leones glacier (see box, page 275) or flying over the ice field (see box, opposite). Most hotels can arrange tours in the region, such as the marble caves of Puerto Río Tranquilo or rafting on the Baker at Puerto Bertrand – see page 274 for more information. For more exotic tours, see those offered by Kalem Patagonia (see below).

Tour operators

Kalem Patagonia Los Alerces 557; /// fattier.trams.nurseries; \ 9 4296 4723, 9 7391 7881; e turismokalempatagonia@gmail.com; f turismokalempatagonia. Born in Mallín Grande & based in Guadal, Pascual Diaz is an excellent guide & his tours are some of the most interesting in the region. The quality of service & attention to detail are impeccable: picnics include a tablecloth, decent cups, a freshly prepared meat & cheese platter, a small bottle of wine (& the traditional whisky with glacial ice when visiting a glacier), fresh fruit, etc. His 'off-the-shelf' tours include trekking to the Ventisquero Leones ($110,000 pp, min 4 people); a 2-day trip to the glacier sleeping overnight in a refuge on a peninsula in front of the glacier, with ice-climbing ($160,000 pp, min 4 people); a fossil trail ($35,000 pp ½ day, min 4 people). Other tours include horseriding around Mallín Grande (½- to multiple-day treks; priced accordingly); a 2-day trek to the Escondido glacier near Mallín Grande; the 12-day horseride from Cochrane to Villa O'Higgins (the ruta los pioneros); the Paso San Carlos trails (page 308); & the 10-day trek between Villa O'Higgins & El Chaltén via the Southern Ice Field. This last trip goes initially to Candelario Mancilla (as with the 'standard' route), but then heads up towards the Ventisquero Chico & up to the Garcia Soto refuge on the Southern Ice Field & then down to Chaltén. The optimal number of trekkers is 4, in sufficiently good physical condition for over a week of trekking without horses. Pascual is also able to offer tailor-made

tours, including far off the beaten track to both ice fields, & alternative routes through Parque Patagonia. He has his own 4x4 van, a satellite phone for emergencies in remote regions, & for a reasonable additional fee can offer transfers. For example, he can pick passengers up at Puerto Río Tranquilo, take them to the Ventisquero Leones (1 complete day) & drop off at Cochrane. Service-oriented, experienced, punctual & returns phone calls when possible – highly recommended & good value. Pascual speaks basic English, but other guides in the company speak English & French. Takes cards.

Patagonia Arisca 2km east of Guadal; \ 9 7650 6769; e ilango.aaron@gmail.com; w patagoniaarisca.com. New tour operator based in Guadal, working in collaboration with Otras Huellas (see box, page 50) & Mirador de Guadal (page 274). Interesting team of passionate local & international guides from as far afield as Germany, India & USA, offering tours off the beaten track. In addition to the standard day trip to the fossils they offer multi-day horseriding trips to the fossils including camping; following the old gaucho trails between Bertrand & Guadal; a 4hr round trip to the spectacular Maqui waterfalls; & perhaps of greatest historic interest, a half-day trip to an abandoned zinc & copper mine above the village – it is hard to imagine this region as a mining hub, but such mines litter the coast of the lake, & this is one of the more accessible ones to visit.

Where to stay and eat Most visitors may prefer to push on to Chile Chico, but there are some accommodation options should you become stranded. As well as the options listed, **Hospedaje Amigos** (cnr of Volcán Hudson & Los Pioneros,

Mallín Grande; ///arrowed.surpluses.pudding; ↘9 9094 2563) offers a room for $15,000, including breakfast and a hot shower. A simple dinner increases this by a further $4,000, but given the absence of a restaurant in Mallín Grande, and only minuscule and informal shops invariably closed, this is a decent option within the village (use of their kitchen also available). Of the hotels in and around Puerto Guadal, **El Arrayan**, **El Mirador de Guadal** and **Terra Luna** all have good restaurants.

🏠 **El Arrayan Lodge & Restaurant** (2 apts) 1km east of Guadal, 100m up road X-881 to Laguna La Manga; ///hyphen.composites.camouflages; ↘9 9122 0499; e elarrayanpuertoguadal@gmail.com; 🅕 elarrayanguadal. This is both a fine restaurant $$$$ & top-quality accommodation for 2 or 3 people. Excellent construction & great views across the lake, a short stroll to the village & even closer to the restaurant, each apt has a mini kitchen (basically to make tea or coffee), laundry, private parking & good b/fast included, but no Wi-Fi. The owner, Pablo, has lived in Guadal all his life & can help with any tours, logistics or information. The restaurant competes with the best in the region – the speciality is seafood, but caters for any dietary request (with notice). Good range of local ales, fresh coffee & particularly tempting puddings. $$$$

🏠 **Lodge El Mirador de Guadal** [map, page 241] (10 rooms) 2km east of Puerto Guadal on the road to Chile Chico; ///unseated.outvoted.stilted; ↘9 9234 9130; e reservas@elmiradordeguadal. com; w elmiradordeguadal.com; ⊕ Oct–Apr. The finest accommodation in Guadal, owned by a Dutch/Chilean couple. Extremely nice standalone rooms in wood-cabin style (without kitchens) each with a deck & stunning views over the lake. Large comfortable beds & wood-fired stoves for heating. The finish is top-notch & the complex has lake access & a beach. The lodge has a rustic boat made by hand in Caleta Tortel out of local cypress. Full b/fast included, & the restaurant also serves dinner in a delightful building, also with views over the lake. The centre of town is a short drive or stroll. Wi-Fi in the restaurant only, ample parking & laundry. TVs are notable for their absence, deliberately to encourage a total disconnection from the outside world. The lodge can arrange various activities in the area, including trips to the marble caves, Maqui waterfalls, glaciers, horseriding, boat trips on the lake including to the Ventisquero Leones ((see box, opposite; via jet boat rather than the longer hike), treks to the local fossil beds & more. Dutch,

English, German & Spanish spoken. Reservations required. Accepts credit cards & can receive bank transfers to Chilean or European accounts. $$$$

🏠 **Patagonia Acres Lodge** [map, page 241] (10 cabins) 5km east of Mallín Grande, 30km east of Guadal; ///headed.curdling.maverick; ↘9 6224 5873; e jcharrison@patagoniaacres.com; w patagoniaacres.com. One of the finest places to stay along the entire southern shore of Lago General Carrera. Fully equipped, comfortable cabins for 4 or 6 people, with spectacular views over the lake & small decks to enjoy the sunset, access to a beach below & kayak rental possible. The property has its own jetty for launching boats, a games room with table tennis & a number of hiking trails within the 160ha property. Gym, jacuzzi & hot tub available, & even includes a rustic 9-hole golf course (clubs available without charge). Owned by an Arizonan family who also sell parcels of land on the property. All services provided, including laundry, Wi-Fi, etc. Can also arrange off-site activities & airport transfers. While for some the distance from Guadal (40km) & Chile Chico (70km) might be a disadvantage, the benefits include utter privacy & the tranquillity of the lake. Accommodation prices are reasonable for this calibre of lodge, at between US$160 & US$200 per cabin, depending on occupancy. This price includes b/fast, fishing equipment & mountain bikes. Lunch & dinner are available ($$$). There are 5km of trails on the property, making the lodge ideal for families. Also offer 3-, 4- & 5-night packages including accommodation, food, various activities, guides & all transport. Accept credit cards & PayPal. $$$$

✳ 🏠 **Terra Luna Lodge** [map, page 241] (cabins, rooms, domes, a house & a treehouse – 80 people max) 1km east of Puerto Guadal; ///exec. bigger.hardest; ↘9 8449 1092, 9 3456 5217; e info@terraluna.cl; w terraluna.cl. A bewildering range of accommodation options, this lodge will appeal to most tastes: from simple, rustic cabins to surprisingly nice hotel-style rooms,

Your Patagonia in a bottle

Tepaluma® Patagonian Distillery

Carretera Austral KM 350, La Junta, Patagonia Chilena

www.tepaluma.com | contact@tepaluma.com

f ○ tepaluma

PLEASE DRINK RESPONSIBLY

a fantastic treehouse accessed by ladder, & a luxurious jacuzzi cabin overlooking the entire lodge & lake. The rooms themselves are cosy with fully equipped bathrooms, lovely views over the lake, & a positively homely atmosphere. Ideal for families, solo travellers or as a romantic break, & because the rooms/cabins are relatively dispersed they also offer a degree of privacy despite the relatively large nature of the complex. There's also a restaurant (**$$$$**), lake access & endless activities – there is little reason to leave the premises at all. Prices are also surprisingly reasonable, ranging from approximately US$80/ night for a couple, up to US$200 for the house which sleeps 6. The treehouse is US$150/night &

sleeps 2. The lodge boasts a spa (sauna, massages & hot tub), a projector, a bar/restaurant (with disco lights upstairs if absolutely necessary), laundry & Wi-Fi. The menu of the day is $20,000. The latest addition is a pizzeria, novel in these parts – $8,000–13,000 for a decent pizza by the lake. However, most interesting are the tours on offer. They can arrange the standard tours in the region (canopy, marble caves, horseriding, various treks, mountain biking, fishing, fossil tour, rafting on the Río Baker), including transfers, but also have their own jet boat able to explore the lake & go up the Río Leones towards the Fiero & Leones glaciers (see box, below). This does involve some mild trekking, & the lodge has a zodiac on the Lago Leones

VISITING VENTISQUERO LEONES

One of the various glaciers protruding from the Northern Ice Field, or more precisely, from the San Valentin Ice Field, is the Ventisquero Leones. This flows into the Lago Leones, which flows in turn into the Río Leones. The entry point to the trek to the glacier is 28km south of Puerto Río Tranquilo (shortly after the bridge, somewhat unimaginatively named the Leones Bridge). The journey begins with a 4x4 drive of approximately an hour, at which point it is no longer possible to proceed in a vehicle. Although not technically challenging, reaching the Ventisquero Leones involves some modest effort – perhaps 3 or 4 hours of trekking, as opposed to sitting on a boat most of the day (as at the Ventisquero San Rafael). In part as a result of this, the cost of reaching the Ventisquero Leones is currently about half that of a trip to the Ventisquero San Rafael.

The public and well-marked trail passes through two private properties for approximately 9km on mostly flat ground to the edge of the lake. At this point the glacier is clearly visible, but is some 11km away on the other side of the lake. There are two boats servicing the route across the lake: that of Pascual Díaz (page 273), and that of Terra Luna Lodge (see opposite). It's worth keeping in mind that some operators offering this trip go no further than the lake's edge, but it's really worth crossing the lake to the snout of the glacier.

The glacier appears initially to be deceptively close, perhaps in part because there is no point of reference from which to gauge distance. Only as the boat chugs towards the glacier does the true distance gradually emerge, as the glacier slowly grows larger and larger.

This glacier is so remote and relatively unknown that encountering another person is highly unlikely. The boats are able to approach the glacier safely (unlike at the more popular Ventisquero San Rafael; page 267) – so close, in fact, that it is possible to view the subtleties of the ice wall in detail without a zoom lens. The picnic spots, too, are so close to the edge of the glacier that in the utter silence, you can hear the cracking and groaning of the ice. Terra Luna reach the glacier either by jet boat or helicopter. Kalem Patagonia (page 273) trek and then have a boat to cross the lake, also offering overnight options.

10

able to approach the glacier directly – this is a far quicker & less arduous means to arrive at the spectacular Ventisquero Leones compared with the slower route involving a longer trek (page 273). English, Spanish & French spoken. Particularly good option if travelling with kids. Accepts credit cards. All-inclusive packages available. **$$$**

🏠 **Hospedaje Janito** (8 rooms) Las Camelias 169; ///subtotal.desired.firm; 📞9 9775 8659; e rosario.reyes727@gmail.com. Great backpacker place particularly if eating there as well. Operating since 2012 with a good vibe & run by a fun owner, the best budget hostel in town. 5 dbls, 1 sgl, 2 trpls, all shared bathroom ($15,000 pp, plus $4,000 extra for b/fast). Rooms are basic, but the food is great – depending on the day of the week & the number of guests there might be a lamb roast ($15,000), otherwise the usual Chilean fare plus cazuelas ($10,000–15,000) & a daily menu for $8,000. No alcohol but can bring your own. **$$**

🏠 **El Pionero** (3 cabins) Los Lirios; 📞9 9496 5397. Surprisingly pleasant cabins a block from the main plaza for 3–6 people ($50,000–70,000), great views towards town or lake from windows in the larger cabin, though it has a slightly smaller kitchen. Lovely balcony, garden for kids to play in, towels & kitchen kit all included – just a simple, sweet, rustic cabin that might easily be overlooked. No email, no credit cards, wood-stove heating, but does have Wi-Fi. Best budget cabins in the village. **$–$$**

🏕 **El Condor Viajero** (Camping for 35 people) By eastern gate to village; ///buzzwords.wardrobes.smoothest; 📞9 7604 1806; e campingcondorviajero@gmail.com; 📘 campingcondorviajero. Excellent camping a few blocks from the centre of the village, immaculately cut lawn among fruit trees (eat what you like), 2 bathrooms with decent hot water, fires not permitted but amazing quincho with full kitchen & wood-stove heating, 4 tables for 4–6 people each, so no need to cook outdoors. Even has a fridge. 1 central BBQ area, & a good hanging rack to dry clothes. Has good Wi-Fi & connections for motorhomes, pay with card. $6,000 pp to camp ($4,000 for kids under 8), $4,000 for a load of laundry, & $4,000 extra for electrical connection for a motorhome – all very reasonable for the quality. Small shop sells pasta, bread, dairy products, dried fruits, cereals, soya meat, etc. **$**

✘ **Café Restaurant El Tehuelche** Southeastern cnr of the plaza; ///rowdy.tidally.ambushes; 📞9 5718 2598; 🕐 noon–22.00 daily. Good coffee, cakes, quiches, pastas, & usual Chilean range of seafood & vegetarian options. Has a piano that anyone can play, without any prior experience apparently, & a play area for kids. Reasonable ice creams for pudding. Fine for a quick bite, but expensive. Takes credit card, which you might need. **$$$**

✘ **Restaurante Casa Vieja Costanera** Los Guindos 332; ///vanity.patriotism.regattas; 📞9 7800 7333; 🕐 13.00–22.30 daily. Simple restaurant opposite the ECA store which doubles as a bar, serving fries, a daily menu, pizza, *pichangas* & sandwiches. Limited range of local ales & regional wines. Wi-Fi. Also have cabins. **$$**

CHILE CHICO After Coyhaique and Puerto Aysén, Chile Chico is probably the next largest town in the region. It has a pleasant microclimate, receiving less rain than elsewhere, and is slightly warmer. However, besides pottering around the pleasant town, doing a little shopping and withdrawing money from the ATM, filling up with petrol and grabbing a bite to eat, there is relatively little in town to entertain visitors for long. Most either head towards Argentina, or into the Parque Patagonia (Jeinimeni sector, page 282).

History Some 10,000 years before modern-day settlers started occupying the land around Chile Chico, indigenous groups such as the Tehuelches inhabited this region. In 1902, after the 1881 treaty between Argentina and Chile which defined the borders, Chilean migrants who had been living on the Argentine side of the border started to arrive, settling in several regions of Aysén including Chile Chico. In 1909 a group of migrants set up home on the southern shore of Lago General Carrera attracted by the peculiar microclimate of the region which they found similar to the central region of Chile, allowing for the cultivation of grains and fruit and raising of livestock. This was their new homeland, their small country which henceforth became known as Chile Chico ('little Chile'). Despite the isolation the settlers built their houses with the intention to put down firm roots. In 1914 they officially requested permission to occupy the land and developed a small village.

Owing to the relative prosperity of the region farmers were drawn to the area with the intention of establishing cattle ranches. In 1917 an advertisement appeared in a national Chilean newspaper announcing the sale of public lands by the Chilean state. In a dubious auction the land around Chile Chico was awarded to Carlos von Flank who represented the powerful and wealthy landowning consortium Braun & Menendez. At first they tried to negotiate with the settlers to sell their land and livestock. The price they offered, however, was very low and no deal was reached. It was then decided to evict the settlers. The settlers organised to stop their eviction led by Antolin Silva Ormeño, known as 'the general'. The first encounter with police was amicable. The settlers were determined to defend the land they had fought so hard for and a group of only ten surrounded the police camp at sunset to give the impression there were many of them. Frightened, the licensees and police officers left and sent word to Santiago that numerous bandits had threatened them and forced them to evacuate.

Another police contingent of 30 was sent to the area led by a young lieutenant. Meanwhile the settlers prepared their defence and sent a delegation to Santiago to plead for their rights to the territory they had been granted. A group of 40 settlers took up arms to face the police in the disputed zone. The police withdrew, claiming it was impossible to attack their fellow Chilean citizens who had done nothing wrong, had made their humble homes there and were flying Chilean flags made of clothing and rags. The lieutenant was sacked and a new police force was sent, leading to violence and the burning of houses of the settlers, some of whom were imprisoned. The first clashes occurred after one settler was killed. A group of 50 settlers opened fire and killed three police officers, wounding another and taking 12 hostage. As a result the police, von Flank and his partners, fled to Argentina on foot.

Von Flank upped the political stakes by falsely claiming that the settlers were invading Argentine territory, prompting the Argentine government to send 122 men and three officials towards Chile Chico to put an end to the supposed invasion.

The settlers, meanwhile, travelled to Buenos Aires and on to Santiago where they spoke with the Minister of the Interior who ordered the immediate end of all official activities against the settlers and withdrawal of all armed forces from the area. He decided to expire the lease of the land that had been awarded to von Flank, finally recognising the rights of the settlers. The Argentine troops had arrived at the border but were recalled. The settlers were finally able to celebrate their victory. These events were later called 'The War of Chile Chico'.

On 21 May 1929 the official foundation of Chile Chico took place. Initially the inhabitants raised livestock, but commerce and transportation developed due to the proximity to the lake and roads leading to the Atlantic. Chile Chico became the centre of distribution of wool produced around Lago General Carrera, as well as an access point to the Río Baker. The first railroads in the region were made by settlers, including routes through Paso de las Llaves (now the highway along the south of Lago General Carrera) and later from Puerto Ibáñez and the Levicán Peninsula, providing access to the markets of Coyhaique. However, the biggest contribution to the development of the area was Chile Chico's acquisition of iron boats that moved goods on several routes on the binational Lago General Carrera. At first it was mainly products for import and export that were transported, subsequently passengers too.

Owing to the abundance of lead and zinc in the soil, in 1940 Chile Chico became the major intermediary for mining and mineral exports and experienced its first true boom. Many restaurants, hotels, theatres and other establishments emerged. Sadly this 'golden age' didn't last as trails in the region north of Chile Chico were widened and a road connected Puerto Ibáñez with Puerto Aysén, the main maritime port of the entire Aysén region. Chile Chico's role as a transportation hub abated. The situation was worsened by the subsequent closure of the mines.

More recently Chile Chico has found another 'goldmine'. Because of its favourable climate it now grows and exports cherries. The difference in timing of the cherry season between the central area of Chile and that of Lago General Carrera enables growers to extend the productive season and gives them an important advantage to buyers in Europe and Asia. Tourism is another sector that saw continued growth as a result of the increased popularity of the Carretera Austral.

Following World War II, approximately 30 Belgians emigrated to Chile Chico, some descendants of which still live in the town, and the European influence is visible in the architectural styles of some of the older houses. For those interested in history it is worth staying either at El Engaño (page 281), where the historian Danka Ivanoff lives; or the Hostería de la Patagonia (page 281), run by one of the daughters of the original Belgian settlers. Danka Ivanoff has written ten books covering various aspects of the history of the region. The book *Cuando Éramos Niños en la Patagonia* (*When we were Children in Patagonia*) is available in the Hostería de la Patagonia, recounting the lives of the Belgian children growing up in Chile Chico.

CHILE CHICO – EYE OF THE COVID STORM

No single location along the Carretera Austral was as badly impacted by the pandemic as Chile Chico. While updating this second edition, the overall rate of business closure across the region was approximately one in seven enterprises. Coyhaique was higher, at roughly one in five, and Puerto Montt suffered about one in four businesses closing. However, in Chile Chico it was almost one in every three businesses. Of four tour operators functioning in early 2020, only one has survived. Three of the original eight restaurants have vanished, and one of the seven hotels. At the time of writing many of the businesses included here were barely surviving.

The main reason the village was so catastrophically hit was its dependence upon tourism, particularly visitors entering/departing to Argentina. Not only were tourist levels dramatically reduced during the pandemic, but the closure of the border meant that even Chilean tourists had little reason to venture off the Carretera towards Chile Chico. Even passive traffic from those traversing the Carretera, not for tourism, bypassed the village. It appears those wishing to soak up the magnificent views from the south of the lake would venture only as far as Puerto Guadal and then return to the Carretera. Finally, there have been constant problems with the ferries crossing the lake, one of the main means to reach/depart Chile Chico.

Updating the Chile Chico section of the book was depressing, and it remains to be seen what will remain of the village after the mediocre 2021/2022 season.

Getting there Chile Chico is notorious for poor logistics. Buses to and from the town are small, few and infrequent. The boat to Puerto Ibáñez (page 60) is often full, particularly for those wishing to travel with a vehicle in high season. Shuttles over the border run more frequently, stopping at Los Antiguos (Argentina), which is well connected with Perito Moreno, from where a wide range of buses travel north towards Esquel and Bariloche, south towards El Chaltén and Calafate, and east across the steppe towards the Atlantic and Comodoro Rivadavia. Hitchhikers and those attempting to connect with the Carretera Austral to/from Chile Chico via public transport routinely moan about logistical problems along this section.

About the route

Mallín Grande to Chile Chico (71km; 1½hrs; rough gravel) This is a treacherous road; unsuspecting drivers may be tempted to risk higher speeds along decent compact gravel, only to be met with vicious sections of loose gravel, major corrugations and pot-holes. There are some steep inclines and descents, often along cliff edges without protective railings – this is not a good section to drift off the road.

The road initially passes through dense forest, but gradually transforms into drier, sparsely vegetated steppe as the arid Argentine Patagonia approaches. Be aware that this road is extremely bendy and be ready for oncoming vehicles; take care as the precipices are very close to the road, tumbling hundreds of metres into the lake. Occasional landslides may mean there are rocks scattered across the road, which also passes through a number of dynamited rock sections where it is not clear whether two cars could pass each other. Cerro Castillo is periodically visible in the distance across the turquoise lake. Even in summer snow is possible along the upper sections of the route. It is worth driving slowly, not only to avoid an accident, but also to absorb the vistas. There are countless photo opportunities, but few places to park a car safely: however tempting, do not stop on a bend.

Shortly before Chile Chico the road passes **Lago Verde** (not to be confused with the town and lake also called Lago Verde further north), with stunning views over the lake and towards the snow-capped mountains, spoiled somewhat by an open mine.

The landscapes approaching Chile Chico are positively lunar: rocks jut out in bizarre formations and poplar trees are twisted into awkward angles by the relentless wind. Beyond Lago Verde the road veers straight east, losing sight of the lake for perhaps 20km and passing some minor marshlands before arriving at Chile Chico on the lakeshore.

Chile Chico to the Argentine border (5km; 5mins; paved) This stretch is passable in any vehicle. The border is open all year from 08.00 to 20.00. The paved road continues 8km to the first Argentine town of Los Antiguos and a further 65km to Perito Moreno. **Taqsa** (☏+54 9 296 641 9615; w taqsa.com.ar) and **Chaltén Travel** (☏+54 11 5199 0476; w chaltentravel.com) both offer long-distance buses within Argentina, both passing through Los Antiguos. Following the collapse of a local tour operator there is currently no public transport between Chile Chico and Los Antiguos. Enquire locally – this is such an important connection for the village that a new operator will inevitably emerge. Failing that, it is a 13km taxi ride.

By public transport This stretch of southern Chile is difficult for both hitchhiking and public transport. Prior to the pandemic there were a few **buses** a week both north to Coyhaique (via Guadal, Puerto Tranquilo and Cerro Castillo) and south to Cochrane. However, all routes are currently on hold (early 2022).

10

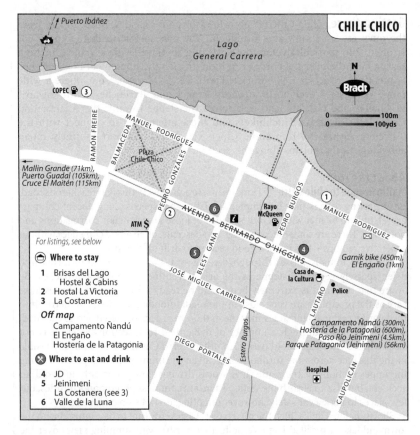

CHILE CHICO

↑ Puerto Ibáñez

Lago General Carrera

N

Bradt

COPEC ☐ ③

MANUEL RODRÍGUEZ

RAMÓN FREIRE

BALMACEDA

Plaza Chile Chico

← Mallín Grande (71km),
Puerto Guadal (105km),
Cruce El Maitén (115km)

PEDRO GONZALES

AVENIDA BERNARDO O'HIGGINS

ATM $

②

⑥

ℹ️

Rayo McQueen

PEDRO BURGOS

①

MANUEL RODRÍGUEZ

✉️

⑤

BLEST GANA

④

Garnik bike (450m),
El Engaño (1km)

JOSE MIGUEL CARRERA

Casa de la Cultura 🏛

● Police

LAUTARO

DIEGO PORTALES

Estero Burgos

Campamento Ñandú (300m),
Hostería de la Patagonia (600m),
Paso Río Jeinimeni (4.5km),
Parque Patagonia (Jeinimeni) (56km)

✝

Hospital

🏥

CAUPOLICÁN

0 ━━━━━ 100m
0 ━━━━━ 100yds

For listings, see below

⬒ **Where to stay**
1 Brisas del Lago
      Hostel & Cabins
2 Hostal La Victoria
3 La Costanera
Off map
      Campamento Ñandú
      El Engaño
      Hostería de la Patagonia

❌ **Where to eat and drink**
4 JD
5 Jeinimeni
      La Costanera (see 3)
6 Valle de la Luna

In high season it is easy to become stranded along the south of the lake for hours, if not days. For details of getting here by **ferry** from Puerto Ibáñez, see page 60.

Tour operators

Garnik Bike Baquedano 151; ///tempt.deceives. dither; 📞 9 9949 6899; e ciclismogarnikbike@ gmail.com; ⏰ 09.00–20.00 Mon–Sat. Rent, repairs & spares. Range of touring tyres, seats, pumps, helmets, bottles & able to solder. The owner, Patricio, claims to be the #1 bicycle fanatic in all of Chile Chico, & this is most probably true.

Since the collapse of most other tour operators in Chile Chico, Patricio has taken up the slack & offers bike tours, as well as pure transport options to Jeinimeni Park. He has a minibus to carry passengers & bikes into the park, & for those wishing to do the 4-day trek towards Cochrane, Patricio can drop off at the trailhead.

 Where to stay *Map, above*

🏠 **La Costanera** (8 apts) Manuel Rodríguez 7; ///unofficial.softies.blueprint; 📞 9 6519 9448, 9 4095 7890; e reservas@costanera-apart.cl. A modern, luxury apartment hotel with views over the lake of Chile Chico. Good for families. Private bathrooms, Wi-Fi, cable TV, parking, fully equipped kitchen & restaurant (page 282). Next to the departure point for the ferry. Expensive, but

potentially a price worth paying if smooth travel is a priority. $$$$$

🏠 **Brisas del Lago Hostel and Cabins** (7 rooms, 3 cabins) Manuel Rodriguez 443; ///plunder.stumbling.indeed; 📞 67 241 1204, 9 8462 6289; e brisasdellago@gmail.com; w turismobrisasdellago.cl. Basic accommodation 1 block north of main street. 1 sgl, 6 dbls/twins with shared bathrooms. Basic b/fast included, Wi-Fi & parking available. Functional but lacking in character. The cabins are better, for 2, 4 or 5 people, with partial views over the lake. Fully equipped, including cable TV (only in the restaurant in the main hostel), Wi-Fi, limited parking. A short walk to the centre. Takes cards. **$$$**

☀ 🏠 **El Engaño** (8 cabins) 1km east on coastal road from Chile Chico; ///clues.bisects. astonished; 🗲 9 9134 8162, 9 7889 4007; e elengano.spa@gmail.com; w turismoelengaño. com. Excellent, fully equipped modern cabins for 4–5 people ($70,000–90,000) very close to the lake & with views across to Cerro Castillo, but with trees protecting the cabins from the often ferocious wind. The term 'spa' does not refer to massage/ sauna but is the legal structure of the company (as in 'ltd' or 'inc'). Facilities include 2 hot tubs, ample parking, laundry service & a quincho. Can also arrange tours in the region including fishing trips, & pre-booking ferry crossings to Puerto Ibáñez. However, the highlight of this hostel is that the mother of the owner is none other than Danka Ivanoff Wellmann, a well-known historian in the region. Visitors interested in the history of the Carretera may be able to have a chat with Danka, & her books are available at the reception (see page 312 for more on her book about the mysterious cemetery in Caleta Tortel). Fine cabins, excellent value if 4 or 5 people & a truly golden opportunity for those interested in the history of the region, but best with private transport. **$$$**

🏠 **Hostal La Victoria** (11 rooms) O'Higgins 210; ///logos.jovially.precautions; 🗲 67 241 1344, 9 9132 3826; e lavictoria@outlook.com. A reasonable & centrally located option, perhaps a little overpriced for the rather thin walls & ceilings, but modern & comfortable. All rooms with private bathroom. Decent b/fast included, communal sitting area, free use of kitchen, & able to arrange transport in the region. **$$$**

☀ 🏠 **Hostería de la Patagonia** (5 rooms, 1 boat, camping) Chacra 3A Camino International; ///marvels.development.pronounces; 🗲 67 241 1337, 9 8159 2146; e hdelapatagonia@gmail.com;

w hosteriadelapatagonia.cl. A beautiful, tranquil setting with views over a pleasant garden. Located slightly outside of town on the lake side of the road towards the border. Spacious rooms for between 1 & 4 people, with comfortable beds, wide windows & decent private bathrooms. Also offers camping for a modest $6,000 pp including bathrooms, hot water & electricity outlets. The truly unique feature of this farm-stay option is a large boat in the garden, which has been converted to a fantastic cabin complete with bathroom & a small kitchen (1 dbl & 3 sgl beds). The house is one of the original settler homes, partly resembling a museum, originally built in 1953. The owner is a direct descendant of the Belgian settlers (page 278) & speaks French. Great b/fast included, with yoghurt, cereals & homemade bread & jams, ham, cheese, eggs, fruit juice, etc. Garden has a pizza oven & parrilla, as well as a hot tub. Great dining/communal room, Wi-Fi & laundry. Good option for bikers as has large private off-road parking & plenty of space for cyclists to tinker with their bikes. A short stroll into town. Very fine accommodation for a reasonable price. Also has bikes for rent. Deposit usually required. Takes credit cards. **$–$$$**

🏠 **Campamento Ñandú** (9 rooms) O'Higgins 750; ///deflation.laughs.derails; 🗲 9 6779 3390; e contact@nanducamp.com; w nanducamp.com. Very good hostel with a range of accommodation options from dorm beds (US$20, shared bathroom) to a family room for 5 with private bathroom (US$75), & everything in between. Old-school hostel to meet fellow travellers that seem to be phasing out nowadays, run by a friendly family who know the region well & can organise tours in the region & particularly within Parque Patagonia where the owners have a tourism concession. Good for families, has a garden, bicycles & climbing wall, & is slightly outside the relative sprawl of Chile Chico. B/fast is available for a small fee, but there's a full kitchen. Laundry available. Unusually this is also the only accommodation we know where the owners also speak Japanese. Best option at this price point. Takes credit cards & ample parking. **$**

✗ Where to eat and drink *Map, opposite*

✗ **Jeinimeni Restaurante** Blest Gana 120; ///blemishes.polisher.folks; 🗲 9 4222 6537, 9 6768 3399; 🕐 13.00–midnight Mon–Thu, 13.00–02.00 Fri & Sat, 13.00–16.00 Sun. The best restaurant

in town, often packed, wise to reserve, great atmosphere & unusual wood/brick construction. Excellent seafood options that actually deviate from the standard fare, an extraordinary *paila marina* (seafood soup), very good steaks, sushi, empanadas, sandwiches, tablas (platters), cocktails & the local Hudson ale. $$$

✕ La Costanera Manuel Rodríguez 7; ///unofficial.softies.blueprint; ☏ 9 6519 9448, 9 4095 7890; e reservas@costanera-apart. cl; ☉ 11.00–23.30 daily. Excellent food in La Costanera hotel. Specialises in pastas, & also has pizzas, fish & meat, good coffee, cakes, imported & artisanal beers & an excellent wine collection. $$$

✕ JD Restaurant O'Higgins 455; ///motoring. gearbox.stoats; ☏ 9 8239 5490; ☉ 07.00– midnight Mon–Sat; good & fast restaurant open all day & even later as a bar only. Usual Chilean fare plus sandwiches, pizzas, a lo pobre dishes, a massive pichanga for $9,000. Early happy hour, no need to reserve, outdoor seating, fresh ground coffee, D'Olbek beer on tap. $$

✕ Valle de la Luna Northwest cnr of O'Higgins & Blest Gana; ///regard.fumbled.locals; ☏ 9 8192 2455; ☉ 13.00–15.30 & 19.00–22.30 Mon–Sat. Mid-range family restaurant popular with locals & with space for 40 people. Serves decent *lomo a lo pobre*, positively good salmon but meat dishes are nothing special. A range of wines is available; no-frills décor. Offers a menu of the day for $7,000; à la carte is notably more expensive & not such good value. Lunch $, dinner $$

Other practicalities There is an **ATM** (Banco Estado) on Pedro Gonzalez 112 just north of the central plaza (///reefs.tinkers.filling), and a COPEC **petrol station** by the harbour (///manure.paraffin.affably). The **tourist information centre** is barely worth visiting for the lack of information available, while the **Casa de la Cultura** occasionally has some local artwork or cultural events (on O'Higgins), and boasts a rather unusual boat parked on the road as a historic relic from the golden era when Chile Chico was an important transport hub. The boat, *Andes*, was bought from England in 1922 and remained in operation until the early 1990s. It was the principal means of transport for those living around the lake, particularly prior to the construction of the road.

Mechanic
Rayo McQueen Pedro Burgos 20; ///toymaker. shrugging.decades; ☏ 9 7730 3373; ☉ 09.00– 13.00 & 15.00–19.00 Mon–Fri, 09.00–13.00 Sat. Able to do most car & motorbike repairs, but note that he doesn't do welding, & doesn't have a scanner for motorbikes. Spare parts available, & those that need to be ordered from Coyhaique can arrive within 24hrs. Has experience with KTM, BMW, Kawasaki & Honda. The only bike mechanic in town. Also works with 'Bruno', another car mechanic who also has a tow truck. Has a limited range of tyres for sale.

PARQUE NACIONAL PATAGONIA (Jeinimeni sector; e benjamin.molina@conaf.cl; w conaf.cl/parques/parque-nacional-patagonia; $8,200/4,100 foreigners/Chileans; free for children under 11; $10,000 per campsite in addition to entry fee) This national reserve is up there with the finest parks in the region, with a stunning trek all the way to the Roballos border crossing with Argentina, the headquarters of Parque Patagonia or to Cochrane. Established in 1967, the Jeinimeni sector (originally a national reserve rather than a national park) extends for 161,100ha and was merged into Parque Patagonia on 11 December 2018. Flora and fauna abound – a variety of woodpecker species, condors, black-chested buzzard-eagles, huemul and guanacos. Only the very fortunate will spot the elusive puma.

Getting there Access to the park is from the main road connecting Chile Chico to the Argentine border. Approximately 1km east of Chile Chico (///detriment.furred. managed), the X-753 heads 55km south to the park entrance (///sings.mitigates. only). The road is rough gravel with some minor river crossings. Garnik Bike (page 280) are currently the only operators with transport to the park, although more will

THE SENDERO PIEDRA CLAVADA *(9km; 3hrs; easy)*

En route to Jeinimeni, just 25km south of Chile Chico (ie: approximately halfway to the main park entrance) is the Sendero Piedra Clavada **hiking trail**. Parking is available off the main road at the trailhead. The trail forms a loop, and easily can be completed in under 3 hours. Although technically within the national park there is no park ranger here. This trail serves as a decent warm-up for the trek through the park, and it is possible to do in a single day from Chile Chico for those not continuing on to the park proper.

The route first passes an unusual 42m-high rock pillar formed by millennia of wind erosion (the 'nailed stone') before coming to a 1,145m-high panoramic viewpoint towards Lago General Carrera (the 'portezuelo'). Next, you reach the 'Cueva de los Manos' where prehistoric hand paintings and images of guanacos can be seen, estimated to be between 8,000 and 10,000 years old, before finally reaching the Valley of the Moon (an arid landscape) some 2.5km from the trailhead. A recommended day trip from Chile Chico, especially for those not tempted by the multi-day trek to Parque Patagonia.

likely emerge when tourism rebounds. Taxis are expensive and, as this road is rarely transited, hitchhiking is difficult. Those staying the night in Chile Chico might be able to plead with a hotel owner for a lift.

The main road continues 20km past the trailhead for the Sendero Piedra Clavada to the main park entrance, where the entry fee is paid.

Where to stay The only formal **campsite** in the park is less than 1km from the main park entrance, at the northern edge of Lago Jeinimeni. Facilities include a table and benches with a roof, fire pit, wood and bathrooms. The crystal-clear, lake-fed stream by the campground is full of trout. The ranger lives in the park, but if he's not around it is possible to park outside the office, pitch your tent in the clearly marked camping sites and pay later or the next day.

Hiking in the park (and beyond) The **maps** provided by CONAF have all trails marked. All trailheads and detours are well signed and adequately maintained.

From the campsite, the **Sendero Mirador trek** (1.6km round trip; 15–30mins; easy) heads west on a well-maintained trail through the lenga forest to a viewpoint above the lake. Here, trekkers are rewarded with a southerly panoramic view of the beautiful, dark blue Lago Jeinimeni set against the rugged, multi-coloured mountain range (the rocks are made up of different minerals).

There are **two other hikes** along this stretch, the first of which leads to another viewpoint on the south side of the lake (1.8km round trip; 15–30mins; easy), showing a similar perspective to the first viewing platform but this time with a northerly view of the lake. The second goes to Lago Verde (5.2km round trip; 1hr; easy) – not to be confused with the Lago Verde just west of Chile Chico, or the Lago Verde near La Junta. It passes Laguna Esmeralda after 400m and crosses the Río Desagui, before continuing for a further 2.2km to the southeastern extreme of Lago Verde. The views over the lake are superb – this is an excellent place to pause and appreciate Mother Nature at her best, or do a spot of trout fishing.

Hiking from Jeinimeni through Parque Patagonia (47km; 23hrs over 3 days; medium) This is a highly recommended trek with stunning alpine mountain

10

scenery, passing glaciers, lakes and pristine native forest. There are no dangerous high mountain passes and most of the trek is sheltered from the Patagonian wind with deep canyons scoured out by glaciers and huge, almost-vertical rock faces towering up to the sky. A high level of fitness is required to trek the 8–10-hour days with a backpack, tent, food and gear suitable for this environment. The trail entry and exit access points make this an ideal trek to do one-way to save doubling back and covering the same ground again.

Day 1: Park entrance to Valle Hermoso campsite (15km; 8hrs; medium)
The trailhead starts from the campground beside the CONAF office at the reserve entrance. Cross the bridge over the Río Jeinimeni next to the campground and walk along the southern shore of Lago Jeinimeni. This is a flat lenga-forested section with views of the lake and the surrounding mountains. After 3km is a **detour** to a wonderful view over the lake, which is worth the effort. A **second well-marked detour** to the southern shore of Lago Verde via Laguna Esmeralda lies at the western end of **Lago Jeinimeni** shortly before Laguna Esmeralda. After **Laguna Esmeralda** is the first knee-deep river crossing – walking poles or a stick will come in handy. The trail continues up a stony riverbed with numerous stream crossings but most can be negotiated without having to remove trekking boots. A **third detour** leads to the eastern shore of Lago Verde. The trail continues for a tough section along the riverbed with no visible trail markers. Look for a low point in the mountain range to the left that is covered in trees: a small red arrow on the riverbank points to where the trail leaves the riverbed towards a short but steep pass, from which there is an amazing view of Lago Verde. A stick or trekking poles will assist in the steep descent to Lago Verde, particularly at the deeper river crossing over to the northern shore (14km from the starting point). From this point, the trail continues for an hour along the riverbed and through the lenga forest to the **campsite**, with a basic toilet and small hut for cooking and eating.

Day 2: Valle Hermoso campsite to Valle Aviles second campsite (10km; 6hrs; medium)
Shortly after the campground, hikers can head right (northwest) for a 90-minute **detour** to the **Ventisquero Estero**. This is a walk up a stony riverbed to the glacier-fed lagoon. On a sunny day, the views over the lagoon towards the glacier might be worth the effort for those with spare time. The main trail continues along an uncomfortable boulder-laden section of riverbed with multiple stream crossings until it veers left and joins the **Valle Aviles**, which passes snow-capped mountains and glaciers. There is a slight climb up over a low valley pass followed by a descent into the Valle Aviles with amazing mountain scenery in all directions. After 1½ hours' trekking through a bush-clad valley, there is a bridge where the Lago Escondido overflow meets the Valle Aviles watershed, across which you'll find the first, very basic, **campsite** in the new park. From this point, it is 24km to the end of the trail at Casa Piedra in the Valle Chacabuco, so it is worth stopping here. Alternatively, it is possible to push on to a **second basic campsite** 1 hour further down the Valle Aviles.

Day 3: Valle Aviles second campsite to Casa Piedra campsite (22km; 9–10hrs; medium)
From the second campsite, the trail continues along the eastern side of the **Valle Aviles** through lenga forests with broad views of the valley. After an hour's walk, there is a swift-flowing river crossing over to the western side of the valley, shortly after which you'll come to a small hut that can be used as an emergency shelter if required. From this point the landscape changes from lenga

forests to the drier, windswept native pasture lands of the steppe – keep an eye out for guanacos and Andean condors. Some 30 minutes past the hut you'll come to the deepest river crossing: between knee- and waist-deep for the average person (subject to climatic conditions). The trail continues for several hours until a spectacular swing bridge that spans 30m over a 34m-deep canyon. This is also the northernmost point of the Aviles loop which starts and finishes at Casa Piedra, with excellent views of the glaciated landscape. The trail then heads a long way down towards a second swing bridge across the Río Chacabuco and 30 minutes later ends at the **Casa Piedra campground**, 25km from the park headquarters along the main border road between Argentina and the Carretera Austral (///gleans.chalked. remarry). Traffic is limited – you can try hitching, but be prepared to walk. It is flat and beautiful, passing large lagoons full of birds including ducks, white-necked swans, flamingos and other wildlife. The regenerating grasslands are now home to many guanacos.

A further trek to Cochrane through the Tamango sector of Parque Patagonia
The southern edge of the Lagunas Altas Trail in Parque Patagonia is very close to the northern boundary of the Tamango sector. It is possible to walk from the trail to the northernmost trails in Tamango which connect to Cochrane itself; however, the trail connecting the two parks is unmarked and not yet officially open. Seek advice from the staff at Parque Patagonia before attempting this.

Jara Beach Approximately 7km west of Chile Chico, on road X-763, is a signpost pointing north to Jara Beach (///tong.tariff.brashly). Follow the road a further 10km to a dead-end. Leave the car here and enter an abandoned campground on a stunning stretch of sandy beach, with some shelter under the trees, a semi-functioning bathroom with cold showers and flushing lavatories. Apparently this was once a municipal campground, and the reception area is a positively upmarket building for a campsite, but also abandoned. One of the best campsites for miles to wild camp, with lovely views over the lake on a slightly sheltered inlet.

⊕ AS THE CONDOR FLIES

Chile Chico is 570km south of Puerto Montt, and 280km north of the border to El Chaltén south of Villa O'Higgins. The southbound condor flying via Chile Chico is thus two-thirds of the way to the end of the Carretera Austral.

Part Four

THE SOUTHERN CARRETERA AUSTRAL

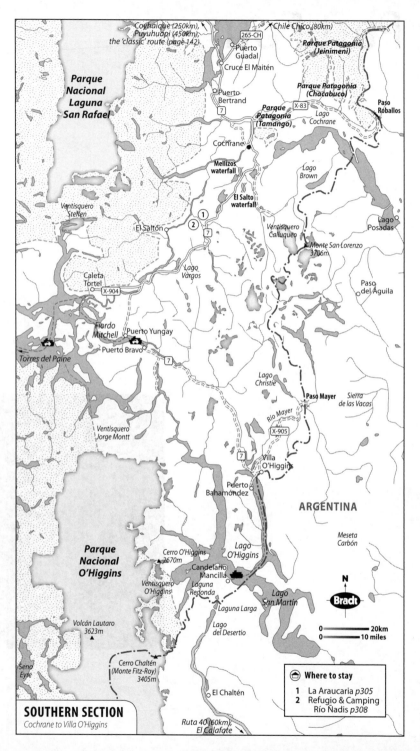

Coyhaique (250km),
Puyuhuapi (450km),
the 'classic' route (page 142)

Chile Chico (80km)

265-CH
Puerto
Guadal
Cruce El Maitén

*Parque Patagonia
(Jeinimeni)*

**Parque
Nacional
Laguna
San Rafael**

Puerto
Bertrand

7

*Parque Patagonia
(Chacabuco)*

X-83

Paso
Róballos

*Parque
Patagonia
(Tamango)*

Lago
Cochrane

Cochrane

*Mellizos
waterfall*

Lago
Brown

*Ventisquero
Steffen*

El Saltón

*El Salto
waterfall*

1

2

7

*Ventisquero
Calluqueo*

Lago
Posadas

*Monte San Lorenzo
3706m*

Caleta
Tortel

X-904

*Lago
Vargos*

Paso
del Águila

*Fiordo
Mitchell*

Puerto Yungay

Puerto Bravo

7

Torres del Paine

*Ventisquero
Jorge Montt*

*Lago
Christie*

Paso Mayer

*Sierra
de las Vacas*

Río Mayer

X-905

7

Villa
O'Higgins

Puerto
Bahamóndez

ARGENTINA

**Parque
Nacional
O'Higgins**

Cerro O'Higgins
2670m

*Lago
O'Higgins*

*Meseta
Carbón*

Candelario
Mancilla

*Ventisquero
O'Higgins*

Laguna
Redonda

Laguna Larga

*Lago
San Martín*

N

Bradt

*Volcán Lautaro
3623m*

*Lago
del Desertio*

0 ————— 20km
0 ————— 10 miles

*Seno
Eyre*

Cerro Chaltén
(Monte Fitz-Roy)
3405m

El Chaltén

⌂ **Where to stay**

1 La Araucaria *p305*
2 Refugio & Camping
   Río Ñadis *p308*

SOUTHERN SECTION
Cochrane to Villa O'Higgins

Ruta 40 (60km),
El Calafate

11

The Deep South: Cruce El Maitén to Caleta Tortel

For those doing the 'classic' route along the Carretera Austral, Cruce El Maitén is the southernmost point of the journey, before heading east towards the Argentine border. For those hardy souls continuing further south, the first village after the Cruce El Maitén junction is Puerto Bertrand, source of the thundering Río Baker, and launch pad for a number of more adventurous treks towards the ice field. To the south and east is the magnificent Parque Patagonia, one of the most ambitious private conservation projects on the continent, which merged with Jeinimeni and Tamango national reserves in 2017 to form a park to rival even Torres del Paine.

Next comes Cochrane – an up-and-coming town in southern Chile. Previously little more than a backwater, before being touted as the proposed epicentre of the controversial hydro-electric plans on the rivers Baker and Pascua (see box, page 220), Cochrane is now finding its feet as a hub for tourists, with a superb array of activities on its doorstep. Continuing 126km further south, Caleta Tortel is an atmospheric village with a slightly spooky history and is unique for having been constructed entirely on wooden boardwalks. It also serves as a good base to visit two glaciers as well as a mysterious graveyard.

While the Carretera Austral can hardly be described as 'the beaten track', the section north of Cruce El Maitén is *relatively* discovered. From this point south, traffic thins, road quality worsens, and distances between inhabited locations increase.

PUERTO BERTRAND

Blink and you may miss Puerto Bertrand, a small village of around 80 souls. Located at the dramatic southern extreme of the lake of the same name with the looming Cordon Contreras Mountains for a backdrop, this is the origin of the Río Baker, Chile's largest river in terms of volume of water. Lago General Carrera flows into Lago Bertrand, and the Carretera Austral follows the Río Baker south to Cochrane and to the eventual delta at Caleta Tortel. Thus Puerto Bertrand arguably deserves a slice of the fame that the Río Baker receives.

The village is famous as a trout fisherman's paradise, with excursions either on Lago Bertrand itself, or on the Río Baker. It is also a base for horseriding, rafting on the river, trekking towards (and even on to) the Northern Ice Field, and kayaking on the lake.

The Río Baker narrowly escaped becoming Chile's largest hydro-electric project in history, as fierce resistance from the local community finally persuaded the Chilean government not to dam the river (see box, page 220). The river discharges an average

FINDING THE BEST EXIT FROM THE CARRETERA AUSTRAL

For those without a private vehicle it is possible to cross the border into Argentina at El Chaltén further south (page 328), thus allowing exploration of the deep south before leaving the Carretera Austral. This is our recommended route. However, for those with a private vehicle, the options are more complex. The southernmost border crossing passable in a vehicle is Paso Roballos in Parque Patagonia (page 300), but exiting the Carretera here potentially means skipping superb scenery further south, including Caleta Tortel and Villa O'Higgins. The car/pedestrian ferry (page 311) from Puerto Yungay/Caleta Tortel to Puerto Natales, gateway to Torres del Paine, opens up a new route for Patagonian travel, avoiding the need to pass through Argentina. This is our recommendation.

of 870m³/s – to put this into perspective, the River Thames in London discharges under 70m³/s, so for a river of only 170km in length, it is astonishing.

The church in Puerto Bertrand was built by Padre Ronchi (see box, page 161).

HISTORY The first settlers of Puerto Bertrand arrived in the 1920s and dedicated themselves to sheep farming, but the village was not formed until the 1940s. According to the village's records, the village itself was formed when two families of original settlers, the Sanzana and Esparza families, donated part of their lands so that the Río Baker Estancia (known as Valle Chacabuco and owned by Tompkins Conservation until converted into Parque Patagonia) could have access to the water for loading their sheep. The actual limits of the donated land fell into dispute, a subject which still hasn't been fully resolved to this day. The settlers of Puerto Bertrand lived off livestock farming and forestry. The Río Baker Estancia also employed a large number of settlers as farm hands. This vast estancia was owned and run – to various degrees of financial success – by Lucas Bridges, an Englishman born in 1874 in Ushuaia, Argentina, the son of an English missionary.

In its heyday, the estancia had 85,000 sheep over 500,000ha, until 1964, when the Chilean government under the new President Eduardo Frei Montalva reappropriated the land instead of renewing its lease, distributing it among local families. This process of land appropriation was reversed from 1973 onwards under the regime of Augusto Pinochet.

In the 1980s, Puerto Bertrand made several important advances. In 1982 the first village council was made official, which allowed them to approach the state for financial assistance, much needed due to the drop in wool prices which was severely affecting the local economy and forcing several landowners to sell their land.

The village came together as a community to build a health centre, under the guidance and motivation of Father Antonio Ronchi (see box, page 161). Running water and electricity also reached Puerto Bertrand around this time. The Foundation for the Development of Aysén (an NGO dedicated to promoting economic and social change in the region) also intervened with assistance in education, business management and technical training, specifically related to farming and other needs of the local community. In 1986 the Carretera Austral reached Puerto Bertrand, connecting it with Chile Chico.

Puerto Bertrand has two organisations in charge of its tourism sector: the government-run Comité de Desarrollo Turístico (Tourism Committee), and the privately run Red de Turismo Rural Río Baker (River Baker Tourism Network).

While the former claims to have greater interests in the local community, the latter has greater resources and infrastructure, and the two organisations have had several disagreements over who should run the village's local tourism industry. Today, the peace and tranquillity of Puerto Bertrand, surrounded by nature at its most pristine, show little sign of the struggles and conflicts that its hardy settlers have lived through over the years.

GETTING THERE There is no public transport specifically to or from the village, but buses between Cochrane and either Chile Chico or Puerto Río Tranquilo and up towards Coyhaique will stop at the junction to Puerto Bertrand, which is approximately 100m from the village.

About the route
Cruce El Maitén to Puerto Bertrand (14km; 25mins; gravel) Some 14km of consolidated gravel road connects Puerto Bertrand with the Cruce El Maitén. Shortly after the junction, the road climbs along the eastern shore of the small but picturesque Lago Negro. The viewing platform on the right is one of the iconic views of the Carretera Austral, followed by the (recommended) Camping Cerro Color (page 270).

Approximately 20km south of Puerto Bertrand, just past the confluence of the rivers Nef and Baker when travelling south, is a detour to the right (south) – El Manzano Pasarela (///feast.argument.asking). This is an alternative, and very scenic, route to Cochrane suitable only for those in a high-clearance car, if not a 4x4. However, this bypasses the turning to Parque Patagonia and on to Paso Roballos, thus is not ideal for those wishing to visit either.

This detour initially passes a bridge over the Río Baker, and then continues on the south/west of the river through farmland. There are no services, no restaurants and only one hotel along this stretch (Baker Domos, page 292). The road is poor quality, with steep inclines, bare rocks, occasional horses and other animals in the road, and is not suitable for all vehicles. Perhaps because of the altitude reached, the views are more impressive than those from the Carretera Austral, taking in mountains not visible from the main route. A novelty river crossing over the Río Baker concludes this detour some 7km north of Cochrane (///cackle.disbanded.cagey). The 'boat' is called *Balsa Baker* and is an ingenious pulley system that transports up to two cars at a time across the river using only the force of the river. It runs from 08.30 to 18.00 with a break for lunch, and is free. The road reconnects with the Carretera Austral at ///lagoon.soother.semi.

TOUR OPERATORS
Monte Campamento Amador Esparza; ///implode.atoning.kitty; 📞 9 8723 2288, 9 8831 7360; e info@montecampamento.cl; w montecampamento.cl. Veteran guide in the region Arcadio Soto & his family offer a range of tours: fly-fishing on the lake ($25,000/hr); a 3hr boat trip across Lago Bertrand to the union with Lago General Carrera (the 200m-long bridge on the Carretera Austral just north of El Cruce de Maitén, $25,000 pp); a zodiac trip downstream to the Baker/Nef confluence (page 294, $20,000 pp, min 4); a full-day navigation across Lago Bertrand to Lago Plomo, with views of the Soler glacier, a short trek to see some waterfalls & then return to a gorgeous sandy beach for lunch before heading back to Bertrand ($45,000 pp, inc lunch); & a trek to Cerro Campamento itself – a short boat ride across the lake followed by a trek through forests of coigue, lenga & ñirre to a viewpoint of the Soler glacier (full day, $50,000 pp). All tours include the ability to quiz Arcadio on the fascinating history of the region. He also has a restaurant offering a decent $12,000 menu of the day (🕐 09.00–15.00 & 18.00–midnight); a small hostel (private

11

bathroom, 2 dbls for $50,000, 2 quads for $70,000, b/fast inc); & they run the Minimarket Hielo Sur (coffee, cheeses, dairy products, pasta, dried fruits, souvenirs, groceries & tourist information) on the plaza.

Rafting Buena Vista On the beach in the village; ☏9 9518 3300, 9 7881 4999. Class III rafting trips on the Río Baker with a snack at the end. Provide all equipment (wetsuits, helmets,

life jackets) & offer warm showers afterwards. Approximately 1½hrs on the river, & the total trip is around 2½hrs ($25,000 pp). Can organise boat trips to Lago Plomo or the Ventisquero Soler (small boat for up to 7 passengers, larger for up to 20) & have kayaks, stand-up boards & pedalos for rent by the hour. Also have 2 4-person hot tubs for rent on the other side of the lake; arrange 3hrs in advance for the water to heat up.

WHERE TO STAY The 10km of the Carretera Austral south of Puerto Bertrand is home to several lodges and cabins along the river's edge catering to most budgets and offering excellent fishing options. Options within Bertrand itself are more limited.

Baker Domo Lodge (4 domes) Across Pasarela El Manzano; 19km south of Puerto Bertrand (turning at ///feast.argument.asking); ☏9 5728 1034; e info@bakerdomolodge. com; w bakerdomolodge.com. Domes set in a picturesque landscape, with the Río Baker & untouched rolling hills stretching as far as the eye can see. The domes sleep up to 3 people, have a bathroom, & the obligatory spectacular view. Trekking tours including Parque Tamango & Parque Patagonia, horseriding & fishing tours are available (prior notice necessary). Private transportation, English-speaking guides & a detailed knowledge of the local area are all on offer. B/fast included with homemade bread. Dinner available (US$50 pp cash only) of lamb, salmon & hare, but prior notice necessary. Bar open 20.00–23.00, no Wi-Fi, wood-stove heating. US$150/dome, US$200 for 3 people. Takes cards, reservation & a 30% deposit is required. Delightful, a tad overpriced but isolation comes at a cost. $$$$$

Borde Baker Lodge (7 rooms) 8km south of Puerto Bertrand; ///whichever. dealings.emperor; ☏9 9583 1308, 2 2585 8464; e administracion@bordebaker.cl; w bordebaker. cl. Superior dbl rooms overlooking the Río Baker, appear rustic on the outside but modern & comfortable on the inside. All rooms have great views of the river & mountains, & are oriented such that other rooms are invisible, maintaining an intimate environment. Top-quality private bathrooms, goose-feather duvets, LED lighting, & both firewood & gas heating. The wooden, elevated pathways that connect the rooms with the main building & dining area are reminiscent of Caleta Tortel. Excellent b/fast inc. Wi-Fi available. The on-site restaurant offers an excellent wine

list & the open kitchen allows guests to watch the chef prepare gourmet delicacies ($$$$). A great place for quiet & solitude with exceptional service. Credit cards accepted. All-inclusive packages available. $$$$$

Parador Loberías del Sur Puerto Bertrand (5 rooms) 4km south of Puerto Bertrand; ///voltage.overgrown.consents; ☏67 235 1112; e recepcion@loberiasdelsur.cl; w loberiasdelsur.cl/puerto-bertrand. Perched along the Río Baker, this is a recent addition to the Loberías del Sur portfolio with a quality to match. 35km north of Parque Patagonia & 8km to the confluencia (page 294), it's a strategic base from which to explore. 3 dbls, 1 twin & 1 trpl, all finely furnished with great bedding, private bathroom, cable TV, Wi-Fi. B/fast with local ingredients included, laundry available. A lovely building that feels more like a private house than a hotel, with cosy communal areas, all surrounded by trees & the river, a terrace with great views & a path around the property down to the river, where there are 2 embarkations. Offer fishing, trekking & horseriding, & can arrange rafting, in addition to the various tours offered by Loberías (page 205), in particular Calluqueo glacier just south of Cochrane or the marble caves just to the north of Bertrand. The property has a decent restaurant but dinner & lunch should be arranged in advance at the time of making a booking (reservations via head office). Otherwise eat in Puerto Bertrand. $$$$

Rápidos del Río Baker (5 cabins) 3km south of Puerto Bertrand; ///corks.unfinished. singing; ☏9 5666 1893, 9 9218 1140; e info@ rapidosdelriobaker.com; w rapidosdelriobaker.cl; ⏰ Sep–Apr. One of the more economical cabins along this stretch of the Río Baker, these are simple

& slightly dated but utterly peaceful & with access to the river. Sleep 4 or 6 people. Set among trees & built with brick & wood, they have new terraces facing the river. The kitchen is adequate, hot water is fine, & there is patchy internet in some cabins. The restaurant can be booked with substantial anticipation, & they have 2 zodiacs for guided fishing trips on the Río Baker. Heating via wood stoves, cooking with gas. If the restaurant is closed there are shops or restaurants in Bertrand, which may be open. Stock up in advance – more suitable for self-catering. **$$$$**

⚐ **Mary's Cabin** (1 cabin) West corner of plaza; ☎ 9 9777 2097; e mamogavero@yahoo. com. Fantastic newly built cabin with 2 dbl beds for up to 4 people ($100,000) & a roaring wood stove to keep warm & dry clothes after a day of trekking. Mary, the delightful owner, is originally from the USA, has lived in Bertrand for 23 years, & is able to help with any questions or tours in the region. Excellent bathroom with great rain-shower, fluffy towels, excellent beds, a freshly baked loaf of bread in the morning, off-road parking, patchy internet (in the entire village), & might do laundry if you ask nicely. Set within the native forest, but with a lake view & utterly peaceful. Highly recommended, especially for those who like dogs & cats. **$$$–$$$$**

⚐ **Bertrand Lodge** (3 cabins) Coastal road, by the pier; ///misused.dancer.picky; ☎ 9 3248 4214, 9 7946 3810; e bertrandlodgepatagonia@ gmail.com; w patagonianow.cl. Quality wooden cabins for 2, 5 or 6 people ($90,000/160,000/180,000), well-equipped kitchen & lake view. No Wi-Fi & b/fast not included, but available in the restaurant ($5,000). Small restaurant/café (⊕ 09.30–22.00) with excellent food (ceviche,

steak, salmon, roast lamb, & a decent pisco sour). One of the best places to stay & eat in the village. Takes credit cards. **$$–$$$**

⚐ **Hospedaje Buena Vista** (2 rooms, 4 cabins) Neff, 150m above beach; ///opted. accountancy.clogging; ☎ 9 7881 4999, 9 9518 3300; e cabanasbertrand@gmail.com. As the name suggests, all accommodation with views over the lake. Dbl & twin room in the main house, both with private bathroom ($30,000/room). Cabins for 3, 4 & 6 people ($50,000/70,000/80,000), all with 1 dbl bed & sgls, full kitchen & bathroom. Ample off-road parking, no cable TV, patchy Wi-Fi, laundry available for small fee, take cards. They also run the rafting operation on the beach. B/fast not inc. **$$**

⚐ **Residencial Los Coihues** (5 rooms) Amador Esperanza 265 (on the plaza beside the church); ///summoned.bleats.absurd; ☎ 9 4495 6563; e evelynpasitamartinez@gmail.com; ⊕ all year. A basic but clean backpacker hostel. Shared bathroom, laundry service, ample parking & Wi-Fi. A decent b/fast is $5,000 extra, with eggs. Good value. **$**

Å **Camping Centro las Lengas** (16 sites, 9 with roof) ///highrise.antibiotic.poses; ☎ 9 3220 7603; e centro.laslengas@gmail.com; w centrolaslengas.cl. Cool campground 200m from the lake & a short stroll to the village, sites have their own water, electricity, BBQ with firewood & light, bathrooms for men, women & those with disabilities, all with hot showers. Washing machine & communal fridge available. Motorhomes $60,000/night, camping/night is $28,000 for 1–3 people, or $48,000 for 4–6 people. Rent bikes & kayaks. Plans to install a food truck & offer rafting trips. **$**

✖ **WHERE TO EAT AND DRINK** There are few formal restaurants in Puerto Bertrand. Tour operator Monte Campamento also operate a restaurant (page 291). The restaurant in Bertrand Lodge (see above) is definitely worth a visit.

✖ **McPatagonal's Costanera** ☎ 9 5735 1701; e flor29@villegas@hotmail.com; ⊕ 10.00–22.00 daily in high season. Continuing the trends seen across all of Patagonia, Bertrand has adopted not 1 but 2 upmarket foodtrucks. This one, on the shore, is run by Frosinia & Claudio, with a limited range of good-quality sandwiches including a vegetarian option, juices & tea/coffee. **$$$**

☀ 🖳 **Coihue Café** 8km south of Puerto Bertrand; ///accompany.bulldozing.secures; ☎ 9 7878 1267, 9 9076 7676; e coihuecafe@gmail. com. Just north of the Borde Baker Lodge lies an unusually good café, in a slightly bizarre location. Sit on the deck overlooking the river & order coffee, tea, biscuits, juices, cakes or homemade ice cream & be pleasantly surprised. Also do a full b/fast,

11

lunches & dinners by reservation. Run by Sofia & Tomás, a Chilean couple who quit the rat race in the north to set up something small & peaceful, & they have succeeded with aplomb. The café was picked up by *Financial Times* journalist Claire Wrathall, whose article on the Carretera Austral, otherwise positive, lamented the lack of good coffee. Stumbling across this café she commented, 'Café Coihue – named after a distinctive species of Andean beech – serves the real deal, the best by a mile of our trip, not to mention a fine line in cakes and toasted sandwiches, the basis of most meals hereabout. It also has a superb location overlooking Río Baker'. Global fame indeed. $$

SIGHTSEEING AND EXCURSIONS Activities in Puerto Bertrand revolve around mountains and water. In addition to fishing, rafting on the Río Baker is popular, with tour operators in Bertrand or based in the lodges further south. Any accommodation in this region can arrange a local guide for water-based activities. Hiking towards the ice shelf is possible, but generally less formal than in other areas, without marked trails maintained by CONAF. It is essential to obtain local information (and ideally a guide), and is more suited to experienced trekkers and mountaineers.

There are two **river confluences** between Puerto Bertrand and Cochrane. The first, where the rivers **Nef and Baker** meet (12km south of Bertrand; ///uplifting. catsuit.fruit), is particularly spectacular – a ferocious waterfall plunges 10m before the differing colours of the two rivers swirl together dramatically as the Baker heads further south. It is clearly signposted with parking facilities (free entry) on the west of the Carretera Austral 20km south of Puerto Bertrand or 30km north of Cochrane; a small trail leads down to a viewing platform. The second, lesser-known confluence is the union of the rivers **Chacabuco and Baker**, accessible from the Carretera Austral via a short walk west where the road towards Paso Roballos and Parque Patagonia heads east from the Carretera Austral.

PARQUE NACIONAL PATAGONIA

(w conaf.cl/parques/parque-nacional-patagonia; ⊕ park: all year, lodge & campgrounds: Oct–Apr; $8,200/4,100 adult/child) Nomenclature is confusing here, depending on whether discussing the park pre- or post-merger. Formerly there were three parks: Reserva Nacional Jeinimeni (south of Chile Chico); Reserva Nacional Tamango (north of Cochrane); and the region in between these two parks, Chacabuco Valley, which was acquired by Tompkins Conservation (TC; now called Rewilding Chile) in 2000. Following the donation of this last section to the Chilean state in 2017, all three parks were merged into one, collectively called Parque Nacional Patagonia, and subdivided into three sectors: Sector Jeinimeni in the north, Sector Valle Chacabuco in the middle, and Sector Lago Cochrane/Tamango to the south.

The Río Chacabuco and the main road connecting the Carretera Austral to Argentina at Paso Roballos (page 300) run through the Valle Chacabuco sector. The 3,045km² Parque Patagonia extends from Cochrane almost to Chile Chico and is one of the highlights of the entire Carretera Austral, increasingly challenging Torres del Paine (in the Magallanes region) as one of the premier parks of the Americas. For more on the work of Kris and Doug Tompkins, see the box on page 134.

TC developed important infrastructure within the park including the main headquarters, the lodge, the restaurant, accommodation for staff and management, a school, roads, offices, and scientific facilities. Most materials used in construction were sourced locally and recycled where possible. Food is organic and sourced locally. Six bridges were constructed to facilitate the trekking trails.

Parque Patagonia is located in one of the few east–west valleys in Chilean Patagonia. There are three main trails (Avilés, Lagunas Altas and Lago Chico) and a number of shorter trails (eg: Vega, Confluencia), but new trails are opening imminently (Los Gatos, Furioso, etc). The park offers unspoiled wilderness, extensive wildlife, excellent trekking, and luxury accommodation for those with decent travel budgets. For the rest of us, the campgrounds are more than adequate. Note that it is not permitted to light fires in the park, or indeed any park in Patagonia (Argentine or Chilean), due to the ease with which forest fires can begin. Camp stoves are essential.

HISTORY The Valle Chacabuco had been used by Tehuelches for centuries, if not millennia. A number of archaeological sites discovered in the region, and the various cave paintings on both sides of the border, are testimony to ancient civilisations living in these regions. In 1906 William Norris reached the Río Baker from Argentina via the Valle Chacabuco on his fateful journey to Caleta Tortel (see box, page 312).

In 1908 the Compañia Explotadora del Baker leased the land around Valle Chacabuco from the Chilean government to set up a large-scale sheep farm, managed by Lucas Bridges. From the outset the estancia struggled to make a profit, forcing Bridges to increase the density of sheep. Overgrazing further reduced profitability, and pushed the estancia into debt. Shareholders of the Sociedad, including Bridges' own family, began selling their shares. The lease expired in 1964 and the government did not renew it. Under the agrarian reform of President Eduardo Frei the Sociedad was liquidated. The land was appropriated by the government and given to local families. In 1967 both Tamango and Jeinimeni national reserves were formed, but the Valle Chacabuco, the land between the two, was still privately owned.

In 1980 Pinochet claimed the entire Valle Chacabuco from these families and sold it at auction to a Belgian landowner, Francisco de Smet, for US$0.5 million. The overgrazing was so severe – with parts of the valley so arid and windswept that they resembled desert – that de Smet was once again unable to turn a profit from livestock. Cheaper Australian wool further lowered the international price of wool, and many estancias across Patagonia were unable to compete. Large-scale sheep farming was simply not viable. De Smet sold the 173,000-acre estancia to TC in 2004, for US$10 million.

TC gradually bought up neighbouring (and equally unviable) estancias. Their first course of action to restore the various ecosystems was to remove all fences and livestock, so that native animals could roam freely. Livestock were sold gradually so as not to depress prices and thus harm the livelihood of other farmers in the region. Invasive plants were removed by an army of volunteers, and native grassland was replanted. Gradually native species, pushed to the brink of extinction, began to bounce back. It is now estimated that Valle Chacabuco is home to 10% of the world population of huemules. Pumas, previously hunted by ranchers (illegally – the puma is a protected species), were also allowed to roam freely, and fears that they would multiply in number and devastate the native huemul population have proved unfounded. TC embarked on an ambitious project to tag and monitor pumas in order to study their behaviour and discovered that the greatest enemy to the endangered huemul was in fact dogs from the nearby town of Cochrane.

As the grasslands began to show signs of recovery, so too did the guanaco population, which in turn attracted more pumas. Pumas remained the vilified enemy of local ranchers and allowing pumas to roam freely was disliked by many. Evidence from the tagging project dispelled such myths: the puma population within the park was stable, and individuals were territorial. Local ranchers were quick to blame Valle Chacabuco for their sheep lost to pumas but were slow to produce evidence supporting their claims (such as sheep carcases), and even slower to admit illegally hunting pumas themselves.

Doubtless pumas did occasionally eat sheep and TC sought a solution to this problem. They began breeding guard dogs (great Pyrenées) that had demonstrated for centuries an uncanny ability to protect herds from predators. When the puppies are only 20 days old they are integrated into the herd, drinking sheep milk and sleeping on sheepskins. A rigorous training programme takes approximately a year, and the dogs successfully guard their herd with almost 100% success. Valle Chacabuco had a corral that suffered not a single loss of sheep to pumas since the guard dogs were introduced. The dogs are now provided to local ranchers, and puma kills have declined dramatically.

Recognising that livestock was the foundation of the local economy, as well as the main source of employment to many people in and around Cochrane, TC offered all former employees of the estancia ongoing employment as park rangers or conservation workers, some of whom still work in the park today.

GETTING THERE Parque Patagonia is most easily visited with a private vehicle or bicycle, as the trails are far apart from one another and the park headquarters, lodge and campground are 11km east from the main junction with the Carretera Austral. There is no public transport to the park headquarters, although all buses along the Carretera Austral must pass by the main junction. However, private vehicles may offer rides within the park.

If making a reservation at the lodge, they can help with arranging a taxi from Cochrane if required.

About the route
Puerto Bertrand to Parque Nacional Patagonia (43km; 1hr; gravel) The gravel road from Puerto Bertrand to the junction leading to Parque Patagonia, and on to Cochrane, is mostly good quality. There are no services along this section, but two points of interest: La Confluencia, the short trail and lookout over the confluence of the Baker and Nef rivers (page 294), and the alternative route to Cochrane (which bypasses the park altogether; page 302). The main road through Parque Patagonia and on to the Paso Roballos border crossing is the X-83, which joins the Carretera Austral 16km north of Cochrane or 32km south of Puerto Bertrand (///gatherings. graduated.impatient). It is a further 11km to the main park buildings (///sustain. unhinge.vending), or 72km to the border.

The Carretera runs parallel to the Río Baker, which is visible for large sections of the journey until turning off to Parque Patagonia. Be aware of guanacos on the road.

WHERE TO STAY AND EAT There is only one **hotel** in Parque Patagonia, and three formal campgrounds in this sector (others are available in the Tamango and Jeinimeni sectors). Camping is possible only in designated areas. The lodge and restaurant are expensive, considering the minor logistical inconvenience of bringing food from Cochrane (the nearest town with any shops for stocking up on supplies). For those on even a reasonable daily budget the camping and cooking combination will save a lot of money. Given the array of activities in the park, this is perhaps not the best location to splash out on expensive accommodation, only to spend most of the day up a mountain. However, budget constraints aside, this is superb accommodation in a unique setting, with a reasonable restaurant.

There is also a handicraft **shop** in the main park building selling a range of products from the region, including knitwear, honey, wooden bowls, baskets, linen products, etc, as well as books and maps. However, for camping equipment and basic food supplies, stock up in Cochrane.

🏠 The Lodge at Chacabuco Valley

(6 rooms) Parque Patagonia headquarters; e reservas@vallechacabuco.cl; ⏰ Oct–Apr. This is a splendid building made entirely from recycled wood & stone from the quarry within the park. Rooms accommodate 2, 3 or 4 people, & it is essential to reserve in advance. Each room is unique, finished to a high standard, with decent hot water, comfortable beds & a desk. The views from the rooms are generally towards the southern side of the valley, so you can watch wildlife from your bed. The main sitting area, where an excellent b/fast is served (included – every conceivable item available including eggs to order, in apparent unlimited supply),has a small bar, huge windows facing the valley & large comfortable sofas. There is a wide range of coffee-table books, mainly published by the Tompkins & focused on nature & conservation. The internet connection is a tad slow. Remove shoes at the door, as the wood & tiled floors scratch easily – there is underfloor heating to prevent cold feet! In summary, this is without a doubt one of the finest accommodations along the entire Carretera Austral, & an ideal launch pad for trails in the region. The downside? All this comes at a high price: rooms range from US$150 pp (quadruple occupancy) up to US$350 (sgl occupancy). A very pleasant treat, but an extravagant one if planning to spend most of the day hiking mountains. **$$$$–$$$$$**

🏕 Stone House Campground

(Camping Casa de Piedra) (7 covered quinchos, various uncovered, rarely fills up) 25km east of Parque Patagonia HQ; ///gleans.chalked.remarry; ⏰ Oct–Apr. No reservations, operates on a first-come-first-served basis. Basic facilities, solar showers, start/end point for Avilés trek. **$**

🏕 West Winds Campground

(60 sites) Behind park HQ; ///instrument.rift.midnight; ⏰ Oct–Apr. No reservations – operates on a first-come-

first-served basis, but rarely fills up. Complete bathrooms, decent sinks for washing dishes, & facilities to wash clothes, but the water is tepid at best. However, given the lack of alternative accommodation in the park, and the modest price ($5,000, paid in the headquarters), this is a small gripe. Sites around the edge have covered tables & benches. The main campground is verdant lush grass, sufficient to lure guanacos for a quick bite. It can get surprisingly cold in the campground at night so be sure to have a decent tent & warm sleeping bag, even in Jan. No electricity. **$**

🏕 Alto Valle Campground

(8 sites with quincho shelters) 28km east of park HQ; ///ourselves.reissues.punters; ⏰ Oct–Apr. No reservations – first come first served, near base of Lago Chico trail close to the border. Includes 2 group sites, bathrooms & solar showers. Free.

🍴 Bar and Restaurant El Rincón Gaucho

Parque Patagonia HQ; ⏰ Nov–Apr 13.00–14.00 & 20.00–22.00 daily. This place has somewhat of a monopoly within the park &, as such, while this is a lovely restaurant in a delightful setting, it's perhaps not the best value for money. The building was constructed to the same high quality as the lodge, with hypnotising huge black-&-white photographs of animals & Mount San Lorenzo along the interior walls, & a view towards the east of the valley through the main windows, where there will invariably be a few dozen guanacos grazing. Picnics can be ordered in advance, consisting of a sandwich, fruit & cookies; or a simple set lunch (US$20). Dinner is again a set menu varying daily, generally consisting of a salad, main course & dessert (US$35). Wine is overpriced. Budget-conscious visitors may be better off in the campground eating pasta! Nonetheless very good quality food & service. English spoken. **$$$$**

THE MAIN TRAILS There are currently three main trails in the park extending 113km in total, with more scheduled to open. From the junction with the Carretera Austral to the Argentine border, the road is 72km passing through many areas worth exploring as well as the trailheads of the Avilés and Lago Chico trails. Maps are available in the park headquarters and are worth obtaining. The trails are generally well marked with the exception of the Lago Chico trail.

In addition to the abundant grasslands that bear no resemblance to the former arid overgrazed estancia purchased in 2004, native species are once again flourishing here. Lakes along the main road through the park are teeming with birds, including flamingos. Black-faced ibis are also common (*Theristicus melanopis, bandurria* in Spanish), and relatively unafraid of humans. Their distinctive long beaks enable them to eat worms and insects, and they are often seen wandering around grassy sections probing for their dinner. Another bird often seen in the lakes is the black-necked swan. The park is also frequented by one of the smallest owls in the world – the Patagonian pygmy owl; but this is not strictly nocturnal and thus easier to spot. However, they are small and well camouflaged. Also, perhaps surprisingly, Austral parakeets are quite common, but seem brightly coloured and tropical for such a region – this is the most southerly parrot in the Americas.

Guanacos are so abundant as to border on becoming a nuisance! Do not be surprised to wake up in West Winds campsite and find a nosey guanaco sniffing around your tent, and take care driving along the main road. Andean condors are slowly returning to the park. As carrion-eaters, they lack talons for hunting, and the increasing guanaco population is an integral part of their diet. The park does not use pesticides – such chemicals previously hampered the development of condor chicks. Vizcachas (*Lagidum viscacia*) are also common. Previously hunted for their meat and fur, they are now flourishing. Their greatest natural predators are foxes and pumas, but having made their homes in inaccessible cracks in rocks, their dexterity and loud warning calls, they are able to survive.

Other fauna include culpeo foxes and the hairy armadillo. Somewhat like a small ostrich, the lesser rhea is also relatively common and can often be seen running in a state of seeming panic with no particular destination in mind. The park is also home to approximately 30 pumas, but sightings are rare.

The rewilding programme of TC is actively working with four species within the park. Beyond monitoring pumas and the endangered huemul deer, they expect to release an Andean condor in late 2020. The most ambitious programme is a reintroduction centre for Darwin's rhea (*ñandu* in Spanish), a species that was almost locally extinct. Since the start of the programme the rewilding team has reintroduced 60 individuals. They are mostly found in the grasslands towards the border but over time are expected to disperse throughout the valley. Through radio collars, monitoring key species offers important data on wildlife populations, their hunting habits and territory.

The **Avilés trail** (47km; 23hrs over 3 days; medium) is described in detail from page 283. The southern portion of this trail can also be visited as a day trek (16km; easy), and forms a loop travelling on both sides of the Río Avilés, thus no need to backtrack on the same path. Note that the trailhead is 25km west of the park headquarters. Also note that if doing the full trek through the Jeinimeni sector this ends at the northern park entrance 55km south of Chile Chico.

The **Lagunas Altas trail** (23km loop; 1 day; medium) begins at the West Winds campground close to the park headquarters and takes a full day. It winds through forests and passes a number of lakes, with views across the Valle Chacabuco. This is probably the most accessible trail for those without private transport, as it begins and ends close to the park headquarters. It ascends the southern side of the valley and reaches the border of Sector Tamango. Keep eyes peeled for Andean condors. Eventually this trail will extend further south to the shore of Lago Cochrane and then head southwest to the Río Cochrane and on to Cochrane. Currently, however, this is an unmarked trail. Confident and well-equipped mountaineers may be able to complete this alone, or hiring a guide in Parque Patagonia may be possible (ask in the reception, or email the park in advance). A shorter trail, **La Vega** (7km; easy) connects the West Winds campsite with the park headquarters, passing the cemetery where the grave of Doug Tompkins can be visited.

The **Lago Chico trail** (26km from main road, 14km with 4x4 to trailhead; ½–full day; medium) is not well marked, but is fairly straightforward. The trail begins 40km west of the park headquarters and is thus easier for those with a private vehicle. From the trailhead at La Juanina do not attempt to drive up the path in anything other than a decent 4x4. As with the Lagunas Altas trail, the trek begins by ascending the southern side of the valley, initially on a gravel road through a forest (7km one-way, easy). Over the ridge the view is stunning, looking out towards Lago Cochrane with Monte San Lorenzo behind. From this point, there are no further trail marks, so take care – there is no mobile-phone coverage. However, the lake provides an obvious point of reference as long as you remember how to return to the ridge at the correct location for the return descent. Expect to see large herds of guanaco, and the forested sections provide ample birdwatching opportunities. The loop trail is apparently 12km, but we got entirely lost and never found the trail; instead we used the lake as a reference. It is possible to bushwhack to the shore of Lago Cochrane. If in a decent 4x4 and able to ascend the initial gravel road, this may be a half-day trek. However, for those walking the gravel road, and particularly those intending to approach Lago Cochrane, this is a full day. Unless you're intending to camp, be sure to return to the ridge before dusk. The trail is not technically demanding, but the lack of markers may mean this trek is more suitable for those with some mountaineering experience or those with a guide.

Other trails include La Confluencia, a pleasant and easy 3km stroll from the park entrance on the Carretera down to the union of the rivers Baker and Chacabuco.

PARQUE PATAGONIA MUSEUM (Free entry if have paid to enter the park, otherwise $2,000 pp) Within the visitor information centre is one of the most impressive museums of all the Carretera Austral (admittedly competition is not stiff on this topic). The museum explains the history and geography of the park, but presents a far broader overview of the key conservation issues facing the planet, in line with the deeper ecological views of the Tompkins, and with thought-provoking, interactive and audio/visual displays. Terrifying images of overpopulation and waste; the history of the planet from 5,000BC to the present day; mankind's impact on land and sea; and a particularly sobering display of species extinction from 1800, projected to 2040. There is a thorough description of the different geologies of the park, the population and use and abuse of the Chacabuco Valley since the first known inhabitants (approximately 8,000 years ago), and a broader look at the settlement of Patagonia. The final exhibit is a 180°cinematic video (in English and Spanish) that takes a sharp look at mankind's tendency to dominate, extract, exploit and hold all other species to ransom – for those that are familiar with the writing of Doug Tompkins it is as though he is narrating the video, and it does contain an interview with Doug. An important museum that is worth spending a couple of hours in, and as with most infrastructure built by the Tompkins, it is tastefully constructed with high-quality exhibits and good descriptions.

THE SCENIC ROAD THROUGH THE PARK TOWARDS THE BORDER The road through the park connects the Carretera Austral with Paso Roballos to Argentina. Even if you've no plans to cross the border, it's worth driving this road, as it passes a number of important sights as well as numerous lakes and opportunities to observe wildlife. This route follows the Valle Chacabuco, with towering mountains on both sides, verdant vegetation following decades of overgrazing, and abundant animals and birds. This was a historical entry point to the region used by the early pioneers. As with the trails, it is worth picking up a map at the park headquarters or downloading one from the website (page 294). If not using the park facilities or trekking in the park, use of this road does not require paying the park entrance fee.

The entire route is 72km one-way from the junction with the Carretera to the Argentine border, on gravel. Beware of animals on the road. Traffic is sparse. While a 4x4 is not strictly necessary, a high-clearance car is advisable, particularly if crossing into Argentina. From the park headquarters, 11km east of the junction, this would be a 122km round trip, possible in a day; if you're combining this with either of the trails along this section (Avilés or Lago Chico) it will be a long day. From Cochrane, 16km south of the junction, this would be a 168km round trip. Also consider that the nearest petrol station is in Cochrane.

At the park entrance is the confluence of the rivers Baker and Chacabuco (La Confluencia trek, page 294). As soon as you enter the park, guanacos are abundant. The initial 8km are of limited interest, until Valle Chacabuco becomes visible. Shortly thereafter lies the park headquarters offering the only formal accommodation in the entire park, and the only restaurant.

Continuing east towards Argentina the road passes **Lago Cisnes** and **Laguna de los Flamencos** (meaning 'swans' and 'flamingos' respectively). Both lakes are of interest to ornithologists, and indeed, the entire park is a birdwatcher's paradise. Again, guanacos are abundant in this region. Some 25km further east of the park entrance is the **Puesto Casa de Piedra (Stone House Campground)**, the trailhead north along the Avilés trail towards Jeinimeni. A further 15km east is La Juanina – a small gathering of houses, formerly part of an old estancia, now used by park employees. This is the trailhead for the **Lago Chico trail**. Within walking distance of La Juanina is the original 100-year-old house used by Lucas Bridges. This has been restored to its former glory and converted into a museum in 2020 (free entry). Danka Ivanoff (page 278) was consulted in the process of restoring the house as the main historian of the region, having published the definitive history book on Lucas Bridges.

NOTE

This is currently the southernmost border crossing on the Carretera Austral by car or motorbike – the more southerly border crossings are pedestrian-only. However, the ferry from Puerto Bravo/ Caleta Tortel (with or without vehicle) to Puerto Natales is an alternative means to leave the Carretera Austral further south, but is not an international border.

The landscape begins to transform at this point, with the first signs of arid steppe. Vegetation becomes scarcer, with fewer to no trees, just shrubs. Approximately 10km east of La Juanina is the **Chilean border control**, although it is a further 10km to the Argentine border.

The province of Capitán Prat covers 37,242km², has a population of approximately 4,000 inhabitants and consists of three communes: Cochrane (the provincial capital), O'Higgins and Tortel. It is the southernmost province in Aysén, and the extreme southeastern corner of it penetrates south of the 49th parallel. Cochrane itself is sleepy, but has a delightful plaza, and a smattering of shops and restaurants, as well as a petrol station and the last ATM before Argentina or Puerto Natales for those continuing south.

HISTORY The Valle Chacabuco and the region surrounding what is now Cochrane was discovered in 1899 by the explorer Hans Steffens as he traversed the Río Baker for the first time. In 1908, the Sociedad Explotadora del Baker, owned by Magellanic cattle farmers under management of Lucas Bridges, acquired the land within the valley in order to construct a large-scale sheep farm (Estancia Chacabuco).

The town of Cochrane originated in 1929 as a small settlement to house farm employees. It was originally called 'Las Latas', and located within the estancia, 8km east of the junction with the Carretera Austral heading towards Argentina, in what is now Parque Patagonia. However, the shareholders of Estancia Chacabuco disliked the proximity of the village and decided to move its inhabitants claiming that a lack of water was the principal reason. The new village was called 'Pueblo Nuevo' (New Town) and it was from here that the present town grew. It was formed in 1930 by government order.

The town was later renamed Cochrane to honour Thomas Cochrane, 10th Earl of Dundonald, a British naval captain and radical politician who made great contributions to Chilean independence (see box, below).

(see box, below)

THOMAS COCHRANE

Following a career in the British Royal Navy, Cochrane was elected to the House of Commons in 1806. He campaigned for parliamentary reform and his outspoken criticism of the war and corruption in the navy made him powerful enemies. After being convicted in the Great Stock Exchange Fraud he was expelled from parliament in July 1814, stripped of his knighthood, fined £1,000 and humiliated in a pillory.

His naval career, however, was far from over. Cochrane arrived in Valparaiso, Chile in 1818 when the country was preparing for its battle for independence. On 11 December 1818, upon request of Chilean leader Bernardo O'Higgins, Cochrane became a Chilean citizen. He was appointed Vice Admiral and took charge of the Chilean navy in Chile's war of independence from Spain.

Cochrane developed a taste for battles for independence, and in 1823 took command of the Brazilian navy in their quest for independence from Portugal. In 1827 he helped Greece's independence from the Ottoman Empire. In 1831 his father died, and Cochrane inherited the earldom. He returned to the British navy the following year. His knighthood was finally restored in 1847 by Queen Victoria. He died in 1860, and is buried in Westminster Abbey. The Chilean navy hold a wreath-laying ceremony at his grave in his honour each year in May. In 2006, the Chilean navy acquired a Type 23 frigate from the British navy (formerly the HMS *Norfolk*) and named her *Almirante Cochrane*.

The Deep South: Cruce El Maitén to Caleta Tortel   COCHRANE

11

The town of Cochrane was officially inaugurated on 17 March 1954, with ten houses in total. The streets and sites of Cochrane were finally laid out in 1955 by three land surveyors: Carlos Pizarro Araneda, Germán Pozo and Fernando Malagueño. On 26 October 1970 the municipality of Cochrane, which then belonged to the Department of Chile Chico, became part of the Baker Department together with the villages of Villa O'Higgins and Caleta Tortel. Esteban Ramírez Sepúlveda became its first governor. In 1975 a new province was created, Capitán Prat, and Cochrane became its capital.

GETTING THERE
About the route
Parque Patagonia to Cochrane (16km; ½hr; gravel) This section is gravel, mostly of good quality. The road narrows as it winds along the Río Baker beneath. Be aware that guanacos may stray into the road. The view down to the valley is wonderful, with the rich autumnal colours of grasslands and other vegetation. There is a petrol station at the entrance to Cochrane.

By bus Cochrane recently had the novel idea to build a bus terminal. Previously buses left from the owner's house. The terminal has vastly simplified matters. Several buses go north to **Coyhaique**, including **Buses Don Carlos** (☏ 67 221 4507; depart 07.00 Tue, Thu, Fri & Sat, return 09.30 Mon, Wed, Thu & Fri) and **Buses São Paulo** (☏ 67 252 2470; depart 06.30 Mon, Wed, Fri & Sun, return 09.00 Tue, Thu & Sun). **Buses Marfer** (☏ 9 7756 8234) go to Chile Chico at 08.00 on Fri, returning at 16.00. **Buses Katalina** (☏ 9 9932 4320, 9 7989 5669) go from Cochrane to Tortel (depart 10.00 Thu, Fri & Sun, return 14.00 same day (Thu & Sun) and 16.00 Fri). **Buses Cordillera** (☏ 9 5641 1858, 9 8134 4990) go from Tortel to Cochrane (depart 08.00 Mon & Thu, return 18.00 same day). **Buses Glaciares** (☏ 9 7754 7214, 9 3428 2348) go from Cochrane to Tortel (depart 11.00 Tue & Wed, return 15.00 same day, & 14.00 Fri & Sun, return 17.30 same day). **Buses Gardi** (☏ 67 239 1845) offer buses from Cochrane to Villa O'Higgins (depart 08.00 Mon, Wed & Sat, return Tue, Thu & Sun – call to check times).

The website w municochrane.cl/turismo/transporte is fairly up to date with bus times and routes.

TOUR OPERATORS
Jimmy Valdes Baigorria ☏ 9 8425 2419; e lordpatagonia@gmail.com; w lordpatagonia. cl. Highly recommended guide focused on 2 main routes – the multi-day Ruta de los Pioneros trek from Cochrane to Villa O'Higgins (one of the definitive trails in southern Chile, guide recommended), & treks around San Lorenzo & the Ventisquero Calluqueo. Various tours offered for all skill levels, including advanced trekking. Very professional & experienced guide capable of veering way off the beaten track, safely.

Katenke ☏ 9 8209 4957; e katenke@outlook. com. A hidden gem run by veterinarian Cristian Restrepo, out the back of Café Tamango. Cristian is a certified PADI Open Water instructor & a licensed operator of water activities. He offers full scuba-diving courses in Lago Cochrane, as well as recreational dives in the lake. He also speaks English. The water in the lake & river is unbelievably transparent – unlike many of the glacial lakes of marvellous colours but limited visibility – & he even offers a snorkelling trip down the Río Cochrane. It begins walking distance from the café, & while the swim is 3.5km it ends walking distance from the café again. The price, $40,000 pp, includes all equipment hire with decent 7mm wetsuits suitable for the temperature of the water, which ranges from 10 to 12°C. It also includes all safety training, & is available to people without any prior experience (as long as they can swim!). Floating down the river with the absolute minimum of effort is as much a meditation as a swim. At times the river narrows & the forest encroaches sufficiently to create an almost tunnel-

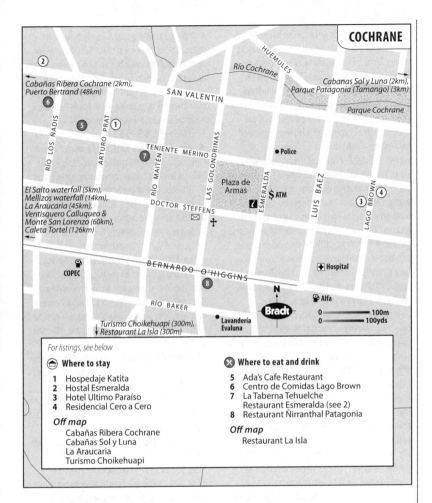

Cabañas Ribera Cochrane (2km),
Puerto Bertrand (48km)

Río Cochrane

HUEMULES

SAN VALENTIN

Cabañas Sol y Luna (2km),
Parque Patagonia (Tamango) (3km)

Parque Cochrane

RÍO LOS NADIS

ARTURO PRAT

TENIENTE MERINO

RÍO MAITÉN

LAS GOLONDRINAS

ESMERALDA

LUIS BAEZ

LAGO BROWN

Police

Plaza de
Armas

ATM

El Salto waterfall (5km),
Mellizos waterfall (14km),
La Araucaria (45km),
Ventisquero Calluqueo &
Monte San Lorenzo (60km),
Caleta Tortel (126km)

DOCTOR STEFFENS

BERNARDO O'HIGGINS

COPEC

Hospital

RÍO BAKER

N

Alfa

Bradt

0 — 100m
0 — 100yds

Turismo Choikehuapi (300m),
Restaurant La Isla (300m)

Lavandería
Evaluna

For listings, see below

Where to stay

1 Hospedaje Katita
2 Hostal Esmeralda
3 Hotel Ultimo Paraíso
4 Residencial Cero a Cero

Off map
Cabañas Ribera Cochrane
Cabañas Sol y Luna
La Araucaria
Turismo Choikehuapi

Where to eat and drink

5 Ada's Cafe Restaurant
6 Centro de Comidas Lago Brown
7 La Taberna Tehuelche
Restaurant Esmeralda (see 2)
8 Restaurant Ñirranthal Patagonia

Off map
Restaurant La Isla

like effect. The depth ranges from 50cm to 10m, with some fun opportunities for swimming the furthest distance possible in a single breath! The riverbed varies from rocks to a clay base, a variety of reeds, minor cases of didymo, occasional tree trunks, endless trout, & a range of colours (on a bright day). The tour is best done in the morning, and takes a total of 3hrs door-to-door including training, with about half of this spent in the water. For the more adventurous, the tour can also be done at night, with torches. Although drifting along a river might not be the most obvious tour in

the region, for those fancying a change from treks, lakes, horses & glaciers this is a surprisingly fun, relaxing adventure, well executed by a competent guide. Cristian is also active in maintaining the cleanliness of the river & periodically arranges days of manual refuse collection with children from the local schools. A highly recommended tour.

Ultimo Paraíso (see below) Fishing with Carlos from the hotel of the same name along the Río Cochrane. US$400/day for 1–2 people including lunch. (Dry) fly fishing for brown & rainbow trout, spinning for coho & king salmon.

WHERE TO STAY *Map, above, unless otherwise stated*

✳ 🏠 **Hotel Ultimo Paraíso** (7 rooms)
Lago Brown 455; ///forums.discussions.reflex;
📞 67 252 2361, 9 8900 0654, skype nela.

francia; **e** hotelultimoparaisochile@hotmail.es;
w hotelultimoparaiso.cl; ⏰ all year. Delightful
accommodation run by an English-speaking

Spanish couple, Carlos & Nela, who have lived in Cochrane for 2 decades. Wi-Fi, Direct TV, laundry service & one of the best b/fasts on the entire Carretera Austral with cheese from La Junta & eggs to order. Quiet, spacious rooms which are warm in winter, cool in summer. The rooms can be adapted to sgl, dbl or trpl occupancy, & are made mostly of cypress, all with well-equipped bathrooms. Wood stoves in each room for the winter, & tasteful pictures of the region adorn the walls. Wonderfully comfortable beds to rest weary bones after hundreds of kilometres on bumpy gravel. Carlos is a dedicated fisherman & can advise on the top spots to hook a fish, as well as the usual tours in the region. They are not formal operators (although Carlos can easily be persuaded to offer a fishing trip), but know the reliable guides, & are happy to help. The full b/fast includes homemade Spanish delicacies. Also has a pleasant but small garden, & a cosy bar/sitting area. Prices may be high by Cochrane standards, but this is the only truly quality place to stay in town. Strict reservations policy; essential in peak season. Credit cards accepted. **$$$$**

🏠 **Cabañas Ribera Cochrane** (2 cabins); ///enlists.constituted.patch; 📞 9 8199 7633; e patagoniawulf@gmail.com; w cabanas-ribera-cochrane.negocio.site. Excellent 4-person cabins a little out of town. Take the Carretera north – 500m out of town there is a road to the left. Follow this road 1.5km to a red gate. Sited on the Río Cochrane, you can literally fish from the (large) garden, go for a leisurely swim, or take the kayak for an evening meander along the river. Excellent beds with proper duvets, double-glazed windows for the winter, Direct TV, Wi-Fi & fully equipped (washing machine available). Wood-stove heating, BBQ in the garden, dining area & separate sitting area. The best cabins in, or slightly outside, Cochrane. US$155/120 in high/low season. **$$$–$$$$**

🏠 **Cabañas Sol y Luna** (3 cabins, 2 apts) 1km towards Reserva Nacional Tamango; ///bookkeeping.acquisition.fleeting; 📞 9 8157 9602, 9 6900 1114; e xime.mardone@gmail.com; w turismosolyluna.cl; 🕐 all year. Good-value, high-quality 4-person fully equipped cabins and 2-person apts. Slightly out of town (15mins' walk) but offering utter peace & quiet, sauna & outdoor hot tub under the Patagonian stars to relax weary bones (additional cost). Well furnished

with pleasant sitting area & lovely garden. No restaurant, so stock up in town. Wood stoves for heating, laundry available, Wi-Fi & parking. Family business & can help arrange local tours. Head north on Luis Baez (past mate-shaped building). Over bridge & then veer right towards Reserva Nacional Tamango. Recommended. All cost $75,000/night. **$$–$$$$**

☀️ 🏠 **Hospedaje Katita** (12 rooms) Arturo Prat 536; ///enraging.spruce.slugged; 📞 9 7881 0631; e gonzalezvasquezanamaria@gmail.com; 🕐 Oct–Apr. One of the better budget options in Cochrane. Simple, clean, adequate bathrooms, basic b/fast inc. No laundry, communal area with TV downstairs, very friendly & chatty owner. Will remind visitors of grandma's house, & the owner, Alicia, fits the profile perfectly, having lived in the house for 53 years. Located 2 blocks from the central plaza just around the corner of Ada's restaurant (see opposite). Lavatory paper occasionally in short supply but frequent reminders to Alicia can rectify this. Wi-Fi available, off-road parking. **$$**

🏠 **Hostal Esmeralda** (7 rooms) San Valentin 141; ///parroted.protected.transcribed; 📞 9 6212 4687. Basic accommodation in 6 sgls & 1 dbl above the rather good restaurant downstairs (see opposite). Private or shared bathroom. Credit card, Wi-Fi, no laundry. **$$**

🏠 **Residencial Cero a Cero** (12 rooms) Lago Brown 464; ///relaxed.limps.edgier; 📞 67 252 2158, 9 7607 8155; e ceroacero@gmail.com. A clean, well-run hostel. The thick new mattresses ensure a good night's sleep & are a pleasant change from the thinner & narrower mattresses that most hostels offer. The carpeted rooms are spacious with good natural light. 8 rooms have private bathrooms (4 twins, 3 dbls, 1 trpl), the rest have shared bathrooms (twin & dbl). Decent b/fast, Wi-Fi, central heating. **$$**

🏠 **Turismo Choikehuapi** (3 cabins) 300m past COPEC; ///bikes.sternest.released; 📞 9 9888 5256, 9 7643 8952; e opazomorales@gmail.com; w cabañascochrane.cl. Given the quality of the restaurant on the same property (La Isla, excellent), it is little surprise these cabins are also great. Sleeping 4, 5 or 6 people & ranging in price from $60,000 to $70,000 accordingly, the cabins are fully equipped right down to decent cutlery & plates. All the usual goodies – Wi-Fi, decent hot water, good sitting & dining area. Only notable absence is laundry, but that is available 500m from the cabins (page 306). Very cosy, great for families & set within a large garden. Offers b/fast in the restaurant next door for $5,000 pp – in all likelihood visitors to these cabins will also visit the restaurant for lunch or dinner. **$**

⅄ La Araucaria [map, page 288] 45km south of Cochrane; ///resets.parkland.garnished. This campsite is situated 3.5km from the Carretera Austral on a gravel trail at the northern end of the Barrancoso Bridge – a minor detour for cyclists or trekkers, which isn't excessively hilly & is definitely worthwhile. This is the entry point for the Cordon Los Ñadis region (page 308). It is a fantastic campsite with spectacular views

towards snow-capped mountains. Also has a small refuge with a bed, but a viable option for those with a sleeping bag & mat in the event of a downpour. The owner, Marisol, grows her own fruit & vegetables for sale to visitors, & can also prepare an asado (there is an outdoor & a covered BBQ area). No mobile-phone coverage, but contact can be made from the Municipality in Cochrane (radio frequency VHF4580). 1 trail on the grounds, but ample opportunities to explore the region. This is an original pioneer ranch. Offers horse treks in the region, & has homemade wool products for sale. A bargain at $3,000 pp, ample room, cold showers, simple kitchen available, & simply stunning views. **$**

✕ WHERE TO EAT AND DRINK *Map, page 303*

✕ Ada's Café Restaurant Teniente Merino 259; ///fleeced.allege.busies; 📞 9 3387 1959/60; e adascaferestaurant@gmail.com; ⏰ 12.30–15.30 & 19.30–midnight daily. One of the biggest restaurants in Cochrane with a large menu covering lamb, fish, chicken, pizza, & more. Good meats & asado. Good selection of wine, beer (bottled & draught), & cocktails. Excellent service, clean, & popular with both locals & tourists. Good with kids. Bustling atmosphere when busy in this otherwise sleepy town. **$$$**

✕ Centro de Comidas Lago Brown Los Ñadis 535; 📞 9 8827 4507; e rinacarmen@gmail. com; ⏰ 12.30–21.30 Mon–Fri. Sandwiches, pichangas, pizzas, steak, salmon, milanesa. Beer & wine selection including D'Olbek on tap. Clean & modern, but lacking in character. Food is reasonable, standard Chilean fare with sizeable portions. **$$$**

✕ Restaurant Esmeralda San Valentin 141; ///parroted.protected.transcribed; 📞 9 6212 4687; ⏰ 11.00–16.00 & 19.00–23.00 daily. One of the better options in a town with a few options. Menu includes meat, chicken, salads, fish & other standard Chilean fare. Decent wine & beer. The lomo fogón is the speciality of the house, a steak with spicy sauce of merken, peppers & garlic, highly recommended ($11,000). Budget hostel upstairs (see opposite). **$$$**

✳ **✕ Restaurant La Isla** 300m past COPEC; ///bikes.sternest.released; 📞 9 9888 5256; e opazomorales@gmail.com; ⏰ Jan & Feb 13.00–16.00 daily, other months w/ends only. A contender for best restaurant in Cochrane, the

lamb has become legendary. Reservation not usually required, capacity for 30 people but does fill up in high season. Seasonal Patagonian food, rotating menu daily, but always with a salmon, vegetarian, lamb & meat option. The lamb is some of the best on the Carretera Austral with seasonal vegetables & fantastic sauces. Excellent range of desserts, local beer (del Meyer & Arisca), homemade bread, good service & a nice vibe – highly recommended. The motto of the restaurant is 'something more than good food' – & it achieves this. Food aside, the building is lovely, set within a garden & is technically on an island. The cabins are also excellent, & there is a small shop selling local products. **$$$**

✕ La Taberna Tehuelche Teniente Merino 372; ///dings.bedtime.rescues; 📞 9 6628 3961; ⏰ noon–23.30 (later Fri & Sat, earlier Sun). Brewpub & the best nightlife in Cochrane, massive *tablas* for 2 people could feed a horse ($16,900). Lively atmosphere, locals & foreigners alike. Good range of beers brewed on site as well as rotating regional beers, fairly typical pub food, décor thematic of the region. Live music & even bingo offered occasionally. **$$**

✕ Restaurant Ñirranthal Patagonia Av Bernardo O'Higgins 650; ///mellows.panel. lovable; 📞 9 7878 2621; e terecata_cu@hotmail. com; ⏰ 10.00–23.00 daily. A bustling little place located a block off the plaza. The menu has all the classics: beef, chicken, pork, lamb, conger eel, merluza & salmon. What distinguishes Ñirranthal is its surprising variety of sauces compared with elsewhere. Diners can choose their dish a lo pobre, with merquen (chili pepper), pepper sauce, mushroom sauce, caper sauce & shrimp sauce. Omar, who is co-owner with his wife Teresa, insists that if you're arriving late in the day & call ahead, they'll stay open for you. Good Patagonian fare. Opening hours can be irregular, so either call ahead, or have a backup plan. Takes credit card & foreign currencies except Argentine pesos. $$

OTHER PRACTICALITIES The ATM (Banco Estado) on the plaza is a vital visit as there are none further south, and the next ATM to the north is in Coyhaique or Chile Chico. Be sure to fill up with **petrol** while in Cochrane at COPEC (cnr Arturo Prat & O'Higgins; ///chug.pretzels.query): the next petrol station to the south is in Villa O'Higgins, at least 224km, or in Puerto Río Tranquilo to the north, 111km. There is a Petrobras petrol station 1km out of town as you enter from the north. There are **shops** in Cochrane, but only for common supplies. If you get to **Lavandería Evaluna** (Río Baker 3; ///dinky.clod.interest; ✆9 9126 4284; ⊕ daily) early enough, laundry can be ready the same day.

Repairs

Alfa Bernardo O'Higgins, opposite the hospital; ///salary.instrument.arena; ✆9 9212 7663; e marvinarriagada@yahoo.com.ar. Basic mechanical repairs & service including light fabricating & soldering. Has a small supply of spare parts for common brands. No motorbikes (there is no motorcycle mechanic in town). Tyres, batteries, has car scanner. For punctures, call Don Segua ✆9 6691 6303).

SIGHTSEEING AND EXCURSIONS Cochrane offers a surprising range of activities, growing each year. The snorkel trip down the Río Cochrane is simply sublime and a relaxing way to spend a couple of hours (page 302). Fishing trips can be arranged through Hotel Ultimo Paraíso (page 303).

Parque Patagonia – Sector Tamango (w conaf.cl/parques/parque-nacional-patagonia; $8,200/4,100 foreign adult/child, $4,100/2,100 Chilean adult/child) Although part of Parque Patagonia, this sector retains its old name locally. This sector is nearly 7,000ha and located 6km northeast of Cochrane. The reserve is bordered by the Tamango, Tamangito and Hungaro mountains on three sides and the Río Cochrane and lake to the southeast, and has a dry temperate climate in the summer but snow in the winter. Principal flora includes lenga and coihue trees, Ñirre (*Nothofagus antarctica*), calafate, mata verde and chaura shrubs. The large Andean condor is sometimes spotted here, as well as the southern lapwing, great grebes, black-crowned night herons and kingfishers, plus various migratory birds. Foxes and guanaco are common, and it is also possible to spot the elusive huemul. The park also has a resident population of pumas, and it is possible to observe the Patagonian skunk and the hairy armadillo.

There is a basic CONAF **campsite** at the park entrance beside the crystal-clear waters of the Río Cochrane ($6,000 pp). A small map is available from the park entrance where you pay the entrance fee.

There are **two main treks**. The first, **El Hungaro** (16km round trip; 7–9hrs; medium), goes to Bahía Paleta along the shores of Lago Cochrane. This is a full-day excursion and offers the best chance to see the huemul in the wild as they are relatively protected in the park. The second trek, **Las Correntadas** (7km round trip; 3–4hrs; easy/medium), runs along the northern bank of the Río Cochrane to a viewing point where the river enters Lago Cochrane. There are numerous viewing points over the crystal-clear river, reportedly one of the most transparent in the world. It is possible to take a small boat trip up the Río Cochrane to the lake (ask in headquarters for details). For the more adventurous, there is also a trail directly to the Valle Chacabuco and on to the Parque Patagonia headquarters. Ask at the park headquarters for details and a map. Trekkers can arrange a guide from the park entrance. The trails are well marked and maintained, but a guide can give an interesting insight into the huemul deer and how they are trying to protect them, as well as helping to identify birds and trees within the reserve.

Ventisquero Calluqueo and Monte San Lorenzo At 3,706m, the ice-covered Monte San Lorenzo is the second-highest mountain in the region and straddles the Argentina–Chile border roughly 60km south of Cochrane. Major work is being put in to the access road, which was previously only suitable for 4x4s. There are two approaches, one that leads to the attractive Ventisquero Calluqueo which itself touches the small Lago Calluqueo, and the other to the Fundo San Lorenzo and on to the Refuge Toni Rohrer that serves as the base camp for ascents of Monte San Lorenzo. To get to the refuge, it is best to arrange a horse in Cochrane or directly from the Soto family. Luis Soto lives on a small farm at the base of the mountain and getting in contact with him is no easy task – ask at the tourist information booth on the central plaza.

To get there from Cochrane, head south approximately 6km and turn left on a gravel road just before Laguna Esmeralda. The scenic drive borders Laguna Esmeralda to the east and follows the Río El Salto until reaching a fork in the road after about 25km. To the right is the road to the Ventisquero Calluqueo, which is a further 20km along a mostly single-lane gravel road until the trail to the lake starts. To the left is the road to the Soto farm where the trail starts up the valley to the Refuge Toni Rohrer. Until the new road is finished, this road is a rough 4x4-only track that slowly deteriorates. Buses Cordillera traverse this route twice a week (page 302).

The drive to the **Ventisquero Calluqueo** takes under 2 hours, but crossing the small lake requires the services of Jimmy Valdes Baigorria who keeps a small boat on the lake (page 302), or a slightly longer trek if the boat is not available. Finding the start of the trail is not particularly easy. Once the glacier is visible the road starts uphill, and the condition deteriorates rapidly. There is just enough room to turn a car around. The trail itself is a short 20 minutes to the lake. The boat ride across is about 1 hour one-way, where there is a pleasant area for a picnic and taking pictures.

The hike up **San Lorenzo** is technical, requiring ice gear and skis, and takes at least three days. Once at the Soto farm, the refuge is another 3 hours' walk and has enough space for around 20 people. From there it's at least 8 hours up to another campsite near the Ventisquero Agostini, and then another 12 hours on ice and over crevasses to the summit. This is a challenging climb for professional mountaineers.

Mellizos waterfall A dramatic 10-minute detour, the impressive Mellizos waterfall is 14km south of Cochrane on the Carretera Austral heading towards Caleta Tortel (///fame.redoubts.rocketed). Park at the bridge over the Río El Salto and walk 100m to the west, along the river. Take extreme caution as there are no guard rails: the rocks are slippery, it's a vertical drop into fast-moving water tumbling over a rock-filled waterfall, pounding through a gulley.

El Salto waterfall in Valle Grande From Cochrane it's 5km to El Salto – a majestic waterfall on the Río El Salto (///eligibility.skims.masterful). Head south on the Carretera and turn right just past the rodeo after the bridge over the Río Cochrane on to a well-maintained gravel road (X-892, ///insufficient.scrapes. minders). Wind through a picturesque valley until reaching a suspension bridge.

Hans Steffen was one of the first, and most legendary, explorers in the region. His first expedition involved discovering a trail between what is now Cochrane and the mouth of the Río Baker, almost a century before the Carretera Austral connected these regions. The principal purpose of the expeditions was to discover the potential for developing and exploiting this region. Based on Steffen's report the Sociedad Explotadora del Baker leased the land around the Río Baker, including the Chacabuco Valley in what is now Parque Patagonia, to develop sheep and cattle ranches. Under the management of Lucas Bridges various routes were discovered in the region in order to transport animals from the fertile grazing lands around the Baker to the Pacific. The Paso San Carlos is a particularly precarious part of these trails, carved into a 590m-high cliff and only 1–2m wide in places. This was the principal route for the development of the entire region, and in recognition both of the engineering feat accomplished, and the historical importance of this pass, it was declared a National Monument in 2014.

Cross the bridge on foot and find the path off to the left that leads to several viewing areas to appreciate the voluminous cascades. The round trip can also be walked in around 6 hours from town or cycled in about 4 hours.

Las Huellas del Paso San Carlos Some 45km south of Cochrane from La Araucaria (page 305), the gravel track (X-902 technically) continues into the little-known region of Cordon Los Ñadis. The main strategic location from which to explore this area is **Refugio & Camping Río Ñadis** [map, page 288], 7km beyond Araucaria, crossing a rickety bridge that might not appear car-worthy, but is. The refugio is run by Lili and set within a 500ha working ranch. Lili can arrange and guide the trek to the San Carlos Pass. She has dormitory-style accommodation for ten people with kitchen, hot water, ample camping, and a great quincho built around a tree. Lili sells bread, tea, fruit and vegetables to visitors. It is a full-day horse ride to visit the pass ($30,000 pp), and there are also two hiking trails in this sector (Caracol and Inmigrante). It is possible to cross the Río Baker south of the pass and visit 'El Gaucho del Baker', the only other accommodation in the region, from where two other trails begin (Río Ventisquero and Las Truchas). There are other trails, and one campground, on the south of the Río Baker, but these require a boat to cross the river – Lili can arrange this. Note that there is no internet or mobile-phone signal in this region – the only form of communication is via radio or satellite phone. In order to facilitate communication Johana Muñoz, based in Cochrane and in contact with those who live in this region via radio, can be reached on ☏9 9941 0799. The only source of information on the region is on their Facebook page (🛉 Huellas del Paso San Carlos), including a map of the region. The main purpose of visiting this area is for some remote trekking and visiting the pass, and to enjoy a relatively undiscovered part of the Carretera Austral.

Cochrane is 645km south of Puerto Montt, and 190km from the border to El Chaltén south of Villa O'Higgins.

Caleta Tortel is certainly worth a visit. However, the first edition of this guidebook listed Tortel as one of the top ten highlights of the entire Carretera Austral, an honour denied the village in this edition. This decision was taken on the basis of four factors: insufficient infrastructure to support the ever-expanding number of tourists; overpriced accommodation and food, beyond what might be considered reasonable given the relative isolation of the village; the visitors' centre at the Isla de los Muertos might be functional but has limited the eeriness of the graveyard; and the quantity of rubbish, abandoned boats, engines lying by the side of the boardwalks left to oxidise and general contamination have created a slight sense of abandonment. The village is, nevertheless, still worth visiting, and is an obligatory stop for pedestrians taking the ferry to or from Puerto Natales, but a day trip might suffice.

If staying, the logistics of getting to a hotel with a suitcase can be a challenge. There is no ATM but finally there is a COPEC petrol station in the village. Mobile-phone coverage is disastrous, WhatsApp is the most reliable means to communicate, and the nearest decent shop is in Cochrane. There is one mechanic just outside the village on the way to the aerodrome (Juan; ☏ 9 9536 3379). Trips to the glaciers require a substantial boat journey. Glaciers further north are comparably magnificent but less isolated, more accessible, slightly more crowded but potentially cheaper to visit. Undoubtedly the village retains a unique charm and the graveyard is worth a visit, particularly if combined with a kayak trip. There is only one decent hotel, and it fills up fast. For those staying at Entre Hielos Lodge, and particularly visiting the surrounding area on their boat, Caleta is a lovely village at the very upper end of the price scale. For those on a tight budget and unlikely to visit the glaciers accessed from Caleta Tortel, pushing north to Cochrane or south to Villa O'Higgins might be wiser.

The commune of Tortel, within the province of Capitán Prat, covers an area of approximately 21,000km², slightly larger than Wales, and has only two populations: Caleta Tortel and Puerto Yungay. The total population is a little over 500 people (versus 3.1 million in Wales). Vast parts of the commune are protected – to the south lies the Parque Nacional O'Higgins containing a large part of the Southern Ice Field; to the north lies the southern extreme of the Parque Nacional Laguna San Rafael and the limit of the Northern Ice Field; and to the west lies the remote Reserva Nacional Katalalixar, accessible only by boat.

Caleta Tortel is built almost entirely on boardwalks at the base of the mountain around a series of small bays. The sea is visible through the planks beneath your feet, and the boardwalks extend for kilometres. Houses were gradually built above the first houses, up the side of the mountain, involving a series of steep stairs weaving chaotically between houses and trees. Even small plazas with playgrounds have been built on these boardwalks. Thanks to this architectural design, every house has a view over the bay, and out to the Baker Canal. There are no cars or horses in Caleta Tortel, and it is not suitable for wheelchairs or anyone with limited mobility. Park your car or bicycle, or descend from the bus, at the upper part of the village, ideally put a rucksack on your back (suitcases are not so convenient), and descend the stairs to the main village. There is a water taxi service available upon request – ask at the tourist information centre.

Besides being a truly astonishing village, the main points of interest in this commune are the relatively accessible glaciers in both ice fields – Caleta Tortel is located close to the estuary of the Río Baker, which feeds into the Baker Canal out to the Pacific, and separates the two ice fields.

11

Although not visible (or accessible, to a great extent) from Caleta Tortel, the village is not far from the (in)famous Golfo de Penas. The Navimag ferry (see box, page 29) sails between Puerto Natales and Puerto Montt, mostly along interior canals, but it does sail in the open ocean at Golfo de Penas, one of the roughest stretches of sea in the world responsible for endless tales of seasickness and prolonged visits to the bathroom! The relatively new ferry between Puerto Natales and Caleta Tortel/Puerto Bravo traverses the Baker Canal and heads south along the Canal Messier between the O'Higgins and Katalalixar parks to the west of the Southern Ice Field, avoiding the Golfo de Penas. Opinions are divided as to whether the ferry has been beneficial for the charm of isolated Caleta Tortel, and whether the infrastructure is capable of supporting more visitors.

HISTORY This region was first inhabited by indigenous nomadic canoeists called the Kawésqar, who have since almost entirely vanished. The last remaining members of this group live in Puerto Eden, one of the most remote inhabited locations in Chile – along the Messier Canal to the west of the Southern Ice Field at approximately the latitude of Monte Fitz Roy. The first documented case of a European 'discovering' this region is Hernando de Magallanes in 1520. Various subsequent expeditions in search of the Lost City of the Césares (see box, page 116) visited the region, and interest in the Río Baker Estuary attracted a number of explorers in the late 19th century, including the famous German explorer Hans Steffen in 1898. In 1901 the Chilean government awarded a concession to Juan Tornero to populate the region with 1,000 families, which led to the formation of the Compañia Explotadora del Baker, and eventually to the mysterious death of some 70 Chilote workers, some of whose graves are visible on the famous Island of the Dead (see box, page 312) – one of the greatest mysteries of all of the Carretera Austral, and a major tourist attraction in Caleta Tortel.

Various companies remained in the region attempting to exploit the abundant timber resources until the early 1940s, when a series of fires largely rendered the region uninhabitable. The Chilean Armada established an outpost in what became Caleta Tortel in 1955, and development continued at a leisurely pace, including a small landing strip, until the village was formally founded in 1981, with under 300 inhabitants. Development continued, with a renewed municipal building and school, construction of additional boardwalks, drinking water, sewage works, a small hydro-electric plant, a library, a covered central plaza (it rains extensively in Caleta Tortel), and various piers for boats. In 1999 work began on the 23km road connection to the Carretera Austral, completed in 2003.

Famous priest Father Ronchi (see box, page 161) built the church, FM radio station and set up several productive projects in Caleta Tortel. Testimony of this is the hull of the boat, which he brought to improve the transfer of passengers and stimulate activities of timber production. Although the boat is no longer in use today and its condition has deteriorated, its shell is still intact. Outside one of the well-known chapels is a life-size wooden statue of Father Ronchi in honour of his memory.

In 2000 Prince William spent ten weeks in Caleta Tortel on an Operation Raleigh trip – the inaccessibility of the village largely kept the media at bay, and the locals, though aware of who the prince was, treated him no differently from anyone else. He received no special favours on the project: chopping logs, lighting fires at 06.15 and making porridge for the team of 16, all of whom slept on the floor in sleeping bags in a communal room – a far cry from the prince's usual accommodation. Details as to his actual activities are scarce, but included working in the community, painting schools as well as trying his hand as a DJ for Radio Tortel. Kate Middleton did a similar trip the following year.

Besides hosting future kings, the main economic activities of the region are the extraction of cypress, tourism and a limited amount of agriculture. The car and pedestrian ferry service to Puerto Natales began in 2017, when it finally became possible to travel between the regions of Aysén and Magallanes without having to travel via Argentina, trek across the border from Villa O'Higgins (without a car), or charter an expensive private boat.

GETTING THERE
About the route
Cochrane to Caleta Tortel (126km; 2½hrs; gravel) From Cochrane the road heads south approximately 103km on gravel to the junction for Caleta Tortel (///elitist.qualifier.painters). From here it is approximately 23km further to Caleta Tortel to the west, or on to Puerto Yungay, where the boat crosses the Mitchell Fjord to Río Bravo for the final stretch of the Carretera Austral, to Villa O'Higgins (another 100km). To the initial junction the road is fairly decent gravel with occasional steep descents and ascents, often along vertical cliff edges. Although the road is not as well travelled as more northerly sections of the Carretera, occasional oncoming vehicles may be in the centre of the road and travelling at speed. Long sections of this road are raised, thus take extra precaution to avoid a wheel going over the edge – it is often better to stop entirely until oncoming vehicles pass. The road is spectacular, with high snow-capped mountains above and the thundering Río Bravo below. One particularly photogenic moment is the confluence of the rivers Bravo and Colorado, although take care pausing on the blind corners to take a photo. When the road grader has recently traversed it can be particularly treacherous. There are no imminent plans to pave this section.

By bus Buses Katalina (🕿 9 9932 4320, 9 7989 5669) go from Cochrane to Tortel (depart 10.00 Thu, Fri & Sun, return 14.00 Thu & Sun, 16.00 Fri). **Buses Cordillera** (🕿 9 5641 1858, 9 8134 4990) go from Tortel to Cochrane (depart 08.00 Mon & Thu, return 18.00 same day). **Buses Glaciares** (🕿 9 7754 7214, 9 3428 2348) go from Cochrane to Tortel (depart 11.00 Tue & Wed, return 15.00 same day, & 14.00 Fri & Sun, return 17.30 same day). **Buses Isabel** offer a thrice-weekly service between Caleta Tortel and Villa O'Higgins (page 322).

By ferry Transbordadora Austral Broom (see page 37 for detailed information) go from Puerto Yungay/Caleta Tortel to Puerto Natales weekly (Sat; departs Puerto Yungay (with cars) at 20.00 or Caleta Tortel (pedestrians only) at 23.00, arriving Puerto Natales at 16.00 Mon (44hrs, via Puerto Eden), returns 05.00 Thu, arriving Caleta Tortel (pedestrians) at 22.00 Fri or Puerto Yungay (cars) at 01.00 Sat). TABSA have a small office behind Borde Río Expediciones (page 60), but it is rarely manned other than when the ferry arrives/leaves – it's easier to book tickets via w tabsa.cl or by phone.

TOUR OPERATORS
Borde Río Tortel Expediciones Sector Centro; ///huddle.arched.commercially; 🕿 9 9940 8265, 9 3452 8586; e borderiotortel@gmail.com; 🛈 Borderio Tortel Expediciones. 4 main tours offered by Enrique Fernandez. All kit, wetsuits, snacks & hot drinks are provided from his base in the centre of the village by the *plaza de armas*, which has changing rooms, bathrooms, & a place to leave luggage if necessary. The first is to the Isla de los Muertos directly by boat (2½hrs,

11

A mere 20 minutes by boat from Caleta Tortel, in the Río Baker Estuary, lies the mysterious **Isla de los Muertos (Island of the Dead)**. Prior to the formation of the village of Caleta Tortel, the only inhabited spot in this region was on the northern shore of the estuary, called Puerto Bajo Pisagua, a few hundred metres from the graveyard. The intrigue surrounding this small graveyard has become one of the most enduring legends in the region, and there is still no definitive explanation of why nearly 70 people died on the island in the winter of 1906, 28 of whom were buried in anonymous graves marked only with a cross.

The following summary is taken from a superb book entitled *Caleta Tortel y su Isla de los Muertos*, written by the well-known historian Danka Ivanoff Wellmann – see pages 278 and 344 for more details.

The Chilean government had awarded 13 concessions in the region of what is now the commune of Tortel as early as 1893, despite the lack of even a basic map, let alone a population. A wealthy businessman named Mauricio Braun was interested in the region for possible exploitation of timber, and acquired the rights from one of the concession holders, Juan Tornero. The first investigative sorties were not overly optimistic regarding the possibilities, but Braun did not despair. Bringing other partners into the venture, they stumbled across a young, adventurous British explorer called William Norris in Buenos Aires. He was promptly hired by the Compañia Explotadora del Baker to investigate the region, establish a cattle ranch, and to find a direct route from Argentina to this isolated region on the other side of the Andes. On the first trip, in early 1905, armed with an ill-defined number of co-explorers, some horses and a substandard map, Norris managed to find Puerto Bajo Pisagua by following the Río Chacabuco (through the future Parque Patagonia), and travelling down the Río Baker. Braun had sent a number of men to Bajo Pisagua to meet Norris. These men, and others soon to arrive, were to work on improving the route from Argentina until Norris's return in April the following year, when he would bring the animals. In Norris's 1939 account of events is a wonderful description of the contrast between the arid Argentine side of the border and the verdant Chilean side, and his optimism for the region:

> There are no words to describe the contrast between the east and west. The east is a torrid, rocky and windswept desert. The west is a territory with water, covered with forests and meadows, with an excellent climate and very little wind in the valleys. Very near the coast, within reach of the river [Baker], are millions of cypresses in very good condition…I think the Baker Valley, when the outside world eventually discovers it, will be the best place in South America. The central valleys and higher regions are the best for raising sheep and cattle. There is grass, water and trees everywhere, sufficient to build many cities. In the lowlands good vegetation is unlimited.

With a sufficiently persuasive story for Braun, Norris returned to Argentina to buy the animals required to establish a local industry, which would also exploit the local timber. He had assured those who remained in Bajo Pisagua, under the interim control of Florencio Tornero (brother of the former concession holder), that he would return by April 1906. Accompanied by thousands of cattle and horses, the second journey was a little more complex and delayed for bad weather. Norris eventually arrived on 15 May that year to La Colonia, further upriver, where he installed the animals. Tornero was under strict instructions to return the employees to Chiloé before the winter, but when Norris travelled down to Bajo Pisagua he was surprised to find the entire team awaiting him, hungry and tired. What subsequently occurred that winter of 1906 is the subject of much debate.

Some have suggested the men were poisoned by the company in order to avoid paying them. Others say they were accidentally poisoned by a toxic liquid required to wash sheep that had contaminated the food on the rough journey by sea to Bajo Pisagua. But neither story holds up to reason. Why would the company kill its staff, only to have to replace them thereafter? And why would they have brought such toxic liquids if there were not yet any sheep in the region? And yet the 'poison story' remains the dominant account of what happened to this day. So why did so many people die at Bajo Pisagua that winter?

In June 1906 Tornero had waited for a passing boat on an island for 12 days, surviving on shellfish alone. He finally caught a boat to Punta Arenas and immediately arranged for a northbound boat to pick up the group, but the boat sank in the Magallanes Strait with five crew and vital cargo destined for Bajo Pisagua. He then arranged for a second boat from Talcahuano to rescue the group, but a devastating earthquake struck Valparaiso on 16 August and the boat was requisitioned and sent to Valparaiso to assist with the rescue effort. But this does not explain why he had not made greater efforts to get the men off the island before the winter. The men were seafaring Chilotes, and Norris mentioned in his memoirs a relative abundance of animals in the region (including guanaco and ostrich). How is it these men had not decided to fish and hunt for food as supplies dwindled? And perhaps the greatest tragedy of all – Norris had begged some men to help him row upstream to where the cattle were located in order to obtain food, but for fear of missing the boat they so eagerly awaited to take them off this dreaded island, none agreed to help. And if the men were murdered, why were they buried in individual graves? But if exhaustion, starvation and scurvy were the culprits, who built the coffins, dug the graves and made the crosses? Why did Norris not detail the events in his memoirs of 1939, but only in a private letter to his uncle written in 1906? And yet, even in this private account, he failed to mention that he was nearly lynched in Chiloé when he finally managed to rescue some of the Chilotes to their island, as described in an account written by a friend of his. Or was her account flawed? And why is one of the crosses inscribed 'Here lie the bodies of Margarita Gallardo and her son Anselmo' dated 1915, some nine years after the fateful winter in question?

In late September 1906 the surviving members were able to return to Chiloé, although 12 died on the journey. The following year many of these survivors returned to work in Bajo Pisagua, with Norris, employed by the same company. Had these survivors believed the company had attempted to murder them, how likely is it that they would return the following year? The company never paid Norris for his work.

We may never know what truly happened in Bajo Pisagua in 1906. Stories of mass murder attract attention and sell boat trips to tourists, but starvation and scurvy are the most likely explanations for the events of that fateful winter. But they are not the *only* explanations.

11

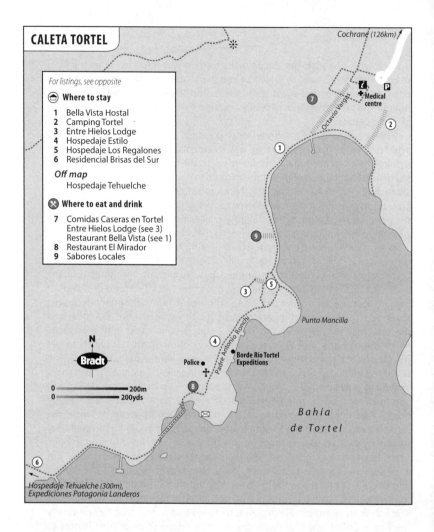

Cochrane (126km)

For listings, see opposite

Where to stay

1 Bella Vista Hostal
2 Camping Tortel
3 Entre Hielos Lodge
4 Hospedaje Estilo
5 Hospedaje Los Regalones
6 Residencial Brisas del Sur

Off map
   Hospedaje Tehuelche

Where to eat and drink

7 Comidas Caseras en Tortel
   Entre Hielos Lodge (see 3)
   Restaurant Bella Vista (see 1)
8 Restaurant El Mirador
9 Sabores Locales

Medical centre

Octavio Vargas

Punta Mancilla

Padre Antonio Ronch

Borde Río Tortel
Expeditions

Police

Bahía de Tortel

Bradt

N

0 ———— 200m
0 ———— 200yds

Hospedaje Tehuelche (300m),
Expediciones Patagonia Landeros

$10,000 pp, min 6 people). Enrique is an expert on the local flora & fauna & can give a detailed insight into the legends & superstitions of the locals. The 2nd tour is to the Isla de los Muertos by kayak, via a waterfall & boats abandoned by the first settlers, navigating along the lesser tributaries of the Río Baker Delta (5hrs, $35,000 pp, min 2 people, highly recommended). The 3rd tour is kayaking along the beach (2hrs, $20,000 pp). The 4th tour is also a full day, to the glacier Steffen ($70,000 pp, min 7 people), including light trekking within the Katalalixar reserve. Enrique lives in Tortel, so tours are possible all year, but Sep–May are the most common months. Can also arrange tailor-made kayak &

boat trips. His attention to detail is impeccable – rare in these parts.

Claudio or Paulo Landeros Playa Ancha; 9 8238 6781, 9 7704 2651; e paulolanderos800@ gmail.com, Claudio.landeros@live.cl; Expediciones Patagonia Landeros C. These brothers offer boat trips to the Montt or Steffen glaciers ($110,000 pp, min 7 people, max 12). As they were born near Ventisquero Montt they know it very well, & can note how it has retreated over their lifetimes. As licensed tour-boat operators, life vests are included, & their boat is sufficiently fast to do the round trip to either glacier in a day & still have time to explore. Conditions permitting it may be possible to climb on to an iceberg near the snout of Ventisquero Montt. The tour also includes a light trek on the mainland towards the Ventisquero Montt where huemules are fairly common. Includes the usual whisky with glacial ice, in abundance. The trip to Ventisquero Steffen includes the boat transport & the guided hike to the snout of the glacier. As they are in opposite directions, you cannot visit both glaciers in 1 day, although it is possible to combine either with a stop at the graveyard. Trips solely to the graveyard $10,000 pp (min 6). They are somewhat chaotic, & while they suggest booking in advance, it can be hard to reach them in practice. However, they have been doing the trip for a decade & know the region well. It is helpful to stay at their sister's hostel, Brisas del Sur (page 316), as she acts as something of a co-ordinator for the brothers, who are often out of contact.

Entre Hielos Lodge Sector Central; ☏9 9579 3779, 9 9599 5730; e contacto@entrehielos.cl; w entrehielos.cl. Offering 3 main tours, principally to residents of the hotel (see below), operated by the lodge itself, ie: not subcontracted. The boat holds up to 12 passengers & prices are per boat regardless of numbers. A day trip to Ventisquero Steffen (with trekking) is US$150 pp (min 6), or a 2-day option sleeping on board for US$337 pp (min 4), with no additional hotel charge for this night. The 2nd tour is to the Montt glacier (US$150 pp, min 6). The final tour is a full day to the Katalalixar archipelago & Isla Merino Jarpa, including trekking to a lake (US$150 pp, min 6). Note that their boat is extremely comfortable, with a full kitchen on board.

WHERE TO STAY *Map, opposite*

✻ 🏠 **Entre Hielos Lodge** (6 rooms) Sector Central; ///stutters.pile.subscription; ☏9 9579 3779, 9 9599 5730; e contacto@entrehielos. cl; w entrehielos.cl. Simply put, the finest place to stay in Caleta Tortel, & is reasonably priced by Tortel standards although might stretch the budget for some travellers. It is located approximately 5mins along the main boardwalk after the descent from the car park, & is signposted to the right up a few steep sets of stairs – not at all suitable with large suitcases – keep an eye open for the signposts on the way up. The lodge does not actually offer much of a view over the ocean, but towards the forest. Rooms are impeccable, clean & comfortable, with fully equipped bathrooms (shower only). Great beds & utterly peaceful. The owners, Maria Paz & Noel Vidal, have excellent knowledge of the region (Noel is from Caleta Tortel), & they have their own boat to offer tours (see above). Complete b/fast inc (fresh ground coffee, fruit juice, eggs to order), great pisco/calafate sours, decent wine list, Wi-Fi, laundry, comfortable sitting area with a range of books. Dinners are offered on request & the lodge has its own chef, thus qualifying as possibly the best restaurant in town, but with a price to match ($$$) – open to the public by prior reservation. The restaurant has featured in *Gastronomia Patagonia*. English spoken. Reservations obligatory all year, & a 30% deposit is required. Min 2-night stay. Accepts credit cards. $$$$

🏠 **Hospedaje Los Regalones** (5 rooms) Sector Rincon Bajo; ///gating.cherries.buyers; ☏9 4010 7582; e los_regalones@hotmail. com; ⊕ all year. An improvement over cheaper options, but still with thin walls. The rooms, all dbl or twin with private bathroom & basic b/fast included, are spacious & comfortable, with carpet & decent finishing. Views of ocean from the dbl rooms. Laundry offered, but no internet. TV in the communal areas where b/fast is served. It is centrally located in the village, watch out for a sign pointing to the right at the end of the boardwalk of the central section. A unique feature is that the entire building appears to sway slightly each time someone climbs the stairs, not enough to make one dizzy, but simulates the effect of being at sea – perhaps deliberately for a village built almost in the ocean itself. Although the price is slightly over most competitors at $75,000/room, the marginal benefit is obvious. Deposit required, & fills up in Jan & Feb. $$$$

🏠 **Hospedaje Tehuelche** (8 rooms) Sector Juntillo; ///lurched.outnumber.flossing; ☏9 9691 7129; e hospedaje.tehuelche@gmail.com. Being at the very end of the boardwalks has the advantage of this place being the last to fill up in high season. If you don't have a reservation it might be wise to call ahead to see if they have space, as it's a long way back if not. They can also arrange a boat pickup if lugging bags this distance is not appealing. It's also pretty quiet at this end of town. Most rooms have a view over the bay, Wi-Fi, central heating, good showers & even offers laundry service. We heard far more footsteps than the guests in the hotel could possibly justify, leading us to think this hotel might be haunted. It is, after all, the closest hospedaje to the Isla de los Muertos. Ghosts aside, one of the better value places to stay in Tortel. Dbl/twin with/without shared bathroom $60,000/50,000, sgl from $17,500. **$$$**

🏠 **Residencial Brisas del Sur** (8 rooms & 1 cabin) Sector Playa Ancha; ///newsdesk.lazier. followers; 📞 9 5688 2723; e valerialanderos@ hotmail.com, brisasdelsur@gmail.com; 🕐 all year. Another budget option. The downstairs dbl is worth avoiding at all costs – the bathrooms are upstairs & involve walking outdoors, often in the rain, & the ceiling is so thin that those upstairs chatting may as well be in the room itself. The upstairs rooms, however, are positively pleasant, with private bathrooms & a lovely view out to sea. There is a small communal sitting area where b/ fast (basic but included) is served. Although a little far from 'downtown' Caleta Tortel, the major advantage of this hostel is that the owner, Valeria, has 2 brothers both with boats & offering tours to the glaciers & the graveyard (see opposite). Because the brothers, Claudio & Paulo, are often out of mobile-phone coverage Valeria acts as a de facto tour operator for their trips. Valeria's husband, Ruben, also has a small boat suitable for visiting the graveyard but not the glaciers. Wi-Fi & laundry. **$$$**

🏠 **Bella Vista Hostal** (7 rooms) Sector Rincon Bajo; ///flattered.jilted.redevelop; 📞 9 6211 7430. Centrally located, basic accommodation perfect for backpackers. Thin walls & rowdy guests can make for a potentially disturbed sleep, but the beds are comfy & being located above a restaurant is convenient. Sgl & dbl rooms with shared or private bathrooms. A very basic b/fast included with eggs available for an extra charge. Neither laundry nor Wi-Fi. **$$**

🏠 **Hospedaje Estilo** (6 rooms) Zona Municipalidad; ///pranksters.handed.motivate; 📞 9 8255 8487; e zuri1_67@hotmail.com. Comfy bedrooms, some with excellent views to the sea. The rooms are traditional, but well furnished, & excellent for families. There is a matrimonial suite available ($80,000) which has a balcony & a large floor-to-ceiling window with views over Caleta Tortel. The restaurant serves fish, mussels, steak & king crab, as well as wine, beer & pisco (**$$$**). Deposit of 75% required (made by bank transfer). Laundry service available at an additional cost. Open all year. Sgl, twin & dbl rooms, all with private bathrooms. B/fast inc. **$$**

⛺ **Camping Tortel** 📞 9 7897 3626; e campingtortel@gmail.com; w campingtortel. cl. 5 covered & 10 regular sites ($6,000/4,000) on wooden platforms, nails provided to anchor tent to ground if required, mini kitchen provided (bring own plates, etc), bathrooms with hot water, close to the main car park, reservation advised in high season, good view over village & a slice of the bay, sink to wash clothes, solar lighting at night. **$**

✖ WHERE TO EAT AND DRINK Map, page 314

Entre Hielos Lodge offers dinners to non-guests with reservations, and is one of the best restaurants in the village. Others include:

✖ **Sabores Locales** Sector Rincon; ///mayonnaise.riches.gloomier; 📞 9 9087 3064; e saboreslocalesdetortel@gmail.com; 🕐 13.00–23.00 low season, 08.00–11.00 & 13.00–midnight high season. Serious competitor for the 'best restaurant in town' award. Lovely view from an elevated wooden building, all ingredients sourced locally where possible, good service & friendly atmosphere. Located at the west end of the main bay in the village, close to the centre, up a flight of stairs from the main boardwalk. The owner, Maritza, is a true Caleta resident, & knows all the history, tours & the unusual places to visit.

She has artisanal beers, when available, including the local brew from Tortel. Salmon is the speciality of the house, but the menu includes all standard fare from the region, with fruit & vegetables from her organic garden, including nalca & calafate. A couple will pay $45,000 for a decent meal with wine – not the cheapest restaurant in town, but worth a splurge. **$$$$**

✖ **Restaurant El Mirador** Sector Central; 📞 9 5597 8649; 🕐 08.00–23.00 Mon–Sat, 13.30–midnight Sun. A new bar/restaurant in Caleta Tortel that serves pizza, salmon ceviche & the usual range of Chilean fare (salmon, chicken, empanadas, seafood stew, lamb). 3-course menu of the day for $12,000. There is an excellent view of the sea from the tables near the window, but the rest of the restaurant is light, open & has a lively, intimate atmosphere. They also serve coffee, wines & cocktails. $$$

✗ **Comidas Caseras en Tortel** Rincon Alto; ☏ 9 9506 1909; ⊕ all year noon–22.30 Mon–Sun. As the name suggests, this is traditional Caleta food. Located on the Octavio Varga boardwalk coming down from the car park towards Tortel, this relatively new restaurant offers possibly the finest views in town. Specialities are salmon, gnocchi, cazuela, lamb & soups, served with local greens & homemade bread. They also serve coffee & hot chocolate. The owners, Loida & Juan, provide great service, & the location is ideal. $$

✗ **Restaurant Bella Vista** Sector Rincon Bajo; ☏ 9 6211 7430; ⊕ noon–20.00 Mon–Sat. Great views, as the name suggests, & abundant servings at this family-owned restaurant just a short walk on the boardwalk from the main stairs that come down from the parking area. Regional cuisine, including salmon or steak a lo pobre at $10,000, or pastas & stews around $8,000 & salads. Regional beers, reasonable wine selection & lovely terrace. $$

SIGHTSEEING AND EXCURSIONS Merely pottering about in Caleta Tortel, particularly on a sunny day, is a worthy activity. Explore the upper boardwalks, some of which offer sweeping views over the village – walk to one of the few landing strips in the world accessed by a boardwalk! There is also a loop track (2hrs; medium) to the **mirador** or **viewing platform** above the town, from which you will see spectacular 360° views of the village, Río Baker and the Baker Canal. For this, take the boardwalk to the landing strip and turn left on to a well-marked trail after 100m. This circuit trail enters the far end of the town again in Playa Ancha at the western end of town close to the campsite. Alternatively, trek up to the hydro-electric power plant for a view over the village (45mins one-way; marked; the trail starts at the eastern edge of the village). There are more ambitious treks close to Tortel, but these are neither marked nor offered as formal tours, but the more adventurous trekkers may wish to seek local advice and head off into the wilderness. The trekking potential in this region is huge, and trails will likely open up over the coming seasons.

The **glaciers** are a highlight, but might stretch the budget of some visitors – they are far from the village and fuel costs are high. The glaciers around Puerto Río Tranquilo (San Rafael, page 267, and Leones, page 275, for example) are more economical. However, if you can find a decent-sized group, the price may be reasonable. Glacier trips can be combined with trips to Caleta Tortel's mysterious **graveyard** situated on the Isla de los Muertos in the estuary of the Río Baker, although a visit to the graveyard alone is well worth the effort and reasonably priced.

Isla de los Muertos For those interested in the history of the entire region of the Carretera Austral, a boat trip to the graveyard is highly recommended. Before you go, read as much as possible about the events of 1906 (see box, page 312) and then speak to some residents about their opinions – this will only serve to further increase the mystery, or mythology, of the graveyard. A pleasant alternative to taking one of the regular boats is to go by kayak (page 314).

Jorge Montt and Steffen glaciers The **Ventisquero Jorge Montt** is stunning, accessible, and rarely visited. A round trip from Caleta Tortel takes most of the day, but can be combined with a trip to the Isla de los Muertos (page 312) on the way back. The journey itself is stunning, as the boat weaves through a seemingly endless series of islands and peninsulas. Eventually some small icebergs will come into view, and rounding the final curve the full splendour of the glacier emerges. This is the most northerly glacier of the Southern Ice Field, and its rapid retreat

11

means that icebergs are abundant so it is not possible to approach the nose of the glacier. However, from the relative distance of the boat it is possible to appreciate the scale of the ice shelf above, which is not always the case with other glaciers. The size is awe-inspiring.

The Patagonian glaciers are retreating faster than in any other region on the planet. NASA estimate that the rate of ice-thinning more than doubled here between 1995 and 2000 compared with 1975 and 2000. A December 2011 study by glaciologist Andrés Rivera used time-lapse photography to measure the retreat from February 2010 to January 2011, and discovered the glacier was retreating at 13m per day. A historical map dating back to 1898 reveals the glacier has retreated nearly 20km. Rivera's updated analysis suggests the glacier retreated a further 2.7km from 2011 to 2018.

Opinions differ regarding the extent to which mankind is responsible for the disappearance of such glaciers, but less so in the case of the Ventisquero Jorge Montt. In January 2012 a man was detained in Cochrane for stealing 5,000kg of ice from the glacier to use in cocktails in Santiago de Chile.

Despite the slightly depressing environmental implications, the glacier is truly spectacular, and it is possible to disembark from the boat and walk along the eastern side of the canal towards the glacier, where huemules are often spotted.

Caleta Tortel is sandwiched between the Northern and Southern ice fields, together comprising the third-largest ice field on the planet after Greenland and Antarctica. To the north of Caleta Tortel lies the most southern glacier of the Northern Ice Field – **Steffen**. It ends in a lagoon from which the Río Huemules is born. It is named after Hans Steffen, the German explorer of Aysén. A trip to the Ventisquero Steffen takes an entire day, and unlike the Ventisquero Montt to the south, involves a 14km round-trip hike. Steffen is also in retreat, but not to the extent of Montt (2.1km from 1987 to 2010, 2.3km to 2019). The journey from Caleta Tortel first passes the Río Baker Delta, and then heads north up the Fiordo Steffen. At the entrance to the fjord it is possible to see an **abandoned saw mill** – timber was the main driving force of the early settlers. The fjord veers east, at which point the glacier becomes visible beyond the estuary of the Río Huemules. The boat will go upriver to the beginning of the trek. A guide is advised, and usually doubles as the boat owner. Neither of these glaciers is well visited, Steffen involves a little more effort, is even more isolated, and passes through more extensive vegetation. It is a longer day compared with Montt, and thus harder to combine with the trip to the Isla de Los Muertos on the way back.

⊕ AS THE CONDOR FLIES

Caleta Tortel is 705km south of Puerto Montt, and a mere 140km from the border to El Chaltén south of Villa O'Higgins.

12

Exiting/Entering the Carretera Austral: Villa O'Higgins and beyond

Few visitors venture this far south: there is no border crossing south of Cochrane suitable for private vehicles. For those with a car, there is no choice but to double back up to Cochrane or take the ferry from Puerto Yungay to Puerto Natales, gateway to Torres del Paine. The road quality in the region is poor with steep inclines and, while the **Ventisquero O'Higgins** is impressive, for those who have already visited the more northerly glaciers, perhaps the final section from Puerto Yungay to Villa O'Higgins can be skipped.

For those without a vehicle, cyclists included, it is not only possible but highly recommended, to traverse this final section and push on through to Argentina. The 100km road from Puerto Bravo to Villa O'Higgins is dramatic, as it traverses some high mountains and runs alongside impressive rivers, but there is relatively little to do en route until arriving at Villa O'Higgins. For more adventurous, independent **mountaineers** there are some ambitious multi-day hikes skirting the Southern Ice Field. The truly dedicated hiker can actually trek from Cochrane to Villa O'Higgins without using either the Carretera Austral or the ferry, but this is a week-long, remote trek and not for the faint-hearted!

The **border crossing** itself is an undisputed highlight, being as it is one of the most exciting and unusual border crossings in the Americas – but be prepared for delays and plan ahead. Weather is a significant variable when making this crossing, so tight schedules are a risky bet for this leg of the journey.

Ultimately the Carretera Austral is not simply a region, but a bridge connecting northern and southern Patagonia and, at least for now, Villa O'Higgins is the end (or beginning) of the Carretera Austral.

However, the ferry connection between Puerto Yungay/Caleta Tortel and Puerto Natales now means that it is possible to travel the length of Chile without the ignominy of having to pass through Argentina. This fundamentally alters tourism in southern Patagonia. Previously Calafate and El Chaltén were obligatory stops on the way between the Carretera Austral and Torres del Paine. Now this is no longer the case, are they really worth visiting? The Perito Moreno glacier near Calafate is beautiful, but does it really compare with the array of glaciers along the Carretera Austral? Trekking around Fitzroy permits some eye-catching photography, but unless intending to actually make the climb, photos in Torres del Paine or Cerro Castillo are equally impressive.

12

VILLA O'HIGGINS AND AROUND

The picturesque region around Villa O'Higgins is rugged – dominated as it is by dramatic rivers and glaciers, but it is also relatively inaccessible. As such, despite the ample trekking options in this area, most visitors spend their time here planning their onward journey north or south. Villa O'Higgins is the last **border crossing** into Argentina along the Carretera Austral, for those without a vehicle. The border crossing is only open in the summer (1 November–30 April) and can only be used by pedestrians and cyclists. Information relating to this crossing is scarce and many believe it's not actually possible to get into Argentina from here, thus page 328 describes in detail the precise means to cross this important border to El Chaltén (Argentina). For those with patience and budget available, it is possible to take a short but spectacular flight over the ice field here, but the weather is volatile and the prices are punchy (page 322).

HISTORY Long before the first explorers arrived, the region of Villa O'Higgins was inhabited by several indigenous groups, such as the Aónikenk who were also called Patagones (and later Tehuelches). They lived in small groups of about 20 people that were linked by blood relations and were expert hunters of Patagonian fauna. They were nomadic and had simple, easily movable homes, mostly made of animal skins. Nowadays these indigenous groups have completely disappeared due to several factors: persecution by landowners of various nationalities; diseases such as syphilis, measles and tuberculosis; and alcoholism.

The first explorers travelled to the region for scientific and geopolitical reasons. In 1877 two Argentine explorers, Francisco Perito Moreno and Carlos Moyano, named the huge lake they stumbled across after the hero of Argentine independence, San Martín. The Chileans later changed the name to Lago O'Higgins, after their own independence hero, Bernardo O'Higgins, who commanded the fight that freed Chile from Spanish rule. The eastern arm of the lake lies within Argentine territory where the San Martín name persists to this day. In 1899 the river outlet was explored by Hans Steffen, a prominent German geographer who was carrying out border studies for the Chilean government. In 1902 a British mediator equally divided the lake between Chile and Argentina.

Once these remote territories were discovered it didn't take long for the first settlers to arrive. The Chilean government accelerated the settlement process by granting farming concessions. In addition to the people attracted by these concessions, European settlers started to arrive on their own account.

Around 1965 an incident between the Chilean and Argentine police, fuelled by ongoing land and border disputes in which a Chilean officer died, encouraged the Chilean president to strengthen sovereignty in the region. That same year inhabitants of the river mouth of the Río Mayer set out to build a landing strip to enable them to receive supplies and support from the main urban areas in Chilean Patagonia, and to reduce dependency upon Argentina. The works were completed at the end of winter 1966. On 20 September of that same year several authorities arrived from Aysén and Magallanes for the official foundation of Villa O'Higgins.

In the years that followed settlers were given ownership titles and the village started taking shape. A primary school was founded as well as a health clinic and a gym. Subsidies were granted for the construction of houses for the settlers. In 1980 Villa O'Higgins became a municipality which allowed for the further development of the area and catered to the needs of the local inhabitants. In 1983 the village started to generate its own electricity. In 1992 the municipality of Villa O'Higgins had 337 inhabitants and construction of a road connecting Villa O'Higgins and Puerto Yungay began, being finally completed seven years later. Up until that point O'Higgins was accessible only by air from Coyhaique or by boat from Argentina. When the road was opened in 1999 new services such as a paved landing strip, internet and satellite telephone became available. It got access to improved electricity and better-quality drinking water.

Currently Villa O'Higgins has around 600 inhabitants and marks the end point of the Carretera Austral. Tourism has taken off and is becoming increasingly important for the local economy. The village is now firmly on the backpackers' map due to its strategic location near the popular Argentine trekking capital of El Chaltén. A new road has been built to Río Mayer, in Chile, as there are pending plans to open a border crossing, but work has paused on the Argentine side of the border, rendering the crossing impassable. The Chaltén border crossing is only open in the summer months. An all-year border crossing connecting Villa O'Higgins with Argentina via the Río Mayer will be an important landmark in the history of the village.

El Chaltén, in Argentina, was not founded until 1985, principally to establish a permanent Argentine population in this region of constant border disputes.

GETTING THERE AND AWAY
About the route
Caleta Tortel to Villa O'Higgins (144km; 5hrs including ferry; challenging gravel) Head north from Caleta Tortel on the only possible road out of the village, towards Cochrane. After 23km (///elitist.qualifier.painters) the road continues northeast to Cochrane (103km), or south towards Puerto Yungay (21km), the ferry and on to Villa O'Higgins. From this junction south the road quality notably deteriorates. Some of the inclines are brutal, and this is certainly not the easiest section for cyclists. The road terminates at **Puerto Yungay** (///truancy.basket. writing) on Mitchell Fjord, where the only means to cross the 8km to **Puerto Bravo** (///buying.lutes.reporters) is on the *Padre Antonio Ronchi* ferry. The crossing is free, and as long as passengers arrive before the scheduled last departing ferry of the day they are guaranteed to cross even if the boat must return from the other side (page 60). At either end of the ferry connection is a small hut that is open 24/7 and it is possible to sleep without cost in these waiting rooms. At Puerto Yungay there is also a small cafeteria and one of only two monuments to Pinochet – the other is in La Junta.

It is 100km from Puerto Bravo to Villa O'Higgins, with few opportunities to sleep along the way, although wild camping is possible (of interest to cyclists in particular). The road begins on the south side of Mitchell Fjord, and is initially relatively flat. After 9km is a turning to the right (ie: south, ///unadjusted.crooks. case) signposted 'Río Pascua 25km' or 'Ventisquero Montt 64km'. Despite this apparently clear direction, the road ends at a precarious cliff and does not reach the glacier. The road is of modest interest (it is certainly beautiful, with some dramatic views of lakes and landslides), but it is not entirely clear why it was built, as almost no-one lives along this section. The road does reach the **Río Pascua**, but it is not clear how the road could ever reach Ventisquero Montt. It appears the signpost was completed long before the road itself. The main road then follows sections of the rivers Bravo and Colorado and passes a number of lakes. This is one of the more challenging sections of the entire Carretera Austral and all the quieter for it.

There are no detours until 6km prior to Villa O'Higgins, when a turning to the left signposted 'Estancia Las Margaritas' on the X-905 leads towards the **Paso Río**

12

Mayer and on to **Lago Christie** (page 327). The final stretch to O'Higgins is paved and relatively uneventful, until greeted by the first houses and the petrol station at the edge of the town. Fill up – it's 224km to Cochrane.

By air Aerocord flies twice a week from Coyhaique. Although this is a spectacular flight and subsidised by the state, priority goes to local residents and the flight is invariably full. In peak season it is nearly impossible for non-residents to get a seat on the nine-seater plane. The only means to buy a ticket is by visiting or calling their Coyhaique office (page 218).

By bus There is no public transport along the Río Mayer detour towards the border, nor to Lago Christie. It is possible to cross the border to/from El Chaltén by public transport (buses and boats combined with some light trekking). **Buses Isabel** (cnr Lago Cisnes & Río Bravo; `\`9 7870 1956, 9 8812 1610; ///nomadism.toiletries. flab) offer a route to Caleta Tortel (depart 08.30 Mon, Thu & Sat, return 16.30 same days). Make sure to buy this ticket as soon as possible from the office, as no reservations over the phone are taken, and in high season the bus fills up quickly. **Buses Gardy** offer buses from Cochrane to Villa O'Higgins (depart 08.00 Mon, Wed & Sat, return Tue, Thu & Sun – call to check times). Tickets can be bought (and the bus leaves) from the office of Aires del Sur. Up-to-date bus timetables can usually be found in the window of the tourist information office.

TOUR OPERATORS Note that to cross the border requires two tour operators: one of two in Argentina to cross the Lago del Desierto, and one of two in Chile to cross the Lago O'Higgins. Note also that this route is currently in a state of flux as of early 2022.

Chile

Aires del Sur Adelaida Vargas 497; `\`9 93578196; e airesdelsur14@gmail.com; ◼ Transportes Aéreos del Sur. An excellent service, offering spectacular flights over the Southern Ice Field in a Cessna P206 (high wing for better views). Flights last 1hr & the principal pilot, Vincent Beasley, doubles as the tour guide. Spanish, English, French & German spoken. The price is US$240 pp based on 5 passengers for trips purchased in Villa O'Higgins – tickets bought through agents will cost slightly more. The Southern Ice Field is only 8mins' flight from the landing strip in Villa O'Higgins, so very little time is spent in transit. This bird's-eye view allows passengers to see countless glaciers, including Jorge Montt & O'Higgins, as well as the lesser-known Pascua, Oriental, Bravo, Lucia, Mellizo Sur, Ambrosio, Rosa, Gaea & Chico. Other options include flights over the legendary Monte Fitz Roy & Cerro Torre, & Volcán Lautaro. It is also possible to fly to the Northern Ice Field (longer transit), or to Monte San Lorenzo closer to Cochrane. At 3,706m San Lorenzo is the 2nd-highest peak in Patagonia (after San Valentin, 3,910m), itself boasting a number of glaciers. Depending on the desired flight path, & also to serve clients crossing from El Chaltén (Argentina), a 2nd landing strip south of Candelario Mancilla is also used, & is closer to Fitz Roy and Lautaro. The plane has a wing-mounted GoPro capable of filming the entire flight in HD for an additional fee. It is also possible to fly to Candelario Mancilla – a useful alternative if the boats are not functioning. The flight is only 40mins round trip, but the cost also depends on the weight of luggage – typically US$250 pp for 3 passengers with luggage. Weather is a major factor in this region – it is wise to have a day or 2 of flexibility, but it is not hard to find things to do around Villa O'Higgins. Clearly this is not a budget option, but when one considers the logistical difficulties of operating a plane in this region, the proximity to the spectacular scenery, & the uniqueness of witnessing sights usually only visible in Antarctica, this is well worth squeezing into a budget if at all possible. Flying over the 3rd-largest expanse of ice on earth is a highlight of any trip to South America (page 327). Also offer tours of the 2 treks in Parque

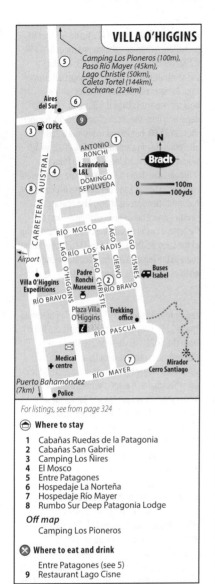

VILLA O'HIGGINS

Camping Los Pioneros (100m),
Paso Río Mayer (45km),
Lago Christie (50km),
Caleta Tortel (144km),
Cochrane (224km)

For listings, see from page 324

Where to stay

1 Cabañas Ruedas de la Patagonia
2 Cabañas San Gabriel
3 Camping Los Ñires
4 El Mosco
5 Entre Patagones
6 Hospedaje La Norteña
7 Hospedaje Río Mayer
8 Rumbo Sur Deep Patagonia Lodge

Off map
   Camping Los Pioneros

Where to eat and drink

   Entre Patagones (see 5)
9 Restaurant Lago Cisne

Santiago, Alta Vista & Mirador del Valle ($20,000 pp) & kayaking in the region with all equipment provided ($40,000 pp). Accept credit cards.

Fly Fishing Villa O'Higgins (see Entre Patagones, page 324) Alfonso offers half-day & multi-day trips to rivers & lakes in the region, including lakes Tigre, Cisnes & Ciervo, the river that drains from Lago Cisnes & the Colorado Sector (near the Paso Río Mayer). Classes available for beginners, both in fly-fishing & recreational

fishing, including use of a Cataraft (3hr trip $70,000, full day $180,000).

Lancha Alberto Lorenzo Lago Christie before COPEC; ///deed.intersection.heaving; ☏ 9 7377 3706; e albertolorenzo1956@hotmail.com; ⏱ 10.00–13.00 & 15.00–20.00 Mon–Sat. 22-person boat from Puerto Bahamóndez to Candelario Mancilla (depart 08.30 Mon, Wed & Sat, return 16.00; $45,000 pp). Operates early Jan–end Feb. Can also go to the O'Higgins glacier if there is sufficient demand, but not in conjunction with Candelario Mancilla service ($110,000 pp return). Cash or card – those arriving from Argentina can pay by card upon arrival in Villa O'Higgins. Has shuttle bus between the port & Villa O'Higgins, synchronised with boat ($2,500 pp).

Las Ruedas de la Patagonia Antonio Ronchi Lote 28; ///muralists.involves. defending; ☏ 9 6627 8836, 9 7604 2400; e turismoruedasdelapatagonia@gmail.com; w turismoruedasdelapatagonia.cl. Operates a crossing from Puerto Bahamóndez to Candelario Mancilla (depart 08.00 Mon, Wed & Sat, return 16.00 same days; $45,000 pp each way), entirely weather dependent & often delayed or cancelled. Also operates a shuttle bus between Villa O'Higgins & Puerto Bahamóndez synchronised with boat arrival/departure (30mins; $2,500 one way). Also offers accommodation (page 324).

Villa O'Higgins Expeditions In front of the aerodrome at the northern entrance to town; ///unbearably.limo.milestone; ☏ 67 243 1821, 9 8210 3191; e info@villaohiggins.com; w villaohiggins.com. The most comprehensive tour operator & information source in town. Owner Hans Silva knows everything worth knowing about Villa O'Higgins & the region. They can help set up the entire crossing to/from Argentina or simply make reservations for the boats. Their website has updated information on accommodation & services in Villa O'Higgins including public transport, & works closely with the community to give them a web presence. Take credit cards.

Argentina

Exploradores Lago del Desierto Av San Martin 55, El Chaltén; ///whiner. doormats.untouched; ☏ +54 9 296 646 7103; e chalten@receptivochalten.com; w exploradoreslagodeldesierto.com. Reliable company operating a boat across Lago del

Exiting/Entering the Carretera Austral: Villa O'Higgins and beyond   **VILLA O'HIGGINS AND AROUND**

12

Desierto & buses between El Chaltén & Lago del Desierto for nearly a decade. Tickets available from their office in El Chaltén (cash or card), or on the boat (cash only). Currently there is only 1 scheduled boat departing from the south of the lake at 10.00, reaching the north at 11.00 and returning promptly, guaranteed daily Oct–Mar inc. A late-afternoon crossing may operate in 2022, but currently this morning-only service means it is impossible to travel southwards from Villa O'Higgins to El Chaltén in 1 day. The northward journey is theoretically possible in a single day. Buses depart El Chaltén at 08.00 and 11.00, 1½hrs to south side of Lago del Desierto, returning at 16.00 and 18.00. Lake crossings cost US$40 each way, bus is US$20 each way. Also offer trekking tours to the Vespignani glacier located halfway along the lake.

Zona Austral Av Miguel Martin de Güemes 84, El Chaltén; ///homages.ballrooms.mogul; ☎+54 9 2902 490535, +54 2966 721113; e info@ zonaaustralturismo.com; w zonaaustralturismo. com. Another established operator with a boat service across Lago del Desierto, currently departing from the south shore at 10.00, northern shore at 11.00, but intend to resume a 2nd afternoon crossing around 17.00 in 2022, which would facilitate reaching El Chaltén from Villa O'Higgins in a single day. See website. Co-operate with Exploradores Lago del Desierto if 1 company has insufficient/excess space. Also operate a shuttle service between El Chaltén & Lago del Desierto, a hostel & camping at the southern edge of the Lago del Desierto (page 332), & offer various tours in the region. Well-functioning website enables reservations online, cards taken.

🏠 WHERE TO STAY *Map, page 323*

🏠 **Rumbo Sur Deep Patagonia Lodge** (12 rooms) Carretera Austral km1, 240; ///feathers.wisteria.lament; ☎9 4217 7577; e info@rumbosurdeeppatagonia.com; w rumbosurdeeppatagonia.com. Modern & elegant, this B&B lodge is the highest-quality & most expensive accommodation in Villa O'Higgins. With fantastic mattresses & duvets, a full gourmet buffet b/fast, 2 wood-heated communal hot tubs, & wall-sized double-glazed windows overlooking the mountains in every room, refined travellers can find comfort in this village at the end of the road. Built in 2012, all rooms have a full private bath & Wi-Fi. The clubhouse is a large cosy space that serves as the b/fast area & is a fine atmosphere for relaxing by the fire or chatting over a cup of coffee or glass of wine. The bilingual & friendly staff can help organise excursions. English spoken. Reservations are recommended at least 30 days in advance & can be made through their Santiago office or on their website. US$130/140/160 sgl/dbl/trpl. Accepts credit cards. **$$$$**

🏠 **Cabañas Ruedas de la Patagonia** (4 rooms, 6 cabins) Antonio Ronchi Lote 28; ///muralists.involves.defending; ☎9 6627 8836, 9 7604 2400; e turismoruedasdelapatagonia@ gmail.com; w turismoruedasdelapatagonia. cl; 🆕 Cabanas Las Ruedas Angélica. Higher-end, well-insulated cabins set on a quiet street backing on to the bush-clad mountain range,

run by tour operator Las Ruedas de la Patagonia (page 323). Located directly towards the hills from the COPEC service station. The smaller dbl-bedroom cabin resembles a honeymoon suite with elegant linen curtains & is suitable for wheelchairs. A wagon-wheel window from yesteryear is a unique feature for all these bungalows. 2 cabins for 4, the 2 larger cabins sleep 5 & 6 people respectively. Sat TV, Wi-Fi & BBQ area are included. A decent b/fast consisting of juice, yoghurt, cereals, cheese, fruit, ham & jams is available for an extra $5,000 pp. Quincho available, and can arrange asado for larger groups with anticipation. Reservations with 50% deposit. Accepts credit cards. **$$$**

🏠 **Cabañas San Gabriel** (12 cabañas) cnr of Lago Christie & Río Bravo; ///tens. interjection.earths; ☎9 6210 2400, 9 3269 4341; e sangabrielcabaña@gmail.com. Cabins for 2–10 people, with shared or private bathroom available. Access to a shared kitchen for all cabins. Run by a family with a long history in Villa O'Higgins who also run 2 mini markets, these cabins are scattered around 2 different blocks & range from new to rustic. They have 2 cabins about 2km out of the village for travellers interested in agritourism. With their wide selection, families or groups could find something suitable. Cabañas have cable TV & wood-stove heating. **$$$**

🏠 **Entre Patagones** (8 cabins) Carretera Austral; ///dislocate.fixate.uplifting; ☎9 9498

0460, 9 6621 5046; e info@entrepatagones.cl; w entrepatagones.cl. Reasonable cabins located at the northern entrance to Villa O'Higgins before the COPEC petrol station, run by master fisherman Alfonso Díaz. Also home to possibly the best restaurant in the village (see below). The cabins sleep 2 to 5 people with a simple kitchen, decent bathroom with reliable hot water & comfortable beds. Ample off-road parking, not that crime in O'Higgins is a big concern. B/fast is not included & the internet connection is lousy – even worse than the rest of the village. 2 cabins have a TV. Deposits normally required, but call to negotiate if this is a problem, & be sure to confirm a reservation shortly before arrival. Alfonso also offers fishing trips. **$$$**

🏠 **Hospedaje La Norteña** (8 rooms) Calle Nueva 1; ///birthdate.many.magpie; 📞 9 7547 1721; e silvia_cuevas@live.cl. Food can be prepared to order for guests. There are private ($35,000 for 2 people) rooms with shared bathrooms & shared rooms ($18,000 pp). Laundry, central heating, Wi-Fi & a basic b/fast (bread, eggs, coffee & tea) included. The hospedaje is very traditional, with correspondingly small beds & chipboard walls, but the overall effect is cosy. **$$$**

☀ 🏠 **Hospedaje Río Mayer** (4 rooms) Río Mayer 202; ///utterly.copybook.delimited; 📞 9 8154 1418; e venis1960.guinao@gmail.com. A family hostel run by Venis Guinao, the daughter of one of the pioneers to Villa O'Higgins. Venis is a mine of information on the town, & chatting with her over b/fast can answer many of your questions on Chilean culture, the history of Villa O'Higgins & day-to-day life before connection with the outside world through the Carretera. Basic b/fast includes eggs, freshly baked bread, cheese, tea & coffee. 1 sgl, 3 dbls, laundry possible, no Wi-Fi. Cash only. **$$**

🏠 **El Mosco** (3 dorms, 8 rooms, 2 cabins & camping) Carretera Austral s/n just south of COPEC; ///worksites.hamsters.window; 📞 9 7658 3017; e patagoniaelmosco@yahoo.es; w patagoniaelmosco.com; 📘 El Mosco Jorge. The most popular place in town for backpackers, cyclists & budget travellers. The owner (Orfelina Barriga) & staff are very well informed on the region & can provide ample, top-quality information about tours & access to/from O'Higgins. The dormitories sleep 6 people each & are perfectly comfortable ($12,000 pp); a sgl is $25,000; 3 comfortable dbls/twins with private bathroom ($50,000) or 2 with shared bathroom ($35,000); the 2 trpls cost $60,000 & have private bathrooms. For an additional fee a sauna & hot tub can be fired up. The cabins are for 4 or 6 people ($45,000 per cabin, $5,000 per extra person). They have a fully equipped wood-stove heated kitchen with a fridge. Camping is also available at $7,000. All guests have Wi-Fi & access to a well-equipped large kitchen. Also doubles as an agent for local tour operators, including tours to Lago O'Higgins, treks to El Mosco refuge, the Submarino & El Tigre glaciers, & can advise on the longer treks into the glacier of the Southern Ice Field & the trek all the way to Cochrane (Ruta de los Pioneros). A lovely & popular hostal run by very helpful people. **$–$$$**

⛺ **Camping Los Ñires** (approx 40 sites) Carretera Austral s/n, beside COPEC petrol station; ///proverbial.frothing.nourishing; 📞 9 4070 3450. A large centrally located campsite with shade from mature native trees. Kitchen & eating area, 6 toilets, hot water, & facilities for washing clothes. $5,000 pp. No reservations. **$**

⛺ **Camping Los Pioneros** (20 sites) Located 100 yards down the road to the cemetery at the northern entrance to the village; ///unbeaten.velcro.decoupled; 📞 9 4261 7410. Hot water, 2 bathrooms & use of the family's kitchen. More of a back garden than a campsite, but flat ground & sheltered from the wind. $5,000 pp. **$**

✗ WHERE TO EAT AND DRINK *Map, page 323*

☀ ✗ **Entre Patagones** Northern limits of town, on Carretera Austral; 📞 9 9498 0460, 9 6621 5046; e info@entrepatagones.cl; w entrepatagones.cl. Of the same owner as the cabins & fishing outfit (page 323), this is a fair restaurant by Chilean standards & a positively decent restaurant by O'Higgins standards. The set menu is approximately $10,000 pp including a starter, main course & pudding, changing daily. Typical dishes include trout, chicken, steak, cazuela, pizzas, empanadas & cakes. Reasonable range of wines & beers. Popular. A new cerveceria has been opened by Entre Patagones next to the restaurant, with artisanal beers from Coyhaique, sandwiches & 'tablas'. **$$$**

✗ **Restaurant Lago Cisne** Calle Nueva # 1; ///fats.hydrated.husbands; 📞 9 6673 2734; w restaurantlagocisne.cl. About the only other place to eat, good range of food from meat & lamb to stews, seafood, sandwiches & kuchen. Slow-cooked lamb asado is the speciality of the house.

Local ingredients where possible, daily menus & decent place for b/fast also. $$$

OTHER PRACTICALITIES There is a COPEC **petrol station**, but **no ATM or bureau de change** in town. The one **laundry** is Lavandería L&L (Lago Christie; ///charms. disarmed.flapjacks; ☏9 8817 2361; e carmelitas_60@gmail.com) for $6,000 per load. For more information on the treks in the area visit the information centre at the entrance to the Mirador Cerro Santiago.

For basic car and tyre repairs there are three **mechanics** in Villa O'Higgins, each with slightly different skills and tools but usually able to cobble together a solution to most problems: Delmiro Quinto (☏9 3393 7035); Juan Carlos Barrientos (☏9 3432 8196); or Gandy Castillo (☏9 9694 6880).

SIGHTSEEING AND EXCURSIONS Within Villa O'Higgins there are relatively few highlights. Besides some basic shopping in small stores, or visiting the museum, most activities are outside the village. **Fly-fishing** and **birdwatching** are popular activities, possible both with and without a guide (see page 322 for tour operators). **Trekking** options relatively close to the town include to the **Mirador Cerro Santiago**, just 30 minutes (1km) from Villa O'Higgins on a well-marked trail, which overlooks the village, the native bush and the mountains in the background. The trail continues for another 40 minutes to a second viewpoint with stunning views of

THE SOUTHERN ICE FIELD

Treks to the Southern Ice Field are only for highly experienced people with excellent navigation abilities, otherwise a guide is required (CONAF and local hotels have contact details of qualified guides).

For those with backcountry experience and time on their hands, the area around Lago O'Higgins is a relatively unexplored paradise of mountains, rivers, native forests and glacier and ice-field views. This area is extremely remote and should only be visited if you feel comfortable with navigation and off-trail travel, carrying enough supplies for eight to ten days as well as some level of Spanish-speaking ability. Keep in mind that you may be at least a couple of days' travel away from any medical attention in case of an emergency, so be sure to register with the Carabineros and let people know where you are going.

Almost all land in this area is privately owned, so it is extremely important to ask for permission first and contact landowners via radio beforehand (or through one of their relatives who can usually be found in Villa O'Higgins) to make sure you are permitted to walk on their land. The landowners themselves should be the first port of call as they are usually the best people to ask about potential routes and conditions of trails, when they exist. CONAF can also provide some information too. Most of the trekking is only accessed by a long walk and/or infrequent boats that are often delayed by weather, so flexibility and an abundance of time is key. If you don't feel comfortable on long-term treks and navigating in unfamiliar terrain with a high potential for inclement weather, it's strongly suggested to go with a local guide. Other, shorter-term treks are also available near Villa O'Higgins itself; ask at the tourist office and/or CONAF for more information.

the surrounding mountains, rivers, lakes, bush and glaciers. There are treks to the viewpoint of the Mosco glacier and the Río Mosco. The round-trip Mosco glacier trek takes 11 hours (10.2km), and is of medium difficulty. The Río Mosco trek takes 9 hours (8.6km) and is also of medium difficulty. Both treks are marked, but it is wise to use a guide to go to the Mosco glacier (see box, opposite).

The short detour (driving only, no public transport) to **Lago Christie**, northeast of town and approaching the Paso Río Mayer (not passable with vehicle), is a pleasant day trip through stunning scenery, passing a delightful chapel built by Father Ronchi (about 20km northeast of junction), before reaching the lake itself. For more advanced, multi-day treks towards, or on to the ice shelf, consult the CONAF office (see box, opposite). These are not standardised tours, often involve quite some planning, and are suitable only for experienced mountaineers. Rescue services in this remote region are extremely limited.

The two key highlights around Villa O'Higgins are **crossing the border** towards El Chaltén and visiting **Ventisquero O'Higgins**. Unfortunately, since the collapse of the Robinson Crusoe tour operator there is no scheduled boat to the glacier, and charter trips are expensive (page 328). For those with a more generous budget, a **flight** over the ice field is a treat – the only other places in the world where such a spectacular perspective is possible are Greenland and Antarctica. By comparison, this flight will seem like excellent value for money! Aires del Sur are the only operator in town (page 322) offering this service.

Back in town, the **Padre Ronchi Museum** (main plaza; ///profile.mojitos.unlike; ☉ 10.00–18.00 daily) is a small, quaint museum located in a restored chapel that was originally built under Father Ronchi's supervision in 1977. Most of the exhibits have signs in Spanish about the history of Father Ronchi (see box, page 161) and the early settlers around Villa O'Higgins. His bedroom with some artefacts is at the back. The museum is, however, of limited interest to those not yet familiar with the history of Ronchi and his legendary status in the Aysén region.

Paso Río Mayer and Lago Christie – a detour

This is a pleasant, scenic detour for those with a high-clearance vehicle, beginning 6km north of Villa O'Higgins (X-905; ///orangey.jades.vocals) and passing a number of glaciers en route to the lake. A gravel road of 45km leads to the Argentine border at Río Mayer and on to Lago Christie. The road passes a small **chapel** built by Father Ronchi and still lovingly maintained. It incorporates an unusual roof-construction called *canogas* – interlocking hollowed-out tree trunks. The road continues to the Chilean border post where it is theoretically possible to cross into Argentina using the Paso Río Mayer. However, there is no vehicular bridge across the river on the Argentine side. Occasionally it might be possible to cross in a high-clearance 4x4 when the river is very low, ie: in winter. This section involves multiple river crossings. From the Chilean border control (///bustled.knots.vanished) it is only 5km, as the condor flies, to Ruta 81 and the Argentine border control (///twos.slewed.booking), a further 53km to the junction with the Ruta 35 (///referrals.yield.combing), and then 50km to the Ruta 40 at the Las Horquetas junction (///farmyard.musicianship.wooed). It is wise to obtain local information before attempting this rarely used crossing – condors may traverse this crucial 5km stretch in minutes, but cars and trekkers attempting this crossing have frequently required rescuing. If requiring assistance, in Argentina call Gendarmeria (☏+54 2963 432033) and in Chile call Carabineros (☏67 256 7196).

It's a shame this border crossing is not more practical: in the winter months, when the El Chaltén crossing is closed, this could be the obvious terrestrial alternative for residents of Villa O'Higgins. The Paso Río Mosco to the south of Villa O'Higgins is also impassable, but theoretically it is possible to reach Estancia Tucu Tucu. Again, not a practical option.

From the Chilean border post at Río Mayer the road continues north perhaps 5km to the shore of **Lago Christie**. This is a pleasant drive involving one minor river crossing. The road follows the river emerging from the lake passing some small **waterfalls**, with ample **wild camping** options along the way. Lago Christie is a beautiful, remote lake and a delightful place to wild camp and explore the area.

Ventisquero O'Higgins – a detour

Ventisquero O'Higgins – a detour Ventisquero O'Higgins can be seen either by boat or a several-day trek from Candelario Mancilla. Travellers are rewarded with a magnificent, up-close view of one of Patagonia's largest glaciers. Upon approach, the boat passes floating icebergs, and the tongue of the glacier spills off the Southern Ice Field into the lake. The 100m-high jagged walls protrude out of the lake and the sounds of the 'calving' glacier resonate like thunder. The front face is about 3km wide, making it one of the biggest accessible glaciers in Patagonia. Lago O'Higgins reaches depths of 836m (the deepest point is close to the glacier), making it the deepest lake in the Americas (Lago General Carrera secures the #2 spot at 586m).

Until 2020 the O'Higgins glacier was easily visited by taking the Robinson Crusoe boat and could be combined with going to/from Candelario Mancilla. Alas Robinson Crusoe was an early casualty of the pandemic, arguably not helped by local competitors with smaller boats. The boat was sold first, and now operates in Tierra del Fuego. The Robinson Crusoe tour operator closed, and the hotel was eventually sold, and continues to operate as Rumbo Sur Deep Patagonia Lodge. The glacier is now only possible to visit via an expensive charter boat and only when weather permits. Currently two boats serve the route between Villa O'Higgins and Candelario Mancilla – it remains to be seen whether there is sufficient demand post-pandemic to offer a scheduled detour to the glacier. Perhaps more worryingly for the village, it also remains to be seen whether there are sufficient visitors at all given the glacier has become inaccessible to most, and there is a smoothly functioning ferry between Caleta Tortel and Puerto Natales offering visitors a seamless means to travel from the Carretera Austral and Torres del Paine. Experienced trekkers can still visit the glacier (see box, page 326), and the flight over the ice shelf is well worth considering despite the cost (page 322).

⊕ AS THE CONDOR FLIES

It is 57km from the centre of the plaza in Villa O'Higgins to the border crossing towards El Chaltén. Puerto Montt is 778km, almost perfectly north. The condor flying directly from Puerto Montt to this border crossing would face a daunting 833km journey!

CROSSING INTO ARGENTINA *Map, opposite*

From Villa O'Higgins there are only two practical ways out: north along the Carretera Austral, or south to El Chaltén in Argentina.

The border crossing between El Chaltén (Argentina) and Villa O'Higgins (Chile) is a great option for hikers and cyclists, and one of the legendary border crossings of the continent. Called the 'Portezuelo de la Divisoria' border in Argentina, it goes by the name 'Dos Lagos' in Chile. Crossing the border here is the only way to traverse the Carretera Austral in its entirety without doubling back since the next practical border crossing is north of Cochrane (page 300).

Take extra food for the crossing (in case of delays) and cash in local currency as there is no bank, exchange office, or ATM in Villa O'Higgins (in fact, there isn't one until Cochrane further north), and most establishments do not take credit cards or Argentine pesos.

For those coming from Argentina, plan on a bare minimum of US$50 per day in cash, while for those entering Argentina from Chile, the first town with facilities (including an ATM) is El Chaltén.

The crossing could previously be done reliably in one day. Since the pandemic there are fewer crossings of both Lago O'Higgins and Lago del

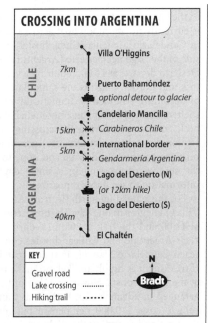

Desierto in Argentina. The journey across the border usually involves one night camping or securing a bed in Candelario Mancilla. However, this is not a simple crossing – delays or cancellations of the boats, particularly across Lago O'Higgins, are common. Do not attempt this journey unless you have a few days' leeway. The only means to cross Lago O'Higgins is currently by boat with **Las Ruedas** or **Lancha Alberto Lorenzo** (page 323), or by charter flight with **Aires del Sur** (page 322). Crossing the Lago del Desierto in Argentina is usually done by boat, of which there are two operators – **Exploradores** (page 323) and **Zona Austral** (page 323) – although it is possible to walk around the lake. As explained in detail below, this involves six separate stages (two buses, two boats and trekking across the physical border). There are no services along this stretch, but the availability of pack horses means that even those with bulky luggage can do this crossing.

THE CROSSING (NORTH TO SOUTH)
Stage 1 – Villa O'Higgins to Puerto Bahamóndez (7km)
A good gravel road that hugs the edge of the Río Mosco. This can be walked or cycled, but watch out for cars coming round blind corners. Keep your eye out for the 'Fin de la Carretera Austral' sign in Puerto Bahamóndez, marking the official end (or beginning) of the Carretera Austral. For those coming from the south, anyone on the ferry is assured a place on this bus to Villa O'Higgins. Las Ruedas de la Patagonia and Lancha Alberto Lorenzo (page 323) operate shuttles between Villa O'Higgins and Puerto Bahamóndez synchronised with their boat departures and arrivals. If flying with Aires del Sur the flight departs from Villa O'Higgins, not from Puerto Bahamóndez.

Stage 2 – Puerto Bahamóndez to Candelario Mancilla (1½hrs)
The ferry across Lago O'Higgins has views of the Argentine and Chilean sides of the lake. For those heading south towards Argentina there is ample time for the obligatory visits

to the Chilean and Argentine border police (Stages 3 and 4 respectively), but there is currently no afternoon boat across the Lago del Desierto (Stage 5), thus a night in Candelario Mancilla (Chile, hostel or camping) or wild camping at the north side of the Lago del Desierto (Argentina) is inevitable. The boat across the Lago del Desierto departs at 11.00, requiring a very early start if attempting to do the 20km trek and border controls the same day. Once in Candelario Mancilla the chance of becoming stranded is dramatically reduced as the Lago del Desierto is more sheltered and the boat runs more reliably than the Lago O'Higgins boat. However, both companies offering the crossing of Lago del Desierto (Zona Austral and Exploradores Lago del Desierto) previously operated an afternoon service from north to south around 17.00 and hope to resume this service in 2022, facilitating the southward crossing in a single day – check their websites for up-to-date information to see if this is possible.

For those heading north (ie: from Argentina) it is theoretically possible to reach Villa O'Higgins in one day. The boat arrives at the north shore of Lago del Desierto at 11.00 and the trek is 20km (5–6hrs trekking), excluding the time required to clear Argentine and Chilean border controls. For cyclists this is enough time to reach Candelario Mancilla in time to catch the 16.00 boat to Puerto Bahamóndez. If trekking it is highly unlikely to make the connection, especially with any delay at the border posts. However, 15km of this 20km trek can be done in a vehicle if arranged in advance with Ricardo at Candelario Mancilla (see box, below). This vehicle costs $10,000 per person but notably increases the chance of catching the boat and spending the night in Villa O'Higgins as opposed to in Candelario Mancilla or camping.

For those travelling north and intending to catch the 16.00 ferry the same day it is highly advisable to communicate with the boat operators (Las Ruedas or

CANDELARIO MANCILLA

Candelario Mancilla (///allowing.system.hissy) is actually the name of the first settler in this region, the founder of a small **estancia** (also of the same name) that is still run by his descendants and who mainly make a living from farming, tourism and logging. There are three shared rooms (each with 1 dbl & 2 sgls) available on a first-come-first-served basis ($15,000 pp), and a campsite ($5,000 pp) with hot water, an oven and a communal table in the kitchen. The family cook homemade meals for tourists (b/fast $6,000, lunch & dinner $10,000). They do not sell additional provisions, so those travelling north are advised to bring extra supplies in case of ferry delays. Ricardo and Nancy (\9 5422 8151, 9 9126 7007; e naguvogt@gmail.com) live in Candelario Mancilla, and run all the services offered. Ricardo can be difficult to contact due to the lack of signal in Candelario Mancilla. He offers transport in a vehicle only to the Argentine border ($10,000 pp, min 2 people, additional $5,000 pp for baggage. Transport to the border by horse with a guide is $40,000 pp (min 2 people), and an additional $40,000 with luggage. In theory it is possible to arrange for Ricardo to come to the border with his vehicle or horses to provide transport back to Candelario Mancilla, but this depends on being able to contact him in advance. This might be particularly useful for those trekking from Argentina and hoping to reach Villa O'Higgins the same day – it is only possible to make this connection if the 15km stretch from the border to Candelario Mancilla is done in a vehicle.

lberto Lorenzo) in advance. However, always be prepared to spend a day or two in Candelario Mancilla if the boat is unable to offer this transfer due to poor weather. This is one region where some form of satellite communication device would be very handy (see page 72 – we use the Garmin inReach Mini). If not intending to catch the boat the same day, either sleep in Candelario Mancilla or wild camp on the north side of Lago del Desierto – either way there is ample time to catch the 16.00 ferry the next day.

Stage 3 – Candelario Mancilla to the border (15km, 3½hrs hiking) The view of Lago O'Higgins from the vantage point above Candelario Mancilla has it all. The snow-topped mountains seem to slide into the aquamarine lake, while rivers and streams wind through the forest. The hike reaches the border police (⊕ 09.00–20.30) 1km uphill from Candelario Mancilla, an obligatory stop for those entering or leaving Chile. It then gains altitude quickly, winding its way up a gravel road to a dense forest where it levels out, passing a small landing strip and Laguna Redonda until reaching the formal border 2km further on. This is all along a clearly marked trail, almost impossible to get lost.

Stage 4 – The border to Lago del Desierto (5km, 2hrs hiking) This area was still in dispute between Argentina and Chile up until recently, and Chile would like to claim all the land between Lago O'Higgins and Monte Fitz Roy as theirs. Argentina has little motivation to relinquish this land or put in a road. The trail is well marked, involves stream crossings and moderately steep inclines. The track is passable by foot and horse but is muddy in wet conditions and there are several short sections where bikes will need to be carried a few metres across a stream or over fallen trees. The border police are on the north shore of the lake (⊕ 09.00–20.30) – knock on the door or attempt to find someone if out of hours. When travelling north towards the border there are multiple trails that could lead to confusion. Ask the border guards for clarification. When travelling south the trail inevitably leads to the border guards.

The campsite next to the Argentine border police closed in 2020, although wild camping is permitted. No food or services are available. Several nice shady spots with good protection from the wind can be found and there is plenty of fresh water available.

Stage 5 – Crossing Lago del Desierto
By boat (1hr) On a good day several glaciers, including the Vespigniani and the Huemul, are seen to the west in the Vespigniani mountain range, and the northern face of Fitz Roy sometimes pokes through the clouds when looking south. Lago del Desierto (Desert Lake) is named either for being an uninhabited area, or from the fact that there were no fish in the lake before being introduced by humans. Fishing and additional treks are available from the north of the lake. Exploradores (page 323) and Zona Austral (page 324) operate the only boats across Lago del Desierto (northbound at 10.00, southbound at 11.00), although both companies intend to offer a second service in the afternoon in 2022 should there be sufficient demand.

Alternative route – Hiking around Lago del Desierto (12km, 5–6hrs) For experienced hikers it is possible to trek along the lake. A trail on the east side of the lake follows a track that has some steep uphill scrambling, downhill sliding sections and doesn't always follow the coastline due to some rugged cliffs. To the west looking over the lake, hikers can appreciate views of Fitz Roy, the Huemul and Vespigniani glaciers while walking through a lush, ancient forest, with trees measuring up to 15m in height. The trail is poorly maintained but well marked with yellow signs. It is impossible with a bicycle, but for a small fee bicycles can be put on the boat and collected at the other side. Note that this trek passes through private property and at both ends of the trail are instructions that must be adhered to in order to ensure that this trek remains open to the public. In particular, it is not permitted to camp anywhere along the trail; remain only on the main trail with the yellow signs – side trails off the main trail are private; it is not permitted to do the trail with animals (horses, dogs, etc); and under no circumstances may fires be lit – this is a remote region resplendent with flammable materials and access is difficult – any fire could have catastrophic implications.

Stage 6 – Lago del Desierto to El Chaltén (40km, 1½hrs)
Additional treks, such as to the Huemul glacier (45mins; easy), are available from this point. Departing from the southern shore of Lago del Desierto, the first 20km is a dirt track that would be difficult for small cars in wet conditions. The next 20km to El Chaltén is a decent-quality gravel road. The scenery along the way varies from lush forest to dry steppe, and most buses will make a short stop at the raging Saltos del Río de las Vueltas waterfall about 5km from the lake. This is a pleasant waterfall, but hardly a highlight of Patagonia. Various shuttle buses service this segment (page 322), although it is usually easier to use Exploradores or Zona Austral for both the boat crossing and the shuttle to/from El Chaltén.

WHERE TO STAY Accommodation is extremely limited between Villa O'Higgins/ Candelario Mancilla and El Chaltén. Wild camping is permitted, and often the only option. Many choose to camp on the north shore of Lago del Desierto, and accommodation and camping is available in Candelario Mancilla (see box, page 330). Four options exist around the south shore of Lago del Desierto:

Aguas Arriba Lodge (6 rooms) Located halfway down the east coast of Lago del Desierto; ///verbatim.iterative.patios; +54 911 4152 5697, +54 911 6134 8452; e info@ aguasarribalodge.com; w aguasarribalodge. com; ⊕ Nov–Mar. Offers all-inclusive packages in their eco-friendly establishment & serves as a great basecamp for some exclusive fly-fishing or hiking in the area, including to the Huemul & Vespigniani glaciers. The lodge is reached by boat or a 3hr walk from the south coast of the lake (a little under 3hrs from the north side; medium difficulty). All food, boat transfers, etc, included – a magnificent treat for those leaving the Carretera Austral, or a fine introduction for what lies in store for those heading north. US$700 pp, min stay 2 nights. $$$$$

Patagonia Eco Domes (4 domes) Midway between El Chaltén & Lago del Desierto; ///fielder.aligning.fixable; +54 9 2966 463386/990; e patagoniaecodomes@gmail.com; w patagoniaecodomes.com. Spectacular domes, part of recent glamping trend, unique views over Fitz Roy, full private bathroom, gourmet food included in price (dinner, b/fast, lunch box). Solar powered, only USB electricity connections (no 220V), no internet/mobile-phone connection, can pay by card with anticipation, otherwise cash only at domes. Take any transport between El Chaltén & Lago del Desierto & ask to be dropped off. Chance to totally unwind & disconnect from outside world, run by a charming Argentine couple who can advise on all travel in Argentine Patagonia as well as crossing to Villa O'Higgins. US$240–350/dome, up to 3 people. $$$$$

Hostería & Restaurante Punta Sur (6 rooms) South side of Lago del Desierto; ///reminding.invests.glam; +54 9 2966 721113; e info@zonaaustralturismo.com; w hosteriapuntasur.com.ar. Operated by tour operator Zona Austral this hostel operates Oct– mid-Apr. All twin rooms with private bathroom, US$40 per couple, dinner US$7 pp. Basic b/fast inc. Also offer a range of tours around the lake. Good website enables online booking, no need to call/ email, take cards. $$

⊼ **Camping Lago del Desierto** Southern shore of Lago del Desierto; ///reminding.invests.glam; 🗘+54 9 2966 721113; w zonaaustralturismo.

com/camping-lago-del-desierto. Basic camping facilities, water, bathrooms with hot water, cooking/eating area, electricity only for lighting. Operated by Zona Austral, decent website enables online booking, takes card. $

TRANSPORT TO/FROM EL CHALTÉN

Confín Viajes Av Lago del Desierto 436, El Chaltén; ///indulge.radial.chanting; 🗘+54 9 2962 409045. Private transfers US$80, for up to 4 people.

Exploradores Lago del Desierto (page 323) Depart El Chaltén 08.00 & 11.00 daily, return 16.00 & 18.00. Can be booked in advance (US$20 one-way).

Frontera Sur 🗘+54 9 2966 1544 5210. Depart El Chaltén noon daily, return 17.00 (high season – earlier in low season).

Zona Austral Depart El Chaltén 09.30 & noon daily, return 16.00 & 17.30 (US$10 one-way).

EL CHALTÉN (ARGENTINA)

The 'trekking capital' of Argentina, but just another stop on the road for the seasoned Carretera traveller. Every year hordes of tourists flock to hike routes in the shadow of Mount Fitz Roy (11,171ft). The town came to fruition in 1985 as a result of a border dispute between Argentina and Chile as a statement of intent, with government buildings built far beyond the appropriate requirement of a small settlement. Now, the town exists solely for tourism. There are plenty of bars, restaurants and accommodation options available but be sure to book in advance in high season. Supermarkets with basic provisions stay open late. There is an ATM, petrol station and laundry.

MOVING ON FROM EL CHALTÉN

Bus-Sur El Calafate: bus terminal, offices in all destinations; 🗘61 261 4224, +54 2902 494680; e info@bussur.com; w bussur.com. Buses to/ from El Calafate & Puerto Natales, from Puerto Natales to Torres del Paine & Punta Arenas, & to Ushuaia. Do not serve El Chaltén or Lago del Desierto.

Chaltén Travel Av Libertador 1174, El Calafate; Av Guemes 7, El Chaltén; 🗘+ 54 11 5199 0476, +54 2962 493392; e contacto@chaltentravel.com; w chaltentravel.com. Transfers to/from downtown El Calafate & daily to Bariloche.

Taqsa Antonio Rojo, cnr Cabo Gimenez, El Chaltén; 🗘0800 333 1188; w taqsa.com.ar. Buses to/from El Chaltén to El Calafate & El Calafate airport, as well as routes to the rest of Argentina including Bariloche, Ushuaia, Los Antiguos (for access to the Carretera Austral at Chile Chico) & Río Turbio for access to Puerto Natales & Torres del Paine).

Taxi Condor 🗘+54 2902 492802; w taxicondor. com.ar. Private transport to/from El Calafate airport, takes cards.

Transporte Las Lengas El Calafate: airport counter & El Chaltén: Viedma St 95 & bus terminal, window 6; 🗘+54 9 2902 414310; e info@lengas. com; w lengas.com. Transfers between El Calafate airport & El Chaltén, synchronised with flight arrivals & departures.

Turismo Zaahj El Chaltén bus terminal; 🗘+54 2902 491631; e zaahj@entelchile.net; w turismozaahj.co.cl. Buses to/from Calafate & Puerto Natales, Calafate & El Chaltén, & from Calafate directly to Torres del Paine.

Zona Austral Av Miguel Martin de Güemes 84; ///homages.ballrooms.mogul; 🗘+54 9 2902 490535, +54 2966 721113; e info@ zonaaustralturismo.com; w zonaaustralturismo. com. Office ⏰ 07.30– 21.00 daily. Buses daily from El Chaltén to El Calafate 08.00 & 18.00, & El Calafate to El Chaltén 08.00 & 18.00 ($30 one-way). Calafate airport to El Chaltén servicing any flight ($10). In high season they offer a daily bus to/from Puerto Natales, 3 times per week in low season ($30 pp).

To El Calafate El Chaltén is situated close to El Calafate – a useful transport hub with buses north, south and east, and an airport with flights to Ushuaia, Buenos Aires and Bariloche. Calafate is also the jumping-off point for visits to Ventisquero Perito Moreno, although this is not such an attraction for those heading to/from the spectacular glaciers along the Carretera Austral. The road from El Calafate airport to El Chaltén is paved, with spectacular views of the pampa and glacial blue rivers near Lago Argentina.

To Torres del Paine For those without a vehicle wishing to connect the Carretera Austral with Argentine Patagonia and continue to Torres del Paine, El Calafate is the best place to take a bus back into Chile.

To Bariloche For those hoping to access the Carretera Austral further north (most likely via Chile Chico), the key route is on Argentina's Ruta 40 towards Bariloche. This is a main highway running broadly parallel to the Carretera Austral on the Argentine side of the Andes, and is *mostly* paved. A good public transport option from El Chaltén is Chaltén Travel (page 333), and the trip between El Chaltén and Bariloche takes two days and makes some intermediate stops. The halfway point is the village of **Perito Moreno**, which is close to the Cueva de las Manos (Cave of the Hands, a UNESCO archaeological site). Some of the hand paintings found here date back more than 9,000 years.

From Perito Moreno various shuttles head west via Los Antiguos, Argentina (with Chaltén Travel or Taqsa bus), to **Chile Chico** in Chile – a main entry/exit point to the Carretera Austral (page 276). This route is offered from mid-November until Easter and costs approximately US$100 (12hrs). Out of season the bus frequency reduces drastically, and in high season buses fill quickly so it is wise to reserve a seat in advance.

The **border crossing to Chile at Cochrane** (Paso Roballos, page 300) is not possible with public transport, and the road between Ruta 40 and the actual border is rarely transited, so this is not an ideal border crossing for those without a private vehicle (or bicycle). Consequently, many use the **Los Antiguos/Chile Chico border crossing** (page 279), and not wishing to double back on themselves, skip the southern section of the Carretera Austral. For those without a car, the strong recommendation of this book is to cross directly into Chile from El Chaltén and to continue north along the entire Carretera Austral. For those wishing to cross back into northern Argentine Patagonia (Villa La Angostura, Bariloche and so on), the most convenient border crossing is Cardenal Samoré, northeast of Puerto Montt.

North of Perito Moreno, Ruta 40 continues on to **Esquel**, **El Bolson** and **Bariloche**. Each of these cities also serves as an entry/exit to the Carretera Austral.

Appendix 1

ISLANDS AND VILLAGES INACCESSIBLE BY LAND

We intended to expand the scope of the second edition of this guide to include the outlying islands and less accessible parts of the mainland that have no direct connection with the Carretera Austral and which were omitted from the first edition. Ayacara (on the west of the Huequi Peninsula, accessible only by boat or plane), and Raúl Marín Balmaceda (technically an island, albeit reached by road from La Junta and a free, regular 5-minute ferry), are already included in the main text. However, due to ferry cancellations and Covid-19 restrictions we were unable to visit the other outlying regions. Rather than exclude them entirely, we include only a brief description.

Most such villages lie along the Naviera Austral slow ferry route connecting the island of Chiloé with Puerto Chacabuco (w navieraustral.cl/cordillera). The villages and ferry routes are visible on the map of the Classic Route (page 142). In north–south order, the ferry passes **Melinka** (roughly 60km south of Chiloé and 60km west of mainland Chile); Raúl Marín Balmaceda (page 167) and then **Villa Melimoyu** and **Puerto Gala**; it then continues to Puerto Cisnes (page 186) and **Puerto Gaviota** (on the south shore of Isla Magdalena National Park where the Puyuhuapi Canal meets the ocean, 3 hours' sailing west of Puerto Cisnes); and **Puerto Aguirre** (a further 2 hours south, on the Canal Moraleda, the last stop before arriving at Puerto Chacabuco, page 202). Beyond Puerto Chacabuco there are no such settlements until leaving the region of Aysén. The ferry from Puerto Yungay/Caleta Tortel (page 319) passes one final village before reaching Puerto Natales – **Puerto Eden**, the northernmost inhabited place within the Magallanes region, beyond the usual definition of the Carretera Austral but briefly described nonetheless.

It is hard to overstate the degree of isolation of these villages. Santo Domingo, an even smaller village between Melimoyu and Raúl Marín, is home to just one family. Mobile phone coverage is patchy to non-existent. Transport is weekly at best. For those with limited time, or pending flight connections, this region might not be ideal. For those willing to invest the time, these are some of the least-visited, most pristine regions of Chile.

In 2014 an excellent travelogue of the Carretera Austral was published by the regional government of Aysén. Alas it was not updated, but remains one of the best descriptions of the fjords and channels to the west of the Carretera Austral. Those wishing to visit this region should read *Chapter 3* of this travelogue, freely available at w issuu.com/patagoniapordescubrir/docs/libro_issuu_ingles.

MELINKA AND REPOLLAL Technically Melinka is the most populous island in the region of Aysén, given that Chiloé itself is not within Aysén. With roughly 1,800 inhabitants it is at the very north of the Guaitecas Archipelago and has been capital of the archipelago since 1979. It was named in the 1860s by Felipe Westhoff, a Lithuanian timber tycoon exploiting the cypress trees of Guaitecas (*Pilgerodendron uviferum*) who named the island after his sister, Melinka Westhoff. Access is via small plane (Pewen Chile and Aerocord fly directly from La Paloma in Puerto Montt; page 126), by Naviera Austral ferries from Quellón or Raúl Marín Balmaceda on the slow Cordillera route, or from Puerto Cisnes or Quellón on the faster ferry (**w** navieraustral.cl/cordillera-corta).

All **activities** revolve around the sea: kayaking, short hikes, whale/dolphin watching, visiting local boatbuilders and artisans. It is the gateway for private trips to Jechica Island (**w** islajechica.cl). There is a petrol station and a bus crosses the island to a smaller village called Repollal offering endless seafood and cordero stew.

Additional information is available at **w** turismo.muniguaitecas.cl.

Where to stay   Melinka has a number of hotels.

↑ Residencial Vista Hermosa (7 rooms, shared bathroom) ///fairness.dethrone.machinery; ✎ 9 7659 8539; **e** pmonterotarino@gmail.com. A number of restaurants, shops & a bar (Puerto Piratas). It was reportedly home to legendary Pirate Ñancúpel who was executed in 1888 for various murders & robberies in the Guaitecas region. $25,000 pp. B/fast inc. **$$$**

↑ Ruca Chonos   Coastal road; ///carpal. cathode.winded; ✎ 9 6588 9248; **e** psoto@ alapatagonia.cl. The largest accommodation on the island with capacity for 60 people. $15,000–40,000, with b/fast, lunch & dinner available for a fee. **$$**.

VILLA MELIMOYU   Founded in 1983, the village currently boasts 53 inhabitants. Sandwiched between Raúl Marín and Puerto Gala, the only means to arrive via public transport is on the slow Naviera Austral ferry (**w** navieraustral.cl/cordillera), otherwise by private boat from Raúl Marín or Puerto Gala, or a charter flight to the landing strip. This is a breathtaking location with views over the canals, to islands, mountains and the Melimoyu volcano (2,440m); there is endless wildlife but limited infrastructure – self-sufficiency is a useful trait here.

Activities include bicycle trails of 10km, various trekking routes including to Río Marchant (fly-fishing, 4hr round trip) and all the way to Gala (7km immersed in giant Nalca plants).

Where to stay   Other accommodation options in the village are Cabañas del Bosque (✎ 9 7263 3306), Melimoyu Austral cabins (///symptom.tucking.rationing; ✎ 9 9591 5105) and Melimoyu Verde cabins (///sage.stoats.reading; ✎ 9 5701 1556).

↑ Hostería Melimoyu   (Private & shared bathroom for up to 20 people) ///tawdry.seclude. ruling; ✎ 9 5400 7038; **e** hosteriamelimoyu@ gmail.com; **f**. This is about the only place to eat if not self-catering, with most food sourced locally. $22,500 pp including b/fast, other meals available for a fee. The same owners run

Melimoyu Ecocamp, a fantastic 2-level dome for up to 5 people with amazing views towards the sea ($100,000/night). Wi-Fi, a huge deck, solar lighting & a small fridge. Located 4km south of the main village on the trail to Seno Gala (///mascara.assurance.busying). **$–$$$**

PUERTO GALA   Another village emerging from the hake/abalone craze of the 1990s, formally founded in 1999, the village is a series of small harbours. It has a viewpoint, a lovely white sand beach (Playa Bonita) and a 30m waterfall (15min

PUERTO GALA ON THE BIG SCREEN

The 2001 film *Fiebre del Loco*, loosely translated as *Abalone Fever*, is an obscure and charming film that touches on some core historical elements of southern Chile and is set in the isolated community of Puerto Gala. Very few films have been based in the region of the Carretera Austral, let alone the outlying islands, and beyond the obvious relevance for visitors to the region, this is simply a great Chilean movie. English subtitles appear unavailable, but the film can be streamed online for free at w archive.org/details/La.Fiebre. del.Loco. (note the final full stop at the end of the URL). It was directed by Andrés Wood Montt, of the Montt dynasty (page 82), won various awards and featured in the Toronto International Film Festival.

The background is a Chilean gold rush – fishermen flooding to isolated coastal locations to furiously hunt the latest fad in fishing, principally hake and abalone. High prices from the mainland and overseas, and poverty in the south, encouraged fishermen to live in so-called 'nylon-camps' – quickly erected homemade tents – fish all hours possible, and some of these communities settled and remain to this day. Gala is one such case.

The movie begins with an oblique description of Puerto Gala: '17,146km southeast of Tokyo'. The slightly convoluted plot revolves around a shady Japanese investor called Fujimori attempting to corner the abalone supply of Puerto Gala. The political trajectory of the village, along with its moral compass, is comically narrated via the local priest and *de facto* mayor. His daily radio show attempts to connect and guide the community, utilising a slightly crude radio play with strange parallels to the real world. Movie buffs will detect similarities with the 1989 Canadian movie *Jesus of Montreal*.

Offering double the going rate for abalone, Fujimori sparks a fishing frenzy. This promise of financial rewards leads to a group of prostitutes arriving in the village by bus carried on a makeshift raft (Gala being an island), docking in the village just as Sunday prayers are underway seeking blessings for the community. Some of the wives and mothers living in the village greet these new arrivals with scepticism, and the antics that ensue are hysterically funny, tragic and insightful in equal measure. An excellent film and essential watching if visiting the more isolated islands, best appreciated by those with a good command of Spanish and Chilean slang.

trip by boat, camping permitted), with a sea lion colony close by. On nearby Chita Island there are archaeological remains of the ancient Chono people who used to live and fish here.

Where to stay Other options, all with shared bathrooms and food available, are: **Hospedaje Macalú** (\ 9 5644 8798), **Hospedaje El Galeón de Manuelito** (\ 9 9253 7717) and **Hospedaje Pamela** (\ 9 5665 9134).

Hospedaje Nómade (6 rooms, shared bathrooms) \ 9 7714 8640, 9 9086 0244; e josesoto.gala@gmail.com. US$40 pp, all food included – ceviche, *cancato* (salmon or eel with cheese & sausage), freshly baked bread, etc.

PUERTO GAVIOTA Legally founded in 1999, this is a small fishing village with a school. Early settlers arrived fleeing persecution under the dictatorship. There were

117 inhabitants in 2002; by 2017 this had declined to only 65 – one of the lesser-inhabited places in the region. The village is connected by boardwalks reminiscent of Caleta Tortel, and has one restaurant based out of Doña Galicia's hostel.

The village has a pleasant beach. Fishing is the main activity, and it is possible to join fishing trips. Industrial fishing and reduced quotas are threatening this last remaining economic activity. Sea life, including whales, is abundant. There is a trek to a lookout above the village, and to some caves, or a 6km kayak trip (or trek) to nearby Puerto Amparo.

Where to stay

Doña Galicia (2 cabins) ☎ 9 9120 1328. Each cabin can accommodate 3 people. $25,000 pp, food available.

Miguel Acosta (4 rooms) ☎ 9 9085 3511. Each room can accommodate 3 people ($20,000 pp, b/fast inc). Also a cabin with 2 beds ($45,000 daily).

PUERTO AGUIRRE Located at the southern extreme of Isla Las Huichas, a mere 65km from Puerto Chacabuco, Puerto Aguirre is a relative metropolis with 539 inhabitants according to the 2017 census, two schools, a small landing strip, a Naviera Austral office, basic medical services, a football pitch, a church, a petrol station, various shops and even a bus service between the two inhabited parts of the island. First inhabited by Chilotes logging cypress trees at the beginning of the 20th century, the village was formally founded around 1940 and is now almost exclusively focused on fishing, especially salmon farming. The village has views of the Macá volcano (2,960m); sea lion colonies nearby; endless kayak options (guided trips with Pachanca Kayak; ☎ 9 9216 3339; e Cerda.vladimir@gmail.com; also rent, but only in the bay). In addition to the scheduled Naviera Austral slow route, ferry company Mar y Magia run four times a week from Puerto Chacabuco (tickets available at the UniMarc supermarket in Puerto Aysén; ☎ 9 9825 5817; e ramon.nauduam@naudutrans.cl). Charter flights also possible.

There is a 10-minute walk to a viewpoint above the village where the entire island and fjords are visible, or a 2km CONAF trail called La Poza. Food available in shops, not restaurants.

Where to stay

Cabañas Aysén (3 cabins) ☎ 9 5699 3406, 9 7871 3732; e ovando85@gmail.com. Cabins for 2 or 3 people. $60,000 per cabin daily with washing machine & quincho.

Hostal don Beña (16 rooms) ///schemers. truly.communal; ☎ 9 9318 2392; e bbalboa@live. cl. Shared bathrooms. ▪ ; $34,000 pp. $$$

PUERTO EDEN One of the remotest regions in South America and the only inhabited place on Wellington Island. With no landing strip, Puerto Eden is accessible only by ferry, 14 hours south of Caleta Tortel or 27 hours north of Pueto Natales. There are only 250 inhabitants, and the main economic activities are timber and shellfish. Formally founded in 1969 when the itinerant community decided to settle in one fixed location, this is the last predominantly Kawésqar community remaining, although the region has been inhabited by their ancestors for at least 6,000 years. Located in very damp rainforest, with ample opportunity to spot huemul, sea otters, sea lions and birds.

Where to stay

Hospedaje Eden ///recycling. crouches.aquarium; ☎ 9 6626 4663. The only

accommodation option in Puerto Eden. Entel phone service available.

Appendix 2

LANGUAGE

BASIC VOCABULARY

Hello/Goodbye	*Hola/Adios*
Good morning/afternoon/night	*Buenos días/buenas tardes/buenas noches*
How are you?	*¿Como está?*
well/very well	*bien/muy bien*
good, OK	*bueno*
yes/no	*sí/no*
of course	*claro*
please/thank you	*por favor/gracias*
Excuse me (I need to pass)	*Con permiso*
Excuse me (sorry)	*Disculpe*
You're welcome	*De nada*
It's a pleasure to meet you	*Mucho gusto*
today/tomorrow	*hoy/mañana*
yesterday	*ayer*
Sorry	*Lo siento/perdón*
What?	*¿Qué?*
When?	*¿Cuando?*
Why?	*¿Por qué?*
How?	*¿Cómo?*
a lot/much	*harto*
here/there	*aquí/ahí*
open/closed	*abierto/cerrado*
large/small	*grande/pequeño*

BASIC PHRASES

Where is…?	*¿Dónde está…?*
What's this street called?	*¿Cómo se llama esta calle?*
Where are you from (your country)?	*¿De dónde es?*
How far is it to…?	*¿A que distancia…?*
How much does it cost?	*¿Cuánto vale?*
May I…? Is it possible…?	*¿Se puede…?*
I am English/American	*Soy inglés/norteamericano*
I don't understand	*No entiendo*
Please write it down	*Por favor, escríbalo*
Do you speak English?	*¿Habla inglés?*
Is there a doctor nearby?	*¿Hay un médico por acá?*
I need to call an ambulance	*Necesito llamar una ambulancia*

DIRECTIONS

left/right	*izquierda/derecha*
north/south	*norte/sur*
east/west	*este* or *oriente/oeste, occidente* or *poniente*
northeast/northwest	*noreste/noroeste*
ATM	*cajero automático*
airport	*aeropuerto*
bus stop	*parada*
border crossing	*paso/frontera*
cove	*caleta*
fjord	*fiordo*
forest/woods	*bosque*
glacier	*ventisquero*
hot springs	*termas*
ice flow	*témpano*
jetty/pier	*embarcadero*
lake	*lago/laguna*
mountain	*cerro/pico*
mountain range	*cordillera/sierra*
next to	*al lado de*
national park	*parque nacional*
national reserve	*reserva nacional*
opposite	*frente*
path (trekking/horseriding)	*sendero*
pass (over mountain)	*portezuelo*
port	*puerto*
river	*río*
road/highway	*camino/carretera*
main highway	*ruta*
shelter/mountain hut	*refugio*
street/avenue	*calle/avenida*
viewpoint/lookout	*mirador*
Are there buses to…?	*¿Hay buses a…?*
A ticket to…?	*¿Un boleto/pasaje a…?*
How can I get to…?	*¿Como puedo llegar a…?*
When do buses return from…?	*¿Cuando vienen los buses de…?*
Where is the nearest place to buy petrol?	*¿Donde está el lugar más cercano para comprar nafta?*
Where is the nearest telephone?	*¿Donde puedo hacer una llamada?*
Can you show me on the map?	*¿Me lo puedes mostrar en el mapa?*

ACCOMMODATION

single/twin/double	*sencillo/doble/matrimonial*
en suite/shared bathroom	*con baño (privado)/con baño compartido (communal)*
camping	*camping*
hotel	*hotel*
hostel	*hostal/residencia/hostería/hospedaje*
Do you have a room?	*¿Hay un cuarto?*

The following words are used in Chilean Spanish, though not in other Spanish-speaking countries.

carabineros	Chilean police (*gendarmería* = Argentine border police)
Chilote	from the island of Chiloé
guagua	baby
huaso	Chilean gaucho, or cowboy
luca	one thousand Chilean pesos
palafito	traditional architectural style dating back to 19th-century Chiloé. Wooden houses built along the shore, often brightly painted, increasingly converted to shops or hotels.
re-	very (*re-barato* = very cheap)

CAMPING EQUIPMENT/SUPPLIES

camping fuel	*bencina blanca*
cooking stove	*estufa*
drinking water	*agua potable*
camp fire	*fogón*
firewood	*leña*
tent	*carpa*
sleeping bag	*bolsa de dormir*
hardware store	*ferreteria*
casserole	*cazuela*
Can I camp here?	*¿Puedo acampar acá?*
Can I make a campfire here?	*¿Se puede hacer fuego acá?*

Transport

4x4	*cuatro por cuatro*
bicycle	*bicicleta*
car	*auto*
ferry/small ferry	*barcaza/balsa*
motorcycle	*motorcicleta*
petrol	*gasolina*
puncture repair	*gomería/vulcanizadora*
paved/gravel/dirt road	*pavimentado/ripio/tierra*
map	*mapa*
seat belt	*cinturón de seguridad*
pot-hole	*bache*
landslide	*derrumbe*
alluvial flood (landslide with mud)	*aluvión*
My car/motorbike/bicycle has broken down	*Se rompió mi auto/moto/bicicleta*
I have a puncture	*tengo un pinchazo*
How is the road?	*¿Como está la ruta?*

CHILEAN DISHES AND LOCAL SPECIALITIES

a lo pobre	meat, fish or chicken dish served with a salad/vegetable, a fried egg and chips
cancato	grilled salmon with melted cheese and tomato
chimichurri	meat condiment based on garlic, parsley, oregano, vinegar, oil and other spices
chorrillana	chips with meat, frankfurter, fried egg and fried onion
congrio	conger eel
cordero al palo	whole lamb slowly roasted on a crucifix
curanto	Chilean dish of seafood, meat and vegetables traditionally cooked in a hole in the ground, originally from Chiloé
kuchen	savoury snacks and pastries/cakes of German influence
mate	tea drunk through a metal straw, mainly in Argentina but also in southern Chile
milanesa	escalope of chicken or beef, coated in breadcrumbs and fried, similar to schnitzel
nalca	giant rhubarb plant; the stalk is edible when cooked
paila marina	seafood broth
pichanga	chips covered with meat, sausage, cheese and vegetables (*chorrillana* = a subtle variety)
salchipapa	chips with diced sausage
tablas	plate of cold meats/cheeses etc

FOOD AND DRINK

beef	*vaca/ternero*		ham	*jamon*
beer	*cerveza*		hot dog	*completo*
bread	*pan*		lamb	*cordero*
breakfast	*desayauno*		milk	*leche*
burger	*churasco*		lunch	*almuerzo*
butter	*mantequilla*		potatoes	*patatas/papas*
casserole	*cazuela*		roast	*asado*
cheese	*queso*		shellfish	*mariscos*
coffee	*café*		steak	*churrasco*
dinner	*cena*		tea	*té*
egg	*huevo*		water	*agua*
fixed menu	*menú del día*		wine	*vino*
hake	*merluza*			

Can I make a reservation?	*¿Podría hacer una reserva?*
When do you open/close?	*¿A qué hora se abre/cierre?*
A table for XX people	*Una mesa para XX personas*
Do you take credit card?	*¿Se puede pagar con tarjeta de crédito?*
The bill, please	*La cuenta, por favor*
Do you have vegetarian food?	*¿Hay comida vegetariana?*

NUMBERS

0	*cero*		3	*tres*		6	*seis*
1	*uno*		4	*cuatro*		7	*siete*
2	*dos*		5	*cinco*		8	*ocho*

9	*nueve*	13	*trece*	17	*diecisiete*
10	*diez*	14	*catorce*	18	*dieciocho*
11	*once*	15	*quince*	19	*diecinueve*
12	*doce*	16	*dieciseis*	20	*veinte*

Appendix 3

FURTHER INFORMATION

BOOKS
History and culture

Astorga, Emilia and Saavedra, Sebastian *Istmo de Ofqui* Ñire Negro Ediciones, 2016. An excellent history of the Isthmus of Ofqui, an obscure and inaccessible stretch of land with a curious past and massive implications to this day. Written by the couple who offer the only tours to the Isthmus.

Chatwin, Bruce *In Patagonia* Vintage Books, 1998. The classic Patagonian read, arguably the first book to popularise Patagonia since its first publication in 1977.

Chenut, Jean *Cuando éramos niños en la Patagonia* Pehuén Editores, 2006. Account of the early Belgian settlers to the region around Lago General Carrera. Packed with extensive black-and-white photos.

Darwin, Charles *The Voyage of the Beagle*. Darwin's pathfinding account of his 1831–36 expedition on the HMS *Beagle*, covering regions along the Carretera Austral. Originally published in 1839.

Guevara, Che *The Motorcycle Diaries*. Che Guevara never made it south of Osorno, so the book does not encompass any region of the Carretera Austral, but is one of the definitive travel books of the entire South American continent.

Hudson, William Henry *Idle Days in Patagonia*. Early account of flora and fauna of the region.

Ivanoff, Danka *Caleta Tortel y su Isla de los Muertos* Fundación Río Baker, 2012. The finest account of the mystery surrounding the graveyard at Caleta Tortel and a good introduction to Lucas Bridges. Mrs Ivanoff has written a number of other books about southern Chile, including parts of the Carretera Austral. Indeed, those staying at the El Engaño cabins (page 281) in Chile Chico are afforded the privilege of meeting and chatting with Mrs Ivanoff. Her books are available in Chile Chico, Coyhaique and Perito Moreno (Argentina), and her book of the war of Chile Chico is available for free download on w memoriachilena.cl. She has also written an account of the history and mythology of Butch Cassidy and the Sundance Kid, just across the border in Cholila, Argentina.

Ludwig, Luisa *Puyuhuapi – Curanto y Kuchen* Kultrun, 2013. A 'book of histories' – a heart-warming account of the early pioneers of Puyuhuapi and the surrounding region, written by the daughter of one of the first pioneers. A wonderful insight into the early life of the first villages, intertwined with early 20th-century European history.

Ludwig, Luisa and Falkwoski, James *Where the Andes Meet the Sea* Ñire Negro, 2017. English translation (abridged) of *Puyuhuapi – Curanto y Kuchen*, with a foreword by Hugh Sinclair. One of the only history books specifically about the Carretera Austral, written by a resident, available in English.

McEwan, Colin *Patagonia: Natural History, Prehistory and Ethnography* Princeton University Press, 2014. This book describes how the intrepid nomads of Tierra del Fuego Patagonia confronted a hostile climate and learned how to live there. It provides an overview of the history of the land and its people. A fascinating look into the people Darwin met while on the *Beagle*.

Moss, Chris *Patagonia – A Cultural History* Signal Books, 2008. An engaging overview of the literature, legends and history of Patagonia, with some sections relating to the region spanned by the Carretera Austral.

Murphy, Dallas *Rounding the Horn: Being the Story of Williwaws and Windjammers, Drake, Darwin, Murdered Missionaries and Naked Natives* Basic Books, 2005. Some overlap with the Carretera Austral, but possibly the most amusing, well-written account of deep Patagonia, combining maritime history, exploration, the first contact with the indigenous residents, and a thumping account of the exploration of the channels of the extreme south.

Pucci, Idanna *La Italiana de Patagonia – Homenaje a Eugenia Pirzio Biroli*. A fascinating account of the life and works of the long-serving mayor of Puerto Cisnes, including many first-hand accounts of her life. Written by her niece, in Spanish and Italian, available directly from the author (e idannapucci@gmail.com).

Vargas, Francisca and Venegas, Verónica *Aysén: Muertes en Dictadura: Historias de Ausencia y Memoria* Editorial LOM, 2017. A disturbing account of the 19 people executed or disappeared during the military dictatorship in Aysén, with often harrowing descriptions of how their families uncovered the truth.

Guides and maps

Aysén – an Undiscovered Patagonia 2014. An early, collaborative guidebook that contains marvellous anecdotes, mysteries, recipes of exotic dishes and decent maps. The project was financed by the Regional Government of Aysén and developed by the Center for Patagonia Ecosystem Investigation. Available for download (in English) at w issuu.com/patagoniapordescubrir/docs/aysen_an_undiscovered_patagonia.

COPEC *Chiletur Zona Sur* COPEC, 2021. Definitive road atlas of the region, best up-to-date maps available of the region. Limited additional information. Covers the entire southern region from Santiago to Tierra del Fuego.

Beccaceci, Marcello D *Natural Patagonia* Pangaea, 1998. This book takes readers on a panoramic journey through one of the world's most magnificent and varied landscapes, explaining its formation and the remarkable animals and flora that thrive in the rugged reaches of Patagonian Argentina and Chile.

Bradt, Hilary and Pilkington, John *Backpacking in Chile and Argentina plus the Falkland Islands* Bradt Enterprises, 1980. One of the earliest Bradt guidebooks and arguably the forerunner to this Carretera Austral guide.

Jaramillo, Alvaro *The Birds of Chile* Princeton Field Guides, 2003. Features concise identification-focused text positioned opposite the superb colour plates to allow quick and easy reference. There are over 470 species detailed, including all breeders, regular visitors and vagrants.

Pike, Neil and Harriet *The Adventure Cycle-Touring Handbook* Trailblazer, 2015. The definitive guide to planning for an extended cycling trip.

Pixmap Cartografía Digital *Chile's Lake District: Puerto Varas–Ensenada–Cochamó*. Double-sided map useful for trekking in the region; one side 1:100,000 map covers Lago Llanquihue with Puerto Varas and the area to the east, the other side 1:75,000 map further south, extending from the Reloncaví Estuary and Puelo eastwards to the El León border. Available from Stanfords (w stanfords.co.uk).

Zegers, Claudio Donoso *Arboles Nativos de Chile*. A useful tree identification guide for Chile's main native trees with commentary in English and Spanish. Produced for CONAF (Chile's national park administration) and available at their information office in Santiago.

Contemporary travel

Crouch, Gregory *Enduring Patagonia* Random House USA, 2003. Excellent mountain-climbing book covering some regions encompassed by the Carretera Austral.

Krull, Robert *Solitude: A Year Alone in the Patagonian Wilderness* New World Library, 2009. Although slightly south of the most southerly point of the Carretera Austral, this intriguing book describes a year living in total isolation on an uninhabited Chilean island. Survival and enlightenment in equal measure.

Reding, Nick *The Last Cowboys at the End of the World* Crown Publishing, 2001. A fascinating, insightful and witty account of living with Chilean gauchos in Cisnes Medio (near Villa Amengual).

Walker, Justin *The Dictator's Highway* Lulu.com, 2015. The only travelogue of the Carretera Austral, superbly written, eloquent, witty and accurate. Great read; the only criticism is that the author was predominantly hitching and thus does not manage to venture off the main Carretera Austral to some of the lesser-known regions.

Other

Orrego, Juan Pablo and Rodrigo, Patricio *Patagonia Chilean ¡Sin Represas!* Definitive text (in Spanish) of the struggle to prevent the damming of the Pascua and Baker rivers. Available from w patagoniasinrepresas.cl.

FILMS

Bear Story Dir. Gabriel Osorio, 2014. Winner of the Academy Award for best animated short in 2015, this film is a moving portrayal of life under the military dictatorship, explaining some of the traits visible in Chilean culture to this day: ▶ watch?v=HG4He0HP1Tk

La Fiebre del Loco Dir. Andrés Wood Montt, 2001. An excellent tragi-comic film about the remote village of Puerto Gala during the seafood rush of the 1980s. Full movie available at w archive.org/details/La.Fiebre.del.Loco.

NEWSPAPERS AND MAGAZINES The main newspaper in Coyhaique, with news of the region, is *El Divisadero*. A good magazine available in most large towns (ie: Coyhaique, Puerto Aysén, Puerto Montt or in Chiloé) is *Destinos*, with cultural/culinary/touristic information of the southern region of Chile. *Patagon Journal*, w patagonjournal.com, is an excellent English language travel magazine focused on (Chilean) Patagonia.

WEBSITES
News

w **aysenenlinea.cl**
w **diarioaysen.cl/regional**
w **eldivisadero.cl/home**
w **elportaldeaysen.cl**
w **radiosantamaria.cl**
w **redaysen.com**

Weather

w **meteochile.gob.cl** Weather forecast for all larger towns and cities in Chile. This website has satellite images and a very good link to the opening hours and current state of border crossings.

Conservation

w **conaf.cl** This is Chile's national park administration website. It contains maps and information about all its parks and reserves. The website is in Spanish with only the rules and regulations section also in English.

Other conservation NGOs in the region:

w **anihuereserve.com/index.html** Reserve protecting flora and fauna around Raúl Marín Balmaceda.

w **aumen.cl** NGO focused on nature conservation, scientific investigation and awareness raising regarding Aysén Province.

w **ciep.cl** Scientific research centre focused on sustainable development of Aysén.

w **codeff.cl/maule/aysen** One of the first conservation NGOs in the region, active in campaigning for the protection of flora and fauna.

w **parquekatalapi.cl** A small park close to Puerto Montt offering workshops and courses related to nature.

w **patagoniasinrepresas.cl** News on developments in the ongoing challenge to protect rivers in the region.

w **reforestemos.org** Environmental foundation focused on Chilean native forests.

w **rewildingchile.org** and **tompkinsconservation.org** Dedicated to the creation of national or provincial parks, protection of wildlife, land restoration and local development.

Tourism

w **bicyclepatagonia.com/carretera-austral** One of a number of blogs dedicated to cycling the Carretera Austral.

w **horizonsunlimited.com** Motorbikers' hub, with local contacts, routes, etc.

w **otrashuellas.cl** Foundation dedicated to promoting travel along the Carretera for those with physical or cognitive disabilities.

w **outdoorroamers.com/cycle-the-carretera-austral** Abundant information for those wishing to cycle the Carretera Austral.

w **sernatur.cl** The Ministry of Tourism website, with all contact details for local offices where maps, etc, are usually available.

Index

Page numbers in **bold** indicate main entries and those in *italics* indicate maps.

INDEX OF ADVERTISERS

THE BRADT STORY

In the beginning

It all began in 1974 on an Amazon river barge. During an 18-month trip through South America, two adventurous young backpackers – Hilary Bradt and her then husband, George – decided to write about the hiking trails they had discovered through the Andes. *Backpacking Along Ancient Ways in Peru and Bolivia* included the very first descriptions of the Inca Trail. It was the start of a colourful journey to becoming one of the best-loved travel publishers in the world; you can read the full story on our website (bradtguides. com/ourstory).

Getting there first

Hilary quickly gained a reputation for being a true travel pioneer, and in the 1980s she started to focus on guides to places overlooked by other publishers. The Bradt Guides list became a roll call of guidebook 'firsts'. We published the first guide to Madagascar, followed by Mauritius, Czechoslovakia and Vietnam. The 1990s saw the beginning of our extensive coverage of Africa: Tanzania, Uganda, South Africa, and Eritrea. Later, post-conflict guides became a feature: Rwanda, Mozambique, Angola, and Sierra Leone, as well as the first standalone guides to the Baltic States following the fall of the Iron Curtain, and the first post-war guides to Bosnia, Kosovo and Albania.

Comprehensive – and with a conscience

Today, we are the world's largest independently owned travel publisher, with more than 200 titles. However, our ethos remains unchanged. Hilary is still keenly involved, and **we still get there first**: two-thirds of Bradt guides have no direct competition.

But we don't just get there first. Our guides are also known for being **more comprehensive** than any other series. We avoid templates and tick-lists. Each guide is a one-of-a-kind expression of an expert author's interests, knowledge and enthusiasm for telling it how it really is.

And a commitment to wildlife, conservation and respect for local communities has always been at the heart of our books. Bradt Guides was **championing sustainable travel** before any other guidebook publisher. We even have a series dedicated to Slow Travel in the UK, award-winning books that explore the country with a passion and depth you'll find nowhere else.

Thank you!

We can only do what we do because of the support of readers like you – people who value less-obvious experiences, less-visited places and a more thoughtful approach to travel. Those who, like us, take travel seriously.